IMAGINING A
GREAT REPUBLIC

IMAGINING A
GREAT REPUBLIC

Political Novels
and the Idea of America

THOMAS E. CRONIN

ROWMAN & LITTLEFIELD
Lanham • Boulder • New York • London

Published by Rowman & Littlefield
A wholly owned subsidiary of The Rowman & Littlefield Publishing Group, Inc.
4501 Forbes Boulevard, Suite 200, Lanham, Maryland 20706
www.rowman.com

Unit A, Whitacre Mews, 26-34 Stannary Street, London SE11 4AB

British Library Cataloguing in Publication Information Available

Library of Congress Cataloging-in-Publication Data
Names: Cronin, Thomas E., author.
Title: Imagining a great republic : political novels and the
    idea of America / Thomas E. Cronin.
Description: Lanham, Maryland : Rowman & Littlefield, 2018. | Includes
    bibliographical references and index.
Identifiers: LCCN 2017019698 (print) | LCCN 2017043444 (ebook) | ISBN
    9781538105726 (Electronic) | ISBN 9781538105719 (cloth : alk. paper)
Subjects: LCSH: Political fiction, American—History and criticism. |
    Politics and literature—United States. | Politics in literature.
Classification: LCC PS374.P6 (ebook) | LCC PS374.P6 C76 2018 (print) |
DDC
    813.009/358—dc23
LC record available at https://lccn.loc.gov/2017019698

♾™ The paper used in this publication meets the minimum requirements of
American National Standard for Information Sciences—Permanence of Paper
for Printed Library Materials, ANSI/NISO Z39.48-1992.

Printed in the United States of America

For Tania, Alexander, Allegra, Asher,
and Pam—with love.

CONTENTS

PREFACE

A nation without historians or storytellers would be like a people crippled by amnesia, confused about who they are, where they came from, and where they are going. A resilient, self-renewing society, by contrast, consults the past in service of imagining its aspirational future.

We live in uncertain times. We have been shaken by 9/11, a major recession, and a stunning backlash election. Inequality persists. Racial and geographic divides endure. Civic participation is low and voters are often poorly informed. Partisan bickering, especially in Washington, D.C., has become debilitating. The promise of the American Dream, for many, remains elusive. America is a rich, powerful, and unprecedented nation; yet our efforts to come together and live up to the ideals outlined in our Declaration of Independence have taken a surprisingly long time. The future direction of our country is uncertain.

From the time our nation was first created, fiction writers and storytellers have captured our coming of age and tried to imagine what America could someday become. These writers have tried to explain us to ourselves and point the way toward a self-renewing dynamic constitutional republic.

Harriet Beecher Stowe, Harper Lee, Toni Morrison, Robert Penn Warren, Henry Adams, Upton Sinclair, Sinclair Lewis, John Nichols, John Steinbeck, Joseph Heller, Michael Shaara, Joe Klein, Philip Roth, and many of their colleagues have been our tribal storytellers. They have been moral and civic consciousness raisers as we have navigated the zigs and zags, the successes and setbacks, and the slow, awkward evolution of the American political experiment.

Fiction may be imagined stories or sometimes even lies; yet these stories also tell us true things, jolt us, push us to try harder, and try to make us understand each other. They can make us laugh at ourselves while also teaching us that we have to work with one another—and even love one another—before we can love America.

This book is an analysis of the fictional literature on American politics. It is a study of American poli-lit, and I hope that it will encourage more people to read poignant American novels that teach us who we are and, more important, by encouraging even more creative and sensible political collaboration, who we can someday be.[1]

Another goal in my reading of these novelists has been to help us understand the rich, yet often competing, political narratives in America's fictional tradition. As I will argue, we have multiple American narratives, just as we have multiple and often competing American Dreams.

Thomas Jefferson may have been reaching for the stars; still, he imagined, on our behalf, a vibrant and effective constitutional republic. A republic where Americans could enjoy life, liberty, economic opportunity, and upward social mobility—where everyone would be treated equally under the law and those who governed needed to earn the general consent of the governed.

Democratic republics had been tried. But their success was poor. John Adams was pessimistic and warned in addition that they had a way of committing political suicide. James Madison cautioned that a major challenge in the new republic would be dealing with factions that would surely emerge. Have and have-nots would always exist, he warned, and they would inevitably band together and oppose one another.

America, as noted, has become a remarkably rich and powerful nation. Still it remains a work in progress when it comes to equality, inclusiveness, tolerance, and striking a balance between liberty and community. The idea of America emphasizes this country as a land of opportunity where the condition of your birth should not predetermine your life and the blessings of liberty. The great jurist Louis Brandeis warned that we can have concentrated wealth in the hands of the few or we can have a constitutional democracy, but we cannot have both.

Undaunted reformers and writers—including many discussed in this book—view America's challenges as opportunities sometimes brilliantly disguised as intractable problems. William Faulkner and Norman Mailer, among others, argue that good fictional storytelling can often be more revealing—and even more truthful—than nonfiction or journalism. The best fiction writers understand truth wears many masks.

Gifted novelists help us remember our past and remind us of our social and moral obligations to one another. Yes, novelists write to entertain and to make money. Yet they can also rally readers to a cause, change our attitudes, make us laugh at ourselves, and change the way we do politics.

Most of these writers implicitly, if not explicitly, imagine a better, more idealistic republic. Reading, rereading, and "interviewing" these novels—especially in these trying times—encourages us to imagine as well as work toward a more mature, spirited, and resilient American constitutional republic.

Americans are understandably proud of our memorials to Jefferson, Lincoln, and Washington. We are proud, too, of the U.S. Capitol, the majestic Supreme Court building, and the White House. We are inspired by the U.S. Constitution and the Bill of Rights (even if many citizens do not fully understand these documents). But the strength and vitality of the American political experiment lies in the hearts and minds of the people. If Americans lose faith, stop caring, and stop believing in the possibilities of self-government and constitutional principles, our monuments and sacred documents will be meaningless.

We pledge allegiance to the flag and that "for which it stands." But we also have to understand our past and take responsibility for the progress of the nation. Giving up on politics is not an option. We have duties as well as rights. That's the deal. Shirking obligations also is not an option.

That's the verdict of most of the novelists I examine in this book. The great poet Walt Whitman eloquently made this point toward the end of his "By Blue Ontario's Shore" (1867):

O I see flashing that this America is only you and me,
Its power, weapons, testimony, are you and me.
Its crimes, lies, thefts, defections, are you and me,
Its Congress is you and me, the officers, capitols, armies, ships are you
    and me.
Its endless gestation of new states are you and me.
The war (that was so bloody and grim, the war I will henceforth forget),
    was you and me,
Freedom, language, poems, employments, are you and me,
Past, present, future, are you and me,
I dare not shirk any part of myself,
Nor any part of America good or bad. . . .

This book discusses dozens of important American political novels. The following novels are treated at length in chapters 3–7.

American Novelists as Political Storytellers

The Novelist as Political Agitator
    Harriet Beecher Stowe, *Uncle Tom's Cabin* (1852)
    Upton Sinclair, *The Jungle* (1906)
    John Dos Passos, *The 42nd Parallel* (1930)
    Sinclair Lewis, *It Can't Happen Here* (1935)
    John Steinbeck, *The Grapes of Wrath* (1939)
    Richard Wright, *Native Son* (1940)
    Ayn Rand, *Atlas Shrugged* (1957)
    Edward Abbey, *The Monkey Wrench Gang* (1975)
    Philip Roth, *The Plot Against America* (2004)

The Novelist as Political Consciousness Raiser
    Mark Twain and Charles Warren, *The Gilded Age* (1873)
    Henry Adams, *Democracy: An American Novel* (1880)
    Winston Churchill, *Mr. Crewe's Career* (1908)
    Helen Hunt Jackson, *Ramona* (1884)
    Robert Penn Warren, *All the King's Men* (1946)
    Harper Lee, *To Kill a Mockingbird* (1960)
    Fletcher Knebel and Charles W. Bailey II, *Seven Days in May* (1962)
    John Nichols, *The Milagro Beanfield War* (1974)
    John Grisham, *The Appeal: A Novel* (2008)

The Novelist as Political Satirist
    Hugh Henry Brackenridge, *Modern Chivalry* (1792–1815)
    Nathanael West, *A Cool Million* (1934)
    Richard Condon, *The Manchurian Candidate* (1959)
    Joseph Heller, *Catch-22* (1961)
    Gore Vidal, *Washington, D.C.* (1967)
    Hunter S. Thompson, *Fear and Loathing in Las Vegas* (1971)
    Christopher Buckley, *Supreme Courtship* (2008)

The Novelist on the Campaign Trail
    Hamlin Garland, *A Spoil of Office* (1892)
    Howard Fast, *The American: A Middle Western Legend* (1946)
    Edwin O'Connor, *The Last Hurrah* (1956)
    Eugene Burdick, *The Ninth Wave* (1956)
    Andrew Tully, *Capitol Hill* (1962)
    Joe Klein, *Primary Colors* (1996)

The Novelist as Political Anthropologist

Horatio Alger, *Ragged Dick* and other novels (1860–1890s)

Herman Melville, *Billy Budd* (1891)

Margaret Mitchell, *Gone With the Wind* (1936)

Allen Drury, *Advise and Consent* (1959)

Billy Lee Brammer, *The Gay Place* (1961)

Michael Shaara, *The Killer Angels* (1975)

Toni Morrison, *Beloved* (1987)

Norman Mailer, *Harlot's Ghost* (1991)

Ward Just, *Echo House* (1999)

Joseph S. Nye Jr., *The Power Game: A Washington Novel* (2004)

1

AMERICAN POLITICAL
STORYTELLING

A nation's political culture is shaped by the storytelling we share with
one another—about heroes and villains, character and courage, disappointments and dreams. American political novels are part of that narrative.
They remind us of who we have been, what we stand for, who we might
become, and help explain us to ourselves.

Great storytelling has played a central role in the Western intellectual and political tradition. *The Iliad* and *The Odyssey* are epic archetypal
storytelling classics. *King Lear*, *Othello*, *Hamlet*, and *Julius Caesar* were
a few of Shakespeare's memorably instructive stories about leaders and
politics. Cervantes's *Don Quixote* made us laugh at would-be leaders and
ourselves.

Legends, myths, and handed-down stories are often an ensemble of
fact and fiction. "Where fact leaves off and fiction begins is difficult and
frequently impossible to determine."[1] In a John Ford–directed film classic,
The Man Who Shot Liberty Valance, the town's newspaper publisher is asked
whether he is going to correct a long-held, yet misinformed, local belief.
"No, sir," Mr. Peabody famously responds. "This is the West, sir. When
the legend becomes fact, [we] print the legend."[2]

Legendary fiction often describes what ought to have happened instead of what did. Storytellers give us hero protagonists the human heart
ceaselessly yearns for and as often matches them with rogues and scoundrels
we yearn to scorn.[3] Whatever the case, imagination and embellishments
included, such stories get passed down in ways that shape identities, memories, and aspirations.

An example of elaborating on legend separated, if not divorced, from
fact is Margaret Mitchell's *Gone with the Wind*. It is a page-turner romantic

thriller; yet it conveys a nostalgia and political interpretation of slavery, plantation life, and the Klan that misrepresents what happened.

Another example is *Lincoln*, Steven Spielberg's earnest 2013 Hollywood celebration of President Abraham Lincoln. Film viewers are left with the misleading impression that Lincoln had long championed the end of slavery and the passage of the Thirteenth Amendment and that he, almost alone, was the redeeming hero of democracy's moral passion play. He even dies for our national original sin. But as most biographers and historians have explained, Lincoln was notably late to this parade and, though he deserves considerable credit, there was a much larger cast of leadership catalysts. They include black leaders and rebellious slaves, abolitionists, the early women's movement, activists in the Underground Railroad, the speaker of the House and others, including Harriet Beecher Stowe, discussed later in this book, who were out front, and they were often more courageous and get too little credit in this otherwise pleasing "Great Man Theory" Hollywood biopic. No matter: Lincoln, known today as the Emancipator and the man who freed the slaves, is part of the well-established American narrative.

Novelist David Guterson, author of the splendid *Snow Falling on Cedars* (among other works), said it was helpful for him to imagine humanity allegorically as a small, weary tribe that was assailed on all sides by enormously threatening forces. His image is a bit melodramatic; yet his story about the importance of stories is well worth noting:

> It is winter and the people are cold and starving, many have died and others are sick, there is no food to be had, the days are dark, cruel enemies are closing in. The sun has set and the wind has come up and the cries of children can be heard. In desperation the tribe gathers around the warmth of a fire which will shortly go out, for there is little fuel to be had. And when the chiefs and spirit keepers are all done speaking and silence has fallen across the land, all will turn to the tribe's storyteller, not just to be swept away, transported out of troubled times by the sheer force of a well-told story, but more importantly because without stories, stories that inspire those who hear them to carry on with the work of sustaining what is best in human beings—without stories, there is no tribe.[4]

Mythical stories are strikingly alike in diverse cultures. Every tribe has heroes and customs and rituals, and, as humanist Joseph Campbell suggests, "It has always been the prime function of mythology and rite to supply the symbols that carry the human spirit forward."[5] Novels are part of this transfer.

Mythology has been variously understood as a primitive explanation of the world of nature, as allegorical instructions for living, as a collective set of dreams, as profound metaphysical insights, and as divine revelation to humans. "Mythology," believes Campbell, "is all of these."[6] Myths get intertwined with legends, and legends morph into aspirations. America, perhaps because of its polyglot and supposed melting-pot composition, is a mother lode of legends, aspirations, and dreams.

American novelists, of course, are especially challenged to discern what, if anything, is peculiarly American in our storytelling narrative. One strain of thinking resulted in Horatio Alger Jr.'s aspirational novels celebrating hard work and upward mobility.

At the core of American storytelling is *The Adventures of Huckleberry Finn*. Twain's is a much-layered narrative of America's painful coming of age. His genius was in capturing plain-talking fugitives in search of freedom, common sense, and basic morality. Twain invents Huck and Jim and their adventures along America's central river, and we are inspired, at least in today's reading, to believe that people of diverse backgrounds can live, play, explore, create, and dream together, and they—and maybe all of us— can escape the wrongheaded prejudices of our darker past.

Huck became an American hero because his journey along the Mississippi was one of self-discovery and moral awakening. "He slowly puts aside the prejudice that he's been taught, embraces Jim, and—in the book's greatest climax—decides he'll just go ahead and burn in hell if that's the cost of helping his friend." What we admire about Huck, political scientist Jim Morone suggests, is that he "learns to treat everyone with respect," whereas his father and most of the other people we meet in the novel "are always working the angle that will get them ahead and the hell with the consequences for everyone else."[7]

In our national tribal stories, we learn not only about Huck Finn but also about Atticus Finch and Scout, Tom Joad, John Galt, Uncle Tom, George Washington Hayduke, Scarlett O'Hara and Rhett Butler, Bigger Thomas, Joe Mondragón and Ruby Archuleta, and about public officials such as Willie Stark, Frank Skeffington, Arthur "Goddam" Fenstemaker, Marine Colonel Martin Casey, and Pepper Cartwright.

Novelists also provide plenty of rogues and scoundrels such as Simon Legree, the Klan, the McCarthyites, the carpetbaggers, the Ladd Devine Development Company, Krane Chemical, the railroad interests, big oil, big meatpackers, big California farmers, segregationists, fascists, Communists, political bosses, national planners, and plenty of wayward politicians and their consultants.

THE ROLE OF THE NOVELIST

Novelists like to believe that they have a "lifetime office" as opposed to politicians who come and go. Poets and fiction writers like to imagine they are the unacknowledged legislators of the world, or at least its conscience. They strive to make us remember the past, as Toni Morrison did, and to serve as a conscience, as Harriet Beecher Stowe and Upton Sinclair did. The brash Norman Mailer even claims good fiction could be "more real" and "nourishing to our sense of reality than nonfiction." And novels, E. L. Doctorow claims, "tell us the secret meaning of places and things as well as our morally immense human secrets."[8]

Most political novelists have had some political experience, come from political families, or have been journalists covering the political process. Among novelists discussed in this book, Hugh Henry Brackenridge, (American) Winston Churchill, and John Grisham served as state legislators. Henry Adams, Harper Lee, Gore Vidal, and Christopher Buckley came from political families. John Steinbeck's dad became an elected county official. John Nichols's father worked for the CIA, a first cousin was governor of Massachusetts, and an ancestor was a signer of the Declaration of Independence. Hunter S. Thompson ran for sheriff in Pitkin County, Colorado. Former governor Dick Lamm of Colorado coauthored a novel I discuss later in this book. Many were political journalists or magazine writers. Some emerged from Hollywood screenwriting and publicist backgrounds. Two were speechwriters for top Washington elected officials. Three were Rhodes Scholars. Herman Melville held a low-level patronage job as a New York City customs house inspector, while Joe Nye served as a high-level national security advisor.

Most political novelists have had "box seats" in watching America as it struggled to make constitutional democracy work. They have seen and worked with heroes and scoundrels and the many more complicated players in between. They have seen courage and phoniness, leadership and hypocrisy—and they capture the diverse array of personalities and contradictory realities that shape the American Experiment. They understand, in short, that we are inconsistent, contradictory, and *human*. They understand, too, that even as we love the idea of America, we are prouder of what this country can someday be than of what it has often been.

Writing political fiction is a demanding craft; yet it can occasionally capture the essence of politics and the quintessential American politician, whom Christopher Lehmann once described as an "unstable compound of means and ends, virtues and sins, righteousness and vanity."[9]

MOTIVATIONS

Most of the novelists discussed in this book were implicitly, if not explicitly, motivated by idealism for what America could become. Most write about disappointments or the darker side of the American Dream. Yet almost all of them wanted their country to better understand the past in order to better deal with our challenges. A youthful John Dos Passos wrote that "we must strike once more for freedom, for the sake of the dignity of man," and Thomas Wolfe suggested "the true discovery of America is before us. I think the true fulfillment of our spirit of our people, of our might and immortal land is yet to come."[10]

Ayn Rand wrote novels because her stories would be more readable and effective in getting her readers to value the kind of country she wanted to live in and that she hoped her readers would also want. The purpose, she said, was "to create for myself the kind of world I want, and to live in it while I am creating it; then, as secondary consequences, to let others enjoy this world, if, and to the extent that they can."[11]

Toni Morrison dedicates her prize-winning *Beloved* to the "Sixty Million and more" Africans and their descendants who died as a result of the Atlantic slave-trade crossing. Her storytelling was aimed at making sure African Americans did not forget their story, their wretched treatment, and how they coped with what she called the "unspeakable unspokens" and others have called America's "original sin."

What motivates political novelists? Most writers, including political novelists, write because it is fulfilling and because it gives them a "buzz." Most writers also have to earn a living. Hence, they learn how to attract readers—paying customers. "I wrote [*The Monkey Wrench Gang*] for the money," admitted Edward Abbey. "But I also hope there's art in it." He also bluntly told a *New York Times* reporter, "All serious writers want to make money. All writers want to be famous. All writers want to make love to beautiful women."[12]

Abbey also said that he wrote to entertain his friends and to exasperate those in authority: "I write to record the truth of our time as best I can see it. To investigate the comedy and tragedy of human relationships. To oppose, resist, and sabotage the contemporary drift toward a global tech-nocratic police state."[13]

Novelists such as Gore Vidal and Christopher Buckley captured read-ers through satirical stories. Harriet Beecher Stowe and Helen Hunt Jackson wrote heart-wrenching sentimental stories, but they, like John Steinbeck, John Nichols, and Isabel Allende after them, intentionally wrote fiction aimed at encouraging people to understand and love one another more.

Some novelists, such as Upton Sinclair, Helen Hunt Jackson, Toni Morrison, Robert Penn Warren, and Richard Wright, force us to remem-ber the past, no matter how disturbing it may be, because understanding and assessing the past, they believed, leads us to a more humane and en-lightened future. The function of the writer is to confront, reveal, unmask, unpack, and explain reality.

Novelists write to share the truth of what they have learned and what they have observed. Many novelists insist that political mistakes and corruption be honestly recounted. Stowe and Sinclair wrote "purpose novels" intending to change the way their fellow citizens thought about slavery and worker exploitation. Novelists Rand, Heller, and Abbey wrote to warn readers about sclerotic bureaucracies, misguided national planners, and threats to freedom.

Jack London, John Dos Passos, John Steinbeck, Richard Wright, and Hunter S. Thompson wrote to alert Americans to the shortcomings and illusions of the Horatio Alger mythology. Nathanael West, Sinclair Lewis, and Philip Roth wrote to jar people from complacency and to alert readers to the possibilities and horrors of fascism.

Protest novels are written because, in George Orwell's words, authors have a "desire to push the world in a certain direction" and want to portray a more just or ideal society. Orwell, who wrote *1984* and *Animal Farm*, among other works, explains how his early experience "forced" him into becoming "a sort of pamphleteer." His first job was as an Indian Imperial policeman in Burma, and he witnessed excruciating exploitation and imperialism. He next became poor and despondent, and then, he says, came Hitler, Franco, and fascism of every kind. Hence, "Every line of serious work I have written since 1936 has been written, directly or indirectly, against totalitarianism and for democratic socialism. . . . It seems to me nonsense, in a period like our own, to think that one can avoid writing of such subjects."[14]

Stowe wrote *Uncle Tom's Cabin* because she had seen the brutal deg-radation of the American black family. She was indignant and sufficiently outraged, especially at the Fugitive Slave Act, to write her protest novel.

Dos Passos and Steinbeck wrote what are called proletarian novels, works that celebrated workers and the dispossessed. They wanted "to tell truth to power" and to stir up public sentiment for either socialism or a new, more just and compassionate political system.

Joseph Heller in *Catch-22* (1961) and Kurt Vonnegut in *Slaughterhouse-Five* (1969) wrote to help us understand the mindlessness and horror of war. Ray Bradbury wrote *Fahrenheit 451* because he had read Arthur Koestler's *Darkness at Noon* and understood that to burn books was to burn authors, and to exterminate authors was to deny our own humanity. "Who, if not writers, are to condemn their own unsuccessful governments," wrote Aleksandr Solzhenitsyn. "In the struggle against lies, art has always won and always will. Conspicuously, incontestably for everyone."[15]

Novelist Ayn Rand says she wrote *The Fountainhead* (1943) and *Atlas Shrugged* (1957) because she was appalled at the diminution of freedom under an increasingly planned and overregulated national government. Her motive, Rand explained, was to celebrate creative, liberty-loving entrepreneurs such as Howard Roark and John Galt as ideal human beings. They were protagonists and heroes and moral examples for showing what is possible. "It is those few that move the world and give life its meaning—and it is those few that I have always sought to address."[16]

Edward Abbey wrote his spirited *The Monkey Wrench Gang* to inspire and mobilize environmental warriors to take to the barricades to halt the degradation of his beloved Southwest. He gleefully accepts his role as an agitator, and his fiction and nonfiction are intentionally indignant and political. Abbey saw himself as a Paul Revere–Thomas Paine warrior against tyranny and for preserving his cherished Southwestern wilderness. His is an almost fanatical plea:

> The wilderness should be preserved for political reasons. We may need it someday not only as a refuge from excessive industrialism but also as a refuge from authoritarian government, from political oppression. Grand Canyon, Big Bend, Yellowstone and the High Sierras may be required to function as bases for guerrilla warfare against tyranny. What reason have we Americans to think that our society will necessarily escape the world-wide drift toward totalitarian organization of men and institutions?[17]

Richard Condon's *The Manchurian Candidate* deals with political tyranny as well, and captures the political paranoia of the 1950s as vividly or more than nonfiction treatments.

Melville wrote *Billy Budd* because he felt compelled both to explain the "back story" about the legend of Billy Budd and to educate us about the hard choices leaders have to make as they try to navigate the eternal contradictions of good and evil. Melville appreciated the paradoxical nature of leadership and bureaucracies. He understood that we live in an insolubly dialectic world. Leaders, Melville wanted his reader to learn, are frequently caught between "apparently external and autonomous opposites such as good and evil, heaven and hell, God and Satan, head and heart, spirit and matter."[18]

Some novelists acknowledge a spiritual or ideological calling to save the world or redeem the American Dream. Stowe, Sinclair, and Steinbeck are illustrative. They are motivated to tell their stories because without their work there is no moral compass, and perhaps no tribe.

Morrison, in the foreword to *Beloved*, writes, "I wanted the reader to be kidnapped, thrown ruthlessly into an alien environment as the first step into a shared experience with the book's population—just as the characters were snatched from one place to another, from any place to any other, without preparation of defense."[19]

Most of these novelists were motivated to encourage readers to support altruistic causes and politicians, to explain the often hard and temptation-strewn challenges politicians have to deal with, and to understand the inevitability of conflicting interests that characterize American political culture. Novelists don't go into detail about these conflicts. But novelists understand that, although most Americans are proud of Washington, Lincoln, the Roosevelts, and other American icons, they simultaneously view politics as a tawdry, tricky, and dishonest profession.

American attitudes, novelists appreciate, are a paradoxical tangle of pride in good old "American exceptionalism" along with a feisty belief in the motto: "Go Fight City Hall."

THE NOVELIST LENS

Novelists invariably need a dilemma or a conflict to fuel a plot. Protagonists get imagined, and we are sucked in as we follow their efforts to navigate the challenges of surviving, prospering, or stumbling.

A common theme in American fiction is about how greed and private interests are too often put ahead of the public interest. Political novelists often view themselves as akin to investigative reporters, detectives, or even as a shadow or opposition government.

Most writers embrace the challenge, to paraphrase Aleksandr Solzhenitsyn's Nobel Prize speech, to sense more keenly than the rest of us the beauty and harmony of the world and the harm people and governments have done to it, and poignantly let their readers know.[20]

Hemingway once told an interviewer that a writer without a sense of justice would be better off editing the yearbook of a school for exceptional children than writing fiction. "The most essential gift for a good writer is a built-in shockproof shit detector. This is the writer's radar and all great writers have it."[21]

The American political novel may be primarily written to entertain us; yet, with Emerson, good writers want to be renouncers of lies, restorers of truths, and undaunted advocates of what communities, and the nation, ideally might become.

They remind us that people are a mixture of good and bad—that's part of the human condition. Novelists do not give us perfect politicians, because perfect politicians do not exist. Nor do they give us perfect citizens. Things are, novelists remind us, complicated and, in politics, the shortest distance between two points is seldom a straight line.

Novelists can bring politics alive and make us more intrigued with (if not necessarily approving of) the political profession. Novelists make us understand that truth wears many masks. Yes, there are shady rogues and bribes, blackmail and hypocrisy, but there are also Huck Finns and Atticus Finches, Arthur Fenstemakers, Ruby Archuletas, Guy Montags, soldiers like Joshua Lawrence Chamberlain and Colonel Martin Casey, and young attorneys like Arthur Vane who inspire us to make the American Experiment work.

Novelists have a special gift of making us imagine the emotional states of their characters, and this makes it easier to identify with the characters and the challenge of public problem solving.

Novelists, in common with screenwriters, are drawn to writing about conflict rather than collaboration. They usually concentrate on portraying a few central figures, and can seldom do justice to the crucial role social and political movements play in bringing about change. And rarely do novelists treat or explain the degrading "money chase" politicians have to master to win political office. Further, few novelists capture the importance and complexity of regulatory or bureaucratic politics that are now such a part of the modern state.

Readers generally appreciate that novelists, in common with film-makers, embellish and distort historical events or known people to make their narratives work. Part of this is necessary to entertain us. Part of this is necessary to highlight and condense. Social scientists want evidence, facts, and footnotes. Novelists give us moods, imagination, speculation, and intrigue. Novels, like films, are not the best medium for facts. Moreover, as Federico Garcia Lorca noted, "At the heart of all the great art is an essential melancholy."

American literature is full of stories that invite counterstories. For every Horatio Alger story that celebrates hard work, sincerity, and rags-to-respectability legends, there are works by Upton Sinclair, John Dos Passos, John Steinbeck, Richard Wright, and Hunter Thompson that share alternative narratives. Ayn Rand wrote to refute the Jack Londons, Edward Bellamys, and Upton Sinclairs, along with the allure and threat of idealized Communist theory.

BIASES AND PERSPECTIVES

The hardest part of designing this book was choosing which novels to include. Several thousand novels have been written about American politics. My sample had to be selective. I wanted to examine celebrated political novels, but I also wanted to explore lesser-known and neglected novels that help us understand politics at different levels of government, in different branches, in different regions, and at the distinctive phases of politics.

Literary merit was secondary to novels that helped readers understand the realities and complexity of politics. My bias was to discuss novels that remind us that governing and societal leadership in America can be monstrously hard—and that governing invariably involves imperfect leaders, imperfect followers, and imperfect political structures constantly striving to adapt to change and to help Americans live up to lofty aspirations. I also had a bias for novels that were fun to read, either because the authors give us compelling, memorable characters or because the plot was suspenseful and politically telling.

Another bias is that I believe politics in America, and everywhere, is inevitable, necessary, and desirable, and that politicians—elected and unelected—are the indispensable horse traders, coalition builders, and agreement negotiators we recruit to keep our sprawling and pluralistic society functioning.

Here are a few themes that guided my reading and that emerged from re-reading and comparing these works in an effort to discern larger enduring American narratives:

1. American political novels, it is said, age poorly. This is sometimes true, and inevitably novels—or at least most—become period pieces. Yet a political reading of the novels selected helps illuminate the politics of earlier eras, and they collectively remind us of the fragility and growing pains of our efforts in constitutional democracy. They also remind us that defining the public interest or the public good is a challenge. The problem is that there is seldom just one public. Novelists help us understand that politics is sometimes a clash between right and right, that sometimes what is good or right comes from people who are only partly right, and perhaps from people who are not necessarily good. Further, sometimes what we as a society want to do in the short run is not necessarily what should be done for the public good in the long term.

2. American political novels, as a group, underscore how hard it is to have "good" politics and bring about artful agreements in a social culture that generally disdains politics and politicians; yet few of the novelists discussed in this book give up on politics. What they yearn for, as all of us do, is for more enlightened political activists and for a citizenry that cannot be gamed by big money, phony zealots, negative campaigns, misused technologies, and deceptive spin masters.

3. Many of these novels jolt us in their detailed exposés of flawed politics or even tragedies. Yet there is often a subtext of optimism or even redemption: that Americans can improve upon their political system and can redeem the promises associated with the Jeffersonian American Experiment.

   Political novels portray flawed politicians and the shortcomings of our political processes; however, they can also serve as a reverse advertisement. "This may be what we get," most seem to be saying, "but we can do better." We should learn, novelists imply, from these stories so we might transcend toxic politics.

   One role of the writer, most of these novelists believe, is to unmask clichés and tropes, to confront duplicity, bullies, fear, and horrors, and help us take stock of these realities.

4. Every tribe has its rituals, its heroes, its villains, and its stories. America, like every tribe, has a complex political culture that is an ensemble of narratives we tell about our past, some of which celebrate people we admire and others that rebuke us for our shortcomings.

History and social scientists record, with some inaccuracy, what Americans have done in the past. However, fiction, writes John Steinbeck, "tells or tries to tell, why they did it and what they felt and were like when they did it."[22]

Further, as noted, most of these novels teach us about the exacting challenges that come with trying to make constitutional democracy live up to its promise. They likewise teach, sometimes indirectly, that we cannot have republics or representative democracy without politics and politicians. The two go together. That's the deal.

ON READING AMERICAN
POLITICS AND AMERICAN NOVELS

Politics is a process of mediating among clashing interests. There are always contending factions—group, ethnic, religious, economic, and regional interests. Factions and partisan divisions are everywhere.

Most of us have a tangled composite of political values. Some are consistent; some are contradictory. For example, we may want national leadership, but we don't want anyone to tell us what to do. We may want a balanced budget but not Social Security and defense spending cuts. We favor liberty *and* equality, free speech *and* religious tolerance, and limited government *yet also* strong national defense (see figure 1.1).

Politics, as writers from Machiavelli to Madison teach us, is about getting power, maintaining it, and using it to manage factions, tensions, and our inevitably conflicting values and dreams. Political leadership, when things work out, helps us reconcile and navigate a multiplicity of contending political aspirations (see table 1.1).

Politics is rarely about achieving perfect justice and more about bringing about a sense of balance, social harmony, and ideally as much progress as is achievable for as many people as possible. Politics, like diplomacy, is typically a long, tedious, and boring process of small steps, adjustments, and compromised incrementalism among these conflicting interests, values, and dreams rather than dramatic *High Noon* or *The Monkey Wrench Gang* confrontations.

Most of us hold overlapping or contradictory political values. That's fine. But it makes it hard for politicians who are trying to be responsive. And it becomes the purpose of politics to reconcile and balance these values to lessen conflict. Figure 1.1 shows how many of our political objectives are in tension with other values. It is hard to rank order these values. Each has its merits. Each has its advocates.

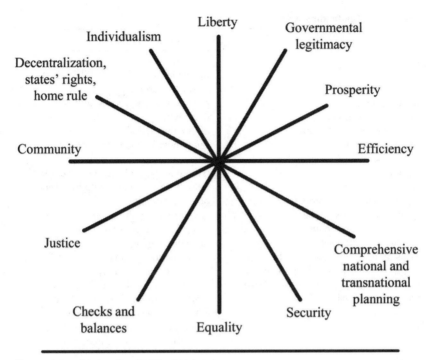

Figure 1.1. Contending Political Values

Similarly, Americans have many variegated dreams. The idea of America is often a composite and umbrella construct for our aspirations. (See table 1.1.) We are raised to respect competing dreams even if we prioritize one over another. Politicians have to function on a reality of dueling values and dreams.

People dislike politics for a number of reasons. We are impatient with all the bickering and with how long it takes to get things done. People also view politicians as having the potential power to manipulate the rules of the game and change, unfairly, how things of value are distributed. The "power games" and the political maneuvering and horse trading appear distasteful and problematic to most people. We also disdain politicians because they are the convenient scapegoats for taxes, regulations, conscription, and perceived or real losses of privacy.

Yet politicians are the people we need to work out acceptable compromises and treaties that keep us from shooting one another. The challenge for them is how to do these tasks in a society that celebrates individualism, privacy, home rule and decentralization, and free-market capitalism and, simultaneously, disdains politics and politicians.

Table 1.1.   Contending American Dreams

The American Way	The American Testament
liberty	equality
freedom	justice for all
rugged individualism	*E pluribus unum*
private property	community, commonwealth
limited government	progressive taxation
achievement, merit, excellence	affirmative action
survival of the fittest	safety nets for the vulnerable
"leave me alone"	generosity
republic	participatory, inclusive civic culture
reward the work ethic	help those who can't help themselves
representative government	political equality
government by expertise	government by the people
American exceptionalism	American realism/pragmatism
unfettered capitalism	regulated capitalism
"This land became great not by what government did for the people but what the people did for themselves."	"America must educate every individual to his or her capacity, eliminating ignorance, prejudice, hate and the
"Anyone can make it if they work hard enough!"	squalor in which crime is bred. We must also protect against the economic catastrophe of illness, disability, and unemployment."

POLITICS AND THE CHALLENGE OF NARRATIVE

One of the toughest challenges for American politicians is to devise an appealing personal narrative. It can be a liability if they are too wooden, too insincere, and too inclined to get us into war. The politician's greatest task is to make us think he or she is like us, and will listen to us, hear us, and understand our story. We are raised to admire "Honest Abe" and our founding president who supposedly could not tell a lie. We like fresh faces; yet, simultaneously, we don't want to risk our communities or nation with people who don't know how to manage and lead.

An enduring paradox in democracies is that we yearn for "leaders" but not politicians. But any would-be political leader must first be a politician who can win elections. Americans conveniently forget that their favorite presidents were also politicians.

We expect politicians to represent interests and to protect and promote our interests. We also want politicians to educate us. Listen to us, but paradoxically also lead us. Act on behalf of our immediate self-interest; yet also act on behalf of what will be best for us. Call on us to make sacrifices, we seem to say, but only when this is urgent.

Everyone who has seen Jimmy Stewart's iconic performance in the movie *Mr. Smith Goes to Washington* understands that patriotism and a sense of wanting to make history can be a call to public service. Would-be politicians believe they can help people, solve community problems, and enrich the quality of life for people in "their tribes." Compassion and an earnest do-gooder attitude are usually involved in motivating any politician.

Political activists and politicians come in all shapes, sizes, and with a distinctive agenda. Each has to reframe themselves and invent their own distinctive political narrative. Below is a framework for helping to differentiate and understand the varied roles political activists perform in the American system.

A FRAMEWORK FOR UNDERSTANDING "POLITICIANS"

It is useful to consider as politicians those who traffic in political ideas and are involved in political change as well as those who run elections and hold elected positions. Political ideas and calls for political change come from a variety of places. They typically go through a series of iterations before becoming embraced by pluralities, majorities, and elected officials.

I like to imagine that political ideas are generated, incubated, and parented by a heterogeneous variety of politically minded agents, by what might be called "off-Broadway" or even "off-off-Broadway" players before moving to the big theater.

Policy change typically requires political leadership or brokerage in at least three phases: ideas are often formulated, invented, or parented in Act I. In Act II, they are refined and amended, and support for the ideas is mobilized. In Act III, power brokers attentive to changing attitudes modify emerging proposals still further. Act II agents likely water down the ideas to make them acceptable to majorities, and, gradually, the ideas generated in Act I and lobbied for in Act II get enacted and eventually implemented. Civil rights, women's suffrage, and health care insurance for the poor are examples of issues that painstakingly progressed through these stages or acts.

Russian playwright Anton Chekhov suggests that playgoers should take note of whether there is a gun on a theater set's wall in Act I. If there is a gun up there in Act I, he suggests, it is likely to go off in Act III. It's like the old adage that where there is smoke, there is probably fire. Similarly, people who want to understand politics should look as much (if not more) to the possible guns and smoke and the early stages of political change as to the talk and action of *Meet the Press* political celebrities.

Table 1.2. Framework for American "Politicians," Broadly Defined

Act I	Act II	Act III
Agitators, disrupters	Consciousness raisers	Power brokers
Rebels, dissidents	Coalition builders	Office holders
Crowd gatherers	Alliance educators	Elected officials
Inventors, idea people	Lobbyists, mobilizers	Government advisors
Policy prophets	Policy advocates	Policy announcers
Movement founders	Movement organizers	Political party leaders

Major political change and innovative policies seldom spring fully formed from those in high political office. Politicians are nudged, if not pressured, by grassroots movements and dissidents to consider new ideas. This has repeatedly been the case in American public policymaking. Dissatisfied colonials over a ten-to-twenty-year period sparked the American Revolution. Change was also sparked by abolitionists, environmentalists, tax-reforming libertarians, and civil and gay rights movements. Change typically comes up through the citizenry rather than down from the elites.

In the American Revolutionary period, it was grassroots activists in central Massachusetts and then people like Sam Adams, Patrick Henry, and Thomas Paine who saw the need for change, agitated, and rebelled in what I call classic Act I behavior. They initially resisted British taxes and regulations. Farmers like George Washington fumed over excessive regulations on their crops and their trade. Then they gathered in crowds, gave impassioned speeches, and stirred things up as they performed an indispensable catalytic role in igniting the Revolution.

The talents needed in Act I political activities are different from those required in implementing a cause or governing, and, later on, protecting policy gains. Agitation and mobilization necessarily give way to more traditional leaders (in the case of the American Revolution, to the Washingtons and Jeffersons) and later to those who build the foundations for the new world order (in the case of the American Revolution, to Alexander Hamilton, John Adams, and James Madison).[23]

ACT I POLITICIANS

Historians sometimes suggest there is a "crank" theory of political change, implying that it is the cranks, disrupters, or even outcasts on the fringe who come up with novel ideas that mainstream officials are slow to embrace.

Such cranks, rebels, or rogues are unburdened with "conventional wisdom"; they dream of what ought to be and gleefully ignore pragmatism.

Act I people often exist, at least initially, in leaderless groups. They promote visions and challenge prevailing norms. Act I folks prod fellow citizens to live up to ideals of freedom, equality, and social justice for all. They often celebrate integrity, community, and authenticity. Act I actors see themselves as the renouncers of lies and the restorers of truth. For example, NSA contractor Edward Snowden intentionally broke laws to reveal what he deemed pernicious invasions of privacy in the name of national security.

In the case of the nineteenth-century civil rights movement, Act I leaders were devout abolitionists who believed everyone deserved equal rights under the law, regardless of their race or gender. William Lloyd Garrison and Wendell Phillips were not running for office. They wrote and lectured to change public attitudes. Garrison was a scourge and conscience of his generation.

Act I activists often operate in ways the majority considers reckless. John Brown at Harpers Ferry was considered a fanatic. Physician Jack Kevorkian, an early champion of physician-assisted suicide, was jailed for a decade for political beliefs that were in advance of his time. Early suffragettes chained themselves to the White House fence or were arrested as they illegally voted, and many were jailed. Extreme environmentalists are often considered vandals and terrorists. Tea Party activists are readily dismissed.

Still, many social, economic, and political breakthroughs have welled up from Act I policy heretics or "prophets" before they receive serious attention in the more accepted Act II stages of political and policy evolution. Act I "stirrer-uppers" are often the people who trigger the debates over what public policies should become.

In sum, Act I political agents are dissidents, crowd gatherers, rebels, and disrupters. They are gadflies like Socrates, idealists like Gandhi, mavericks like Thomas Paine, and prickly agitators like Malcolm X and members of the Boston Tea Party (especially as the latter were viewed from London).

ACT II POLITICIANS

Act II political agents understand the principles and goals that Act I people espouse; yet they modify these ideas in ways that will broaden the base. They are organizers, mobilizers, activist lobbyists, preachers, or teachers with an interest in articulation policy objectives.

Susan B. Anthony, Martin Luther King Jr., and even U2's Bono are Act II politicians. They are alliance builders who rally people to a policy cause. They build and bring pressure on elected officials. They bring people together in anticipation of what their country could and should be.

Their goals are seldom accomplished in short periods. Abolitionists became involved in a two-generation campaign. Suffragettes waged even a longer struggle. Libertarians know theirs is a long-term effort. Climate-change reformers likewise know that easy and early victories are unlikely. Act II politicos seek to educate the public and to raise consciousness by arguing the validity of an idea, no matter how long it will take.

Rachel Carson's *Silent Spring* educated millions of readers about the need to use agricultural chemicals with greater caution. After her consciousness-raising classic was published, she faced an outburst of public reaction and an especially harsh backlash from chemical companies. But she quietly stood by her findings, and as Harriet Beecher Stowe had done a century earlier, her classic helped fuel grassroots political change.

Act II "politicians" seldom run for political office; they seek to change the thinking of officials and electorates. One exception was U.S. senator Bernie Sanders, who, while he did serve as a mayor, a member of Congress, and a presidential candidate, portrayed himself as a radical populist advocate for egalitarian policies. The power of Act II types lies in their ability to swell the ranks on behalf of new ideas, new reforms, or new paradigms.

They are pragmatic intermediaries who, though seldom part of the mainstream of the establishment, are nonetheless savvy enough about the way the political system works that they can recruit converts and bring pressure on the system. They can translate fresh approaches and new values into at least tentative legislative or administrative propositions that can be entertained, if not entirely embraced, by top power brokers.

Act II types are coalition builders and consciousness raisers who take the ideas and innovations of Act I types, understand their potential, and make them into viable causes. In the case of the American Revolution, it took military leaders like George Washington and public relations alliance-building geniuses like Thomas Jefferson to put the revolutionary spirit of the disorganized Act I protestors into a galvanized strategic movement that could rally anti-British forces and mobilize them into battle.

Conservative antitax and anti–gun control movements have also had their share of Act II political agents rallying people to their policies. Act II types defy facile left and right labels. Cindy Lightner, who founded Mothers Against Drunk Driving, was initially only an outraged mother whose daughter was killed by a drunk driver. Her Act I impulses were to storm

City Hall and be furious at the lenient prosecutorial system. She learned, however, that organizing thousands of other mothers was the practical way to get heard by elected officials. She became an Act II activist and eventually changed multiple laws at all levels of government, including the national drinking age.

If Act I types can be called cranks, agitators, rebels, and revolutionaries, Act II types are usefully characterized as intermediary catalysts and "evolutionaries."

ACT III POLITICIANS

Act III politicians are pragmatists, adjusters, and incremental fixers (using fixer in its positive sense). They are elected officials, top advisors, and the financial and political power brokers who operate at the center of our political systems.

Act III politicians are typically transactional bargainers. They gauge public and legislative sentiment for what is doable. They are attentive to Act II movements and often refashion and modify Act II agendas in politically achievable or acceptable ways.

Officials performing in Act III are cautious. Their legitimacy depends on electability, and thus they view themselves largely as delegates, as agents on behalf of their parties or the larger general public. They fear being in advance of their time, of being too far out in front. They recognize Act I, and even Act II, activists are primarily motivated by principles and their conscious and by the truth as they see it. In contrast, Act III individuals feel responsibility to what's doable, practical, achievable, and acceptable to broad majorities.

Act III politicians balance and reconcile competing claims about how best to serve the public interest. Leadership, as performed by Act III types, is interpretation. Act III politicos continually read the public pulse. An Act III politician focuses more on relationships with constituents and the gradual and incremental adjustments that need to be made rather than on grand ideas or ideals.

One of the important realities about politics is that a vibrant society needs all kinds of politicians, elected and nonelected, the cautious as well as the dreamy agents of protest and reform. They are needed to perform in a whole variety of scenes and acts that make up the large theater of politics. Context, culture, and institutions matter, but so do "politicians" in all areas and in every stage of public policy development.

My suggested framework and discussion here is not to celebrate political actors in one act as opposed to another. Creativity and leadership can be, and need to be, provided in every act. I also believe the individuals can be hybrids of Act I and II, or of Act II and Act III, or may be an Act I activist on a certain issue but more of a coalition builder or even establishment figure on other issues. Many people change over time as well. Obama, for example, went from being a community organizer to president. George Washington served in the British military before commanding troops against the British. Bernie Sanders was a pragmatic mayor before he became a crusading populist egalitarian.

A TYPOLOGY OF AMERICAN POLITICAL NOVELS

The idea that there are different types of political leadership (Act I, Act II, and Act III) encouraged me to consider that American political novelists can similarly be understood as offering variegated political narratives, some more agitational and others more moral or civic awakening in content. Still others help explain past and present political beliefs, customs, and patterns.

Novelists are generally viewed as left of center in their political views. And most are. But novelists range from being politically radical to conservative libertarians. Some novelists are largely apolitical.

Ernest Hemingway once said writers are often gypsies without a clear allegiance to any party or even nation, though Hemingway himself took sides in the Spanish Civil War. J. D. Salinger apparently told an unwelcome admirer who showed up at his New Hampshire sanctuary's mailbox that he had no advice for the gentleman who was seeking life advice. "I'm a fiction writer, not a counselor," Salinger said in shooing the fellow away.

Salinger might also have said he had no political advice as well and pointed to essays of his, like "Franny," which is mostly about manners and relationships. Yet there are those who contend politics is found everywhere: in families, business, unions, the military, the cultural world, and elsewhere. "Marxists," novelist Mary McCarthy notes, "say that all novels are political, especially those like Jane Austen's that avoid the subject, thus lending tacit support to the status quo."[24] Novelist George Orwell goes even further, arguing that "all issues are political issues" and moreover "politics itself is a mass of lies, evasions, folly, hatred and schizophrenia."[25] Take that!

My interest is in the space between "everything is political" and "I couldn't care less about politics—I'm only a fiction writer." Political and economic ideas often arise in good fiction. But as Robert Penn Warren correctly warns, "The economic and political men are not the complete man and other concerns may still be important enough to engage worthily the attention of a writer—such concerns as love, death, courage, the point of honor, and the moral scruple."[26] Much of Hawthorne, Hemingway, Fitzgerald, Joseph Conrad, and Henry James, for example, are about people learning to live with themselves, with defining themselves, and are not directly preoccupied with politics and political ideas.

The novels treated in this book are works written by American authors consciously trying to tell us about our politics and the idea and ideals of America. They write to help us understand who it is that we are and who it is that we might become. These novelists write because there is a lie, myth, or fraud they want to expose or a story they feel compelled to share, even if it's also true that most of these authors also wanted to produce a work of art.

Singer-composer Bruce Springsteen spoke to this muse: "I was very conscious of being an American musician and addressing the issues of the day," said Springsteen. "There was a sense that the flag was up for grabs [he is referring especially to the post-Vietnam 1970s and 1980s], that you had to stake your claim to its meaning and to the kind of country you wanted your kids to grow up in."[27] His "Born in the USA" and "Ghost of Tom Joad" are examples of his desire to connect with American history and be among those who, like Woody Guthrie, Bob Dylan, and John Steinbeck, were unafraid of treating American political ideas and history in their art.

Political novelists are political storytellers with a purpose. They write about an America they know, but in most cases they are also writing about and imagining an America that is an unfinished project. The American Experiment, most seem to be telling us, is just this: an experiment is not a guaranteed product—it has to be reinvented and revitalized on a regular basis.

Steinbeck visited Russia on at least three occasions. He read Russian history and tried to understand its politics. But he allowed that "I could not have had access to Russian thinking" unless he had also read Dostoevsky, Tolstoy, Chekhov, Pushkin, Turgenev, and others.[28] Similarly, to understand the American mind and American politics requires a reading of our great essayists and poets such as Thoreau, Emerson, and Whitman, watching notable films such as *Citizen Kane, Dr. Strangelove, 12 Angry Men, Mr. Smith Goes to Washington,* and *The Fog of War,* and reading novels such as those discussed in this book.

Harriet Beecher Stowe, Upton Sinclair, and Richard Wright were Act I novelists. They had a cause. They wanted to challenge America to live up to its aspirational creed. Novelists Ayn Rand and Edward Abbey wrote novels celebrating Act I political activists. Novelists Hamlin Garland, Winston Churchill, and John Nichols wrote novels celebrating Act II organizers and change makers. Novelists Billy Lee Brammer, Allen Drury, Fletcher Knebel, and Charles W. Bailey wrote to celebrate Act III politicians, those in the political arena trying to make political systems work. Joe Klein's *Primary Colors* similarly depicts an Act III politico engaged in a messy pragmatic election campaign for the White House.

Most novels can be analyzed along the spectrum of Act I to Act III political agency. Similarly, they can be viewed along a spectrum of agitation to acceptance, and as moralizing about how we should act to merely reporting human nature as it is.

Novelists who write as agitators are provocateurs and rebels. They have a distinctive cause and propose in their novels' clear-cut solutions. Other novelists are more detached observers, functioning as anthropologists explaining a foreign culture. These novelists show us the intricate interconnections in a political culture, suggesting crunchy questions about politics and political leadership. Other political novelists are consciousness raisers, less confrontational and less certain about solutions than the agitators. These authors bring to life both sides of an issue and make us aware of the roots of conflict. Still other political novelists write as satirists, poking fun at the foibles and weaknesses of politicians, making us laugh but at the same time sending a message about things that are not working.

Many political novels are blends of these pure types. For example, a novel may be agitational while using satire to make its point. This is the case in Sinclair Lewis's *It Can't Happen Here*, Edward Abbey's *The Monkey Wrench Gang*, and Ayn Rand's *Atlas Shrugged*. Political novels may also be satirical and make us laugh at politicians, and at ourselves, while at the same time bringing to light important problems, as observed in Richard Condon's *The Manchurian Candidate* and Nathanael West's *A Cool Million*. Political novelists may be storytellers first, conscious of the entertainment value of their work, but, as noted above, most also care about larger purposes—trying to end prejudice, corruption, favoritism, small-mindedness, or demagoguery.

Gone with the Wind similarly defies easy categorization. It is a panoramic historical romance; yet it is also an epic narrative about a distinctive people and place caught up in the tumultuous swirl of war, anguish, slavery, and clashing political values. It is part Tolstoyan and part Homeric. Although Margaret Mitchell may not have intended her work as a political novel, it regularly addresses political choices, ideologies, and local and national political conflict. Moreover, racial politics is a constant backstory.

Table 1.3. Illustrative Types of Political Novels

Agitators	Consciousness Raisers	Satirists	Anthropologists
Protest novel	Reform novel	Parody	Reflection novel
Proletarian novel	Anticorruption novel	Lampooning	Inside stories
Libertarian novel	Social and civic awakening novel	Ridicule	Explanatory novel
Proanarchy novel	Investigative reporting novel	Mockery	Remembrance novel
"Paul Revere" novel		Sardonic	Novel on the paradoxes of politics and leadership
Moral awakening novel			

Note: This framework, or typology, can also serve, to an extent, as a spectrum, where those on the left have more answers than questions and those on the right side of this ledger are preoccupied with political dilemmas, paradox, and questions. More heroes or would-be heroes are suggested on the left and more complexity and enigma on the right.

So how can it not be, among other things, including nostalgic memories of antebellum southern society, read as a political novel as well?

THE NOVELIST AS POLITICAL AGITATOR

This is the easiest fictional genre to identify. Authors of agitational novels address a specific political failing. They raise questions; yet they also suggest answers. They have an agenda. They point to what needs fixing. They call for action, new attitudes, new policies, changed times, and a spirit of insurgency.

Thus, Harriet Beecher Stowe writes that the Fugitive Slave Act of 1850 was wrong and that slavery must be ended. Hers is a book aimed at rallying people, especially Protestant women, to the abolitionist cause. She seeks to tug on her readers' hearts and wants dramatic, not gradual, change.

Upton Sinclair's *The Jungle* is both a proletarian and an indignation novel. How can we treat our most vulnerable people so miserably? How can we proclaim life, liberty, and equal justice for all and exploit people the way the meatpackers and Chicago political elites were doing? He writes not only to enlist support for better regulations but also to shame Americans into recognizing that this unfairness was a by-product of our existing economic values. He is an unabashed proselytizer for socialism.

Steinbeck's *The Grapes of Wrath*, like most agitational novels, telegraphs what is right and especially what is wrong. It preaches. It urges its readers, and all of America, to consider restructuring the political and economic system. And it sympathetically portrays a protagonist who has tried to follow the rules and work hard but, in despair, turns to violent resistance to the system.

Richard Wright challenges readers to understand the dehumanizing racism that makes a mockery of the American Dream. His *Native Son* is an example of both brutal realism and a call for radical political change.

Ayn Rand's *The Fountainhead* and *Atlas Shrugged* are agitational in a different way. Her novels are calls for resistance to what she regards as an increasingly oppressive Socialist-leaning national government, and a call to arms—a call to the barricades.

Edward Abbey's *The Monkey Wrench Gang* celebrates libertarianism similar to that of Ayn Rand's, although from a different ideological direction. Abbey's novel is a vigorous defense of individualism and, at times, even anarchy.

Rand, Abbey, Stowe, Sinclair, Wright, and fellow agitational novelists write with an authorial confidence of what needs to be done. They are interested in not only exploring the problem but also pulling us out of complacency and pushing us to an overhaul—often a radical overhaul—of the existing system.

Readers of political novels should seldom expect objectivity, detailed documentary references, or intellectually refined, analytical expositions in such novels. This is especially true of the novelist as political agitator. They are on a mission. They deliberately disturb the peace. They intentionally want to stir things up, agitate, protest, and preach.

Unlike J. D. Salinger, who, as noted, claimed he was merely a fiction writer, "not a counselor," agitational fiction writers might respond, "Yes, I'm a fiction writer—but contemporary political and social practices are unacceptable. Things have to change—and here's what must be done."

THE NOVELIST AS POLITICAL CONSCIOUSNESS RAISER

Consciousness-raising novels are a common type of political novel. The novels identify the defects in the political system—bribery, spoils, over-the-top lobbying and manipulation, prejudice, greed, deal making, pay-to-play politics, and other forms of favoritism. But these novelists want readers to understand both the complexities and the quandaries of the issue. Consciousness-raising novelists can be reformers and civics teachers.

Consciousness raisers, especially when compared to the agitational novelists, tend to have more questions than answers. And they favor remedial reforms such as civil service laws and electoral and judiciary improvements as opposed to the agitators' call to arms.

Henry Adams's *Democracy* is a prime example of consciousness raising. He uses his protagonist, Mrs. Madeleine Lee, to get "to the heart of the great American mystery of democracy and government. Is government by the people possible? Is American government an improvement on governance elsewhere?" Mrs. Lee finds, Adams relates, that America had most of the failings of other governments as well as a number of its own. The idealistic Adams laments that too many well-educated people remain aloof from the business of government. He also bemoans the kickback or pay-to-play system.

If Adams "exaggerated some facts, or over-emphasized others, he has done so," writes Morris Speare, "to make certain that he has driven an essential truth home."[29] Namely, that Americans needed to reaffirm their commitment to the American political experiment. America needed to elect better people. America needs better procedures, like civil service reform, to safeguard the integrity of the constitutional experiment. Adams is still a believer. He shares his hopes in the words of one of his secondary characters: "I believe in Democracy. I accept it. I will faithfully serve and defend it. I grant it is an experiment, but it is the only direction society can take that is worth taking."

Harper Lee's best-selling *To Kill a Mockingbird* is another example of consciousness raising. Her moving fictional memoir of her small Alabama hometown tells of two individuals who had been systematically "otherized." One, black sharecropper Tom Robinson, was falsely accused and convicted of raping a young white woman. A second, Boo Radley, was a much-maligned recluse who apparently was housebound by his family for childhood indiscretions or perhaps because of an abusive father.

Lee uses these representational personalities to discuss how important it is to accept one's neighbors' failings while still standing up for one's own values. She also describes how an act of courage can isolate one from the rest of a community. *Mockingbird* is a call for a more tolerant, more accepting, and more inclusive society.

David Guterson's *Snow Falling on Cedars* (1994) is yet another consciousness-raising meditation on the nature of pride and prejudice and the need for greater tolerance and communitarian understanding. Lee and Guterson are storytellers first, yet moralists as well. They encourage us to transcend racism and xenophobia and understand our mutual obligations to one another as fellow human beings.

Best-selling novelist John Grisham offers us a straightforward "good guys" versus "bad guys" scenario in *The Appeal*, as he does in a number of his other novels, such as *The Rainmaker*. However, his goal was to get his readers to understand state judicial elections and the consequences of the antiquated way nearly half of the states still elect state Supreme Court justices. He identifies a problem, discusses it in colorful detail, and outlines logical political reforms. Grisham, like most consciousness raisers, concludes: It does not have to be this way.

John Nichols's *The Milagro Beanfield War* is an example of the political novelist as consciousness raiser, satirist, and political anthropologist, with a good dose of agitational spirit thrown in. It was, along with *The Manchurian Candidate*, one of the most difficult of these novels to categorize. Nichols offers entertaining and satirical portraits of local rogues, a county sheriff, and a malevolent land developer. His capturing of the local Milagro Hispanic cultural community rivals that of cultural classics like *Village in the Vaucluse*, *Middletown*, or Clifford Geertz's South Asian anthropological surveys.

But *The Milagro Beanfield War* also raises important questions about our political system. How do marginalized people participate in our political system? How do the poor get heard? What type of political organizing and local protest is needed to retaliate against corrupt deal making that businesses and political elites often get away with? Nichols does not explicitly promote a political reform agenda, but his story (which has a temporary happy ending) points to stark deficiencies in the way politics is done at state and local levels.

Another novel that defies easy classification is Robert Penn Warren's *All the King's Men*. It forces the reader to see how political power can intoxicate. It shows what happens when normal checks and balances don't work as well as intended, and it raises more questions than it offers answers. Profiling the ragged edges and rough tactics of hardball politics, Penn Warren asks whether it takes unscrupulous methods to get good programs enacted. His novel revisits the icy political realism made famous in Machiavelli's *The Prince*; yet it also suggests the troubling allure of toxic leaders. Warren masterfully describes Louisiana politics in the 1930s with a special emphasis on personalities and ideological clashes. His fictionalized populist governor, Willy Stark, mobilizes the underclass and then proceeds to blackmail entrenched business and political elites to do business with him. This is politics as transactional and quid pro quo dealing.

King's Men is also about political overreach and ego. Warren shows vividly how political leadership—the life of politics—is attractive and exhilarating. But we also see that even if political power is used to make good things happen, it can simultaneously dehumanize and degrade the person who wields it.

Consciousness raisers may write with political purpose, but their métier is complexity—and perplexity. Novelists, says the British writer George Orwell, are often driven "by some demon whom one can never resist nor understand." He adds that for him, writing a novel "is a horrible, exhausting struggle, like a long bout of some painful illness."

But even if there are no sure answers or magical policy solutions, consciousness raisers share political spirit and purpose. Again, Orwell explains, "I see that it is irrevocably where I lacked political purpose that I wrote lifeless books and was betrayed into purple passages, sentences without meaning, decorative adjectives and humbug generally."[30]

THE NOVELIST AS POLITICAL SATIRIST

Contemporary novelist and social commentator Christopher Buckley is a raucously funny political satirist. In his laugh-out-loud political novel *Supreme Courtship*, he takes on the U.S. Senate and its pretentious confirmation hearings. His novel is especially snarky in its roasting of former U.S. senator Joe Biden, who, in this semi–*roman à clef*, serves as a pompous, loquacious chairman of the U.S. Senate Judiciary Committee.

The novel is entertaining; yet it has a mission. Buckley lampoons pretentious and self-righteous legislators and justices, but he also suggests that the American system of presidential-congressional separation of powers may be dysfunctional.

Gore Vidal's *Washington, D.C.* ridicules the rise of a John F. Kennedy–like U.S. senator who positions himself to run for the presidency. Vidal makes us laugh at how we do politics, but he also raises important questions about the deal making that characterizes presidential politics in the mid-twentieth century.

Mark Twain, Henry Adams, and Richard Condon are among the many novelists who take on power wielders and politicos. When it comes to the powerful and political leaders, Twain once wrote, "The human race has one really effective weapon"—and that is laughter. "Against the assault of laughter, nothing can stand." Twain may have been only partly right. But bringing down the high and mighty has been an age-old pastime, and American political novelists have enriched this tradition.[31]

Political satire pokes fun at our political customs. We want honesty, candor, and transparency from our elected officials; yet elected politicians' survival regularly demands discretion, cunning, and occasional vagueness, if not outright dissembling. When politicians fail or dash our unrealistic expectations, we are disappointed and even angry. Political satire is one way to gain a small revenge.

The satirical novelist mocks hypocrisy, the abuse of power, extreme ideologies, and self-importance, and exposes injustices, prejudices, and corruption. Few readers who encounter Edward Abbey, John Nichols, Nathanael West, Richard Condon, Joseph Heller, or Hunter S. Thompson will forget the hilariously drawn characters in these novels—George Hayduke, Joe Mondragón, "Shagpoke" Whipple, Ellie Iselin, Raoul Duke, and John Yossarian.

Yet beneath most of the parody and satire in these novels lurks an unexpressed hope for a better, more enlightened politics; for better, more responsive, and humane bureaucracies; for improved policy outcomes; for justice and equality. Behind these stories is a latent idealism, the belief that the American political experiment can be made to work, and that by recognizing the flaws in our system and transcending selfishness and materialism we might better understand what needs to be fixed.

THE NOVELIST AS POLITICAL ANTHROPOLOGIST

Some of the best American political novels investigate the human dynamics within a particular political arena. Allen Drury, for example, in *Advise and Consent*, takes us behind the curtain and into the private lives, and even bedrooms, of U.S. senators. He describes Senate hearings and floor debates and explores the personal worries, anxieties, and demons that shape how senators and, in turn, the Senate function. Drury does it through fiction, but his novel explores the Senate in fresher and more believable ways than textbooks or biographies are able to do.

Novelists Ward Just and Joe Nye capture the life of Washington power brokers. These novelists are political anthropologists, investigating the fundamental architecture and structure of the tribal customs in American politics. The task of the political anthropologist is to make sense of how people behave in certain environments. Twain did that in his *Adventures of Huckleberry Finn*. Solzhenitsyn does it by describing life in the Soviet gulag. Thoreau did it by describing his solitude away from town.

Political anthropologists, including Herman Melville, Margaret Mitchell, Norman Mailer, Billy Lee Brammer, Michael Shaara, and Joe Klein, penetrate the culture of an institution: a presidential campaign, a large bureaucracy like the CIA or the State Department, a navy warship, a Civil War battle, or a defeated South during Reconstruction.

Unlike novelists as agitators or as consciousness raisers, novelists as political anthropologists explore and dwell more on the irony and paradoxes of politics. They note that we say we are a nation of laws and not of men, but that we conveniently break or at least bend the law when it serves our ends. We celebrate honesty and integrity but accept that deal making and compromise is necessary to serve large public goals.

These anthropologists frequently offer what noted anthropologist Clifford Geertz called "thick descriptions" and "local knowledge."[32] These novelists are less interested in answers than in sharpening questions and picking apart the often-competing factors that motivate politicians and shape public policy.

Herman Melville's *Billy Budd* is an analysis of the difficult choices faced by a leader. Melville understood, as do Mailer, Just, and Klein, that leadership cannot be fully understood or explained: there are always rough edges, always "back stories," always competing interpretations of events. There are many kinds of leadership, and leaders invariably are human and share the same weaknesses and limits of ordinary human beings.

Edwin O'Connor's *The Last Hurrah* is a sympathetic portrait of an aging big-city machine boss. The aging mayor of "Boston" has many flaws; yet he has also done much good for his city. In fact, O'Connor suggests, the mayor's methods may be better than those of his likely alternative. Similarly, Robert Penn Warren's Willie Stark is woefully problematic, but he had noble purposes and was a promising agent for Louisiana's voiceless.

I turn next, in chapter 2, to nine competing narratives that emerge from my political reading of these celebrated American novelists and their rich storytelling.

2

THE TRIBE OF THE EAGLE AND
ITS POLITICAL NARRATIVES

Tribes, cultures, and nations need motivational and inspirational stories. We celebrate pioneers and ancestors distinguished for their noble achievements and character. We admire their spirit and yearn to become like them.

We also need stories about the tests and trials our tribe has endured, and the mistakes that were made. We need these stories so we can learn from them and adapt to the future appropriately.

American fiction writers have provided us with multiple narratives, some celebrating the American political experiment, and many that remind us, sometimes painfully, of the gap between the aspirational idea and ideals of America and reality.

Our notable novels, films, and songs simultaneously depict what we have been and what we might become. An implicit, if not explicit, theme is that we the people and our leaders need to rededicate ourselves to the ideals of a more generous, communitarian, constitutional republic.

Here are a few representative novels, movies, and songs of political instruction and political motivation: *To Kill a Mockingbird, The Jungle, Grapes of Wrath, Killer Angels, Uncle Tom's Cabin, Snow Falling on Cedars, It Can't Happen Here, Ragged Dick, Mr. Smith Goes to Washington, Catch-22, Twelve Angry Men, Ramona, The Milagro Beanfield War, Beloved, Fog of War, Dr. Strangelove,* "The Battle Hymn of the Republic," "We Shall Overcome," "Tom Joad," "This Land Is My Land," "Born in the U.S.A," and "The Star-Spangled Banner."

The American culture is hardly monolithic. It is comprised of multiple and sometimes contrarian themes. We love "up from adversity" and "coming of age" narratives. We are beguiled by Horatio Alger stories of orphaned street urchins who strive to be somebody. We love the Huck

Finn escape story and his coming to terms with who he is and the ultimate American dilemma. We love the freedom theme variously addressed by authors as different as Walt Whitman, Ayn Rand, and Jack Kerouac. And we are mesmerized by the national rebirth and renewal messages in Lincoln's "Gettysburg Address" and Martin Luther King's "I Have a Dream" address.

Americans have a tendency, like people everywhere, to think ours is the best country and the best history mainly or merely because it is our history. As will be discussed, we are often tempted to believe we are the chosen, or "almost chosen," people with a providentially blessed mission to provide the rest of the world an exemplar for achieving freedom, liberty, and equality of opportunity.

Americans and America's founders regularly asked for God's blessings, and many believed God had some role in placing the United States between two great oceans to refute the fatalistic notion that republics, as with Greece and Rome, are destined to fail. Thus the additional aspiration for America to serve as a redeemer nation.

But many American writers remind us that no nation is unique or sacred, and that our continuing efforts to invent a resilient constitutional democracy remain an experiment—one that continually needs more progress.

The American Founders may have been dreamers, but they were also realists: they understood previous republics had floundered and succumbed to corruption, greed, and oligarchy. They were pragmatists who understood human nature and the countless temptations to abuse power and depart from republican virtues.

Historian Arthur M. Schlesinger Jr. reminds us, for example, that the U.S. Constitution was hardly the product of immaculate conception and that the founders were hardly saints. "No people who systematically enslaved black men and killed red men could be innocent . . . No nation founded on invasion, conquest, and slaughter could be innocent." They were defiant optimists as well as pragmatic realists willing to gamble on reinventing the way people could govern themselves.[1]

American storytelling includes writers who talk about America as destiny, as an experiment, and a number who make us laugh at our hypocrisy, our failings, and our inability to live up to our aspirations.

There is no one American Story. Just as we have competing notions of the American Dream we have competing fictional accounts of what has transpired in America. Horatio Alger's America is markedly different from Richard Wright's narrative about Bigger Thomas. Toni Morrison seems to inhabit a different nation than that depicted by Margaret Mitchell in *Gone with the Wind*.

Richard Condon and Robert Penn Warren remind us of the paradoxes of power and the hard challenges of making constitutional democracy work. The fictional accounts by Sinclair Lewis, Nathanael West, Philip Roth, and Fletcher Knebel and Chuck Bailey warn us about the fragility of the American republic.

Mark Twain jokes in his autobiography that "it is the will of God that we must have critics and missionaries and Congressmen and humorists, and we must bear the burden."[2] Yet it is the critics and humorists who are often the most helpful in explaining us to ourselves. Writers such as Twain, along with Joe Klein, Gore Vidal, Christopher Buckley, Joseph Heller, and Hunter S. Thompson, penetrate and puncture our illusions and delusions. Satirists make us laugh because most satire, they remind us, is about important matters.

We love the possibilities and patriotism suggested in *Mr. Smith Goes to Washington* or Michael Shaara's *The Killer Angels* and the rugged individualism celebrated in John Wayne movies and Ayn Rand's celebration of American entrepreneurs.

But we also yearn for stories that help explain our past—both good and bad. Thus *Grapes of Wrath*, *Native Son*, *Ramona*, *Gone with the Wind*, *Snow Falling on Cedars*, and *Killer Angels* have won huge audiences by portraying harsh realities that characterize America's maturation.

Americans also have a penchant for reading the alarm-bell-ringing dystopian fiction that warns of imagined constitutional breakdowns and failures. Nathanael West, Sinclair Lewis, Ray Bradbury, and Philip Roth are just a few of the notable contributors to this American narrative. Their work is often read along with Canadian Margaret Atwood's best-selling *The Handmaid's Tale* and the Brit Aldous Huxley's frightening *Brave New World* and his countryman George Orwell's equally worrying *1984* (published in 1949). Many of these works grew out of the horrors of watching the rise of Stalinism, fascism, emotional nationalism, and nativism.

Many of our stories celebrate the American spirit or the American Dream, but many stories celebrate lawbreaking or "doing bad" on behalf of trying to bring about some greater good. Thus Americans loved the television series *The West Wing*, which celebrates idealistic White House political leadership on behalf of constitutional and progressive ends; yet they also liked a later series, *House of Cards*, which portrays political leaders engaged in lies, manipulation, self-preserving Machiavellian maneuvering, and narcisstocracy rather than acceptable constitutional governance.

We are individualistic, yet sometimes communitarian. We believe in free speech but incline to political correctness if religions, races, or gender are being slighted. We favor political equality and equality before the law; yet we similarly favor a form of capitalism and campaign financing that encourages inequality. We favor privatization, home rule, and decentralization except when we want national security, environmental protection, and the kind of comprehensive planning that will provide for public safety, clean air, clean water, and safe roads and airports. We favor checks and balances and federalism but dislike gridlock and ineffective governmental responses to hurricanes, droughts, epidemics, and disasters. We want to believe that the American Dream and the American spirit are alive and well; yet we are sensitive to, and worried about, policies that seem to be undermining the American Dream.[3]

A close reading of dozens of American political novels suggest at least nine relatively distinctive thematic narratives. Many writers make use of more than one narrative, the better to connect with their readers who have been raised with a fusion rather than a singular American Story.

Most of us, as discussed, share multiple American Dreams and cherish values that sometimes collide with one another. We not infrequently favor some candidates or issues in our hearts and others in our heads. We also change our minds, from time to time, or "evolve" about what should be the top priorities of our nation.

What follows are cluster categories that help us understand most of the enduring narratives developed in American fiction. These will necessarily be presented in broad strokes. They are residual and suggestive and more thematic than explanatory. Collectively, however, they help us understand who we have been, why we are the way we are, and, perhaps also, rekindle our imagination of what we might become.

COMPETING AMERICAN POLITICAL NARRATIVES

1. The "City on a Hill" American Exceptionalism Narrative
2. The America as a Pragmatic Experiment Narrative
3. The "Leave Me Alone" Individualism Narrative
4. The "We Are All in This Together" Communitarian Narrative
5. The "Going Rogue" or Breaking the Law for the Greater Good Narrative
6. The Laughing at Political Hypocrisy and Paranoia Narrative
7. The Dystopian Fear of Authoritarianism and the Collapse of Constitutionalism Narrative

THE "CITY ON A HILL" AMERICAN EXCEPTIONALISM NARRATIVE

A venerable part of the American political belief system, notably for Americans of European heritage, has been the phrase ",we shall be as a City upon a Hill," a paraphrase of Jesus's Sermon on the Mount, borrowed in 1630 by Puritan leader John Winthrop while still aboard the ship *Arbella* headed for Boston.

Winthrop, it seems, was not necessarily boasting that he and fellow Puritans were "chosen" or "blessed" but that the eyes of the world would be closely watching them and their new settlement. Similar colonial communities were floundering; some had disappeared altogether. Theirs would succeed, Winthrop counseled, only if they worked hard, worked together, and had a disciplined, unified spirit.

Winthrop and his fellow Puritans were fleeing the corrupt tyranny of Charles I and saw themselves akin to the children of Israel seeking their own promised land, one that would allow them their religious freedom. They believed they had God's blessing for their moral journey, but, as noted, Winthrop emphasized to his flock that they must do God's work or else be shamed in the eyes of the world. This aspirational coming-to-Boston sermon has been often borrowed, stretched, and metaphorically adopted as an early illustration of the American idea, the American Dream, and America's exceptional pioneering spirit.

Settlers in Boston and elsewhere eventually succeeded in commerce, self-governance, and a newfound independence. Winthrop was right that the world was watching. And there developed over the next century an emerging nationalism that what was going on in these colonial states might, or should, become a model for people elsewhere. This nationalism was at least partly messianic. We will be judged, Winthrop insisted, on how we live our lives and how we would stand tall in service to God as well as to one another. Thus this spiritual and moral belief system became, at least in the eyes of many, the foundational anchor of American exceptionalism.

America's European settlers remained loyal British citizens for several generations. That changed with the Boston Tea Party, Lexington and

Concord, and the American Revolution. That revolution and the aspirational creed outlined in the Declaration of Independence transformed the experimental settlements of John Winthrop and others.

Americans, including Jefferson, repeatedly asked that "God Bless America," and many Americans came to believe that Providence had designated Americans as exceptional people whose government and political ideals could and indeed were obligated to play an unprecedented, if not indispensable, role in world affairs. Many Americans, citing Jefferson, claim that God, not government, granted our rights and liberties. Alabama Supreme Court justice Roy Moore, for example, contends that America was founded on "the God of the holy scriptures."[4]

The phrases *the American Dream* and *American exceptionalism* are twentieth-century creations—yet the central themes that everyone, regardless of circumstances, should be able to make it in America, and that American ideals of freedom, liberty, and justice for all should be a model for the rest of the world, have been evolving over the history of the Republic. In short, most Americans love to view their nation as an exceptionally blessed and exceptionally noble political exemplar for the rest of the world.

It is part of the election script in America that would-be leaders will expand the American Dream of prosperity and equality of opportunity for as many people as possible. Suffrage was extended to non-landowners, to blacks, to women, and to younger people.

Novelist Horatio Alger Jr. (1832–1899) wrote more than a hundred novels celebrating the possibility that determination, hard work, and being mentored by already successful people was an ideal formula for making it in America. Alger's name entered our vocabulary "as a synonym for the country's creed: that no matter how deprived your circumstances, your fate is determined by your attributes and your behavior; not by whatever hardship or injustice the social order imposed."[5]

There are many, too, who believe that the American republic has become both essential and singularly stunning. Inspired by the revolutionary ideal that we are endowed by God with certain inalienable rights, we have become the exemplar of freedom's possibilities. Dick and Liz Cheney claim America has "guaranteed freedom, security, and peace for a larger share of humanity than has any other nation in all of history. There is no other like us. There never has been. We are, as a matter of empirical fact and undeniable history, the greatest source for good the world has ever known."[6]

Alger's novels did not claim that every person would succeed; yet his happy endings for his typically orphaned teenage protagonists telegraphed an optimistic faith in the American political and capitalistic experiment. His message was not, as is often misconstrued, that everyone who strives will go from rags to riches, but that striving and virtue plus luck and mentoring will enable some, and possibly many, young people to overcome what Machiavelli called *fortuna*. Alger wrote from the perspective of one who shared the Jeffersonian and Emersonian faith in the American Experiment. His stories of young people who believed in themselves and developed tenacity in the face of threats and adversity are, in some ways, an allegory for the coming-of-age American political experiment in the tumultuous Gilded Age.[7]

The American idea is that most Americans should be able to make something of themselves and that upward mobility is the ideal. That's why we love the stories of Benjamin Franklin, Alexander Hamilton, Abraham Lincoln, Andrew Carnegie, Booker T. Washington, and, in more recent times, Harry Truman, Ronald Reagan, and Barack Obama. America's favorite novel, *The Adventures of Huckleberry Finn*, is a coming-of-age story about an essentially orphaned youth setting out on a journey of self-discovery, personal growth, and freedom. And the bonus is that he does noble deeds along the way.

Horatio Alger stories were almost entirely about young Caucasian males. Scores of novelists have satirized that type of American Dreamism and the storybook democracy or storybook capitalism it seemed to celebrate. Mark Twain satirized Alger. Nathanael West's *A Cool Million* (1934) was an undisguised parody of Algerism. Richard Wright's *Native Son* (1940) was a bleak rebuke of Alger. Hunter S. Thompson's *Fear and Loathing in Las Vegas* has the subtitle *A Savage Journey to the Heart of the American Dream* (New York: Random House, 1971), and it is a sardonic commentary on American Dreamism. Michael Moore documentaries are more of the same.

Americans want to believe in the American Dream; yet everyone knows that race matters, educational opportunities matter, and that family wealth and the tax code confer advantages on the already privileged.

Contemporary American angst about politics, government, and Wall Street is in good part rooted in a sense that social mobility and equality of opportunity have become stunted. The American Dream, for many, is more elusive than in the past. Many Americans fear upward mobility is more myth than reality.[8]

Moreover, few nations have copied or adopted our constitutional presidential-congressional shared-powers form of democracy. The "Westminster" or British parliamentary system is the preferred model. None have copied our electoral college or convoluted and patchworky presidential nominating procedures.

Notions of American exceptionalism may have also unwittingly encouraged white supremacist doctrine, Manifest Destiny, and an imperial temptation (as in Athens, Rome, and London) regarding territorial expansion and regime change policies. Novelists Harriet Beecher Stowe, Helen Hunt Jackson, and Toni Morrison remind us of our racist past. And novelist Nathaniel Hawthorne, along with other nonfiction writers, remind us that our sometimes sainted Puritan ancestors were a sadly repressive, intolerant crowd.

Still, most Americans want their nation to champion opportunity and equality at home and freedom and liberty abroad. We want to believe America is special and can become an even more just, compassionate example of constitutional self-governance.

A favorite passage in the many novels I have read is Michael Shaara's imagined pep rally talk, which his Colonel Joshua Lawrence Chamberlain gives to fatigued and reluctant soldiers on the eve of the Battle of Gettysburg. Chamberlain tells his Union troops they are fighting for something new, noble, and special. They were fighting to set other people free. "This is free ground," he said as he was positioning his brigade. "All the way from here to the Pacific Ocean."

> No man has to bow. No man is born to royalty. Here we judge you by what you do, not by what your father was. Here you can be something. Here's a place to build a home. It isn't the land—there's always more land. It's the idea that we all have value.

There can be no denying that America has always had an aspirational and semi-messianic narrative that America is blessed not only in physical natural resources and incomparable beauty but also with noble intention about the sacredness of life, liberty, equality, and justice for all.

America has been a remarkable political and economic story. Its Declaration of Independence, Constitution, Bill of Rights, and Gettysburg principles and its many economic inventions and achievements have made it a superpower and magnet for immigrants. Americans are proud of their history—despite its blemishes—because it is their history and their narrative. It is understandably part patriotism, part nationalism, and part Atticus Finch in *To Kill a Mockingbird*, part Joshua Chamberlain in *Killer Angels*, part Jimmy Stewart as U.S. senator Jefferson Smith in *Mr. Smith Goes to Washington*, part Ragged Dick, Luke Larkin, Andy Buck, and Phil the Fiddler in Horatio Alger novels, part John Wayne in *The Searchers* or *The Man Who Shot Liberty Valance*, or at the Alamo or with the Green Berets, or Harrison Ford as president in *Air Force One* or Will Smith in *Independence Day*. Every country yearns for heroes and a narrative that includes optimism, dreams, and aspirational rhetoric.

There are those who are uneasy with or reject the notion of American exceptionalism, yet believe in the proposition that America is not just a vital and even great nation but also an idea. Celebrity Irish U2 singer Bono notes, "Ireland is a great nation, a beautiful nation, filled with great people—but it is not an idea. America is an idea."

We also need a patriotism, as will be discussed, that understands our shortcomings and challenges, along with recognizing that most of these cannot be addressed without effective national planning and governance.[9]

THE AMERICA AS A PRAGMATIC EXPERIMENT NARRATIVE

A patriotic belief in national righteousness and providential destiny (together with American Dreamism) has and will continue to be a major, if not dominant, narrative in American political culture.

But there has also been a pronounced pragmatic tradition in America. Pragmatists such as William James and Reinhold Niebuhr correctly warn that people here, as everywhere, are corruptible and that America, like every previous political experiment, is always on probation, always a work in progress. To paraphrase U.S. Supreme Court Justice Oliver Wendell Holmes: Constitutional democracy is an experiment, as all life is an experiment. And an experiment can fail.

It is wonderful that Americans hold themselves in uncommonly high regard. Every nation is entitled to its own national pride and patriotism. Yet no nation has a monopoly on the ultimate truth or the ultimate way of life. America's challenge is not to claim to be exceptional but to govern and conduct itself in ways that earn such acclaim.

Realists and pragmatists caution that exaggerated notions of American exceptionalism can be dangerous. They say, as earlier noted, that believing the founders of our country, who wiped out Indian nations, propagated slavery, and gave us the electoral college, were the greatest geniuses in the world is flawed logic at best.

The American Experience has shown that like every other people, our country has "interests real and fictitious, concerns generous and selfish, motives honorable and squalid." Providence, writes Arthur Schlesinger, "has not set Americans apart from lesser breeds. We too are part of history's seamless web."[10]

Several novelists have analyzed versions of America's original sins. Helen Hunt Jackson's *Ramona* (1884) reminded Americans of the racist and exclusionary treatment of indigenous Americans. The important writings of Harriet Beecher Stowe's *Uncle Tom's Cabin* (1852) and Toni Morrison's *Beloved* (1987) confronted the American myopic claim that ours was a land of liberty and freedom for all. By enslaving so many millions, white Americans had essentially mocked the notion that ours was the land of innocence, righteousness, and a "City as upon a hill" worth emulating.

Mark Twain and Henry Adams examined the political culture of Washington, D.C., in the post–Civil War era. Both found politicians and a government failing to live up to the aspirations of the American creed. Twain and Adams depicted a Washington of political schemers more interested in their reelection than in the national interest.

Adams has his protagonist, Mrs. Madeleine Lightfoot Lee, outraged by the vanity and moral somersaults of her friends in Congress (*Democracy: An American Novel* [1880]). Adams's protagonist loses her faith in the masquerade of America's democratic government. She discovers "that it was nothing more than government of any other kind." A cynical, or perhaps realistic, diplomatic friend explains to Mrs. Lee, "You Americans believe yourselves [wrongly] to be exempted from the operation of general laws."

Hamlin Garland, a product of the naturalist school of American fiction, examined life and politics in a Midwestern state in the 1870s and 1880s. His earnest, Alger-esque young farmer became a state legislator and is repulsed by the corruption, duplicity, and immorality he sees at his state capital. He fears for his soul and for the American republic, as he learns many of his colleagues are conniving thieves. He despairs of the Grange, the major political parties, and even his career as a legislator, and he joins in a new populist movement building a People's Party.

Upton Sinclair, writing in the naturalist tradition and as an early example of "muckraking" (in *The Jungle* [1906]), mocks the political and business elite of Chicago and has his protagonist advocate for an overthrow of the existing system and an embrace of socialism. Sinclair, foreshadowing Bernie Sanders, concluded the American political experiment had failed the working class and had become more of an oligarchy than a constitutional democracy. Howard Fast's *The American* (1946) similarly despairs of a corrupted political system that mistreats its farmers, miners, and laborers.

Other novelists similarly warned that the American political experiment is fragile and not necessarily destined to preeminence or permanence. Nathanael West's *A Cool Million* (1934), Sinclair Lewis's *It Can't Happen Here* (1935), and Philip Roth's *The Plot Against America* imagine and warn that fascism could take hold. Richard Condon's *The Manchurian Candidate* (1959) warns that Americans, no less than people elsewhere, can be brainwashed, and cherished democratic institutions can be subverted.

Fletcher Knebel and Charles Bailey's *Seven Days in May* (1962) sounds a different warning for those who become overly complacent with America as a mission with heavenly protection. They write of a plausible military coup in which U.S. military leaders decide that national security interests are too important to be left to elected politicians. Theirs is a compelling warning of potential Ceasarism and the ever-present challenge to the ideal of civilian control over military operations.

The realism and naturalism of Robert Penn Warren, Richard Wright, Eugene Burdick, and John Grisham are a few others who remind us of the gap between exaggerated versions of America as a glorious destiny and America regularly challenged as a political experiment. These novelists wanted to believe with Ralph Waldo Emerson that "the office of America is to liberate, to abolish kingcraft, priestcraft, caste, monopoly, to pull down the gallows, to burn up the bloody statute-book, to take in the immigrant, to open the doors of the sea and the fields of the earth," but they understood that racism, inequality, oligarchical tendencies, and an often ill-informed public were a constant challenge for America as it tried to produce sensible leaders and policies that would address societal problems.

The naturalists and the pragmatists love their country as much as anyone else, and indeed some of them held that America was the greatest country and the most ambitious experiment in constitutional self-governance; yet their stories remind us that America remains a work in progress. They wanted to help us imagine a just, more inclusive, more generous republic—and thus they reject Pollyannaish and pious chauvinistic boasting as diversionary, if not delusional (not to mention offensive to every other nation).

THE "LEAVE ME ALONE" INDIVIDUALISM NARRATIVE

If most Americans embrace, or want to embrace, the shining city on a hill or American Dream narrative, there is an almost equal fondness in our culture to celebrate quirky, nonconformist individualism.

Our Fourth of July is almost sacredly referred to as Independence Day. The Declaration of Independence, honored on that annual holiday, declared not only that life, liberty, and the pursuit of happiness were fundamental rights but also that people had the right and even the obligation to sever their social and political contract and rebel if state oppressors violated individual rights.

Shortly after America earned its independence, a political debate broke out over the proper role of the nation-state. Some, like Alexander Hamilton and James Madison, argued for a stronger compact of the former local colonies. But there were almost equal numbers who decried nationalization and centralization and championed limited government, states' rights, and decentralization. The Anti-Federalists may have failed to stop the ratification of the U.S. Constitution, but they succeeded in getting a reasonably strong Bill of Rights. And, importantly, they began a prolonged debate over the proper reach of government that has helped define American politics.

A Whiskey Rebellion staged by western Pennsylvanian farmers in 1794 challenged newly imposed federal taxes as early as the George Washington presidential administration. Washington and Hamilton quickly crushed these rebels, but they had to deploy thousands of federal militiamen to defeat these early nonconformists.

The Civil War was fought in large part over states' rights. Advocates of laissez-faire economics have long fought for individualism and market capitalism and against unwanted governmental regulations.

Libertarianism and even some forms of anarchism from John Brown at Harpers Ferry to Edward Abbey's Monkey Wrench Gang to Cliven Bundy's Nevada-based "war" on the U.S. Bureau of Land Management are illustrative.

America's transcendental philosopher, Ralph Waldo Emerson, preached a doctrine of self-reliance, independence, and individualism. "Whoso would be a man must be a nonconformist," wrote Emerson. It is, he continued, not only proper but also important to be yourself and experiment with ideas, even if you might be misunderstood: "Pythagoras was misunderstood, and Sophocles, and Jesus, and Luther, and Copernicus, and Galileo, and Newton, and every pure and wise spirit that ever took flesh." He added, "To be great is to be misunderstood."[11]

Emerson's young friend Henry David Thoreau practiced and extended what his mentor preached. Thoreau cherished his individualism so much he literally walked away from his small community and tried, at least for a year or so, to live alone—divorced from politics, government, and even minimal community responsibilities.

He was appalled at his country for condoning slavery and for the Fugitive Slave Act. He opposed the Mexican War, and he scorned the politicians and lawyers who comprised the state. Some say he was an outcast. Others viewed him as the ultimate transcendental individualist. Save for supporting the abolitionists and enjoying friendly berry hunts or canoe trips with friends, Thoreau was a civic and social withdrawer. The inspirational Thoreau was also priggish and somewhat of a grump. He was a libertarian verging on anarchist. He unrealistically held "that government is best which governs not at all."

Thoreau was an intellectual forerunner to novelist Ayn Rand—suspicious of government, elitist, and devoted to individualism. He cared little for philanthropic activity and projected an antipathy for the majority of people, whose pathetic lives bored him.

Thoreau critic Kathryn Schulz scolds him for writing "a fantasy about escaping the entanglements and responsibilities of living among people."[12] A nation composed of fierce individualists like Thoreau "would not, it is true," writes Schulz, "need much governance. But such a nation has never existed."[13] His was, in short, a delusional escape from the implied obligations associated with the Hobbesism, Lockean, or Jeffersonian social contract.

Still, Thoreau remains a staple of high school English courses and an American icon for his obvious love of nature along with his celebration of civil liberties and limited government as a response to political or communitarian regulation. We may appreciate that a Thoreau-styled democracy would be dysfunctional for contemporary society; yet the romance of Thoreaueanism and our love of "westerns" and wilderness pioneers lives on in the American political culture.

Ayn Rand, Edward Abbey, and, to a lesser extent, Joseph Heller, Jack Kerouac, and the gun-, drug-, and privacy-loving Hunter S. Thompson echoed his themes.

American novelists have embraced this celebration of the nonconformist, the rebel and those who would challenge the status quo. With Huckleberry Finn's refusal to turn slave Jim over to the authorities, and to accept—according to his "sivilizing" mentors—that he will go to hell, American culture was changed forever.

Ayn Rand wrote novels celebrating nonconformist entrepreneurial individuals and their righteous battles to evade or transcend what she deemed injurious and mindless state regulations. Her Howard Rourk, Henry Reardon, Dagny Taggart, and John Galt were ideal types of creative, self-reliant geniuses who stand up to statism. Her writing helped to inspire libertarians,

Tea Party activism, and semi-anarchistic cults opposed to government. Her message was blunt: government undermines freedom, creativity, and innovation. We can make America great again only if we practice self-reliance and resist most forms of government regulation.

Novelist Edward Abbey, inspired by Thoreau and poet Walt Whitman, gave us additional fictional exemplars of antistate libertarian individuals who waged metaphorical wars against both government and big corporations. Joseph Heller's memorable protagonist John Yossarian in *Catch-22* bravely struggles to defend his individualism in the face of oppressive bureaucracy. Hunter Thompson's fictional Raoul Duke specialized in irreverence and breaking conventional norms. Margaret Mitchell's twin protagonists Scarlett O'Hara and Rhett Butler famously defy those who would regiment them. They glory in being independent, irreverent, and defiant. The individualistic streak in our culture is inherently embedded and undeniable, and is one of the many reasons that governing is such a challenge in America.

Nevada rancher Cliven Bundy and his sons waged militia conflicts with the federal government in Nevada and Oregon. They read the Constitution, and especially its Tenth Amendment, as divinely inspired. They fervently believe that because they helped to settle the West and put their stamp on it, in a Lockean sense, they are entitled to the rights to use the land free of federal interference.

Bundy adheres to a strict constructionist interpretation of constitutionalism, libertarianism, and conservative Mormonism. He and his family are activists inspired by the spirit of Thoreau, Rand, and Abbey—and, although he is in distinct minority, he is not alone.[14]

Individualists and those who celebrate individualism, especially as personified in Thoreau, John Galt, the Monkey Wrench Gang, and dedicated Tenth Amendment activists like the Bundy family, question the state and its efforts to regulate, tax, conscript, and "govern" the land that they believe was "made for you and me."

THE "WE ARE ALL IN THIS TOGETHER" COMMUNITARIAN NARRATIVE

Even John Winthrop in his "City as upon a Hill" sermon emphasized that his fellow pilgrims would have to stand united and work together in harmony.

Just as liberty and freedom are fundamental American values, egalitarianism and communitarianism are also part of the American DNA. Harriet

Beecher Stowe's *Uncle Tom's Cabin* was a plea that America could not boast about freedom and humanitarianism and Christian ideals if it simultaneously enslaved millions of its countrymen (including fellow Christians like Tom). Her message was that we dehumanized ourselves in dehumanizing our African American brothers and sisters. An America where so many remained enslaved could not possibly be an America that claimed to be the land of the free. She was a pioneer among the many American writers who debunked the fantasy tales about contented, happy slaves and compassionate, doting plantation owners.

Stowe praised the occasional white family that sympathized with Uncle Tom or who sheltered a runaway fugitive in Ohio. But her larger plea was for an American republic that would end slavery and begin to understand our shared communitarian obligation to one another as fellow human beings.

Novelists Hamlin Garland (in his *A Spoil of Office*), Upton Sinclair (in his *The Jungle*), Howard Fast (in *The American*), and John Nichols (in his *The Magic Journey*) celebrate those who would unite and fight against machine politicians and oligarchs. Their open advocacy for populism, socialism, or a progressive Democratic Party emphasized communitarian obligations as a much-needed counterbalance to the American ethos of fierce individualism and heartless capitalism.

Another powerful American fictional work celebrating communitarianism is John Steinbeck's *The Grapes of Wrath*. His Joad family members strive to make something of themselves. They are forced to pull up stakes and head West; yet they—in common with the spirit of the American Dream—imagine that hard work and perseverance will permit them to transcend what they believe is their temporary adversity.

But the Joads endure repeated setbacks. They are bullied, rebuked, and scammed by heartless corporate farmers and public officials. Steinbeck celebrates small acts of kindness; yet these humanitarian gestures are usually proffered by those who are also struggling to survive, not those who could readily afford to be philanthropic. Steinbeck has his main protagonists wondering why such a rich country has lost its soul. Why, in this country that boasted about equality of opportunity and the rights of man, could there not be a more capacious spirit of sharing and caring and love?

Ma Joad in *Grapes* is portrayed as a nurturer, a feeder, a unifier, and especially a sharer. She holds the Joad family together and is a striking contrast to the absence of community and humanity in the larger society.

Steinbeck said he didn't like people to be hurt or hungry or dispirited; yet that's what he saw in the migration of Okies to California. Steinbeck

never worked out a coherent strategy for what was needed in those tumultuous years of the late 1930s. But his protagonists see the limits of narcissistic individualism and the negative side effects of unregulated monopolistic
practices.

Tom Joad wonders aloud to his mother why we can't "work together for our own things" and all farm our own land. He is moved by his
friend—the ex-preacher Jim Casy—who has concluded that we don't have
individual souls, but rather each of us has just a small piece of a great big
(communitarian) soul.

Tom Joad sets out to organize on behalf of those who are poor, voiceless, and been left behind. Steinbeck concludes his novel by having Tom's
sister, Rose of Sharon, who has just birthed a stillborn child, share breast
milk with a famished old man who might otherwise starve. Steinbeck calls
for redemption, sharing, giving, and community. His was a plan not to
reject but to repair an American republic that had lost its way.

Novelist John Nichols celebrates a Hispanic-American community
that comes together to support one another and to defend one of their
own who they believed was being unduly harassed by corporate and political elites. *The Milagro Beanfield War* wonderfully captures a slowly emerging sense of community as the people of Milagro rally around a quirky,
beleaguered local rogue named Joe Mondragón. He may or may not have
broken a local ordinance, but he is targeted, harassed, and probably unfairly
punished by state and local barons. Nichols gives us a fictionalized portrait
of a sleepy community of individualistic characters who are awakened to
their common interests, their common heritage, and the necessity to work
together to preserve their way of life.

Harper Lee, in *To Kill a Mockingbird*, calls for tolerance and respect for
everyone regardless of their skin color or their quirkiness. Hamlin Garland's
A Spoil of Office describes how backcountry Iowa farmers must form new
and more populist alliances if they are to have a voice in their state and
national capitals. He vividly portrays a Horatio Alger-esque Bradley Talcott
who gets adopted by a local lawyer and mentored by a fiery, inspirational
feminist. Talcott goes into politics to help his rural farming communities
but is repulsed by the professional politicians in the mainstream political
parties of his day. He and his mentor, who is later his wife, Ida Wilbur,
devote themselves to creating a People's Party that might transcend the
greed, corruption, and individualistic politics of the 1880s.

Congressman Talcott joins his ideological muse Ida Williams at a populist conclave in Kansas and tells the audience he is a farmer: "My people
for generations have been tillers of the soil. They have always been poor.

All the blood in my heart goes out towards the farmer and the farmers' movement. It seems a hopeless thing to fight the privileged classes, with all their power and money. It can be done, but it can be done only by union among all the poor of every class." He becomes enmeshed in the beginning of a great populist reform and explicitly communitarian movement. And his mentor, muse, and now collaborator Ida Wilbur comments that this movement is a "new religion—the religion of humanity."

Novelist Garland and his characters Talcott and Wilbur are here imagining a greater, or at least better, American republic, one turning not to socialism or Communism but to some form of communitarian populism that could help redeem the foundational maxims of America.

Other novelists including Upton Sinclair, Jack London, Edward Bellamy, and Richard Wright encouraged an America that embraced a Marxist or at least Socialist solution to the problems of inequality, racism, and class divide. These novelists won less political support in America, but the communitarian narrative—as championed by Stowe, Lee, Nichols, Steinbeck, Garland, Fast, and to some extent Helen Hunt Jackson—is a persisting melody in the American political culture. These novelists span the political spectrum; however, most believe that the ideal American republic should reconcile support for the enterprise system and market economics with a Judeo-Christian spirit of community, charity, and compassion. Most of them agree with those who contend that America can have concentrated wealth in the hands of a few, or we can have a constitutional democracy, but not both.[15]

THE "GOING ROGUE" OR BREAKING THE LAW FOR THE GREATER GOOD NARRATIVE

American leaders encourage fellow citizens to obey the law and become law-abiding, virtuous civic members of their community. The legitimacy of government derives from the consent of the governed, and a large part of the societal or social contract involves complying with the rules and laws our government establishes.

Yet there is a streak of antigovernment and antiauthoritarianism that is well established and often celebrated in the American political culture. George Washington and his revolutionary colleagues became subversive insurgents and anti-British terrorists in the eyes of the English. Americans nowadays of course believe Washington and his rebels did what they were obliged to do. Ma Joad in *Grapes of Wrath* famously tells her son, who has just killed a man, "You done what you had to do." The idea that you must do what you believe is right "and let the law catch up" is an old, if debated, American maxim.

America has at least a mild love affair with outlaws and rogues. Maybe this is because the Bonnie and Clydes, the Kerouacs and Cassadys, the Al Capones and Godfathers ignore the rules and are symbols (or at least temporary illustrations) of individual freedom. Novelist John Grisham wrote a *New York Times* best seller called *Rogue Lawyer* (2015). His scruffy, gun-toting, drinking, pool-playing, cage-fighter-investing attorney is a defense attorney for thugs and scumbags. But he proudly and defiantly defends his clients because he believes that even outlaws and rogues (like himself) are entitled to a fair trial—and that law enforcement officials, prosecutors, judges, and juries are not always right and in fact often have prejudices. So Grisham's Sebastian Rudd is motivated by his hatred of injustice and those big businesses, big governments, and big politicians who, he believes, don't give a damn about the little people.

Grisham's rogue lawyer is unorthodox, unconventional, and unlikable except that storyteller Grisham has us ultimately cheering for him after he becomes unduly harassed by virtually everyone else in the novel, including the government, drug lords, his ex-wife, and his clients. We come to understand his lonely crusades to be there and lend a voice to his renegade clients.

Mark Twain's Huck Finn was in many respects an outcast teenager—faking events (including his own death), breaking the Fugitive Slave Act, and lying on behalf of his friend Jim. "I don't give a dead rat," Huck roguishly says at one point to his buddy Tom Sawyer, "what the authorities think about it."

Margaret Mitchell's Rhett Butler is still another unsavory, yet ultimately intriguing (if not admired), rogue. He is the antithesis of the good southern gentleman and a fictional counterpart to Mr. Ashley Wilkes in *Gone with the Wind*. He is a fun-loving drinker, womanizer, blockade-running brothel owner who woos, plays with, and ultimately walks away from heroine Scarlett O'Hara. He famously tells Scarlett, "Frankly, my dear, I don't give a damn," and relishes breaking rules and making up his own.

Edwin O'Connor's Mayor Frank Skeffington in *The Last Hurrah* (1956) endears himself to his supporters (and to O'Connor's readers) because of his roguish, patronage-ridden, folksy style of leadership. He is admired as he fights the old establishments in his city. He takes on the leading business, the leading newspaper owner, and even preeminent church leaders who want to defeat him. He considers himself the "people's mayor" and does what he deems necessary to grease his machine so he can stay in office. Skeffington uses intimidation, patronage, and pay-to-play political arrangements; yet his rogueness is—at least in this fictional telling—mostly overlooked, if not admired.

Steinbeck's Jim Casy and Tom Joad are similarly portrayed as willing to break the local laws if that is needed to advance the common good. Edward Abbey celebrates environmental rogues who cheerfully cause damage to public and private property in the name of advancing the public interest. His Thoreauean "badass," George Washington Hayduke, is a rebel with a cause, an ex-Marine out to disturb the peace of those who would develop his beloved Southwest.

Joseph Heller's rogue bombardier John Yossarian is another reader favorite. Yossarian has fought the good war and the good fight and has earned the medals to prove it. But he ultimately goes rogue as he takes on bureaucracy gone astray. He becomes a folk hero in *Catch-22* because he stands up for sanity, reason, and civility.

The Italian Machiavelli five hundred years ago warned that political leaders occasionally must do things we may not admire or condone. He and other political theorists suggest that sometimes doing the right or seemingly virtuous thing may be the wrong thing to do and, inversely, that doing something sinister may be helping the greater good. Thus the use of cunning, duplicity, force, and even killing may, under certain circumstances, be morally and even legally justified. A "rogue" leader may be doing the right thing in utilitarian terms but still be guilty of breaking the law.

Washington broke the British laws. Lincoln bent the U.S. Constitution. FDR and Harry Truman used hard force, sometimes debatably. Obama violated international law by commanding the Navy SEALs to enter Pakistan and kill Osama bin Laden—yet Americans cheered him on.

Lincoln campaigned in 1860 saying he only wanted to stop the spread of slavery, not end it. FDR campaigned saying he would balance the budget. LBJ, earlier in his career, kept a distance from civil rights reform but times and his constituency changed and he later helped enact landmark civil rights legislation. All of these leaders were cunning and deployed manipulative strategies to get things done. Are these examples of "doing bad for the greater good"? They are certainly examples of assertive leadership deployed against political adversaries—intended to advance the public interest.

Robert Penn Warren's *All the King's Men* revisits these never-ending questions about the darker or the roguish side of American politics. His fictional governor, Willie Stark, is notably well intentioned, yet roguish in the extreme. He bribes, intimidates, and becomes ultimately a malicious, unsavory, and subversive political operative. And yet he achieves some good things. Warren celebrates Stark even as he warns us about Starkism.

Americans are fascinated by roguish spies and "going rogue" special agents who deliberately work the dark side—often courageously—to protect American national security. Norman Mailer's long and little-read *Harlot's Ghost* (1991) celebrates CIA operatives carrying on clandestine activities to win the Cold War. Ward Just's *Echo House* talks wistfully of those who worked in the OSS and similar clandestine operations after World War II. The television series *24* gives us the patriotic, heroic special agent Jack Bauer, who regularly puts his life on the line and operates "on the dark side" to save the American president or the American people.

We are likewise fascinated by CIA, Navy SEALs, and American sniper agents who fulfill our yearning for patriotic "superman" or "national spider-man" performances. A whole library of Tom Clancy, James Patterson, Richard Clarke, and David Baldacci novels thrill us with their depictions of "black operatives" to whom the government invariably grants deniability.

We have a long history of both fictional and historical narratives that celebrate those who lie, break the law, and resort to violence. Nat Turner and John Brown were early examples. Robin Hood steals from the rich to share bounty with the poor. Huck Finn does what he has to do to protect himself and his friend Jim. Abraham Lincoln dissembles and denies civil liberties because he deems it to be in service of the greater good. Women suffragettes and civil rights activists, like the now revered Rosa Parks, occasionally broke the laws in their day, and did so unapologetically knowing that they were helping in necessary causes to upgrade the law.

Popular culture provides countless examples of audiences cheering on rogues and lawbreakers. In the iconic *Godfather* novels and films, audiences are fascinated with how the Corleone family goes about its business. The Netflix series *House of Cards* focused on a ruthless Machiavellian political couple who lie, cheat, steal, and commit murder.

We sometimes celebrate "bad boys" or the "badass" in professional sports as well as in some forms of music. The Rock 'n' Rock Hall of Fame group NWA succeeded by emphasizing an antiauthority, and even anti–law enforcement, narrative. America loved Willie Nelson no matter what he was smoking. Hunter Thompson's followers love him for his rogue lifestyle and his Gonzo writing style. Jack Kerouac's Neal Cassady is likewise idealized because of his Dionysian, speed freak, con man roguish mystique. The Japanese Nissan auto company named one of their cars Rogue, presumably to appeal to young, freedom-loving buyers.

Ayn Rand's antigovernment entrepreneurs are yet another example of fictionalized celebrations of those who revolt against the established political order. It plays on the always latent, if not inherent, cynicism and suspicion about politicians and government.

A "rogue elephant" is one that roams apart and separates from the herd. That is what GOP candidate Trump did in his 2016 nominating race. Part of Donald Trump's initial political appeal in 2016 was his willingness to play the role of being an antipolitics, "shake up the status quo," "drain the swamp" maverick. Former governor Sarah Palin, in her early endorsement of Trump, specifically noted, "He's been going rogue left and right. That's why he's doing so well. He's been able to tear the veil off this idea of the system."

So there is an enduring fascination with unruly or wayward people who are, at least to some extent, incarnations of individual freedom. Some are rascals or scoundrels. Some march to the music of a different drummer. Some help us imagine a wilder, more Dionysian version of ourselves.

It is important not to celebrate breaking the law, going rogue, or "going Galt" as a noble end in itself. We are usually pleased when the Al Capones and Bonnie and Clydes, however they may have fascinated us, get brought to justice. Most of our better fiction writers understand that roguish law breaking divorced from worthy purposes is merely manipulation and deception, and, in the extreme, self-aggrandizement and repressive tyranny.

Those who try to imagine a great or at least a better American republic want citizens who have character and integrity and are willing to champion redemptive ideas of achieving common goals that speak to the valid aspirational wants and needs for all Americans.

THE LAUGHING AT POLITICAL HYPOCRISY AND PARANOIA NARRATIVE

Most satire is about important things. We laugh at politicians and at politics because elections matter, leadership matters, liberties and rights matter, and public policy outcomes matter.

Sometimes we laugh as an alternative to crying. One of America's first satirists, Hugh Henry Brackenridge, made us laugh at the trials and tribulations of frontier democracy in the 1790s because he was concerned about whether the American political experiment could work. He worried about the way votes could easily be bought and the impatience citizens had with the slow-moving legislative and judicial processes. He successfully makes us laugh at politics and human nature—yet he imagined a more exalted American republic.

Mark Twain and his coauthor Charles Dudley Warner, in their *The Gilded Age* (1873), ridiculed the hypocrisy of the fraudulently pious U.S. senator Abner Dilworthy. Dilworthy poses as a Sunday school teacher who loves his country but is a Gilded Age schemer, just like the many land developers and pay-to-play politicians of the unregulated Reconstruction Era politics. Both Washington and New York City vied for the title of "Corruptionville" as the authors offer a discouraging portrait of political and business leadership of the period.

Henry Adams's *Democracy: An American Novel* (1880) similarly paints a disheartening picture of how money, greed, and ambition compromise a leading candidate for the American presidency. But Adams didn't write just to expose what he had observed. He mocks the hypocrisy of those who claim to be the stewards of the public interest. He pricks the pretentious and the pompous in the corridors of power. Adams writes of an American republic that has lost its way. He makes us laugh at it; yet he is obviously deeply troubled by the decline of statesmanship and rectitude.

Christopher Buckley's *Supreme Courtship* (2008) unmasks a U.S. senator who is supremely self-centered, calculating, and pompous. His Senator Dexter Mitchell is an artfully drawn caricature of an elected official putting personal privilege and self-promotion over public interest considerations. Buckley makes us guffaw at Mitchell's pretensions, and we laugh even harder when his adversaries get revenge.

Joe Klein's fictional southern governor Jack Stanton in *Primary Colors* (1996) is still another politician who wants to do well, and who knows how to play the game, but who is also a hypocrite when it comes to lying or negative attacks on a foe when his electability is tested. We laugh as he deceives his aides and himself and as he wiggles around being high-minded at one moment and a dishonest sleazebag at the next. We both laugh *and* cry when he rationalizes that a politician just has to do these unsavory things because "it's the price you pay to lead." Klein's Stanton puts it about as bluntly as it can be put:

> Only certain kinds of people are cut out for this work—and, yeah, we are *not* princes. Two thirds of what we do is reprehensible. This isn't the way a normal human being acts. We smile, we listen—you could grow calluses in your ears from all the listening we do. We do our pathetic little favors. We fudge when we can't. We tell them what they want to

hear—and when we tell them something they don't want to hear, it's usually because we've calculated that's what they really want. We live an eternity of false smiles—and why? Because it's the price you pay to lead.

Gore Vidal's Clay Overbury in *Washington, D.C.* (1967) is similarly portrayed as presenting himself—indeed, selling himself—as a marketed commodity: as an electable person rather than a principled policymaker. Vidal gets sardonic as he unpacks the trickery and frauds of new television-era politics.

Novelists like Upton Sinclair and Richard Wright do not extensively discuss the political machines of their fictionalized Chicago. But when political operatives such as party bosses, prosecutors, or even ward healers are described they are invariably viewed as part of a self-serving oligarchical political economic machine—a machine that is entrenched and dedicated to preserving the status quo that benefits the haves.

American historian Richard Hofstadter wrote a provocative essay on "The Paranoid Style in American Politics" that talks about the periodic nativist conspiracies that America has experienced. These conspiratorial groups or movements are typically viewed as arising because their members are worried that the American republic will be done in by external assaults on America—from Communists, illegal immigrants, radical Muslims, or whatever.[16] Paradoxically, however, the American Revolution was a resistance movement and, some contend, a conspiracy against their British rulers. Then, too, the Anti-Federalists of the early 1790s feared a conspiracy at work when leaders such as Hamilton and Washington were pressing for a more centralized union and the adoption of a U.S. Constitution.

Both Sinclair Lewis in *It Can't Happen Here* (1935) and Nathanael West in *A Cool Million* (1934) write of fictionalized fascist takeovers of American politics. These groups are characterized as racist, prejudicial, anti-Semitic, and irreverent when it comes to Bill of Rights' protection of civil liberties. Lewis and West were doubtless influenced by what had taken place in Russia, Germany, and Italy, and they were using fiction to warn about the potentially looming paranoia in Depression-wracked America. Ray Bradbury's *Fahrenheit 451* (1953) is yet another consciousness-raising novel warning us of paranoid regime intent on both book burning and the suppression of dissent.

Richard Condon's *The Manchurian Candidate* (1959) is a brilliant satire about an apocalyptic conspiracy to overthrow the American republic. Condon ridicules a Joseph McCarthy–esque U.S. senator and his sinister wife as perplexingly serving as double agents who both lead a nationwide anti–Communist crusade and are undercover operatives of the Soviet empire. It is a masterpiece of espionage and paranoid political intrigue. Condon makes us laugh at the political hysteria of the 1950s and worry about the way American political institutions can falter so much in their assigned responsibilities.

America, like most cultures, has a tradition of laughing at its leaders—in part to reaffirm our democratic values and in part to mock those who exercise power over us. Many of our best novelists portray politics and a political class that are not living up to what we should get from a representative democracy or a government by and for the people.

Most of these novelists have higher aspirations for the American republic, and they enjoin us to imagine elected officials who will rise *above* bribery and pay-to-play, conventional, transactional politics—officials who will listen to everyone regardless of their campaign contributions and will conduct themselves with civility and integrity.

THE DYSTOPIAN FEAR OF AUTHORITARIANISM AND THE COLLAPSE OF CONSTITUTIONALISM NARRATIVE

Americans had rebelled against King George III and their colonial royal governors. The American Revolution was a war of liberation, for liberty, and against monarchy, authoritarianism, and submission. Thus it is hardly surprising that an important component of American political literature is the fear of the collapse of constitutional democracy and republicanism. In many ways this is a sister narrative to our fear of paranoia or the rejection of politics as a means to solve our societal problems. Yet it is also in many ways a literary narrative with a distinctive life of its own.

As noted earlier, the British novelists Aldous Huxley and George Orwell are two of the best exemplars of these fears. Hungarian-born British novelist Arthur Koestler, in his *Darkness at Noon* (1940), is another example of the understandable fears of an authoritarian nightmare.

Nathanael West's *A Cool Million* (1934) was a satirical example of dystopian fears. Sinclair Lewis's *It Can't Happen Here*, published the next year, describes an imagined fascist takeover of America and the immediate dismantling of citizen rights and liberties and the evisceration of our checks and balances system.

The Plot Against America by Philip Roth (2004) imagined a gradual collapse of constitutionalism under a President Charles A. Lindbergh who had defeated Franklin Roosevelt in 1940. Lindbergh pursues an "American First" isolationist foreign policy and permits, if not encourages, an atmosphere of anti-Semitism.

Noted science fiction writer Ray Bradbury's *Fahrenheit 451* (1953) depicts a dystopian future in which reading, books, and critical thinking are banned. His unforgettable "fireman" protagonist, Guy Montag, is employed not to put out fires but to use hoses of kerosene not only to burn books but also to burn houses containing books. "Burn 'em to ashes, then burn the ashes" is his team's mantra.

Bradbury is a master storyteller whose warning is that in the process of burning books, society can burn authors and the intellectual tradition. But, as Bradbury makes clear, this form of authoritarianism leads to losing our shared history and to forgetting (if not denying) our own humanity. In the end Bradbury gives us a hopeful redeeming finale where the classics are memorized and preserved for future generations. His *451* is a love letter to books, storytelling, and the gift of the classics. As Neil Gaiman writes in the sixtieth anniversary edition of *Fahrenheit*, "If we lose these (the books Bradbury is celebrating), we lose our shared history. We lose much of what makes us human. And fiction gives us empathy: it puts us inside the minds of other people, gives us the gift of seeing the world through their eyes. Fiction is a lie that tells us true things, over and over."[17]

Another celebrated science fiction writer, Ursula Le Guin, gave us a dystopian short story that was a parable about how we developed into a heartless people willing to live with the trade-off of letting a few people suffer life's worse indignities so the rest of us could not only pursue but also live a life of happiness. Her masterpiece, "The Ones Who Walk Away from Omelas," warns us of the choices our society has to make if it wants to avoid the corruption of the American soul.

Knebel and Bailey and Richard Condon, in their novels *Seven Days in May* and *The Manchurian Candidate*, warn us about a future where constitutionalism could be sabotaged. And Joseph Heller's *Catch-22* warns us about a future that is undermined by a crippling bureaucratization and regimentation that also threatens our shared humanity. Philip K. Dick's *The Man in the High Castle* (1962) is still another alt-history that makes us remember that both our past and our future could be far different from the one we are struggling to make work.

One of the many gifts of the dystopian narrative is that it forces readers to remember the exalted purposes of the American political experiment—and to be alert to those forces or political agents that betray our constitutional and Jeffersonian aspirations. The best of this genre forces us to reexamine our assumptions, our values, and our political practices.

THE PARADOX OF POLITICS NARRATIVE

Blessed are the politicians who admit to being politicians and the people who both take politics seriously and understand the inevitability, necessity, and desirability of politics. Governing is a burden as well as a privilege. Politics is the art of managing community and societal conflict and mediating among contending group interests. Politics is rarely about achieving perfection and more routinely about trying to bring about the possible, the achievable, and the desirable for as many people as possible.

Democratic constitutionalism relies on an acceptance by both the majority and the minority that the elected majority has a right to govern; yet it also relies on the conviction that the majority will exercise its rights with a due regard for minority interests.

Politics, as many of our novelists such as Penn Warren, Burdick, O'Connor, Condon, Adams, Brammer, Knebel and Bailey, and Klein make clear, is not always pretty; however, politicians and political activists are the necessary agreement negotiators we need to keep a diverse, pluralistic society functioning.

Several American political novelists understand the character and the paradoxical demands of politics. Billy Lee Brammer's little-read *The Gay Place* portrays a fictionalized Lyndon Johnson serving as a governor of Texas in the 1950s. Brammer had been a veteran Austin political journalist and an LBJ speechwriter. He captures the excitement, exhilaration, and messiness of politics. He shares the paradox that politics invariably brings out virtues as well as vulnerabilities.

Brammer, along with Edwin O'Connor and Joe Klein, discusses how principled purists get to live with their ideals, but they don't get much done. Brammer's Governor Fenstemaker advises his political mentee that "you do what you *have* to do. . . . You need to make the best of a not-so-bad bargain. Give a little. . . . The first principle is that you've got to learn to rise above principle." As Joe Klein's fictional governor Jack Stanton says, "it's the price you pay" to be a leader.

Politics, many of our fiction writers write, is messy and full of temptations—biting the apple of power and the adrenaline rush that accompanies it changes everyone who gets into that "room," and the changes are sometimes narcissistic and ravenous (see Andrew Tully's *Capitol Hill*, Allen

Drury's *Advise and Consent*, and Robert Penn Warren's *All the King's Men*); yet the best of politicians effectively help the republic navigate competing interests in order to arrive at something approximating the public interest. The best of politicians help us do good on a large scale.

In a constitutional republic, there is a continuing tension between competing truths, cherished values, and conflicting American Dreams. That's part of free speech and liberty. It is the job of politicians to help us reconcile and balance our contending aspirations—freedom and equality, individualism and community, idealism and pragmatism, free-market capitalism and communitarian compassion.

In Joe Nye's instructive *The Power Game: A Washington Novel* (2004), one of the political operatives advising a presidential candidate says, "Politicos ain't angels, but don't knock 'em. Somebody's got to do the hard work of putting a coalition together. . . . Otherwise there'd be anarchy. Like the Balkans and the Middle East."

Nye's protagonist Peter Cutler learns, "Straight talk that pleases one group scares the hell out of another." And, "We need politicians who can blur people's differences if we're going to get anything done." Constitutional and democratic politics works, Nye has his operative say, "when there's politicians who can overcome our differences."

Politicians need, by definition, to be ambitious and get up on the public stage. Part of what politicians have to do is posturing, acting, and showmanship. They are forced by the system to be self-promoters and to boast that they can make a difference. Politics is always an admixture of personal striving and personal competitiveness pitted against rivals who are similarly advocating for both their public policy choices and the claim that they would be the preferable elected leader.

The political marketplace—campaigning and the semi-permanent campaigns between elections—invariably gets loud and sometimes raucous. Politics is not for wallflowers, and it is mostly an unsentimental profession. John Grisham, in his *The Appeal: A Novel* (2008), depicts an especially loathsome campaign in which his bad guys use unfair tactics and questionable financial backing to subvert a political election. Joe Klein and Edwin O'Connor capture election realities, including the good, the bad, and the embarrassing.

Daniel Patrick Moynihan once said "elections are not our finest hour," and what he probably meant is that serious policy answers cannot be reduced to bumper sticker slogans and that claims and charges too often get exaggerated during elections. He may have also been referring to the fact that Americans haven't figured out how to level the playing fields in the way we design our electoral arrangements. Though we can make claims for America as an exceptional political experiment for self-governance with bills of rights and an independent judiciary, we are still trying to improve on systems such as gerrymandering, the electoral college, and the mudslinging attack-ad politics so embedded as part of our political culture.

Few Americans approve of election arrangements in which the winners lose and the losers win. Few Americans believe in pay-to-play kickback politics. And sadly, an overwhelming number of Americans believe that elected officials disproportionately listen to and enact policies that favor the already well-to-do.

We need the most honest and effective politicians we can get who are willing go into politics and win elections to restore the integrity and effectiveness of our political system. As Sinclair Lewis's protagonist in *It Can't Happen Here* (1935) makes clear: giving up on politics is not an option. And as John Nichols's heroine, Ruby Archuleta, exemplifies, people have to organize, petition, and make their voice heard if they want to achieve progress and desired results. Progress more often results from Act II activists bringing pressure on Act III synthesizers than the other way around.

The "ideal" politician is typically a Hollywood or storybook creation, perhaps a combination of Jimmy Stewart in *Mr. Smith Goes to Washington*, Harrison Ford in *Air Force One*, Henry Fonda in *Young Abe Lincoln*, and Bradley Talcott in *A Spoil of Office*. The ideal politician is heroic and capable of pleasing the common people, all the time. Such a person, we might fantasize, could make conflicts disappear, never have to engage in compromise, can eliminate taxes, and guarantee rags-to-riches happiness for everyone. Such people don't exist. And if they did, it would be possible only in a small, homogenous community where everyone shared the same ideas, ideals, and interests. But the very liberties Americans cherish invite diversity, conflict, and clashing ideas about how we should be governed.

There is yet another paradox of politics. There are purists who scorn compromise of any kind and naïvely dream of some nonpartisan nirvana. But those who want to take the politics out of politics incorrectly think that their nonpartisan, nonpolitical, would-be heroes would always be right and the public generally wrong.

"Compromise" is wrongly considered a dirty word. But politics everywhere is about "give and take" and trying to find common ground. It is not about compromising morals or principles, it's usually a matter of achieving something rather than making no progress at all. Bluntly put, politicians are necessary to grease the creaky, clashing gears and wheels of our public bureaucracies. Even our political system needs a little grease, or perhaps olive or flaxseed oil, to help us navigate our way among our largest political challenges. Beware taking compromise and wheeling and dealing and politics out of politics. Compromise, debate, and deliberation and give-and-take are the oxygen of constitutional democracy.

As most of the novelists treated in this book believe, politics may be a disorderly and boisterous way to conduct the public's business, but you can't have a democracy without politics, and you can't have politics without parties, competing factions, and contending candidates.

Herman Melville and Robert Penn Warren, among others, emphasize that life is full of contradiction and paradox; yet, regardless of the ambiguities inherent in life, people have to act, politicians have to make choices, and leaders have to make decisions.

Those who are antipolitics or who don't care for politicians are giving up on the grand experiment of the American republic. Politics is the lifeblood of constitutional democracy, and it is the price we pay for aspiring to achieve a resilient constitutional democracy. Politics is at the very heart of a representative republic. It is to democracy what the experimental method is to physics, what melody is to music, what the imagination is to poetry.

THE IMAGINING A JUST, GENEROUS, AND GREAT CONSTITUTIONAL REPUBLIC NARRATIVE

The men who signed the Declaration of Independence, said Abraham Lincoln, intended to establish aspirational benchmarks "for a free society which should be familiar to all, and revered by all, constantly looked to, constantly labored for, and even though not perfectly attained, constantly approximated, and thereby constantly spreading and deepening its influence and augmenting the happiness and value to all people of all colors everywhere."[18]

Harper Lee's fictional Atticus Finch in *To Kill a Mockingbird* reminds us of the maxim that our courts "are the great levelers, and in our courts all men are equal." The courts, this temporary public defender says, are "the one place where a man ought to get a square deal . . . be he any color of the rainbow." Alas, Harper Lee's fictionalized Tom Robinson fails to receive fair justice at the Maycomb, Alabama, courthouse. And we are regularly reminded that this founding maxim is too often still an aspiration rather than an achievement.[19] Yet it is still part of our dreamed idea of America.

Freedom, dignity, equality, and the right to personal happiness are maxims in the Declaration and Constitution. They have not been achieved for everyone over the course of American history, but we still embrace them as markers of what we want to achieve.

Novelist Michael Shaara has his Union officer, Joshua Lawrence Chamberlain, evoke a related aspiration as a means to rally his reluctant charges just before the consequential battles at Gettysburg. Chamberlain tells his troops the reason they are fighting is not for loot, or for pay, or for some king. They're fighting, he says, to set other men—African Americans—free. "It's the idea that we all have value, you and me, we're worth something more than dirt. I never saw dirt I'd die for, but I'm not asking you to come join me and fight for dirt. What we're all fighting for, in the end, is each other." Chamberlain apologizes for sounding preachy, "but I thought . . . you should know who we are." Most of our best political novelists preach, at least a little, and, like Shaara's Chamberlain, they write to let us know who we are and who we could become.

Novelists such as Sinclair Lewis in *It Can't Happen Here*, Richard Condon in *The Manchurian Candidate*, and Philip Roth in *The Plot Against America* warn us about paranoid and rogue counterfeit leaders who can threaten constitutionalism.

Fletcher Knebel and Charles Bailey, in *Seven Days in May*, warn that our Constitution's promise of civilian control over the military cannot be taken for granted. Their fictional General James Mattoon Scott plans and plots a military coup. He claims that the unpopular incumbent president has been too soft in his foreign policies and has irresponsibly impaired military morale. Scott nominates himself as the Caesar America needs. Fortunately, a brave and loyal Marine colonel warns the White House, and the coup d'état is averted.

President Lyman Jordan concedes that top dedicated military officials should always be afforded the opportunity to share their policy recommendations. "But once the President and the Senate, as the responsible authorities, make a decision, then my fellow citizens, debate and opposition among the military must come to an end. That is the way of war: the commander solicits every possible view from his staff, but once he decides on his plan of battle, there can be no disputing it. Any other way would mean confusion, chaos and certain defeat. And so it also must be in the councils of government in Washington." *Seven Days in May* was both a plea for the importance of constitutionalism and a warning against Caesarism and the undue political influence from the military and the military-industrial complex.

The American novelist Winston Churchill, in his consciousness-raising novel *Mr. Crewe's Career* (1908), has a young attorney, Arthur Vane, reminding his father and the president of a major railroad and his fellow New

Hampshirites that one can support capitalism and the Republican Party while also being in favor of honest elections and fair practices in the process. Progressive politics, he says, is rooted in the exhalted precepts of the American republic. Elected officials should be able to go about their deliberations free of intimidation by railroad barons and other special interests.

Churchill, like Henry Adams and Hamlin Garland before him, wrote to rally the civic and moral conscience of fellow Americans. They called out elected officials and political donors who abuse American policymaking processes. No special interest, they are saying, has the right to intimidate or hold monopolistic control over the legislation process.

Churchill's progressive hero wants us to take our founding ideals seriously.

> Surely, we cannot have commercial and political stability without commercial and political honor! If, as a nation, we lose sight of the ideals which have carried us so far, which have so greatly modified the conditions of other peoples than ourselves, we shall perish as a force in the world. And if this government proves a failure, how long do you think the material interests of which you are so solicitous will endure? Or do you . . . Perhaps not. But it is a matter of importance, not only to the nation, but to the world, whether or not the moral idea of the United States of America is perpetuated.

Americans take justifiable pride in the political, constitutional, and economic success of the nation, not as sacred, proscribed destiny but as an enormously promising political experiment.

The American idea, or American creed or testament, is what we want America to be. The American way is what we do in the meantime, it's who we are—imperfect human beings with imperfect institutions struggling to be better—always imagining that we might and can become better. Among all our competing political narratives, imagining a more just, inclusive, generous American constitutional republic remains our most energizing political narrative.

The next several chapters discuss in detail the differing ways novelists approach politics and the American political culture.

Chapter 3 treats American novelists who wrote as provocateurs—prodding us and advocating that America needs to rededicate ourselves—reconsecrate, to use Lincoln's phrase—if we are going to find our way. Among these are some of America's most memorable novels. Unfortunately, space limited me to an appraisal of a mere nine examples; yet these are suggestive of a trove of similar agitational fiction.

3

THE NOVELIST AS
POLITICAL AGITATOR

Political novelists write for a variety of purposes, including to entertain
and to make money. But some also write to provoke, preach, and
encourage political and moral awakening. Harriet Beecher Stowe, John
Steinbeck, Richard Wright, Ayn Rand, and Edward Abbey, for example,
entertained; yet they also pushed readers to think and act differently.

Writers treated in this chapter intentionally wrote about people or
causes they deemed disenfranchised. Twain's memorable Huck Finn shares
a journey of self-discovery and, ultimately, a moral awakening. Finn decides that he will lie to his family and anyone else rather than betray his
black friend, Jim.

"Like Huckleberry Finn," writes Edward Abbey, every American
writer must sooner or later make a choice "between serving the powerful
few or the disorganized many, the institutions of domination or the spontaneous, instinctive, natural drive for human liberation."[1]

For Abbey, this meant the writer had to become political: revealing
truths, often unpopular truths, to their readers and especially to those in
power. Inspired by Walt Whitman's mantra of "Resist much, obey little,"
Abbey crusaded against traditional, sentimental, and sacred cows which, in
his case, spanned the political spectrum.

Aleksandr Solzhenitsyn reminded fellow writers that it was their responsibility to sense more keenly than others the beauty and truths and
ideals of the human condition and to communicate these to their fellow
citizens. Writers and artists, he added, likewise had a special obligation to
expose falsehoods. "Falsehood can hold out against much in this world, but
not against art."[2]

It is in this sense that the novelist as agitator has a lot in common with
the Act I political activist. The American agitational novelist, as a societal

political critic, wants to say things that would otherwise be ignored or silenced. They write to urge Americans to live up to their ideals. They willingly write on behalf of weak or even nonexistent opposition movements.

They become, at least in several cases, a one-person band, a literary political troubadour disturbing the peace or "muckraking." To the extent they challenge conventional wisdom and the existing order, they invite being considered a "nuisance," a "troublemaker," a "charlatan," or even subversive. Such epithets, for most of them, were a badge of courage. Few of them worried about being in advance of, or at odds with, their times.

Stowe, Sinclair, the early Dos Passos, Lewis, Steinbeck, Wright, Rand, Abbey, and Roth each, in different ways, wrote agenda-pushing protest novels. One was inspired by her faith and her repulsion for the nightmare of slavery. Some wrote about inequality, societal justice, and the promise of egalitarian political uprising. Sinclair Lewis's was a call to arms against a possible fascist takeover in America. Roth's *The Plot Against America* imagined an America where anti-Semitism ran rampant under an "American First" President Charles Lindbergh. Rand and Abbey wrote from a libertarian, antistatist political stance.

What did they have in common? They understood that political fiction could be deployed as a political weapon, that the power and influence of the pen could have agency. These authors are merely representative of a distinctive political fiction genre. One helped enlarge the ranks of the abolitionists. Two inspired political cults, and all enjoyed a wide readership.

AMERICA: LAND OF THE ENSLAVED[3]

"Yer mine, now, body and soul," says Simon Legree, American fiction's most malicious slave owner, who has just purchased a black slave named Tom for twelve hundred dollars. "No! No! No! My soul ain't yours, Mas'r! You haven't bought it—ye can't buy it! It's been bought and paid for, by one that is able to keep it—no matter, you can't harm me!" So declares American fiction's most famous slave, Uncle Tom, in Harriet Beecher Stowe's celebrated novel *Uncle Tom's Cabin*.

Stowe (1811–1896) was one of thirteen children. Her father was a prominent Congregational minister, as were six of her brothers and her husband, Calvin Stowe. A sister was an early advocate for women's rights. Though born and raised in Connecticut, Stowe spent many years in Cincinnati, Ohio, across the Ohio River from Kentucky, then a slave state. She had been neither a political activist nor an abolitionist before writing *Uncle*

Tom's Cabin. She was preoccupied with raising six children and assisting her husband in his career as a biblical scholar. She supplemented the family's meager income by writing for magazines and newspapers.

Two developments changed Stowe. One was the passage of the Fugitive Slave Act, adopted by the U.S. Congress in 1850. This act, building on earlier law, essentially said it was unlawful to aid or abet runaway slaves. Moreover, it allowed slave owners to lawfully reclaim fugitive slaves no matter to which state they had fled.

Second, she had come to know several former slaves as well as fugitives. She and her husband helped shelter and assist some. And she had become increasingly disturbed by how they were treated.

Stowe, because she was a woman, could neither vote nor run for political office. Yet she could write. She decided first in magazine stories, and then in this novel, to make clear her moral and political objections to the fugitive slave regulations and, even more important, to the destruction and dehumanization of the black families in the South.

How did she go about her research? She interviewed fugitive slaves escaping into Ohio. She read some of the biographical narratives of former slaves, including one by Josiah Henson. She was influenced by abolitionist writings such as Theodore Weld's *American Slavery As It Is* (1839). And she had probably read Richard Hildreth's *The Slave: or Memoirs of Archy Moore* (1836). She made at least one trip into neighboring Kentucky to observe the conditions in which slaves were used. She also benefited from firsthand accounts from one of her brothers, who worked in New Orleans. All this informed her, but hers would be a fictionalized narrative as she could obviously only imagine what it might have been like to live as a slave.

Stowe wrote her novel two years before Solomon Northrup (1808–1863) had his graphic nonfiction, *Twelve Years a Slave*, published. His is an especially moving story of how, as a free man living in New York, he was drugged, kidnapped, and forced into slavery in Louisiana in the 1840s. His narrative served as the basis for the prizewinning 2013 Hollywood film of the same name. Much of Stowe's fictional material is similar to Northrup's: slave auctions, family breakups, whippings, and the dehumanizing brutalities.

More on the Fugitive Slave Act: northern abolitionists strenuously opposed this law. Most southerners, especially plantation owners, vigorously defended it. Abraham Lincoln (1809–1865), two years older than Stowe, was a rising politician in Illinois at the time. Lincoln, the political pragmatist, believed the Fugitive Slave Act was the law and had to be enforced.

Lincoln, from everything we have learned, opposed slavery and would later fight to prohibit its expansion into western states. Yet Lincoln was conflicted when it came to racial equality. He opposed interracial marriage and considered blacks inferior to whites. For a long while, including into his presidency, Lincoln championed the policy of deporting free blacks to Africa or Caribbean nations. He was never an abolitionist; he believed strident northern activists were in too much of a rush to end an institution he hoped might die a natural death. Lincoln, well into his White House years, complained about being falsely accused of being an abolitionist.

Between 1830 and into the 1850s, a few thousand slaves escaped to the North in search of freedom. The Underground Railroad, which assisted in these escapes, infuriated the South and was a major catalyst for the Fugitive Slave Act.

It was one of the ironies of this period that the South, which used "states' rights" as a major argument for leaving slavery in place, turned to the federal government in the Fugitive Slave Act to provide national enforcement of their inhumane practices. So much for their opposition to a strong national government.

Lincoln may not have liked the Fugitive Slave Act, but he went along with it, as a great many northerners and westerners did, as a means to preserve the union.

Lincoln's "moderate" policy stance reflected the views of Illinois's white male voters and helped him win elections to the state legislature, a term in Congress, and later the 1860 Republican nomination over the expected nominee U.S. senator William Seward. Most biographers, as suggested, conclude Lincoln was personally haunted by the injustices of slavery. Yet, when he ran for president in 1860 (eight years after *Uncle Tom's Cabin* had become a national best seller), he ran on a platform that left the institution of slavery undisturbed in states where it existed.

Stowe, as noted, had not been affiliated with the abolitionist movement. It might have been risky for her and her family to be an abolitionist when she was living in Cincinnati in the 1840s. But the abolitionist movement was at least a generation or two old when she took up her pen. One of the heroic leaders of the abolitionists was the Boston-based William Lloyd Garrison. He edited and published *The Liberator*, a magazine with a small circulation that excoriated slavery and especially opposed the American Colonization Society, an association of well-intentioned business and philanthropic leaders who wanted to help emancipated blacks settle in Africa. Garrison believed blacks were Americans and deserved freedom at home. Garrison led a lonely campaign in the 1830s and 1840s. He was later joined by Wendell Phillips, who provided oratorical strength to the abolitionists.

Prominent elites denounced the abolitionists as reckless, radical, subversive, and anti-American. But Garrison was a tenacious zealot, willing to give his life for the fight against slavery. If Garrison, Phillips, and other abolitionists were motivated by moral and religious convictions, it is hard nowadays to remember that most northerners and even a majority of the clergy opposed them.[4]

"At the outset, Garrison had naturally assumed that these servants of Jesus would eagerly embrace the Negro emancipation," writes Charles A. Madison. "A few ardent souls did heed his call and became devoted lieutenants. But the large majority of divines rejected either his uncompromising principles or his leadership with unctuous scorn."[5]

It is also difficult nowadays to imagine the political culture of the 1840s and 1850s. To be an abolitionist was to be considered a radical. Moreover, antislavery supporters were not of one mind. Some were gradualists, some "immediatists." Some, like Stowe's father, favored compensating slave owners for freeing slaves. Others favored compensating slaves, not plantation owners. The movement was rife with both visionaries and competing ideologues. Little consensus existed on what today we believe was one of the most profound moral issues America ever faced.

Stowe may not have been an activist before the Fugitive Slave Act, but this law was, for her, a bridge too far. It was incompatible with her interpretation of Christian values. God, she said, inspired her, and although she made clear she did not consider herself a prophet, she did see herself as an instrument of Christian righteousness.

Slavery, she believed, was a crime against humanity. This new law was an unjust law, and she would do everything in her storytelling capacity to get the Act and slavery overturned. Like Sophocles's Antigone, Stowe said laws that violate the natural law of God were sinful and unjust. For Stowe, the promises so eloquently stated in the Declaration of Independence were both an American and a Christian ideal, and individual bigots, as well as the country, scarred by the original sin of slavery, now had to overcome this unacceptable past through new laws and a new morality.

Stowe relentlessly calls on morality to make her case; yet she also invokes America's aspirational principles to bolster her argument. At one point, she has a fugitive slave, who has been caught and returned to his master, cry out:

> What laws are there for us? We [black Americans] don't make them, we have nothing to do with them; all they do for us is to crush us, and keep us down. Haven't I heard your Fourth-of-July speeches? Don't

you tell us, once a year, that governments derive their just power from the consent of the governed? Can't a fellow think that hears such words? Can't he put this and that together and see what it comes to?

Politicians are barely mentioned in *Uncle Tom's Cabin*. One exception has an Ohio state senator explaining to his wife that he and his colleagues have just passed state legislation, apparently mirroring the Fugitive Slave Act, that forbids aiding and abetting runaway slaves. Senator John Bird suggests this was, he believed, the Christian and kind thing to do. His short, timid, and usually deferential wife virtually explodes at this: "Now, John, I don't know anything about politics, but I can read my Bible; and there I see that I must feed the hungry, clothe the naked, and comfort the desolate; and that Bible I mean to follow."

"You ought to be ashamed, John!" adds Mary Bird. "Poor, homeless creatures! It's a shameful, wicked, abominable law, and I'll break it, for one, the first time I get a chance—and I hope I shall have a chance, I do!"

Thus does an apolitical, passive housewife become politicized and indeed soon welcomes and shelters a courageous mother who had escaped over a thinly iced Ohio River. Mary Bird, Stowe's law-breaking heroine, admirably shames Senator Bird into being her accomplice in breaking the very legislation he recently passed in the state legislature.

Stowe, here and elsewhere, is writing as both Christian preacher and anti–Fugitive Slave Act politician. Like Mary Bird, she couldn't reconcile her faith with the mean-spirited heartlessness of slavery. Her goal was to shame not just the Senator Birds but also mothers everywhere; Christians, both northern and southern; and all the fence-sitting Lincolns of the day to have the moral courage to reject unjust laws and inhumane practices. Her clarion call for moral awakening was aimed at the heart of middle-class Protestants—especially at fellow mothers like her who could understand the horrors of their spouses and children being "sold down the river," thus undermining the sacred integrity of one's family.

But Stowe's passion is not limited to changing people's attitudes. She actually celebrates lawbreakers. She celebrates those who courageously fled across the Ohio River to freedom. She celebrates, as in the Bird family case, those who aided and abetted fugitives. She even favorably depicts an escaped slave who shoots at a slave-catching bounty hunter searching for fugitives.

Stowe's novel depicts Tom, his friends, and his slave master. Tom is a tall, broad-chested, manly African American, a father, husband, devout Bible-reading Christian and a much-trusted and effective superintendent on his master's Kentucky farm. "Uncle Tom," as his family calls him, lives in a small log cabin next door. "There was," writes Stowe, "something about his whole air self-respecting and dignified, yet united with a confiding and humble simplicity."

Tom's master falls on tough economic times and, despite pledges to set Tom free, sells him to a slave broker who will sell him "down river." Tom is horrified, but he stoically accepts his fate, saying that "it's better for me alone to go" than any of his master's other slaves, and better his sacrifice than for the farm to be broken up and sold.

Tom is bought and manages for a while to serve in families that treat him well. He becomes a companion to a dying young white girl, "Little Eva," who befriends him and, in a tear-jerking episode, pleads with her father to free his slaves. The horrors of slavery are so great, Eva says, that she can now imagine "why Jesus wanted to die for us." Little Eva says that she, too, is willing to die, "if my dying could stop all the misery [of slavery]."

But Tom is sold again. His new master, Simon Legree (one of American fiction's most villainous pariahs), a transplanted Vermonter in Louisiana, strips Tom of his belongings and tries to strip him of his faith and dignity: "I'm your church now! You understand—you've got to be as I say." Tom is assigned backbreaking cotton-picking chores. He is treated miserably; yet his spiritual convictions only grow. In the end, he dies a martyr's death rather than reveal to the cruel Legree the whereabouts of two fellow slaves who have escaped.

Stowe says of Tom's unwavering faith, "Uncle Tom felt strong in his God to meet death rather than betray the helpless." Tom becomes a Christ-like, redeeming figure, forgiving both the godless and miserable Legree and the black overseers assigned to beat him to death. "What a thing it is to be Christian!" Tom says as he lies dying.

"Like Jesus he suffered agony inflicted by evil secular power," reflects historian James McPherson. "Like Jesus, he died for the sins of humankind in order to save the oppressors as well as his own people."[6] Stowe's nineteenth-century Protestant Americans may have understood that message better than more secular and perhaps more cynical readers today.

Stowe's book was hated in the South; yet it was an underground best seller in Charleston and elsewhere. Dozens of books refuting *Uncle Tom's Cabin* were hurried into print. Stowe received threatening mail (and, by one account, a package containing the ear of a slave). She was accused of slander, falsehoods, and distorting the facts; of writing in a sentimental, melodramatic style; and of unrelenting preachiness and sensationalist propaganda. U.S. Supreme Court Chief Justice Roger Taney blamed her and her novel for fomenting the political hate that led to the Civil War.

Her great achievement in *Tom's Cabin* is that she effectively debunked the plantation legend southern planters had put forth for decades—namely, that their slaves lived happy, healthy, and satisfied lives. Stowe refutes these myths with her vivid stories. She makes the case that American slavery enslaved the American republic as a whole. Every slave owner who dehumanized African Americans dehumanized themselves in the process. And those in the rest of the country who just stood by were, in many ways, complicit and co-conspirators in the moral compromising of the American political experiment.

Literary critics faulted Stowe's novel for the sentimental excesses that brought readers to tears. Tom's forgiveness of his enemies is unworldly. Simon Legree is unbearably villainous and both Tom and Little Eva unbelievably saintly. "Artistically the novel is very bad," writes Joseph J. Blotner. "Its structure sprawls, its melodrama creaks, and its sentiment oozes over hundreds of pages peopled more often by cardboard figures than believable human beings."[7] Yet sentimentalism, most critics now agree, was a demand of the time. Moreover, Stowe was a woman with a mission. She was on a political, not a literary or artistic, mission.

She was criticized for understating the horrors caused by slavery. Toni Morrison's majestic *Beloved* and Colson Whitehead's *The Underground Railroad* are two of many treatments that would later more graphically assay the tragic practices and consequences of slavery. She was criticized for appearing to support the idea of deportation. At one point near the end of the novel, a former slave and his family migrate with evangelical fervor to Liberia. African Americans rebuked Stowe's suggestions about colonization, saying, in effect, "We are here and here we will remain." They rejected deportation and championed emancipation.

Critics have also complained that her "Uncle Tom" inspired the caricature of an uneducated, docile, ignorant black man, too ready to accept his inferiority, too eager to please his white master—a stereotype and gratuitous minstrelization. They likewise rejected Stowe's recourse to racist explanations about the traits of her black characters and for relying on stereotypes of the era.

"*Uncle Tom's Cabin* is a very bad novel," wrote novelist James Baldwin. Stowe was, he said, not a novelist but an impassioned pamphleteer merely pointing out the obvious and making people feel guilty. Moreover, Baldwin contended, Stowe's *Uncle Tom* was written mainly to make people feel virtuous or righteous for reading it. Finally, he said, her depiction of Tom is of a man "robbed of his humanity and divested of his sex."

Critics also complained about Stowe's tone, or voice, her righteous indignation and lack of sophistication or irony. She is accused of telling other people's stories. How could a white woman comprehend the plight of blacks? And "if her natural compassion had for the first time transformed slaves from an abstraction into human beings, it rendered them as not more than children."[8]

Stowe may have used other people's stories as her sources, "but what drove her to write was her outraged response to slavery," explains a supportive Roxana Robinson. "She had the right to that response. Isn't it better that Stowe wrote her book, instead of staying respectfully mute because the stories were not hers to tell?"[9]

Tom's Cabin may well have been artistically defective, but it was politically consequential, read by millions, and is considered the most influential novel in American history. It helped in framing the abolitionist arguments against slavery and against the Fugitive Slave Act. When Lincoln met Stowe in 1862, he allegedly told her that her book had undoubtedly helped trigger the Great War. Even if that story is apocryphal, *Uncle Tom's Cabin* was an effective political weapon, a compelling national sermon whose message was told through a vivid narrative at a time when most of the nation's elected political leaders were unconscionably quiet.

Uncle Tom's Cabin, regardless of its literary liabilities, was a volley heard round the world. The novel was also a best seller in England, whose commercial interests, especially the cotton trade, favored the South. The effect of the best-selling novel probably reinforced England's inclination to remain out of the war. Historians say the book was also effectively used in the campaign that helped enact England's Reform Act of 1867 and in the arguments for the emancipation of serfs in Russia.

Today, *Uncle Tom's Cabin* is a celebrated part of American political history. It is the most enduring novel about American slavery. It may have had more political influence than any other novel in America. Literary critic Lawrence Buell notes that other notable American novels expressed moral seriousness, but *Cabin* stands alone as an example of "its enlistment of art in the service of activism."[10]

Stowe is now widely recognized not only for her courage but also as a feminist pioneer. Stowe was an unelected middle-aged homemaker and mother who riveted the nation's consciousness. Her agitational storytelling provided crucial moral fervor to the leadership efforts of Garrison, Phillips, and others as the American Experiment faced its greatest test. Stowe foreshadowed Toni Morrison's *Beloved* when she wrote that there were mothers "whom the accursed traffic had driven them to the murder of their own children."

Stowe never apologized for her moralistic sentimentalizing. If anything, she reminded readers that "nothing of tragedy can be written, can be spoken, can be conceived that equals the frightful reality or scenes daily and hourly acting on shores beneath the shadow of American law, and the shadow of the cross of Christ."

She has a friend from Tom's old Kentucky master's family kneel at Tom's grave and vow, "Oh, witness, that from this hour I will do what one man can to drive this curse of slavery from my land." The cause she describes as George Shelby's is obviously Stowe's cause as well. In the end, *Tom's Cabin* tellingly reminded Americans, as Sinclair, Dos Passos, and Steinbeck later also do, of their shared obligations to each other as human beings.

Stowe was not explicitly political: she did not call out elected politicians or urge people to vote a certain way. Her message was more about changing moral than political attitudes, though she relentlessly rails against the Fugitive Slave Act. Stowe's intent is simply put in her preface: "The object of these sketches is to awaken sympathy and feeling for the African race, as they exist among us; to show their wrongs and sorrows, under a system so necessarily cruel and unjust as to defeat and do away with the good effect of all that can be attempted from them." She succeeded. Other American novelists, such as Melville, Twain, Hemingway, or Steinbeck, have now been more widely read around the world, but "no American novel has come close to matching *Uncle Tom's Cabin*'s impact." This single book, says Lawrence Buell, "changed the world. Of what other [American] novel could the same be said?"[11]

Stowe's passionate story about a humble black man and the injustices of slavery reminds us that political leadership comes from many different voices. Stowe is exhibit A that people without fame, money, or elected office, or even the right to vote, can exercise consequential political leadership.

JUNGLED AMERICA[12]

To you, the toilers, who have made this land, and have no voice in its councils! To you, whose lot it is to sow that others may reap, to labor and obey, and ask no more than the wages of a beast of burden, the food and shelter to keep you alive from day to day. It is to you that I come with my message of salvation, it is to you that I appeal.

These "Debsian" words were music to the soul of the long-suffering Jurgis Rudkus, an immigrant from Lithuania, who had migrated with his family to Chicago in search of a better life.

Upton Sinclair (1878–1968) was a prolific novelist and pamphleteer, one of socialism's most committed political activists, and one of the best examples of the muckraking school of American Realism. *Muckrakers* was the term, initially used by critics, describing journalists and novelists who exposed corporate and big-government corruption.

The Jungle ("the *Uncle Tom's Cabin* of wage slavery") shocked American readers with its detailed descriptions of the poverty of the working-class poor. It also details worker exploitation by the meatpacking industry and predatory politics in turn-of-the-century Chicago.

Sinclair, educated at City College of New York and Columbia University, spent several weeks in Chicago in 1904 researching the living and working conditions of employees in the meatpacking industry. He worked (incognito) in one of the plants as an embedded employee and came away with even more disturbing findings than expected. His searing political fiction was first published in serial form in 1905 in a prominent Socialist weekly, *Appeal to Reason*. His novel, *The Jungle*, dedicated to "the working man of America," was published in 1906, when he was twenty-eight years old.

Sinclair pulls no punches. He depicts factory owners who are as heartless and cruel as Harriet Beecher Stowe's infamous Simon Legree. He finds government food inspectors who are either incompetent or bought off. He finds union bosses and political ward bosses thriving in a sea of graft, bribery, kickbacks, and the pay-to-play politics Chicago, unfortunately, is still known for. Building codes are disregarded. The judicial system is corrupt. Meatpacking industry titans seek to maximize profits. They use every part of an animal, even entrails or diseased pieces that should have been considered unfit for consumption. Anything left on the factory floor—blood, dirt, and even a hapless worker—would be shoveled into the sausage-making machines.

Sinclair grew up reading Horatio Alger Jr. novels about the rags-to-respectability American Dream. But he had also read *Uncle Tom's Cabin* and had, apparently, become a passionate, exuberant, "born again" Socialist. He was an unapologetic Socialist for the rest of his life. His writings are rightly associated with those of Frank Norris, Theodore Dreiser, Edward Bellamy, and Jack London, all of whom wrote about the need for collective action on behalf of the dispossessed proletariat.

Jungle is variously described as a protest novel, a sociological study, social realism, or as Socialist propaganda. It is all of these, a proletarian novel *par excellence*, combining investigative journalism with a sentimental account of a fictional hardworking immigrant. It is also agitational political fiction and an indictment of the failures of unregulated capitalism. In the end, it is a moralistic and political call for a more humane social system, and in political leadership terms, it was an Act I agenda-setting book foreshadowing the Progressive Era.

Critics complained the first half of the book was overly sensational and fatalistic and his last chapters too naïvely optimistic—a dreamy celebration of a revolution leading to a Socialist nirvana. Sinclair, however, was not writing for the critics or for English teachers—his aim was to critique the overly rosy American Dream exceptionalism of the era and to arouse a complacent middle America and inspire working-class solidarity. A classic agitation novel, it is explicitly intended to win sympathy for Chicago's as well as America's voiceless poor. It highlights a problematic side of American capitalism and trumpets the promise of socialism.

His Social Darwinian storytelling has those on top succeeding as predators of their desperate prey on the bottom. This world of unfettered capitalism is likened to a jungle, where predators thrive and the prey struggle to survive under the "iron heel" of heartless, exploitive corporations.

The metaphor of the jungle, writes Christopher Phelps, refers to "the ferocity of dog-eat-dog competition, the barbarity of exploitative work, the wilderness of urban life, the savagery of poverty, the crudity of political corruption, and the primitiveness of the doctrine of the survival of the fittest, which led people to the slaughter as surely as cattle."[13]

Sinclair's Chicago is a jungle of political deal making and con artists:

> The city, which was owned by an oligarchy of businessmen, being nominally ruled by the people, a huge army of graft was necessary for the purpose of effecting the transfer of power. Twice a year, in the spring and fall elections, millions of dollars were furnished by the businessmen and expended by this army; meetings were held and clever speakers were hired, bands played and rockets sizzled, tons of documents and reservoirs of drinks were distributed, and tens of thousands of votes were bought for cash.

Sinclair sees a widespread system that corrupted virtually every part of civil and economic society: "All of these agencies of corruption were banded together." The police captain would own the brothel he pretended to raid. Machine bosses would pay scabs to foil a workers' strike. Voting fraud was routine. Political henchmen were put on the city payroll for "no-show" jobs. A gigantic Racing Trust, mostly known for its elaborate scams, appeared to own the state legislature and many newspapers.

Sinclair depicts politics in this "Butcher of the World" city as the antithesis of storybook, government-by-the-people democratic constitutionalism. His Chicago was a corrupt political and economic system rigged to serve the wealthy and to exploit the people at the bottom. One of my students wrote a paper on *The Jungle* and aptly titled it "Chicago: Corruption at Its Finest, Meat at Its Poorest." This student also joked that Chicago doesn't have its "Windy City" nickname because of the fierce winds coming off Lake Michigan so much as because of the Chicago politicians who were constantly blowing hot air, causing a breeze that "tears through the city."[14]

Sinclair's social realism was aimed at documenting the travails of those who naïvely believed in the illusions and fantasies of American Dreamism. Industrialization and corporatization had, Sinclair declares, changed the way owners and managers treated workers. The twentieth-century corporation had a lot in common with feudalism and plantations. And those who suffered most, he says, were immigrants who had sacrificed to travel long distances in search of jobs in what they believed would be the land of promising new opportunities.

> Here was a population, low-class and mostly foreign, hanging always on the verge of starvation, and dependent for its opportunities of life upon the whim of men every bit as brutal and unscrupulous as the old-time slave drivers; under such circumstances immorality was exactly as inevitable, and as prevalent, as it was under the system of chattel slavery. Things that were quite unspeakable went on there in the packing houses all the time, and were taken for granted by everybody.

His storytelling is often more an investigative documentary than fiction; yet the fiction format allowed him to generalize beyond his data, get readers intrigued with his protagonist, engaged in the protagonist's wanderings and fate, and curious about what will happen both to him and to America. A nonfiction report would probably not have become the blockbuster best seller *Jungle* became.

Jungle has little subtlety. Sinclair tells his story through the seamy experiences of Jurgis Rudkus. Jurgis and his wife, Ona, live in a festering slum. He works in backbreaking jobs in unsanitary conditions. He has a few fellow Lithuanian immigrant friends, but otherwise he experiences a "reverse welcome wagon." He is scammed at work and conned into buying a shoddy residence with so many strings attached that he soon loses it. His wife and relatives are "compromised" by their bosses or forced into prostitution.

When Jurgis is maimed on the job, he is laid off, even though his employer's factory was responsible. Jurgis loses his wife and son. He lives on the streets and is arrested as a tramp, and his soul becomes "filled full of bitterness and despair." Jurgis lives "like a wounded animal in the forest; he is forced to compete with his enemies upon unequal terms." He lives, Sinclair writes, in an unforgiving world. There were few antipoverty programs helping people like him, though it should be noted that the duly celebrated Jane Addams had begun her Hull House and some pioneering social settlement projects around this time.

Jurgis "saw the [so-called] world of civilization then more plainly than he had seen it before; a world in which nothing counted but brutal might, an order devised by those who possessed it for the subjugation of those who did not."

What amazes the reader today is how wide ranging Sinclair's documentary-style novel is—the result of just seven weeks of participant/observer fieldwork in Chicago's depressing Packingtown neighborhoods.

Sinclair wrote *Jungle* in part as an exposé of the inhuman and hypocritical meatpacking industry. Readers were nauseated to learn of the way food processors prepared and packaged their food. The unsanitary food message, he later recalled, hit people in their stomachs. But Sinclair's larger purpose was to criticize unregulated capitalism and marshal support for the Socialist movement. *The Jungle* failed to achieve these more central objectives, as its ideological message was harder for most readers to digest. Most Americans wanted to believe in some variation of the American Dream as expounded in the Horatio Alger novels. Capitalism, for most, had practically become synonymous with democracy, and few readers could identify with Jurgis's conversion to socialism.

Sinclair beguiles us early in the novel with Jurgis's unwavering belief in the American Dream; yet his odyssey ends with an unwavering faith in democratic socialism. *The Jungle* was the first book in which Sinclair wholeheartedly embraced socialism. His hapless protagonist is rescued and transfixed by a messianic call to socialism. Stumbling by accident onto the scene of a political rally, Jurgis is mesmerized by a crusading Socialist who proclaims, "For I speak with the voice of the millions who are voiceless! Of them that are oppressed and have no comforter!"

Sucked into the vortex of this Socialist dream, Jurgis soon loves his new comrades and bellows out "The Marseillaise" as he learns about strategies for organizing Chicago workers. He also meets Lucas, who had been an itinerant religious preacher, now teaching that the churches, including the Vatican, have become perverted into serving the powerful rather than ordinary people. Jesus, Lucas tells him, would disown these modern churches. Jesus, after all, was "the true founder of the Socialist movement, a man whose whole being was one flame of hatred for wealth, and all that wealth stands for." Jurgis is exposed to a variety of Socialist visions—some utopian, others more pragmatic. He embraces the pragmatism of a campaign operative and proceeds to seek votes from like-minded fellow immigrants in the Chicago area.

Sinclair hardly invented the idea of socialism in America. European Marxism was already more than two generations old, and a U.S. Socialist Party had begun in 1901. In 1904, a year or so before *The Jungle* was written, Eugene Debs, a veteran union leader and riveting orator, ran as the Socialist candidate for U.S. president. (Debs won four hundred thousand votes, 3 percent of the total votes cast. Eight years later, in 1912, Debs would win 6 percent, but that would be the zenith for American Socialists.)

The socialism celebrated in the last chapters of *Jungle* was doubtless inspired by "Debsian" oratory. Democratic socialism, it claimed, would be the true road to freedom and happiness. The working class needed to adopt a new class-consciousness, one that would remind them of their rights and obligations. They also needed to understand the virtues of common ownership and democratic management. People must shed their habit of supporting the traditional, but now irrelevant, political parties. Socialism was, in Sinclair's words, "the new religion of humanity—or you might say it was the fulfillment of the old religion, since it implied but the literal application of all the teachings of Christ."

Debs's democratic socialism would redefine the American Dream to empower the working classes and give everyone an opportunity to share in the nation's economic success. Sinclair, like Debs, welcomed being called an agitator. The role of the dissident, both believed, was to channel workers' discontent and indignation in politically pragmatic directions.

This exposé of the inhumane conditions in Chicago's Packingtown had an impact. President Theodore Roosevelt, who prematurely criticized Sinclair as a "crackpot" and sensationalist "muckraker," altered his view after the book triggered a huge outpouring of support for improved meat inspections and regulations. Roosevelt even invited the young Sinclair for lunch at the White House. (Chicago sausage was likely not on the menu.) Congress enacted some minimal, watered-down food laws. About sixty years later, President Lyndon Johnson reinvited Sinclair, then eighty-nine, to witness the signing of a new meat inspection law.

Critics point out that, despite Sinclair's powerful message so long ago, corporate meat producers are still oligopolies, still recruiting immigrants and minorities, and still competitively driven by the bottom line. But they are more regulated, and the nation has gradually become more informed about food quality and safety.

The eccentric Sinclair wrote about eighty novels, including exposés of the coal and oil industries. He also ran unsuccessfully for public office several times, usually on the Socialist Party ticket. But in 1934, at the height of the Great Depression, he changed registration and became the Democratic candidate for governor of California. He ran on an ambitious redistributive public policy platform called "End Poverty in California," or EPIC. The program, personally drafted by Sinclair, called for a progressive income tax; pensions for widows, the disabled, and the elderly; and a variety of partnerships between industry and workers aimed at creating more jobs and better utilizing idle land and factories.

The blunt and often prickly Sinclair was an unnatural politician. He tried in vain to get political support from Franklin Roosevelt, but FDR and most of his advisors viewed Sinclair as too radical. Republicans, business leaders, and Hollywood moguls targeted him as a socialist and Communist rabble-rousing firebrand. He acknowledged his socialism but vigorously denied any belief in Communism. Sinclair analyzed his defeat in an unusually candid firsthand postcampaign memoir.[15] In a three-person race, Democrat Sinclair won 38 percent of the vote, losing to the incumbent Republican.

Several publishers, perhaps not surprisingly, rejected *The Jungle* because it was considered incendiary. Doubleday agreed to publish it only if the company's lawyer verified the general conditions Sinclair described. The lawyer confirmed the awful conditions, as did a subsequent White House–appointed task force. Doubleday was also encouraged to publish it when twenty thousand people pledged to purchase a copy of the book.

Literary critics have often belittled *Jungle* as breathless muckraking journalism and propaganda. It likewise gets faulted for its sentimental moralism and its insensitivity toward blacks. The novel is frustratingly vague on what socialism is and how it would help. The naïve predictions about electoral success and the exhortation that "Chicago will be ours!" obviously missed the mark. Still, *Jungle* remains one of America's most pedagogically powerful political novels. It makes readers reflect on their political and economic assumptions. Its harsh indictment of conventional American politics and unregulated laissez-faire capitalism is among the most riveting examples of American realism.

In Sinclair's defense, political fiction writers rarely provide solutions to major public policy problems. The most we can usually get are helpful analyses (or, as in his case, documentation) of public policy problems. And they can make us think about and imagine a more ideal American Experiment. In this Sinclair succeeds.

The Jungle became a best seller at home and abroad, and its storytelling is embedded as part of the American narrative. It is continuously reprinted and regularly read, especially by high school and college students.

DEPRESSION-ERA WANDERINGS[16]

> Fainy, you're a bright boy . . . I wish I could have helped you more; you're an O'Hara, every inch of you. You read Marx . . . study all you can, remember that you're a rebel by birth and blood. . . . Don't blame people for things . . . blame the system. And don't ever sell out to the sons of bitches, son. . . . All right, go on. . . . Better cut along or you'll miss your train.

That's Uncle Tim O'Hara's advice to a young Fenian O'Hara Mc-Creary as he sets out on his life's journey from Chicago in Dos Passos's *42nd Parallel*, his first of three novels that chronicled the early decades of the twentieth century.

Dos Passos believed his job as a novelist was "to capture the snarl of the human currents of his time." His *USA* trilogy, 1,450 pages long, is considered one of the most inventive political novels in American literature.

John Roderigo Dos Passos Jr. (1896–1970) was one of the more gifted, fascinating, and complicated political storytellers of his time. He was the illegitimate son of a wealthy, politically well-connected Wall Street attorney, a counsel to major banks and corporate interests. His father, a Catholic with Portuguese heritage, chose not to get a divorce but maintained a longtime affair with his son's mother, a wealthy southern aristocratic widow, Lucy Madison. Their son, called "Josh Madison" until age sixteen, when he assumed his father's name, had a privileged, yet strained, upbringing. He and his mother traveled a lot, with long stays in Europe. It was, he later lamented, "a horrible childhood," a "hotel childhood." But it was a worldly (if sheltered) childhood.

Dos Passos was educated by tutors, at a British boarding school, and later at Choate and Harvard, where he migrated easily to writing and editing. He described himself as meek, shy, and unathletic; yet he basked in the praise he earned as a young writer for his school publications. Writers and poets, including E. E. Cummings, became his friends.

As a professional writer, he tackled major subjects: war, alienation, capitalism, socialism, Communism, trade unions, the New Deal, Jefferson, Wilson, demagogues, the Horatio Alger aspirations, and the promise of "our storybook democracy." He was a pacifist and fiery Socialist in his younger years; however, his evolving disenchantment with both Russian Communism and New Deal statism led to his becoming, in later years, a conservative Republican.

Dos Passos was a literary lion for decades. Despite his shyness, he was addicted to travel and enjoyed a friendship with Ernest Hemingway, with whom he sometimes hunted, fished, and partied. He was iconoclastic and almost deliberately irreverent in his writings. He rarely worried about offending political or literary interests.

In his early years, Dos Passos identified less with the privileged class of his father, whose financial support he depended on, or his Choate and Harvard classmates, and more with antiestablishment "workers' struggle" movements such as the Socialists, anarchists, and militant labor unions. His first novel, *Three Soldiers*, was a stark condemnation of war.

He regularly wrote for the left-leaning *New Masses* and actively joined with literary luminaries such as Upton Sinclair and Dorothy Parker in denouncing the arrest and conviction of Socialists Nicola Sacco and Bartolomeo Vanzetti. He protested on behalf of striking miners, and his anticapitalism led him to an infatuation with the Russian experiment. He spent nearly a half-year in Russia in 1932, examining what was taking place there. He returned to America more ambivalent than converted, though he did vote for the Communist Party presidential ticket in the 1932 election. He said he never joined the Communist Party, but he plainly had friends who did—and, like many intellectuals at the time, he was searching for alternatives to the seemingly failed (or at least stalled) American Experiment.

The 42nd Parallel was written as an agitational message-sending novel. It was an intentional mockery of the Horatio Alger dream and the illusion of equal opportunity for all. Its dozen or so fictional biographies suggest the American Dream was, for most people, misleading, if not a fantasy.

Parallel has no unified plot and employs four seemingly disconnected formats for examining the themes and events in the twentieth century's early decades. Dos Passos describes working-class Americans as generally unhappy, if not disillusioned, and struggling to make a living. He employs "newsreels" at regular intervals, which are snippets from newspaper headlines or advertisements. He also offers short biographies of prominent heroes and villains. And perhaps influenced by James Joyce or Thackeray, he offers stream-of-consciousness autobiographical authorial commentary on his own coming of age. Some readers loved these innovative features; others criticized them as too clever or as disruptive trickery. But collectively, they provide a probing (if somewhat convoluted) political commentary of the times. Some critics faulted Dos Passos for not being Marxist enough. Others disparaged him for his concentration on whites and the exclusion and occasional derogatory attitude toward minorities.

In *Parallel*, a young protagonist, "Mac" McCreary, hears Upton Sinclair deliver a lecture about the brutalities of the Chicago stockyards. Soon afterward, Mac learns about the Industrial Workers of the World (the IWW or "wobblies") and their workers' rights campaign. Mac, a sometime printer, learns that the day has come to start building a new society, one "in the shell of the old and for workers to get ready to assume control of the industries they'd created out of their sweat and blood." The exploiting classes, his new mentors tell him, will be helpless against the solidarity of the whole working class. Workers had to realize that fights for better wages, for free speech, for improved living conditions, were merely the first steps in the larger fight for the revolution and the coming "cooperative commonwealth." One organizer also informs him that revolutionaries postpone marriage and children until after the revolution.

An inspired McCreary goes to work for the union, first in the mines of Nevada. He sees himself as a comrade in a fierce uphill battle: a young revolutionary, joining whomever will help overthrow despotic oppressors. Later, he joins the Zapata revolution in Mexico.

In Mexico, he finds himself adept at engaging as well as drinking with the workers, the trade unions, the *partido laborista* and *agraristas*. Yet, before long, Mac is co-opted by women, financial obligations, and the lures of the middle class. He gradually loses faith in the revolution and at one point utters, "Aw, hell! Let's sell out and go back to the States."

McCreary and friends are described as adrift without a compass, just as Depression-era America was. Stories about long, wandering journeys date back to Homer's *Odyssey* and beyond. Typically, there is a clear goal or unifying cause in such journeys. Dos Passos's goals are more implicit and distant. His are presumably Socialist-inspired goals of a fair representative government and a more just economic system.

Many of Dos Passos's characters in *Parallel* are drifters and voiceless malcontents, by-products of the new industrial age. Charley Anderson from Fargo, North Dakota, is one of these confused and restless wanderers. A mechanic, Charley bumps around a lot, and at one point he joins the AFL union and gets curious about politics. "He decided he'd read the papers more and keep up with what was going on in the world. What with this war, and everything you couldn't tell what might happen." Charley believed working stiffs like himself had to stick together and fight for decent living conditions, and "the time was coming when there'd be a big revolution like the American Revolution, only bigger and after that there wouldn't be any bosses and the workers would run industry."

But Charley, like the Socialist movement in which he is a lowly private, gets repeatedly buffeted by unfriendly bosses and bad luck. One boss complained that his Socialist and revolutionary ideas were the talk of "a damn foreigner" and that he "ought to be ashamed of himself, and that a white man ought to believe in individual liberty and if he got a raw deal on one job he was goddam well able to find another." Charley Anderson, like many Dos Passos characters, drifts around America, searching for a decent job, love, and an always vague, ill-defined, and ill-organized "revolution."

A more sinisterly drawn Dos Passos character is J. W. Moorehouse, who had initially meandered his way through a couple of marriages and a variety of minor jobs before making it as a Madison Avenue public relations counselor to corporate titans. His mandate, for which he is handsomely compensated, is to take on the Socialists and sentimentalists in the labor unions and preach about the prosperity of the American Dream. He wheels and deals with political and corporate chieftains to dampen revolutionary sentiments and later to channel America's energies into defeating the Germans during the first World War.

Dos Passos satirizes J. W. Moorehouse, his rise to riches, and Chamber of Commerce boosterism. Morehouse is a marked counterpoint to the fanciful Socialist dreaming of the Mac McCrearys and Charley Andersons. Dos Passos is especially sarcastic about the new public relations profession and characterizes them as middlemen business agents who add little or no productive value to society.

Dos Passos's sentiments decidedly lie with the underdogs, lost souls who yearn for a second American Revolution that will remedy the heartless injustices of the Industrial Revolution. But the author is well aware of the challenges facing Act I political activists. He had seen this firsthand. He was raised as a privileged member of the establishment and knew that the Rockefellers, Morgans, Wall Streeters, and special interests had the upper hand. And just as union organizing is gaining some traction stateside, a new world war comes along to unite the country in patriotism and to disarm pushes for workers' rights. One of the novel's more cynical theorists explains, "It's a plot of the big interests, Morgan an' them, to defeat the workers by sendin' 'em off to war. Once they get you in the Army you can't howl about civil liberty or the Bill of Rights. . . . They can shoot you without a trial, see?"

What is Dos Passos telling us? *Parallel* is an ideological attack on phony civic boosterism, privileged elites, the exaggerated myths of prosperity and the American Dream. It, like the writings of Upton Sinclair, Jack London, and Frank Norris, celebrates underdog yearnings of the invariably disorganized workers. It is also brutal social realism, recognition that political organizing without resources and without friends in high places is an invitation to frustration. Act I activists are typically viewed in every society as disruptive agitators. Dos Passos's would-be reformers, however, are consistently hapless, unfocused, divided, and largely ineffective.

Dos Passos chronicles frustrations about the prevailing incentives that encourage people to "sell out to the sons of bitches." These "sons of bitches" are, unmistakably, corporate and political leaders. He laments the "dirty smell of politics," at one point lacerating William Jennings Bryan as having "a silver tongue in a big mouth," while somehow overlooking that union organizing, anarchism, and revolutions are also political activities. Perhaps, in his view, a "smell-less" form of politics?

The American Dream is, of course, an enduring theme in American literature. Thanks to Sinclair, London, and other novelists, we see those who, for a number of reasons, are unable to participate in it. That's also the Dos Passos story. He is a novelist and also a sociologist, anthropologist, social analyst, and political critic. *42nd Parallel* is a novel of political estrangement, rife with narratives of betrayal, malaise, and indignation about the social injustices that are the by-products, he contends, of capitalism. Novels of political estrangement pay less attention to politicians and their institutions and more attention to ordinary people, people whose choices and freedoms are devitalized by the dominant establishments of their time.[17]

Several noted writers, including Hemingway, Steinbeck, and Mailer, considered Dos Passos's *USA* trilogy among the best writing in American literature. His writing made him famous, but not especially wealthy. His literary devices of using newsreels, short biographic sketches, and his own authorial "camera's eye" are inventive. Steinbeck doubtless borrowed from this for his "interchapters" in *The Grapes of Wrath*.

Dos Passos went on to write a negative fictionalized account of FDR and what he called "the Raw Deal," *The Grand Design* (1949). He appreciated some of the benefits of the New Deal, and he had voted for FDR in 1936, but he loathed the centralization that came with sweeping executive power. The novel denounces the "concentration camps" for Japanese Americans and the Big Power (United States, Russia, and Britain) negotiations that divided up the globe, and were, he believed, a setback for liberty.

As his disenchantment with Communism and New Dealism grew, so did his interest in Jeffersonian notions of limited government. This led to his pro-Jefferson *The Head and Heart of Thomas Jefferson* (1954). Eventually, in his fifties, he became an ardent anti-Communist and wrote disparagingly about the New Left. Yet, throughout his political evolution from socialism to libertarian conservatism, there were certain continuing themes. Robert C. Rosen suggests that Dos Passos

> first came to oppose capitalism through his distaste for industrialism and his hatred of war; later he came to accept American society through his hatred of communism, in which he saw many of the evils he once attributed to industrial capitalism itself: the concentration of power, the crushing of the individual, the aggression of war. The same intense individualism that gave rise to his radical criticisms of the Communist Party in the 1930s made him an enemy of the increasingly powerful and bureaucratic modern liberal state after the war. Through all of his work runs an anger born of misplaced faith. Wilsonian liberalism, American communists, trade unions, the New Deal, his country's efforts in World War II—all disappointed him. However much he yearned to love his "chosen country," he remained its tireless critic, always the rebel, ready to attack whatever he perceived to be "the interests."[18]

In *42nd Parallel*, Dos Passos captured the disillusionment of the times and shared vivid, if disheartening, stories of people struggling to find their way. Dos Passos similarly struggled to find his way politically. He achieved notoriety as a writer; yet he restlessly searched, in common with many Americans, for a more satisfying political philosophy and a more admirable American republic.

WARNING: FASCIST ALERT[19]

> The tyranny of this dictatorship isn't primarily the fault of Big Business, nor of the demagogues who do their dirty work. It's the fault of Doremus Jessup! Of all the conscientious, respectable, lazy-minded Doremus Jessups who have let the demagogues wriggle in, without fierce enough protest.

These are the sad conclusions of the Vermont small-town newspaper editor Doremus Jessup in Sinclair Lewis's dystopian *It Can't Happen Here*.

Can't Happen envisions FDR's defeat in 1936. The nation's economy teeters on the edge of collapse, anxieties soar, and constitutional democracy crumbles. Impatience and fear reign. In January 1937, an American-style fascist regime (yet with a deceptive veneer of Mark Twain folksiness) takes over the country. This anti-Roosevelt ticket won by promising share-the-wealth schemes, nativist antiminority fears, and the promise of decisive "Make America Great" leadership.

How bad does it get? The novel describes an appalling, shocking political and social nightmare. The charismatic new president, Berzelius "Buzz" Windrip, a former Democratic U.S. senator (a fictionalized composite of a racist Huey Long and a Hitler), comes to office heading up the American Corporate State and Patriotic Party. His populist-leaning party championed "Forgotten Men" and had promised that everyone would be granted several thousand dollars a year and nobody could earn more than $500,000. Windrip loves mass rallies and railing against the fake news of the mainstream media. This radical new party immediately abolishes other parties, abolishes states, and creates eight provinces. He also disempowers Congress and the courts, declares martial law, censors the media and the arts, burns "seditious" books, closes down suspicious universities, and begins campaigns against blacks and Jews. A year or so later, this transformed America, spearheaded by its militant followers, called the "Minute Men," invades Mexico.

Lewis's protagonist, Doremus Jessup, owns and edits a small newspaper, *The Daily Informer*, in Fort Beulah, Vermont. He is a proud member of the local school and library boards, and, of course, the Fort Beulah Rotary Club. Lewis describes Fort Beulah as an innocent, drowsy town, "a town of security and tradition, which still believed in Thanksgiving, Fourth of July, Memorial Day, and to which May Day was not an occasion for labor parades, but for distributing small baskets of flowers."

Jessup considers himself a well-read, civic-minded reflective moderate; yet he also possesses a kind of quirky libertarian individualism. He admires fellow New Englanders like Henry David Thoreau and is skeptical about governments, especially "big solution" schemes. By his own account, he has a "tentative" temperament.

Then comes the Great Depression. And with it, even in small-town Vermont, comes a diminished faith in the American Dream: "The Horatio Alger tradition, from rags to Rockefeller, was clean gone out of the America it had dominated." American exceptionalism fails to carry the day. It happened in Germany. It happened in Italy. It was now, in Sinclair's story, happening here.

Harry Sinclair Lewis (1885–1951) grew up in rural Sauk Center, Minnesota. His father was a respected local physician, and Harry (he would drop the Harry and call himself Sinclair—he was "Hal" or "Red" to his friends) attended local public schools and prepped at Oberlin Academy in Ohio before going to Yale University. According to biographers, he was tall, gangly, acne prone, and often lonely in his youth. At Yale, he never felt "accepted" but was a frequent contributor to the *Yale Courant* and *Yale Literary Magazine*. He took a few weeks off from Yale in 1906 to work in Upton Sinclair's utopian cooperative colony, Helicon Hall, near Englewood, New Jersey. Lewis was enchanted with socialism at the time, but he quickly migrated back to Yale.[20] Upton Sinclair and Jack London were his early heroes. Lewis briefly joined the Socialist Party in 1911 and 1912.

After Yale, Lewis worked in the New York publishing world and became a freelance writer with frequent publications in national magazines. This led to his writing novels, and at a relatively young age, his *Main Street* (1920) and *Babbitt* (1922) (which satirize American boosterism, commercialism, and middle-class hypocrisy) won acclaim. More novels followed, and he became the first American to win the Nobel Prize for Literature (1930).

The events in *It Can't Happen Here* (1935) reflect the tumultuous political developments taking place in Europe and in the United States. Hitler and Mussolini had come to office in Germany and Italy through national elections. America was still in the grip of economic hardships from the Great Depression, and there were great fears about what would happen here.

Populist demagogic U.S. senator (and former Louisiana governor) Huey Long had broken with FDR and was setting out to challenge him in the 1936 election. Long promised major redistributive programs to help the working classes and poor. His "share our wealth" platform excoriated big business as the source of the evil besetting America. (Lewis's book was completed just before Long was assassinated in Baton Rouge.)

Long was not alone. Prominent populists and preachers of the time were also repudiating FDR and attacking Wall Street and the bankers. These populists called for subsidies for the elderly, more steeply graduated income taxes, and an array of programs to address poverty and inequality. Upton Sinclair's 1934 California campaign for governor and his famous EPIC (End Poverty in California) plan was one of the many transformational plans being discussed. The Detroit radio priest Rev. Charles Coughlin, whose programs had an estimated forty million listeners, blasted FDR and formed the National Union for Social Justice. Coughlin issued sweeping denunciations of what was wrong in America. He eventually became an isolationist and anti-Semite.

It Can't Happen Here is, as noted, a dystopian doomsday forecast. Fascist alert! It *can*, Lewis is shouting, happen here. Wake up, Americans, before it's too late! His is a political-message-sending book. Lewis wanted to rally responsible Americans to become involved to prevent a fascist America. A "mind-your-own-business" or Thoreauean approach to citizenship, he warns, can only lead to disaster.

His Doremus Jessup describes the situation: "First they came for the Socialists, and I did not speak out—Because I was not a Socialist. Then they came for the Trade Unionists, and I didn't speak out—Because I was not a Trade Unionist. Then they came for the Jews, and I did not speak out—Because I was not a Jew. Then they came for me—and there was no one left to speak for me."

Jessup, who believed he was safely ensconced in isolated, bucolic Fort Beulah, learns his lesson the hard way. He writes an editorial criticizing the new Windrip regime and is immediately arrested, intimidated, and forced to recant. But this he cannot do for long. He soon joins an ill-organized resistance movement and tries, in vain, to escape to Canada.

The once-smug individualistic Rotarian is now forced to rethink his notion of citizenship. Despite his "tentative" temperament, he is now belatedly politicized and radicalized. His long-suffering wife, Emma Jessup, beseeches him to stay out of politics. That is, she exclaims, "no occupation for a gentleman!" But Doremus is aghast at hearing of mass executions and concentration camps in the United States. Then the regime's local authorities shoot his son-in-law.

Jessup joins others in putting out *The Vermont Vigilance*, an illegal underground resistance rag that exposes national and local "un-American" atrocities. At one poignant point, his now-widowed daughter sneaks into local drugstores and inserts *The Vigilance* inside *Reader's Digest* magazines.

In earlier days, Jessup had disdained rabble-rousers, utopias, and radicals. "Blessed be they," he had opined, "who are not Patriots and Idealists, and who do not feel they must dash right out and Do Something About It." Now, however, he understands agitation and violence are sometimes warranted. The aggressive, occasionally violent abolitionists, and even the tragic slaughter of the Civil War, he reflects, were necessary "because easygoing citizens like me couldn't be stirred up otherwise." "It's my sort, the Responsible Citizens who've felt ourselves superior because we've been well-to-do, and (we thought) 'educated,' who brought on the Civil War, the French Revolution, and now the Fascist Dictatorship. . . . Forgive, O Lord! Is it too late?"

It Can't Happen Here chronicles Jessup's journey from respected "big gentleman" on Main Street to a reborn "conviction" activist, committed to a second American Revolution. The newly activist Jessup is arrested and sentenced to seventeen years in prison. He is taken off to Dartmouth College in Hanover, New Hampshire, which has been converted to a prison. His new politics of estrangement lead him to shout, "Now I know why men like John Brown became crazy killers."

Eventually he is sprung from jail. This time, he successfully navigates his way to Montreal, where he enlists as a resistance fighter. He becomes a spy and organizes for the cause to reclaim America. The novel ends as various coups are taking place in Washington, D.C., with Jessup still an Act I resistance fighter now operating in the upper Midwest.

Lewis's account of the fascist national leaders is often over-the-top satire (his literary trademark) as they stumble in their efforts to deliver on their share-the-wealth efforts. In fact, the Windrip presidency utterly fails to restore prosperity, redistribute wealth, and make America great. The new regime becomes increasingly centralized, imperial, and infected with graft and corruption. Eventually, the generals oust the president and secretary of state. The ghoulish regime is inept as well as evil.

Can't Happen covers the imagined years of 1937 through 1939. This what-if novel is chillingly bleak. It is a fiction writer's political manifesto, calling on respectable Americans to reject civic passivity.

The novel was a direct response to the events of the day and was doubtless influenced by his wife's experiences in Europe. Lewis's second wife, Dorothy Thompson, had covered and interviewed Hitler in the early 1930s in her role as a foreign correspondent and had witnessed Hitler's racist and anti-Semitic scapegoating, propaganda, and persecutions. American intellectuals debated whether fascism might come to America. FDR and his advisors privately viewed Huey Long as the most dangerous man in America. They also feared the rising military star General Douglas MacArthur.

Roosevelt understood the cruel appeal that Long and similar share-the-wealth demagogues on the left had for those whose careers and dreams had been dashed by poverty. He worried about their haranguing methods and especially their unscrupulous use of fear, hate, envy, and specious appeals of lavish handouts. FDR also worried about potential demagogues who might arise on the right. He specifically told aides this could come from a person such as MacArthur:

> There was latent, he thought, not far below the uneasy surface of our
> disrupted society, an impulse among a good many "strong" men, men

used to having their way, mostly industrialists who directed affairs without being questioned, a feeling that democracy had run its course and that the totalitarians had grasped the necessities of the time. People wanted strong leadership; they were sick of uncertainty, anxious for security, and willing to trade liberty for it. That was the thesis.[21]

Roosevelt's and Lewis's worst fears did not come to pass. FDR was reelected in 1936 by nearly 61 percent of the popular vote, and he carried all states except for Maine and, ironically, Vermont.

A noted novelist as political storyteller had spelled out in gripping terms what could happen if Americans complacently shirked political involvement. In bleak narrative, Lewis, performing a Paul Revere role, proclaims it could be worse than his readers imagined.

Can't Happen attacks both complacency and idealism. "There will never be a state of society anything like perfect!" his protagonist proclaims. He learns belatedly that the perfect can be, as an old saying puts it, the enemy of the good. "Is it just possible," he wonders, "that the most vigorous and boldest idealists have been the worst enemies of human progress instead of its greatest creators?"

Literary critics were rough on *It Can't Happen Here*. It was faulted for sentimental and plodding dialogue, heavy-handed satire, corny and one-dimensional characters, intellectual incoherence, and pretentious patriotism. Much of this is true. Lewis never thought of it as one of his best novels.

But *Happen* was a commercial success, and it was a serious political statement by a celebrity writer. It remains an important book for students of American politics. It helps explain an enormously troubling moment in American history, and it once more illustrates how a writer can make us think, and can help, in Orwell's words, "to push the world in a certain direction."

Some observers have suggested that America has two constitutions: one for peacetime and a much more restrictive one for wartime. We learned about this even from the sainted Lincoln, who among other things suspended *habeas corpus* during the Civil War. We learned it anew when Japanese Americans were sent to internment camps in the early 1940s, and with the permanent establishment of the Central Intelligence Agency in the late 1940s and the blacklisting and rumormongering of the House Un-American Activities Committee (HUAC) and McCarthyism.

Lewis died (in Rome) at the height of the McCarthy era. Were he alive now, he would hardly be surprised by the passage of the U.S. Patriot Act, the establishment of a Department of Homeland Security, extraordinary rendition policies, "enhanced interrogation" programs, or the sweeping data-mining activities of the National Security Agency. He would probably have celebrated Edward Snowden's 2013 revelations about government snooping as more patriotic than criminal. And he doubtless would have been repulsed by Russian interference in the 2016 presidential election.

Lewis's message still matters. No matter how corny his characters or how implausible his doomsday scenario in *Can't Happen*, Lewis's warnings remain relevant. Indeed, it again became a best seller in 2017 as comparisons were being made between Lewis's president Buzz Windrip and President Donald J. Trump. Both played off the fears of working-class white people. Both discredited the media. Both emphasized nativist and emotional nationalism. Both made unrealistic campaign promises. Both won support during economically unsettling times.

Beware, Lewis is saying, the allure of toxic leaders scapegoating minorities and bearing utopian solutions. A generation later, Richard Condon's valuable novel *The Manchurian Candidate* (perhaps somewhat inspired by *It Can't Happen Here*) was yet another warning that undesirable political changes *can* happen here. Ray Bradbury's *Fahrenheit 451* raises similar dystopian fears. Still later Knebel and Bailey's *Seven Days in May* warns us about the possibility of military coups in America.

Americans are impatient with government and politicians. Support for jingoistic and imperial adventurism jostles with mindless xenophobia. National politics often reflect a public increasingly cynical and frustrated with partisan stalemate. Lewis's message is threefold: We might not recognize it when it is happening. Beware the cult of the magic-pushing simplistic leader. And don't wait until it is too late—don't give up on politics. Politics needs to be the preoccupation (Emma Jessups's lament notwithstanding) of everyone who cherishes constitutional democracy.

IN SEARCH OF GRAPES AND HUMANITY[22]

Wherever they's a fight so hungry people can eat, I'll be there. Wherever they's a cop beatin' up a guy, I'll be there . . . I'll be in the way kids laugh when they're hungry an' they know supper's ready. An' when our folks eat stuff they raise an' live in the houses they build—why, I'll be there.

These are Tom Joad's parting words to Ma Joad as he heads off to fight for those who, like his Okie farm family, have been dispossessed of their land and livelihoods and set adrift in a world where they are ill prepared to survive.

Hamlin Garland's messianic Ida Wilbur in his *A Spoil of Office* (1892) declares, "Wherever a man is robbed, wherever a man toils and the fruits of his toil are taken from him; wherever the frosty lash of winter stings or the tear of poverty scalds, there the principles of our order reaches."

Tom's words are similar to the iconic Socialist Eugene Debs, who had earlier proclaimed, "While there is a criminal class I am in it; while there is a soul in prison I am not free." And they are also derived from the labor-organizing songs of Joe Hill and others. Joad's defiant pledge has been later memorialized in various ballads, most notably by Woody Guthrie's "Tom Joad" and Bruce Springsteen's "The Ghost of Tom Joad."

These are examples of how politicians, novelists, and songwriters influence one another; tribal stories get absorbed in the political culture, often in an unconscious process of assimilation.

John Steinbeck (1902–1968) won the National Book Award, the Pulitzer Prize, and, in 1962, a Nobel Prize for his stinging account of the Joad family's struggles to stay together as they coped with the disruptive changes and uncertainties of a Depression-wracked America. It made the thirty-seven-year-old novelist famous and set off a firestorm of controversy. It was immediately attacked or disputed by corporate agricultural organizations, many Californians, many Oklahomans, and countless church groups and most Republicans.

But it has been a huge best seller in America and around the world. It is among the most acclaimed political narratives of the past century, and it served as the basis for a prize-winning Hollywood film starring Henry Fonda as Tom Joad and directed by the legendary John Ford. (Steinbeck was pleased by the film's faithfulness to his novel, even if it softened its sharper political message.)

In short, *Grapes* was "burned and banned, borrowed, smuggled," and bought, read, and reread.[23] It became one of America's most celebrated novels.

The Grapes of Wrath is not a story about traditional election or institutional politics. It is a protest novel in the tradition of Stowe's *Uncle Tom's Cabin* and Sinclair's *The Jungle*, a bottom-up, politically themed fictional documentary dramatizing oppression, inequality, and placelessness. It accuses political elites of being bought off by corporate interests. It especially indicts corporate agricultural interests for greed and heartlessness.

It is a call for a more just economic and political system. It builds upon Steinbeck's earlier fictional *In Dubious Battle* (1936), nonfictional news reporting on the "harvest gypsies" and related field research, and it is an angry book, aimed at its readers almost as if it was an ultimatum. It is also a sometimes heart-wrenching spiritual conversation, challenging Americans to rediscover shared communitarian obligations. Much of the novel can be read as an ethical treatise about what it is to be a human being—a human being with a heart.

As the story begins, young Tom Joad has just returned home to his family's small farm in Sallisaw, Oklahoma. He has served a four-year term in McAlester State Penitentiary for killing a man in a bar fight (it was, we understand, done in self-defense), and now he expects to help his parents work on their farm. He returns home, however, to find his family bankrupted by the Depression and the Dust Bowl environmental disaster. The banks have foreclosed, and the Joads have been forced off their small farm. But the bank owns the mortgage on the land. The bank's local representative apologizes to the Joads but can only suggest, "Why don't you go on west to California? There's work there and it never gets cold."

The Joad family had worked their land for at least four generations. They were proud of their hard work. They were proud of their American heritage and were exemplars of the Jeffersonian vision of small farmers as a centerpiece of the idea of America.

So who was it that was taking away their land? Climate change and poor farming practices played a role. But Steinbeck's characters feel they are being displaced by a faceless and heartless invisible hand. "It's the bank. It's the monster," they are told. But, the tenant farmers reply, aren't the banks only made up of men? "No you're wrong there—quite wrong," a local acquaintance explains. "The bank is something else than men . . . it's the monster. Men made it, but they can't control it." And so the tractors, driven by a friend's son, come rolling down the road to destroy their homes. A seemingly compassionless system uproots and displaces the Joads.

The Joad entourage—about thirteen people (and a dog), including two frail grandparents and a newly pregnant sister, with her new husband, an uncle, and with their former preacher, Jim Casy—pack up an old, overloaded jalopy of a Hudson truck and set out, Exodus style, for California in search of their American Dream—jobs, opportunity, and a home.

"Jus' let me get out to California," Grandpa Joad says. "Gonna get me a whole big bunch of grapes off a bush or whatever, an' I'm gonna squash 'em in my face and let 'em run off my chin." Muley Graves, a neighbor of the Joads, wistfully tells them, "I ain't going. This country is no good, but it's my country. No you all go ahead. I'll jus stay right here where I b'long."

Theirs becomes a bleak odyssey across southwestern America. Okies are unwelcome along Route 66. The Joads have little money; Grandpa and Grandma Joad die along the way. A brother and brother-in-law desert the family.

The real Joads, fictionalized here, were some four hundred to five hundred thousand desperate refugees fleeing the Great Dust Bowl region headed West ("lighting out for the territory," in Huck Finn's phrase) in search of a hoped-for paradise.

Once in California, the dreamed-of land of milk, honey, oranges, peaches, and grapes, the Joads experience one disaster after another. Few jobs are available, and growers are able to hire workers for nonliving wages. They are tricked, exploited, abused, and scorned. "Well, Okie use 'ta mean you were from Oklahoma. Now it means you're a dirty-son-of-a-bitch. Okie means you're scum."

Nearly everyone is hostile. Worker exploitation is a day-to-day reality. Migrants in the labor camps develop hopelessness as they learn the system is stacked against them. Ma Joad stoically holds together what is left of the family because, as she says, it is all they have.

Steinbeck speaks best through his characters: the slowly maturing Tom Joad, the ex-preacher Jim Casy who is ultimately murdered for organizing a migrant workers' strike, and the indomitable Ma Joad, the iconic nurturer, teacher, and spiritual communitarian who tries in vain to keep her family hopeful and together.

On one level, *Grapes* was Steinbeck's variation on the biblical Exodus story—a diaspora of displaced and dispossessed Dust Bowl victims as they trekked along Highway 66 in search of promise, hope, community, and opportunity. On another level, this is a story about young Tom Joad and his coming of age. He had been a temperamental and carefree youth who lived for the here and now. He loved his family; yet he was mostly self-absorbed and something of a drifter.

We meet him when he has just become a parolee, and we watch him become a fugitive and then an outlaw. He moves from being relatively naïve to developing a commitment to fight injustice. Tom may be only in his mid-twenties, but his education and maturation come fast, and it is as if he is "called" to transform himself into an agent for those who suffer.

Tom and his mom confront xenophobic hatred. Out West an officer tells them, "Well you ain't in your country now. You're in California, an' we don't want you goddam Okies settling down."

Tom's path toward self-actualization and purpose is gradual. He is quiet, yet quick to sense the prejudice and duplicity of the people he and his family meet. "We ain't no bums," Tom says. "We're looking for work. We'll take any kind a work."

He seethes with anger when he learns the big farmers deliberately recruit far more workers than they need so they can lower their wages. Or when they burn or destroy their crops to force smaller farmers out of business. He learns, too, that the big farmers put troublemakers on blacklists that will likely make them unemployable or maybe even jailed. "So we take what we can get, huh, or we starve; an' if we yelp we starve."

The more he learned about the obviously rigged system the more Tom becomes angry. Finally he bursts out, "I ain't gonna take it. Goddamn it, I an' my folks ain't no sheep. I'll kick the hell outa somebody." He gradually concludes, "They's a mean thing here. The folks here is scared of us people coming west, an' so they got cops out trying to scare us back."

Tom also learns that anyone who the farmers don't like is called an agitator or red. He hears about a farmer who says, "Goddamn reds is driving the country to ruin." "We got to drive the reds out." The discussion turns to who exactly is a "red." And it is said, "A red is any son-of-a-bitch that wants thirty cents an hour when we're paying twenty-five." Tom's friends respond to hearing this story by saying, "Hell, we're all reds." Tom laughs a little and adds, "Me too, I guess."

In the end Tom wanders outside of one of their camps and meets up with the strike leaders, including his old friend Jim Casy. Casy is clubbed to death by one of the strike-breaking hired guns for the farmers. Tom retaliates by killing Casy's assailant. Tom is wounded and branded with facial scars. He tells his mom and soon realizes he better flee so the family will not be punished. Ma Joad assures Tom that he has done the right thing but wishes that he didn't have to go.

In one of Steinbeck's tear-jerker passages, Ma Joad insists in their briar patch hideout that Tom take her last $7 and flee to somewhere like Los Angeles, where he can escape capture from those poised to kill him. Tom reluctantly takes the money and bids her farewell. But as he does so, Tom experiences a spiritual and political awakening inspired by both the family's humiliating experiences and the now-deceased Casy. The transformed and energized Tom commits himself to getting people to stand together, to work together, to yell together and lift each other up. He hasn't worked it out in any coherent plan, but he now believes, as Casy had counseled, that "a fella ain't got a soul of his own, but only a piece of a big one."

Tom Joad may be the protagonist in *Grapes*, and Ma Joad may be the most admirable character, but family friend and ex-preacher Jim Casy is the most compelling person in Steinbeck's host of characters. Jim Casy had been a charismatic and rowdy ("tom-cattin'") preacher for the Joads and their greater community back home in Oklahoma. Early in the novel we learn that Casy no longer believed in Christian notions of sin. "There ain't no sin and there ain't no virtue. . . . There's just stuff people do. It's all part of the same thing. And some of the things folks do is nice, and some ain't nice, but that's as far as any man got a right to say."

So Casy becomes nonjudgmental and now rejects simplistic Manichean definitions of virtue and sin. He has lost his traditional religious views, just as many of his fellow Oklahomans and Americans were beginning to have doubts about their faith in America, the American Dream, and the ideals of the American political experiment.

Casy says, "I lost the spirit." Where he once had faith, "I ain't so sure anymore." He becomes an ex-preacher without a church. Jim Casy's "Come to Jesus" epiphany occurs after he left his traditional church calling. He develops an ethical perspective on what is happening to the Joads and America. Greed has corroded and impoverished the American soul. Told about a person, perhaps like William Randolph Hearst, who owned vast lands in California, Casy replies that if that guy "needs a million acres to make him feel rich, seems to me he needs it 'cause he feels awful poor inside hisself." He later says that he senses that most of what causes trouble in America stems from people who hoard the wealth and fail to share the blessings of the land with those in need.

Steinbeck, through characters like Casy, distances himself from organized religion (and at one point actually makes fun of the "Jesus lovers"). He is nonetheless concerned with spiritual and ethical concerns.

Casy is Steinbeck's spokesman for communitarian values:

> I got thinkin' how we was holy when we was one thing, an' mankin' was holy when it was one thing. An' it only got unholy when one mis'able little fella got the bit in his teeth an' ran off his own way, kickin' an' draggin' an' fightin'. Fella like that bust the holi-ness. But when they're all workin' together, not one fella for another fella, but one fella kind of harnessed to the whole shebang—that's right, that's holy.

Is Casy (and Steinbeck) suggesting that the American political system and American capitalism privilege individualism over community? Probably.

At one point, Casy takes the rap to protect his friend Tom, who was on parole back in Oklahoma but had violated the conditions of his parole by leaving the state. Casy is arrested and, after a brief stint in jail, is run out of town. But he soon finds a new calling—helping to organize farm workers with the aim that they can earn a decent wage and enjoy humane working conditions.

Casy meets up with Tom and tells him that when he was in jail he had further developed his understanding of human nature. Most of his fellow jailmates were there because "they stole stuff; an' mostly it was stuff they needed an' couldn' get no other way. Ya see?" Tom didn't understand. But Casy went on, "Well, they was nice fellas, ya see. What made 'em bad was they needed stuff. An' I begin to see then. It's need that makes all the trouble. I ain't got it worked out."

Casy now believes the voiceless, homeless, and exploited can only redress their grievances if they band together, unite, organize, and demand fair wages and fair conditions. He tells Tom, as noted, that we do not have singular individualist souls; we are interconnected and interdependent and are merely one part of a larger unified soul.

To some this egalitarian communitarian "preaching" doubtless sounded socialistic or even communistic. Yet Casy and Steinbeck are more probably arguing for the right of workers to organize unions and bargain with their employers. Further, Steinbeck was simply calling for the same basic rights Franklin D. Roosevelt would outline a few years later in his aspirational Second Bill of Rights.

Ma Joad is proud of her family and proud of America. We're Joads, she boasts. We look up to nobody. Grandpa's grandpa "fit in the Revolution." We're farm people. She's a nurturer and feeder and morale booster. She is an indomitable spirit and has an uncommon adaptability. "Rich fellas come up an' they die, an' their kids ain't no good an' they die out. But we keep a'comin'. We're the people that live. They can't wipe us out; they can't lick us. We'll go on forever, Pa, 'cause we're the people."

Ma never whines and seldom complains. She is obviously unnerved that Tom killed Jim Casy's murderer. "But," she comforts, "you done what you had to do." She is grateful for the small kindnesses that come her way. At one point Ma celebrates that love and humanity are more likely to come from the impoverished than the privileged. "I'm learning one thing good," she said. "Learning it all a time ever'day. If you're in trouble or hurt or need—go to poor people. They're the only ones that'll help—the only ones." Ma is suggesting, as Steinbeck seems to believe, that those distant bankers and megafarmers removed from the marginalized cease to feel their pain and cease to treat them with compassion.

Ma Joad's strength and perseverance are an inspiration to her family and to Steinbeck's readers. And it is her guidance that leads to the redemptive act by her often difficult daughter Rose of Sharon. Rose had been pregnant since they had left Oklahoma nine months ago. But her child is stillborn.

Ma and Rose of Sharon and what's left of the family are, because of dislocation and floods, crowded into a barn next to an old man who is dying from starvation. Rose, with her mother's encouragement, breastfeeds the old man in a profoundly symbolic gesture of rebirth. It suggests that even out of horrible times such as stillborns and starving can come hope and redemption. Editors tried to talk Steinbeck out of this ending, and it doubtless made some readers squeamish, but it celebrates humanity and human sharing in an especially poetic way. Steinbeck celebrates Ma and Rose of Sharon as he also honors Jim and Tom for their willingness to fight injustice.

Steinbeck also makes a point of including nearly a dozen cameo incidents when working-class people aided the Joads. Empathy and compassion came from plain folks, not from the elite. By dehumanizing their workers, corporate barons dehumanized themselves. But real people—the Wilsons, a waitress named Mae, some truck drivers, a federal camp warden, and a company store manager—helped the Joads and affirmed Steinbeck's central theme that people need to help one another and that the best approach to the human condition is to understand that we're all in this together—that there is "one big soul" that connects and encompasses all of us.

"We're proud to help. . . . People needs to help," says Mrs. Sally Wilson, who helped the Joads on Route 66. This, too, was a Steinbeck theme. Helping one another is what makes us human and ethical beings.[24]

Did *Grapes of Wrath* celebrate Communism or even democratic socialism? Probably not. Rather, it is a call for restraints on unbridled capitalism and monopolies. It asks simply that the exploitative and dehumanizing aspects of capitalism be appropriately regulated.

Steinbeck denied that he was a Socialist or Communist. He joked that he was rarely a joiner after having been in Boy Scouts and the Episcopal church choir in his youth. He viewed himself as a writer, and a writer who had important stories to tell. Writers are charged, Steinbeck later said in his Nobel Prize acceptance speech, "with exposing our many grievous faults and failures, with drudging up to the light our dark and dangerous dreams for the purpose of improvement."[25] He also said writers should celebrate man's capacity for gallantry, courage, compassion, and love, even going so far as saying that "a writer who does not passionately believe in the perfectibility of man has no dedication, nor any membership in literature."[26]

Political historian James MacGregor Burns agrees that *Grapes* advocated for neither Communism nor any coherent political or economic program. It was "rather a mystic union of Emerson's transcendentalism, Whitman's mass democracy, and Jefferson's agrarian populism. It beckoned readers back to the time when men and the land were one; when greed yielded to selflessness," and cites one of Steinbeck's memorable lines "for the quality of owning freezes you forever into 'I,' and cuts you off forever from the 'we.'"[27]

Steinbeck's sympathies are, of course, transparent. A few years before writing this novel, in Steinbeck's hometown of Salinas, striking lettuce farm workers had been crushed by corporate growers, bankers, utilities, and politicians, many of them friends of his parents and parents of his Salinas High schoolmates, making life miserable for the imported workers (especially Filipinos) the locals, paradoxically, needed to harvest the region's abundant crops.

Steinbeck wrote a series of news articles about the abusive conditions migrant workers faced in California's Central Valley. He also wrote a novel, *In Dubious Battle*, in which he describes an ill-fated Communist Party–led apple pickers' strike against orchard owners in central California. In one of the most reflective "interchapters" in *Grapes of Wrath*, Steinbeck warns that the corporate owners should have learned from studying history that "when property accumulates in too few hands, it is taken away," and "repression works only to strengthen and knit the repressed."

Wrath is a gripping political parable about America's capitalistic system. The persevering Joads are inspired by the American Dream; they have been self-sufficient homesteaders, and they are earnest, family oriented, and Bible reading—even if they are individually a bit quirky. But Steinbeck suggests the Joads' hopes of participating in the American Dream are virtually doomed by the rigged social and economic system they must try to compete in.

America's capitalistic system needs to be restructured, the novel suggests, if there is to be any hope for fairness and justice for people like the Joads who are willing to work hard. We need leaders willing to reject a "system that lets people live like pigs," willing to fight for the right of people to organize and to earn decent wages. The novel briefly celebrates a model workers' camp established by the New Deal Resettlement Administration, where the Joads find temporary relief. This is an affirmation of FDR's efforts to find a way to mitigate Depression-era misery.

In 1934, novelist and Socialist Upton Sinclair had surprisingly captured the Democratic nomination for governor of California. He won 38 percent of the vote in a three-way race against two mainstream politicians. Sinclair outlined detailed policy proposals to end poverty in California. His ideas were considerably to the left of FDR and somewhat along the "share the wealth" ideas of Huey Long or the socialism of Eugene Debs. FDR politely met with Upton Sinclair at Hyde Park, New York, but FDR provided no political help. Sinclair was a case of a fiction writer becoming a full-fledged Act II politician, aggressively seeking an Act III elected office.[28] He soon retreated to his more natural Act I agitational fiction and pamphleteering.

Steinbeck was aware of all the political debates going on in populist and anxiety-ridden California and New Deal America. He had read Upton Sinclair, Jack London, and John Dos Passos. But in 1934, he was still struggling to become an established writer. He understandably and rightly viewed himself as a fiction writer and not as a politician or public policy advisor. He would share a broad tapestry indicating the need for new directions. His role in *Wrath* is that of a storyteller whose characters and his often political interchapters speak for him. Steinbeck hints at (yet stops short of) prescribing specific policy solutions.

He did tell friends, as he was writing *Wrath*, that "I've done my damnedest to rip the readers' nerves to rags." He was motivated in this decidedly "purpose novel" to shame "the greedy bastards who are responsible." Steinbeck was, predictably, accused of being a Socialist. The Associated Farmers of California also attacked him as a propagandist for Communism. As in the case of *Uncle Tom's Cabin*, anti-*Wrath* books were hurried into press. One anti–*Grapes of Wrath* film was titled *Plums of Plenty*. A novel, *Grapes of Gladness*, was among many responses.

But Steinbeck's message was heard. A U.S. Senate committee was formed to investigate how migrant workers were being treated. Subsequent federal initiatives, such as Medicare, Medicaid, unemployment programs, job-retraining programs, food stamps, Head Start, and Pell grants have attempted to provide more of a safety net and educational opportunities for America's poor.

Steinbeck probably held back political and policy prescriptions for what should be done for a number of reasons. First, he yearned to be accepted and respected as a fiction writer. Second, he was raised as a conservative and very much the product of the middle class. He was a solid student and decent athlete at Salinas High School (home of the Cowboys). He went to Stanford University. His parents were stalwart civic and social participants in what Sinclair Lewis would have called small-town Main Street Babbitt Americana. His father was a manager of local mills and active in the Masonic Lodge. His mother was a schoolteacher, and his parents attended the neighborhood Episcopal church, where young John even served as an altar boy. His father also served for a decade as the elected treasurer of Monterey County. In later years, his parents owned a small getaway cottage in Pacific Grove near the ocean. He had grown up in a Republican family, a Republican county, and a Republican state, and he attended Leland Stanford and Herbert Hoover's Republican-leaning Stanford University. In many ways *Grapes* was a scolding manifesto critical of his parents, neighbors, former schoolmates, and hometown.

Steinbeck had friends who were Communists. His first wife, Carol, registered briefly as Communist in the mid-1930s, and they visited Moscow in the summer of 1937. But, and this is speculation, John Steinbeck personally worried about being dismissed as an anti-American Communist. A preeminent villain in *Grapes* was the Associated Farmers of California, founded in 1934. Their primary goal was to advance the interests and profits of corporate farmers. A secondary goal was to "smoke out" and vilify Communist troublemakers who were instigating labor strikes among the farm workers. Steinbeck obviously villainized the farmers and the political allies and chides them for monopolistic economic practices and brutal, thuggish intimidation of those who tried to represent the Okie refugees and their like. They would crush these workers just as they crushed their grapes.

Steinbeck has his characters and his narrative make his case for political change.

Just as Tom Joad lacked a coherent plan as he set out to "be there" for voiceless little people, so Steinbeck's plan for what should be done in California and elsewhere is invariably implicit rather than explicit. Echoing Upton Sinclair's End Poverty in California (EPIC) initiatives, Steinbeck wonders why millions of acres went underused when so many needy families would desperately want to have just a few. He plainly detested the collusion of wealthy corporate interests and public officials who intimidated the poor.

Steinbeck was pleased when his wife suggested the "Grapes of Wrath" title because he viewed his books as a "kind of march," and he liked the biblical and political implications. The source of the novel's title proclaims a reckoning and a revelation. Taken most immediately from Julian Ward Howe's "The Battle Hymn of the Republic" and more distantly from the Bible, the relevant verse proclaims, "Mine eyes have seen the glory of the coming of the Lord/He is trampling out the vintage where the grapes of wrath are stored." *Wrath* describes the seeds of wrath and fury that haunt the oppressed, and it implies a judgment day for the oppressors will inevitably come. Thus the Joads' plight is linked to African American struggles for emancipation, and California farmers have symbolically enslaved themselves as they enslaved their crop-picking serfs. Readers, he reasoned, knew the "Battle Hymn" and might link his message with the traditions of the American Revolution. Moreover, this "disarms in advance," he hoped, "any accusation of radicalism and will weld the American reader to the subject matter more completely."[29]

The novel, while describing the bleak despair of the Joads' situation, still has an optimistic, if muted, message that America can and must rededicate itself to the country's communitarian and constitutional ideals. His main point is: It does not have to be this way. Don't give up on the ideals of equal opportunity and justice for everyone. In common with Roosevelt (whom he supported) and Upton Sinclair (whom he doubtless admired), Steinbeck condemns capitalism's failed practices but simultaneously encourages us to imagine a better way, where more Americans share in the blessings of liberty. The reckoning may not yet be at hand. But it will come. Our system is temporarily flawed, but Steinbeck seems to be saying it can be mended. This part of his message may be subordinate to his more agitational faulting of existing practices—but it is there, and a careful reading of *Grapes* concludes Steinbeck's is an ethical, empathetic, and pro-American narrative.

Steinbeck's postsecondary career was a series of false starts and improvisation. At Stanford (1919–1925) he studied English, biology, and history, and took at least a couple of writing courses. But he took long absences and never completed his degree. Throughout high school, college, and for about a decade afterward, he did a dozen odd jobs: farmhand, laboratory assistant, highway crew member, watchman, bricklayer, caretaker, and trout hatchery assistant. But he kept on writing. A short stint in journalism in New York City didn't work out. Much of his early story writing was rejected, or else he personally deemed his work unworthy of publication. It took nearly a decade after leaving Stanford to achieve success.

He found his writer's voice only when he returned to the Salinas, Monterey, and San Jose area. And this voice was that of a storyteller who identified with the working-class people of his home region. *The Pastures of Heaven, Of Mice and Men, Tortilla Flat, The Grapes of Wrath, Cannery Row,* and, later, *East of Eden* captured real people and special places as only a local could. He was especially gifted at describing the human condition, human frailties, and the hardships of marginalized people.

Steinbeck was virtually ostracized for two generations in his old hometown of Salinas. They tagged him as a lefty or worse. In his later years, he became a New Yorker and an establishment celebrity figure—a far cry from his one-time image as an angry radical. He became a close friend of Adlai Stevenson. He attended John F. Kennedy's inauguration as a special guest. He was an overnight guest in LBJ's White House. A lifelong Democrat, he was an ardent supporter of Stevenson, Kennedy, and Johnson.

Grapes simultaneously shined a light on capitalism's failings while encouraging us to imagine a better way, a more communal America where everyone who wants to work hard might share in the blessings of liberty. He understood that Americans lived and breathed and functioned by paradox. "We are not satisfied. Our restlessness, perhaps inherited from the hungry immigrants of our ancestry, is still with us," he wrote in the mid-1960s. "We have never sat still for long; we have never been content with a place, a building—or with ourselves." Finally, he reflects, "We have failed sometimes, taken wrong paths, paused for renewal, filled our bellies and licked our wounds; but we have never slipped back—never."[30]

One critic faulted Steinbeck for unfairly pitting "complex good" against "unmitigated, unbelievable evil." Another critic labeled it "middle-brow" fiction. These same complaints can be made against most protest novels. Fair-mindedness and "balance" are splendid values in university research, but the "novelist as agitator" has different and competing motivations. Their one-sidedness is part of their mission, the mission of making a case and disturbing the peace, or as Steinbeck put it, to rouse his readers from complacency.

Readers should not turn to political novels, and seldom do, to find objectivity and carefully documented research. Some novels merely entertain us; some make us laugh. Others intentionally tug at our emotions and make us think. Steinbeck does this.

Another occasional complaint about *Wrath* was that it focused exclusively on an Anglo family at the same time that Latino, Asian American, and African Americans were probably even more ill treated than the "Okies." The charge is fair. But in focusing on his fictionalized Oklahoma family, Steinbeck may have more effectively spoken to the heart of the American Dream and captured a greater audience. For the Joads were believers—evangelical, if not churchgoing—and quintessential heartland Americans. They weren't foreigners; they weren't outsiders. They were like most of Steinbeck's intended audience.

Yet another complaint was Steinbeck's use of "interchapters," or "inner chapters." Steinbeck shared with friends that these chapters "have been pommeled," but he defended them as a counterpoint to his description of the Joads' journey and travels. Critics said they were disruptive and perhaps too much of a gimmick. Steinbeck replied that they were pace changers, but the basic purpose was to hit the reader below the belt. With the rhythms and symbols of poetry one can get to a reader—open him up, and while he's open introduce things on an intellectual level that he would not or could not receive unless he was opened up. It is a psychological trick, if you wish, but all techniques of writing are psychological tricks.[31] These chapters were more poetic, philosophical, and even biblical compared to the rest of the book. They were reflective pauses. "The interchapters pull a reader off the main road and allow consideration of the long stretch, the big picture."

Steinbeck's agitational protest novel has plenty of reformist zeal in it and, as discussed, its messages at times seem to embrace socialist, if not Communist, themes. Tom Joad's now famous "words to Ma are a sermonic call for grassroots collective engagement," writes biographer Susan Shillinglaw. But the Tom Joad/John Steinbeck message here "is an egalitarian notion that reverberates throughout American politics and history and letters—not a communist but a democratic idea. United we stand."[32]

Franklin and Eleanor Roosevelt read and celebrated *Grapes*. Eleanor was motivated by it to undertake a fact-finding tour of several migrant-worker camps. She rejected criticism that *The Grapes of Wrath* was anti-religious or un-American. In a June 1939 nationally syndicated column ("My Day"), Eleanor Roosevelt simply wrote, "It's a profoundly religious, spiritual and ethically urgent book." Millions of readers have agreed.

BASTARD SON IN A RACIST, EXISTENTIAL WORLD[33]

"I never wanted to hurt nobody . . . I hurt folks 'cause I felt I had to; that's all. They was crowding me too close; they wouldn't give me no room," a doomed Bigger Thomas tells his defense attorney in Richard Wright's landmark *Native Son*.

Twenty-year-old protagonist Bigger Thomas had dreamed of becoming a pilot, but he was an impoverished young black man in a decidedly segregated Chicago struggling with the Great Depression. "I was trying to do something else. But it seems like I never could. I was always wanting something and I was feeling that nobody would let me have it. So I fought 'em. I thought they was hard and I acted hard." He also muses, "Maybe they right in not wanting us to fly, 'cause if I took a plane up I'd take a couple of bombs and drop 'em sure as hell."

Wright's disturbing novel begins with Bigger Thomas reflecting on his virtually caged existence in Chicago's segregated South Side: "They don't let us do nothing. The white folks . . . We live here and they live there. We black and they white. They got things and we ain't. They do things and we can't. It's just like living in jail. Half the time I feel like I'm on the outside of the world peeping in through a knothole in the fence."

A proud, defiant, volatile, scared, and confused Bigger accidentally kills white Mary Dalton and intentionally kills his black girlfriend Bessie Mears in a burst of rage against the caged imprisonment he dwelt in. "I didn't want to kill! But what I killed for, I am! It must've been pretty deep in me to make me kill! . . . What I killed for must've been good!" Bigger shouts. "When a man kills, it's for something . . . I didn't know what I was really alive in this world until I felt things hard enough to kill for 'em."

Richard Wright's controversial masterpiece is part sociology, part psychology, part a lengthy Marxist riff, and also an existentialist-influenced political protest novel. It is variously described as a novel about institutional racism, the human condition, and the human heart. It is a novel that forces African Americans to consider the cost of submission, and everyone to recognize the price of inequality and injustice. It is in the tradition of celebrating, or at least trying to understand, defiant loner renegades (akin to Steinbeck's Tom Joad, Dostoyevsky's Rodion Raskolnikov, Abbey's Monkey Wrench Gang, and even Twain's Huck Finn) who violate laws in protest of what they consider to be social injustices.

In literary frames, *Native Son* is an anti–*Uncle Tom's Cabin* novel. Where Tom was the epitome of Christian acceptance and forgiveness, Bigger Thomas scorns religion and rejects society's efforts to exploit, tame, dehumanize, and devitalize him. It is as well an ironic parody of Horatio Alger novels. "In a supremely ironic inversion of the central act of the Alger myth, Bigger does not fall in love with and marry the boss's daughter, but instead kills her, decapitates her, and incinerates her in a furnace," writes literary commentator Robert Butler. Wright's reversal of the Alger narrative, Butler says, telegraphs two arguments. That American capitalism fails to work for black people and other minorities—a point Upton Sinclair had made two generations earlier (especially in *Jungle*). Further, the Marxist Wright "emphasizes that blacks and other minorities must overturn American capitalism, pushing for radical changes that will ensure they can become 'native sons' who fully share in the democratic possibilities of American life."[34]

"Over and over he had tried to create a world to live in, and over and over again," Wright writes, Bigger "had failed."

Richard Wright's (1908–1960) Bigger Thomas is one of American fiction's most sullen, alienated, and troubled young men. He is recently released from reform school. His nagging mother disparages him. "Boy," Mrs. Thomas says, "I wonder what makes you act like you do." "Bigger, sometimes I wonder why I birthed you . . . we wouldn't have to live in this [rat-infested] garbage dump if you had any manhood in you."

A welfare agency finds Bigger a job as a chauffeur for a white real estate tycoon. On his first day on the job he is assigned to drive the family's spoiled daughter, Mary, to an evening engagement. She directs Bigger away from her supposed engagement and secretly meets up with her Communist boyfriend, Jan, with whom she parties and drinks for most of the night. Bigger is forced to join them. Mary and Jan tell Bigger they believe in equality for blacks, that they're on "your side." They discuss the political revolution they are active in and urge Bigger to join them. It is all pretty confusing to Bigger—this unexpected fraternizing and proselytizing. "Was they laughing at him? Were they making fun of him?"

Bigger drives them home. Jan leaves them. Bigger, who is almost as drunk as Mary, has to struggle to carry her to her bedroom. But as he puts her to bed he is essentially seduced by her or perhaps was in the process of seducing her. It is blurry. Mary's blind mother suddenly appears and questions her late homecoming. Bigger tries to quiet Mary by putting a pillow over her face and winds up accidentally suffocating her.

Mary is killed, and the dazed and overwhelmed Bigger carries her to the basement in a trunk and grotesquely puts her body parts into the furnace. Bigger devises a plot to frame Mary's Communist friend Jan. His plan is to make the Daltons believe that Mary was kidnapped by the Communists and that they have to pay a handsome ransom fee to retrieve her. Bigger involves his girlfriend, Bessie Mears, in this implausible scheme, but he winds up killing her when he believes she may back away from the deal and squeal on him.

After his plan is ruined with the discovery of Mary's body in the furnace, Bigger goes on the run. He is hunted down by the Chicago police and soon winds up in the Cook County jail, indicted for alleged rape and murder. *Native Son* is a brutal story, depicting a young, urban African American who is convulsed with fear, hate, revenge, and inarticulate rage against both white and black America, against religion, and against the system. He may be a native son, but he believes he is hopelessly enslaved in this so-called land of the free. Bigger doubtless felt more like America's bastard (as opposed to native) son.

He hates his mother for her addiction to religion and his girlfriend for her addiction to whiskey. He fears and hates white people because they have the political and economic power to degrade people like him: "They keep us bottled up here [in the Black Belt] like wild animals." He yearns to be free, to be respected, to be human, to discover himself in the larger, more prosperous world that he sees in the movies—"to be allowed a chance, to live like others, even though he was black." "They don't let us do nothing," Bigger explains.

"We black they white. They do things and we can't. It's just like living in jail." Or, he might have added, on a plantation.

Later celebrated African American novelists like Ralph Ellison and James Baldwin pay tribute to Wright's path-breaking book; yet they believe Bigger Thomas is depicted as too depraved a monster, too inhuman—in effect, merely another hard-to-digest caricature of the worst images of the African American. Wright's other black characters are similarly portrayed as deficient in character or integrity. Wright's intended audience was white, and he may have intentionally exaggerated his narrative to shock his readers. He succeeded; yet black writers understandably felt his depiction of black life in America was overly bleak and ungenerous.

Noted literary critic Irving Howe proclaimed, however, that "the day *Native Son* appeared, American culture was changed forever." Yes, it was obsessed with violence and its protagonist is engaged in pervasive self-hatred, but even "in all its crudeness, melodrama and claustrophobia of vision, Richard Wright's novel brought into the open, as no one ever had before, the hatred, fear and violence that have crippled and may yet destroy our culture."[35]

Native Son defies easy categorization. It is a complex blend of the literary naturalism fashionable in Wright's younger years. It also has elements of a gothic novel. Wright was a member of the American Communist Party before and during the time he wrote this novel, and there is definitely a Marxist theme in *Son*. There are glimpses, too, of black nationalism, though these are not well developed. Finally, Wright's fascination with existentialism is clear as he describes his new kind of hero, a tragic hero who has both come of age and come to a belated self-awareness that is decidedly protagonist centric.

A few comments about Wright himself help clarify the narrative in *Native Son*. Richard Nathaniel Wright was born on the Rucker Plantation near Roxie, Mississippi. He was the grandson of slaves and the son of an illiterate sharecropper. His maternal grandfather had briefly fought in the Union Army; yet he never received the veteran's pension that he believed he was due. His mother and maternal grandmother primarily raised him.

He briefly lived in an orphanage and regularly worked odd jobs, including hotel bellhop, delicatessen delivery boy, and golf club caddy. Wright was a high school dropout but a voracious reader. H. L. Mencken's writings influenced him, and he went on to read Hawthorne, Melville, Poe, Dreiser, Conrad, Dostoyevsky, and Ibsen. He also read Horatio Alger and dime-store crime novels.

He moved to Chicago when he was nineteen. He worked as a postal clerk, street sweeper, at a South Side boys club, and in various Work Progress Administration (a New Deal program) projects that allowed and even encouraged him to write. He had begun writing as a mostly self-taught teenager.

He became attracted to the Communist Party, which he joined for about a decade, though he said he was often irritated by the secrecy, factionalization, and regimentation that came with party involvement. "I tried to be a Communist," he would later say, and he believed in many of its aspirations. His fascination and subsequent disillusionment with the party is discussed at length in his chapter in Richard Crossman's edited book *The God That Failed* (New York: Bantam Books, 1959, 103–46).

Wright, in a reflective essay, "How Bigger Was Born" (reprinted in the appendix of most editions of *Native Son*), explains his protagonist is a composite of many defiant "Biggers" whom he met as he was growing up in the South, and others he met on the streets of Chicago and in the labor movement. He recalls that the Bigger Thomases he knew in the South were the only blacks "who consistently violated the Jim Crow laws of the South and got away with it, at least for a sweet spell." Sadly, Wright notes, these Biggers were often later "shot, hanged, maimed, lynched, and generally hounded until they were either dead or their spirits broken."

Wright discusses how the post–Civil War America devised countless Jim Crow tricks and rules to keep blacks economically and politically submissive. This was, he believed, America's inexcusably sick game of robbing African Americans of their humanity and agency. This is what precisely leads the novel's Bigger Thomas to feel that his humanity has been stripped by an environment and a system that hated his blackness—and that his world was regulated by the color of his skin. As a product of both the South and Chicago, Wright grew up listening to the laments of alienated and dispossessed blacks: "I wish I didn't have to live this way. I feel like I want to burst." And "God, I wish I had a flag and a country of my own." And from an African American World War I veteran: "What in hell did I fight in the war for? They segregated me even when I was offering my life for my country."

Wright understood that some blacks successfully won entry into America's middle class, but he wanted to tell the story of the more numerous disinherited "native sons" who so often, during the Great Depression, found themselves exiled in a no-man's land. "He was an American because he was a native son; but he was also a Negro nationalist in a vague sense because he was not allowed to live as an American. Such was his way of life and mine; neither Bigger nor I resided fully in either camp."

Wright's goal in *Native Son* is less to exonerate Bigger, and people like him, than to condemn the conditions that created him. Social contract theory suggests that he surrender some rights in exchange for safety and for governance that serves the broader public good. Yet there are few, if any, options for the very poor and dispossessed to, like Thoreau, opt out of a singularly one-sided social and political covenant. Escape for Bigger was a myth. There was no Walden Pond to retreat to, nor was it feasible to pick up and move to another country that treated its citizens with greater fairness and dignity. Bigger did the only thing he thought he could do to escape from the system so that he could be himself.

Wright's Bigger is intentionally hard to understand and even harder to like. But Wright's overarching point is that our social and political and criminal justice systems are also hard to understand and in need of major repair. Just as Steinbeck had concluded, Wright is also saying that it does not, and should not, have to be this way.

Wright does not—in his third-person narrative—necessarily agree with Bigger's intense hatred of white people, nor does he condone Bigger's brutal killings. Yet he understands how Bigger feels dehumanized by white people and why his fear and shame translates into an indiscriminate hate, even for those who try to befriend him. Wright, through Bigger, suggests that the American Dream is largely a white construction, out of reach for most blacks who live in the back alleys of even our greatest cities.

Wright's *Native Son* is part of the literary tradition of naturalism. Naturalists, partly influenced by Charles Darwin's theory of evolution, believed social environment and one's heredity influenced one's character and behavior. The French novelist Émile Zola and American writers William Dean Howells and Theodore Dreiser were major exemplars of this literary school. Naturalists intentionally exposed the harsh or brutal realities of life—poverty, racism, classism, prejudice, corruption, and violence.

Wright wanted to tell the truth of the Bigger Thomases who had to struggle in their unwanted no-man's land. "The most that I could say of Bigger was that he felt the need for a whole life and acted out of that need; that was all." Wright explains, "To those who wanted to kill him he was not human, not included in that picture of Creation; and that was why he had killed it. To live, he had created a new world for himself, and for that he was to die."

Later black writers such as Ralph Ellison, James Baldwin, Toni Morrison, and Colson Whitehead provided additional and often more nuanced variations on this theme. A more contemporary nonfiction African American writer, Ta-Nehisi Coates (in his *Between the World and Me* [New York: Spiegel and Grace, 2015]), revisits some of Wright's themes.

Coates writes that his ancestors came to America in chains and that even today African Americans live in fear of being physically assaulted or crushed. "To be black in the Baltimores of my youth is to be naked before the elements of the world, before all guns, fists, knives, crack, rape, and disease." That nakedness, Coates writes, is not an error, nor pathology. It is "the correct and intended result of policy, the predictable upshot of people forced for centuries to live in fear. The law did not protect us." Coates, like Wright and Morrison before him, writes that in America it is traditional to "destroy the black body" and to make it hard for blacks to participate in the American Dream.[36] That's what *Native Son* professed and protested.

A deeply psychological theme in *Native Son* is derivative of the gothic tradition in American fiction. Robert Butler suggests that:

> The world as seen through Bigger's mind is a continuous nightmare filled with rats, "ghosts," eerie cats, rotting buildings that resemble skulls and city streets that are strange labyrinths leading nowhere. Such a world triggers in the hero the same kind of fear that suffuses Poe's fiction and the same kind of guilt that pulses through Hawthorne's stories. Like Melville, Wright was shocked by his recognition of the dark underside of American life and was not fooled by its bright but shallow optimism.[37]

Critics sometimes fault *Native Son* for merely being Marxist propaganda, and indeed its Marxian aspirations are readily apparent.

Mary Dalton's Communist boyfriend encourages Bigger to consider Communism and explains to him the need for a proletarian uprising to overthrow capitalism. "After the revolution," Jan Erlone simplistically intones, "it'll be ours. But we'll have to fight for it." After the revolution, "There'll be no white and no black, there'll be no rich and no poor."

Boris Max, a devout Communist Party member, volunteers to serve as a defense counsel for the arrested Bigger. He understands his client will probably be given the death penalty. Max might have tried to push for an insanity defense. Instead, he tries to argue that Bigger's punishment should be "merely" a life in prison.

The first person Bigger trusts is Max, whom he informs, "I don't reckon I was ever in love with nobody," presumably himself included. Bigger pours out his life story.

> Mr. Max, a guy get tired of being told what he can and can't do. You get a little job here and a little job there. . . . You don't make enough to live on. . . . You just keep on moving all the time, doing what other folk say. You ain't a man no more. . . . The white folk, they own everything. They

choke you off the face of the earth. . . . They like god. . . . They don't even let you feel what you want to feel. They after you so hot and hard you can only feel what they doing to you. They kill you before you die.

Max prepares and delivers what some writers refer to as his "The Guilt of the Nation" defense address, essentially suggesting that while his client may indeed be guilty, so are the rest of us. Max's major intent, as noted, is not the exoneration of Bigger Thomas but a condemning of the unforgivably rotten conditions that shaped him. Boris tries to put institutional racism and the problematic relations between blacks and whites on trial. Bigger Thomas may be Chicago's public enemy number one, but he is a product of a sick society that is at least in part responsible for creating him. If Bigger was a monster, Max argues, he was the creation of American capitalism and American society and Chicago. America, Max contends, is on trial.

Critics claim that the defense counsel's rambling riff is less related to Bigger's case and may indeed be less helpful to him than an awkward elaboration of Wright's personal Marxist ideological thinking.

A few excerpts from the Boris Max defense of Bigger Thomas:

- In him and men like him is what was in our forefathers when they first came to these strange shores hundreds of years ago. We were lucky. They are not. We found a land whose tasks called forth the deepest and best we had; and we built a nation, mighty and feared. We poured and are still pouring our soul into it. But we have told them: "This is a white man's country!" They are yet looking for a land whose tasks can call forth their deepest and best.
- He murdered Mary Dalton accidentally, without thinking, without plan, without conscious motive. But after he murdered, he accepted the crime. And that's the important thing. It was the first full act of his life; it was the most meaningful, exciting and stirring thing that had ever happened to him. He accepted it because it made him free, gave him the possibility of choice, of action, the opportunity to act and to feel that his actions carried weight.
- We are dealing here with an impulse stemming from deep down. We are dealing here not with how man acts toward man, but with how a man acts when he feels that he must defend himself against, or adapt himself to the total fear imposed on him by the natural world in which he lives.
- Your Honor, remember that men can starve from a lack of self-realization as much as they can from a lack of bread! And they can murder for it, too!

- The truth is, this boy did *not* kill! . . . He was *living*, only as he knew how, and as we have forced him to live. The actions that resulted in the death of those two women were as instinctive and inevitable as breathing or blinking one's eye. It was an act of creation!

Boris Max's claim here is that inevitable social forces were at work, and that the tragedies caused by Bigger Thomas need to be understood as the result of the inequalities and injustices of our economic and political systems. This was, in the event, a hard sell, and the judge rejects it.

If Wright's defense counsel puts things in simplistic terms, the state's attorney, Mr. Buckley—who, as it happens, is in the middle of a political campaign to win reelection—frames his case against Bigger in an equally simplistic way. His case:

I shall not lower the dignity of this Court, nor the righteousness of the People's cause, by attempting to answer the silly, alien, communistic and dangerous ideas advanced by the defense.

Every decent white man in America ought to swoon with joy for the opportunity to crush with his heel the wooly head of this black lizard, to keep him from scuttling on his belly farther over the earth and spitting forth his venom of death.

Buckley calls Bigger a demented savage, a liar, and a rapist, and he demands that the judge sentence Bigger to be executed.

It is unclear how sincere Wright was in portraying his elaborate Marxist defense of Bigger. Wright, we know in retrospect, was ambivalent about simplistic Marxist answers. There is doubtless some ambivalence and perhaps some irony in Wright's characterization of Boris Max.

There is also ambivalence in Wright's occasional references to black nationalism. His narrator has Bigger wonder if it would be possible to unify blacks so they could overthrow their oppressors: "Dimly, he felt that there should be one direction in which he and all other black people could go whole-heartedly; there should be a way in which gnawing hunger and restless aspiration could be fused. . . . But he felt that such would never happen to him and his black people, and he hated them and wanted to wave his hand and blot them out." Yet Bigger, and probably Wright too, had only vague hopes of this possibility. So despite glimpses of black nationalism, *Native Son* leaves these ideas to be developed by the Malcolm X's and others who would come later.

If Wright wrote in the spirit of naturalism, emphasizing the brutally deterministic realities conditioning Bigger's existence, he also conceived his protagonist as an existential hero. Bigger may be traumatized by his poverty, neurotic fears, and his yearning to be tough and subversive, but, in Wright's telling, Bigger is searching to discover both himself and meaning in an otherwise absurd world. He had, in existentialist terms, to create himself, to find his own freedom, to make decisions based on subjective rather than rational inclinations.

Bigger Thomas rejected conventional ideas of religion and morality because, like Max, he believed these were used by the powerful to either control people or encourage submission. He defends himself as a rebel, a fugitive, an outlier, and invents his own destiny as he confronts both oppressive whites and submissive blacks.

Wright tries to get his readers to understand Bigger's psychological yearning to free himself from fear and transcend the meaninglessness of his existence. He was black, poor, uneducated, despised, and denied the chance to become someone. Once arrested he was threatened, bullied, and accused of having raped and murdered Mary Dalton. But, as noted, the killings, he believed, had somehow freed him: "Toward no one in the world did he feel any fear now, for he knew that fear was useless; and toward no one in the world did he feel any hate now, for he knew that hate could not help him."

> In all his life these two murders were the most meaningful things that ever happened to him. He was living, truly and deeply, no matter what others might think, looking at him with their blind eyes. Never had he had the chance to live out the consequences of his actions; never had his will been so free as in this night and day of fear and murder and flight.

Bigger's compulsion to rebel and to kill in *Native Son* morphs into a somewhat implausible, yet humanizing, journey to understand himself. His incarceration and introspective dialogue with his attorney transform Bigger's status from a victim to that of a new kind of existential, if tragic, hero. "This achievement of selfhood," writes Robert Butler, "does not allow Bigger simply to transcend the force of environment; after all, he is still in jail and will soon be executed by the state."[38] But Bigger is portrayed, in the end, as having come to terms with himself. Wright suggests his tragic hero, at least according to this sympathetic interpretation, is experiencing a form of spiritual growth along with a long-delayed self-awakening.

Wright feared being branded as a propagandist. But he felt compelled to show what racism and unregulated capitalism had done to the young blacks he had worked with in his various jobs, especially in his work at the South Side Boys' Club. In his "How Bigger Was Born" essay, Wright shares, bluntly, that the rich white people (like the Daltons) who paid him to mentor young blacks did not "give a good goddamn" about these kids.

> They were paying me to distract Bigger with ping-pong, checkers, swimming, marbles, and baseball in order that he might not roam the streets and harm the valuable white property which adjoined the Black Belt. I am not condemning boys' clubs and ping-pong as such, but these little stopgaps were entirely inadequate to fill up the centuries-long chasm of emptiness which American civilization had created in these Biggers. I felt that I was doing a kind of dressed-up police work, and I hated it.

Wright privately admired that many of his young charges intentionally broke the law and caused trouble.

Native Son is contemptuous of Chicago's politics and judicial system. Wright describes its politicians as stirring up racial hatred. He condemns the powerbrokers and realtors who connive in redlining and charging higher rent in black neighborhoods.

Wright is doubtless speaking through his Marxist Boris Max when he has Max say:

> The hunt for Bigger Thomas served as an excuse to terrorize the entire Negro population, to arrest hundreds of Communists, to raid labor union headquarters and workers' organizations. Indeed the tone of the press, the silence of the church, the attitude of the prosecution and the stimulated temper of the people are of such a nature as to indicate that *more* than revenge is being sought upon a man who has committed a crime.

He then goes on to say the antiblack and antiproletariat hysteria has been deliberately incited by the prosecutor, the mayor, the governor, and other elites to suppress any type of rebellion, strikes, or subversiveness.

At one point, defense attorney Boris Max asks whether Bigger ever sought help from black politicians to redress the grievances he and others in his neighborhood had obviously felt. Bigger says, "They wouldn't listen to me. . . . They almost all like the white people, when it comes to guys like me. They say guys like me make it hard for them to get along with white folks."

> Did you ever hear any of your leaders make speeches?
>
> Yeah [said Bigger]. At election time.
>
> What did you think of them?

Aw, I don't know. They all the same. They wanted to get elected to office. They wanted money, like everybody else. Mr. Max, it's a game and they play it.

Why didn't you play it?

Hell, [said Bigger] what do I know? I ain't got nothing. Nobody'll pay attention to me. I'm just a black guy with nothing. I just went to grammar school. And politics is full of big shots, guys from college.

Didn't you trust them?

I don't reckon they wanted anybody to trust 'em. They wanted to get elected to office. They paid you to vote.

Did you ever vote?

Yeah, I voted twice [said Bigger]. I wasn't old enough so I put my age up so I could vote and get the five dollars.

You didn't mind selling your vote?

Naw; why should I?

You didn't think politics [asked Max] could get you anything?

It got me five dollars on election day.

Wright dismisses politics here as a game and an unlikely medium for poor people, especially poor black people, to achieve representation, not to mention public policy remedies. Politics, he implies, is when white folks do deals to trade property and exploit the poor that pay.

Son was faulted, as noted, for being less a work of art than a mere protest novel—a lengthy pamphlet praising Marxist ideas and scornful of the naïve Horatio Alger narrative. Its writing style similarly was criticized as often flat in prose and implausible in some of its plot development. Yet no one denies that Wright's characterization of Bigger Thomas was a major achievement. The parable of Bigger is a haunting one for both black and white people. Celebrated African American writer James Baldwin said, "No American Negro exists who does not have his private Bigger Thomas living in his skull." And few white readers could continue to cling to black stereotypes once portrayed in the writings of Harriet Beecher Stowe or the plantation myths of Margaret Mitchell, whose best-selling *Gone with the Wind* was published just four years earlier. (Wright's message, as suggested, was simultaneously an attack on Horatio Algerism and a description of a parallel universe to the depictions in Stowe and Mitchell.)

A generation later, Martin Luther King Jr. would write from his Birmingham jail cell that African Americans had been waiting for more than 340 years for their constitutional and God-given rights. King could imagine a great American republic, but he spoke not only of the fictional Uncle Toms or Bigger Thomases but also for millions of Americans when he complained that white Americans had for too long asked black Americans to be patient and just wait a few more years or decades.

> Perhaps it is easy for those who have never felt the stinging darts of segregation to say, "Wait." But when you have seen vicious mobs lynch your mothers and fathers at will and drown your sisters and brothers at whim; when you have seen hate-filled policemen curse, kick, and even kill your black brothers and sisters, when you see the vast majority of your twenty million brothers smothering in an airtight cage of poverty in the midst of an affluent society; when you suddenly find your tongue twisted and your speech stammering as you seek to explain to your six-year-old daughter why she can't go to the public amusement park that has just been advertised on television and see tears welling up in her eyes when she is told that Funtown is closed to colored children. . . . When your first name becomes "nigger," your middle name becomes "boy" . . . and your last name becomes "John," and your wife and mother are never given the respected title "Mrs." . . . when you are forever fighting a degenerating sense of "nobodiness"—then you will understand why we find it difficult to wait.[39]

King was hardly seeking forgiveness for the crimes of a Bigger Thomas, but he was calling for a country that lived up to its pledge of equality before the law and equality of opportunity. "There comes a time when the cup of endurance runs over and men are no longer willing to be plunged into the abyss of despair. I hope," he said to fellow Americans, "you can understand our legitimate and unavoidable impatience."

Richard Wright lacked King's ability to weave together the plight of the African American with America's spiritual principles and constitutional aspirations. But *Native Son* was an effective political and social protest novel. It had an impact on American political culture. If it failed to win followers for the Communist Party in America, it led to an awakening of Americans to their native sons who live lives with few breaks, much rage, and little hope. Bigger, readers invariably conclude, is America's "native son" to the extent that he is a by-product or even a creation of racism and oppression.

Wright was talented, angry, and radical, and *Son* was intentionally written to disturb the peace. It still does, and its brutal characterization of life on Chicago's South Side still has relevance. Note Spike Lee's *Chiraq.* Also, "Paranoia" is a chilling reminder of *Native Son.* It is the second track on Chance the Rapper's 2012 mixtape, *Acid Rap,* another harsh look at Chicago's South Side. Chance's lyrics say, "They murder kids here/Why you think they don't talk about?/They deserted us here . . . they'll be shooting if it's dark or not/Down here it's easier to find a gun than it is to find a fucking parking spot." There are several shootings every day in Chicago (more than seven hundred in 2016). Chance, like Wright, is an artist trying to call attention to injustice, violence, and rage.[40]

Wright's legacy and enduring reputation as a great fiction writer remain because, as Andrew Delbanco reminds us, of "his unprecedented ability to convey the horror of being black in America, especially in that time and place."[41]

Bigger Thomas yearned to connect with other people, to play some part in the common human struggle. In his jail cell, Bigger wonders:

> If he reached out with his hands . . . reached out through the stone walls and felt other hands and touched other people, reached out through the stone walls and felt other hands connected with other hearts . . . would there be a reply? . . . Just to know that they were there and warm! Just that, and no more; and it would have been enough, more than enough. And in that touch, response of recognition, there would be union, identity; there would be a supporting oneness, a wholeness which had been denied him all his life.

The condemned Bigger is perhaps trying to imagine a postracial country and a postclass world where "the sun's rays melted away the many differences, the colors, the clothes and drew what was common and good upward toward the sun."

His attorney and even Mary Dalton's boyfriend somehow forgive Bigger, and in his own dreams Bigger yearns for a time and for a country that can transcend racial profiling, dehumanization, and bigotry. In the end, Bigger Thomas, and presumably Richard Wright, are striving to reimagine an America with equal opportunity for everyone.

GOING GALT[42]

> The only proper purpose of the government is to protect man's rights, which means: to protect them from physical violence. A proper government is only a policeman, acting as an agent of man's self-defense, and,

as such, may resort to force *only* against those who *start* the use of force. The only proper functions of government are: the police, to protect you from criminals; the Army, to protect you from foreign invaders; and the courts, to protect your property and contracts from breach or fraud by others, to settle disputes by rational rules according to *objective* law.

So declares fictional maverick physicist and inventor John Galt (echoing some of the sentiments of political economist Adam Smith) in a lengthy radio address aimed at President Thompson, the U.S. government, and the American people.

But a government that *initiates* the employment of force against men who had forced no one, the employment of armed compulsion against disarmed victims, is a nightmare infernal machine designed to annihilate morality; such a government reverses its only moral purpose and switches from the role of protector to the role of man's deadliest enemy.

Ayn Rand's (1905–1982) best-selling celebration of entrepreneurism and what she calls "objectivism" is Wagnerian in style, intensity, and grandiosity. She writes to condemn the regulatory state, collectivism, and any form of socialism that might inhibit rugged individualism and creativity.

Her book, part political satire, part political philosophy, and part political manifesto, not only condemns Communism, socialism, and the regulatory state but also serves as a call to the barricades, a call for a Tea Party revolution sixty years before the Tea Party became an American political phenomenon. She outlines a utopian political economy that is a broadside attack on progressivism, collectivism, and even the most conservative versions of a welfare state.

She describes politicians and bureaucrats as looters and scumbags. Rand targets political planners who want to nationalize, regulate, and control what, she insists, should be left to the free market. Her government officials are cartoonish in their quest for power and control, as well as hopeless in their misunderstanding of creativity.

Rand's president, Mr. Thompson, whom she calls merely "head of state," is clueless about what should be done in troubled economic times. He defers to his advisors who prescribe more taxes, more regulation, and further nationalization. When the president and his government are ultimately threatened by both a major depression and a strike of the nation's creative industrialists, Thompson clumsily tries to co-opt Rand's hero John Galt and his fellow strikers.

The president tells his advisors, "We'll make a deal with him [Galt]." He adds, "We will have to compromise. We'll have to make a few concessions to big business, and the welfare boys won't like it, but what the hell!—Do you know any way out?" His aides sheepishly object, "But his ideas . . ." suggesting that Galt's vision of economic policy is unacceptable to them. The president, contemptuously portrayed here as the ultimate pragmatic cipher, retorts, "Who cares about ideas?"

But any notion of co-opting Galt ends when the industrialist begins to propose his economic prescriptions, which include abolishing income taxes and firing all federal bureaucrats. Tensions in the nation's capital escalate quickly, as both sides nervously stare across the aisle at a political adversary wholly unlike themselves, as well as down the barrel of an impending, wholesale economic meltdown. Now in too deep, and feeling as though he is backed into a corner, Rand's evil President Thompson instructs his secret operatives to begin physical torture on Galt in order to "condition" submission. This also fails when Galt's friends employ Navy SEAL tactics to rescue him from his remote torture chamber. Galt's fugitive coalition retreats to a fictional Galt's Gulch, a self-contained mysterious valley somewhere in the middle of Colorado, which serves as the base of operations for their planned takeover of the country. Rand leaves a lot to the imagination as to exactly when or how the coming takeover might take place.

The strength of the book, and a large bulk of its more than 1,100 pages, is Rand's loving portrayal of a handful of disciplined, driven, and ingenious business people. Chief among them is the aforementioned John Galt, Rand's iconic inventor and political philosopher. *Atlas* also celebrates fictional railroad tycoon Dagny Taggart, a fearless woman devoted to making her grandfather's railroad, Taggart Transcontinental, a prime example of American business genius. She is cold, intense, and beautiful. She disavows her spineless brother, who is her nominal supervisor, and she falls in love occasionally—but only with like-minded superhero entrepreneurs.

Another of Rand's exalted captains of industry is steelmaker Henry Rearden, who invents a new, cheaper, more durable form of steel and is a ruthlessly effective chief executive officer. Rearden loathes government regulation and stalwartly defends his individualistic and profit-making motivations. Rearden, in Rand's adoring portrait, is akin to the mythical Atlas who willingly carries the industrial world on his shoulders.

Rearden's wife urges him to be practical and make concessions to the government: "I think you should abandon the illusion of your own perfection, which you know full well to be an illusion. I think you should learn to get along with other people," she says. "The day of the hero is passed. This is the day of humanity, in a much deeper sense than you imagine. Human beings are no longer expected to be saints, nor to be punished for their sins. Nobody is right or wrong, we're all in it together, we're all human—and the human is the imperfect."

Rand loathes such pragmatism and rejects the idea that the day of the hero is over. She has heroes, and they are nongovernmental, rugged, private sector entrepreneurs. Such is apparent when Rearden, in front of a federal judge while on trial for trumped-up charges, says:

> I work for nothing but my own profit—which I make by selling a product they need to men who are willing and able to buy. I do not produce it for their benefits at the expense of mine; and they do not buy it for my benefit at the expense of theirs; I do not sacrifice my interests to them, nor do they sacrifice their interests to me; we deal as equals by mutual consent to mutual advantage—and I am proud of every penny that I have earned in this manner. I am rich and am proud of every penny I own. I have made my money by my own efforts, and in free exchange through the voluntary consent of every man I dealt with—the voluntary consent of those who employed me when I started, the voluntary consent of those who work for me now, the voluntary consent of those who buy my product.

Rearden refuses to apologize for his success or money: "If this is evil, make the most of it." And, for emphasis, he adds, "If it is now the belief of my fellow man, who call themselves the public, that their good requires victories, then I say: The public be damned, I will have no part of it." Then, to make a long story brief, the government blackmails Rearden over an affair with Dagny Taggart, thereby winning his cooperation while not dampening his ideological fervor.

Most of Rand's narrative expands on the virtues of unfettered laissez-faire economics. Her heroes are libertarian true believers. Her villains are hopeless, pathetically toxic sentimentalists. "There are two sides to every issue," she writes. "One side is the right and the other side is the wrong, but the middle is always evil." Before you can identify something as gray or middle of the road, she explains, you first must know what is black and what is white, because gray is merely a mixture. When you learn that one alternative is good and the other is evil, the middle is unjustifiable. There is no reason for choosing any part of what you know to be evil. Rand deals in Manichean absolutes. Political parties, for her, are debased with blatant and unacceptable contradictions.

Rand celebrates the pursuit of truth and suggests that the same genius and disciplined reasoning that inspires great composers and poets similarly motivates people who invent electric motors, run great mines, or discover how to exploit our national resources.

It is impossible to do justice to most of Rand's ideas here, but they include a political philosophy that celebrates reason and disdains religion, faith, myth, or conventional spirituality. "His own happiness is man's only purpose." She sides with the antigovernment strikers in *Atlas Shrugged* who are revolutionary in their goals as well as their means. She goes to great length to inspire her readers to honor creative business heroes. Get the Washington politicians, she admonishes, and their looting (a favorite word) central planners with their cannibalistic philosophy completely out of the way. "Give up and get out of the way," she has one of her heroes say.

Rand grew up in Russia and watched the Communist takeover while she was a teenager. Her father's pharmacy was nationalized, and her upper-middle-income family learned firsthand the effects of Orwellian and *Darkness at Noon* statism. She studied philosophy, history, and screenwriting, and she was able to immigrate to Hollywood, where she began a career of writing for films and stage before becoming a novelist.

Atlas inspired the formation of the Libertarian Party, even though Rand distanced herself from it—no doubt because of some of its contradictions and compromises. One of her disciples and friends, Alan Greenspan, became a top presidential advisor and longtime chairman of the Federal Reserve Board. Rand's philosophies inspired Republicans Ron and Rand Paul. She would have been pleased by congressman and 2012 Republican vice presidential nominee Paul Ryan's Republican convention speech that denounced the false promises and misdeeds of the nation's "central planners."[43]

Businessmen Ted Turner, Mark Cuban, and Whole Foods founder John Mackey said Rand influenced their entrepreneurial careers. Several of Donald Trump's cabinet and White House staff noted *Atlas* as a formative influence. In short, *Atlas*, along with Rand's lesser-known works, inspired one of America's more distinctive political cults.

This novel has also been blasted as a godless screed for mindless and mean-spirited capitalism. Some critics dismiss it as the simplistic work of an ideologue who willfully misunderstands the necessity of political consensus building. It is also criticized by those who believe that Rand completely ignores and underestimates the government planning and leadership that Hamilton, Clay, Lincoln, and both Roosevelts provided, which at crucial times guided, enriched, and may even have saved America's capitalistic system.

Her harshest critics dismiss her libertarian beliefs as merely a form of fascism with a cosmetic face-lift. Her unfettered capitalism and "rational selfishness" are equivalent, these critics complain, to letting corporations rule in a system with little or minimalistic safeguards for the public interest. She was effectively, her critics say, in favor of a return to the Gilded Age.

Her book was surprisingly criticized in the conservative *National Review*. Their reviewer understood her plea for limited government but called her an atheist with a flawed and dangerous hedonistic message. Religious conservatives such as William F. Buckley Jr., founder of the *National Review*, criticized Rand and her writings. It should come as little surprise, then, that most of Rand's modern-day following is made up of secular conservatives and libertarians. Religion scholar Stephen Prothero reminds people that this libertarian (or "objectivist," as Rand called herself) icon was prochoice, antireligion, and glorified permissive extramarital liaisons.

> In Rand's Manichaean world, it is not God vs. Satan, but individualism vs. collectivism. While Jesus says, "Blessed are the poor," she sings hosannas to the rich. The heroes of *Atlas Shrugged* are captains of industries such as John Galt. The villains are the "looters" and "moochers"—people who by hook (guilt) or by crook (government coercion) steal from the hard-won earnings of others.
>
> Turning the tables on traditional Christian morality, Rand argues that altruism is immoral and that selfishness is good. Moreover, there isn't a problem in the world laissez-faire capitalism can't solve if left alone to perform its miracles.[44]

Rand was obviously against many things. She denounced religion, statism, socialism, Communism, liberalism, and most of what a government does. She saw no need for the United Nations. Her desire was for a society, and a politics, largely without politicians. Her objectivist philosophy envisioned a concept of man as a heroic being, with personal happiness and "rational self-interest," as the moral purpose of life. Productive achievement was the noblest activity, and reason the only absolute.

Rand liked to view herself as a radical, not an anarchist, even if some of her heroes acted as revolutionaries. She understood, as noted, that there had to be police to protect people from criminals, military to protect the nation from invaders, and legal institutions to settle contractual disputes according to objective laws. Anarchy would entail the breakdown of law and order but could not be a viable guiding political philosophy.

She insisted her objectivism was not the same as conservatism. She did not want to preserve the present system but to change it at the root.

As one of her disciples explained, "In the literal sense of the word, we are *radicals*—radicals for freedom, radicals for human rights, radicals for capitalism."[45]

If she inspired widespread, influential political cults, Rand herself was a political loner. She supported Republican Wendell Willkie in 1940 and Barry Goldwater in 1964. And she was active in some anti-Communist groups. She admired Austrian economist Ludwig von Mises, but she believed even her favorite economists compromised too much. She was mostly prickly and combative, even with would-be allies like economist Friedrich Hayek. She dismissed President Ronald Reagan, the GOP's patron saint of free enterprise, as a lightweight. Rand's faith in egoism and a doctrine of rational self-interest—that people have few, if any, obligations beyond a respect for the freedom and rights of others—is understandably appealing to many people who disdain taxation, regulations, and bureaucratization. John Galt made his entrepreneurial costrikers recite the following oath when they joined his Colorado commune: "I swear by my life and my love of it that I will never live for the sake of another man, nor ask another man to live for mine." That is hard-core Randianism, and it has a life of its own, in part as a variation of Horatio Alger stories, in the American political narrative.

Rand's second most famous novel was *The Fountainhead* (1943), which she said was rejected by at least twelve publishers. They thought, she said, it was too intellectual and too controversial. But she lived to see it, like *Atlas*, become a best seller.

She writes in a later introduction to *Fountainhead* that it was not her purpose as a novelist to present heroes who were without flaws, but rather the ideal man. She wanted to proclaim the spirit and glory of what was possible. "It is those few," like her fictionalized architect Howard Roark, "that move the world and give life its meaning." She elaborates on the explicit need for a certain type of political economic system as a prerequisite for the nurturing and empowerment of her ideal, creative heroic individualist.

> Since my purpose is the presentation of an ideal man, I had to define and present the conditions which made him possible and which his existence requires. Since man's character is the product of his premises, I had to define and present the kinds of premises and values that create the character of an ideal man and motivate his actions; which means that I had to define and present a rational code of ethics. Since man acts among and deals with other men, I had to present the kind of social system that

makes it possible for ideal man to exist and to function—a free, productive, rational system which demands and rewards the best in every man, and which is, obviously, laissez-faire capitalism.[46]

Rand was both a political philosopher and a fiction writer, who believed the purpose of her fiction was to create "for myself the kind of world I want and to live in it while I am creating it," and then secondarily to let readers enjoy this same world if and to the extent that they could.

Literary critics were generally harsh on Rand for writing overly long and melodramatic novels. Some called them sophomoric, shrill, and "retro fantasy." Others faulted her for portraying her ideal types as unbelievably beautiful, brilliant, and decisive, whereas her villains were unbearably unattractive in every way. Her characters, although often memorable ideal types, are mysteriously interconnected, and her plots verge on being gothically convoluted.

But her fans praised her writing as compelling and inspirational. Her books have sold at least forty million copies, or more, and several remain best sellers. Rand's *Atlas* is among the most commercially successful, influential, as well as controversial American political novels.

Rand's political vision has inspired millions, and her uncompromising criticism of the welfare and regulatory state and her call for unrestricted personal freedom are, and will remain, enduring ideological themes in American politics.

GOING HAYDUKE[47]

"Always pull up the stakes. . . . Anywhere you find them. Always. That's the first goddamned general order in the monkey wrench business. Always pull up the stakes." So proclaims George Washington Hayduke, the eccentric twenty-five-year-old Green Beret Vietnam veteran who is the most colorful and charismatic member of the Monkey Wrench Gang. "My job," says Hayduke, "is to save the fucking wilderness. I don't know anything else worth saving."

Hayduke is a burly, beer-drinking, raucous, irreverent "badass" prankster in Edward Abbey's best-selling 1975 cult novel, *The Monkey Wrench Gang*, about enviro-rage. His character was inspired, at least in part, by Abbey's friend, the naturalist Doug Peacock, who lived among the Yellowstone grizzly bears for several years after returning from military service in Vietnam. Abbey also writes of Hayduke, "A lot of Shawnee blood back in there, maybe, somewhere."

Abbey (1927–1989) dedicates his book to the eponymous Ned Ludd, the machine-smashing British weaver who, in 1779, tried to slow down the pace of industrialization; his type became known as Luddites. But Abbey is mostly inspired by his own love affair with the Southwest—especially Arizona and New Mexico and the canyonland of southeastern Utah.

Though raised in the Appalachian part of Pennsylvania, Abbey hitch-hiked and camped in the Southwest as a teenager. He returned there after his military service at the end of World War II. He spent much of his time, when not in Albuquerque, Santa Fe, or Tucson, hiking and camping in the canyonlands region. A seasonal employee of the U.S. National Forest and Park Services for about a dozen summers, he enjoyed long, solo excursions into the region's remote areas.

Abbey's feisty iconoclastic brand of environmentalism is captured in a 1983 letter he sent to an "Earth First!" gathering:

> Climb those mountains, run those rivers, explore those forests, investi-gate those deserts, love the sun and the moon and the stars, and we will outlive our enemies, we will piss on their graves, and we will love and nurture and who knows—even marry their children.

Abbey had a career-long intellectual interest in anarchism, a form of political activism known for subversive insurrection and mayhem. As a Fulbright Scholar at Edinburgh University, he wrote a research thesis titled "A General Theory of Anarchism," and a few years later, at the University of New Mexico, he wrote a master's thesis on "Anarchism and the Moral-ity of Violence."

He told *Mother Earth News* in 1984:

> I'm something of an anarchist, because I learned long ago to distrust the government . . . and not only the government, but all big institutions: big business, big military, big cities, big churches, big labor unions . . . any institution that grows so large that it's no longer under the control of its membership. My kind of anarchism is no more than democracy pushed as far as it can be pushed, government by the people, decentral-ized in all its forms.[48]

Hayduke's co-conspirators in the Monkey Wrench gang include Doc Sarvis, a fifty-year-old Armenian-born physician who works as a surgeon in Albuquerque and whose hobby is blowing up or torching highway billboards. His auto's bumper sticker proclaims, "God Bless America: Let's Save Some of It." Like Hayduke, and Abbey, Sarvis develops a relentless passion for preserving the wilderness of the Southwest. He acts as the gang's philanthropist banker, financing their Don Quixote–style eco-vandalism. Sarvis's girlfriend, twenty-eight-year-old New Yorker Bonnie Abbzug (the only female in the gang), is strong-willed, independent, sensual, and somewhat of a hippie. The fourth member of the gang is thirty-five-year-old Joseph Fielding Smith, a Jack Mormon who has wives in different parts of Utah. As a riverboat guide on the Colorado River, Smith is away from home for long periods of time. He is known, fittingly, to friends and his three wives, as "Seldom-Seen Smith." Smith, a kindred libertarian spirit, readily joins with his compatriots to retaliate against the region's transgressive intruders. He especially shares the gang's hatred of the Glen Canyon Dam (on the Colorado River near Page, Arizona). "I hate that dam," he says. It "flooded the most beautiful canyon in the world."

Dictionaries define a monkey wrench as a hand tool with adjustable jaws for turning nuts of various sizes. A second informal definition, origin unknown, is something disruptive, as in "that threw a monkey wrench into our project." "Monkey wrenching," in Abbey's usage, is nonviolent disruption of, or resistance to, the destruction of natural diversity and wilderness. Monkey wrenchers are warriors with a messianic zeal in a crusade to protect and preserve the wilderness. Abbey preached that the desert wilderness was our true home, and since it was threatened with invasion and senseless pillage, preservationists like his gang have the right and even moral obligation to defend this sacred "home."

The villains of the story are the U.S. Bureau of Land Management (which Abbey calls the U.S. Bureau of Livestock and Mining), the U.S. Forest Service, the U.S. Bureau of Reclamation (which Abbey snarkly renames the U.S. Bureau of Wrecklamation), the dam builders, Exxon, Peabody Coal, Anaconda, Georgia Pacific, Utah's San Juan County Search and Rescue Committee (led by the creepy hypocrite Mormon bishop J. Dudley Love), and other kindred allies intent on "Californicating" the wilderness of the great Southwest. The gang's mantra is "keep the Southwest like it was." These unruly characters are not Sierra Club or Audubon Society liberals, content merely to "leave no footprint." They are gun-loving, freedom-loving libertarians. Their unifying philosophy is that of insurgency. They don't like government, even "good government," and they don't like progress. They don't even like tourists. Automobiles, Abbey elsewhere quipped, already have their national park—the interstate highway system.

The gang's ultimate goal is to blow up the Glen Canyon Dam. They agree to undertake easier projects first. "I'd like to knock down some of their power lines they're stringing across the desert. And those tin bridges up by Hite [across the Colorado River]," says Hayduke, "and the goddamned road-building they're doing all over the canyon country." Doc Sarvis adds, "And don't forget the billboards. And the strip mines. And the pipelines. And the new railroad from Black Mesa to Page [in Arizona]. And the coal-burning plants. And the copper smelters. And the uranium mines."

In a wonderful satirical twist, Doc Sarvis adds, "And the people who throw beer cans along the highways." But this turns out to be too much for his friends. "I throw beer cans along the fucking highways," says Hayduke. "Why the fuck shouldn't I throw fucking beer cans along the fucking highways?" Seldom-Seen agrees: "Hell, I do it too. Any road I wasn't consulted about that I don't like, I litter. It's my religion." "Doc," explains Hayduke, "it's liberation." Doc comes around, or at least acquiesces, to his new friends' point of view.

Doc seems, however, to prevail when it comes to the gang's decision-making procedures. They wouldn't take votes: "No voting. We're not going to have any tyranny of the majority in this organization," Doc declares. "We proceed on the principle of unanimity. What we do we do all together or not at all. That is a brotherhood we have here, not a legislative assembly." Doc adds, "Friends, I don't believe in majority rule. You know that. I don't believe in minority rule, either. I'm against all forms of government, including good government. I hold with the consensus of the community here. Whatever it may be. Wherever it may lead. So long as we follow our cardinal rule: no violence to human beings." Doc's libertarian principles doubtless reflect those of the novelist. Indeed, each of his gang members, though they differed in their embrace of violence, illustrated Abbey's views.

The gang agrees they will try to halt various development projects; yet they will not physically hurt anyone. But blowing up and "monkey wrenching" corporate projects define their agenda. Hayduke, who had been trained as an explosives expert in the military in Vietnam, takes a special delight in concocting demolition scenarios. "What's more American than violence?" he asks. "Violence, it's as American as pizza pie." Environmental activist Bill McKibben described Hayduke as "a sort of Henry David Wayne."

The American Dream of economic prosperity and materialism, the gang members believe, is destroying not only the environment but also the American soul. Abbey depicts this merry and motley band of eco-defenders as Robin Hood–style idealists, engaging in countervandalism, contending the real vandals are the "looting" developers and the "jellyfish" government agencies facilitating development. His eco-raiders were both inspired and obligated to go rogue to serve a higher obligation. They were an example of doing bad for the greater good. To fight off the criminality of wilderness development was, in their view, a fight for humanity.

Much of the novel, describing a year or so in time, consists of wickedly satirical descriptions of the gang's adventures—car chases, close calls with security agents, intricate and dangerous explosives. One of their first projects is to sneak into a construction site at night and destroy bulldozers by cutting electrical wires and filling gas tanks with sand and corn syrup. This is their warm-up for dynamiting bridges and burning a helicopter. These acts of sabotage are committed in the name of liberty and Mother Earth. And, of course, the bad guys are akin to an invasive vine or pest—heartless despoilers of everything beautiful.

One of Abbey's fictional local villains was the Mormon bishop Love, who heads up the San Juan County Rescue Committee. It turns out he is also a politician and developer—two of Abbey's arch adversaries. Seldom-Seen Smith had helped defeat one of Love's swindling deals. Here is Abbey as his snarly best:

> Bonnie comments, "I thought he was a Bishop."
> Seldom replies: "Well that's on Sundays and Wednesday church-study nights only. Rest of the time he's neck deep in real estate, uranium, cattle, oil, gas, tourism, most anything that smells like money. That man can hear a dollar bill drop on a shag rug. Now he's running for the state legislature. We got plenty like him in Utah. They run things as best they can for God and Jesus, and what them two don't want why fellas like Bishop Love pick up. They say it's a mighty convenient arrangement all around. Jesus Saves at eight and a half percent compounded daily, and when they make that last deposit they go straight to heaven."

Abbey has an uncanny way of pulling in his readers, just as Mark Twain did describing Huck Finn's adventures on the Mississippi or John Steinbeck did chronicling Tom Joad's road to becoming politicized. Midway through the novel, many, if not most, readers find themselves cheering on the gang, hoping they succeed—or at least hoping they don't get caught.

Abbey struggled to make his characters real and likable. As he notes in his journal, "And I want the reader to like these people—nay, to love them. Otherwise the whole novel will fall on its face. . . . They've got to be lovable—even heroic—perhaps tragic. How? O Muse of Novelists, bring me thy wit and wisdom, thine grace and understanding!"[49]

Eventually, however, three of the gang do get caught and settle down, after paying some fines and serving lenient sentences, to a much more normal life in Green River, Utah. Hayduke, thought to have been killed, surprisingly reappears at the end of the book—perhaps symbolizing perseverance and triumph.

In the tradition of Harriet Beecher Stowe, Upton Sinclair, and John Steinbeck, *Monkey Wrench* captures a spirit of idealism and the culture and character of a region. George Washington Hayduke is an unforgettable "alternative" political rogue—an uninhibited, opinionated, crude, fearless, and often reckless Act I political agitator, willing to do whatever it takes to protect the Southwest wilderness he loves.

Critics of *Monkey Wrench* fault Abbey for celebrating vandalism, law breaking, and eco-terrorism. One Arizona newspaper called it "eco-pornography." Abbey, however, defended his gang's activities as a form of civil disobedience, as patriotic as the legendary agitators who threw tea into the Boston Harbor. Abbey's pranksters, he added, kill machines, not people. It is the "moral duty" of a serious writer, Abbey said, "to act as a social critic of one's country and culture, and as such, to speak for the voiceless."[50]

The sometimes prickly "Cactus Ed," as friends called him, jokingly referred to himself as a half-time environmentalist, a part-time crusader, and a halfhearted fanatic. "I'd be a liar," he told an interviewer from *Outside* magazine, "if I didn't admit that I enjoy being a troublemaker. I like provoking people."[51] He also liked to say that society is like a stew and that it had to be stirred up so the scum doesn't rise to the top.[52]

Some readers are understandably put off by Abbey's gratuitous racist, sexist, and ethnic slurs. For example, in talking about one remote Arizona town, he suggests, "That town is *asking* for trouble. And they're even trying to make Christians out of the Indians. As if the Indians weren't bad enough already." My students were mostly forgiving of Abbey's rudeness, saying it was language as permissible art in conveying the authenticity or even raw charm of his central character. Regardless, it's still gratuitous and off-putting.

In *Monkey Wrench* and a handful of other novels, as well as in his iconic nonfiction personal reflections *Desert Solitaire: A Season in the Wilderness* (1968), Abbey could be cranky, inscrutable, racist, and sexist. "Damn the torpedoes, full speed ahead. I've been willing to be dismissed as a crank and a crackpot simply for the pleasure of saying exactly what I really do believe."[53] Abbey became a fierce opponent of illegal immigration and an ardent supporter of population control. Some critics noted a similarity of his political asides to the rhetoric of white supremacists and right-wing militia.[54]

Political conservatives have long opposed the creation of natural parks. In the 1970s a so-called Sagebrush Rebellion flourished for a while, urging states to reclaim federal lands for state and local usage. A "take-back-the-land" or reclamation movement continued well into the twentieth century. Edward Abbey would be amused, though upset, by latter-day Sagebrush militants, like Ammond Bundy's Citizens for Constitutional Freedom. Their goal, they say, is "to get the logger back to logging, to get the rancher back to ranching; to get the miner back to mining." That wasn't what Abbey favored.

Both Abbey and the armed Bundy militias in Nevada and in Oregon have a misguided sense of Western economics. The federal government, as Abbey would point out, more often than not has subsidized the ranches of the West. And few states can afford to manage existing federal lands. Further, the federal government has usually been a reasonable steward of western lands. "Demonizing the federal government and trying to resuscitate the past may have its demagogic appeal," writes James Surowiecki. "But the old West is gone, and it isn't coming back."[55]

Abbey is sometimes remembered as much for his faults as for his gifted writing and love of the Southwest wilderness. "Abbey," writes biographer David Gessner, "suffers from both excessive criticism—from those who see him as a sexist, racist, xenophobic—and excessive love, from those readers of what Luis Urrea called 'the Abbeyite Order.'"[56]

But Abbey was a consummate storyteller who melded environmentalism and anarchy in a compelling and novel way. He was a twentieth-century Thoreauean, who took seriously Thoreau's explanation that "if a man does not keep pace with his companions, perhaps it is because he hears a different drummer. Let him step to the music which he hears, however measured or far away." Abbey shared Thoreau's antipathy for politicians. He liked Thoreau's snarky maxim, "Oh, for man who is a *man*, and, has a bone in his back which you cannot pass your hand through."

Thoreau found his hero in John Brown, who acted, rather than just ranted, on his convictions. Abbey created his hero in his gang, especially in Hayduke. Hayduke epitomizes the libertarian spirit that challenges every hierarchy, every institution, every unnecessary fence and barrier. Abbey agreed with Thoreau that success and happiness needed to be redefined. He was more of a rebel than Thoreau, and he had a more sweeping political cause. "Some might see something adolescent in this rebellion against the way things are. But going against and staying against," writes David Gessner, "requires a deep bravery, a ballsiness, a commitment."[57]

The iconoclastic Abbey understood the paradoxical nature of his crusade. On the one hand, he appreciated the elitist part of excluding others from enjoying the great Southwest he had come to love. But he also liked to acknowledge his hillbilly heritage of having grown up in Appalachian southwest Pennsylvania. "I am a member of Rednecks for the Wilderness," he boasted.

> I call myself . . . not a conservationist and environmentalist but a wild preservationist. My motto is, not simply, keep it like it is, but like it was. I am a reactionary . . . one who can seriously entertain the proposition that in many ways the so-called primitive societies, the hunting and gathering way of life, may have been immensely superior to our own.

Abbey's writings are credited with inspiring the Earth First! environmental movement and the more fanatical Earth Liberation Front. Earth First! not only took as its emblem the monkey wrench but also adopted as one of its slogans "Hayduke Lives!" Yet Abbey's novel also inspired more moderate, law-abiding environmental movements. Persistent and growing coalitions are slowly forming around various environmental causes, from removing unnecessary dams in the West to statewide mileage requirements for automobiles to state and national proposals for reducing carbon emissions. The men of Abbey's gang—Doc, Bonnie, Seldom-Seen, and the indomitable Hayduke—have become political heroes for irreverent environmentalists, even if the gang is seen as a bunch of criminals and eco-terrorists by industry, developers, and government agencies.

Abbey wrote a follow-up novel, *Hayduke Lives!*, that continues with more tales about the gang. He also wrote a cheerleading foreword to *Ecodefense: A Field Guide to Monkeywrenching* (Tucson: A Ned Ludd Book, 1958 and 1987), edited by Dave Forman and Bill Haywood.

Few readers will consider *Monkey Wrench* a literary masterpiece, but it is an inventive and readable American saga and an iconic lament for the old American West in the wake of industrialization and mass tourism. (It has had a fan base of teenage and young adult readers, who might be reading Salinger's *Catcher in the Rye*, Rand's *Atlas Shrugged*, or Steinbeck, Hemingway, or Bradbury novels at the same time.) It is also a heartfelt homage to the beauty of the Southwest—to the yucca, black-bush, junipers, willows, sage, cottonwoods, mesquite, and purple asters, and to the canyon-wren and great horned owls who live there. Paradoxically, his gang may have wanted to discourage conventional tourism, but Abbey's celebration of the Southwest desert and canyonlands has been a magnetic invitation for millions of visitors who invariably want to see both America's "wild west" and Abbeyland before they are paved over.

Whatever its literary merits or faults, *Monkey Wrench* stands as a powerful story of a small group of people whose love for the land—"We *stand* for what we stand on"—led them to radical political action.

Edward Paul Abbey was a complicated individual. His paternal grandfather immigrated to America as an Aebi and changed it to Abbey. His father, Paul Revere Abbey, was a farmer and Socialist. Ed was a student of classical philosophy and an admirer of Tolstoy, Thoreau, Proudhon, and Kropotkin. His heroes included Garrett Hardin, Pete Seeger, Paul Ehrlich, Amory Lovins, and Barry Commoner. His favorite writers included Cervantes, Tolstoy, Twain, Whitman, Zola, Dostoyevsky, Melville, Steinbeck, Robinson Jeffers, Bertrand Russell, and Hemingway.

Abbey agreed with Hemingway's maxim that the most essential gift for a good writer is a built-in, shockproof shit detector. "This," said Hemingway, "is the writer's radar and all great writers have had it."

Though Abbey didn't mention him, he wrote with a similar motivation as the great Aleksandr Solzhenitsyn, who held, "Who, if not writers, are to condemn their own unsuccessful government as well as society itself. . . . Writers and activists can do more: they can vanquish lies! In the struggle against lies, art has always won and always will. Conspicuously, incontestably for everyone." Abbey would have said, "Amen!"

This Thoreau "bad boy" of the desert had, as noted, a penchant for insulting people, including noted writers, most politicians, Mormons, Indians, Mexicans, and women. He also had a thick file kept on him by the ever-suspicious FBI. He was both a happy warrior and a stinging contrarian: "I really am an anarchist and libertarian, a true believer in personal liberty, spontaneity, diversity, power decentralized in all forms, pure democracy."[58]

Abbey's attitudes have won a significant following. And his *Monkey Wrench Gang*, once viewed as mostly a cult novel, is read, along with *Desert Solitaire*, as recommended reading, especially for young people growing up in the American West. Abbey is read because he had an imaginative storytelling style that is appealing and entertaining. He was obviously having fun as he wrote, and readers feel this.

What kind of American republic would Abbey have liked? In this he was somewhat of a reactionary. He wanted population control, a halt to immigration, smaller families (which he didn't help), and little or no development. He had nostalgia for a simpler, preindustrial, pretechnology revolution past. He was, as noted, an elitist, selfish, libertarian anarchist. Like the also shy, irreverent Thoreau, he was more a withdrawer than a joiner. He saw himself as a fighter for humanity; yet he was never sure whether humanity cared for what he was fighting for. This didn't bother him. He would do what he was convinced was right—and he hoped most people would understand, and maybe, as one of my narratives puts it, the law would someday catch up.

A few years after writing *Monkey Wrench*, Abbey famously crusaded against the BLM and called for reducing the number of cattle on public lands. Eat less beef, he urged. Restore our sacred West with buffalo, antelope, big horn sheep, wolves, and mountain lions. Overgrazing, for Abbey, was the same as strip mining and the reckless damming of rivers.

Even Abbey doubtless imagined a more just, more sensible American republic, but in the meantime he and his libertarian eco-defenders had to reframe the nation's priorities and to preserve what they believed was one of the most precious and sacred of the nation's assets. Note that whereas most novelists in this book encouraged people to accept and love each other more, Cactus Ed primarily wrote to promote a love of place—his beloved desert wilderness.

Abbey was more than a preservationist rogue. He was a committed oppositionalist. He was as close to the writer as politician and preacher as it comes. He was a philosopher about the wilderness. The wilderness and desert, he liked to say, need no defense; they only need more defenders. The wilderness he loved could help restore our authenticity—"What Americans did wrong, deserts seemed to do right."[59]

He also understood the ironies and paradoxes of his craft: "Art, especially literary art, requires and thrives upon contradiction, paradox, human difficulty. An ideal society, if ever realized, would put people like me out of business. As perhaps we should be. There are no writers in Heaven, I imagine."[60]

NEWARK KID'S NIGHTMARE[61]

"Fear presides over these memories, a perpetual fear. Of course no childhood is without terror," wrote prize-winning novelist Philip Roth (1933–), "yet I wonder if I would have been a less frightened boy if Lindbergh hadn't been president or if I hadn't been the offspring of Jews."

Roth's *The Plot Against America* (2004) is about the temptation to look for scapegoats, about prejudice toward the marginalized, and about the potential deterioration of the basic values we hold dear in the American republic. *Plot* is in the tradition of Jack London's *The Iron Heel* (1908), Nathanael West's *A Cool Million* (1934), Sinclair Lewis's *It Can't Happen Here* (1935), and several of George Orwell's works. It is painfully disturbing. And it is exceedingly well written save for its ragged and hard-to-follow last fifty pages.

Roth's use of the word *plot* deserves discussion. First, there is the threatened "plot" of Hitler taking over the world. Second, there is a plot by the "America First" isolationists led by Lindbergh and Henry Ford to take over the Republican Party and then the U.S. government. Third, there is the demonizing of the Jews and the emphasis on "us-versus-them" thinking, not unlike what occurred in 2016 and 2017, when Mexicans and Muslims were demonized by Trump and his supporters. Finally, and perhaps central to Roth's novel, is the evolving threat to democratic values and constitutionalism as rights gradually diminished and civility and political processes were subverted. His use of the word *plot* may well be employed here as an umbrella term subsuming all of the above.

Roth's narrator protagonist is a grade school boy "coincidentally" named Philip Roth. Young Phil lives in an all-Jewish working-class neighborhood in Newark, New Jersey, and we learn almost everything we want to know about his insurance-selling father, Herman; his devoted mom, Bess; and his talented, yet often prickly, older brother, Sandy. They live in a rented second-story apartment and are just scraping by as the 1940s begin.

The Roths are Democrats and Franklin Roosevelt supporters. Roosevelt had helped navigate the country during the worst years of the Great Depression. He condemned German Nazism and Italian fascism. He had several Jewish advisors, and he seemed to understand that America and everyone anywhere was threatened by the horrible treatment of Jews and marginalized people in Germany.

Roth's fictionalized Phil shares, in vivid detail, his memories of the presidential election of 1940. He is only seven years old and in third grade. But this is what he believes took place.

Everyone assumed FDR would be renominated in July and reelected in November, though there was concern that he would be breaking the two-term tradition established by presidents Washington and Jefferson. But then the Republican Nominating Convention is held in Philadelphia. The Republican Party, at least in Roth's imagined alternative history, was deeply divided. They were inclined to nominate an internationalist such as Wendell Willkie, or possibly Thomas Dewey or Michigan U.S. senator Arthur Vandenberg. However, the growing isolationist and antiwar bloc of Republican conven-

tioneers withheld their support for the internationalists. They yearned for a
patriotic outsider who could challenge FDR, who they feared might team up
with Winston Churchill and the Brits and lead us into another world war.

The Republican convention was deadlocked until the twentieth ballot. And then things happened. Famed aviator and celebrated isolationist
Charles A. Lindbergh makes an unanticipated dramatic entrance onto the
convention floor at 3:18 a.m. And Senator Gerald P. Nye of North Dakota,
a rabid isolationist, nominates Lindbergh. A near-exhausted convention
embraces Lindy as their potential game-changing nominee.

Every American knew that back in 1927 this then twenty-five-year-
old, handsome, brave, and courageous aviator piloted *The Spirit of St. Louis*
in a successful and historic solo flight from New York across the Atlantic
Ocean to Paris. It took thirty-three hours and thirty minutes, and it turned
Lindbergh into an instant hero and celebrity. President Calvin Coolidge
awarded him the Distinguished Flying Cross and commissioned him a
colonel in the U.S. Army Air Corps Reserve. Lindbergh later became a test
pilot and consultant to aviation companies.

Lindbergh married Anne Morrow, who became a best-selling author.
Tragedy struck when a son of theirs was kidnapped in 1932. Craving privacy,
they lived for many years in a small English village. But Lindbergh, both on
behalf of the U.S. government and probably on his own, visited nearby Germany several times in the late 1930s. He was apparently not alarmed by the
genocidal policies then being put in place. He was, young Roth remembers
accurately, awarded the Service Cross of the German Eagle—a gold medal-
lion with four small swastikas. This was an authorized gesture by Hitler—
a token of Germany's respect and friendship for their American friend.

For this and perhaps other reasons, Lindbergh became an admirer of
Hitler and the German people and, when he returned to the United States
in the late 1930s, he became an advocate of the America First Committee,
an association that sought to prevent the United States from entering the
new war in Europe.

Roth's fictionalized 1940 presidential election features Lindbergh telling American voters, "Your choice is simple. It's not between Charles A.
Lindbergh and Franklin D. Roosevelt. It's between Lindbergh and war."
Lindbergh campaigns across the country, dramatically flying his own plane,
emphasizing that he is the candidate who will best preserve the American
republic, and he'll do this by preventing America from taking part in an
unnecessary world war.

Most Jews, or so the Roths believed, were worried that Lindbergh's
isolationism was too convenient a mask for Nazi sympathies. Lindbergh

and his supporters faulted the Jewish community for encouraging FDR to enter what they called "the Jewish War." Philip's father was incensed at these political developments. He and most of his Jewish friends were solidly for Roosevelt.

But there were a few outliers among the Jews who tried to make the case for Lindbergh. One of these exceptions turns out to be a prominent conservative rabbi from their own city of Newark. Rabbi Lionel Bengels- dorf not only endorsed Lindbergh but also became a surrogate speaker and champion for him. He understood that Jews were victims of hate crimes, especially in Germany, but he reasoned that going to war would somehow make things even worse. This is how Roth's Bengelsdorf put it at a packed Madison Square Garden political rally:

> This is not America's war. . . . This is Europe's war. It is one of a thousand-year-long sequence of European wars dating back to the time of Charlemagne. It is their second devastating war in less than half a century. And can anyone forget the tragic cost to America of their last war? The number of our dead—tell me, President Roosevelt, will it be merely doubled or tripled, or will it perhaps be quadrupled? Tell me, Mr. President, what sort of America will the massive slaughter of in- nocent American boys leave in its wake?

Bengelsdorf then acknowledges the persecution of Jews in Germany, but he is not persuaded that this warrants America going to war:

> Of course, the Nazi harassment and persecution of its German Jewish population is a cause of enormous anguish to me, as it is to every Jew . . . I oppose their treatment with every ounce of my strength, and so too does Colonel Lindbergh oppose this treatment. But how will this cruel fate that has befallen them in their land be alleviated by our great country going to war with their tormentors? If anything, the predicament of *all* of Ger- many's Jews would only worsen immediately—worsen, I fear, tragically. Yes, I am a Jew, and as a Jew I feel their suffering with a familial sharpness. But I am an American citizen, my friends. I am an American born and raised, and so I ask you, how would my pains be lessened if America were now to enter the war and, along with the sons of our Protestant families and the sons of our Catholic families, the sons of our Jewish families were to fight and die by the tens of thousands on a blood-soaked European battleground?

One of the charms of *Plot* is that novelist Roth tells this story through the eyes and "re-memories" of a likable and completely innocent young boy who may not yet be living the American Dream but still believes in it. We learn about Phil's stamp collection, his rivalry with his older brother, and his ordinary day-to-day routines of coming of age in working-class America. Roth captures this ethnic community, its struggles, its joys, and its inevitable squabbles.

But even young Roth's polite, pleasant, and protected youth could sense the chilling threats to Jews and constitutionalism that were gradually unfolding before his young eyes. Fear and unsettling politics lurked in the larger background—even for a seven-year-old.

In Roth's alternative scenario, Lindbergh unexpectedly defeats Roosevelt in a landslide election in November 1940. It was an upset win by a charismatic outsider, and just as in 2016, the experts got it wrong. Republicans also enjoyed great victories in the House and Senate elections. The New Deal came to a halt, and an isolationist foreign policy replaced the moderate internationalism of FDR. People had voted for change, for a hero, for a handsome, charismatic new face distinguished for his courage and "graceful athleticism." He was also known for his promise to keep America out of war and for his anti-Semitic sensibilities. (The nonalternative facts of 1940, of course, are that FDR won a third term with 54.7 percent of the vote to Wendell Willkie's 44.8 percent. Roosevelt swept the electoral college by a 5 to 1 margin.)

Back to *Plot*. Lindbergh is now president. Former U.S. senator Burton K. Wheeler, a maverick isolationist from Montana, becomes vice president. Famed automobile inventor and builder, and America First leader, Henry Ford of Detroit is made secretary of the interior.

One of the first major initiatives by the Lindbergh administration is to negotiate peace treaties with Germany and Japan. The first agreement, with Hitler, is sealed diplomatically in Reykjavik, Iceland, and dubbed the "Iceland Understanding." It is essentially a noninterventionist peace pact. In short, the United States will stay out of Hitler's way. A second pact, "The Hawaiian Understanding," arranged in Hawaii, agrees to a similar noninterventionist policy with imperialist Japan.

Lindbergh's Nazi sympathies become even more transparent when Hitler unilaterally ignores the Hitler-Stalin Non-Aggression Pact of 1941. Hitler simply invades Russia. And what does Lindbergh do? "With this act," Lindbergh lamely intones, "Adolf Hitler has established himself as the world's greatest safeguard against the spread of Communism and its evils. If the German army is successful in its struggles with Soviet Bolshevism . . . America will never have to face the threat of a voracious Communist state imposing its pernicious system on the rest of the world."

Meanwhile, on the home front, several programs are established in the U.S. Department of Interior. A euphemistically named "U.S. Office of American Absorption" is set up. One of its programs encourages Jewish youths to go to work, for the summer or possibly longer, in the American heartland in order to learn how mainstream Americans live. Sandy Roth, Phil's older brother, cheerfully enrolls in this program and comes back from his Kentucky apprenticeship "more patriotic" and more supportive of Lindbergh.

An even more draconian program is developed aimed at getting Jewish men like Herman Roth to move to middle America. "Homestead 42" is the name of this not-so-subtle Jewish dispersal program. It will remind some readers of the Indian removal programs of a century earlier or the Japanese internment camps set up and operated by the Roosevelt administration from 1942 to 1945.

Met Life, Herman Roth's employer, which is cooperating, or perhaps collaborating, with this new U.S. Office of American Absorption, assigns Mr. Roth a new position in the Midwest. He agonizes about this "offer" but decides to refuse it and resigns from the company. Now he has to work in a lower-paying, more menial job in his older brother's grocery store.

Further, members of the Roth family are questioned and harassed by FBI agents, as if some of them are being judged as unpatriotic or disloyal Americans. Thus the already marginalized Roths are led to believe they are suspect outsiders living in their native homeland.

Herman Roth, Phil's dad, rightly perceives creeping fascism taking place in his home of the brave and the free. He sees Lindbergh's treaty making and pacifism as giving Hitler a free pass to do what he wants—including eventually establishing Nazi leadership in Great Britain. He sees Jews in Germany and in Russia, and perhaps everywhere, enduring hate crimes and genocide. He is alarmed by "Homeland Security" strategies being pushed by the Lindberghs and Fords.

Philip's father is not himself a political activist, but he speaks his mind and his fears about what is happening. He feels America is sliding away from sensible positions, turning its back on our friends and making wrongheaded alliances with enemies. "You know what it means, son? It means destroying everything that America stands for." Meanwhile, Lindbergh supporters are stepping up both rhetorical and physical attacks on Jews. They chant "Keep America Out of the Jewish War." Intimidating Jews is widespread and seemingly tolerated.

An unlikely resister steps up to challenge Lindbergh and Lindberghism. New York City–based radio and newspaper commentator

Walter Winchell, himself a Jew, becomes a strident critic of the increasingly isolationist and anti-Semitic nation. Winchell, at this stage of his career, was wealthy and mostly a celebrity gossip columnist, but he had an audience of millions.

Winchell's strong, outspoken criticism of Lindbergh motivated FDR to come forward and rebuke the White House. The only thing we must now fear, FDR told a Madison Square Garden rally of dissenters, is

> the obsequious yielding to his Nazi friends by Charles A. Lindbergh, the shameless courting by the president of the world's greatest democracy of a despot responsible for innumerable criminal deeds and acts of savagery, a cruel and barbaric tyrant unparalleled in the chronicle of man's misdeeds. But we Americans will not accept a Hitler-dominated America. Today the entire world is divided between human slavery and human freedom. We—choose—freedom!

Winchell stepped up his attacks on Lindbergh. Soon his radio program is terminated as his corporate sponsors refused to underwrite his programs. Then William Randolph Hearst cancels Winchell's syndicated newspaper columns. The Roth family, longtime Winchell listeners and readers, are appalled to watch as Winchell is silenced by the powers that be.

But Winchell, in his newfound, undaunted Act II political coalition-building role, announces he will run for the presidency—and he announces this two and a half years *before* the 1944 elections—even before the 1942 congressional midterm elections are to take place.

Winchell barnstorms around America. But as he takes his case to the country, he is met with belligerent and sometimes violent supporters of the Lindbergh regime. There are brawls in Boston and riots in Detroit. There is even a fight between Phil's father and his cousin Alvin.

Walter Winchell is assassinated while at a political rally in Louisville, Kentucky. He is slain, we learn, by a suspected American Nazi Party member in collaboration with the Ku Klux Klan. Winchell is hailed as a martyr, as thirty thousand mourn his death in Manhattan. But the anti-Lindbergh resistance is temporarily silenced and anti-Semitism grows. Fear spreads among Jewish communities. It even prompted in the Roth neighborhood the establishment of a Jewish Provisional Police, a voluntary "Minute Man" corps to provide for their own neighborhood security.

Roth's depiction of this hastily organized band made up of local high school dropouts is a humorous counterpoint to the larger and more ominous dystopian theme of his novel:

These were local boys without any of the ideals that were embedded in the rest of us, who'd already begun to emanate an aura of lawlessness as afar back as the fifth grade, inflating condoms in the school toilet and breaking into fistfights on the 14 bus and wrestling till they bled onto the concrete sidewalk outside the movies, the ones who, during their years in school, parents directed their children to have nothing to do with and who were now in their twenties and occupied running numbers and shooting pool and washing dishes in the kitchen of one or another of the neighborhood's delicatessen restaurants. To most of us, they were known, if at all, only by the hoodlum magic of their supercharged nicknames—Leo "the Lion" Nusbaum, Knuckles Kimmelman, Big Gerry Schwartz, Dummy Breitbart, Duke "duke-it-out" Glick—and by their double-digit IQ scores.

President Lindbergh's response to Winchell's assassination is to personally fly to Louisville to give a brief reassuring talk to people there. Lindbergh says there is nothing to fear: "Our country is at peace. Our people are at work. Our children are at school. I flew down here to remind you of that. Now I'm going back to Washington, so as to keep things that way." It is a brief and characteristically laconic message.

Lindbergh's plane, however, mysteriously disappears en route back to Washington. Search parties fail to find any evidence of a crash. Vice President Wheeler assumes the job of acting president amid growing paranoia and hysteria.

Here is where Roth's novel becomes disjointed, confusing, and (some would say) bizarre. Roth introduces several competing theories of Lindbergh's disappearance. One explanation disclosed suspiciously by German state radio is that Lindbergh was kidnapped by a major Jewish conspiracy aimed at taking over America. This announcement triggers intensified anti-Semitic rioting and leads to the arrest by the Wheeler administration of many prominent Jewish leaders and newspaper reporters. Anne Morrow Lindbergh, the former First Lady, is detained at Walter Reed Medical Center, apparently in the psychiatric ward. Martial law is introduced. Even FDR is taken into custody "for his own protection." The Bill of Rights is ignored.

Other theories of Lindbergh's disappearance, including his voluntary surrender to the Germans, are offered. Roth's own fictionalized chronology is also altered here. But Acting President Wheeler, who presides in office for a mere eight days, takes authoritarianism to its zenith.

Meanwhile, in Newark, the Roth family is further unhinged by the killing of one of their close friends and looming pogroms that seem to be escalating around the country. Around this time a confused, now nine-year-old Phil plans to run away, perhaps to Boys' Town in Omaha. This doesn't happen.

Plot Against America ends with Lindbergh's wife, Anne Morrow Lindbergh, defiantly escaping her "protectors" at Walter Reed and, with the help of her Secret Service aides, sneaking back into the White House. She realizes the constitutional disaster that has taken place. She, with borrowed and imagined authority, calls for the removal of Acting President Wheeler. She also, apparently acting according to the Presidential Succession Act of 1866, calls upon the secretary of state to serve as president.

Mrs. Lindbergh suspends the martial law that Wheeler had imposed. She calls for the release of the recently imprisoned Jewish leaders. And she interprets the Presidential Succession Act as allowing for the nation—under unusual circumstances like this—to hold a special presidential election and calls for this to be done to coincide with the scheduled congressional elections of November 1942.

Novelist Roth turns Mrs. Lindbergh into a much-needed redeemer heroine, and Roosevelt Democrats quickly dub her "Our Lady of the White House." First Lady Lindbergh addresses the stunned nation as follows:

> The present administration has a history of repeated injustices and usurpations, all having in direct object the establishment of an absolute tyranny over these states. This government has been deaf to the voice of justice and has extended over us an unwarrantable jurisdiction. Consequently, in defense of those inalienable rights claimed in July of 1776 by Jefferson of Virginia and Franklin of Pennsylvania and Adams of Massachusetts Bay, and by the authority of the same good people of this United States, and by appealing to the same supreme judge of the world for the rectitude of our intentions, I, Anne Morrow Lindbergh, a native of the state of New Jersey, a resident of the District of Columbia, and the spouse of the thirty-third president of the United States, declare that the injurious history of usurpation be ended.

We have suspended our disbelief here as the First Lady almost magically—as well as majestically (yet with dubious "presidential power")—brings Wheeler's reign of terror to an end. Her restorative actions and words apparently also bring an end to the worst features of the Lindbergh nightmare.

On November 3, 1942, Franklin Roosevelt is once again elected as president. Democrats take over the U.S. House and U.S. Senate. Then, in Roth's inverted chronology, the Japanese attack Pearl Harbor and the United States enters the war in both the Pacific and Europe.

Critics can understandably fault Roth for a hard-to-digest and semi-happy ending. Constitutionalism is restored; yet the United States becomes involved in a monstrous war. We hear little more about young Roth save for his—and our—two-year-long nightmare coming to an end.

Roth is a great writer, and his is a chilling, painful, and powerfully instructive narrative. Scapegoating and political paranoia are realities, especially in economically stressful times. Most of what Roth writes is believable, and, sadly, much of what he writes did take place in other nations.

Roth's *Plot* deserves to be read by a wide audience—and read along with the kindred novels of Jack London, Nathanael West, Sinclair Lewis, Robert Penn Warren, Toni Morrison, Ray Bradbury, David Gutterson, and Canadian Margaret Atwood.

Roth has told interviewers that *Plot* was written less as a warning than as a reminder of what could have happened here in America and what tragically did happen to marginalized minorities in so many other nations. It is also a reminder of the fragility of our constitutional processes. The incremental deterioration of democracy and republicanism can begin—like leaking gas—quietly and without much notice. The darker impulses in human nature can bring out meanness, intolerance, and hate crimes. The history of the world is all too revealing of these.

Roth's novel leaves us with several questions. How likely, then or in our day, is Roth's scenario? The answer is—enough to take it seriously. What was the link between isolationism and anti-Jewish sentiment? There was a definite link at that time. And it is one of the enduring realities of America that our treatment of Indians, African Americans, and waves of immigrants from the Irish to Syrians is marked by prejudicial, if not brutish, practices.

What are the larger implications of Roth's narrative for the American political experiment? First, there is always the possibility of the tyranny of the majority, or the tyranny of those who have won election to our national positions in the federal government. Balancing majority authority and minority rights will always be a central challenge in America. And, as noted, despite all the exceptional advantages Americans enjoy, our experiment in constitutional democracy will always be an experiment, a work in progress and a challenge requiring vigilance by large numbers of civic activists. Experiments can fail—as the history of the world attests.

Roth pays credit to the Lindbergh plot resisters, including Walter Winchell, FDR, and ultimately Anne Morrow Lindbergh. But he also, in his own way, honors the Herman Roths and the neighborhood Jewish

Provisional Patrol as part of the necessary concerted group agency needed to thwart authoritarianism. Roth deserves credit for reminding us, even as he entertains us, that a nation—even with our exalted constitutional aspirations—can drift away from its principled moorings.

Roth's brilliant *The Plot Against America* will remain timely as long as America exists—and it not surprisingly gained an expanded readership in the aftermath of President Donald Trump's Islamaphobia, populist nativism, and renewed "American First" appeals. A hopeful, optimistic, and liberating spirit will always have to contend with the dark, foreboding fears of despair, intolerance, and prejudice. *Plot* can be read as agitation, as consciousness raising, and as rich, contextual local anthropology as it beautifully captures a struggling, yet proud, American family, in a special place and at a special time. It will, regardless of how we categorize it, endure as one of America's compelling political novels.

We turn next in chapter 4 to consciousness-raising American political novels. They, too, can be considered "purpose novels." But they are written less to jolt the reader than to expose some of the flaws in the American political experiment. Let's not overly boast that we are exceptional, these novelists seem to be saying. Instead, let us recommit ourselves and the nation to greater integrity, to greater fairness, and to more vigilant constitutional practices.

4

THE NOVELIST AS POLITICAL
CONSCIOUSNESS RAISER

Novelists in every culture have performed in part as reformers and political and moral consciousness raisers. Disraeli, Hugo, Huxley, Orwell, Stendhal, Dostoevsky, Zola, Malraux, and Koestler are a few European examples of this tradition.

Most American political novelists engage in some form of consciousness raising. But the novelists treated in this chapter were notably addressing the need for America to come to terms with trickery, blackmail, political prejudice, and the toxic consequences of political manipulation by big money and political machines or military elites.

Consciousness-raising novelists differ from agitator novelists in that they are primarily calling attention to problematic practices. They often depict an innocent protagonist who is unfairly treated or shocked by how the political system seems to be rigged to advantage the already advantaged.

These authors may not be pushing for radical political change—as agitator novelists are—yet they are typically calling attention to practices that are unacceptable and contrary to the notion of representative democracy, fair play, and equality before the law.

Consciousness-raising novelists are authors with a point of view. They want their readers to be upset with the status quo. They show their disappointment with the political practices they describe, and they regularly signal that Americans should support political reforms and political leaders who might help us achieve our constitutional aspirations.

This chapter is obviously a mere sampling of consciousness-raising political novels. Three are located in Washington, D.C. Three are concerned with state politics, one looking at New Hampshire, a second at Louisiana, and a third is set in Mississippi. Two examine small communities, in Alabama and New Mexico, respectively. One focuses on the Caucasian occupation of Southern California in the nineteenth century.

GILDED AGE HYPOCRISY[1]

"No," said Philip Bolton, "the chances are that a man cannot get into Congress now without resorting to arts and means that should render him unfit to go there. . . . Why, it is telegraphed all over the country and commented on as something wonderful if a Congressman votes honestly and unselfishly and refuses to take advantage of his position to steal from the government."

This is a typical passage from the first novel by Mark Twain (1835–1910) and his friend and Hartford, Connecticut, neighbor, Charles Dudley Warner. Their novel—a scathing, satirical commentary on the largely unregulated scheming and political corruption that defined the post–Civil War Era—sold well. It is not among Twain's celebrated novels, but it was one of the first major political novels set in Washington, D.C. It would be followed by hundreds of D.C. novels by Henry Adams, Allen Drury, Andrew Tully, Gore Vidal, Fletcher Knebel and Chuck Bailey, Ward Just, Christopher Buckley, Joseph Nye, and others. It also did something unusual; it gave a distinctive and lasting name to the era, now understood as post Civil War to the end of the century period.

Most of the satirical criticism in *The Gilded Age* is directed against the greed and lust—for land, for money, for power—of an alliance of western land speculators, eastern capitalists, and corrupt officials who dominate this so-called peaceful post–Civil War time.[2] Twain and Warner capture the euphoric ambitions as well as illusions and dashed hopes of the age.

The "Gilded Age" is a mocking allusion to Athens's Golden Age and implies that beneath the glitter of westward expansion, invention, and the coming of the transcontinental railway, little was golden. Rumor had it that the wives of the authors challenged Twain and Dudley to write something more realistic than the best-selling sentimental novels of James Fenimore Cooper, Horatio Alger Jr., and others of their day.

Gilded Age was their response. Twain's masterpiece, *Huck Finn*, would come a decade later. *Gilded Age* was no masterwork. It is a patchworky collection of convoluted stories, apparently written over the course of just a few months. This shows. Critics rightly complained that the novel failed to jell structurally. This was in part because both authors wrote disparate chunks of the book, with Dudley elaborating on some romances while Twain expounded on corrupt land deals and unscrupulous, sordid political intrigue. Dudley's chapters were workmanlike, while Twain's were full of noise, burlesque, and stinging parody.

Gilded was both consciousness raising and caricature. It acknowledges the liberating, free-wheeling entrepreneurial economic enterprise of the period while exposing the dubious political morality of the day and makes the case that the average citizen is being scammed by the political and economic elites of the day. The clear impression is left that business interests were able to suppress any serious governmental efforts to regulate them.

Before his successful literary career, Twain worked as a typesetter, a steamboat pilot, an unsuccessful gold prospector out West, and a much-traveled reporter. He also served as an aide to a Nevada governor and U.S. senator, briefly living in Washington, D.C., for about a semester (his Washington semester) in the late 1860s. Most of Twain's and Warner's characters are based on people they knew and experiences of family members.[3]

Their senator, Abner Dilworthy, from a nameless Midwestern state, looms large in the novel, portrayed initially as a pious and principled representative. He is well off and well connected. He lives a block away from the White House and is a fixture at capital social events. A large though not tall individual, he is "a pleasant man, a popular man with the people."

Dilworthy had been a Unionist and is a proud Christian who touts a commitment to help the recently freed African Americans. His self-proclaimed guiding principle is "I never push a private interest if it is not justified and ennobled by some larger public good. I doubt if a Christian would be justified in working for his own salvation if it was not to aid in the salvation of his fellow man."

The reader learns, however, that Dilworthy's piety is insincere. We read of his guest sermon to a Sunday school gathering back in his home state. He tells the three-dozen lads present that he grew up poor, that his parents sent him to Sunday school, that he loved Sunday school, and that he hopes they do as well. He credits his Sunday school values as the reason he was elected a legislator and later as governor. His is a self-referential homily, delivered in the third person: "Temptations lay all about him, and sometimes he was about to yield," he shares. "But [then] he would think of some precious lesson he learned in his Sunday school a long time ago, and that would save him." He goes on:

> After a while, the people elected him a representative to the Congress of the United States, and he grew very famous—now temptations assailed him on every hand. People tried to buy his vote; but no, the memory of his Sunday school saved him from all harm. . . .

My precious children, love your parents, love your teachers, love your Sunday school, be pious, be obedient, be honest, be diligent, and then you will succeed in life and be honored of all men. Above all things, my children, be honest. Above all things be pure-minded as the snow. Let us join in prayer.

Alas, our pure-minded, Sunday school–reared senator turns out to be a scoundrel. He was regularly "on the take" from special interests and handed out bribes and favors to secure his reelection by the state legislature. Those same state legislators eventually exposed his bribery and prevented his re-election. His fellow U.S. senators, however, looked the other way at their wayward colleague, who, in spite of his routine proclamations of piety, was apparently so similar to themselves.

Senator Dilworthy was modeled after a particularly sleazy Bible-quoting, protemperance, Civil War and Reconstruction–era U.S. senator, Republican Samuel C. Pomeroy from Kansas. Twain had met him during his days in the capital.

In the convention of the *roman à clef*, the narrative is based on thinly disguised characters and events from the recent past. Twain biographer Phillip S. Foner explains, "It is through the career of Senator Dilworthy, who for public consumption, 'glibly links the name of God Almighty with his purposes,' while privately he will touch no bill until a fat retainer's fee is guaranteed, that Twain most effectively exposes hypocrisy of so many wealthy, deeply religious men of the Gilded Age."[4]

Among the fascinating characters in *Gilded* is Laura Hawkins, a strikingly beautiful young woman from a disadvantaged past. She has some ill-fated early romances and a short-lived "marriage" to an already married, handsome former Confederate officer. But she wins the attention of the aforementioned Senator Dilworthy when he is visiting her state (well before his political fall) and gets invited to come and live with the Dilworthy family as a kind of niece. Under the senator's guidance, she also becomes a fixture at Washington political and social events. She quickly becomes a shrewd and financially successful lobbyist.

Laura uses her considerable charm and physical attractiveness to influence members of Congress to support various measures championed by Dilworthy. Among these is a measure that would designate a huge swath of undesirable land (some seventy thousand acres) in East Tennessee for a university, which of course would be paid for by federal funds—and which, coincidentally, would make Laura Hawkins, who is part heir to this land, rich. Twain's own family had similar lands for which they had high hopes, which in his case went unfulfilled.

She teases her clients, members of Congress, with multiple wiles and a surprising political acumen, though apparently *not* with sexual favors. She breaks hearts, yet wins votes. There is a vivid scene in which she threatens a representative with blackmail. He walks away muttering that he is up against a "beautiful devil"; yet he votes as she had requested.

Our femme fatale, however, soon encounters a new, apolitical challenge concerning the only man she had ever loved. Colonel Selby, the former Confederate officer and Laura's ex-husband, has come to Washington on business, his family in tow. She confronts him and demands he leave his wife and remarry her. Laura has become adept at getting her way with men. Though she is able to keep many of Washington's most powerful men wrapped around her finger, Selby is her Moby Dick and she is possessed "by a fever of love and hatred and jealousy."

Orphaned as a child and betrayed by Selby as a young woman, winning back this officer represents for Laura the conquest of her deep-seated issues with abandonment and self-worth. Selby flees to New York; she follows, and shoots him. A theatrical trial ensues, and she is miraculously acquitted on the grounds of temporary insanity. Twain and Warner use the shooting, imprisonment, and trial chapters to mock both the corrupt and boss-run Tammany Hall political machine and the judiciary.

In the end Senator Dilworthy is defeated and disgraced. Laura Hawkins, who is alternately a potential heroine and a figure cursed by the crass materialism of her family and her age, dies an ignominious death. And the Hawkins-Dilworthy fraudulent land-swap university bill similarly meets defeat in the Congress. So, in a way, bad guys and bad deals meet their just desert.

Gilded Age is a profile of Grant-era follies with brief romantic interludes. But the larger message here is that Washington, D.C., was a slimy political cesspool of intrigue and lost innocence. The newly unified Americans looked westward and dreamed of prosperity and expansion. But just as many speculators and their golden ambitions failed during the period, so also, we are told, there were countless political failures. Twain and Warner ask the question American political novelists regularly raise: Is it a question of our government falling into the hands of bad people, or are our politics, our governing system, our representatives, and maybe even our people, unable to cope with the inherent paradoxes of political power and constitutional democracy?

While *Gilded Age* doesn't explicitly detail conspiratorial governmental plots against the people, it suggests that land speculators, railroaders, shipping interests, and their friends regularly manipulated Congress for their own benefit. Beware, the authors urge, the dishonesty, the phony patriotism and pietism of those who pretend to be the public's "representatives" in Washington. Beware, too, get-rich-quick schemes that defined this buccaneering and restless era of westward expansion and yearning conquest.[5]

Mark Twain was more a storyteller and national satirist than a profound political thinker. He had a Midwestern and perhaps even youthful idealism that people were honest and that the American republic was a valid and promising political experiment. He was a Lincoln Republican and accepted capitalism as the way America conducted its business. But in his sections of *Gilded* he writes as a reporter who is discouraged, if not alarmed, by the excesses and violations of the golden rule.

Gilded is an exposé, sometimes bitter, sometimes cynical, sometimes comical, of the darker side of American exceptionalism and pay-to-play machine politics (in both parties). The Dilworthy and Hawkins stories, along with their hilarious huckster pal Colonel Beriah Sellers, epitomize a narrative of betrayed innocence. These characters know that what they are doing is wrong, but they are unapologetic and mostly unashamed.

Gilded predates the heyday of the Populist movement and takes place long before the coming of Progressivism; yet it at least implicitly foreshadows the call for sensible national regulations that would lessen political corruption and deceptive, fraudulent business practices.

Gilded is not an example of the novelist as political agitator. Yet it is a good example of the novel as consciousness raising. It is an amalgam of satire, ridicule, storytelling, and a sophisticated attempt to capture the spirit of the times.

Both Twain and Warner hoped that the American people and their elected leaders could act more honorably. Who, they asked, is looking out for "the common good" of the young nation? Is this the kind of political system that Washington, Jefferson, and Madison had devoted their lives to invent and preserve?

This should have been a triumphant period for the Republican Party. With Lincoln at the helm, they had won the Civil War. Republicans, when Twain and Warner wrote, controlled the White House and the Congress. Both Twain and Warner were Republicans. But they were obviously disheartened by the political practices they watched in Washington, D.C., and New York. Americans, these consciousness raisers are saying, deserve much better, and thus their lampooning, fictional account of the post-Lincoln political and social landscape.

Gilded Age, as noted, is not a masterpiece. No one nominates it as a great American novel. Still, it is worth reading because it was cowritten by the celebrated Mark Twain, whose *Huckleberry Finn* is one of our greatest American novels. It is also worth reading because it, perhaps sadly, captures an important period in American political culture. Many contemporary readers remark that *Gilded*'s subtitle, *A Tale of Today*, remains appropriate or relevant for some of the political and economic practices of our era as well. *Gilded* should be read along with Henry Adams's *Democracy* (1880) and Hamlin Garland's *A Spoil of Office* (1892), both of which were written just a few years later and similarly address the gap between our high hopes for the American Experiment and less exalted realities.

MADELEINE LEE COMES TO D.C.[6]

"The ease with which Ratcliffe alone had twisted her about his finger, now that she saw it, made her writhe, and the thought of what he might have done, had she married him, and of the endless successions of moral somersaults she would have had to turn, chilled her with mortal terror. She had barely escaped being dragged under the wheels of a machine. . . . When she thought of this, she felt a mad passion to revenge herself on the whole race of politicians, with Ratcliffe at their head."

So thinks Madeleine Lightfoot Lee, our protagonist in Henry Adams's *Democracy: An American Novel*, after being told of the corrupt pay-to-play shenanigans of her once potential husband, U.S. Senator Silas P. Ratcliffe from Peoria, Illinois.

Madeleine Lee, a rich, worldly thirty-year-old widow, had come to Washington, D.C., in the 1870s to meet the nation's leader. She wanted to understand the inner workings of American government. What was the quality of the men who shaped it? Was constitutional democracy possible? Where was the American Experiment headed? And, she seemed to be asking herself, was there a role she might play?

Henry Adams (1838–1918), great-grandson and grandson of U.S. presidents, was the son of a distinguished diplomat and congressman. Henry Adams himself served as a diplomat, reporter, magazine correspondent, congressional aide, and became a noted historian. He was uncommonly well connected and lived in Washington during the ill-fated Reconstruction era and the notably inept U. S. Grant presidency. He closely observed the "leadership" of Rutherford Hayes, Chester Arthur, and James G. Blaine. He would later write a monumental nine-volume history of America during the Jefferson and Madison eras. Still later he wrote a best-selling and prize-winning introspective autobiography, *The Education of Henry Adams*.

Democracy, often cited as a preeminent work within the American political canon, was published anonymously in 1880 because its *roman à clef* format might have gotten Adams sued by political officials who saw themselves depicted in the book. (It was not until after his death that he was officially identified as the novel's author.)

Central characters are Mrs. Lee and the leading Republican U.S. senator of the day, Silas P. Ratcliffe, known colloquially as "the Prairie Giant." Lurking in the background is a woefully empty cipher of a president who seems a mockery of American election arrangements.

Mrs. Lee is as curious and idealistic as she is beautiful. Tired of New York and Europe, she comes to Washington to understand the heart of American governance, how political leaders perform their duties, and whether a respectable government was possible in a representative democracy. Mrs. Lee is fascinated with political power: How is it obtained? How is it exercised? In whose interest? And, perhaps, how might she acquire power?

Madeleine Lee takes her political education seriously. She frequently visits the Senate gallery to listen to debates. She regularly reads the *Congressional Record*. She studies the lives and legacies of American presidents. Her initial reaction is that of disappointment. Most of our "leaders," she concludes, are shallow, melancholy failures, and the nation has spent most of its history overrun by swollen egos craving flattery. Men of principle are rare. "Surely" she resolves, "something must be done to check corruption. Are we forever to be at the mercy of thieves and ruffians?"

Because of her beauty, intelligence, and money, she soon becomes a popular hostess in her home across from the White House. (Adams had lived in the same neighborhood.) Her parlor becomes a much-sought-after haunt of politicians, diplomats, and intellectuals. And Adams's novel in many ways is a witty and satirical comedy of manners.

Mrs. Lee becomes infatuated with the larger-than-life Senator Ratcliffe, a fifty-year-old widower, who just missed winning the Republican presidential nomination and is, at the same time, the most influential leader in Congress. He is a gifted orator, a crafty political pragmatist, and "not without good looks." He loves power and still yearns to become president. "The pleasure of politics," he readily acknowledges, "lay in the possession of power."

What's more, Ratcliffe is a committed partisan. To him, the nation's interest and his party's (Republican) interest are one and the same. He believes great progress can only be achieved through strong, disciplined political parties. He holds, too, that the morally suspect approaches employed by politicians are generally acceptable as long as ends are relatively sound. He is widely viewed, we are told, as an effective, if not great, statesman.

"The smoothness of his manipulation was marvelous." He has a reputation, which is the essence of politics, for bringing hostile interests together and striking deals. "The beauty of his work," our narrator tells us, "consisted in the skill with which he evaded the questions of principle." He had no sympathy for reformers, moralizers, or political theories.

He loves power. He intends to be president. Yet he is lonely.

He is an accomplished political broker. Power is his goal; principles are secondary. Ratcliffe's immediate goals are to ensure Republican control and to influence, if not outright control, the newly elected president, whom he considers an inexperienced political lightweight. He succeeds and in the process becomes secretary of the Treasury.

Mrs. Lee and Senator Ratcliffe see each other regularly, share secrets and personal matters, and grow increasingly fond of, as well as semi-dependent on, one another. She sees him as a high priest of American politics, and through him she earnestly plans to understand political statecraft. She is determined to figure him out and, in doing so, to appraise the meaning of democracy. She also likely sees in him her own path to power and perhaps even becoming First Lady in the White House. Mrs. Lee's sister and close friends warn, however, that Ratcliffe, despite impressive political success, is an unsuitable partner.

Ratcliffe, as noted, makes no pretense of being a reformer or idealist. He wants a companion, and in Lightfoot Lee he sees not only a wife but also an additional political asset to help him achieve even more power and personal glory. He awkwardly proposes marriage:

> I'm not one of those who are happy in political life. I am a politician because I cannot help myself; it is the trade I am fittest for, and ambition is my resource to make it tolerable. In politics we cannot keep our hands clean. I have done many things in my political career that are not defensible. To act with honesty and self-respect, one should always live in a pure atmosphere, and the atmosphere in politics is impure. Domestic life is the salvation of many a public man, but I have for many years been deprived of it. I have now come to the point where increasing responsibilities and temptations make me require help. I must have it. You alone can give it to me. You are kind, thoughtful, conscientious, high-minded, cultivated, fitted better than any woman I have ever saw, for public duties. Your place is here. You belong among those who exercise an influence beyond their time. I only ask you to take the place which is yours.

Mrs. Lee, intrigued at the prospect of gaining such influence, is inclined to accept. Yet, before she consents, she learns more about Ratcliffe's political past, which includes a corporate bribe that "encouraged" him to change his mind and vote for a pivotal piece of legislation. This leads to an acrimonious showdown in which our pragmatic politico begs forgiveness and even pledges to give up his political career in exchange for her love. His explanations are in vain. The more he talks, the more convinced Lightfoot Lee becomes that Ratcliffe not only lacks courage but also is just another pitiful example of America's failed political experiment. In addition to losing his recent bid for the presidency, she is now convinced, the senator is merely another unprincipled politician who has lost his soul.

It's Ratcliffe's moral somersaults that are, in Mrs. Lee's view, his undoing. "Wealth, office, power are at auction. Who bids the highest? Who hates with the most venom? Who intrigues with the most skill? Who has done the dirtiest, the meanest, the darkest, and the most political work? He shall have his reward."

Mrs. Lee had come to Washington in search of leaders she could admire. She had hoped that America's grand experiment with constitutional democracy would be capable of producing leaders inspired by noble ends, men who would rise above partisanship and personal self-interest. She yearned for the presumed unsoiled days of George Washington (and probably also people like John Adams and his son John Quincy Adams), but Ratcliffe and most of his colleagues dashed such optimistic hopes: "She had got to the bottom of this business of democratic government, and found out that it was nothing more than government of any other kind." Personal ambitions and craving power for power's sake seemed to intoxicate the politicians she put under her microscope. A disillusioned Mrs. Lee flees Washington lamenting that "democracy has shaken my nerves to pieces."

Lightfoot Lee sees through her once admired companion, and her disgust for him sums up her contempt for Ratcliffe's Washington: "The audacity of the man who seemed sublime," who couldn't tell the difference between good and evil, between a lie and the truth. Indeed, "the more she saw him, the surer she was that his courage was mere moral paralysis, and that he talked about virtue and vice as a man who is color blind talks about red and green."

It is easy to identify the author's personal yearnings in this narrative. Adams was searching for public servants like his grandfather and great-grandfather. Instead, he saw the likes of Andrew Johnson, Ulysses Grant, and Senator James Blaine. He saw appalling levels of corruption, extensive "pay-to-play" politics, and rampant patronage abuse. And he feared that exceptional people were not standing for public office as often as in the past because the common voter may have failed to encourage them to do so. In this, Adams may have been sympathetic to Benjamin Disraeli's view that well-bred and educated elites are the least likely to be corrupted. In any event, Adams publicly supported civil service reform and even dedicated the novel's royalties to that cause.

In the end, Adams leaves us with familiar questions: Can one be a successful politician *and* a good person? How can we reconcile high-minded public-interest principles with the political agreement-building process? What can be done to limit the influence of money and bribery?

Adams's despair with the politics of the 1870s is summed up in the jaundiced political philosophy of his antihero. In defense of his unscrupulous machinations, Ratcliffe says:

> If Washington were president now, he would have to learn our ways or lose his next election. Only fools and theorists imagine that our society can be handled with gloves and long poles. . . . If virtue won't answer our purposes we must use vice, or our opponents will turn us out of office.

The parable of Mrs. Lee and her frustrating capital sojourn has a remarkable freshness several generations later. We struggle still with Mrs. Lee's (and Adams's) investigative concerns, fears, and findings. We yearn still for intelligent and honorable leaders who will help the United States function democratically and effectively.

Democracy, as noted, ends with an almost estranged dismissal of America's once promising presidential-congressional separation-of-powers system. Adams obviously sees his contemporaries as pale shadows of his illustrious relatives, and even the Jeffersons and Lincolns who had risen to the White House. And Adams, in common with many of the early and mid-nineteenth-century novelists (e.g., James Fenimore Cooper), is at least mildly suspicious of the possible tyranny of the new majorities. Beware the greedy and unscrupulous politicians—but also the people who have elected them.

Had Adams given up on American democracy? *Democracy* leaves us with that verdict—at least in his "majority report." But he does give us two lesser characters, one a Connecticut congressman and the other a former U.S. minister to Spain and fellow "Back Bay" intellectual and historian, who offer some solace.

His Congressman French champions civil service reform even as the Ratcliffes belittle it. His Nathan Gore, perhaps reflecting Henry Adams's personal views, or at least his aspirational hopes for America, provides what might be called his "minority report."

Mrs. Lee bluntly asks Gore whether he believes in universal suffrage and "do you yourself think democracy the best government?" He is squeamish at being pinned to the wall but quietly affirms, "I believe in democracy. I accept it. . . . Democracy asserts the fact that the masses are now raised to higher intelligences than formerly. All our civilization aims at this mark." Gore concedes, "I grant it is an experiment, but it is the only direction society can take that is worth its taking. . . . Every other possible step is backward, and I don't care to repeat the past."

In the end, there are two Henry Adamses in this well-written, well-crafted novel. The loudest is critical, dismissive, and even condescending toward politics and politicians of his era. The second is his grandfather's son, one with almost unmatched public service DNA; this one wants to believe constitutional democracy can be made, and must be made, to work. The reader has to work harder to hear this second, more understated, political message—yet it is there. I also contend that it is there, or at least latent, in most American novels.

So Mrs. Lee heads off once again traveling to Europe and to do good deeds of her own choosing. But she had met at least a few honest and decent people in the nation's capital. Maybe their day will come. Perhaps, someday, America's public servants will live up to America's highest ideals. At the very least, our Silas Ratcliffe, like his real-life counterpart, the corrupt Senator James G. Blaine, is rebuked in his drive to become president.

NATIVE DAUGHTER MEETS MANIFEST DESTINY[7]

"Pablo," Franciscan Father Peyri advises a Luiseño Indian chief in the novel *Ramona*, "your people will be driven like sheep to the slaughter, unless you keep them together. Knit firm bonds between them; band them into pueblos; make them work; and above all, keep peace with the whites. It is your only chance." Nevertheless, white settlers from the East pour into what Helen Hunt Jackson (1820–1885) had described, sentimentally, as a beautiful, pastoral coexistence between Spanish hacienda dons, gentle Franciscan priests, and hardworking, if poor, Indian villagers.

Jackson had in 1881 written a seething nonfiction indictment of U.S. inhumane treatment of indigenous Americans. Nonindigenous Americans relentlessly pushed westward in search of better farmland, water, minerals, and the good life. But, wrote Jackson, they cheated, robbed, and murdered; repeatedly broke promises; and seldom (if ever) recognized Indian rights such as life, liberty, and the pursuit of happiness. The "first Americans" were exiled or crushed in the so-called land of the free that, as the Eurocentric narrative has it, Christopher Columbus (or perhaps the Vikings?) had "discovered." Congress had enacted the Indian Removal Act in 1830, and that set the tone for the next two generations.

Her nonfiction *A Century of Dishonor* (1881) held that "so long as there remains in our frontier one square mile of land occupied by a weak and helpless owner, there will be a strong and unscrupulous frontiersman ready to seize it, and a weak and unscrupulous politician, who can be hired for a vote or for money, to back him."[8]

This nonfiction work was written as a strident consciousness-raising tract to educate fellow Americans about broken promises and questionable confiscations of tribal lands. "She revealed that the government had almost never protected the Indian against private outrage," wrote historian Allan Nevins. "She proved that its constant vacillation, its endless changes of policy, had produced the same effects as gross brutality. Federal authorities were forever uprooting the Indian; one sardonic chief whose people had been removed six times within one generation remarked that he thought it time the government put them upon wheels."[9]

Jackson sent a copy of *A Century of Dishonor* at her own expense to members of Congress and to leading clergy. She unapologetically tried to shame political leaders and fellow countrymen into recognizing they had blood on their hands. But her investigative analysis won scant attention and meager readership. It was the work of an amateur historian, and it deliberately accentuated the negative; yet it received positive reviews in leading newspapers. Jackson, however, was disappointed in the sales. She had underestimated the prejudice most of her fellow citizens held toward Native Americans.

Jackson, now in her early fifties, was a widely published and respected poet, as well as a short story and travel writer. Ralph Waldo Emerson had hailed her as one of America's leading poets. She also wrote books and essays for children. She decided now that she must turn to fiction writing to attract a larger audience. People might read a novel, especially one that contained a suspenseful melodramatic romance, when they would not read a serious book—especially about the Indian question. She had tried to influence and educate people's consciences directly but concluded, rightly, that people would ignore an inconvenient report such as hers.

She was motivated in turning to fiction in part because Harriet Beecher Stowe had done it so successfully a generation earlier. In fact, she told friends that if she could do for the Indians even one-hundredth of what Stowe had done for black Americans, she would consider it a serious contribution. So she conceived and wrote *Ramona*. She said, "I didn't write *Ramona*, it was written through me." She poured all her energy and "lifeblood" into the novel. She died a year later.

Her heroine, Ramona, is a beautiful mixed-race person; her father was a dissolute Scottish sea captain and her mother an Indian squaw. She was abandoned and left in the caring hands of a Spanish family in Southern California sometime in the 1840s. But because of deaths, she was bequeathed to the wealthy Spanish Moreno clan somewhere in what we now know as Ventura County.

Ramona was raised Catholic in an expansive and orthodox Spanish hacienda setting. She was cheerful, loyal, caring, and well liked by everyone, save the matron of the clan, Señora Moreno, who looked down upon Ramona because of her impure mixed heritage: "I like not these crosses. It is the worst, and not the best, that remains."

Jackson's novel centers on Ramona falling in love with her Romeo—who is, alas, a pure-blooded Indian by the name of Alessandro Assis. Alessandro is, of course, uncommonly handsome and a talented sheep-shearer and horse trainer, a talented singer and violin player, and an emerging leader of his Luiseño tribe in Temecula, a few days ride to the southeast. Jackson's fictionalized Alessandro is a manly and handsome fantasy male conveniently crafted, no doubt, for her Victorian women readership.

Señora Moreno objects to their relationship and threatens to banish Ramona if she marries this, in her eyes, unworthy Indian. She also says she will give greatly valued jewels that Ramona's biological father had left for her to the church if Ramona were to marry Alessandro.

Even Alessandro, despite being profoundly in love with her, tells Ramona that any prospective life with him and his fellow Indians would likely be one of frustration, poverty, and dire challenge. He warns they could be hunted as if wild beasts. "But," she protests, "I too am an Indian, Alessandro!" She adds that she would rather die than be left behind by her lover. "Oh, Alessandro, take me with you!"

Jackson beguiles her readers to fall in love with both the sweet and very Christian Ramona and the hardworking and compelling mission-inspired Catholic Alessandro. Their love is wondrously rich, but, alas, they are forced to elope and forsake the luxury of hacienda life to forge their own path as Indians.

They set out for Alessandro's tribal community, only to learn that it has been destroyed and taken over by the plundering and greedy new white settlers who claim the state and federal courts have ruled the land is theirs. Alessandro's father, Pablo, dies in heartbroken shock, and the surviving fellow tribesmen become fugitives in inhospitable canyons.

Alessandro concludes that when Americans buy or confiscate Mexican lands, they proceed to remove the Indians as if they were dogs. They say, he adds, "we have no right to our lands," even though their Mexican owners "promised them to us forever."

His favorite Franciscan priest, Father Salvierderra, tries to console Alessandro by saying we—the Indians and the Mexicans—are all alike helpless in their hands: "They possess the country, and can make what laws they please. We can only say, 'God's will be done,' and he crossed himself devoutly, repeating the words twice."

Alessandro also crosses himself and repeats the padre's words. Yet he wonders aloud, "Then, again, how come it be God's will that wrong be done? It cannot be God's will that one man should steal from another all he has. That would make God no better than a thief, it looks to me. But how can it happen, if it is not God's will?"

Alessandro and Ramona are fated to wander in an odyssey of despair and impoverishment. The whites keep invading, and their judiciary keeps handing down edicts decreeing formerly Indian territory to belong to the newly arrived settlers. "They are a pack of thieves and liars, every one of them!" cries an anguished Alessandro. "They are going to steal all the land in this country; we must all just as well throw ourselves into the sea, and let them have it."

Jackson's heroic Alessandro is her stand-in for hundreds of thousands of indigenous people who had been long oppressed and removed by Manifest Destiny, which inspired the conquerors of the American West.

Jackson's love story between Ramona and Alessandro is her seductive medium for her renewed efforts to educate Americans about a long list of shameful abuses of Indian rights.

Jackson had never been an activist for abolition or women's suffrage. She was a well-bred, well-educated Victorian Calvinist, and generally able to live the life of a creative literary professional. Her father had been a professor of religion and classics at Amherst College. Her childhood and lifelong friend was poet Emily Dickinson. She went to boarding schools for privileged young women and later became friends with literary giants such as Emerson, Henry Longfellow, and Thomas Wentworth Higginson.

Her first husband, Edward Hunt, was a top-ranked West Point graduate and later worked for the Army Corps of Engineers and the Union Army. He was also decidedly conservative and believed blacks were inferior and should be deported to Africa. He even wrote a white supremacist monograph. He died in a Civil War–related accident in 1863.

Jackson probably didn't share her husband's views, and she told friends she admired Stowe's *Uncle Tom's Cabin*. But she had expressed disdain for activist women—women who went about lecturing and were dedicated to political causes. She also expressed contempt for politicians. Her second, and affluent Gilded Age Republican (a banker and railroad promoter) husband, William S. Jackson, unsuccessfully sought election by the Colorado state legislature to the U.S. Senate. Helen was opposed and relieved when he lost. She made her distaste for politics clear:

> Human nature being what it is, I believe that our "institutions" will always bring to the surface of political power the scum of the land: now I know these are unpopular beliefs—and I rarely air them: but you have forced me to declare myself. To see my husband in that crew of liars and pickpockets will almost kill me: and to breathe the air myself will be a perpetual moral typhoid fever.[10]

However, several factors transformed Helen Hunt Jackson from being an anticause and antipolitics literary celebrity into a political crusader and muckraking activist.

Her friends and biographers point to a lecture she attended in Boston in late October 1879. Ponca tribal chief Standing Bear, along with two Omaha Indians and Thomas H. Tibbles, a reporter for the *Omaha Daily Herald*, was on tour to educate Americans about injustices to Native Americans and to raise funds to assist the displaced Ponca tribe.

U.S. policies had moved the Ponca westward from the ancient lands. Then when gold was discovered in the Black Hills the Ponca were unceremoniously ordered to leave these new lands and resettle to Indian Territory some thousand miles south.

Standing Bear refused to leave and was jailed. He fled and was arrested again. Standing Bear's people suffered tremendous losses as they journeyed southward. In the fall of 1877, however, he and other tribal leaders petitioned the U.S. government and met with President Rutherford B. Hayes and Interior Secretary Carl Schurz to plead for a return to their old reservation. Their requests were rejected. They then tried to find a redress to their grievances in Nebraska and federal courts.

Jackson's encounter with Standing Bear was a political awakening that led to her writing magazine and newspaper articles advocating on behalf of the Ponca. She raised money for them and badgered friends and the Secretary of the Interior to help reverse the brutal policies of Indian removal. Her efforts led to a U.S. Senate investigation and some favorable editorials—and later some fiscal compensation to the Ponca.

A second influence on Jackson is that she had moved to Colorado in the mid-1870s and married William S. Jackson.

White settlers had come to Colorado as part of the "winning of the West" and were in search of farmland, silver, and gold. Indians, Jackson learned, were viewed as "in the way." Jackson studied the Sand Creek Massacre of 1864 in which hundreds of peaceful Cheyenne and Arapaho had been murdered.

Most Coloradans had celebrated this and similar "revenge" killings of Indians because they contemptuously viewed Indians as harassing white expansion and trade. Helen Hunt Jackson took exception to what she believed was unjust, un-Christian, and, though she didn't use the word, genocidal policies.

Jackson traveled around Colorado and tried to understand the plight of the miners and the Indians, and she developed the view that the Indians lived an existence that was often worse than the American slaves had experienced.

She became a contrarian and a literary and political maverick. She had always been known by her friends as moody, impulsive, and inconsistent. She also suffered from depression and a variety of health ailments. But now a liberated H. H. Jackson became a fiery policy advocate. She became obsessed and perhaps possessed. She explained to a friend:

> I have done now, I believe, the last of the things I have said I would never do. I have become what I said a thousand times was the most odious thing in the world, "a woman with a hobby." I cannot help it. I think I feel as you must have felt in the old abolition days . . . I believe the time is drawing near for a great change in our policy toward the Indians.[11]

Jackson was bravely taking on conventional American political thinking. George Washington and Thomas Jefferson had condoned Indian removal. Chief Justice John Marshall had ruled (in *Johnson and Graham's Lessee v. William M'Intosh*, 1823) that "the tribes of Indians inhabiting the country were fierce savages, whose occupation was war. . . . That laws which regulate and ought to regulate in general, the relations between the conqueror and conquered was incapable of application to a people under such circumstances. . . . Discovery gave an exclusive right to extinguish the Indian title of occupancy either by purchase or by conquest." Marshall in 1831 said Indians are in a state of pupilage. Their relation to the United States resembles "that of a ward to his guardian."

Andrew Jackson, well before becoming president, was a noted land speculator and Indian remover in western Tennessee. He famously fought the Chickasaws, the Muskogees, and the Seminoles. Jackson in 1824 said the United States was a country "Manifestly called by the Almighty to a destiny which Greece and Rome, in the days of their pride, might have envied."[12] "[Native Americans] have neither the intelligence, the industry, the moral habits, nor the desire of improvement which are essential to any favorable changes in their condition," Jackson declared in his fifth annual message to Congress on December 3, 1833. "Established in the midst of another and a superior race, and without appreciating the causes of their inferiority or seeking to control them, they must necessarily yield to the force of circumstances and ere long disappear." In 1862, President Abraham Lincoln ordered the hanging of thirty-eight Dakota Sioux in Mankato, Minnesota. Most were holy men and political leaders falsely accused of crime.

Not long after Helen Hunt Jackson's death, a young Teddy Roosevelt, later to be hailed as a legendary progressive Nobel Peace Prize recipient and Mount Rushmore "hero," reiterated that Manifest Destiny policies of Indian removal were as beneficial as they were inevitable. Roosevelt was explicitly racist in many of his views about Indians, though he merely echoed conventional American thinking when he declared that Indians never had any real title of sovereignty over the land they roamed. Their rights to the land, in his view, were illegitimate because they were mainly nomadic.

Most non-native Americans in Helen Hunt Jackson's day assumed the superiority of the "civilized" Caucasian race. They worshipped a white, primarily Anglo-Saxon, Protestant God. Indians, most of Jackson's fellow citizens believed, were treacherous, lazy, inferior, and "not like us."

She rejected these assumptions and stereotypes. She celebrated the hardworking, peaceful, and spiritual attractiveness of her Indians. She of course understood that there had been Indian raids and even several Indian massacres of whites, like at Custer's Last Stand in 1876 or the Meeker massacre in Colorado, but she wanted to believe most of these regrettable incidents were provoked by the whites, and many were. She likewise understood that there were Indians who had alcohol problems and were unreliable. But her travels in Colorado and in Southern California had convinced her that most Indians were peaceful, willing to work hard, and would be fine, law-abiding citizens, and probably even good Christians, if only their land rights and their dignity were respected. Her *Ramona* described and idealized this view.

Helen Hunt Jackson was an undaunted contrarian. She knew she was taking on conventional political beliefs. She knew that most of her neighbors believed "the only good Indian was a dead Indian." Even her second husband tried to get her to back off and, though supportive, considered himself only "half-converted."

But Jackson, in *A Century of Dishonor* and (more famously) in *Ramona*, tellingly took on her fellow Americans. She relished being a nonconformist. She accepted that most people now considered her a meddlesome busybody and crusader. This energized her. She was inspired by one of her literary mentors, and probable love interest, Thomas Wentworth Higginson, a noted Bostonian who in his earlier years had been a stalwart abolitionist, a supporter of John Brown and fugitive slaves. He also had famously commanded the first all African American regiment of freed slaves to fight in the Civil War. He may have been a proper Bostonian, but he was also a fervent progressive spirit, and he regularly offered Jackson encouragement for her writing and for her late-in-life political activism.

She may have been raised in an orthodox Calvinist family, but she became a feisty, independent literary professional, and her spiritual views had shifted to Unitarianism and Transcendentalism. "In my *Century of Dishonor* I tried to attack people's conscience directly, and they would not listen," she explained to a friend. "Now I have sugared my pill [in *Ramona*], and it remains to be seen if it will go down."

She wanted to raise public awareness so the people would lobby their members of Congress. She may have disdained politics, but she now understood the need to be political—to change public opinion in hopes that political officials would respond to new, more tolerant, and pro-Indian attitudes.

Jackson traveled extensively in Southern California. She visited Indian villages and interviewed the Franciscans who ran missionary schools. She even got herself appointed by U.S. Interior Secretary Henry Teller, a friend of her husband, as a special agent to investigate the living conditions of mission Indians.

She and a colleague, Abbot Kinney, completed their Report to the Commissioner of Indian Affairs in July of 1883.[13] They described general conditions of the mission Indians and urged in their recommendations for better and more honest surveys, allocating certain lands to the Indians, providing more and better schools, and providing independent legal advice and useful agricultural equipment. But most important, they called for recognizing the land rights of those who had long lived there—despite the changing political regimes of the Spanish, Mexican, and American empires.

Jackson's novel is often considered primarily a local color piece and a melodramatic, if melancholy, historical romance. It is a charming and page-turning romantic story. Literary critics, however, rated it a second-rate piece of literature. Some said its seductive "chick-lit" romance swallows her public policy message—and there is some truth to this view.

Along with the romance, however, it is an artfully woven political consciousness-raising narrative. *Ramona*, the "American novel in print for the longest uninterrupted time, is scathingly critical of the American mission in the Southwest," writes historian Douglas Monroy. Jackson's readers may fall in love with Ramona and Alessandro, but her consciousness-raising intent was to expose American hypocrisy and meanness and affirm the higher American creed of equality of opportunity, compassion for the less fortunate, and equal justice under the law.[14]

Life as Indians in a Manifest Destiny world would again and again test Ramona and Alessandro's marriage. They regularly had to relocate and constantly struggled. Alessandro grew depressed as he came to believe their saints had deserted them: "They do not pray for us anymore." He warned his wife, "The Americans will destroy us all. I do not know but they will persistently begin to shoot us and poison us, to get us all out of the country, as they do the rabbits and the gophers."

Alessandro grows despondent that the white settlers, with the help of their courts, armies, and Indian agents, are inevitably taking control over the "land that our ancestors are buried in." His father's advice that Indians needed to band together and keep the peace with the whites was no longer even remotely possible.

Ramona urges him to move to Los Angeles or other cities where he can find work, working for white men. He rejects this idea. He yearns, as Jackson implies all Indians yearn, to be free, and to work his own land. They live the life of fugitives. They have a child who heartbreakingly dies, perhaps in part because an Indian agency doctor refuses to make the short journey necessary to reach and assist them. Alessandro and Ramona eventually seek refuge in the ragged San Jacinto Mountains. The novel's narrator notes:

> There was no healing for Alessandro. His hurts had gone too deep. His passionate heart, ever secretly brooding on the wrongs he had borne,

the hopeless outlook for his people in the future, and most of all on the probable destitution and suffering in store for Ramona, consumed itself as by hidden fires.

Alessandro and Ramona became increasingly lonely, scarred, and scared by their betrayal. They succeed in having a second child; yet Alessandro's mind deteriorates. He inadvertently steals a horse in a nearby village, and the owner of that horse, a well-known white ruffian, hunts him down and murders him. "That'll teach you damned Indians to leave off stealing our horses!"

There is some attempt to investigate and possibly punish his murderer. But, as Jackson suggests, the word *justice* has lost its meaning in those parts. Ramona holds his dead body and mourns, with the Christian submission that both she and Helen Hunt Jackson had been imbued with, "My Alessandro is gone to be with the saints; they will listen to what the martyr says."

The end of the novel is anticlimactic and controversial. Felipe Moreno, her foster family's son, with whom she had been raised as a virtual stepsister or step-cousin, discovers Ramona in this moment of dire distress and brings her and her young daughter back to the luxury of the Moreno hacienda. The harsh Señora Moreno has passed on. Ramona is enthusiastically welcomed back to the comforts and elegance of the Moreno estate.

Ramona and Felipe eventually marry and move to Mexico City. He also realized the white settlers were overwhelming the Spanish as well as the Indian cultures they had known and loved. Their moving to Mexico and enjoying the good life there irritated many readers. Some thought that the novel should conclude on a less happy note, with Ramona's life ending in some cruel and bitter fashion. Others point out that Mexico, unlike the new California, was a place that respected diversity and was a country and a culture dedicated to integrating and realizing "e pluribus unum."

Jackson doesn't explain her ending. Maybe Jackson merely yielded to the contemporary demand for at least a relatively happy ending.

She was a storyteller with a message, a novelist with a purpose, a preacher's daughter who in her last five years of life preached the gospel of inclusiveness, fairness, humanity, and equal justice under the law.

Critics call it sentimental and fault it for its one-sided idealizations. Her romantic duo is indeed so admirable, so spiritual, and so physically attractive that they might make even a Hollywood scriptwriter blush. Jackson toys with the reader's emotions—yet she does this intentionally and often in a poetic and lyrical way.

One later critic, poet Denise Chávez, in the introduction to the Modern Library edition of *Ramona* (2005), said she was initially put off by what she perceived "as a clumsy outsider telling the story of a culture not her own," with too many "hyperboles, simplistic and stereotypical extractions, reductions and incomplete histories." However, she reminds us that most of the problems Jackson wrote of are still with us. But Chávez adds tellingly that to speak truth, one must write fiction, just as Jackson poignantly did in her day.[15]

It is also true that Jackson's "research" in Southern California was mainly hearing a mix of folk tales, secondhand stories, and mission-inspired fantasies that the Franciscans might have been able to create a paradisic community of joyous believers (Spanish, Mexican, and Indian) who could prosper and integrate with one another in the region. But, in her defense, *Ramona* was fiction. She knew enough of what had gone wrong. She knew enough about which American ideals were being compromised. Her job, she doubtless believed, was to write a vivid, compelling novel that would change public attitudes. Her novel doesn't provide policy ideas and solutions. Her simple message is that Indians should be treated as humans.

Ramona does raise questions about assimilation programs and the Christianizing Franciscan mission schools. Many Catholics praise Friar Junipero Serra, the now canonized founder of the California Spanish missions, for his dedication to making a place for native people in the region. Yet others contend that he forced Christian beliefs on indigenous people, often brutally, at the cost of their culture. Helen Hunt Jackson did not pick up on this controversy and, if anything, seems to share an overly benign appraisal of the Serra and Franciscan traditions.

The church, however, was of little or no help to our fictional Alessandro. And heroine Ramona sets out, in the end, like her Midwestern contemporary Huck Finn, for a friendlier, less oppressive territory. So much for the Southern Californian Christianization plan.

Ramona never became a huge best seller like *Uncle Tom's Cabin*. But it did become a cult classic. It has gone through hundreds of reprintings. It has been the basis for several films, plays, and a long-acclaimed Ramona Pageant still put on every year in Hemet, California. It is still read, still in print, and still worth reading. It inspired a number of Indian Rights Associations and may have helped with soon-to-pass federal legislation like the Dawes Act, which provided for the modest allotment of reservation land to Indians. Her writings probably also helped encourage an 1891 Act for Relief of the Mission Indians in California.

Ramona "has the indispensable virtue of vitality," wrote historian Allan Nevins. "No one had dealt with that period and theme before; no one indeed has dealt with them since. . . . But the principle factor in the book's vitality is a poignancy of many of its pages. They were written from an overflowing heart, she was aflame with eagerness to expose wrongs, and despite passages of confusion and unreality the book leaves an impression of fiery truth."[16]

But Helen Hunt Jackson's fiery and passionate consciousness raising mostly failed to change the way her fellow countrymen treated Native Americans. Americans continue to "otherize" the surviving first Americans just as they had long enslaved and then mistreated most of the four million black Americans before, during, and after the Civil War. And American motives of Manifest Destiny hardly stopped at our continent's shores. See, for example, Stephen Kinzer's compelling nonfiction account of American foreign policy in the immediate century that followed Jackson's time: *Overthrow: America's Century of Regime Change From Hawaii to Iraq* (New York: Times Books, 2006). Jackson would have liked this work.

Jackson and her *Ramona* were calling on Americans to change. But Americans were reluctant, if not indifferent, to heed her call. Eight hundred treaties with the Indians were only honored unilaterally. The U.S. Senate never ratified half of them, and most of the rest were violated.

"To justify betrayal, usurpation, and rapine—not to speak of atrocious cruelty and murder," writes Peter Matthiessen, "it became desirable to denigrate the native peoples, even the hospitable and faithful allies, as subhuman beings, nomadic savages, with no geographic, political, or moral claim upon their territories."[17]

The American political experiment and constitutional democracy, inspired by the Declaration of Independence and the Bill of Rights, was supposed to be different. Americans want to view our nation as an exceptionally blessed and exceptionally noble political experiment. We understandably criticize German genocide of Jews, Turkish treatment of Armenians, British colonialization of Ireland and India, Japanese abuses in Korea, Vietnam, and China, but we are reluctant or even amnesic in our acknowledging racial and ethnic injustices that were part of the evolving fabric of our own nation.

It was Jackson's dream that Americans would not forget the Indians—would not, in today's colloquialism, "throw them under the bus." Even the week she lay dying she wrote a petitioning letter to President Grover Cleveland:

From my death bed I send you a message of heart-felt thanks for what you have already done for the Indians. I ask you to read my *Century of Dishonor*. I am dying happier for the belief I have that it is your hand that is destined to strike the first steady blow towards lifting this burden of infamy from our country, and righting the wrongs of the Indian race.[18]

Ramona stands with *Uncle Tom's Cabin*, *The Jungle*, *The Grapes of Wrath*, and especially *Beloved* as a reminder that we can and must be more inclusive; a nation that honors life, liberty, the pursuit of happiness, and justice for everyone.

Ironically, it was around this same time that the French people donated the Statue of Liberty that was placed—facing Europe—to symbolize America's presumptive love of liberty, and as the narrative of the time developed, its welcoming of those immigrants yearning for freedom. Helen Hunt Jackson's novel was a call for a "statue of inclusiveness" for those first Americans or indigenous people who had already been here long before the Vikings, Italians, Spaniards, and Pilgrims came.

Cleveland and others did succeed in making some progress. Indian schools and tribal colleges helped. But federal policies kept changing, and marginalization and neglect were too often the pattern. Native Americans have disproportionately suffered from diabetes, alcoholism, tuberculosis, and hate crimes. Suicide rates are shockingly high. Their jail and prison incarceration rate is at least a third higher than the national average.

Mineral rights and casino revenue have brought selective prosperity to some Indians and tribes, but Jackson would doubtless be disheartened by the continual exploitation of Indians in later years.[19]

Jackson's plea for justice for all was an effort to disturb the peace in her day and help explain part of our past to all of us despite our reluctance to want to understand some of this embarrassing past. Readers of *Ramona* should also read novelist Frank Waters's (1902–1995) lyrical novel of the mixed-bred *People of the Valley*, which beautifully describes the joys and sorrows of dispossessed people in Northern New Mexico. His protagonist is Maria del Valle (or Maria of the Valley). She is of the earth, has unexplained (mystical) wisdom, lives wild among goat herds, has sex and children naturally, tends to herbs and folkloric remedies, and gradually becomes the soul of her valley.

The Waters fable can be condensed as follows: Gringos from the East, with their politicians, laws, and engineers, are the evil bringers of progress and woe to the valley in the form of a dam that will eat up much of the land. Maria understands but tries to resist. She shows her people that, in addition to keeping faith in their land, they are only of their own time and must yield to "progress" while still somehow keeping their faith. This is a parable of resistance and survival.

Maria tries to explain to her valley people:

> Faith is not to be dammed. It is not to be measured and meted out when timely. It must be free to penetrate every cell and germ of the whole. For it is the obstructed whole that finally bursts the dam, brings destruction and misery, swamps the temporal benefits of the past.
>
> There are dams. There will be more. But all are temporal and unwhole. For they, like us, are spattered, swept and undercut by our unseen flow—a flow that is stronger than casual benefits, that never ceases to permeate and undermine our lesser father, and which can never be truly dammed.[20]

Waters was part Indian himself, and, in this and several other prize-winning novels, he carries on the spirit of Helen Hunt Jackson and may well have inspired some of the later excellent storytelling by New Mexico–based Edward Abbey and John Nichols.

A more recent novel, more complicated than *People of the Valley* or *Ramona*, but equally scathing, is William T. Vollmann's important *The Dying Grass: A Novel of the Nez Perce War* (New York: Viking, 2015).

STANDING UP TO A NEW HAMPSHIRE MACHINE[21]

"It seems," says railroad tycoon Augustus Flint to the young attorney Austen Vane, "that you have grown more radical since your first visit."

"If it be radical to refuse to accept a pass from a railroad to bind my liberty of action as an attorney and a citizen, then I am radical," replies Vane. "If it be radical to maintain that the elected representatives of the people should not receive passes, or be beholden to any man or corporation, I acknowledge the term. If it be radical to declare that these representatives should be elected without interference, and while in office should do exact justice to the body of citizens on the one hand and the corporations on the other, I declare myself a radical. But my radicalism goes back beyond the establishment of railroads . . . back to the foundations of this government and to the idea from which it sprang."

Mr. Crewe's Career is a consciousness-raising novel by a progressive patrician Republican reformer. Literary critics doubtless read much of it as a sappy, preachy civics lecture. Socialist or even moderately leftish progressives likely dismissed it as too bullish on capitalism and too satisfied with the mere need for modest good government and civic improvement such as the direct primary and lobbying regulations.

The American Winston Churchill's novel may be an overly simplistic fictional account of good versus evil; yet it is a compelling account of a political oligarchy and its perceived invidious consequences. It documents in fictionalized form why the Progressive movement flourished not just in urban centers but also in places such as rural New Hampshire. This is also a close-up analysis of politics by a writer-politician. He understood that every novel is necessarily a compound of fact and fiction. Churchill (not to be confused with the younger Winston S. Churchill in England) is one of a small number of politicians who could write well and who understood politics from personal experience—he spent several years in the New Hampshire state legislature and ran for his party's nomination for governor.

Churchill wrote several romance novels before writing *Coniston* (1906) and *Mr. Crewe's Career* (1908), but these later political novels, as was the case in Benjamin Disraeli's novels, were autobiographical. Churchill's fiction, like Disraeli's, is strikingly convergent with his political initiatives and hopes.[22]

Unlike Jack London or Upton Sinclair, Churchill eschews socialism and rejects the notion that capitalism needs to be replaced by some form of communal ownership. Rather he argues for transparency, more and better forms of political participation, and an end to bribery and favoritism in politics. Churchill is solidly in the tradition of Mark Twain and Henry Adams—disappointed in the politics of his day but even more optimistic than they were that the American ship of state could be righted. And unlike Twain and Adams, Churchill offers us a hero and an implicit advertisement for Teddy Roosevelt–style Progressivism.

Both of Churchill's political novels are noteworthy on another score. Unlike so many other works of American political fiction, they depict Republican political machines.

Winston Churchill (1871–1947) was a U.S. Naval Academy grad, and editor, poet, essayist, and best-selling novelist. Some of his novels sold over a million copies, and this novel about New Hampshire politics was the nation's best-selling novel of 1908.

Mr. Crewe's Career combines three interrelated, yet separate, narratives—two of them capturing contemporary politics, the third a Victorian romance between an earnest and dashing young attorney and the beautiful daughter of a railroad president.

The eponymous Mr. Crewe is a patrician New Yorker who has a summer place in New Hampshire and runs successfully for the state legislature and unsuccessfully for the Republican gubernatorial nomination. He is a principled Teddy Roosevelt Republican who advocates good government and economic reform measures. He is wealthy, uncommonly self-confident, impatient, and vulnerable to the complaint that he is an outsider by virtue of his part-time residency. Churchill, satirizing his semi-autobiographical Crewe as "the People's Champion," has a somewhat sympathetic observer note that "the career of a gentleman in politics is a thankless one in this country," and "if he [Crewe] didn't have such an impenetrable conceit, he might go far, because he learns quickly, and has an industry that is simply appalling. But he hasn't quite the manner for politics, has he?"

Churchill's *Mr. Crewe's Career* describes and parodies his own failed effort to win the Republican nomination in 1906. Like his fictionalized Crewe, Churchill was thwarted by the state political bosses who were under the thumb of the "railroad interests." "Railroad interests" doubtless referred explicitly to the railroad monopoly in New Hampshire, but it is also used here as a metaphorical reference to the corporate monopolies that Teddy Roosevelt was also campaigning against in this era. Insurance companies and big banking interests, among others, were helping to fuel the conservative Republican political engine in New York state and elsewhere. But the Boston-Maine Railroad was Churchill's primary villain in fiction and reality.

Churchill's second, more central story is about a father and son and their complicated political dueling over the way the railroad interest dominated New Hampshire state government. The father is the courtly, well-bred, well-fed, and well-read Hilary Vane, affectionately referred to as "Judge" and "Honorable" (despite holding no judicial or elected political office). Hilary Vane is chief counsel for the "Northeastern Railroad" and oversees the railroad's political machine. He is essentially a fixer and enforcer, helping to lubricate the railroad's domination of the state legislature by means of hefty campaign contributions and free railway passes to supportive legislators. His son, Austen Vane, a preppy and independent-minded graduate of Harvard Law School, reveres his father and joins him in the practice of law. But he soon accepts clients who have been maimed or economically hurt by the railroad that his father serves. Young Vane discovers that the railroad not only "owns the Republican party machine" but also controls the legislature and the State Railroad Commission. He sees how the "Northeastern Railroad" gets away with minimal safety regulations and throttles competition, thus increasing profits and enriching their stockholders. Meanwhile, the consumer, the employees, and the public get short shrift.

Austen Vane confronts his father about these monopolistic practices. The elder Vane dismisses his son's complaints as nonsense. "The railroad employs the best lawyers it can find to look after its interests. I'm one of 'em, and I'm proud of it. If I hadn't been one of 'em, the chances are you'd never be where you are, that you'd never have gone to college and the law school." The Republican Party, he says, realizes the railroad's vital role in the state, and "the prosperity of the road means the prosperity of the state." The leaders of the party, himself included, vigilantly protect both the railroad and the state from "scatterbrains and agitators," like some of Austen's friends.

Austen ultimately concludes that his father is merely a political tool of greedy, self-serving interests. "It's no use, Judge," he says. "If material prosperity alone were to be considered, your contention might have some weight." But, he adds, "the perpetuation of the principle of American government has to be thought of. Government by a railroad will lead in the end to anarchy." His father and his father's client, Austen is now convinced, are inviting the destruction of the American political experiment.

Churchill's novel is dedicated to people in every state who are engaged in the struggle for "purer politics." His is another example of art in the service of a political agenda. Teddy Roosevelt, Elihu Root, and their Progressive allies in New York and elsewhere had already, in the 1890s, been crusading for legal and even constitutional bans on excessive corporate funding of state legislators. Progressive Republican William E. Chandler had been championing similar causes in New Hampshire. Churchill's political novels reflected these political reformers and helped expand their ranks. Young Austen Vane, with Teddy Roosevelt–like vigor, takes on not only his father but also the railroad president, saying the railroad's political practices violate every principle of free government.

Meanwhile, in story number three, young Vane is falling in love with the beguiling daughter of railroad tycoon Augustus Flint. Influenced by both Humphrey Crewe and Austen Vane, young Victoria Flint begins to question her father's political practices. In a blunt rant against politicians, her father responds to her concerns:

> But I do expect you [Victoria] to understand this: that politicians are politicians; they have always been corrupt as long as I have known them, and in my opinion they always will be. The Northeastern is the largest property holder in the state, pays the biggest tax, and has the

most at stake. The politicians could ruin us in a single session of the Legislature—and what's more they *would* do it. We'd have to be paying blackmail all the time to prevent measures that would compel us to go out of business.

The people are "dupes," Flint explains to his inquiring daughter. They're at the mercy of political schemers:

> What little influence I exert politically I have to maintain in order to protect the property of my stockholders from annihilation. It isn't to be supposed . . . that I'm going to see the state turned over to a man like Humphrey Crewe. I wish to heaven that his and every other state had a George Washington for governor and a majority of Robert Morrisses [a distinguished founding father] in the Legislature. If they exist, in these days, the people won't elect 'em—that's all.

In the end, Augustus Flint and his machine easily defeat Humphrey Crewe (Churchill's fictional Progressive candidate for the Republican nomination of governor). But Flint loses his daughter to young Austen Vane, and the couple happily marry at the novel's sentimentally sappy conclusion.

Churchill wonderfully describes a Republican political machine challenged by Teddy Roosevelt–style "good government" reformers. He condemns bad guys as villainous and honors those yearning for political integrity.

Churchill's description of the 1906 New Hampshire Republican Party convention is hilarious and provides one of the best analyses of state politics in American literature. He is a gifted storyteller, and even though he himself was a central figure in the election that year, he had an uncanny and sophisticated eye for the political transactions, tactics, and strategies that regularly took place in political nominating battles. His caricatures of corporate and lobby bosses capture the realities of the era.

Churchill's political ideology is that of a progressive, yet centrist, Republican. He believes in capitalism and concludes that good government reforms of the Progressive movement could make capitalism and constitutionalism flourish. Writing at the same time as Upton Sinclair's *Jungle*, Churchill's novel does not even hint at a need for major economic redistribution, much less socialism. Unlike railroad mogul Flint's lack of faith in politicians and voters, Churchill displays a Jeffersonian faith in democracy and constitutionalism. Churchill's young hero, Austen Vane, suggests that an enlightened public will recognize and reconcile a place for capitalism, alongside their sense of fairness, public safety, and social justice.

Churchill's faith in the Progressive movement and his idealization of Austen Vane may strike contemporary readers as rather quaint. In the end, the novel leaves the reader with an optimism that "the old method of politics which was wrong, although it had some justification in conditions, had gone out" and a "new and more desirable state of affairs has come." Our young hero, Austen Vane (who obviously exemplifies Churchill's ideals), proclaims that "the era of political domination by a corporation and mainly for the benefit of a corporation is over." Hilary Vane, the father, resigns from his position at the railroad. Young Austen, out of respect for his father's last official duties on behalf of Flint, humbly declines an almost assured nomination for governor—presumably postponing this for another day.

Churchill's political novels—*Mr. Crewe's Career* (1908) and *Coniston* (1906)—are period pieces that have been shelved and forgotten. But *Mr. Crewe's Career* gracefully and invaluably captures the politics of an era and still offers useful insights about the challenges of making democratic institutions work in a predominantly market-oriented system. This is a "golden oldie" that entertains, educates, and in many ways, inspires us about the promise and possibilities for the American Republic.[23]

Churchill's novel was a readable crowd-pleaser with a happy—perhaps overly happy—ending. Our hero, Austen, gets the femme fatale. He successfully exposes and shames the monopolistic railroad. He becomes the unofficial new leader of the rising Progressive Republicans. Our faith in democracy is restored and the public interest is poised to triumph. This was the stuff of a best seller in 1908; yet it is also the stuff of consciousness-raising American reformers across time and across the country.

A PROPHET'S RISE AND DEMISE[24]

"Sure, sure, there's some graft, but there's just enough to make the wheels turn without squeaking," says fictional governor Willie Stark from an unnamed state that looks like Louisiana. "Sure, I got a bunch of crooks around here, but they're too lily-livered to get very crooked. I got my eye on them. And do I deliver the state something? I damned well do."

All the King's Men is doubtless the best American political novel, even if Warren urged that it should be read as more than a book about politics. It is a novel as much about human nature, populism, and a journey of self-discovery as it is a work about the harsh realities and paradoxes of political power. Yet *King's Men* is a work very much about politicians and the political culture of a particular time and place. It is also a novel about political irony, how good can sometimes come from bad, and bad can sometimes come from good. "*King's Men* asks," writes David Brooks, "if in politics you have to sell your soul in order to have the power to serve the poor."[25]

The book is, in part, an exercise in Machiavellian philosophizing as the novel's narrator, Jack Burden, an erstwhile political reporter, puzzles over the age-old notion that

> All change costs something. You have to write off the costs against the gain. Maybe in one state change could only come in the terms in which it was taking place, and it was sure due for some change. . . . Process as process is neither morally good nor morally bad. We may judge results but not process. The morally bad agent may perform the deed which is good. The morally good agent may perform the deed which is bad. Maybe the man has to sell his soul to get the power to do good.

Warren's novel is as much about this starkly conflicted "right-hand man" as it is about the once well-intentioned but now increasingly autocratic, self-proclaimed political messiah, Governor Willie Stark.

The governor starts his political career as a self-described country redneck. He had gone to a local Baptist college for a year and served a brief stint in the army. He then studied law (homeschool law) and made a name for himself defending the downtrodden and going after corporate interests and political bosses. When Stark tries to win reelection as his county's treasurer, machine pols get him defeated. Later the machine sets him up in a governor's race as a tool to divide the rural vote.

He is kicked around and turned into a sap by the political machine. Willie seeks revenge. He wants to "be somebody," and he defines this as winning political office, acquiring and exercising power. He is also motivated, or so he claims, by the chance to help the have-nots. They need him, and he tells them it will take one of their own—a "hick" like them in high public office—to bring about justice.

Stark rallies crowds of poor white farmers by playing upon their powerlessness and resentments:

> Friends, red-necks, suckers, and fellow hicks. . . . That's what you are. And me—I'm one, too. Oh, I'm a red-neck, for the sun has beat down on me. I'm a sucker, for I fell for that sweet-talking fellow in the fine automobile . . . nobody ever helped a hick but the hick himself. Up there in town [referring to the State Capital] they won't help you. It is up to you and God and God helps those who help themselves!

Why does Stark go into politics? There is rarely just one reason why people go into politics. Some go into politics merely for the sake of power. Many go into politics because they were "losers" in their earlier social or athletic lives and are trying to redeem themselves—to prove something, to earn respect. Yet others go into politics to make a difference, to do good deeds, or even to change the course of history. Warren's fictional Willie Stark, as with most real-life politicians, went into Louisiana politics because of a blend of these motivations. And power and public office, Willy reasoned, or perhaps rationalized, were prerequisites for making good things happen.

Stark moves to the populist left as he builds his campaign around raising taxes on the oligarchical rich and oil companies. Indeed, a major narrative in *King's Men* is the rise of Willie Stark as the challenger to oligarchs, like Jack Burden's friends and family, that had ignored the wants and needs of the common people. He'll use the revenues from such taxes to upgrade schools, highways, and public health services. He becomes an aggressive New Dealer even before there is a New Deal.

He appeals to mass prejudices, promises a better, more egalitarian future, and offers beleaguered followers convenient scapegoats for their problems. Where he had earlier been a lackluster country bumpkin, fictional Governor Stark evolves into a rabble-rousing political wheeler-dealer. He gives followers something to believe in amid the economic chaos of the times. He provides for some of their needs, and he is more effective than his counterparts in other states. He makes them feel a part of something.

Populist leaders, from Eugene Debs to Bernie Sanders, try to bring followers to a full consciousness of their needs, help convert the resulting hopes and aspirations into practical demands on other leaders and the political system. Our fictional Willie Stark was part of a long tradition—a tradition that continues.

Like other toxic leaders (such as "Shagpoke" Whipple in Nathanael West's *A Cool Million* and "Buzz" Windrip in Sinclair Lewis's *It Can't Happen Here*), Stark skillfully exploits what psychologists call "chronic followers," people who hunger for and willingly follow charismatic and authoritarian politicians. Such followers give themselves to leaders who appear confident, strong, and share their pain. Following such a politician often gives joiners a sense of place, purpose, and makes them feel relevant. The darker side of political leadership can seldom be divorced from the dark side of follow-ship. Politicians, like Stark, can become tyrants on behalf of arguably acceptable goals, and many people—from redneck hicks to patricians like Jack Burden—willingly follow.

Starkism is captured in Willie's declaration to his political base that "your will is my strength" and "your need is my justice." He feels empowered and emboldened to make things happen for them even if the laws have to catch up later. You have to break eggs to make an omelet, and, in Willie's mind, goodness often has to come out of a certain amount of badness.

Stark, similar to the real-life Huey "Kingfish" Long (who inspired his character), *does* care about average people, especially those left behind and voiceless. Like Long, Stark is depicted as a man of destiny, with a spark of leadership genius and even a potential charismatic greatness to him. Somewhere along the way, however, Stark becomes intoxicated by his new status and the always dangerous drug, power. The ambition necessary to gain high office evolves into a pathetic narcissism. His self-confidence becomes a swollen ego. A sense of entitlement takes hold, as he bribes, blackmails, and betrays his political enemies as well as his aides and friends (all the "Kingfish's" men). Ultimately, his drinking, boorishness, vulgar ruthlessness, and constitutionally subversive strategies make him unbearable.

"There is always something," Stark insists, some past mistake or skeleton in everyone's political closet. Jack Burden, now a top aide to the governor, is tasked with digging up dirt and converting it into political support for the governor.

Narrator Burden regularly attempts to understand the political tsunami that engulfs him. "I'm not a politician, I'm a hired hand," he tries to explain. Elsewhere he says, "No, I'm not in politics . . . I've just got a job." In fact, if he loathes the darker side of politics, he also voyeuristically enjoys being influential. He may dislike politicians and the life of politics, but as a student of history and former political reporter, he savors his front-row insider's seat at the formative political battles of his state.

Burden understands that many of the political deals he and his colleagues are engaged in are immoral; yet he deludes himself in believing that his boss is a great man motivated to do noble things. He willingly becomes a multitasking enabler and blackmailer. He rationalizes, as many people in such positions do: "And what we students of history always learn is that the human being is a very complicated contraption and that they are not good or bad, but are good and bad and the good comes out of the bad and the bad out of the good." He (shades of Sophocles' *Oedipus*) is assigned to dig up dirt on the man he doesn't realize is his own biological father, ultimately leading to Judge Montague Irwin's suicide. He even rationalizes when Governor Stark (shades of the *Iliad*) takes Burden's longtime love interest as his mistress. (At least Achilles put on a dramatic pout!) Burden's belief in his boss is regularly tested, to put it mildly, and often tormented—yet he stays. In a Shakespearean-style soliloquy, Burden reflects:

> I must believe that Willie Stark was a great man. What happened to his greatness is not the question. Perhaps he spilled it on the ground the way you spill a liquid when the bottle breaks. Perhaps he piled up his greatness and burnt it like a bonfire and then there wasn't anything but dark and the embers winking. Perhaps he could not tell his greatness from ingreatness and so mixed them together so that what was adulterated was lost. But he had it. I must believe that.

In the end, Jack's closest friend, Dr. Adam Stanton, assassinates Governor Stark (just as "Kingfish" Long was killed by a physician). Stark, his assassin believes, had betrayed Stanton and his family. Perhaps, too, Stanton designates himself as a Brutus-like savior bringing a halt to Stark's Caesarism. Both Willie Stark and Julius Caesar are killed at their respective capitols. There can be multiple interpretations of Stark's demise, as Robert Penn Warren makes it complicated, and delightfully so, despite the tragedy of it all.

At one point our narrator Jack Burden formulates what he calls the "Great Twitch" theory, holding that every action is comparable to a small, uncontrollable twitch on someone's face or body. His dubious "theory" allows Jack to avoid taking responsibility for his actions and to overlook his and his colleagues' shortcomings.

The Twitch theory conveniently masks Jack's aimlessness and general abdication of responsibility. "Being in the room" counted more than character. It is only late in the novel that he rejects the Twitch theory and begins to accept personal responsibility for what has happened to his father, his closest friends, and himself.

Burden's dilemma lay in his admiration of what Governor Stark was trying to do on behalf of the poor and his growing understanding that Stark's now swollen ego had transformed into a dictatorial, amoral ruthlessness. "But nobody had better forget," threatens a sick Willie, "that I'll do what I've got to do. By God, I'll do it if I've got to break their bones with my bare hands."

Stark descended into a downward spiral of drinking, womanizing, and debilitating negativity. His new ambition to become a U.S. senator transformed him to enhanced feverishness, which led to further graft, blackmail, and bullying.

Then his all-star LSU football son, Tom, a notorious juvenile delinquent, became paralyzed and almost died as a result of a football accident.

Stark's much-neglected wife, Lucy, calls Willie out after Willie lamely boasts that he'll name the new state hospital after Tom:

> Those things don't matter. Having somebody's name cut on a piece of stone. Getting it in the paper. All these things. Oh, Willie, he was my baby boy, he was our baby boy, and those things don't matter, they don't ever matter, don't you see?

This chastisement and Willie's seeming epiphany at his almost total loss of integrity apparently inspire him to change his ways. He announces he is going back to live with his wife. He will terminate graft, and especially a kickback-infested contract deal with a pay-to-play businessman.

Warren doesn't exactly explain this transformation, and Willie's time seems to be running out. "Jack, let's get upstairs. I want to tell you something." But while they are on their way, Dr. Adam Stanton assassinates Willie in the great lobby of the state capitol.

Warren's *King's Men*, like the Humpty Dumpty of Lewis Carroll's nursery rhyme, is a combination of a *roman à clef* and an allegory of the fall of a leader from grace, a fall because of the devils of pride, narcissism, and overreach. And just as in the rhyme, all the king's horses and all the king's men (including Jack Burden) are unable to put the driven, consumed Stark back together again.

Most literary critics agree that *King's Men* is not only a masterful, big-message novel about political power and corruption but also one of America's major novels, ranking with, or just behind, the novels of Hawthorne, Faulkner, Melville, Twain, and a small handful of others. Warren earned a Pulitzer Prize for *King's Men* and later won two additional Pulitzers for poetry. The novel has some lyrical passages, as when Jack Burden temporarily "runs away," headed West (like Huck Finn, the Joads, and Kerouac), from the political morass that has engulfed him:

> For West is where all plan to go someday. It is where you go when the Land gives out. . . . It is where you go when you get a letter saying: Flee, all is discovered. It is where you go when you look down at the blade in your hand and the blood on it. It is where you go when you hear that thar's gold in them thar hills. It is where you go to grow up with the country. It is where you go to spend your old age. Or it is just where you go.

What does it take to fight for greater equality, and what are the trade-offs for liberty and freedom? How does power reshape those who acquire it? Ultimately, this is a book as much about the American political experiment as about human nature. We want bold leadership, but we have also learned to be suspicious of leaders who acquire power.

Warren's novel follows the familiar arc of a "Mr. Smith" character who goes to the capital to do good deeds; yet Mr. Stark does so using questionable means, and in the end, implodes. Stark's right-hand man, Jack Burden, shares his fascination with and seduction by Willie Stark. Jack is mesmerized by the good Willie Stark—the fighter for the common people—yet bewildered by the cynical, manipulative, and authoritarian Willie. Jack is for hope, change, and redistributive progress, but he is morally paralyzed when he realizes that he should resist political skullduggery of the worst kind. Warren makes Burden the stand-in for us. What, Warren cleverly (if indirectly) asks, would we have done?

Narrator Jack Burden ultimately "has to lose his innocence to understand the multiplicity and sadness of the truth."[26] Burden also, though belatedly, begins to understand the paradox of power and the monstrously hard challenge of governing responsibly and constitutionally.

Warren heightens our understanding about democracy, the way in which votes can be exploited, and the fragility of constitutional safeguards. His *King's Men* is a complicated set of narratives and subplots, and they are a stark (sorry) warning about political systems. Politics and politicians may be inevitable and necessary, but they are always potentially dangerous. Our corrupt politics, Warren reminds us, are not just about money. It can also be about pride, narcissism, entitlement, and unrequited personal needs. Historians and biographers regularly wrestle with Warren's questions. Thus, there is an age-old debate that tries to distinguish between an *effective* leader and a *good* leader. Some agree with Jack Burden: effective political leaders sometimes have to have dirty hands to achieve good policy results: "Maybe a man has to sell his soul to get the power to do good." This was "the course that [Huey] Long, faced with relentless opposition, felt he had to follow," writes historian T. Harry Williams.

> I believe that some men, men of power, can influence the course of history. They appear in response to conditions, but they may alter the conditions, may give a new direction to history. In the process they may do great good or evil or both, but whatever the case, they leave a different kind of world behind them. Their accomplishment should be recognized. I believe that Huey Long was this kind of man.[27]

Williams contends nearly every political practitioner has to wrestle with the enduring dilemma of reconciling ends and means. Politicians seldom talk about it but understand that they sometimes do certain things in which they do not believe in order to gain power or to stay in power—for without political power they can accomplish few of the things that they passionately favor.[28]

Biographer Richard D. White agrees that Long brought about tangible improvements in the lives of most Louisianans. He helped build roads, bridges, universities, and hospitals, and he helped improve schools and literacy. Yet White also says that Long was cruel and corrupt, a demagogue who packed the state payroll with cronies and savaged political opponents.[29]

Stark was initially motivated to serve the ordinary and voiceless people who first elected him. Power, and being in the spotlight, changed him. He became intoxicated by the seductive fruits of political status and power. He was effective in the short run. He was doubtless both a product and an architect of the corrupt political culture of his place and time. Still, he deluded himself that his admixture of noble and narcissistic ends justified his means. *King's Men* makes it clear that Willie's personal needs eventually dictated both his means and his demise. In cinematic terms, our "Mr. Smith" who goes to Baton Rouge becomes a near monarch with Machiavellian courtiers. Power, we learn once again, can corrupt not only those who receive it but also their Jack Burdens and, to some extent, the political culture at large.

Novelist Robert Penn Warren (1905–1989) was raised in Kentucky and Tennessee and graduated with highest honors from Vanderbilt University. He later studied at the University of California at Berkeley, Yale, and, as a Rhodes Scholar at Oxford University. He was, even though he lived most of his adult years in the North, a proud and dedicated southerner. He grew up in Jim Crow era and was slow to embrace racial equality and desegregation. "African Americans" in *King's Men* are virtually all depicted as "the help" and play insignificant roles in shaping or influencing the politics of that era. *King's Men* portrays women in clearly subordinate positions and is understandably viewed as sexist by modern readers.

Penn Warren spent nearly a decade teaching at Louisiana State University (1934–1942). Huey Long had served as governor before Warren had arrived. He was elected U.S. senator in 1932 and was actively seeking the U.S presidential nomination in 1935 when he was assassinated at the state capitol.

Long had made LSU a top funding priority and had helped jump-start its becoming a reasonably preeminent southern research university. Penn Warren's English Department at LSU directly benefited from this patronage.

In 1935 Warren met Senator Huey P. Long, probably for the first and only time, when the senator came to LSU to brag about how much he had done for the university. Warren thought he was simultaneously a "political genius" and a "buffoon, clown . . . sentimental dreamer, man of ruthless action, coward, wit, philosopher, orator."[30] Long obviously left an indelible impression on the earnest assistant professor of English. Later that year Long would be killed and the mythology of Huey Long was magnified.

The real Huey Long did have a streak of political genius. He was more than a rabble-rouser. He fashioned himself as an authentic champion of the people in a state long dominated by an oligarchy made up of those who controlled cotton, sugar plantations, lumber, shipping, and oil.

Long's "share-the-wealth" program was vintage populism; yet, through effective oratory and wheeling and dealing, he was able to make good on many of his campaign pledges. Robert Penn Warren's novel about Willie Stark neglects or understates Governor Long's clever use of radio, organized efforts to get sympathetic legislators elected, and the starting of his own newspaper, *The Progress*. Long also successfully won the support of a few of the oligarchs and shrewdly manipulated Louisiana's state control of petroleum production.

Long clearly had a Robin Hood morality—at least at the outset, before political and personal finances became mixed. There is little doubt that Huey Long was one of America's most colorful populists who was in the process of becoming a regional political kingpin. FDR is said to have viewed Long not only as a feared political rival but also as one of the most dangerous men in America.

Most nonfiction interpretations of Huey Long miss the complexity of the man. One of the great students of southern politics, V. O. Key Jr., rejects simple theories about Long:

> They range from the theory that he and his crowd were ordinary boodlers to the notion that here was native fascism. Boodling there was, to be sure. Fascism? Huey was innocent of any ideology other than the sort of indigenous indignation against the abuses of wealth clement in the epoch of William Jennings Bryan. The Long phenomenon must be explained in terms of the pathological situation in which he arose, in terms of traditional anti-corporation, plus the genius of the man himself in political manipulation and organization.[31]

King's Men made no pretense of being a biography of Huey Long. The Long story served as a backdrop, and, as Warren regularly said, Willie Stark was "only himself," a fictional political leader who was as much imagined as he was inspired by reality. Penn Warren made no pretense of being a political scientist or much interested in the political process. His professional preoccupation both before *King's Men* and after was poetry, literary criticism, and examining the human condition. Even though he is more popularly known for *King's Men*, he was better known, and highly admired among American literati, for his poetry, his literary analysis of Herman Melville, and his various texts on American literature.[32]

All the King's Men was a best seller, became a successful film, and enjoyed multiple theatrical offshoots. It remains one of America's major novels and is probably, as noted earlier, the essential American political novel. Warren became a mainstay of the English faculty at Yale University and one of America's much honored and revered men of letters.[33] His *King's Men* inspired future writers, political journalists, political scientists, and many who went into politics.

It is criticized for being "overplotted" and melodramatic. It is true that Warren has a storyteller's tendency to wander as he delves into southern history and the creation of various paralleling "doubles" that complicate his story. He, however, rejected the criticism about melodrama, saying that Louisiana was a citadel of melodrama and that he was merely being faithful to the culture he was writing about.

Some critics worried that Warren's novel was, at least in part, an apologia for Long's over-the-top unconstitutional political tactics. Warren rejected this criticism as "innocent bone-headedness." Others would have liked Warren to have written with a more agitational voice—perhaps crusading for vigilance against those who would subvert our Madisonian political procedures. Warren viewed himself as a fiction writer, not a reformer or agitator. His novel has plenty of consciousness raising in it for those who do a close political reading.

King's central question, akin to questions Machiavelli and Shakespeare had previously raised, is whether noble ends can justify dubious or evil means to bring them into being. Penn Warren mostly leaves the answer to this to his readers. He seems to side with Stark's pessimistic view of the "nature of things" and the unfairness of the political system as it was. But Warren also telegraphs his fears about the breakdown of constitutionalism and the moral order.

Warren, whose later career became celebrated, as noted, more for his poetry and criticism, was satisfied with having created a handful of memorable southern political operatives—Willie Stark, Jack Burden, secretary/mistress Sadie Burke, driver and bodyguard Sugar-Boy O'Sheean, politician Tiny Duffy, and Dr. Adam and Anne Stanton—in a specific place and time as they wrestled with ideals and action, rich and poor, good and evil, means and ends, and the paradoxes of political power. *King's Men* triumphs in this achievement. It stops well short of John Adams's stark warning that a democracy never lasts long. "It soon wastes, exhausts, and murders itself," feared Adams. "There never was a democracy yet that did not commit suicide."

Robert Penn Warren is fascinated with, yet concerned about, democracy. He sees its promise and its aspirational hopes; yet he rightly warns that "Starkism" as well as oligarchy will remain as central challenges for the American republic.

ON MOCKINGBIRDS AND WATCHMEN[34]

"The one place where a man ought to get a square deal is in a courtroom, be he any color of the rainbow, but people have a way of carrying their resentments right into the jury box. As you grow older, you'll see white men cheat black men every day of your life, but let me tell you something and don't forget it—whenever a white man does that to a black man, no matter who he is, how rich he is, or how fine a family he comes from, that white man is trash." These are the pained words fictional attorney and public defender Atticus Finch shares with his young son Jem and precocious daughter Scout in Harper Lee's best-selling *To Kill a Mockingbird* (1960).

Protagonist Finch is a fifty-year-old widower in Maycomb, a small southwestern Alabama town in 1935. He practices law and represents his county in the Alabama House of Representatives. He is gentle, meticulous, and caring, a bit of a loner who would rather read than go hunting or fishing or hang out at a local watering hole.

But Lee's novel makes it clear that he loves his family, as well as the ideals and legal reasoning of the American judicial system, and he also appears to understand the aspirational American values of civil rights, civil liberties, and communitarian civility. Indeed, in Harper Lee's radiant prose, the saintly Atticus Finch is the greatest father and public defender in American literature.

Finch is no civil rights activist. He merely believes in the law, and if there is injustice, even in the interpretation of the law, he believes this needs to be changed. He wants to believe that there is at least one place in America where all men are created and treated as equals: "There is one human institution that makes a pauper the equal of a Rockefeller, the stupid man the equal of an Einstein, the ignorant man the equal of any college president. That institution, gentlemen, is a court." In his address to a local jury, Finch adds, "It can be the Supreme Court of the United States or the humblest J.P. [Justice of the Peace] court in the land, or this honorable court which you serve. Our courts have their faults, as does any human institution, but," and here Finch fantasizes, "in this country our courts are the great levelers, and in our courts all men are created equal." Bryan Stevenson's best-seller *Just Mercy* (New York: Spiegel and Grau, 2014) appropriately refutes this claim.

Finch accepts a temporary appointment to serve as a public defender to represent a local black field hand, Tom Robinson, who is wrongly charged with raping a young white woman. Finch contends there is sufficient reason to doubt his client's guilt in what is essentially a he said/she said case. But Finch loses the case. Robinson is convicted on circumstantial evidence by the all-white male jury and sent to a state prison to be hanged. Subsequently Robinson tries to escape and is killed fleeing. (Robinson is a symbol, many literary analysts suggest, of three centuries of injustice toward African Americans.)

Mockingbird is narrated over a four-year period through the curiously mature eyes of Finch's young tomboy daughter, Miss Jean Louise, or Scout, as she is affectionately called. Scout learns at one point from neighbors that her father is a "nigger-lover." She asks him what the term means. He answers her by saying:

> "Nigger-lover is just one of those terms that don't mean anything. . . . It's hard to explain—ignorant, trashy people use it when they think somebody's favoring Negroes over and above themselves. . . ."
>
> "You aren't really a nigger-lover, then, are you?" [asks Scout.]
>
> "I certainly am. I do my best to love everybody . . . I'm hard put, sometimes—baby, it's never an insult to be called what somebody thinks is a bad name."

Atticus understands that cases such as the Tom Robinson defense go to the essence of a man's conscience and that it is the responsibility of lawyers like him to make sure everyone, regardless of circumstance, has effective legal defense in the court of law. He knows that access to a fair trial is not a Democratic or Republican issue, nor a black or white issue—it is a quintessential American aspirational ideal. Fundamental to a constitutional republic should be the principle: Justice should not be rationed.

Lee's Atticus Finch is a portrait of heroic and civic rectitude. Most people, he tells his children, are nice when you come to know them. You never really understand a person until you consider things from this point of view, "until you climb inside of his skin and walk around in it." So, he says, he tries to see the best in people.

Finch understands prejudice and racism. He knows there is a big racial divide as well as segregation and prejudice in Maycomb. He is their popularly elected state representative. Yet he wants to believe that "the one thing that doesn't abide by majority rule is a person's conscience."

Atticus Finch is the moral heart of this nostalgic and inspirational parable. He is Harper Lee's gift to us, a political exemplar. He is "a man who knows himself and, who, therefore can love others."[35] He is, Lee suggests, a giver and a sharer who understands both civil and natural law, and who understands who we are and, more important, who we ought to be.

Lee's novel is a grandchild, in a way, of Harriet Beecher Stowe's *Uncle Tom's Cabin*. *Mockingbird*, written nearly a century after *Tom's Cabin*, and it is a case study in the oppression and Jim Crow racism facing blacks in the South. In some ways *Mockingbird* is also a companion story to *12 Angry Men*, the 1950s television drama that was artfully turned into an award-winning Hollywood film, starring Henry Fonda, in 1957. In *12 Angry Men*, reason ultimately transcends prejudice and the trial ends happily. In David Guterson's award-winning novel *Snow Falling on Cedars* (New York: Harcourt Brace, 1994), a Japanese American is almost wrongly convicted in a similarly prejudicial setting, but, again, justice ultimately prevails. By contrast, in *Mockingbird*, despite Finch's eloquence and courage, justice is not served. Robinson is convicted and Finch is jeered and spat upon, his children threatened and almost killed.

Mockingbird has a secondary narrative about prejudice involving the mysterious "Boo" Radley, a neighbor who lives three doors up the street from the Finch family. Boo is an unknown entity—housebound, outcast by reputation, possibly because of teenage indiscretions but more probably because of mental health problems. The neighborhood children think of him as a type of scary ghost or malevolent phantom. Rumors spread that he eats cats and squirrels. The children try to get him to come out, and joke about his "otherness."

Although Harper Lee (1926–2016) mostly denied her novel was autobiographical, her personal story doubtless shaped *Mockingbird*. Her own father, like Atticus Finch, was a local attorney and state legislator and newspaper editor in the small Alabama town of Monroeville, with a population of around 1,500 in the 1930s, 3,500 in the 1950s, and about 6,000 nowadays, halfway between Montgomery and Mobile. (It voted for Democrats in the 1930s but is solidly Republican nowadays.) He once defended an African American man who was convicted and subsequently hanged. Lee also had a "strange" neighbor like Boo Radley. Her father, like Finch, tried on occasion to deflate his town's KKK racism. Lee later said that Atticus, this case, and her depiction of Boo were merely fictional composites of events and people she observed as she grew up.

But the debate as to how much of the novel is autobiographical is irrelevant. Lee's novel is a poetic and lyrical account of a place and time in the not-too-distant past, and it has become an enduring American parable. Her message, similar to the one Mark Twain suggested in his iconic *Huckleberry Finn*, is that we must try harder to transcend racism and prejudice. Told from a child's perspective, *Mockingbird* exudes a coming-of-age warmth of remembrance, innocence, and caring. Atticus is a southern gentleman who understands even as he does not accept his town's prejudice. At the "High Noon" moment in his defense of Robinson, Finch implores the jury:

> You know the truth, and the truth is this: some Negroes lie, some Negroes are immoral, some Negro men are not to be trusted around women—black or white. But that is a truth that applies to the human race and to no particular race of men. There is not a person in this courtroom who has never told a lie, who has never done an immoral thing, and there is no man living who has never looked upon a woman without desire.

Being able to accept one's friends' and neighbors' weaknesses is what makes Lee's storytelling heartwarming.

Lee wrote *Mockingbird* a few years after the landmark *Brown v. Board of Education* Supreme Court decision (1954), and in the shadow of one of the most famous Alabamans, Justice Hugo Black, who had gone from being a youthful member of the KKK to becoming, for Harper Lee's generation, one of the most consequential progressive judicial voices of the twentieth century.

At the time of her writing, the civil rights movement was strengthening, gearing up for its moral triumphs in Birmingham, Selma, and Washington, D.C. *Mockingbird*, with its message of tolerance, its tug on the heartstrings, and its memorable hero, may have quietly influenced the national political climate of the times as Americans reluctantly embraced the Civil Rights and Voting Rights Acts of the mid-1960s. Yet, as her second novel *Go Set a Watchman* (published fifty-five years later, but written before she wrote *Mockingbird* in the late 1950s) and the voting records of this region over the next generation attest, her home county remained racially divided.

On one level, *Mockingbird* is a Southern Gothic novel. It vividly captures, like her heroes Jane Austen, Eudora Welty, and William Faulkner might have captured, the mood and manners of the small, sleepy town, with its quirky characters, like the mysterious Boo Radley, the rural black and white poverty of the surrounding farmland, and the sweltering heat of southwestern Alabama.

On another level, the novel is a probing account of a still unreconstructed South of *Gone with the Wind*. Beneath the warm memories of childhood, Lee describes the ugly divide between black and white, and, with a sociological eye, the divide between "ordinary" whites and lower-income "white trash." She also reveals the injustices and inhumane treatment still faced by blacks and other minorities. It is also a telling reminder of the price an earnest public defender may have to pay. Finch and his children are threatened as he stoically exercises his civic responsibility. In doing so, the fictional Atticus Finch becomes a patron saint and national poster icon of public defenders. Scout, appropriately named, becomes our young guide, a role model of thoughtfulness and tolerance.

Mockingbird shows how tightly woven is the web of interpersonal connections that make up a small town's society. Community leaders such as Atticus Finch and the town's sheriff understand these connections. In Maycomb, as in the real Monroeville, the family home, her dad's law office, the county courthouse, her church, and her local public school are all just a few blocks from each other.

We learn from Lee's biographers that her father, A. C. Lee (1880–1962), was a local moderate who did, on occasion in the 1930s, stand up to the Ku Klux Klan. But her father only reluctantly adopted some of the pro–civil rights moral views reflected in *Mockingbird*'s Atticus Finch. "Though more enlightened than most, A. C. was no saint, no prophet crying in the wilderness, with regard to racial matters," writes Lee's biographer, Charles Shields.[36] Lee's father, for example, opposed an activist role on behalf of racial equality that some fellow Methodists were advocating for in his church. Like most of his fellow white southerners, he favored racial segregation, states' rights, and limited government.

Harper Lee herself was not a political activist. Commentators suggest she was unenthusiastic in the 1960s about the "Freedom Riders" and the use of federal troops to integrate southern schools of higher learning. She may have been for tolerance, yet was a gradualist.

Lee's understated political outlook is partly captured in her remarks at West Point in the 1960s. She spoke to the first year "plebs" who had been assigned to read *Mockingbird*.

We like to have all our comforts and familiars about us, and to push away that which is different and worrisome. That is what happened to

Boo Radley, and to Tom Robinson. They were not set apart by evil men, or evil women, or evil thoughts. They were set apart by an evil past, which good people in the present were ill-equipped to change.

Then she emphasized, "The irony is, if we divide ourselves for our own comfort, *no one* will have comfort."[37]

Still, Lee writes as a consciousness raiser. We need to understand our past, our biases, our traditions, she suggests—and we need to educate ourselves about our interconnectedness and the importance of being neighbors. This was, of course, much the same message Rev. Martin Luther King Jr. was preaching in Montgomery just a hundred miles away from her hometown. Lee was suggesting that the South and people everywhere needed to grow up and develop the civic inclusiveness and sensitivity modeled by fictional Atticus Finch. This was also a John F. Kennedy message—that we love our country not so much for what it has been, but what it (with more Attics Finches, Harper Lees, and Martin Kings) can and someday will be.

In the famous eponymous metaphor, Atticus tells his son, "I'd rather you shot at tin cans in the backyard, but I know you'll go after birds. Shoot all the blue jays you want, if you can hit 'em, but remember, it's a sin to kill a mockingbird."

> That was the only time [his daughter Scout says] I ever heard Atticus say it was a sin to do something, and I asked Miss Maudie [a neighbor] about it. "Your father's right," she said. "Mockingbirds don't do one thing except make music for us to enjoy. They don't eat up people's gardens, don't nest in corncribs, they don't do one thing but sing their hearts out for us. That's why it's a sin to kill a mockingbird."

There is an exquisite twist on this theme in the last chapters, in which the children are saved by the mysterious Boo Radley. Boo, as noted, was the ghostly neighbor in the children's lives, a subject of fascination and superstition. "Boo was our neighbor," Scout says. "He gave us two soap dolls, a broken watch and chain, a pair of good-luck pennies, and our lives." Late in *Mockingbird*, he apparently kills the vengeful Bob Ewell, who attacked Finch's children as a means of punishing Atticus. The novel is a bit murky about what actually happened. Finch's son Jem might have killed the racist revenge attacker. But the killer, most readers believe, was probably Boo.

Finch reasons that whoever did it should be arrested and subject to the law. But the local sheriff, Heck Tate, argues for a different kind of justice. He claims Ewell fell on his own knife. Then he adds, as much as to acknowledge Boo as Ewell's killer:

I'm not a very good man, sir, but I am sheriff of Maycomb County. Lived in this town all my life an' I'm goin' on forty-three years old. . . . There's a black boy dead for no reason, and the man responsible for it's dead. Let the dead bury the dead this time, Mr. Finch. Let the dead bury the dead . . .

To my way of thinking, Mr. Finch, taking the one man who'd done you and this town a great service an' draggin' him with his shy ways into the limelight—to me that's a sin.

The sheriff is right, says young Scout. "What do you mean?" asks her father. "Well, it'd be sort of like shootin' a mockingbird, wouldn't it?"

Atticus, albeit reluctantly, consents. Harper Lee asks her readers to understand and respect one another. Understand Tom Robinson and Boo Radley and all the "others" and the mockingbirds they represent. Build social, legal, and political communities where everyone in God's creation is treated fairly. Be guided by principled civility.

Some critics have disparaged *Mockingbird*. "I loathe that book," said one English professor friend of mine. Here are charges leveled at *Mockingbird*:

- It has more than its share of Hallmark card and "Mister Rogers" moralistic bromides.
- It has a well-educated white male as the heroic protagonist while portraying African Americans as incapable of acting for themselves. There are no black role models here. Indeed, in a town that is more than half African American, there is virtually no understanding of this "other Maycomb."
- It is full of stereotypic, even cartoonish, characters, except for the Finch family. And the idealized Atticus Finch appears, rather transparently, as a mythologizing bouquet to Lee's father.
- Its faith in human goodness and in human nature is strained and naïve.
- It provides little context about local politics. How, for example, did Atticus get elected to the state legislature in what we are told is a Klan-dominated town? And what did he do there? Did he do anything at all to help the large African American population in his county? Did he do anything to help poor white families?
- *Mockingbird*'s villains are the Klansmen and the uneducated, unemployed town drunk Bob Ewell (the man who falsely accused Tom Robinson of raping his daughter). Ewell, in every way, is the anti-Finch. (He represents the prejudiced dark side of the South.)

This was the Great Depression, when FDR, Huey Long, and Upton Sinclair were championing programs to lift up the Bob Ewells of society. Had the American Dream died among most Maycomb citizens who seemed to live, like Ewell, quiet lives of anger, hate, and desperation?

These are valid complaints. But Harper Lee's consciousness-raising storytelling succeeds in teaching us about racism and the imperfections in our social and political systems. We learn about injustice and outcasts, the innocence of childhood, and the role that dedicated, civically engaged citizens can play in redeeming the American Dream of liberty and equality—especially under the rule of law. This is simultaneously a book about stark realities and aspirational hopes.

Nelle Harper Lee had studied at the University of Alabama and at an Oxford summer session semester before moving to New York City. She worked ordinary jobs in New York as she labored over writing *Mockingbird* and other manuscripts. For decades she would spend half of her year in New York (upper East 83rd Street) and the other half back in Monroeville, where she lived a decidedly quiet life with her older sister, local attorney Alice Finch Lee. Except for serving a few years on the U.S. National Arts and Humanities Council, Ms. Lee seldom, if ever, was involved in public life.[38] We know she regularly attended her family's Monroeville First United Methodist Church, liked to fish, and was reclusive.

A second novel, *Go Set a Watchman*, published in 2015, briefly became a best seller, but no one hailed it as a classic. It sold a remarkable million copies in its first year, doubtless due primarily to *Mockingbird*'s fame. It was apparently written but rejected by her publisher in the 1950s, right before (yet around the same time) that she was writing *Mockingbird*. Most of *Mockingbird*'s fans have not liked *Watchman*. As one of my friends explained, "Hell, I'm not going to read that second novel. I want to preserve my Atticus Finch the way he was!" Most of the locals I interviewed in Monroeville in 2017 said they had not read this second novel or, if they had started it, they couldn't finish it.

Watchman, like *Mockingbird*, is based on life in Lee's fictional Maycomb, Alabama. But if the idealized Atticus Finch in *Mockingbird* is almost too good to be true, *Watchman*'s Atticus is disconcertingly human. He longs for the old South, the one before the Earl Warren Supreme Court.

Watchman, while less charming and less memorable than *Mockingbird*, is politically more instructive. It probes the political values of the white community, and puts under a microscope the "pay-to-play" politics of the courthouse political cabal in a small Alabama county.

Watchman is set in the late 1950s (in contrast to the mid-1930s). Scout's father is now in his seventies. Like many southern white males, he feels threatened by recent events like integration, the demand for equal schools, and by the possibility that African Americans could take over the city hall and county courthouse. Scout, now twenty-six, living in New York City, has become "Yankee-fied." When she visits Maycomb, she can't believe the racism she now hears and observes. "How can they devoutly believe everything they hear in church and then say the things they do and listen to things they hear without throwing up?"

In *Watchman* the Honorable Mr. Finch is a member of the local White Citizen's Council, an organization dedicated to preserving segregation and fighting the NAACP and recent U.S. Supreme Court decisions, especially *Brown v. Board of Education* (1954).

Jean Louise "Scout" Finch is appalled by her father's seemingly new racism. His political views, in Lee's telling, may be equally (if not even more) backward than those of Scarlett O'Hara's in Margaret Mitchell's *Gone with the Wind*.

"Do you want Negroes by the carload in our schools and churches and theatres?" he asks. Finch wants the feds, the courts, and northern liberals to leave them alone. "What would happen if all the Negros in the South were suddenly given full civil rights? There'd be another Reconstruction." The feds, Finch complains, are trampling on the Tenth Amendment to the U.S. Constitution, adding the blacks "down here are still in their childhood as a people."

Scout becomes outraged and calls her dad out as a coward and tyrant. (Her moral outrage calls to mind Antigone railing against her uncle, King Creon of Thebes.) Scout finds that her aunt and uncle, and her sometime boyfriend, share her father's hardened segregationist views. Boyfriend Henry Clinton is a young law associate in her father's law firm who wants to run for the state legislature. Scout asks him why he is in league with the segregationists.

Henry, echoing Atticus Finch's sentiments, says it is expedient, the necessary thing to do. "Have you ever considered that men, especially men, must conform to certain demands of the community they live in simply so they can be of service to it?" Translation: To earn a decent living here you have to accept local norms and practices. "You are," she responds, "a god damned hypocrite." Scout assumes the role of "watchman"—or conscience—yet is treated as the bearer of unwanted criticism.[39]

Alabama famously voted for Dixiecrat Strom Thurmond in the presidential election of 1948 as a response to civil rights platforms of the

Democratic Party that year. It had voted into office some Klan-supported governors in these same decades, and a few years later, it would elect George C. Wallace, who pledged in January 1963 to be "for segregation now, segregation tomorrow, segregation forever." Although *Watchman* doesn't tell their story, large numbers of Americans from South Texas to South Boston similarly feared and opposed the federal government's initiatives in the 1940s and 1950s to enfranchise and empower blacks and poor whites around the country.

Lee's *Watchman* may be about her small town in southern Alabama, but it is also instructive political anthropology. She helps explain political realities of our darker past and the reasons local political elites often act the way they do. Whereas *Mockingbird* was a consciousness-raising inspiration about how we can overcome intolerance, *Watchman* is a frank examination of the persistence of racism.

Lee, unfortunately, conveys little or no understanding in either of her novels of the leadership and politics in the African American community. The novel's fictional town (and Lee's real hometown) was at least 50 percent African American.

The great student of southern politics, V. O. Key Jr., perhaps defensively, summed up southern white political attitudes in his 1949 classic, *Southern Politics*, where he wrote, "A rural agricultural people views with distrust the urban, laboring classes of the North. The almost indelible memories of occupation by a conqueror create a sense of hostility toward the outsider."[40]

Court decisions and the evolving civil rights movement unsettled Harper Lee's hometown and triggered a transformational political realignment in American politics. These effects are still felt today. Alabama whites are overwhelmingly affiliated now with the Republican Party of Jefferson Davis Sessions and Donald Trump. African Americans almost all consider themselves Obama Democrats. Local schools are still segregated; the public schools Harper Lee once attended are now almost all black—whites who can afford it attend private Christian academies.

Mockingbird became one of America's favorite novels because it was highly readable storytelling, reasonably short, and part of the long tradition of aspirational parables urging Americans to live up to founding principles. Who couldn't like the idea that we might someday overcome prejudice, bigotry, and racism? Who couldn't like the idea that good and bad people are not determined by their skin color, or wealth, or religion, or their IQ or even their last name, but by their character? It is character that should count, says Harper Lee. Character above all.

Watchman is a more jarring novel. It reminds us of the disappointingly slow progress in race relations in America. Finch's fictionalized daughter sums it up in her aggrieved lament: "I looked up to you, Atticus, like I never looked up to anybody in my life and never will again." (Ironically, she is now buried three feet away from her dad in the "new section" of their local Methodist cemetery.)

Go Set a Watchman demands that readers "abandon the immature sentimentality ingrained by middle-school lessons about the nobility of the white savior and the mesmerizing performances of Gregory Peck in the film adaptation of *To Kill a Mockingbird*."[41] Atticus had been, for Scout and for all of Lee's readers, a paragon of decency and integrity—and now he talked like Bible Belt political racists Strom Thurmond and George Wallace.

Harper Lee, as noted earlier, was a gradualist, not a civil rights activist. *Mockingbird* is a classic Act II consciousness-raising novel. So is *Watchman*. The shy Harper Lee lived just two months shy of her ninetieth birthday. She never married and shied away from public life, although her novels were plainly progressive, especially for an Alabamian. She did grow more conservative as she aged. Friends described her as a George W. Bush Republican in her older years. Trump would probably have tested her taste for a Republican in 2016, but she passed away before that election.

Watchman will never become a classic; yet it helps explain political realities of our darker past and the reasons local political elites often act the way they do. It also highlights the ongoing challenges for the American political experiment that famously professed at the outset that "all men are created equal."

Mockingbird will remain a classic. Quaint, sentimental, and preachy, it is sometimes wrongly dismissed as a children's book. But "publishing a thinly veiled account of her small Alabama town's grappling with a deeply entrenched racial divide was a bold declaration," writes Margaret Eby.[42] *Watchman* was a still bolder declaration, and not especially welcomed down home in Monroeville.

Critics will continue to chide *Mockingbird* for its clichés and autobiographical tone. But it helped shape the country's political dialogue. It has become one of the most influential consciousness-raising novels and is an important part of America's aspirational communitarian narrative. It has been translated into more than forty languages and has become the best-read novel in American high schools.

Mockingbird and *Watchman* build upon Stowe's *Uncle Tom's Cabin* and Twain's *Huckleberry Finn*. Lee, like Stowe and Twain, implores us to become better people. And like Twain, she tells her growing-up-in-America story through the eyes of a beguiling young person. Her two novels provide a more realistic alternative to the plantation fantasies of *Gone with the Wind*. Lee's works need to be read together with Richard Wright's masterful *Native Son* and Toni Morrison's seminal *Beloved*.

To Kill a Mockingbird was once banned in a Richmond, Virginia, area school district. Lee was taken aback by this. *Mockingbird*, she said, merely spells out a code of honor, a code of conduct "Christian in its ethic." She also could have added "American in its aspirations."

One final note: Harper Lee left us with the message of tolerance and respect for all our neighbors, especially the vulnerable. What is not mentioned in either of her works, however, is that her home, Monroe County (named after President James Monroe), was, a few generations earlier, the tribal grounds of the Creek Indians who were infamously forced, for the most part, to disappear westward by military leaders such as Andrew Jackson.[43]

THE ULTIMATE WHITE HOUSE–PENTAGON SHOWDOWN[44]

"Listen, Mr. President," says Joint Chiefs of Staff Chairman General James Mattoon Scott, "you have lost the respect of the country. Your policies have brought us to the edge of disaster. Business does not trust you. Labor flaunts its disdain for you. . . . Military morale has sunk to the lowest point in thirty years. . . . Your treaty was the act of a naïve boy."

"That's ugly talk, General," replies President Jordan Lyman.

"Those are the facts," Scott says. "The public has no faith in you. . . . Unless the country is rallied by a voice of authority and discipline, it can be lost in a month."

President Lyman demands this rogue outlaw general's resignation. Scott resists, but he eventually tenders it when Lyman reveals that he has discovered Scott's detailed plans to overthrow the nation's civilian authority and replace it with a Scott-led military cabal.

Scott, like Abraham Lincoln's General George McClellan, is popular among the nation's military. And like Douglas MacArthur, who was famously fired by President Truman, he enjoys widespread popularity in the country and in Congress. Readers are told that Scott is a "blend of the best of Eisenhower and MacArthur," and that he enjoys an especially close friendship with California U.S. senator Frederick Prentice, chairman of the Senate Armed Services Committee, and with popular national radio talk show host Harold McPherson (an apparent forerunner of Rush Limbaugh of later years). Prentice and McPherson enthusiastically support General Scott in the effort to fight President Lyman's diplomatic efforts with the Soviets. More important, we learn that they are co-conspirators in General Scott's audacious move to oust Lyman in a military coup d'état.

Washington journalists Fletcher Knebel (1911–1993) and Charles Bailey (1929–2012) wrote this consciousness-raising thriller in the first year of the Kennedy presidency, after the Bay of Pigs fiasco but before the Cuban Missile Crisis. The Cold War was in full force, and right-wing conspiracy theories championed by U.S. senator Joseph McCarthy were a not-too-distant backdrop on the plot. An outspoken John Birch Society supporter, General Edwin A. Walker, had recently been forced to resign. Air Force general Curtis LeMay (who a few years later would be the running mate on George Wallace's presidential ticket) led some people to believe that President Kennedy was wrong not to have used nuclear weapons to support the invasion at the Cuban Bay of Pigs. The nuclear age bred anxiety and fear, and patriotic conservatives in and out of the military were deeply worried about nuclear weapons treaties.

In *Seven Days*, the fictional, liberal Democratic president, Jordan Lyman, acting sometime in the 1970s, has just negotiated a comprehensive disarmament treaty with the Soviet Union. The book describes the treaty as controversial and widely debated but ultimately ratified with appropriate U.S. Senate approval.

Despite this modest success, Lyman's Gallup public approval rating is a mere 29 percent. The president's approval rating is further hampered by his apparent mishandling of a major strike at missile-building plants and by low military morale due to delayed pay and benefit programs. A few opponents in the military have convinced themselves that, despite their sworn oaths of allegiance to the U.S. Constitution, they may have an even higher obligation to protect the American people and save the American way of life.

The popular, handsome, and charismatic Scott doesn't trust the Soviets. He is convinced they will cheat on the Americans and may well launch a sneak attack. "Gentleman Jim," as the general is known, sees himself as the patriot America needs to survive. He is encouraged in the pursuit of an unconstitutional ousting of the president by a few fellow generals and, as noted, by some members of Congress and the media. He deems it his prerogative and his responsibility to bend or suspend constitutional niceties to save the nation and preserve its security and capitalism.

The plot in *Seven Days* is plausible, yet bizarre. A secret base, able to control all military communications, is established fifty miles from El Paso,

Texas. The president is not informed of either the base or its mission. A national Red Alert day is planned where the president will be brought to a concealed bunker under "Mount Thunder," somewhere in the Blue Ridge Mountains. Congress will be in recess, and the vice president, Vince Gianelli, is scheduled to be in a remote Italian village.

Scott's coup d'état unravels over a riveting week in May. A top staffer at the Joint Chiefs understands Scott's antipathy to the U.S.-Soviet treaty but senses this impending coup is a clear violation of the Constitution's civilian control of the military. Joint Chiefs Staff director Colonel Martin J. Casey, a twenty-two-year Marine veteran, feels compelled to circumvent the chain of command and alert the president to what might soon happen. Fortunately, Colonel Casey has an old friend (from college basketball days) who is a top White House staffer. Their friendship (and this is often how Washington works) allows Casey to have a secret nighttime briefing session at the private quarters in the White House with the incredulous, yet attentive, President Lyman.

President Lyman calmly digests Colonel Casey's warnings. Lyman asks Casey how Scott really feels about the recently completed treaty with the Soviets: "He thinks it's a terrible mistake sir, a tragic one. [Scott] believes the Russians will cheat and make us look silly, at best, or use it as a cover for a surprise attack, some night, at worst."

Lyman questions Casey on his own views about the treaty. Casey confesses that he can't really make up his mind about it: "Some days I think it's the only way out for both sides. Other days I think we've been played for suckers." However, he adds, "I guess it's your business, yours and the Senate's. You did it, and they agreed."

Colonel Casey believes that though the military can question the treaty, they shouldn't fight it—especially after it has been ratified and approved. President Lyman is obviously pleased by Casey's understanding of our constitutional procedures.

After Casey's meeting with the president, Lyman and his advisors painstakingly connect the dots over the next few days. This involves a handful of hardball political characters. It also entails high suspense as the president and his counselors try to verify and quell the plot to take over the government the very next weekend.

Much of the detective thriller character of *Seven Days* involves the president's friends and associates spying on Scott, learning about his New York mistress, secretly penetrating the aforementioned undisclosed hidden military command base in the Southwest, meeting with a high-ranking admiral in Gibraltar to confirm Scott's plot, and related Secret

Service investigations. All of this leads to an ultimate showdown between the general and president.

General Scott lashes out at the president's support for that treaty: "We told you time and time again that the Russians would never adhere to the spirit of the treaty. And we emphasized until we were blue in the face that it was folly to sign a document which left a clear loophole . . . I must say further, Mr. President, that it borders on criminal negligence not to take some immediate action. If you persist in that path, I shall have no recourse as a patriotic American but to go to the country with the facts."

President Lyman then confronts Scott with his full discovery of the plotted coup and demands his resignation. Scott hesitates but gives in, especially when the president explains there will be no indictment, conviction, or court-martial; instead, the president will make it clear that top military officials have to accept agreed-upon policies or else step aside.

At a press conference the next day, the president confirms that there has developed a bitter and lingering opposition to the treaty among some of his highest military brass. Lyman uses the occasion to emphasize America's long-cherished history of constitutionalism, especially regarding civilian control over the military:

> I should take a moment here to explain my own concept of the civilian-military relationship under our system of government. I deeply believe, as I know the overwhelming majority of Americans do, that our military leaders—tempered by battle, matured by countless command decisions, dedicating their entire lives to the service of the nation—should always be afforded every opportunity to speak their views. In the case of the treaty, they were given that opportunity.

The president continues:

> But once the President and the Senate, as the responsible authorities, make a decision, then my fellow citizens, debate and opposition among the military must come to an end. That is the way in war: the commander solicits every possible view from his staff, but once he decides on his plan of battle, there can be no disputing it. Any other way would mean confusion, chaos and certain defeat. And so it also must be in the councils of government in Washington.

Lyman goes on to say that these top officers crossed the line by organizing efforts to prevent the implementation of the treaty. This leaves him with no choice, he claims, but to ask for Scott and his associates' resignations. The president then presents a carefully prepared list of successors.

Seven Days in May is a clear warning against undue political interference from the military and the military-industrial complex. Indeed, the novel is prefaced with the oft-quoted warning from President Eisenhower's memorable farewell address (January 17, 1961):

> In the councils of government, we must guard against the acquisition of unwarranted influence, whether sought or unsought, by the military industrial complex. The potential for the disastrous rise of misplaced power exists and will persist. We must never let the weight of this combination endanger our liberties or democratic processes.

Knebel and Bailey make a compelling case that American constitutionalism demands civilian control over the military. Yet the American Revolution is a cherished example of a civil-military uprising against the colonial parliamentary-royal authority of the 1770s. Good leaders and good governments occasionally come about because of military coups (e.g., South Korea). Millions would have loved the coup against Hitler to have succeeded in 1944.

Knebel and Bailey give us a fictional president; yet their Jordan Lyman is more believable than any other president in American fiction. He is regularly challenged in dealing with an erratic and pugnacious Russian leader, Chairman Feemerov. He is at odds with the leader of the AFL-CIO over ending strikes. He doesn't trust some of his own cabinet members, is at loggerheads with even some leading members of his own party, and is candid about being lonely and frustrated. In addition, his wife is away this week, helping oversee their daughter's having a new child. He understands the country is in a foul political mood, and that "people have seriously started looking for a superman." He was compelled, he says, to negotiate his controversial nuclear disarmament treaty because he believed that peace was his top priority and that it was needed to prevent a nuclear catastrophe.

President Lyman is, however, a good listener, and, despite his low public approval ratings, he has the necessary political temperament to deal with both his Soviet counterpart and his power-craving chairman of the Joint Chiefs of Staff. He understands, the authors explain, that he must both save the country and the U.S. Constitution from violent overthrow and keep the American people convinced that it could never happen.

When the people lose their faith in the nation, President Lyman reasons, something much graver might be lost. In his speech to the people, he asserts that the "American people do not believe that any such thought ever entered the mind of any general officer in our services since the day the country began." This is a lie—a fact to which the past six days attest.

Rather than allowing that fear to seep into the minds of the people or to take public responsibility for thwarting General Scott and his co-conspirators, Lyman prefers to obscure the true reason for their forced resignations. He doesn't do this to protect Scott but to prevent the likely firestorm of hearings on Capitol Hill that would ensue. Further, the politically astute Lyman wants to preserve the feeling among the American people that this type of military takeover would never happen here.

Lyman refuses to blackmail Scott by exposing his mistress and her tax return deductions for entertaining him. But two of Lyman's political advisors are not as gentlemanly—they warn the just-fired chairman as he leaves the White House that they might use these transgressions maliciously if Scott considers running against Lyman for president. Lincoln's fired George McClellan famously did run for president against him in 1864.

Knebel and Bailey give us a credible and authentic president. He is idealistic and pragmatic; calm, yet agitated; fatigued, yet resourceful. They humanize the office and the realities of West Wing politics, long before the TV soap opera called *The West Wing*. They are especially good at capturing White House operatives, the head of the Secret Service, and a few of the president's pals, like Georgia U.S. senator Ray Clark. They realistically highlight the paradoxical loneliness presidents endure as the people's leader at the most prestigious 1600 Pennsylvania enclave. Presidents have access to nearly everyone in the country; yet, in reality, they often have only a handful of trusted friends—and of course a loving dog. (Lyman's dog is named Trimmer. "He's a political dog—no convictions, but he's loyal to his friends," jokes the president.)

Knebel and Bailey were veteran Washington journalists. They captured the political anxieties of their time just as Sinclair Lewis's *It Can't Happen Here* captured the fear of fascism and potential constitutional subversion in the mid-1930s.

Literary purists may have too readily dismissed this underappreciated political novel as a melodramatic potboiler. True, some of its plots are hard to imagine, and the magical unraveling of this intended constitutional conspiracy comes together far too conveniently in a matter of days. But this is political storytelling—storytelling with enough authenticity to stay on the *New York Times* best-seller list for nearly a year. In 1964 it became a modestly respectable Hollywood film, with Burt Lancaster skillfully acting the role of our bad guy, General James Scott.

What these writers warn us about remains as relevant in our day as in the 1960s. There will always be political ideologues or fanatics, including some in the military, who are opposed to treaty making that might lessen the likelihood of war. There were strident critics of John Kennedy's modest 1963 arms treaty with the Soviets. President Obama was regularly castigated for his diplomacy-first and multilateral approaches to foreign policy. Presidents Lyndon Johnson and George W. Bush were widely criticized for interventionism. But the noninterventionists invited equal scorn. Knebel and Bailey are sympathetic here to the Kennedy style and to the Eisenhower "military-industrial complex" injunction. Knebel and Bailey anticipated the heated debates about the Obama Doctrine and its criticism from the Cheneys and Donald Trump, among others.[45]

Private military contractors play a major role in the conduct of military operations and play an especially important role in the politics of military budget making. It's not implausible that the future threat of a coup might come from private contractors as from the Pentagon. Fantasy scenarios along these lines have already been scripted.

Seven Days makes its readers consider multiple enemies. First, there are the Communists. Second, there is the concern for the zealot patriot who feels "called" to take over as a savior figure "on horseback." Third, and this is a theme the *Seven Days* movie suggests more than the novel: the enemy may be the nuclear age itself, and all the fear, angst, paranoia, and anxieties such an age guarantees. The Hollywood box office hit *Dr. Strangelove* (1964) evoked similar concerns.

Seven Days in May remains a chilling reminder of the fragility of constitutionalism. It was an effective consciousness-raising novel with a happy ending, along with a heavy—perhaps too heavy—dose of feel-good patriotism. Colonel Casey is promoted to brigadier general and assigned to the White House as the president's Marine aide.

Seven Days gives us a believable and quietly heroic president of the United States. It succeeds, as mentioned, in giving us a realistic sense of the challenges presidents face. And it highlights the need for presidents who have character, patience, and a mature social and political temperament.

This novel is scary in a positive way. It forces readers to appreciate the value of constitutionalism in the age of nuclear weapons. It ends happily. A major constitutional crisis is averted—just in the nick of time.

If Knebel and Bailey give us a happy ending, it is also something of a sappy, civics-book ending. Their president thwarts a military coup, fires four generals, settles a major labor strike, forces the Russian leader to abide by their treaty, and promotes a new energetic team to lead the Pentagon (and perhaps goes on to win reelection—but we are not told that).

Their national Spider-Man fictional hero also reassures his fellow citizens that America's constitutionalism is strong and secure. He outright denies the rumors and whispers that his generals were plotting an overthrow of the American government. "Put aside your fears," he says. "Do not listen to the whispers, for they are wrong."

> This is a republic managed by a President freely elected by all the people. Sometimes the President has been a military man. Sometimes he has been a civilian. It matters not from what profession he may come from; once he is elected, he must assume full responsibility under the Constitution, for the foreign relations and the defense of the United States. He may make mistakes, his decisions may be popular or unpopular, but so long as he remains in office, he may not avoid the responsibility for decision. And it must follow that once he has made a decision—whether for better or for worse—members of the government which he directs must give his policies full support.

President Lyman explains that he requested General Scott's resignation not because of his opposition to the disarmament treaty but because he had persisted in opposing it well after the treaty had become established national policy.

Lyman also feels compelled to defend America's strength and exceptionalism:

> I would close with one final observation. There has been abroad in this land, in recent months, a whisper that we have somehow lost our greatness; that we do not have the strength to win—without war—the struggle for liberty throughout the world; that we do not have the fortitude to face, without either surrender or blind violence, the present challenge of men who would use tools as old as tyranny itself to make the future theirs.
>
> I say to you today that thin whisper is a vile slander—a slander on America, on its people, on the institutions which we hold dear and which in turn sustain us. Our country is strong—strong enough to be a peacemaker. It is proud—proud enough to be patient. We love our good life—love it enough to die for it if need be, or to forgo some of its benefits to help others less fortunate come closer to achieving it.

Knebel and Bailey, who doubtless had heard more than their fair share of rhetorical White House speechifying, have their fictional president conclude (perhaps in satirical mockery):

So, my fellow citizens, go back to this lovely day in May. Do not weep for your country. Do not listen to the whispers. We remain strong and proud, peaceful and patient, ready to sacrifice, always willing to help others who seek their way out of the long tunnels of tyranny into the bright sunshine of liberty. Good-by and God bless you all.

Knebel and Bailey remind us that the American republic is more of a political experiment than a destiny. It may be an exceptional experiment; yet it is always on probation. Nothing can be taken for granted. Leadership matters, as does a firm commitment to constitutionalism. Knebel and Bailey were committed partisans of our constitutional system and to notions of a vigorous presidency, but their novel was a warning against complacency and a reiteration of President Eisenhower's warning about being vigilant against the unchecked influence of military or industrial leaders who might endanger our precious civil liberties or democratic processes.

Their fictional possible overthrow of the U.S. government was a creation of their imaginations. But as they have their fictional president muse at the end of the novel, "with missiles and satellites and nuclear weapons, military commanders could take control of my nation by just pushing some buttons." *Seven Days* remains a powerfully instructive consciousness-raising work.

DAVID BEATS GOLIATH TEMPORARILY IN A NEW MEXICAN VILLAGE[46]

"I knew Joe Mondragón couldn't go through his entire life," says Ruby Archuleta, "without attempting one great thing." Joe Mondragón is a thirty-six-year-old ornery, fun-loving, local rogue in fictionalized "Milagro," a largely Hispanic American village somewhere near "Chamisaville" (Taos, New Mexico), nestled between the Sangre de Christo Mountains and the Río Grande.

Joe is married and has three children, four cows, three horses, ten sheep, one irrigated acre, and an acre or two of pastureland not too far away. He also inherited nearly an acre west of the highway. Obstinate and defiant, he seldom has a steady job, but he is always hustling to make a buck. "He's got such a hot head you'd think he was plucked off a chili plant instead of born natural like the rest of us," says one of his neighbors. "He's one of those little guys likes to beat the shit out of big guys," says a friend. Talented storyteller John Nichols (1940–) depicts Joe as a nonconforming maverick and fearless troublemaker—and a character impossible not to like.

Joe and his neighbors in *The Milagro Beanfield War*, have been worn down trying to earn a subsistence living on the land where the government, usually in cahoots with large landowners, "gathered up the souls of little ranchers and used them to light its cigars." He is upset by "the way permit fees [to graze cattle on Forest Service land] were always being hiked, driving himself and his kind not only batty, but also out of business." He is fed up with having to buy a license to hunt deer on land that his grandfather and his friends once owned. He also notices that a wealthy local developer seems to get special treatment from politicians and government agencies, but nobody seems to care about "little people" like him.

Joe is right. A powerful businessman, Ladd Devine the Third, has bought precious water rights and plans to develop the area—building a golf course, a ski area, and a high-end residential development called Miracle Valley. The Ladd Devine conglomerate sees their project as an opportunity to make a financial killing.

However, the plan requires constructing a dam on nearby Indian Creek. This will raise taxes for locals, who can now barely afford to make ends meet. While Devine promises the project will generate jobs and bring "progress" to the valley, locals remain skeptical, concerned their way of life, hard as it is, will become even more threatened. And as the story unfolds, Joe Mondragón—who is generally irresponsible, and the antithesis of a community leader—engages in a small act of defiance, an act akin to giving the proverbial finger to Devine and his corporate empire.

Joe kicks a water line that runs past the plot he inherited from his father. The line breaks and water flows. Instead of repairing the line, Joe decides to use the unexpected extra water. He plants milagro beans in this small half acre or so. Soon his beans are flourishing. Later, he wonders aloud about whether what he did was wrong: "Maybe I shouldn't have cut that water into that fucking beanfield after all." However, he reasons, the local water barons, real estate developers, and their allies in the state capital are all working together in a kind of conspiracy to exploit his little community. So some small form of rebellion seems justified.

Joe's gesture, however, sends a shock wave over the big-shot developers. They immediately call their friends down at the state capital—the state engineers, the state police, prominent state politicians, and the governor. (The governor is, we later learn, one of the investors in the development.) Pressure is put on the local sheriff to arrest Joe. An undercover state investigator, Kyril Montana, is hired to harass him. All kinds of schemes are hatched to intimidate Joe.

The more Joe is harassed, the more his friends and neighbors, initially skeptical and even scornful, revise their views about what he did. The locals become increasingly resentful of the developers. This does not happen quickly, however. Most people in the village are polite, cautious, and conservative. By nature, they are suspicious and afraid to take a stand. Politics is an unnatural activity for them.

But the feisty and communitarian Ruby Archuleta, who owns and operates a nearby auto body shop and plumbing business, emerges as a stalwart supporter of Joe's beanfield. Hey, she declares, "That beanfield belongs to all of us." And she begins to mobilize people.

Mobilizing Chicanó Milagro is a slow process. A friendly Anglo local lawyer, Charley Bloom, warns that it would be too expensive to fight Devine and his financial backers. Ruby remains undaunted. In a classic move seemingly from a "Local Politics 101" or a community-organizing seminar, she forms the Milagro Land and Water Protection Association and circulates a petition opposing the Indian Creek Dam. The dam, she claims, is designed to profit a few wealthy investors at the expense of the locals.

Archuleta understands the odds are stacked against her, but in the spirit of insurgency, she announces, "We will be like the Vietnamese" (a reference to the Viet Cong guerrillas who at that time were successfully defying the vastly superior-equipped U.S. military):

> If we can scare those bastards up in the canyon and down in the capital, maybe we can get a foot in the door. Because of José—and because of your [lawyer Charlie Bloom] talk in the church—I think some people will sign this petition, and once they sign the petition it will be possible to form as a group.

When the sympathetic lawyer scoffs at her aspirations, Archuleta scoffs right back: "Bullshit. If the spirit is willing I can make a revolution with a bunch of three-legged burros, or a sackful of bullfrogs." Archuleta is yet another example of the maxim that political reform is not for the easily winded.

Nichols's luminous storytelling captures the eccentric characters in this poor rural community. They may live just thirty or forty miles outside of Taos, and just an hour or two north of the capital in Santa Fe, but they live in a traditional rural setting. Surrounded by majestic mountains and plenty of land for hunting, fishing, and outdoor adventures, the community has resisted "progress." In Nichols's telling, the villagers come alive, with all their quirks, foibles, and liabilities. They are authentic and fascinating—especially when contrasted with the privileged, boring, "white bread" city folk. The urban businessmen and politicians may have the money, but, to paraphrase Thoreau, they, at least in Nichols's account, mainly live empty lives of quiet desperation.

Nichols has hilarious satirical riffs about an earnest, yet ineffective, VISTA volunteer, Herbie Goldfarb. An English graduate from CCNY, Herbie has come to do good deeds in impoverished Milagro. A pacifist and conscientious objector, he sees VISTA service as a safer alternative than risking his life serving in Vietnam. Little does he know that he will find his own "war" in Milagro—a war between the "haves" and "have-nots," between the Anglos and the "brown people," between the thugs hired to contain (or even eliminate) Joe Mondragón and the community guerrillas led by the heroic and defiant Ruby Archuleta.

It may not be a conventional war, but as the story unfolds, both sides use a variety of tactical acts of terrorism and counterterrorism. The good guys (Archuleta and the locals) are initially intimidated, but they do not back away from the fight. And the more Joe is harassed, the more they unite as a community.

Nichols's descriptions of Herbie alone are worth the price of the book. And there are at least two dozen characters who are vividly developed, including a wishy-washy, fence-sitting Sheriff Bernabé Montoya, a Smoky-the-Bear carver named Snuffy Ledoux, the crusty old Seferino Pacheco and his forever wandering pig, horse thief Shorty Wilson, Butterfly Love, and the one-armed Onofre Martínez and Milagro's barely surviving senior citizen Amarante Córdova. These locals do a lot of drinking. They know each other's strengths, weaknesses, and idiosyncrasies. They have experienced decades of hardship due especially to their increasing loss of water rights. Many of their sons joined the military and serve in Vietnam. Some of these have died. The novel takes place circa 1972–1973.

There are intraneighborhood squabbles; yet there is also a palpable sense of community, a sense of place. The characters have a certain admiration for each other, "stubborn neighbors surviving on a wing and a prayer, on bootleg liquor, on a half-dozen illegal deer a year, on a handful of overgrazed alfalfa fields." The cultural integrity of this community is an underlying theme of the novel. These people may be poor and exploited, but they have a friendship, pride, and sense of reciprocity that is quaint and admirable.

The novel's villains are vividly described and caricatured. Ladd Devine tops the list. Devine inherited large chunks of land from his father and grandfather, who over the years had successfully bought out struggling farmers and made profitable deals with the U.S. Forest Service, the Bureau of Reclamation, and the U.S. Bureau of Land Management. They cultivated the deal makers at the state capital and shrewdly invested in local banks, motels, and bars.

Devine has a retinue of lieutenants. He motivates them to retaliate against Joe Mondragón, and the retaliation gets bloody. Joe is attacked by goons as he and his friends are shooting hoops at a local elementary school playground. A bullet is fired into his house. Federal and state agents try to arrest him on trumped-up charges.

Nichols's sympathies are transparent. Devine's people are snakes and vultures. Even Devine himself, in a confessional soliloquy, wonders what it all means: "Why was it so important to keep on growing, building, expanding and absorbing and accumulating things and power and making money, and making more money on top of that. What did it all add up to?"

A key turning point in the escalating war occurs when Joe shoots old Seferino Pacheco (owner of the wandering pig). As one local explains the complicated squabble, "Seferino is dying because José Mondragón shot him yesterday after he shot José because José shot to death Seferino's sow who was eating the bean plants in José's old man's beanfield José is irrigating illegally over there on the western side of the highway." The shooting becomes the excuse state authorities have been waiting for, a reason to go after Joe and terminate his rebellion. A manhunt is launched.

Joe, after briefly hiding out, decides to turn himself in. "What am I going to be charged with?" he asks. It turns out witnesses say they saw Joe shoot in self-defense, and Pacheco, who is in fact still alive and recovering, declines to press charges. Upon hearing of his arrest, dozens of Joe's neighbors drive, in a majestically drawn, almost carnival-like scene, to the local jail to make sure law enforcement officials don't rough him up. Joe ends up being charged with a simple misdemeanor and released. Many of his friends and neighbors now sign Ruby Archuleta's petition. Even Devine's wife is sympathetic.

Ruby's petition is as simple as it is heartfelt, but it does the job:

> We, the undersigned residents of Milagro, representing the Milagro Land and Water Association . . . are opposed to the formation of the Indian Creek Conservancy District and the Indian Creek Dam, essentially because these projects are designed to profit a few wealthy landholders and investors at the expense of the poor people who are not going to be able to afford the much higher special district taxes needed to construct the dam.

The governor and allied state officials, unnerved by what is happening in Milagro, back away from Devine's project. "Those damn old-fashioned people are a real thorn," one laments. Another official explains to Devine:

> We had hoped to sneak through the conservancy district and your dam, Ladd, without much hoopla. We underestimated the people's ability to comprehend the complexities and to react against what none of them actually understands, other than instinctively, to this day. I think it would have gone smoothly if not for that beanfield, which was their stroke of luck, or apparently their rallying point.

The governor now concludes that the dam should be postponed, lest the Milagro situation ignite protests in other communities. "I'm not the kind of man who throws an investment out the window," he says. "But at the same time I'm not the kind of man who cuts off his nose to spite his own face either. I fold when I'm not holding a winning hand, and wait for better cards." So the locals have won, at least temporarily.

The Milagro Beanfield War celebrates the local Davids who successfully defy the powerful Goliaths of the corporate world and in the state capital. It also celebrates cultural identity and ethnic cultural integrity. The novel dramatizes the way Act III politicians and governments are willing to collude with the wealthy and too often neglect those who struggle just to get by.

Nichols's rich descriptions of fictional Milagro were inspired by his own experience in Taos, New Mexico. Moving to Taos in 1969, he worked as a journalist and volunteered with a local alliance of irrigation-ditch farmers, trying to challenge a large dam that had been proposed for the region. He met dozens of characters like Joe, Ruby Archuleta, and Seferino Pacheco in and around Taos. He was a keen and sympathetic observer. And he was deeply moved by visiting towns like Costilla in Northern New Mexico that had all but died because their water rights had been bought out and transferred to privileged outsiders. All of his characters, he says, are imaginary composites of people Nichols had encountered. The feisty Act II Archuleta may remind readers of César Chávez, who organized Latino farm workers first in California and then nationwide. Chávez had both successes and failures but became the charismatic face of an important struggle for workers' rights.[47]

In an afterword, published in 1994, twenty years later, Nichols reports that he was decidedly agnostic, anti–Vietnam War, and leftish when he wrote *Milagro*. Between 1965 and 1972, he says, he wrote six very bad "radical" novels that never saw the light of day. For this book to succeed, he realized, he had to make it more readable and include more humor. "I bent over backwards to be humorous as well as politically correct," says Nichols.

He succeeded. *The Milagro Beanfield War* became a cult favorite, and several years later, in 1988, a modestly enjoyable, though financially unsuccessful, film directed by Robert Redford (mostly filmed in the beautiful small town of Truchas, a half-hour south of Taos). Literary critics fault the novel for a certain amount of purple prose and gratuitous swearing, but few can resist Nichols's irreverent, affectionate, and funny storytelling ability and his "thick descriptions" of life, culture, and politics in a small rural community.

Nichols is pretty fluent in Spanish. His comprehension of the Hispanic culture of small-town New Mexican villages is remarkable for a Yankee outsider. He may portray many Milagro citizens as a bit crazy, but readers grow fond of his eccentric villagers. Readers who want an insider fictional narrative about life in a Hispanic American or Chicanó village can supplement Nichols by reading Rudolfo Anaya's evocative *Bless Me, Ultima* (1972).

Anaya gives us a coming-of-age story about Antonio Juan Marez y Luna. Young Tony sees killings, gang fights, and the cultural tensions between relatives who are devout Catholics and those who are skeptics, between relatives who are restless cowboys and more reserved farmers. His parents share different values.

Antonio, like Huck Finn and Tom Joad, searches for what it is to become a man, to become a good person and to understand the human condition. His biggest and most prized mentor is not from his Catholic church, or from his school or his family. She is an older woman named Ultima who accidentally comes to live with his family.

Ultima calls herself a "curander," a healer who collects herbs and roots in the countryside and relies on a trusted owl to help her engage in pagan-inspired healing practices. In a larger sense, Ultima is a communitarian, a seeker of beauty, harmony, and goodness.

She is a mix of Steinbeck's Ma Joad and Nichols's Ruby Archuleta. Ultima is an optimist and positivist. She holds that "good is always stronger than evil. Always remember that Antonio. The smallest bit of good can stand against all the powers of evil in the world and it will emerge triumphant."[48]

Ultima is the healer every community yearns for: "My work was to do good . . . I was to heal the sick and show them the path to goodness." She teaches that the tragic aspects of life can be overcome by a magical strength that resides in the human heart and that understanding life ultimately means having sympathy for other people.

Anaya's novel has its gothic and sentimental moments, but its heartfelt message is a storybook blessing for communities everywhere and is summed up as Ultima is dying and young Antonio asks for her blessing. She places her hand on his forehead and her last words are "I bless you in the name of all that is good and strong and beautiful. . . . Always have the strength to live. Love life, and if despair enters your heart, look for me in the evenings. When the wind is gentle and the owl sings in the hills."

Every community needs its Ultimas, its Ruby Archuletas, its Ma Joads, its Ida Wilburs, its Harriet Beecher Stowes, its Helen Hunt Jacksons, and its Toni Morrisons. Novelist Frank Water's *People of the Valley* (1941) gives us yet another memorably strong woman in his Marie del Valle.

Back to *Beanfield War*. A politics of resistance emerged almost by accident in little Milagro. Joe Mondragón is, as mentioned before, anything but a leader. But when Ruby Archuleta stands up and uses her entrepreneurial skills to help organize his neighbors, Joe's act of defiance, together with her political mobilizing, becomes a game-changing rallying point for the community. The village becomes the squeaky wheel that gets noticed, and together they help prevent their little town from at least this particular exploitation.

The Milagro Beanfield War is delightfully comic as well as consciousness raising. "I hope this book will continue to inspire people and make them laugh," writes Nichols in his afterword, "and if in the process it should also encourage them to overthrow the capitalist system, well, why not."

Nichols's anti–Vietnam War and anticapitalism attitude belies his Puritan and aristocratic heritage as well as his well-mannered preppy/hippie and transcendentalist temperament. He is a genial, generous, and proud descendant of William Floyd, a Declaration of Independence signer from New York. A grandfather was a noted naturalist, and his father, also a naturalist, worked as a Cold War Russian expert for the CIA. A first cousin, William Weld, was a well-regarded governor of Massachusetts and in 2016 a candidate for vice president on the Libertarian Party ticket. Nichols attended Loomis prep school in Connecticut and Hamilton College in upstate New York, where he majored in English and played varsity hockey.[49] He read voraciously.

Nichols was a middling student and somewhat of a prankish rogue in prep school. But his love of writing began in the teenage years. He drafted his first novel in secondary school and another in college. He contributed regularly to his school literary journals.

He spent part of his summer in 1957 in Taos, and in Portal, Arizona, and this had a lasting influence on him. He spent a year in Europe, where he learned Spanish and French. He returned to New York to write: "As a child I felt I had a gift [for writing], I felt like I had this gift when I wrote [two books] in my teenage years." "I was a maniac for writing."[50]

Nichols became an established writer with the publication of his novel *The Sterile Cuckoo* (New York: McKay, 1965), which became a Hollywood film. He visited a friend in Guatemala in 1964, and this radicalized him. He was repulsed by the poverty he encountered and embarrassed by how American corporations, with a bit of assistance from the U.S. government, had turned the country into a miserable American satrapy (his depiction).

He returned to New York more politicized than before and began homeschooling himself in leftist critiques of America—ranging from Charles and Mary Beard to Noam Chomsky, Ida Tarbell, Matthew Josephson, Rachel Carson, and Barry Commoner. As he matured, his inspiration was that "artists need to be activists. A writer's job is to create a defense of this globe. So let's develop a revolutionary consciousness, then take to the barricades in whatever ways we deem ourselves most effective."[51]

Nichols is proud of a later novel he wrote called *The Magic Journey*, where he denounces the rigged political and economic system of his community. He was a Bernie Sanders populist forty years before the Sanders revolution of 2016.[52] He saw this novel as an extension of Penn Warren's *All the King's Men*, Sinclair's *The Jungle*, Robert Moses's *The Power Broker*, and Roman Polanski's film *Chinatown*.

Magic Journey is more ambitious than *Beanfield*. It has more characters, more plots, and spans a forty-year period from the mid-1930s through the mid-1970s. It, like *Beanfield*, gives us a strong, crusading woman. This time it is April McQueen Delaney. She is the well-endowed, spoiled, femme fatale daughter of Chamisaville's most notorious developer. Dale Rodey McQueen is a combination of Ladd Devine and Donald Trump. Nichols has the sensuous April become a bohemian hippie and travel the world before she returns (a bit like Joseph Campbell's heroic journey returns) to her hometown to take on the forces of greed and exploitation.

April joins up with Virgil Leyba, an intrepid and indefatigable local attorney who champions the rights of the dispossessed. Leyba had served as a fighter in Emiliano Zapata's Mexican revolution and fled to New Mexico with five bullet holes. He is both hero and rogue. He is a relentless advocate for the poor and an antagonist of Chamber of Commerce "progress."

Nichols's plots become convoluted when April, "possessed by devil-inspired energies," takes on her dad: "You've run this pathetic dog-eared valley like it was your own personal satrapy. . . . You initiated projects like the Cañoncito Reservoire—knowing they would never hold water—in order to tax poor people off their land and into oblivion!" She becomes her father's greatest antagonist and, in effect, a monkey-wrencher, to use Edward Abbey's term.

Meanwhile, Virgil's brilliant son, Junior, graduates from Harvard Law School and returns home to become the chief attorney for the "bad guy" developers. He becomes his father's chief antagonist.

But alas, our hero, Virgil Leyba, never gives up: "As always, I have hope. . . . People of conscience still exist here." Virgil, as portrayed by Nichols, is the ultimate consciousness raiser. He and April put out an alternative newspaper that excoriates the local business and political machines. Together they resist those who scam the poor Hispanics and Indians.

Magic Journey is an angrier, more sarcastic, and more agitational work than *Beanfield*. Unlike *Beanfield*, it has an unhappy ending. It is an elegy that celebrates those who have the courage and stamina to champion fairness, justice, and to stand up for the voiceless and exploited. *Magic Journey* may live in the shadow of the more popular and more easily read *Milagro Beanfield War*, but it deserves to be read.

Nichols chafed at being tagged as a regional or as a Southwestern novelist. He believed *Milagro, Magic Journey*, and his other works had universal themes. A New Mexico icon, Nichols went on to write more than twenty works of fiction and nonfiction. He went through three marriages and countless health challenges but kept on writing, hiking, fishing and remained young at heart. "My curse, maybe my gift, is that I never grew up. Not even remotely. And somehow I got away with it."

Meanwhile, one should reread, or read for the first time, *Milagro* for the wondrously zesty consciousness-raising novel that it is. It may not be considered part of the American literary canon, but it has earned its place among splendid American political storytelling narratives. It reminds us of how state and local politics works, and it celebrates—as novelists Winston Churchill, Howard Fast, and Harper Lee (at least in *Mockingbird*) had done—feisty, civic idealists. It is, along with his *Magic Journey*, a classic example of full-throated consciousness raising.

One update: In late 2013 hedge fund billionaire Louis Bacon bought Northern New Mexico's Taos Ski Valley. This high-profile entrepreneur and self-proclaimed conservationist aimed to revitalize the area, upgrade the ski resort to attract competitive skiers, and, of course, make money. High on his agenda was to expand the Taos regional airport so it could welcome more elite private jets. Locals grumbled once again that this could involve increased taxes on them most to profit the well-to-do. Others were more optimistic about the already very rich Bacon. Nichols told me he didn't share that optimism and criticized a monstrosity of a hotel that Bacon's interests had erected.

Nichols, as noted, is a descendant of early American founders. He enjoyed all the benefits of upper-middle-class America. Yet he became a populist critic of the American experiment. Still, a close reading of his writings reveals he believed in the American creed of liberty and justice for all. Like his characters Ruby, April, and Virgil, he still had hope—but it is the pragmatic type of a hard-bitten realist who knows the American political experiment needs a lot more Act I and Act II citizen activists. I asked him in a conversation we had at one of his favorite Taos restaurants (in 2016) about his political faith in America. "Yes I am American and, even though my mother was French, I have always felt a debt to our country. But I also have a fucking guilt trip about the fact that America is *the* major problem in the world—we are the biggest consumers, we are doing more damage to the planet and we've been a major imperial power."[53] He allowed that he was sometimes conflicted by the passive role of being a writer; yet he believed that writing of the kind he had done—both fiction and nonfiction—was a form of spirited and creative activism.[54] Nichols was an activist in many ways and rightly notes that "whatever else you accuse me of, it can't be any lack of manic, smartass energy."

Nichols admired writers such as Steinbeck, Harper Lee, and Isabel Allende who, he believed, wrote so that people would love each other more. Writing, Nichols says, has to be more than just earning a living, it must also be about protecting the living. "And always the artist must find hope in a dark situation. That is why we write, create music, paint, or dance."[55]

John Nichols, in common with most of the talented writers discussed in this book, rejects despair, hopelessness, or resignation. One must fight, regroup, and resist.[56] Nichols encourages us to rejoice at the countless possibilities for literature and art to help carve out a different and more imaginative future.

GOLIATH BEATS DAVID IN
MISSISSIPPI SUPREME COURT POLITICS[57]

"Politics was a dirty business where the winners were not always the cleanest guys in town," reflects Krane Chemical chieftain Carl Trudeau. "One had," he adds, "to be a bit of a thug to survive." Trudeau engages in contaminated politics, hires the brightest political consultants money can buy, and, ultimately, wins.

The Appeal was John Grisham's twentieth novel. As in most of his page-turning legal thrillers, there are hapless good people and there are irredeemable bad guys. Trudeau, his corporation, and his dodgy political operatives are unmistakably the bad guys here. This is a David-and-Goliath plot.

Krane Chemical Corporation, based in New York, has been accused of toxic dumping in Cary County, Mississippi, an act alleged to have caused about seventy deaths by cancer and made for undrinkable water. Irrigation systems for the local little league team turn fields brown. The county earns the dubious nickname "Cancer County."

A local state jury had returned a damning verdict accusing Krane Chemical of depositing massive toxic chemicals into a small town's water supply. Wall Street predator Carl Trudeau immediately appeals the case to the Mississippi Supreme Court, where he is told by his consultants that he just needs one more "favorable" vote to override the local court ruling.

Twenty-eight publishers reportedly rejected Grisham's first novel. He has now written more than three dozen, most of them best sellers. Raised in Mississippi, Grisham (1955–) worked his way through a community college and eventually graduated with an accounting degree from Mississippi State University, and later earned a law degree from the University of Mississippi.

He practiced criminal law for a decade, served as a Democratic Mississippi state legislator for several years, has a passion for baseball, and has, according to his résumé, coached little league and taught Sunday school. He says he was influenced by Mark Twain, Steinbeck's *Grapes of Wrath*, and Harper Lee's *To Kill a Mockingbird*. *Appeal* is about victims, lawyers, political consultants, and the Mississippi Supreme Court. It is, Grisham says, "all about politics."

The Krane Corporation sets out to buy itself a friendly new member of the nine-person state Supreme Court. In Mississippi, as in about half the states, including Texas and West Virginia, state judges and justices are elected to lengthy terms such as eight years.[58]

Judges, or so Americans would like to believe, are not politicians in black robes. "Justice," we want to believe, "is not for sale." Judges are not supposed to have a platform or agenda, or promise to do certain things in exchange for votes or contributions. U.S. Supreme Court Chief Justice John Roberts famously claimed judges were like baseball umpires, merely applying rules they did not make themselves. Sure, he says, they play an important role, but it is a limited, and hopefully nonpolitical, one. "Nobody," Roberts said, "ever went to a ballgame to see the umpire." Grisham knows, however, that few judges are wholly disinterested in the political issues of the day and simply mete dispassionate justice uninfluenced by political ideas and the political influences that shape judicial elections.

Grisham's *Appeal* was inspired by legal proceedings in West Virginia when a coal company, Massey Energy, spent more than $3 million in 2004 to elect a "supportive" justice to the West Virginia Supreme Court. Once elected, "their" new justice, Brent Benjamin, conveniently cast the deciding vote in a three to two ruling to overturn a $50 million jury verdict against Massey.

A rival energy company appealed this decision all the way to the U.S. Supreme Court. In a controversial five to four decision in 2009 (note that this was after Grisham's novel had become a best seller; is this a case where a novel may have influenced a court ruling?), *Caperton v. Massey* held, in effect, that Justice Benjamin's failure to recuse himself created an unconstitutional "probability of bias." The majority opinion found the due process claims of the Fourteenth Amendment requiring judges to recuse themselves not only when actual bias has been demonstrated or when a judge has an economic interest in the outcome of the case but also when "extreme facts" credit a "probability of bias."

While Grisham may have borrowed some ideas from the West Virginia judicial elections and lawsuits, his own fictional case of *Baker v. Krane Chemical Corporation* invents its own locale, its own characters, and a more developed good-guys-versus-bad-guys plot.

In Grisham's narrative, millions of dollars, most of it suspiciously laundered, is spent to defeat a moderate incumbent justice, Sheila McCarthy. The Krane Corporation wants her out because it calculates that their pending appeal, if it went against them, could cost them $40 million. And her vote might be for the wrong side.

Enter the political consultants: "When our clients need help, we target a Supreme Court justice who is not particularly friendly, and we take him, or her, out of the picture," says one such briefcase-carrying mercenary. For about $8 million, Trudeau is informed, he can buy himself a Supreme Court justice. He is also told that these campaigns can get pretty bruising. "The truth, Mister Trudeau, is that you really don't want to know how the money is spent. You want to win. You want a friendly face on the Supreme Court so that when *Baker vs. Krane Chemical* is decided in 18 months, you'll be certain of the outcome. That's what you want. That's what we deliver." Trudeau, who's net worth is about $2 billion, knows a bargain when he sees one. So he signs on.

The campaign uses an invented group, "Judicial Vision," to find a white, evangelical lawyer with a clean past who has litigated on behalf of insurance companies. Ron Fisk is their man. The consultants then launch as much mudslinging to demonize the incumbent Justice McCarthy as is legally possible.

Grisham's good guys here are the plaintiffs—lawyers who represent the cancer victims of Cary County. His bad guys are conglomerate-owner Carl Trudeau and his "whatever it requires" political consultants. Grisham reveals the all-too-human flaws in his good guys, but it becomes obvious that his bad guys have zero redemptive qualities.

Trudeau and his unscrupulous consultants win their race in which well-spent money talked. Their newly elected justice implausibly never explores where all his campaign contributions came from. And even though he develops some qualms about his decisive vote in favor of Krane Chemical, he delivers the goods just as the consultants had promised.

Grisham's ingenious storytelling raises familiar questions about sleazy campaign tactics, suspicious financial contributions, and shameless attack-ad politics. It is yet another work that reinforces our now well-ingrained cynicism toward "fat cats," campaign hit men, and the imperfections in electoral politics. But equally (if not more) important, Grisham's is a stinging indictment of the way Mississippi and nearly half the states select their appellate and Supreme Court judges.

A couple of years after this novel, retired U.S. Supreme Court Justice Sandra Day O'Connor called for taking these elections off the ballot: "When you enter one of these [state] courtrooms, the last thing you want to worry about is whether the judge is more accountable to a campaign contributor or an ideological group than to the law."[59]

What O'Connor and Grisham are saying is that the judiciary, unlike legislatures and elected executives, should answer exclusively to the law and to the Constitution. Their message: Our courts must be a safe haven where every citizen, regardless of means, can receive the fairest, most unbiased hearing possible.[60]

The U.S. Supreme Court gave at least a nod in this direction when, in *Caperton v. Massey* (2009), it ruled that the Constitution requires a state judge to disqualify himself or herself when someone with a major personal stake in a case has spent considerable campaign contributions to elect a particular person to the bench. "Otherwise," the Court found, "the due-process rights of other litigants before the court would be violated."[61]

Grisham in *The Appeal*, as well as in many of his novels, is a gifted consciousness-raising storyteller. He gives us satirical caricatures of those in politics. His previous legislative and courtroom background also make him a political anthropologist in the best sense of that phrase. Grisham in *The*

Appeal entertains us at the same time as he makes us rethink the way we go about providing equal justice for all.

While *The Appeal* tells a fictional story of an imagined race for a Mississippi Supreme Court seat, Grisham is plainly making us think about the role of money in every American election. What does it mean for the "American Dream" if "it's all about money," and elections and public policies are unduly influenced by corporations and billionaires? Grisham obviously revisits the central narratives earlier raised by Steinbeck and Harper Lee—namely, that our nation's most vulnerable have to be treated with justice, and that justice should not be rationed because of money or prejudice. Note, too, that Grisham's storytelling parable preceded the soon-to-become much-debated *Citizens United v. the Federal Elections Commission* (2010).

We turn next, in chapter 5, to examining the political novelist as satirical commentator on the American political experiment. Political communities and nations have had political satire for as long as we've had politics. The one breeds the other—and, for the most part, they coexist. A healthy political system permits and even encourages robust political parody, for the best satirists invariably instruct as well as entertain us.

5

THE NOVELIST AS
POLITICAL SATIRIST

Politics and the political process fascinate people because we ask would-be leaders to help us achieve noble common purposes while simultaneously forcing them to engage in political wheeling and scheming that result in only modest progress. When politicians and our political system dash our invariably high expectations, we are disappointed, if not angry. One recourse is to laugh at politics and politicians.

Freud and others contend that satire and jokes are forms of rebelling against authority and can be a way to vent resentment at inequality or oppression and related disappointments. Among the many functions of political satire are: deriding politicians and ideologies we dislike, lampooning the gaffes and incompetence of political officials, mocking hypocrisy, exposing the abuse of power, and reminding us of some absurdities in the life of politics and politicians—especially the comic posturing, cunning, and pretensions that come with political work. American political satire can also be a caustic indictment of American phoniness; it can be a warning about what might happen if social issues (racism, inequality, paranoia, authoritarianism, statism, etc.) flourish or spread.

Political satire leaves a distinct trail that can be traced from the culture that gave us the word *polis*. The Greek comic playwright Aristophanes ridiculed Athenian political leaders and even the later-sainted Socrates to the delight of Athenian playgoers. Cervantes's *Don Quixote* reminded us that life and our aspirations are full of ambiguities and that laughing at our circumstances can be a helpful way to comprehending the human condition. Cervantes made us laugh at both would-be leaders and ourselves.

Jonathan Swift's infamous *A Modest Proposal* (1729) is perhaps the godfather of modern Western political satire. It was an effort to shame the ruling British colonial elite in Ireland, rally the dispossessed Irish Catholic poor, and mock do-gooder schemes. Swift said that since the British were essentially treating the Irish as animals, he satirizes what would happen if the British took the next natural step—namely, that poor Irish one-year-olds be used as food to solve mutual problems. Swift published his pamphlet anonymously for obvious reasons. His remains a trenchant example of political satire. George Orwell's brilliant, satirical novellas (*1984* and *Animal Farm*) about an all-powerful government and the loss of freedom are again derived from imagining, satirically, what might happen if the powers of the state kept growing.

Politics is a ceaselessly demanding and unsentimental profession. We force politicians to promote themselves, make promises, place them in hard-to-win challenging situations, and then mock them for what we assume they could or should have done.

Political satire can entertain, educate, and insult. It can be a form of political resistance. It can also be irreverent, blasphemous, and add to the culture of relentless mudslinging that is so strongly associated with partisan politics. Effective political satirists can help us make sense of the contradictions and paradoxes of the human condition; however, it may also turn us against politicians and politics in general—including desirable politics and the creative noble public official.

Political satirists can be agitators. Many effective satirists, however, are consciousness raisers. Satirists are often at their best when they expose the weakness and vanity of those in positions of authority who have lost humility.

Questioning authority and exposing hypocrisy is an age-old past-time—for novelists, playwrights, and cartoonists. In addition to Aristophanes, Cervantes, Swift, and George Orwell, noted satirists include Voltaire, Mark Twain, Thomas Nast, Will Rogers, H. L. Mencken, Hunter S. Thompson, Jon Stewart, the *Onion*, and the Paris-based magazine *Charlie Hebdo*.

Satire can be an edgy, subversive, and dangerous undertaking. Practitioners of what some have called aggressive "slingshot wit" have been banned, beaten, jailed, and, as was the tragic case of *Charlie Hebdo* Paris staffers in 2015, shot and killed.

America has, with several exceptions, tried to protect freedom for both the ideas and the jokes we hate. Public officials in the United States cannot sue for libel unless they can convincingly establish that false statements were uttered recklessly and knowingly. Governments in America, the U.S. Supreme Court has ruled, may not prohibit satire or the expression of an idea simply because society finds it offensive or disagreeable. Yet every country, including the United States, limits or regulates free speech. An example was the heated debate on the Confederate flag and Confederate memorials as unacceptable symbols.

In earlier days, America famously banned seditious speech: The U.S. Congress in 1798 passed the Alien and Sedition Acts authorizing the president to deport disruptive immigrants and punish the publication of "malicious" statements levied against government officials. Even the much-honored Abraham Lincoln had a record of bullying and perhaps even bribing members of the press.

New York City's legendary political boss, William Marcy Tweed, urged his associates to "stop them damn pictures," referring to Thomas Nast's ridiculing cartoons of him. "I don't care what the papers write about me—my constituents can't read. But damn it, they can see the pictures." The larger point here is that political satire and caricature can be both small acts of political resistance and important signaling of societal civic messages.

Satire, it may be argued, is merely a temporary therapeutic relief or venting against harsh realities or against those in power. This may often be the case, but, on occasion, satire can be a powerful medium for writers and entertainers to protest or advance political agendas. It can be an act of resistance, a conscience, and an opposition or shadow political party. At the very least it helps explain us and our imperfections to ourselves.

What follows is a political reading of seven American novels that are representative examples of American political satire:

- Hugh Henry Brackenridge, *Modern Chivalry* (1792–1815)
- Nathanael West, *A Cool Million* (1934)
- Richard Condon, *The Manchurian Candidate* (1959)
- Joseph Heller, *Catch-22* (1961)
- Gore Vidal, *Washington, D.C.* (1967)
- Hunter S. Thompson, *Fear and Loathing in Las Vegas* (1971)
- Christopher Buckley, *Supreme Courtship* (2008)

Other novelists, treated elsewhere in this book, used satire to help them expose corruption or raise our consciousness, but they are discussed separately because political satire wasn't their chief medium. Some examples of this are Mark Twain, Sinclair Lewis, Edward Abbey, John Nichols, Joe Klein, Philip Roth, and Billy Lee Brammer.

The American political satirists discussed here get us to laugh at politicians, political processes, and the tough challenges of making constitutional democracy work. Collectively, behind their political storytelling lurks the hope for better, more enlightened political leaders; for better, more enlightened citizens; and for improved political and social circumstances. There is, along with laughter and parody, a latent idealism; a belief that the American political experiment must be made to live up to at least many of the exalted aspirations implied in the idea of America.[1]

AN AMERICAN CERVANTES
SATIRIZES FRONTIER POLITICS[2]

> When they laughed upon the one [an honest deacon], they felt an inclination to promote him. But when, again, on the other hand, they saw two kegs which they knew to be replenished with a very cheering liquor, they seemed to be inclined in favor of the other [an unqualified, ignorant Scotch-Irishman]. The candidates were called upon to address the people, and the grave person mounted the stump of a tree, many of them standing round, as the place was a new clearing. His harangue was listened to by some of the older and more sedate. . . . As soon as the man of the two kegs took a stump, he was surrounded by an eager crowd. —"Friends," said he, in the native Scotch-Irish, "I'm a good dimicrat, and hates the Brattish . . . [adding a few other facts]—now all ye that's in my favor, come forit an' drenk."

H. H. Brackenridge (1748–1816) tells us that in this incident, appetite or thirst prevailed. Whiskey, in his view, decided too many elections in his western Pennsylvania. He was undoubtedly correct. Yet it wasn't only frontier yokels who used free liquor for political advantage. A few years earlier George Washington had provided 160 gallons of rum, wine, beer, and punch for 390 votes in his successful Virginia state legislative race.[3]

This was one of many caricatures of frontier democracy in the fledgling new republic. Brackenridge employs irony to mock the often anti-intellectual sentiments of his fellow frontiersmen. Brackenridge admired and even advocated political equality; yet he simultaneously warned of a mindless, ill-informed tyranny of the majority. His aim in *Modern Chivalry*, as well as in his civic career, was to educate people so they could understand the complex citizenship responsibilities that came with democratic constitutionalism.

Brackenridge's storytelling was inspired, in part, by Miguel de Cervantes Saavedra's iconic *Don Quixote (The Ingenious Gentleman Don Quixote of La Mancha)* (published in two volumes, 1605 and 1615), about a fifty-year-old Spanish knight-errant "hidalgo" who set out on a fanciful personal adventure to redress wrongs, help the people, ameliorate abuses, and rectify injustices.

Hugh Henry Brackenridge's storytelling was aimed at promoting rational and deliberative constitution democracy. In contrast to *Don Quixote*, his intent was not to tilt at windmills or assail fantasized enemies but to warn fellow citizens about demagoguery, corrupt practices, and the challenges of implementing a viable and realistic democratic republic.

His method was to combine satirical parable with reflective commentary. His Don Quixote was Captain John Farrago, a middle-aged landowner living on the American frontier who sets out to "see how things were going here and there and to observe human nature."

Henry David Thoreau later famously wrote, "I went to the woods because I wished to live deliberately, to front the essential facts of life, and see if I could not learn what it had to teach." Brackenridge went over the Appalachian Mountains in search of making a living as a young lawyer. He was neither a political philosopher nor a professional writer—but, like James Fenimore Cooper, and Thoreau and Mark Twain, who would follow, he felt compelled to observe the manners and politics of his neighbors to ascertain whether the dream of popular democracy could work.

His was one of the first novels written and published in the new republic. It was America's first notable satirical political novel, and it was one of the first extended analyses of life on the frontier. It is another example of the American thirst for books that document and try to explain us to ourselves. He said he primarily wrote for his own amusement; yet his was also a novel with a purpose. He was an ardent anti-Tory, pro–U.S. Constitution, Republican state legislator, and later a member of the Pennsylvania Supreme Court. Brackenridge's career and writings urged America to live up to its aspirations as the world's pioneering experiment in constitutional democracy. His early volumes were also probably a case of settling scores and meant to rebuke those in his legislative constituency who chose not to reelect him. His biographers say voters may have turned on him in part because he voted on at least one matter differently than he had pledged in his campaign.

Captain Farrago's Sancho Panza is a redheaded, likable Irish lad named Teague O'Regan. Teague is Farrago's valet and horseman and is described as illiterate, ignorant, witless, unscrupulous, and a rogue who is fond of "less refined forms of amusement." One of his few abilities is singing a fine Irish song. Yet despite, or perhaps because of, his ignorance, he has a cocky self-assuredness that emboldens him to aspire to all types of positions. Indeed, O'Regan is clownishly portrayed as constantly putting himself forward to assume jobs for which he is unqualified. They include teacher, legislator, actor, minister, revenue collector, Indian-treaty negotiator, and husband.

His boss and mentor, Farrago, tries to develop Teague's skills and manners and "to indoctrinate him in a knowledge of politics," to little avail. Farrago spends most of his time trying to prevent O'Regan from accepting various invitations to fiasco. At one point the exasperated captain exclaims, "Will absurdities never cease?"

Chivalry is packed with caustic parables. One treats corrupt Indian-treaty scams. Another offers Swiftian satirical dialogue about expanding voter rights to animals. In yet another, Teague O'Regan seeks a federal commission and is appointed by the U.S. president as a tax collector in western Pennsylvania. Unfortunately for Teague, the Whiskey Rebellion was in its most exuberant phase. Whiskey was the region's most cherished product, a main medium of exchange, and, as indicated earlier, a regular lubricant in the political practices of the day. These western farmers regularly turned their wheat and corn crops into commercially valuable whiskey. Locals on their frontier viewed the Alexander Hamilton–inspired excise tax on whiskey the same way Bostonians in the 1770s had viewed the English import tax on tea. So the hapless O'Regan, who tries to enforce the tax on his whiskey-loving neighbors, is tarred and feathered and barely escapes an inglorious exile in the wilderness. Ironically, Brackenridge himself tried to mediate between the anti–whiskey tax crowd and the feds. He wound up alienating both sides and was briefly considered treasonous by the "invading" Hamiltonian troops who had been sent to the region. Washington and Hamilton, it turned out, had little patience for frontier people who disliked their policies. The Whiskey Rebellion was never a violent rebellion, but the rebels were considered by Washington and his allies to be part of the growing "Democratic-Republican" local societies dedicated to promoting the republican ideals of the American Revolution.

Washington, in this instance, called up 12,500 troops and personally marched, along with Hamilton, into western Pennsylvania. It was an overreaction; yet Hamilton had convinced Washington that this rebellion could lead to secession and had to be decisively put out. This "invasion" apparently made Brackenridge even more of a Democratic-Republican opposed to the Federalist ideology and actions of Washington and Hamilton. He shared his Princeton classmate James Madison's view of factions and their reality in politics. Class struggle was part of human nature.

Political divisions will always exist, said the Captain. It is inseparable from the nature of a community. And it is not in the nature of things that power can be long on one side. *The duration depends upon the judgment of using it.* The people will revolt from themselves when they find they have done wrong, and that side which was now the weakest will become the strongest.

Brackenridge was uncommonly well educated. He graduated from Princeton in 1771. He completed graduate studies in theology and later "read law" under a noted attorney in Annapolis. He was an erudite lover of Latin, Greek, and the classics. Yet he was a dedicated small *d* democrat. He believed in the reality and the idealism of political equality. He won election to the Pennsylvania state assembly in 1786 but failed to win reelection a year later. His lament about this is reflected in the following parody of anti-intellectualism.

"They report of me that I am a scholar! It is a malicious fabrication. I can prove it false. It is a groundless insinuation," laments Brackenridge's fictional candidate in public office.

What a wicked world is this in which we live. I a scholar! I am a son of a whore, if I ever opened a book in my life. O! The calumny; the malice of the report. All to destroy my election. Were you not seen carrying books said a neighbor?

Aye, said the distressed man; two books that a student had borrowed from a clergyman. But did I look into them? Did any man see me open the books? . . . I am innocent of letters as the child unborn. I am an illiterate man, God be praised, and free from the sin of learning, or any wicked art as I hope to be saved . . . is there no protection from slander, and bad report? God help me! Here I am, an honest republican; a good citizen, and yet it is reported of me, that I read books.

This sarcastic riff against the learned and competent is part of Brackenridge's larger campaign of encouraging rationality, balance, legal reasoning, and deliberative republican virtues.

Brackenridge's own political views are regularly expressed in the observations of his fictional Farrago. Brackenridge's format was satirical short stories in the tradition of Lucian, Swift, and Cervantes followed by "Observation" and "Conclusion" chapters that were more explicitly authorial. This method of formatting chapters probably inspired Dos Passos's "The Camera Eye" and Steinbeck's reflective "interchapters."

Elsewhere Brackenridge urges the selection of leaders who have judgment, fortitude, and modesty. He rails against demagogues and encourages voters to elect well-informed, judicious public officials. Still, people need to be vigilant about prominent leaders: "It is a truth in nature, and a maxim in philosophy; that from whence our greatest good springs, our greatest evils arise."

He believed in democracy and opposed the property ownership qualification. He was opposed to government by the few; yet he yearned, as most people do, for honesty, intelligence, good sense, and competence. In voting he was a conservative or realistic democrat. Here is an example of his realism:

> A democracy is beyond all question the freest government: because under this, every man is equally protected by the laws, and has equally a voice in making them. But I do not say an equal voice; because some men have stronger lungs than others, and can express more forcibly their opinions of public affairs. Others, though they may not speak very loud, have a faculty of saying more in a short time; and even in the case of others, who speak little or none at all, yet what they say contains good sense, comes with greater weight so that all things considered, every citizen, has not, in this sense of the word, an equal voice. But the right being equal, what great harm if it is unequally exercised? Is it necessary that every man should become a statesman? No more than that every man should become a poet or a painter.

Brackenridge is at his best when he both describes and satirizes the practice of democracy in his rural region. He witnessed too many examples of unqualified people either running for public office or being appointed to public positions. He saw demagogues of various persuasions. He saw, from a distance, the excesses of Hamiltonism and Jeffersonism. "America was engaged in a great and noble experiment," writes Vernon Parrington, and the "success of that experiment depended upon an honest and intelligent electorate; it must not be brought to failure by demagogues through the incapacitation of the voter."[4]

Brackenridge never discusses women or black suffrage. There is virtually no discussion of slavery. Further, his derisive humor, often at the expense of Teague O'Regan, could be read as prejudicial; yet Brackenridge says he himself was half-Irish and celebrated that the Irish people, if not the government of Ireland, supported the great cause of the American Revolution. He meant no disrespect to the Irish or to Ireland, or so he said.

John Dos Passos was a fan of *Modern Chivalry* and would write later that it had "a scorching sense of humor."[5] Literary historian Alexander Cowie writes that Brackenridge's wit and wisdom were aimed at the educated intelligentsia more than at average citizens (though it apparently was popular among readers on the frontier): "It is the font of one of the ripest minds of the country," Cowie writes. "It is an aristocrat among books. Brackenridge's embraced the welfare of the commoner convictions, but his art could not stoop to the level of mass appeal, try as he could."[6]

Brackenridge aimed high. He mixed lampooning tales with classical references and citations from Plato, Plutarch, Horace, and Milton. He quotes at length in Latin, and regularly cites or invents maxims for thoughtful civic life. He also breaks into poetic verse—sometimes several pages in length to illuminate a theme.

Chivalry is engaging but challenging. Still, it is a splendid description of manners and political intrigue in the early days of the republic. His book was "unapproached by any other," writes Carl Van Doren. "Races, elections, rural conjurors, pseudo-scientists, inns, duels, and challenges, treaties and Indians, the American Philosophical Society, the Society of Cincinnati, hedge parsons, brothels, colleges, Congress, Quakers, lawyers, theaters, law courts, Presidential levees, dancing masters, excise offices, tar and feathers, insurrections: all these are displayed in the first part of the book with verisimilitude and spirit."[7]

Brackenridge's portrait of America is a welcome antidote to the library of hero-centric tributes to the nation's founding fathers. He captures candid scenes of rural citizens and communities, people who were often at odds with the newly centralized government and often impatient with the rule of law and the apparatus of impartial electoral and judicial procedures. Brackenridge was a lawyer, legislator, party activist, and judge very much in the middle of the founding generation. His location and ideology put him at the outskirts, embedded in frontier politics rather than in the central cities of New York, Philadelphia, and Washington, D.C., where national leadership developments were taking place. This makes his stories and storytelling all the more valuable as political life in the "big cities" has been more thoroughly documented.

Brackenridge warned against the temptation in a popular sovereignty to elect overly ambitious, unqualified, and unseemly people to positions of public trust. "A stout and unrepentant democrat, he was no visionary to shut his eyes to the unpleasant facts lest they disturb his faith," writes American lit scholar Vernon Parrington. As Brackenridge "considered the turbulent confusions of an America in rough process of democratization, he saw the evils as clearly as the hope, and it amused him to satirize those evils after the manner of Don Quixote."[8]

Brackenridge's fictionalized *Chivalry* was used to attack, at least in delightfully colloquial and caustic art, the rise of demagogues, simplistic ideologies, and ambition merely for selfish ends. He lays bare some of the darker sides of backwoods "coonskin cap democracy." He succeeds at making us laugh at some of our political practices and, in the tradition of Cervantes, at ourselves. He also artfully makes fun of himself and his often wordy and rambling style. But in a larger sense, Brackenridge was one of the first American popular fiction writers who used fiction to help us not only understand ourselves but also imagine a more resilient American constitutional republic.

This book is seldom read or even cited today. It did not become an American *Don Quixote*. It is remembered nowadays, if at all, as one of the nation's first major novels and as an initial standard setter in American political satirical fiction. It did, however, influence American fiction writers in the next few generations, including Cooper and Twain, and later Dos Passos, Lewis, and Steinbeck.

ON DREAMY EXCEPTIONALISM
AND COUNTERFEIT LEADERSHIP[9]

"This is the land of opportunity and the world is an oyster . . . that but waits for hands to open it. Bare hands are best," advises Nathan Whipple to a Vermont teenager.

Yes, "America is the land of opportunity. She takes care of the honest and industrious and never fails them. This is not opinion," he says earnestly—it is faith. "On the day that America stops believing it, on that day will America be lost."

Nathan "Shagpoke" Whipple is Nathanael West's fictionalized former one-term U.S. president who voluntarily retires to Ottsville, Vermont, and to the modest life of a small-town banker. Like his real-life Vermont counterpart, Calvin Coolidge, Whipple preaches the then fashionable bromides made famous in Horatio Alger Jr.'s "success" novels written for juveniles.[10] All it takes is honesty, hard work, and a few breaks. Success is yours so long as you really want it.

Success maxims were embedded in the American Way. Alger had trumpeted them. The hard work from "rags to respectability" platitudes seemed confirmed by the affluence of the Roaring Twenties. "In the glow of the twenties," West biographer Jay Martin writes, "businessmen rode a wave of confidence, made of high tariffs, decreases in tax on upper-bracket incomes, easy corporation regulations, and a favorable share of international markets."[11]

Moreover, President Coolidge in the 1920s famously boasted that the "the business of America is business" and declared, "the man who builds a factory builds a temple—and the man who works there worships there." Coolidge also said "what we need is thrift and industry." The problem for West was that by 1932 and 1933 his father and millions of Americans could not find temples in which to work; for them no jobs were to be had.

Had this optimistic Americana been oversold? Had a naïve belief in American exceptionalism closed people's eyes to the weaknesses of capitalism and the vulnerabilities of democratic constitutionalism? The Great Depression profoundly tested American innocence, idealism, and capitalistic ideology. For West, whose friends considered him an incurable pessimist, the optimism of Alger, Coolidge, and Rockefeller bordered on being a grotesque joke. West (1903–1940) in his third novel regards these sentiments as reductionist clichés espoused by those in power to assuage and manipulate those without it.

Whipple, early in the novel, mentors a seventeen-year-old Vermont lad named Lemuel Pitkin. Lem is a likable, earnest, "strong-spirited lad" with "an honest face." He is the son of an aging and financially ailing farm widow. Lem is all ears and gullible, as Whipple, like Coolidge, lectures that success is yours, young man, so long as you really want and strive for it. Whipple warns innocent young Lemuel:

> You will find in the world a certain few scoffers who will laugh at you and attempt to do you injury. They will tell you that John D. Rockefeller was a thief and that Henry Ford and other great men are also thieves. Do not believe them. The story of Rockefeller and of Ford is the story of every great American, and you should strive to make it your story.

Young Lem is "all in" for this American Dream; yet, as the novel unfolds, his dream, like for so many in the 1930s, becomes an American nightmare. Our hero Lem borrows money from "Shagpoke" to go to New York and earn money (hopefully his fortune), so he can come back to Vermont and pay off the mortgage on his mother's farm.

Cool Million depicts the myopia of American exceptionalism and the betrayal of the American Dream by Wall Street, "international bankers," unions, Communists, and other "alien" interests.

Much of the novel is a mocking parody of Horatio Alger and John D. Rockefeller's sentiments. Critics faulted it for its overly unsubtle caricature of Alger-esque parables. But *Cool Million* was more than that. It also, like Sinclair Lewis's *It Can't Happen Here* published a year later, burlesques a looming *Mein Kampf* moment as restless and anxious Americans lurched right and left in Depression-plagued America.

When "Shagpoke" Whipple's Rat River National Bank in Ottsville falls on hard times early in the Depression, its depositors unceremoniously force our aging statesman out of office and into prison.

Meanwhile, our poor hero Lemuel, on his way to New York, is scammed out of all his money, including Whipple's modest loan, from a thief claiming to have just been left "a cool million" by his father. West's narrator refers to Pitkin as a hero throughout the novel. He is a hero initially because he is pursuing the American Dream—and even after he loses nearly everything, he is presumably heroic in that he keeps on trying.

Thus begins Lem's trail of repeated personal setbacks. He loses an eye, his teeth, his girlfriend, and just about everything save his perseverance. Unlike Horatio Alger heroes, Lem never gets a break—and his one mentor, Whipple, turns out to be a fraud and a political monster.

West satirizes America's exaggerated optimism and contrasts it with a narrative of horrible miseries suffered by his "American boy hero," Lemuel Pitkin. Whatever malady one can imagine eventually befalls "Lem" and his equally harrowed and beleaguered girlfriend Betty Prail. They are cheated, beaten, and exploited by countless charlatans. Meanwhile, ex-president and now ex-con Whipple has soured on an American political system whose praises he previously could not stop singing.

Whipple leaves prison a broken and angry man. Soon after release, he is reunited with his young Vermont protégé. Penniless, they both stand in line at a New York City Salvation Army center, waiting to receive coffee and a doughnut. Whipple tells Lem he's considering running for political office again. His old party, he says, the Democratic Party, has become too socialistic for him. His capacious, yet vague, new vision is to form an insurgent party to represent the homeless, the unemployed, the voiceless middle class, and anyone else left behind.

> The time for a new party with old American principles was, I realized, overripe. I decided to form it; and so the National Revolutionary Party,

popularly known as "Leather Shirts," was born. The uniform of our "Storm Troops" is a coonskin cap like the one I am wearing, a deerskin shirt and a pair of moccasins. Our weapon is the squirrel rifle.

In this way Shagpoke Whipple outlines his Depression-era populism: "This is our country and we must fight to keep it so." America must become American again. He quickly enlists the much-beleaguered but ever optimistic Pitkin. He even appoints him a commander on his "general staff."

A central plank of Whipple's new party is to create jobs—jobs for everyone. Whipple rails against capitalists as well as unions. "We of the middle class are being crushed between two gigantic millstones. Capital is the upper stone and labor the lower, and between them, we suffer and die, ground out of existence."

A fired-up Whipple energizes his followers with racist, xenophobic, fascist, and inflammatory rhetoric:

> We must drive the Jewish international bankers out of Wall Street! We must destroy the Bolshevik labor unions! We must purge our country of all alien elements and ideas that now infest her . . . America for Americans! Back to the principles of Andy Jackson and Abe Lincoln!

Whipple recruits a few followers, but he and his party are quickly forced underground when their rivals, on both the right and the left, the more powerful bankers and the Communists, threaten to eradicate them.

Whipple convinces Lem to join him in his travels West, ostensibly in search of gold, but primarily in a search for Whipple's newly reframed American Dream. The ex-president recruits for his openly fascist and xenophobic crusade along his improvised "campaign trail," with surprising success in the South and West. He and his cult eventually plan a triumphant march on Chicago. "Commander" Lem becomes invested in the cause but is mysteriously assassinated as he delivers a rally speech.

Whipple seizes on Pitkin's assassination as a symbolic election-changing event to galvanize his political following. The reader is left with the impression that none other than the crusading Shagpoke may have arranged this politically convenient death. Lem was, Whipple intones, a decent and honorable and promising young American. He had set out for the big city to "make his fortune," and then had gone westward in search of a new America, but his country failed him (as it would fail Tom Joad and his family in Steinbeck's *Grapes of Wrath*). His first reward was jail, poverty his second, violence his third, and then, finally, a brutal death.

Whipple magnifies Lem's death into a *contrarian inspirational narrative*. The tragedy of Lem Pitkin, he claims, speaks volumes of the right "of every American boy to go into the world and there receive fair play, and a chance to make his fortune. Of industry and probity without being laughed at or conspired against by sophisticated aliens."

"But," Whipple roars, "he did not live or die in vain. Through his martyrdom the National Revolutionary Party triumphed: and America was thereby freed from both Communism and Industrial Capitalism alike. Through the National Revolution its people were purged of alien diseases and Americans became again Americans."

Whipple has miraculously clawed his way back into power. His political cult, animated by the image of its slain hero, holds tremendous sway from coast to coast. And he apparently wins the presidency again—though West leaves this murky. He declares a national holiday in honor of Lemuel Pitkin.

"Hail the martyrdom in The Bijou Theater!" roar Shagpoke's youthful listeners. "Hail, Lemuel Pitkin!" "All Hail, the American Boy!" Here the novel abruptly ends.

West's message is clear: Instead of realigning the country to its highest constitutional aspirations, Whipple uses his political passion and rhetorical skills to espouse racism, statism, and dictatorship. In the end he demands disciples, not citizen constituents. The much-talked-about (and, in West's narrative, laughed-about) American Dream is depicted in Lem's case as the American nightmare. We are led to believe that the dismantling of the American Dream parallels the grotesque dismantling of poor Lemuel Pitkin.

West's dyspeptic treatments of both the venerable Horatio Alger legend and his delusions of fascism disturb the peace. It agitates as well as satirizes. Some critics faulted *Cool* for being unacceptably mocking and, as noted, too unsubtle a deconstruction of Alger-esque platitudes. Little wonder this 1934 novel was largely ignored by a scared, soul-searching America. It would be a few decades before critics such as Yale University's Harold Bloom reclaimed this dark, mocking parable as a valued part of the American canon.

In fairness, Alger regularly emphasized that more than hard work and good character were required to succeed; one also needs good luck, connections, patrons, and perhaps a few breaks to "make it in America." Poor Lem Pitkin had few breaks and an evil mentor-pathon.

Million is less a novel about the life of politics than a satire about the larger ideological debates of the period. It never mentions the big-stage politicians of the day, such as Coolidge, Hoover, or FDR. Yet lurking in its subtext are ideas from a broad range of activists and dissidents such as

Eugene Debs, Huey Long, and the anti-Semitic, fascist-leaning, Michigan-based radio priest Father Charles E. Coughlin.

West writes to warn Americans of phony promises, counterfeit leaders, and simplistic ideologies. He illuminates, as a skilled satirist can, America's awkward odyssey in finding its political soul. West asks fundamental questions and challenges conventional answers: Are Americans willing to live up to promises about fairness and equal opportunities for everyone? Are we able to see through spurious political ideologies that would undermine cherished constitutional values? Are we able to resist the false, fast-talking political prophets and xenophobes who play on fear and prejudice?

> More shrewdly than most of the social prophets of his time, West saw the sudden, surprising upsurge of native Fascist movements as a genuine folk movement which had connections, however distant and indistinct, with fraternal societies, clubs, evangelical religions, patriotic symbols, and the scarcely suppressed American love of authority, tradition, and ceremony. . . . Plans of all kinds were a major form of intellectual restlessness in our history. To list the semi-fascist versions of social security is to catalogue the sometimes comic but always hopeful utopias of the day, most of which made their first appearance just before the publication of *A Cool Million*.[12]

Thus the Ku Klux Klan revived with its mantra (a bit like Whipple's) of "Native, white, protestant supremacy." Anti-Catholic, anti-Jew, anti-Black, anti-Asian, and anti-Communist groups flourished in different parts of the country—the Knights of the White Camelia and William Dudley Palley's Silver Shirt Legion, with their silver shirts no less—all spoke to themes similar to Shagpoke's National Revolutionary Party.

West's narrative was not that original, but his is another example of resorting to fiction to telegraph warnings and perspective.

Critics also fault West for his coarse anger, his slapstick and sardonic dark humor. His parodies of the racist and ethnic fears sometimes border on being less funny and even semi-racist themselves.[13]

Cool Million was, we are told, hurriedly written. West's literary fame was more earned by his *Miss Lonely Hearts* (1933) and *The Day of the Locust* (1939) than from *Cool Million*. He was also noted as a Hollywood screenwriter.

West was the son of Jewish immigrants to New York. He changed his name from Nathan Weinstein to a more Anglicized Nathanael West, as he seemed to distance himself from his Jewishness and first-generation status. He was an indifferent high school student but manipulated his way into

Brown University, where he earned a bachelor's degree in English. He was known to be somewhat of a dandy for his fancy clothes—and he apparently enjoyed the good life. One of his best friends at Brown, S. J. Perelman, married his sister and became a noted American humorist. West dedicated *A Cool Million* to Perelman.

Cool Million is playfully satirical and caustic. It offers a grim view of human nature. Aside from his protagonist hero, the novel is populated with racist, misogynistic, anti-Semitic, and greedy characters. It was written in the same agitational spirit of Sinclair Lewis's *It Can't Happen Here*, Philip Roth's *The Plot Against America*, and Steinbeck's *Grapes of Wrath*. It also has thematic aspects in common with the consciousness raising in Twain's *Gilded Age* and Robert Penn Warren's *All the King's Men*. It doubtless influenced Joseph Heller and Kurt Vonnegut, who in turn influenced Hunter S. Thompson and his satirical writing.

Leadership and power can be used for liberating and empowering purposes. But West reminds us that political power, in the hands of toxic individuals, can lead to authoritarianism and tragedy, and can subvert the promise of a viable American republic.

RIDICULING PARANOID POLITICS[14]

"I told them to build me an assassin. I wanted a killer who would obey orders from a stock in a world of killers. . . . But we have come to the end now, and it is our turn to twist tomorrow for them, because just as I am a mother before anything else, I am an American second to that, and when I take power [she has her sights on the White House] they [the Soviets] will be pulled down and ground into dirt for what they did to you and for what they did in so contemptuously underestimating me." So speaks the politically scheming and villainous Eleanor Iselin, fictional wife of a fictional prominent U.S. senator, in Richard Condon's 1959 cult novel *The Manchurian Candidate*.

She is talking to her son, Raymond Shaw. He is handsome, about thirty years old, and despises his domineering mother. He is also a Korean War army vet who, we are told, was brainwashed by the Chinese and Soviets in a brief imprisonment in a Manchurian prison camp.

Eleanor Iselin, for unexplained reasons, became a double agent with the Soviets even as she and her husband masqueraded as the fiercest anti-Communists in America. Now, we are told late in the novel, if she wins the White House, she will do everything in her power to wipe out the Soviet empire. Can we believe this power-driven, conspiring double agent? Condon's readers have their beliefs and disbeliefs tested in this novel.

Condon has so many jolts and reversals in his plot that it is hard to tell who is telling the truth and what the truth is. That's probably one of his goals. He succeeds in forcing his readers to question everything that anyone in politics says, and especially to be skeptical of simplistic and paranoid sloganeering—to be aware of brainwashing at home as well as from enemies abroad. The novel satirized Communists, anti-Communists, politicians, the media, and the shallow political culture of the period. There are a few moments of political courage, but these are dwarfed by the larger Cold War hysteria.

Condon's convoluted satirical, psychological, and political thriller offers a range of plots and subnarratives, including soldier brainwashing, romance, violence (about a dozen killings, assassinations, or suspicious suicides and disappearances), international conspiracy, dodgy presidential politics, a power-hungry Machiavellian political wife, a ranting and loathsome Joe McCarthy–style U.S. senator, traitors, counterespionage, and a heavy dose of paranoia and political intrigue.

Manchurian Candidate was a best-selling novel that has become enmeshed in American political folklore. A memorable 1962 Hollywood film version, starring Frank Sinatra and Angela Lansbury (among others) and directed and coproduced by John Frankenheimer, won acclaim as a suspenseful political thriller. The film, however, was not a box office success, and it was taken out of circulation for nearly twenty-five years after the assassination of President John F. Kennedy. Yet it has had an intriguing and deserved afterlife as a much-debated American political cult film.

Condon's novel won immediate praise as a wickedly skillful and masterfully told thriller. It was also full of hard-to-believe, fanciful tales. Some called it heavy on nonsensical plots. Others saw it as too sarcastic. Years later the novel is regarded as one of the most respected political fictional classics. The novel's title has become a mainstay in our political lexicon, though often invoked by people who haven't read the novel and are typically clueless about the real Manchurian candidate.

Manchurian was a devastating portrait of the McCarthyism of the mid-1950s and the anti-Communism of an entire generation beginning in the 1940s. Condon makes the compelling and ironic point that the fear of Communism and Soviet dictators might be used to justify and even encourage a homegrown dictatorship. In this sense his narrative is similar to that in *It Can't Happen Here* and West's *A Cool Million*.

Condon (1915–1996) spent his early years as a film publicist for a number of Hollywood studios, including Disney and United Artists. He had witnessed the intimidating House Un-American Activities Committee (HUAC) investigations of Communists or Communist sympathizers in the movie industry, which had begun in the early 1940s. In 1954, Wisconsin senator Joseph McCarthy (the nation's most famous Communist hunter) railed against American Communists and held investigative hearings aimed at exposing Communist traitors in the U.S. Army, the State Department, and elsewhere. McCarthy became the political spectacle of the 1950s and later would be consumed by alcoholism (and perhaps also by the political monster he had created).

The effect of McCarthyism on the film industry and American politics was especially significant. "Firings, fear, fanaticism" was the order of the day in Hollywood in the 1950s. Nervous movie studios "retreated, the HUAC (and McCarthy) attacked, the left was nearly destroyed as Hollywood and film—as an art—declined."[15]

Condon quit Hollywood in 1956 and began writing novels, several of which would become films. *Manchurian Candidate* was his second. He was motivated, he said, to educate people about how politicians can mislead and wrong them. It is a Cold War story of espionage and counterespionage, eventually leading to a macabre Chinese-Soviet plot to assassinate the leading candidate in the 1960 presidential election, and presumably to a White House takeover by pro-Communists agents.

The novel is also, as noted, a bitter indictment of McCarthyism and the paranoid style of American politics in the 1950s. See also the less satirical, yet related, historical fiction *Fellow Travelers: A Novel* by Thomas Mallon (New York: Pantheon, 2007).

Condon's satirical protagonists are Johnny and Eleanor Iselin, who hail from a nameless Midwestern state (such as McCarthy's Wisconsin). Johnny had been an attorney, then a judge, then governor, and eventually, in 1952, a U.S. senator. He is a fictionalized Joe McCarthy, even sharing McCarthy's alcoholism. Johnny Iselin, we are informed, was a sleazy judge known for "merchandizing" justice. He also falsified his military service record to make it look as if he were a hero.

His stepson, Raymond Shaw, loathes Senator Iselin, viewing him as a slimy political scumbag. It is not just that he is a windbag who will say anything to generate publicity. He is also mean-spirited and wholly without integrity. "I know John Yerkes Iselin to be an assassin and a blackguard since my boyhood," Shaw says. "He lives by attacking. He is the cowardly assassin in politics who strikes from the dark and evil alley of his opportunism." He is also, Shaw adds, a threat to national security.

Senator Tom Jordan, a liberal member of Iselin's own nameless political party, is just as blunt in his searing estimate of Johnny Iselin: "I feel loathing toward you and for what you have done to weaken our country and very nearly destroy our party." Jordan vows to bring impeachment charges against the unscrupulous Iselin. Jordan is the honorable counterweight to Ellie and Johnny's detestable politics: he successfully sues Ellie Iselin for defamation of character and slander. It costs her $64,000 and court costs, which Jordan proudly donates to the American Civil Liberties Union, an unsubtle hint about Condon's political views.

This brings us to Eleanor or Ellie Iselin, Senator Iselin's wife and mother of the brainwashed but Congressional Medal of Honor–winning Raymond Shaw. She dominates her son, her husband, and Condon's novel.

She is an imperious mother. "If you don't do this, Raymond," she says before he joins the army, "I will promise you on my father's grave right now that you will be very, very sorry." She engineers her husband's political career and is comically portrayed as a social and political climber. Condon suggests that she had incest with her father, eliminated her first husband, arranged a safe military officer role for her second husband in World War II, and relentlessly lusts for power (and maybe for her son as well).

Readers are told she was heartbroken when her father died and became driven by some maniacal sibling rivalry to outshine and discredit her brother, the better to stand in her father's "shoes and place and memory." This bizarre competition with her own brother somehow fuels Eleanor's craving for power. She is obsessively ambitious: "She sought power the way a superstitious man might look for a four-leaf clover. She didn't care where she found it. It would make no difference if it were growing out of a manure pit."

She and her husband have little regard for constitutional principles. "What's the Constitution among friends?" might have been their mantra. They view the electorate ignorant and necessarily subservient to their superior political agenda. They do everything they can to generate publicity for themselves, including arranging for her son, Raymond, to fraudulently receive the Medal of Honor.

Her dominated and brainwashed son rightly calls Ellie out as a political fraud. She famously replies, "I have to be a fraud. . . . And I have to be the truth, too. And a shield and the courage for all the men I have ever known." Ellie adds, "There is so much fraud in this world and it needs to be turned away with fraud, the way steel is turned with steel and the way a soft answer does not turneth away wrath."

Ellie sees herself as America's savior, which, she believes, is facing a nation-threatening Armageddon. Along the way she formed the "Loyal American Underground," which consisted of a few million "followers" all militantly committed to Senator Iselin and what he stood for. This morphs into a nationalistic superpatriotic "Ten Million Americans Mobilizing for Tomorrow," whose central mission is to win the presidential nomination for Johnny Iselin.

This ruthless Joe McCarthy–styled couple is plotting to take over their party and conspiring with the Soviets to win the White House. Fiction readers and moviegoers are regularly encouraged to suspend disbelief, but Condon may be asking too much. The extent of the bizarre here sometimes strains credibility.

Condon uses this plot to condemn McCarthyism, which in the novel is "Iselinism," and it is here that the novelist's voice emerges. He has an Iselin critic say:

> Iselinism has developed a process for compounding a lie then squaring it which is a modern miracle of dishonesty far exceeding the claims of filter cigarettes. Iselin's lies seem to have atomic motors within them, tiny reactors of such power and such complexity as to confound and baffle all with direct, and even slightly honest, turns of mind.

Ellie helps her U.S. senator husband win reelection for his second six-year term, on November 4, 1958, by the biggest plurality in their state's history.

Senator Jordan sees the Iselin supporters as a part of the country's lunatic fringe. Older Iselin supporters include followers of the demagogic and fascist-leaning Father Coughlin from the previous generation.

Ellie Iselin tries a number of ploys to thwart the opposition to her husband from the opposition wing of their party, led by Senator Jordan. She even strategically arranges for her son to marry Jordan's beautiful daughter, Jocie. This Romeo and Juliet gambit doesn't work, however. "I would spend every cent I own or could borrow to block you," Senator Jordan tells Ellie. "I have contempt for you and fear for you, but mostly I fear for this country." He tells her that he considers her husband, Johnny, merely a "low clown," "but you are the smiler who wraps the dagger in the flag and waits for your chance."

Condon is credited for creating, in his Ellie Iselin, one of American fiction's most notorious female villains. Condon's mysterious "leading" man is Ellie's phlegmatic and largely unlikable loner son Raymond. He graduated at the top of his class at the state university and wanted to become a reporter, and he worked at this until joining the army in 1950.

Raymond becomes a staff sergeant in a combat unit on the front lines in Korea. His platoon is ambushed and captured in July 1951. It is flown to a Manchurian prison camp, where his unit is brainwashed for three or four days. He is singled out for mind control experiments, which train him to kill on command when triggered by the appearance of the Queen of Diamonds in a card pack.

Condon devotes his early chapters to describing the Pavlovian methods used to condition Shaw. Americans in the mid- and late 1950s were fascinated and appalled by the fact that thousands of captured soldiers were brainwashed in some form or another. The example Condon uses here stretches our imagining of what was possible with such mind-manipulating tactics. Shaw's unit is almost magically returned to the allied front lines, and Shaw's captain, also brainwashed, wrongly credits him for saving his platoon and taking out countless North Korean soldiers at the same time.

Shaw, as noted, is recommended for the Medal of Honor. In accepting it he unwittingly becomes a fraudulent prop in patriotic celebrations of his wartime feats. His mother and politician stepfather bask in Raymond's fame and glory. He, however, is disgusted with them and their hogging of the political limelight on this occasion, and he hastily escapes to work for a New York–based newspaper columnist. He works initially as a glorified intern and researcher for this illustrious columnist. His Soviet and American handlers program him to assassinate his boss, which he does, and he immediately inherits his boss's column.

Readers get scant information about what Raymond Shaw writes in his new position as columnist. All we learn is that he disowns the politics of his stepfather, and he is far different in his politics from his parents.

A related subplot involves Raymond Shaw's army platoon leader. This fellow, Ben Marco, suffers from recurring nightmares about their Manchurian imprisonment. Shaw's brainwashers had forced him to strangle one platoon buddy and fatally shoot a second. Marco gradually remembers their improbable capture and brainwashing sessions and even vaguely recalls Shaw's killing of his platoon mates.

Marco, still in the U.S. Army, eventually reunites with Shaw in New York. He befriends the lonely Shaw and eventually confronts him about these deaths and Shaw's strange behavior. Marco secretly begins working with the FBI and CIA to investigate Shaw. He gradually unravels Shaw's "trigger" mechanism (used by his controllers) and confronts Shaw about his mysterious dark side.

"I don't know what is happening to me," Shaw admits. "They are inside my head like you said, aren't they, Ben?" Marco nods. "Can they—can they make me do anything?" Shaw asks of Marco as he tries to fathom his programmed existence. In his "fog of war" confused and controlled state, Shaw involuntarily kills Senator Tom Jordan (the leading obstacle to his stepfather's national political aspirations) and Jordan's daughter, Jocie, who had become his wife. He had earlier assassinated targeted liberals in London and Paris.

Shaw's next proposed assignment is to assassinate a 1960 presidential nominee as he gives his acceptance speech at New York's Madison Square Garden. His stepfather, Johnny Iselin, is the would-be vice presidential nominee.

Ben Marco now knows enough to at least partially reprogram Shaw and suggests last-minute changes in Shaw's assignment. Shaw is asked to stay in touch with and phone Marco. Suspense heightens, as readers are unsure of what to expect.

Shaw, disguised as a priest, climbs to an empty spotlight booth, aloft in the rafters, high above the old Madison Square Garden. He awaits the presidential nominee's acceptance speech as previously assigned by his handlers. In an unexpected turn of events, and contrary to his instructions from his handlers, he assassinates his mother and stepfather instead of the presidential nominee.

Ellie's plot had been for the party's nominee to die in the arms of her husband, who would then presumably become the nominee. He would give a melodramatic and heart-wrenching address and be nominated for president by acclamation. Next would come a November general election victory. Then, if they won the election, she would share the power and the glory and the White House.

Complicated ending: Raymond Shaw shoots himself in the booth. Marco, who gets to the scene just as the Iselins are hit, observes this suicide and says with irony, "No electric chair for our medal of honor man." Did Shaw shoot himself voluntarily? Or was this due to a suggestion or order from Marco? It is unclear.

In the Hollywood film ending of *Candidate*, Shaw blurts out, before he shoots himself, "You couldn't have stopped them. The U.S. Army couldn't have stopped them. That's why I had to do it [killing his mother and stepfather]. That's why [he tells Ben Marco] I didn't get back to you."

What motivated Condon to write this complicated novel? He needed first to make a living, and with this novel he was richly rewarded. His years in Hollywood had educated him about storytelling narrative, and *Candidate* became a humdinger of a psychological thriller—one that seemed artfully designed to become a Hollywood movie.

It is also clear, as noted, that Condon was a product of the politically damaged Hollywood and political left of the 1940s and 1950s. Joe McCarthy was a U.S. senator from 1947 to 1957. In the early 1950s, McCarthy was viewed by many, especially liberals, as perhaps the most predatory political figure in America. He had haunted Truman, the U.S. Army, the State Department, Hollywood, the media, and the universities with his anti-Communist crusade. He had a wide network of allies on the conservative right, and was also a close friend and ally of Joseph P. Kennedy. He dated two of Kennedy's daughters and was the godfather of Robert Kennedy's first child.

Until McCarthy was censored by his Senate colleagues for overreach and unsubstantiated allegations about a large number of Communists in the State Department, most major centrist politicians were intimidated by him. John F. Kennedy avoided crossing or opposing him. Eisenhower excused his public passivity on McCarthyism by allegedly telling associates that he didn't want to "get down in the gutter with that guy." Behind the scenes, however, Eisenhower quietly encouraged McCarthy's opponents.

Condon was obviously motivated to expose McCarthyism and warns, through this ridicule, how profoundly harmful wayward politicians can become. Beware not only of the Communists, he is saying, but also of manipulation originating from our own politicians. We understandably were alarmed at political brainwashing and espionage by our enemies. However, the McCarthy era reminds us of the dangers of homegrown manipulation and fearmongering.

Candidate, carefully read, is a plea to be on guard against Ellie Iselins, no matter what their party affiliation or nationality. Question anyone who becomes intoxicated with political power and especially those who wantonly diminish our civil liberties and the free expression of diverse opinions. Ask tough questions of any crusading politician; fight for the rights of individuals, writers, and even moviemakers to ask tough and probing questions about our government. Question, too, any foreign government that interferes with our domestic elections—a fear that obviously was revisited in 2016 and 2017.

One lingering question: Who is the Manchurian Candidate? Conventional thinking is that it was the brainwashed sleeper agent Raymond Shaw. "They" made him into a war hero—a fake hero, yet a carefully managed one. He was presumably programmed to be the ultimate war hero (like Eisenhower or Kennedy) who might later become a national leader and candidate for the presidency.

But Raymond Shaw was about as apolitical a person as one could imagine. He was, in his own words, "unlovable." He intensely disliked the phoniness and circus antics involved in the political process. Who would have bet on Shaw to become a political candidate? Moreover, there was no programming either in Manchuria or when he was based in New York to transform Raymond into an ambitious or skilled politician. He was, in short, an unlikely politician and candidate.

One view of Shaw is that he is a lonely and forever struggling rebel who is trying to find and reclaim himself. He was a broken, yet somewhat defiant, man seeking to grasp for the last remnants of humanity his programmers could not reach. They had turned him into a robotic drone who would kill on command; yet he knew, especially with Marco's later interventions, that something was wrong.

Maybe in the end Shaw's humanity, a humanity hitherto mostly disguised, triumphs? This is speculation and probably even more Hollywoodish than Hollywood. My Los Angeles–based colleague Michael A. Genovese, author of several works including *Politics and the Cinema: An Introduction to Political Films* (Needham Heights, MA: Ginn Press, 1986), suggests this idea.

Senator Iselin is the only major elected official in Condon's narrative. He is, after all, a former governor and a twice-elected U.S. senator. He may be a divisive and even despicable politico, but he has set his sights on being a national contender even though, as the novel ends, he has had to settle for the vice presidential nomination.

So is he the "Manchurian Candidate"? Possibly, but probably not. He was, the novel makes clear, a rather pathetic puppet controlled by his spouse—and a buffoon and alcoholic to boot. Yet he is the only overt politically viable candidate.

Still another reading contends Ellie Iselin is the real Manchurian Candidate. She was the "do whatever it takes" political force hell bent on getting to the White House. Raymond was her tool. Johnny was her puppet. But she was the ideologue and the real politician. She was cunning, tenacious, and ruthless. Although she would not assume the presidency herself, she would be the power behind the throne—just as she was the architect of Johnny's rise in the U.S. Senate and in his party.

Condon never clarifies who the Manchurian candidate is. Perhaps the "candidate" is someone who is psychologically or ideologically conditioned to seek undisputed control over society. The brainwashed Raymond, the dominated senator, and the toxic Ellie are, in my view, all possibilities.

Much depends, however, on how Condon and his readers define "candidate." Condon purposefully confuses the issue, perhaps deliberately leaving it to the reader to decide. This may have been one of his gifts. We never know from which direction a Manchurian candidate might come. It could come from a "controlled" outsider, or from the lunatic political right or left, or the disguised middle. In the end, the Manchurian candidate is not definitively linked to any of Condon's major fictional-ized characters and may instead refer to the notion of a "brainwashed" or paranoid ideologue who could become subversive to the ideals of our constitutional republic.

Ultimately Condon's *Manchurian Candidate* is a conscious-raising political novel as well as taut satire. It is one of those novels that requires a second or even third reading to unpack its multiple themes. It remains, however, a fictional masterpiece that both encourages sophisticated debate and shares alternative ways to interpret the often complicated American political experiment. I view it as satire, but it is simultaneously a conscious-ness-raising work with some distinctively dystopian elements to it.

SATIRIZING MILITARY BUREAUCRACY AND LIFE[16]

There was only one catch and that was Catch-22, which specified that a concern for one's own safety in the face of dangers that were real and immediate was the process of a rational mind. Orr was crazy and he could be grounded. All he had to do was ask; and as soon as he did, he would no longer be crazy and would have to fly more missions. Orr would be crazy to fly more missions and sane if he didn't but if he was sane he had to fly them. If he flew them he was crazy and didn't have to; but if he didn't want to he was sane and had to. Yossarian was moved very deeply by the absolute simplicity of this clause of Catch-22 and let out a respectful whistle.

"That's some catch, that Catch-22," he observed.

"It's the best catch there is," Doc Daneeka agreed.

This passage from Joseph Heller's *Catch-22* calls attention to paradoxical reasoning that entraps its victim in circular logic. Heller describes a number of absurd, no-win choices in which the desirable choice is made impossible and the rules only serve those who make the rules. In the case of the original catch-22, the commanders manipulate the definitions of sanity and insanity to their advantage. Many soldiers, like our protagonist John Yossarian, yearn to stop endangering their own lives, killing, and seeing their peers killed. However, the only way for a healthy soldier to get out of missions (besides feigning the need for hospitalization—a tactic Yossarian and his liver employ frequently) is to be declared crazy. To prove this, they must ask their superiors; the request to stop flying missions is then classified as sane or rational, necessitating that they fly more missions.

Catch-22 is a book about a lot of things, but especially about the fear of dying, not only at the hands of the enemy but also in the clumsy and uncaring hands of one's own commanders: "The enemy is anybody who's going to get you killed, no matter which side he is on." Yossarian has flown fifty-one bombing missions from his squadron's base in the fictional Pianosa Island in the Mediterranean Sea. His commander, Colonel Cathcart, keeps raising the number of combat missions his men must fly before returning home, believing that getting his men to fly more missions will get him promoted to general. The maddening circularity of catch-22, the very real fear and tragedies of combat, and senselessness of his superiors take a toll on Yossarian. These anxieties mold Yossarian into an entertaining character whose defiant personality wins reader empathy.

Part of Yossarian's appeal is his rejection of unquestioned obedience. Obedience for Yossarian must have an advantage beyond serving a greater cause or upholding his reputation in the eyes of a superior—it must have a *personal* advantage: "It doesn't make a damned bit of difference who wins the war to someone who's dead." Therefore Yossarian refuses to continue endangering his life for a colonel and country in which he is losing faith. "What is a country?" he asks. "A country is a piece of land surrounded on all sides by boundaries, usually unnatural. Englishmen are dying for England. Americans are dying for America. Germans are dying for Germany. Russians are dying for Russia. There are now fifty or sixty countries fighting in this war. Surely, so many countries can't all be worth fighting for."

Yossarian is presented as the sane mind trapped in a line of a mindless or even insane command that has little regard for his life.

Yossarian's foil in the debate between individual interest and interest of a country at war is the young bombardier, Clevinger. Clevinger is a patriotic Harvard grad who believes in justice and a greater good. He cannot understand Yossarian's irreverence toward those higher in command. He argues, "These are men entrusted with winning the war who are in a much better position than we are to decide what targets have to be bombed." While Clevinger shares some of Yossarian's frustration with the continually increasing number of required missions, he accommodates. Clevinger, according to the narrator, "was a very serious, very earnest and very conscientious dope." Yet, Yossarian concludes, he was "one of those people with lots of intelligence and no brains."

Clevinger dies in combat shortly after his arguments with Yossarian. The questions their characters raise are still very much alive: What is the appropriate level of obedience or patriotism in the midst of a country's war effort? Should an individual be willing to die for a cause and line of command they are unsure about? Heller treats Clevinger as idealistic and naïve, especially in comparison to Yossarian, who has come to prioritize his own life over the squadron's success. Could Heller's treatment of Clevinger suggest that there is a place for Yossarian's self-concerned defiance? Or is Clevinger's death a testament to the arbitrary and cold hand of war that exercises no discretion in the lives it claims? In the event, Clevinger's death sends Yossarian into a spiral of bruised bewilderment.

Heller leaves us to contemplate an enduring paradox: war can seem glorious and logical—personal sacrifice in exchange for a "greater good"—while simultaneously be maddening and illogical; countless deaths demanded by uncaring officers for minimal or ill-understood gains.

Other satirical targets of Heller's novel include the lunacies of the military mind in his own squadron. His colonels and generals are portrayed as obtuse narcissists. The list begins with Colonel Cathcart. The colonel continually raises the number of required missions, believing his squadron will be viewed as one with superior endurance and commitment and he will be promoted. Heller makes Cathcart's character loathsome, describing him as "daring in the administrative stratagems he employed to bring himself to the attention of his superiors. . . . He was handsome and unattractive, a swashbuckling, beefy, conceited man who was putting on fat and was tormented chronically by prolonged seizures of apprehension." Cathcart brandishes an expensive cigarette holder at his inferiors. In one memorable scene, Cathcart berates Yossarian for flying over his target twice and not firing the first time. He reasons, "We're trying to be perfectly objective about this. . . . It's not that I'm being sentimental or anything. I don't give a damn about the men or the airplane. It's just that it looks so lousy on the report." In the end, Cathcart manipulates the report by awarding Yossarian a medal for hitting the target the second time, a medal that Yossarian irreverently accepts, attending the award ceremony naked.

Cathcart and fellow officers are hypocrites. They are willing to do almost anything to get their picture in the *Saturday Evening Post* and win a promotion; yet they do not fly any missions themselves. At one point Cathcart plans ostentatious prayer sessions before every mission in hope of drawing attention to his squadron. Cathcart's fellow commanders find inspiration in ostentatious patriotism, designed only to please superiors in Washington. One orders that the fronts of all tents should face directly toward the Washington Monument. Another, Captain Black, requires all soldiers to recite a "Glorious Loyalty Oath" to America, including multiple recitations of the "Star-Spangled Banner" and Pledge of Allegiance. "The important thing is to keep them pledging . . . it doesn't matter whether they mean it or not. That's why they make little kids pledge allegiance even before they know what 'pledge' and 'allegiance' mean."

Catch becomes a veritable *Alice in Wonderland* world with "Dilbert" characters everywhere. Heller's squadron becomes a satirical microcosm for large bureaucracies and organizational idiocies that exist everywhere. It combines Orwellian themes with the madness of *King Lear*.

Mess officer Milo Minderbinder is another jewel in Heller's storytelling. Milo is an uncanny entrepreneur who finds the market, even if it's from the black market, for the freshest food anywhere. He is depicted as the ultimate wheeler-dealer as he trades his squadron's parachutes and medicines to barter for better produce deals. He forms his own syndicate and winds up trading with other companies he has also formed. He regularly sells his product at handsome profits to army mess halls.

Ultimately, Minderbinder is Heller's stand-in for war profiteers. He is prophetic foreshadowing of the military contractors like Blackwater and Halliburton who would reap huge profits in later wars. He buys off his supervising officers by providing them with choice food and drink. His ultimate deal is forming his own private army, which he hires out to the highest bidder. He even contracts with the Germans to strafe his own squadron—at cost plus a 6 percent profit. "What's good for the syndicate is good for the country!" "Frankly," concludes Minderbinder, "I'd like to see the government get out of war altogether and leave the whole field to private industry."

Along with expressing resentment toward war profiteers through characters such as Minderbinder, Heller is particularly bitter in depicting officers who evade responsibility. One of his enduring characters was a hapless fellow with the memorable name of Major Major, who had mistakenly been promoted to the rank of major by an IBM computer error. With confidence and capacity poorly matched for his new position, Major Major directs his assistant to schedule visitors only when he is out of his office. This ploy is symbolic of shirking responsibility, which is all too characteristic of all the officers described. Paraphrasing the famed Shakespearean line from *Twelfth Night*, Heller writes, "Some men are born mediocre, some men achieve mediocrity, and some men have mediocrity thrust upon them; with Major Major it had been all three."

Like Clevinger, Heller uses Major Major to make the reader question obedience for obedience's sake. In describing the evolution of Major's morality, Heller writes, "He was told that he should not kill, and he did not kill, until he got into the Army. Then he was told to kill, and he killed. He turned the other cheek on every occasion and always did unto others exactly as he would have had others do unto him." This, of course, satirizes the Ten Commandments, especially the "golden rule": Why treat others the way you want to be treated if there is little likelihood they will return the favor?

This question is central to Yossarian's plight. He needs *someone* to listen to him, understand his fear, show at least some compassion for his desire to return home. Yet Yossarian is surrounded by commanders who only care about their own promotion, and peers whose own disillusionment, diversions, or insanity prevent them from offering him continued companionship. Why should Yossarian give others his blind faith (others in this case could signify his peers, commanders, or country) when they display little, if any, faith in him?

Yossarian prioritizes his own well-being over the squadron's, necessitated by the reality that the leadership in his squadron has created virtually no inspiration—their actions are only concerned with how to improve their rank and reputation rather than caring for their squadron. Heller describes a social dynamic where self-interest is disguised in acts of patriotism and bravery; he makes us feel the absence of a "common cause" within the squadron.

Yossarian dutifully goes through all the channels to get sent home. He is continually rebuked. His officers, his doctor, his chaplain, and his friends are of no help. He wants his country to win the war, but he has had enough. He feels he has done his fair share. He yearns to go home. He feels trapped by mindless regulation and the unfair increase of mandatory missions. He is asked to fly forty missions, then fifty, and then seventy and ultimately eighty.

"They can do anything to us and we can't stop them."

His supervisors finally view him as a nuisance and as a threat to squadron morale. So they contrive to have him arrested when he is on leave in

Rome without a pass. He is confronted with the choice of being court-martialed or sent home. If he is sent home, however, he must agree to brag about his supervising officers—yet another catch-22. He considers doing this, but he ultimately believes that would be a betrayal of both his squadron and his conscience. So he will walk away and make his way to neutral Sweden. The novel ends before he succeeds.

But in the end Yossarian is defiant. He asserts his individualism in the face of the military machine. His anarchic AWOL break is subversive (akin to John Galt in *Atlas Shrugged*, or Tom Joad in *Grapes of Wrath*, or Edward Abbey's *Monkey Wrench Gang*). Readers cheer him on. A popular 1960s bumper sticker read, "Yossarian Lives!" Just as libertarians believe that John Galt lives and environmental activists cheer on fictional hero George Washington Hayduke.

Heller (1923–1999) grew up in Brooklyn, New York, the son of poor Russian immigrants. At twenty he was in the U.S. Army Air Corp, and at twenty-one he was a B-25 bombardier with the 488th Bombardment Squadron in the 12th Air Force stationed in Corsica. He flew sixty missions and initially felt "something glorious in it." He earned war honors and came home after the war feeling like a hero. He understood World War II was a war of necessity, not a war of choice.

He had also learned about the horrors of war. Many of the stories in *Catch-22* were inspired by his combat experiences in the Mediterranean and his occasional off-duty escapades in Cairo, Rome, and elsewhere. He had experienced the dehumanizing and senseless brutalities and the harsh realities of war. Yet, and here is the double dilemma that his book only begins to address, he simultaneously understood that evil fanaticism of Nazism was an equal, if not worse, evil than war. He understood the pacifist option was not an option in that war. Nonetheless, the characters in *Catch-22* call to our consciousness the overwhelming, appalling, and isolating effects that war can have on a soldier's psychology. It is entirely sane, not crazy, to ask, "Why should I be the one to die?" And those in combat anywhere and at any time deserve to be informed as to why they are at war—and to have officers who "have their back."

Heller came home and, thanks to the GI Bill, studied English at New York University, earning Phi Beta Kappa honors. He then studied at Columbia University and, with a Fulbright award, at Oxford University. He cites a long list of literary influences including Shakespeare, Faulkner, Eliot, Mencken, Waugh, Nabokov, and Louis-Ferdinand Céline's *Journey to the End of the Night*. *Catch-22* is noticeably influenced as well by the satire of Jonathan Swift and Lewis Carroll.[17]

Catch-22 is nowadays read as an antiwar and antimilitary novel. This is in large part because Heller himself became more questioning of war and especially the Cold War rhetoric in the 1950s. It is also because *Catch* mocks so many military leaders who try to make soldiers feel as if they are fighting for an admirable cause while they themselves are shamelessly avoiding responsibilities. Heller wrote this as a part-time writer over several years in the late 1950s. He was upset by McCarthyism and the Korean War and the beginnings of the Vietnam War. His is not an anti–World War II novel, and it is much more than a war novel. It understands the paradoxical evils of war as well as the occasional necessity for war. Its insights on questioning authority, the tolls and fears of war, obedience and reciprocal morality, make it a compelling novel about the human condition.

One effect of good satire is to exaggerate reality and to make us wonder and laugh. Heller uses similar techniques as Nathanael West and Richard Condon had used—and as Jonathan Swift and Cervantes had perfected in their classics. He uses exaggeration and grotesque comedy. Heller "found a way to confront the humbug, hypocrisy, cruelty, and sheer stupidity of our mass society," wrote Robert Brustein.[18]

Heller, writes John Aldridge, "was saying something outrageous, unforgivably outrageous, not just about the idiocy of war but about our whole way of life and the system of false values on which it is based. The horror he expressed was not confined to the battlefield or the bombing mission but permeated the entire labyrinthine structure of establishment power. It found expression in the most completely inhumane exploitation of the individual for trivial, self-serving end and the most extreme indifference to the official objectives that supposedly justified the use of power."[19]

Note that Heller's ultimate villains are not his supervisors but the larger system. It is reminiscent of Steinbeck's discussion of the tractor in the opening sections of *The Grapes of Wrath* and of Ken Kesey's rebellious Randle Patrick McMurphy who resists the manipulative and controlling Nurse Ratched in *One Flew over the Cuckoo's Nest* (New York: Viking, 1962). Kesey liked to note that his nurse character was not the villain but merely the minion of the villain. She's really just a big, old, tough ex-army nurse who is trying to do the best she can according to the rules the "Combine" has given her. Kesey's mental hospital is a bit like Heller's 256th squadron. Dehumanization is the common theme. Satire is the literary tool.

Catch-22 earned mixed reviews and modest sales when first published. It was long, repetitive, and struck many readers as more a collection of sketches than a structured, well-integrated novel. Some faulted it for its slapstick or nonsensical humor. Another likened it to a Jackson

Pollock painting. Others were put off by the rambling descriptions of Nately's whore and her angry efforts to kill Yossarian after he had told her of Nately's death.

Catch-22's female characters are presented in a crude and frustrating way—they are little more than sexual entertainment for Yossarian and his colleagues. Perhaps this is Heller's earnest portrayal of how his soldiers came to objectify women in war. If so, it was repetitious, gratuitous, and offensive, and something he later regretted.

Heller gives us forty characters and countless deceptions, frustrations, and hypocrisies. It is also preoccupied with death, the horrors and the seeming purposelessness of war.

Catch succeeds because Heller captures the existential absurdities and evils of war. He is joined in this by his friend Kurt Vonnegut, whose *Slaughterhouse Five* (New York: Random House, 1969) is a kindred novel that makes us both laugh and cry about war. Heller captured the vulnerability, formality, and self-serving character of those often thrust into leadership positions. Herman Wouk's *The Caine Mutiny* similarly captured an unhinged captain at the helm. The notorious fragging (the intentional killing of hated senior officers by their Vietnam platoons) is another example, as are some of the very human stories shared in Tim O'Brien's wonderful *The Things They Carried* (Cambridge, MA: Houghton Mifflin, 1990).

Instructors at the U.S. Air Force Academy and at other military training schools have used Heller's *Catch-22* along with *Twelve O'Clock High* as they teach future officers about the challenges of organizational leadership and the inevitable dehumanizing aspects of highly regulated life in combat zones.

Highly decorated Marine platoon leader and company commander in Vietnam, and later Democratic U.S. senator from Virginia, James Webb, says he reread *Catch-22* in a foxhole in Vietnam in 1969. This winner of two Purple Hearts and two Bronze Star medals said he devoured the book during a lull in fierce combat that sadly took the lives of many of his men: "It mattered not to me that Joseph Heller was there protesting the war in which I was fighting, and it matters not a whit to me today. In his book, from that lonely place of misery and disease, I found a soul mate who helped me face the next day and all the days and months that followed."[20]

Thirty million people died in World War II. Who can forget the Holocaust, Pearl Harbor, Omaha Beach, Dresden, Tokyo, Hiroshima, Nagasaki, and all the other scenes of horror and tragedy? War is hell. And, as Heller reminds us, war is also often full of bureaucratic contradictions and absurdities.

Heller's book became a best seller in the mid 1960s and 1970s because it resonated with the public anger at the Vietnam War and the win-at-all-costs "fog of war" mentality that guided Lyndon Johnson, Robert McNamara, and General William Westmoreland, among others. H. R. McMaster's *Dereliction of Duty* (New York: HarperCollins, 1997) and Errol Morris's prize-winning documentary *The Fog of War* speak of this unfortunate era in different ways. *Catch-22*'s themes were prophetic: they voiced the angst the nation would later feel in full force in the face of questionable foreign wars.

Presidents and generals simultaneously must love and honor their troops while asking their soldiers to die for their country. (I later discuss Robert E. Lee's soliloquy on this paradoxical trap when I treat Michael Shaara's *Killer Angels* in chapter 7.) They must motivate their troops to defend their country, to defend the values of democracy and freedom. Pericles, Horace, and other classical thinkers spoke poetically about how sweet and noble it is to die for one's country. *Dulce et decorum est pro patri mori*: Sweet and proper it is, to die for the fatherland. In World War II, Dwight Eisenhower, Omar Bradley, and George Patton dwelled on these themes of fighting for freedom, justice, and the idea of America.

But soldiers burn out. The yearn to survive, to be an individual, to be free, to go home again; this is what every soldier, at least after a while, wants. Yossarian felt trapped, abandoned, and uninspired. He had lost faith in his supervisors, and as a result he lost faith in the larger war.

Military life, as Heller makes clear, can be dehumanizing, and everyone has their breaking point. Soldiers have spouses, partners, children, and parents back home. They have their own American Dreams and at a certain point believe they have "done enough." See a similar theme in the civil war novel *Killer Angels*, discussed later.

The job of a leader, in the military as well as everywhere, is to understand people and care about their needs, hurts, and aspirations. And to set the example, Heller's *Catch* leaders flunk these tests. Heller's leaders didn't listen, didn't empathize, and seldom knew how to motivate their troops. And later, when he became a critic of the Vietnam War, Heller believed Johnson and Nixon and our generals were similarly flunking the test.

Heller doesn't give us many answers. But he raises trenchant questions about what kind of people we want to be and what kind of republic we want to live in. His is a triumphant work of satire as well as an intensely serious political work.

War and the way it is waged will always seem maddening. Young men and women undertake treacherous missions, many giving their lives in the process, for minimal or often inconclusive ends. Think Vietnam, or Afghanistan. Yet war can have its glorious moments, with soldiers sacrificing themselves for their fellow countrymen and for exalted "greater good" values. *Catch-22* captures these paradoxes. It is especially effective in explaining the way large, impersonal bureaucracies turn into agencies primarily concerned with their self-preservation. Sometimes the only way to respond, like Yossarian did, is to walk away. Heller's satire is a challenge to every political and military leader that bureaucracies must have heart, soul, sensible purposes, and leaders who listen and lead by example.

ON POLITICAL AMBITION
AND PRAGMATISM[21]

"Politically you play chess. If the polls indicate a move to the left you move to the left. A computer could anticipate your position on any subject," charges Washington journalist Peter Sanford (and probable Gore Vidal stand-in) about his former brother-in-law and now presidential aspirant Clay Overbury.

Sanford adds that Overbury is a hypocrite and opportunist who has traded in principles for cash and glory: "To be blunt, you are not what you seem. Of course most people aren't either, but between what you are and what you appear to be there is a million dollars worth of publicity trying to make us believe that you are a war hero, which you are not, a serious and thoughtful senator, which you're not, a man inspired by the best motives, which you are not."

Both Vidal and his fictional Peter Sanford are envious of the spectacular political rise of protagonist Overbury, who is a thinly disguised John F. Kennedy figure. "Envy," Vidal once noted, "is the central fact of American life." *Washington, D.C.* is a product of both Vidal's apparent envy and his rich grasp of American political realities. Vidal was also known for his quip that "every time a friend succeeds, something inside me dies a little." The reality that the Kennedys were much more successful—at least politically—than Vidal was no doubt a motivating factor in this snarky caricature.

This novel is one of the better examples of American political satire. Gore Vidal proposes no policy or procedural changes for American politics, but he brilliantly dissects the scheming, packaging, and manipulating political culture of the nation's capital.

Eugene Louis "Gore" Vidal (1925–2012) was a prolific writer. He wrote at least two-dozen novels, including the best-selling *Julian* (1964),

Burr (1973), and *Lincoln* (1984), several plays, television and movie scripts, and many nonfiction books as well. His Broadway play *The Best Man* (1960) was a hit on both stage and screen. He was a regular on television talk shows and a gifted essayist known for his irreverence and his aphorific insights in the Montaigne bon mot tradition. Among his many other aphorisms was "the untelevized life is not worth living" and "never lose an opportunity to have sex or be on television."

He was born at West Point, where his father had been an all-American athlete and returned to serve as a flying instructor and assistant football coach. His maternal grandfather, whom Vidal idolized, was U.S. senator Thomas Pryor Gore (a Democrat and isolationist from Oklahoma) who had a significant influence on Vidal. Senator Gore, who had once run for Congress in Mississippi on the Populist Party ticket, served as senator from Oklahoma from 1907 to 1937. Gore Vidal's socially prominent parents divorced when he was young, and this resulted in Vidal's living at his grandfather's elegant home in the Rock Creek Park section of Washington, D.C. He often assisted and read to his grandfather, who was blind. He also served briefly as a U.S. Senate page for his grandfather.

His early education was at elite Washington, D.C., area private schools: the Potomac School, the Landon School, Sidwell Friends School, and St. Alban's School. He was at best a mediocre student. His parents shipped him West for a year to the Los Alamos Ranch School before sending him to the even more elite Phillips Exeter prep school in New Hampshire.

Most of his prep school friends went on to the Ivy League. Vidal joined the army in 1943 and eventually became a warrant officer in the U.S. Army Air Force stationed in the Aleutian Islands. This was the setting for his first novel, written while he was still twenty. By 1945 he had moved to New York and was working for a publishing house and launching his own writing career.

Vidal spent his life in and around politics. He was tutored by his illustrious grandfather and went to schools where the children of politicians and cabinet members were classmates. He grew up learning manners and rituals at the social watering holes of the Washington elite. Later in life he would twice run for office. He won 43 percent of the vote for a congressional seat in New York in 1960 (forever bragging that he won more votes in his district than JFK, who, of course, was at the top of the ticket that year; JFK did, however, win New York State that year and the White House). He ran again in 1982, this time as a candidate for the U.S. Senate Democratic Party nomination in California. He also served from 1970 to 1972 as chairman of the People's Party, supporting Ralph

Nadar for president. In 2004 he endorsed Ohio congressman Dennis Kucinich for president.

He sometimes presented himself as a populist and indeed advocated higher taxation on the wealthy when he ran in 1982. But friends and biographers say that, both by temperament and birth, he was an aristocrat. He savored his role of being an iconoclastic gadfly. He was assertive, arrogant, narcissistic, sardonic, witty, and a larger-than-life—and sometimes out-of-control—personality. He was a tireless self-promoter and relished his role as a scold, a provocateur, and a public intellectual. He was, in addition, among America's best historical novelists, satirists, and iconoclastic ironists.

Gore Vidal's politics, like his personality, were complicated. He was proud of his relation to Jackie Kennedy (they shared a stepfather), and he claimed Jimmy Carter and Al Gore were distant cousins (which he could only loosely document). He loved being a literary celebrity but had long, public quarrels with writers and commentators such as William F. Buckley Jr. and Norman Mailer. He enjoyed social ties with the Kennedys; yet he was once unceremoniously escorted out of the White House when he apparently drank too much and became obnoxious at a state dinner. His Kennedy ties frayed, most especially with Bobby Kennedy, though he enjoyed a long friendship with Kennedy advisor and biographer Arthur M. Schlesinger Jr.

Vidal loved his country; yet he feared that too many of its political leaders were shallow and manipulating. Those who sought political power in Washington, D.C., he believed, had especially selfish and duplicitous motivations. He decried the way the American republic was turning into a less admirable empire. He was, like his grandfather, opposed to what he deemed America's overly militaristic foreign policy. Biographer Jay Parini says Vidal believed the American republic "had not lived up to his expectations, and this upset him deeply."[22]

Vidal thought of politics as an ugly profession, but he reveled in it, and it provided him with an endless supply of characters and political stories. He paradoxically viewed himself as both a patriotic conservative and a radical polemicist.

Back to the novel. Vidal has three leading figures, two of whom hunger to be president. One says, "There was no point in pursuing a career in politics if the ultimate prize was not, at least theoretically, possible."

Vidal's plot is inventive. An aging, yet venerable, senator, James Burden Day, aspires to become president. He is a white-haired, stately conservative Democrat, from somewhere in the Southwest—in other words, someone a lot like Vidal's grandfather. Senator Day, a member of the

Senate old-boys' club, is a potential candidate for the Democratic Party's 1940 presidential nomination. Day won some acclaim for successfully opposing Roosevelt's court-packing scheme in 1937, but, unfortunately for him, World War II came along and the country voted to retain FDR. Day is depicted as an old-school noble public servant who understands politics and is largely devoted to his constituency out West. But, as it turns out with many of Vidal's political actors, Day was once involved in a bribery scandal. Day was a fixture in Washington's social scene but, in return for campaign contributions, arranged a bargain sale of Indian lands in his state to an oil conglomerate, which, in exchange, pledged to back his presidential campaign.

Day's longtime administrative assistant, Clay Overbury (the *roman-à-clef* JFK figure, introduced earlier), learned the craft of politics in Day's office. Overbury loves the old man and knows the senator has mentored him and made his career possible. "I regard Senator Day as one of the finest men I have ever known, and if it hadn't been for him, I might never have got here." Nonetheless, he resigns and runs for a seat in the House of Representatives in their home state. When he wins he immediately sets his sights on running for Day's Senate seat. This would come after he gained, in his words, "appropriate experience." This doesn't take long. "But how was I to know that I'd get the maximum experience two years ahead of schedule?"

Tensions escalate. Should Day run for a seventh term? While Day ponders his decision, Overbury announces his own bid for the seat. Overbury confronts his mentor, telling Day he has evidence about the old bribery scandal and will use it, if necessary, to force Day to retire. In a heated exchange—with overtones of a Greek tragedy—Overbury tells the old man, "I thought it was absolutely impossible. There you were, the most incorruptible man in the Senate, or so I thought. That's why at first I just couldn't believe it. But then I saw how it made sense. That year was your year to go for the top. And we had to have money. And where else could you get so much so fast?" Day responds sardonically, "I'm glad you really admired me."

Day knows the sun is setting on his career. There are shades of Sophocles, Shakespeare, Melville, and Robert Penn Warren next. "He (Day) had treated Clay as a son who would, as was proper in legend, strike him down and take his place." Upended by his ambitious protégé, the senator becomes a broken man and drowns himself in the Potomac.

Overbury is young, handsome, and telegenic, with a craving for popularity and women. He is quickly embraced and funded by established publishers and behind-the-scenes political operatives. Overbury's story line, as noted, resembles John F. Kennedy's. (Somehow Vidal's narrative jumps from the 1930s to the 1950s with little transition.) Vidal's cynicism toward the Kennedys saturates his portrait of Overbury. The fictional Kennedy is depicted as a popularized, movie-star politician with little or no redeeming policy substance.

Vidal apparently loathes the new Washington, D.C., and the media politics that he believes encourages slick, telegenic opportunists. He was probably nostalgic for the Washington of his grandfather, when Congress played a more influential role. Yes, there were bribes and scandals back then too, but Vidal implies that this new Washington had become less focused on the public interest, less concerned with principles, and more about posturing and image maintenance. Television's turning of politics into a popularity contest, with focus on appearance instead of merit, is one of the villains here (a theme also suggested in Edwin O'Connor's *The Last Hurrah*).

Vidal's principled hero is journalist Peter Sanford. Sanford, presumably like Gore Vidal, sees beyond the political games being played. He accuses Overbury of being all profile and little or no courage. "There is nothing to you," laments Sanford, "other than the desire to be first." A similar charge was brought by some intellectuals against Senator John Kennedy in the 1950s, when Kennedy ducked the Joe McCarthy issue and seemed squishy on other hard-core liberal issues such as civil rights.

Vidal seldom disguises his indignation. Politics, in *Washington, D.C.*, is a sleazy, underhanded profession. In his telling, the city is a snake pit of unprincipled and ambitious political subversives. *D.C.* has much in common with Twain's *Gilded Age*, Drury's *Advise and Consent*, and later televised soap-opera treatments such as *House of Cards*—narratives that can be summed up in the aphorism that "the road to power is paved with hypocrisy and casualties."

Hemingway had been an early influence on Vidal, but *Washington, D.C.* was more influenced by Robert Penn Warren's *All the King's Men*, Henry Adams's *Democracy*, and some of Anthony Trollope's droll British political fiction. Gore's own youthful years in D.C. shaped his gossipy and cynical analysis of his hometown. Biographer Parini puts it in perspective:

> This is the new Rome, transmogrified. Gore brings to the material his experience of watching at close hand how politicians operate. He has observed his grandfather moving and shaking hands through the U.S. Senate. He has studied JFK at close quarters. Yet hardly a single character in this world is not—like Gore himself—a narcissist, in desperate

need of reflection. This cynical attitude may owe something to Gore's own failure to thrive in this atmosphere, but his resentment, combined with a satirist's eye for human foibles, generates an entertaining plot despite its failure to reach higher levels of political fiction.[23]

Vidal's satirized politicians are unsentimental and unscrupulous. They are preoccupied less with effective policymaking than with how best to position themselves for the next election.

Vidal is a caustic storyteller. He understands the narcissism, publicity-seeking, affairs, and questionable money transactions that fuel both the political and the social life in the city. He relishes introducing his readers to the adultery, alcoholism, and kindred skeletons seemingly hidden in nearly every Washington closet.

D.C. is, in some ways, a reprise of his success with *The Best Man: A Play* (1960), which examines the complicated personal lives of two "compromised" presidential aspirants. One has marital problems (his wife memorably allows that "politics makes strange bedfellows"), and this candidate suffers nervous breakdowns. The other is accused of pursuing "an imaginary Communist mafia" and of having had a homosexual affair. In the end, a third faceless light-weight gets elected, and Vidal, among many messages, leaves the disquieting impression that sometimes the "best man" is too good for politics.

Vidal characterizes politics as a cynical and bleak transactional enterprise. He is condescending toward politicians and politics, a mind-set perhaps stoked by jealousy of the Kennedy brothers, who had, at least temporarily, mastered the art of politics in the television era. Yet this view belies a pride in his grandfather's accomplishments—a hope or nostalgic reminiscence for a politics based on thoughtful policy debates and honorable transactions.

Ironically, the time in which Vidal was writing *Washington, D.C.*, the early 1960s, was a time when Americans overwhelmingly trusted the federal government to make the right decision on behalf of the public. Vidal's view was a provocative dissent to prevailing public opinion. Today's pundits and political scientists are nostalgic about the late 1950s and early 1960s, when the public trust in government was high—the very period Vidal so skillfully and scornfully satirizes.

Through his political caricatures, Vidal decries that politics from the mid-1930s through the 1950s was largely a matter of keeping track of debts. His Clay Overbury put it bluntly to a newly indebted friend: "So forget about it. Only—don't forget you're living in one of the dirtiest towns in the country, where everybody, officially and unofficially, is watching everybody else, building a case for future use." Vidal's political message: Beware of how political appetites can compromise the ambitious. The necessary drive to win morphs into single-mindedness and a cutthroat competitive spirit that undermines political civility and cooperation.

He bemoans the blackmail, bribery, and also the humiliation that often comes with the territory. Vidal, himself a political wannabe, seems especially appreciative of old Senator Day's warning to Peter Sanford: "Like it [politics], but don't practice it. Of all the lives I can think of, politics is the most . . . the most humiliating." He doesn't offer any coherent remedies, instead romanticizing the detached perspective of his probing and muckraking Peter Sanford.

Vidal wants us to understand that politicians are flawed human beings like the rest of us—perhaps even more so. He wants us to understand that his era's politicians are more easily tempted to convince themselves to compromise their previously held principles.

Vidal is terrific at lampooning the political and social swirl of Washington, D.C.'s, semi-permanent residents. But the dream of representative government requires politics and politicians. While the Peter Sanfords and Gore Vidals might have a superior grasp of what shapes the Washington merry-go-round, it is easy to scorn the grim, shadowy sleaze of Washington and to praise the untainted, detached commentators who of course transcend the scheming. The government requires elected officials to function. The unsatisfying part of the novel is his continual deprecation of politicians without acknowledging that ambition, compromise, and deal making are the indispensable oxygen of their profession, and of democracy.

This is doubtless one of the limits of political satire. Satire is at its core all about caricature, mockery, and making us laugh at people in positions of authority. Satire can be terrific at deflating pompous so-called leaders. Vidal is a master craftsman at this. Yet such criticism shouldn't take away from Vidal's provocative political satire.

The intrigue of Vidal's writing derives from his unusual status as both an insider and an outsider. He was born to the ruling class, often aspired to become an accepted member of it, but was an indefatigable outsider, jealous and indignant, yet also uncommonly perceptive. Vidal was a strong writer, a gifted political storyteller, and a shrewd, if perhaps excessively caustic, observer of the American political experiment.

VEGAS ROAD TRIP IN SEARCH OF THE DREAM[24]

"We were somewhere around Barstow on the edge of the desert when the drugs began to take hold. I remember saying something like 'I feel a bit light-headed, maybe you should drive.'" Protagonist Raoul Duke (the fictionalized stand-in for author Hunter S. Thompson [1937–2005]) assures readers that he and his sidekick attorney (Dr. Gonzo) are well supplied for their trip to Vegas:

> The trunk of the car looked like a mobile police narcotics lab. We had two bags of grass, seventy-five pellets of mescaline, five sheets of high-powered blotter acid, a salt shaker half full of cocaine, and a whole galaxy of multi-colored uppers, downers, screamers, laughers . . . and also a quart of tequila, a quart of rum, a case of Budweiser, a pint of raw ether and two dozen amyls.

Hunter Thompson's fascinating, funny, sardonic, inventive, yet often depressing *Fear and Loathing in Las Vegas* (1971) is on one level a report by a magazine reporter covering two events (a cycle race and a national conference on narcotics) in Las Vegas, Nevada. It also morphs into an often incoherent stream-of-consciousness rant about American decadence and the growing demise of the American Dream. It has become, in part, a cult classic commentary on America's era of "sex, drugs and rock 'n' roll." Its unusual fictionalized writing style—now widely called "Gonzo fiction" and "Gonzo Journalism"—made it a landmark illustration of an alternate form of writing on politics and social culture.

Hunter Thompson's trademark was his roguish Holden Caulfield and Gore Vidal irreverence. His attitude was almost always more important than his narrative. And his attitude was to satirize and prick authority, complacency, orthodoxy, and pomposity. Thompson loved being unpredictable, being an outlier, and circumnavigating rules. His writer friends included Tom Wolfe, Ken Kesey, P. J. O'Rourke, and Christopher Hitchens, though his writing includes elements of Whitman, Thoreau, West, Fitzgerald, Rand, Kerouac, and Henry Miller.

Fear and Loathing is a complicated blend of entertainment, parody, and a diatribe on the bleak cultural and political developments of the late 1960s and early 1970s.

Back to the novel.

"Can you hear me?" Raoul Duke yells to a hitchhiker he and his buddy welcome into their rented red Chevy convertible headed at high speed (literally and figuratively) for Nevada's mecca for gambling and hedonism. Their apprehensive hitchhiker nods. "That's good," said Duke. "Because I want you to know that we're on our way to Las Vegas to find the American Dream." Duke proclaims that this "savage journey to the Heart of the American Dream" is going to be a different kind of trip.

Raoul Duke mumbles that it will be a classic affirmation of everything right and true and decent in the American character. It would be a salute, he boasts, apparently sarcastically, "to the fantastic possibilities of life in this country—but only for those with true grit. And we were chock full of that."

They arrive in Las Vegas pumped up with grit, booze, and, as noted, every conceivable drug. They may be in search of America and the American Dream, but most of the book is an elongated, mostly plotless tale of their carefree, juvenile pranksterism. Duke and his attorney are condescendingly abusive to nearly everyone they meet. They mock hotel and casino employees. They mock police officers. They mock the tourists who come to Las Vegas for their escapist vacations. They mock the locals. They even mock their own boorish road-trip antics.

Duke and Gonzo briefly attend "The Mint 400"—a competitive road race for motorcycles and dune buggies. The real-life Thompson had received an assignment from *Sports Illustrated* to write some brief commentary to accompany the magazine's photographer who was there to capture this classic with his camera. But Thompson (like his fictional Duke) was bored by the event and irritated by the dust the bikers churned up. Elsewhere we learn that Thompson sent *Sports Illustrated* a far lengthier description of the event—which they rejected.

All we learn of this event in *Fear and Loathing* is that Duke and Gonzo quit the event long before it concludes and return to their hotel to attend to their own escapades.

Thompson uses literary interludes or asides to criticize the hippie, drug, and movement politics of the 1960s. He especially rails against Dr. Timothy Leary, the foremost self-designated "high" priest promoter of LSD. Thompson paints Leary as a liar and a quack whose message of "Turn on, Tune in, Drop out" was an insidious message for a generation that needed to be engaged in protest politics rather than dropping out. Thompson also faults counterculture fringe groups of the 1960s like the Manson family and the Rolling Stones's Altamont concert as examples of perverted, and misguided diversionary behaviors.

Here is Thompson's leveling of Leary:

> All those pathetically eager acid freaks who thought they could buy Peace and Understanding for three bucks a hit. But their loss and failure is ours too. What Leary took down with him was the central illusion of a whole life-style that he helped create . . . a generation of permanent cripples, failed seekers, who never understood the essential old-mystic fallacy of the Acid Culture: the desperate assumption that somebody . . . or at least some force—is tending the light at the end of the tunnel.

Thompson had been fully immersed in the California 1960s scene. He had lived for a year or so in Big Sur. He had partied with Allen Ginsberg and Ken Kesey. He had protested the war in Vietnam. He had used LSD and other psychedelic drugs. He also had famously partied and ridden with the Hells Angels motorcycle club. His first major book, the nonfiction *Hell's Angels: A Strange and Terrible Saga* (1969), chronicled his riding with these "outlaws." (In his writing, including the title of his book, Thompson added an apostrophe to the name of the motorcycle gang.)

Thompson, who was clearly a product of the 1960s counterculture, expresses nostalgia as well as a rebuke of that decade. It was an era that had liberated him and had inspired and enabled him to invent a new brand of journalism. But he also expresses how he and many in his generation had had their hopes dashed by the combined pretentious and overly optimistic expectations that emerged in the mid-1960s. He could applaud the free-speech movement, the antiwar movement, and the lifestyle freedoms that came along with drug use and experimental writing—and yet somehow he believed these experiments wasted away as Haight-Ashbury became a tourist mecca and whatever revolutionary spirit existed exhausted itself.

In the most discussed passage in *Fear and Loathing*, Thompson laments both the possibilities and the failures of the 1960s.

> Strange memories on this nervous night in Las Vegas. Five years later? Six? It seems like a lifetime, or at least a Main Era—the kind of peak that never comes again. San Francisco in the middle sixties was a very special time and place to be part of. . . .
>
> There was madness in any direction, at any hour. If not across the Bay, then up to the Golden Gate or down to Los Altos or La Honda. . . . You could strike sparks anywhere. There was a fantastic universal sense that whatever we were doing was *right*, that we were winning. . . .
>
> And that, I think, was the handle—that sense of inevitable victory over the forces of Old and Evil. . . . Our energy would simply *prevail*. There was no point in fighting—on our side or theirs. We had all the momentum, we were riding the crest of a high and beautiful wave. . . .
>
> So now, less than five years later, you can go up on to a steep hill in Las Vegas and look West, and under the right kind of eyes, you can almost see the high-water mark—that place where the wave finally broke and rolled back!

One writer likens Thompson's passage as akin to F. Scott Fitzgerald's *Gatsby* lament on the false sense of hope and possibility encouraged in America's Jazz Age. "Both Fitzgerald and Thompson, each an avowed chronicler of his respective age, believed, at one time, in the possibilities of America."[25] Each also attacked the narcissism, pretentiousness, and melancholy of his misguided generation.

Some readers interpret Thompson's Las Vegas road trip in search of the American Dream as merely a nostalgic quest to rediscover the freedom, sparks, mayhem, and "momentum" they had temporarily enjoyed in Northern California. He had loved that there had been madness, at any hour—and this romp through Vegas was perhaps both recreational and re-creational.

Duke and his partner also attempt to cover (now for *Rolling Stone* magazine) the third annual National District Attorney's Conference on Narcotics and Dangerous Drugs. This is, of course, more than ironic. Two stoned dudes wander around a convention hall full of prosecuting attorneys. They sign in and start listening to presentations and are aghast at how little the speakers know. These attorneys are, Thompson writes, at least a decade behind the times. Hey, they don't even know "mescaline from macaroni." Thompson mercilessly satirizes the district attorneys— yet, just as he had with the Mint 400 cycle races, he is bored by this magazine assignment. His attorney walks out first, announcing, "I'll be away in the casino . . . I know a hell of a lot better ways to waste my time than listening to this bullshit." Duke follows. He and his sidekick keep on overdosing on drugs and alcohol and behaving as though they were *On the Road* with Jack Kerouac and Neal Cassady or are party guests at John Belushi's *Animal House*. They also, and this is murky, are still in search of the American Dream.

Thompson makes several references to Horatio Alger novels, though he gives no evidence that he has read them. Instead, he invokes the Horatio Alger of popular legend that those who work hard and strive should be able to enjoy economic rewards, upward mobility, and the wonderful blessings of liberty.

Thompson shares one bizarre tale of how Raoul Duke and Dr. Gonzo wind up at a café in North Las Vegas. "We're looking for the American Dream," they tell the waitress, "and we were told it was somewhere in this area." They are abusive to the waitress—as they have been to most of the help in Las Vegas. When they ask about the American Dream, however, they learn that it might be nearby.

The waitress asks Lou, the café's cook, "Hey Lou, you know where the American Dream is?" Lou asks, "What's that? What is it?" Gonzo says,

"Well, we don't know, we were sent out here from San Francisco to look for the American Dream, by a magazine to cover it."

> Lou: Oh, you mean a place.
>
> Gonzo: A place called the American Dream.
>
> Lou: Is that the old Psychiatrist's Club?
>
> Waitress: I think so.
>
> Gonzo: The old Psychiatrist's Club?
>
> Lou: Old Psychiatrist's Club, it's on Paradise. . . . Are you guys serious?
>
> Gonzo: Oh, no honest, look at that car, I mean, do I look like I'd own a car like that? . . . All we were told was go till you find the American Dream. Take this white Cadillac and go find the American Dream. It's somewhere in the Las Vegas area.
>
> Lou: That has to be the old . . .
>
> Gonzo: . . . and it's a silly story to do, but you know, that's what we get paid for.
>
> Lou: Are you taking pictures of it, or . . .
>
> Gonzo: No, no—no pictures.
>
> Lou: . . . or did somebody just send you on a goose chase?
>
> Gonzo: It's sort of a wild goose chase, more or less, but personally, we're dead serious.
>
> Lou: That has to be the old Psychiatrist's Club, but the only people who hang out there is a bunch of pushers, peddlers, uppers and downers, and all that stuff.

Gonzo thanks the waitress and Lou. "That's the best lead we've had for two days, we've been asking people all around." Two hours later, they finally arrive at the suggested location only to find that it had burned down about three years earlier.

This club, Thompson leads us to believe, may be metaphorically emblematic of the American Dream. Perhaps the Dream had died? Perhaps it was an illusion—akin to all the *disillusions* of the 1960s, and perhaps also to Gatsby's disillusions.

Around the same time, however, Duke and Gonzo spend time at the Circus-Circus Casino in downtown Las Vegas. Here they learn about the owner, whose dream when he was young was to "run away and join a circus." Now the guy owns the hotel/casino named Circus-Circus. This seems to please Duke—in a weird and confusing way. Here is Duke chatting at the bar with a friend named Bruce Innes at the Circus-Circus:

> "When are you taking off?" Bruce asked.
>
> "As soon as possible," I said. "No point hanging around this town any longer. I have all I need. Anything else would only confuse me."
>
> He seemed surprised. "You found the American Dream?" he said. "In this town?"
>
> I nodded. "We're sitting on the main nerve right now," I said. "You remember that story the manager told us about the owner of the place? How he always wanted to run away and join the circus when he was a kid?"
>
> Bruce ordered two more beers. He looked over the casino for a moment, then shrugged. "Yeah, I see what you mean," he said. "Now the bastard has his *own* circus, and a license to steal, too!" He nodded. "You're right—he's the model."
>
> "Absolutely," I said. "It's pure Horatio Alger, all the way down to his attitude. I tried to have a talk with him, but some heavy-sounding dyke who claimed to be his Executive Secretary told me to fuck off. She said he hates the press worse than anyone else in America."

Thompson messes with us here: Is *Fear and Loathing* primarily a lament for the death of the American Dream? Or a lament for the high-wave moments of the 1960s? Or is this last satiric riff about the hotel owner and the way Duke cruises and carouses about Vegas enjoying incredible freedom and license implying that enterprise, hustle, striving, and ambition are still rewarded in America? He is, probably, playing with us and venting his contempt on both the dreamers and the schemers.

The Circus-Circus Casino owner, the youth who had once wanted to run away and join a circus, now presides over the ultimate Americana carnival and fleecing operation. "Now the owner of a casino," writes commentator Kevin T. McEneaney, "stages every night a mock crucifixion of someone in a gorilla suit spinning atop a neon cross. The owner himself, an icon of the Horatio Alger trajectory, becomes a parodic illustration of the Horatio Alger theme in all its debauched and delusionary grossness. Once the dream is achieved for oneself, one becomes a cynical exploiter of others, fleecing them while entertaining them, with inane and hallucinatory spectacle."[26]

Thompson ridicules the freak show Vegas has become. He mocks the Dallas used car dealers and the Elks Club conventioneers who come to reward themselves in this shrine of hedonism and gambling. Paradoxically, Duke and Gonzo are on a buddy road trip to end all road trips. They wander around irresponsibly in complete stupor. Gonzo rapes an underage girl. They trash their hotel rooms. They are abusive and obnoxious. They don't gamble much; yet we learn from biographies and interviews that Thompson, in addition to being a drug fiend and alcoholic, was a multi-decade gambler—betting on sporting and political events with a passion.

Thompson's editor at Random House had been pressing him for a couple of years to complete a book about the death of the American Dream. Thompson kept a growing file on the topic.

Thompson, who was often broke, paid his bills by doing magazine stories. But he desperately wanted to do another, major book to follow up on his Hells Angels success. Thompson's editor apparently inspired the trope of the death of the American Dream as a loose narrative theme to tie his disparate and ostensibly thin Las Vegas magazine stories together. It was a problematic gambit. But somehow Thompson's clever storytelling and his ingenious writing style made it strangely come together. He says he rewrote it five times, and it was also heavily edited.

There is much to fear and loathe in Las Vegas. This is obvious. It is harder, even if this is the argument Thompson tried to make, to understand Vegas as an epicenter of the American Dream. It is, to be sure, an escapist venue that exploits addictions. But it is also an outlier mega adult entertainment park for middle- and upper-class Americans. It offers the chance for people to hear Frank Sinatra, Barbra Streisand, Debbie Reynolds, Wayne Newton, Eric Clapton, Elton John, and major touring bands and comedians.

Many other nations have Vegases—like Monte Carlo, Cabo, Dubai, Macau, Ios, Mykonos, and so on. Humans yearn for holiday getaways that allow them to escape everyday routines and traditional mores. Duke and Gonzo viewed their Vegas outing with a seemingly similar escapist as well as roguish spirit.

Thompson's is a bitter dirge on Vegas and what takes place there: "For a loser, Vegas is the meanest town on earth." It is a place of illusions and fun-house mirrors. This is not a good town for psychedelic drugs, he writes. "Reality [here] itself is too twisted." Thompson seems to suggest Vegas is a mecca of extreme capitalism and rampant bingeing—and perhaps also a case of unbridled personal freedom. Thompson faults Vegas for its over-the-top commercialization and its promotion of Gatsby-esque dreams of becoming rich, famous, and in love. Here, perhaps, Thompson is likening Vegas to the Horatio Alger stories that, while they intended to encourage hard work and earnest striving, may have misled readers to believe everyone would win life's jackpots without the required discipline, investment, and networking Alger prescribes.

Thompson's lament for the American Dream works only up to a point. It would have been more convincing had he actually read and understood Alger's novels. It would also have been more convincing if his stories and rants were not so contradictory. And, finally, his American Dream bashing would be more compelling if it did not clash so dramatically with Thompson's own personal story and his faith in much of the idea of America narrative together with his love of politics and belief that Timothy Leary and the Haight-Ashbury hippies were dead wrong—giving up on politics and giving up on the pursuit of the American Dream are not, Thompson's life attests, an option.

Hunter Thompson lived the American Dream. He was raised in middle-class Louisville, Kentucky. His insurance-selling dad died when Hunter was a teenager. Hunter's mother became a drinker. He loved to read and write at a young age. He had literary heroes: J. P. Dunleavy, Fitzgerald, Hemingway, Faulkner, Conrad, Robert Penn Warren, and others.

Thompson was a prankster who yearned for attention and regularly got it as well as trouble. He began drinking as a teenager and never stopped. He was in jail at the time of his high school graduation. He joined the U.S. Air Force to lighten his jail sentence.

Thompson would later recall that he dreamed of becoming a writer and novelist; yet he understood that he would have to be a journalist first. But he had the ambition, drive, and optimism of a fatherless Horatio Alger youth.

> I grew up thinking, despite the obstacles presented by the swine, I would be successful no matter what I did. I guess that's one of the things about growing up in the fifties, it never occurred to me that you wouldn't be at least as successful as your parents.[27]

Thompson became an editor of his high school paper and participated as a teenager in a local literary society. He connived a way to spend most of his three years in the Air Force as a sports reporter covering local base teams. He later migrated to New York, Puerto Rico, Latin America, and a handful of other places finding jobs as a sports or public affairs reporter, even doing a stint as a copy boy for *Time* magazine. He never gave up. He kept writing fiction and nonfiction.

His heroes were Fidel Castro, Bob Dylan, and fellow Louisville native Muhammad Ali. Dylan's "Mr. Tambourine Man" was his favorite; he arranged for it to be played at his 2005 memorial service. He liked viewing himself as a combination of outlaw, rogue, anarchist, libertarian, and rugged individualist. He loved guns and gambling. He liked women. Most of all he loved writing and the adrenaline rush of getting published. He had been an angry young man filled with resentment at not being accepted into Louisville. He continued to be an angry, ambitious, and driven adult.

His biographers and his son describe him as a lifelong prankster who was fond of being considered weird and roguish. He liked being different but did not necessarily recommend it to others. He once joked, "I hate to advocate drugs, alcohol, violence, or insanity to anyone, but they have worked for me." He was an abusive husband and father. Everyone around him understood that Hunter's writing and freewheeling lifestyle were his top priorities. They also understood that he could write.

His son, Juan Fitzgerald Thompson, writes in a memoir that he feared and hated his father. His father was abusive to his mother and terrifying to him. Thompson was an unusual dad: "an alcoholic, and drug fiend, a wild, angry, passionate, sometimes dangerous, charismatic, unpredictable, irresponsible, idealistic, sensitive man with a powerful and deeply rooted sense of justice."[28] The son grants that his father was a great writer with a magical sense of words and imagination. He likewise reports that he became much closer to his dad when Thompson was ailing in his later years, but he adds that Thompson was irresponsible and largely uncaring. He was more embarrassed and ashamed of his dad, he writes, until a gradual reconciliation occurred once the son grew into his thirties.

His father, writes the young Thompson, was "both a madman and southern gentleman, a prophet and a hooligan, an idealist and cynic. He loved being the center of attention. He loved that his writing turned into a distinctive brand. He wanted people to wake up, take notice, and read him. He thrived on disruption, unpredictability and thwarting expectation."[29]

Thompson had run for sheriff of Pitkin County, Colorado, on the "Freak Power" ticket a year before he wrote *Fear and Loathing*. He owned a large farm in a paradise valley ten miles west of Aspen. In 1972 he would cover and report on the presidential campaign that eventually pitted George McGovern against incumbent Richard Nixon. His second most famous book was the nonfiction *Fear and Loathing: On the Campaign Trail '72* (1973).

Thompson believed in politics. He was active in local politics and became a friend of national politicians such as McGovern, Jimmy Carter, Bill

Clinton, and John Kerry. (McGovern, Kerry, and Gary Hart came to his memorial service after he committed suicide in 2005.) Thompson believed politics was a means of controlling one's environment and protecting one's freedom. He had loved his extensive gun collection. He was also a property rights advocate who hated the "greedhead" developers he thought were destroying Aspen and his beloved Roaring Fork Valley.

Back to *Fear and Loathing*. Yes, it can be read as a lament for the passing, or the false promises, of the American Dream. But one writer at the *New York Times* saw Thompson's work as mostly that of a bitterly disillusioned idealist.

One of my former students adds:

> Everything in *Fear and Loathing* should be taken with many grains of salt, mainly because the protagonists are too high to provide us with a coherent ideology or even a linear story. However . . . it is striking that neither of them are ever arrested in the book. This speaks to the American value of personal freedom. We want [Thompson certainly believed this] law enforcement to leave us alone until we actively become a danger to others.[30]

Yes, his portrait of Vegas is unflattering. Is it an example of American Dream taken too far? At times Thompson seems to be criticizing unbridled personal freedom in the same manner that he attacks Leary and Manson for being false gurus. Yet *Fear and Loathing* is also a celebration of freedom, free speech, and liberty.

Political scientist Evan Oxman interprets *Fear and Loathing* as offering a vision of "idealistic cynicism," "in which the possibility of achieving the American Dream is at its most worthwhile when it is widely seen as seriously in doubt." Do not read *Fear and Loathing*, Oxman suggests, as primarily a lament for the loss of the American Dream, "but instead as a call to action in the name of that lament."[31]

The problem with the 1960s, Oxman points out, was that a false optimism had convinced many young people to passively ride the escapist wave of drugs, sex, and rock and roll, as if this somehow, mysteriously, might lead to victory. However, the Vietnam War kept getting bigger and worse, and the country got Nixon and Agnew. Thompson, according to this helpful view, is warning his readers to beware false optimism. Beware gurus. Beware escapism and dropping out and disengaging from politics. And beware the direction America was going.

At the end of *Fear and Loathing*, Raoul Duke heads home to Colorado. He stops over in Denver and, perhaps ironically or satirically, likens himself to a reinvented Horatio Alger. Like so much in his novel, it is not entirely clear what he means; yet it just might mean that as he escapes Vegas en route back to his cherished Owl Farm in Woody Creek, Colorado, he, too, is—as many of his friends claimed was the case—living the American Dream. "I took another big hit off the amyl, and by the time I got to the bar my heart was full of joy. I felt like a monster reincarnation of Horatio Alger . . . a Man on the Move, and just sick enough to be totally confident." Perhaps, some say, he admits to enjoying the Dream and the unprecedented freedom his career and country allowed him.

Hunter Thompson was his own best story. He loved life and all its irony and absurdity. He was mostly a self-made man. The Air Force and editors, especially Jann Wenner at *Rolling Stone*, mentored him and acted as Alger-esque benefactors. But it was Thompson's dreaming, surviving, thriving, and his thrill at being a gifted maverick writer that is at the heart of this novel and much of his writing.

His writer friend Christopher Hitchens once pointed out to him that a lot of people still believe that the American Dream is alive and well. Hitchens asked him, "Haven't you lived the American Dream?" Thompson's response was "Goddamnit! I haven't thought about it that way. I suppose that in a certain way I have."[32] Moreover, Thompson liked to say that the United States was probably the only country in the world where he could enjoy so much freedom and quirky independence. Few other countries, he acknowledged, would have tolerated him.

Another important feature of *Fear and Loathing* was its going gonzo. "Gonzo" was a term a *Boston Globe* editor had used to describe Thompson's journalism. It was, people believe, a Boston street term referring to the last person standing at a party of drunks. Thompson liked the term and proudly appropriated it to describe his brand of writing.

Thompson is known today as the father of gonzo journalism and gonzo fiction writing. *Fear and Loathing* was a weird combination of the two. Gonzo journalism is when reporters intentionally make themselves the central figure in their stories. Thompson believed the only way to write honestly about events was to be part of them—yet he felt obliged to be transparent about the role of his subjectivity. He relished, he said, not being the fly on the wall but being the fly in the ointment.

It should be noted here that both Whitman and Jack Kerouac also put themselves in their narratives and are thus earlier or precursor examples of gonzoism. Note, too, that Whitman's *Song of the Open Road*, Twain's *Finn*, and Kerouac's *On the Road* are prime examples of earlier *road* and *rogue* narratives in American literature.

Thompson liked to cite William Faulkner's notion that the best fiction is truer than any kind of journalism. Thompson's writing style often blended fictional storytelling with his brand of participatory journalism. He emphasized that objectivity was nearly impossible and that many great journalists splendidly transcended objectivity—including H. L. Mencken, I. F. Stone, Mike Royko, and Mark Twain.

His brand of gonzo writing used sarcasm, irony, exaggeration, ridicule, humor, and not a little profanity. It often also involved a stream of consciousness, blending fact and fiction in a way that was both creatively and, at times, disconcertingly indistinguishable. He told one interviewer that you can't be objective when you're dealing with passionate situations like politics. "I guess you can. I never have. For instance, if you were objective about Richard Nixon you would never get him or understand him! You have to be subjective to understand Nixon. You have to be subjective to understand the Hells Angels."[33] We can only imagine how he would have approached Donald Trump.

Drugs and alcohol took their toll on Thompson. He also suffered from depression—a subject he and his son exchanged letters about, calling it their "Glum Reaper."

Thompson's masterworks were his nonfiction account of riding and partying with the Hells Angels (1969), *Fear and Loathing in Las Vegas* (1972), and the widely admired gonzo reporting *Fear and Loathing: On the Campaign Trail '72* (San Francisco: Straight Arrow Books, 1973). He wrote other novels and nonfictional works and perhaps as many as a thousand stories and news reports. He was a prolific essayist and letter writer, and also one of the more widely interviewed writers of his day. Some of his notable reporting was on boxing matches and the Kentucky Derby.

Fear and Loathing in Las Vegas remains his signature work. A 1998 Hollywood film was made based on the book. Movie star Johnny Depp won praise for trying to portray Thompson's Raoul Duke. But the cinematic stoned prankster traveling in and around Las Vegas came across as boorish, freakish, and incessantly juvenile. The movie was, understandably, a box office failure.

Fear and Loathing was hailed by some critics as a classic, a "scorching epochal sensation," and one of the few major novels of the 1970s. It gave voice to those in the 1960s and early 1970s who believed that America was losing its way—that the exalted promises of Horatio Alger's legends, the optimism and idealism associated with President John F. Kennedy, or the "highs" associated with movement politics of the late 1960s, were but dashed memories.

Fear and Loathing, as discussed, can be read for a variety of messages. It lives on as a remarkable example of gonzo writing. It is valuable as a chronicle of an unusual time and place. Not a few people, however, who once viewed it glowingly, now view much of it as incoherent rambling more than an insightful explanation of that period, or of America.

Hunter Thompson, while satirizing the idealistic notions of the American Dream, became an example of someone, though troubled and narcissistic, living the American Dream. He lived for nearly four decades in splendid privacy at his Aspen-area Owl Farm. He became one of the most noted and quoted writers of his era. His Aspen and celebrity friends called him "whipsmart" and a great conversationalist despite his posturing as an American "badass." He became an iconic personality in Aspen and earned a Hunter S. Thompson Day, keys to Louisville, and Kentucky Colonel status in the city where he had been jailed and grown up resentful. He also became a feature caricature in Garry Trudeau's long-running comic strip *Doonesbury* (where he was portrayed as "Uncle Duke").

Thompson had political views that were sometimes in conflict with each other. He was, as noted, part anarchist, part libertarian, part progressive liberal, and a sometime NRA member, who was especially proud of his twelve guns. He apparently invented his character Raoul Duke's name by combining Fidel Castro's brother's name (Raoul Castro) with iconic western actor John Wayne's nickname "Duke." He loved the protest songs of Bob Dylan. He admired George McGovern's decency and was depressed when McGovern lost in a landslide.

Thompson considered running for a U.S. Senate seat in Colorado in 1974. He didn't give up on politics. He didn't give up on America. He merely yearned, as he made clear in many of his writings and interviews, for a more just and freedom-loving America. He favored gun rights and the legalization of recreational drugs. He despised the national security state; yet he enjoyed going to national political conventions (even though he got beat up in Chicago in 1968) and covering presidential races. He also supported his friend Oscar Zeta Acosta (Dr. Gonzo in *FLLV*) and his championing of Chicano rights.[34] He loved privacy; yet he loved America and all it bestowed on him.

Thompson held out hope for the American political experiment and even the American Dream even as he satirized them. One of his biggest fans celebrates him:

> That legacy of hope, along with its hilarious critique of abusive power, bumbling national incompetence, and moneyed corruption, secures his position in the pantheon of American letters, as well as his place as the

author of an enduring, singular classic. The laughter that Thompson's work engenders—both literary and political—revives the courage to face contemporary problems that glare at us now with even more Spenglerian doom than when Thompson was alive.[35]

Hunter Thompson understood the flaws of political candidates, the flaws in our political process, and his country's lofty constitutional and social aspirations. In many ways his anger toward certain politicians and about the distance between our American aspirations and our practices fueled his writing, especially his political writings. He kept on writing. He kept on hoping. He kept envisaging, in his own way, an America that might provide liberty and justice for everyone.[36]

ON POMPOUS AND
HYPERPOLARIZED POLITICS[37]

"This is politics at its worst, if that isn't redundant," declares fictional president Donald P. Vanderdamp as he lashes out against the proposed Twenty-Eighth Amendment that would limit a president to a single four-year term.

Vanderdamp has become unpopular, both inside Washington and across the country, because he relentlessly vetoed congressional pork-barrel spending. "Every president's hope is to bring the country and the people together," he explains. "I seem to have accomplished that. I've managed to unite most of you in disapproval of me."

Vanderdamp is a folksy, underwhelming, "church-going, family-oriented, golden retriever-owning Midwesterner" who models himself after his hero, Calvin Coolidge. He loves bowling and, like Coolidge, yearns to retire voluntarily after one elected term. From Wapokoneta, Ohio, he was "as middle American as a slice of white bread." He is so infuriated by what he calls "quite possibly, the worst Congress in United States history" that he decides, on principle, to run again for president. His campaign slogan promise is "More of the Same." He then offers less measured criticism of Congress: "Let me go further, I don't think there's been such a concentration of rascality and unscrupulousness under one dome since the worst days of the Roman Empire."

Christopher Buckley's (1952–) *Supreme Courtship* is one of the funniest novels about American political culture. It is glib and facile, and on a few occasions it features slapstick humor (e.g., *Greet the Press* for NBC's *Meet the Press* and "Retropolitan Club" for Washington, D.C.'s venerable Metropolitan Club, etc.). Yet it is a splendid example of well-crafted American political humor.

The novel includes multiple subplots that capture both the humor and the sad realities of a hyperpolarized Washington. For example, the president is forced to appoint a "Judge Judy" celebrity TV personality to the Supreme Court due to Congress's continual rejection of his nominations. It has a chief justice trying to commit suicide in the Court's sacred Conference Room. Shortly thereafter, the "Chiefy" marries the new associate justice, who had only recently been the star of daytime television's *Courtroom Six*. It has a comical analysis of the genesis and ratification of the Twenty-Eighth Amendment. Another highlight are the stinging parodies of both former U.S. senator Joe Biden and associate Supreme Court justice Antonin Scalia. Biden is the novel's Connecticut senator Dexter Mitchell, and Scalia's *roman à clef* is the fictional Justice Silvio Santamaria.

But there's more. There are superb riffs on Washington "super lawyers" and the personality quirks of clashing justices.

It has cunning asides, such as the author's comic defaming of the capital's "punditariat": "Collective term for the one-seventh of the population of Washington D.C. who opine on political matters on television." Another reworks an old Washington snarky saying: "It is a cliché in Washington that the most dangerous place to find yourself is between a politician and a TV camera or microphone, but in the case of Senator Dexter Mitchell the cliché had acquired a kind of Darwinian perfection. Dexter Mitchell loved and indeed lived to talk. He uttered his first full sentence at the age of fourteen months and hadn't stopped since."

Then there is a political counselor's sarcastic advice given to the ambivalent president who isn't sure whether he wants to win or lose the next election: "Honestly, sir, I don't know what to tell you. . . . If you really want to lose this [election], well, I guess you're just going to have to stop being a leader and start being a politician."

"Members of Congress," the book's narrator satirizes, "understand that their main job, their highest calling, their truest democratic function, is to take money from other states and funnel it to their own."

Vanderdamp, like most presidential candidates, ran saying he would, if elected, change the way business was done in Washington. And because he sees himself as a small-government conservative, he proceeds to veto virtually every spending bill Congress sends him, including gems calling for a Museum of Gluten and an Institute for the Study of Gravel. So he succeeds in challenging Washington, but both Congress and the states, so accustomed to federal pork, become bitter opponents; they didn't want *this* kind of change.

A central drama in Buckley's snarky political satire is a bitter feud between President Vanderdamp and the Joe Biden look-alike Senator Dexter Mitchell, who serves as chair of the U.S. Senate Judiciary Committee. Mitchell is narcissistic and garrulous, and has run for the presidency three times. He also views himself as the most appropriate nominee for the next opening on the U.S. Supreme Court.

Conveniently enough, an associate justice retires. Vanderdamp nominates two worthy candidates in a row, both of whom get grilled, skewered, and rejected by the handsome, yet pompous, Mitchell and his committee.

"Mitchell has asked the president to appoint him, but this the president is unwilling to do." Here the book's narrator informs us that the vain Mitchell, despite some superficial appeal, is just another power-hungry conventional, transactional politician (similar to Gore Vidal's Senator Clay Overbury): "If a computer were programmed to design a president of the United States, it might very well generate Dexter Mitchell. Everything about him seemed, indeed, calculated. And yet, for all his qualifications, Dexter somehow added up to less than the sum of his considerable parts." President Donald Vanderdamp was so peeved at Mitchell for blocking his judicial nominees he "repressed the temptation to storm up Pennsylvania Avenue and insert Senator Mitchell's microphone in an orifice not specifically designed for such purposes."

Partly in revenge and partly in desperation, Vanderdamp implausibly (and there's a fair amount of implausibility, or satirical license, in Buckley's narratives) recruits and nominates TV Judge Pepper Cartwright, a veritable Oprah of cableland's *Courtroom Six*. She is widely popular, beautiful, and a Fordham Law School graduate with at least some prosecuting and local Superior Court judicial experience. A native of Plano, Texas (just call her a "plain old girl from 'Plano'"), she is bright, sassy, wears cowboy boots, and gradually develops Sandra Day O'Connor's winsome touch when it comes to personal relationships. Her no-bullshit honesty makes her instantly likable. Imagine her as some combination of Judge Judy, Sarah Palin, and Jefferson Smith, the unlikely and accidental U.S. senator in the film *Mister Smith Goes to Washington*. Cartwright is reluctant to leave her more lucrative television gig; yet ultimately she is moved by the patriotic sentiment and a pleading president to serve her country.

Buckley gives us a priceless description of nominee Cartwright's courtesy call on Chairman Mitchell. "So let's get to it," she declares. "You're fixing to nail me to a cross like you did those other two [previously rejected nominees]?" Mitchell is taken aback and lamely replies, "That's not the way we do things up here." He is his arrogant and evasive self, until our heroine Pepper Cartwright unloads on him:

> Now, you don't like anything about me, starting with the fact that I'm sitting here in your office, not kissing your ass like you're used to. . . . That's fine. . . . Now I don't know what kind of witch trial you got planned for me, but this being a courtesy call, let me tell you how *I'm* going to play it. I've got the number one-rated TV show in the country. As of this morning—and I checked—Congress's approval ratings are at eighteen percent. So it's my numbers up against your numbers, Senator. And if you and your distinguished colleagues try to pull any shit, I am going to climb up on that nice wooden committee table of yours and beat you to death, one by one with your microphones.

Cartwright dazzles as well as intimidates the Judiciary Committee and sails through both the Committee and the full Senate confirmation process. She joins a divided court, replete with 5–4 decisions: "The Court was as divided as the Korean Peninsula." The Court's division is akin to that between Congress and the White House.

Christopher Taylor Buckley's father, William F. Buckley Jr., was the much-celebrated founder and publisher of *The National Review* and godfather to the conservative movement in the late twentieth century. His uncle, James Buckley, was a U.S. senator from New York. His first father-in-law, Donald Gregg, was a career CIA operative, a White House aide, and U.S. ambassador to South Korea. Buckley himself served as a senior speechwriter for Vice President George H. W. Bush. He has written for, and served as editor of, influential magazines, including *Esquire* and *Forbes*. All of these experiences helped make this Yale honors graduate (and Skull and Bones member, like his father and the George Bushes), a savvy commentator on Washington's political rituals.

Buckley has a pleasing, versatile, conversational style with plenty of dead-on as well as deadpan satirical asides. Among his many successful novels are *Thank You for Smoking* (1994), *The White House Mess* (1986), and *God Is My Broker* (1998). Buckley, like this novel's President Vanderdamp, describes himself as a small-government conservative. He surprised friends and family by endorsing Senator Obama in the 2008 election, explaining his disappointment in George W. Bush's presidency, which was then coming to an end.

Buckley stings with caricatures depicting a capital of politicians who are better at self-promotion than collaboration. The Supreme Court and its practices are put under the microscope and found wanting. Ditto for Congress.

Justice Pepper Cartwright, however, rises to her challenge and becomes, like Senator Jefferson Smith in *Mr. Smith Goes to Washington*, an untainted and presumably "apolitical" heroine. She has an uneasy initiation period where she stumbles, is over her head, and earns the nickname "Justice Lightweight." But she eventually captivates most of her colleagues and even, as noted, marries the chief justice.

Perhaps only legal and political junkies will enjoy Buckley's tale about the Twenty-Eighth Amendment campaign. But it is preciously funny. It is proposed because, as noted, politicians at both the state and the federal level are mad at President "Don Veto" Vanderdamp for his repeated vetoing of pork-barrel legislation.

Vanderdamp rightly understands this amendment wasn't about future presidents. It was about him. His response: "Let me remind the Congress that we already have mechanisms for denying presidents a second term. They're called elections. And—what do you know—we have one coming up just sixteen months from now. If the Congress can't wait that long they could just impeach me, but since my crime consists of trying to force the Congress to be fiscally responsible, I'm not sure that dog would hunt." "So," he declares, "now I am going to run, if only to make a point. I will not be dictated to—nor will I allow future presidents to be dictated to—by what I consider to be, quite possibly, the worst Congress in United States history."

All he really wants to do is to retire to his beloved Ohio village and be with his grandchildren. Nonetheless, he does run, but the Twenty-Eighth is ratified just days before election. Here Buckley gives a Con Law 101 refresher lecture that is faintly similar to *Bush v. Gore* (2000), except this time it is *Mitchell v. Vanderdamp*.

Pepper Cartwright's Supreme Court immediately takes up the case. It boils down, writes Buckley, to two arguments—one technical, the other philosophical.

> The first was the President Vanderdamp's election was invalid because the term limit amendment took legal effect the moment it was ratified by Texas, two days before the election. Mitchell's second argument centered on the larger issues of governance, that is, whether the Court should recognize a validly adopted amendment, or the people's decision in the election.

Cartwright's is the crucial swing vote. But should she recuse herself? After all, she owes her seat to Vanderdamp. Heavy-hitter celebrity litigators are hired to argue both sides. A myriad of obscure court cases are cited by litigators and justices alike.

Finally, Pepper Cartwright writes the 5–4 majority opinion denying the Mitchell claim in *Mitchell v. Vanderdamp.* "In finding for the President," Justice Cartwright writes, "we simply give effect to the principle of popular sovereignty that lies at the heart of our real founding document: 'We hold these truths to be self-evident . . . that whenever any form of government becomes destructive to these evils, it is the right of the People to alter or to abolish it, and to institute new government, laying its foundations on such principles and organizing its powers in such form, as to them shall seem most likely to effect their safety and happiness.'"

"When the going gets tough," she mentions to the chief, "the scared-shitless quote from the Declaration of Independence." Alas, the constitutional system survives. A moderate and sensible vote and unpretentious voice has joined the high court. The dislikable former senator Mitchell fails to become president. President Nice-Guy gets reelected but (graciously) resigns on the last day of his first term, allowing his vice president to replace him for the second term he never wanted.

Buckley's novel has a few notable subtexts. First his characterization of Pepper Cartwright suggests that a commoner from outside the system can provide the reasoned judgment our political system needs. Second, his principled, nonpolitically ambitious "white bread" president seems refreshingly wholesome in a city where everybody every day is addictively consumed with approval ratings and pork for their districts. These plot elements are intriguingly populist, especially coming from the establishment-bred and -wed Buckley. His ability to make us laugh at our elites is in part aided because it comes from one of their own—indeed, as noted, a certifiable Skull and Bonesman Yalie.

In addition to his skilled parody of U.S. Senator Biden, he also irreverently disrobes Supreme Court Justices. He tells us of the supreme jerks, pompous pricks, and even about "nine old farts sending [endless] footnotes to each other."

Buckley's humorous discussion about turning to a TV star to overcome divisiveness in Washington was a prescient foreshadowing of the Republican Party's turning to Trump, the reality TV host, in 2016. Buckley also parodies the proposal, in Dexter Mitchell's presidential campaign bid, of installing land mines along the U.S.-Mexico border to fend off undocumented immigrants. Mitchell supports this; Vanderdamp opposes it.

He neither glorifies nor denigrates the political system. He knows it is much more than a game; yet he also knows it is very much a human and imperfect process. He advocates no structural or constitutional reforms, as law school professors often do.[38] His goal, and he admirably succeeds, was to prick the pompous and make us laugh at both the human condition and our less-than-perfect political experiment. *Supreme Courtship* is a splendid companion to the writings of Brackenridge, Twain, Adams, West, Condon, Heller, Vidal, and Thompson.

Buckley, in a 2015 interview, said he had moved more toward writing straight rather than satirical fiction: "The trouble with trying political satire anymore is American politics have reached the point of being self-satirized." Satire, he said, "is everywhere, especially on TV, and is being brilliantly done."[39]

Buckley is an uncommonly well-informed satirist. He captures the vanity as well as partisan and institutional feuds that come with both our Madisonian system and practical life in D.C. He makes us laugh at politics, politicians, and ourselves; yet his ingeniously witty satire also encourages us to imagine a more perfect union and a more resilient republic.

Buckley is probably speaking for himself when he has his quietly heroic President Vanderdamp say, "Whatever happens, don't give up on America. It's still a great country. It's just a little confused right now."

CONCLUSION

Political satire exposes or pokes fun at politicians, political customs, and institutions. It allows writers to tell political stories they could not normally talk about. Satire, at its best, helps unpack political rituals and the imperfections inherently present in constitutional self-governance.

George Orwell wrote that most issues are political issues and that politics is replete with lies, evasion, folly, and schizophrenia. Sometimes, as in Orwell's case, satire can be one of the best ways to treat these realities.

Still, politics is the lifeblood of constitutional democracy. Democracy is impossible without politics, and politics is impossible without politicians. A healthy society is a place where it is safe for controversial ideas to be freely fought out in the public sphere, where it is safe to be a politician, and a dissenter, a maverick, cartoonist—*and a satirist*. Healthy communities everywhere benefit from humorists with the courage and imagination to deflate pompous politicians to help keep politicians accountable, and to alert us to the excesses and vulnerabilities of democratic constitutionalism.

One final point: Demeaning politics and politicians isn't always a laughing matter. Rich political humor leaves us laughing, curious, and understandably unsettled; yet, as Sinclair Lewis emphasized in *It Can't Happen Here*, and as many other authors have concurred, it should not lead to giving up on politics. Nor should it diminish our commitment to the idea of America.

The next chapter, chapter 6, examines the novelist on the campaign trail—novelists who try, through their storytelling, to help us understand candidates, parties, campaigns, and American electioneering.

6

THE NOVELIST ON
THE CAMPAIGN TRAIL

Central to understanding American politics is coming to terms with
how politicians get elected. Campaigns for political office can be
messy and negative affairs. Candidates run for office wanting to help their
neighbors and to do good, but campaigns and politics tempt candidates to
become expedient and sometimes to become infatuated, if not intoxicated,
with the attention and the game of politics. Novels in this chapter help
explain this behavior.

Standing for public office requires uncommon personal ambition and
typically involves being aligned with a partisan faction or even a political
machine. Elections and campaigns in America are often the least attractive
aspect of our constitutional democracy. Yet democracy is impossible without politics, parties, and elections.

Fortunately, several intrepid fiction writers have tackled election politics. The novels treated in this chapter illustrate how fiction can help unmask the complicated vicissitudes of campaigning in America. These novels
remind us once again that our constitutional and republican aspirations rely
on imperfect political agents and often murky political practices as part of
the deal in self-governance.

Hamlin Garland's *A Spoil of Office* follows the career of an unlikely
farmer-turned-politician, Bradley Talcott. It describes how Talcott's message
evolves from his beginning as an idealistic newcomer in politics to a crusading populist. This novel is less about a specific campaign than about the rise
and challenges of a new political movement: Grange politics and Populism.

Howard Fast's *The American* builds on Garland's story by examining
populism's impact on a governor of Illinois and on the Democratic Party
in the late nineteenth century. Edwin O'Connor's *The Last Hurrah* may be
the best depiction of twentieth-century big-city machine politics. It is part

279

analysis and part nostalgia for old-style politics. Political scientist Eugene Burdick in *The Ninth Wave* gives us a chilling account of election engineering and the ruthless tactics that are sometimes used. Andrew Tully's *Capitol Hill* tells the story of a presidential advisor who succumbs to corruption as he tries to position himself as a running mate or key cabinet advisor to the next president.

Veteran journalist Joe Klein wonderfully captures a presidential primary campaign that takes place in the early 1990s. It is partly satirical but captures presidential campaign realities as well as (or even better than) most nonfiction accounts. It entertains us and raises compelling questions about what it takes to win presidential elections.

A handful of other novels treated elsewhere in this book share similar themes that help us understand campaigning in America. *Mr. Crewe's Career, All the King's Men, The Appeal, The Manchurian Candidate, The Gay Place,* and *Washington, D.C.* can be read as companions to the novels examined here.

PRAIRIE POPULISM[1]

"I have a dream of what is coming . . . I see a time when the farmer will not need to live in a cabin on a lonely farm. I see the farmers coming together in groups . . . I see them enjoying lectures . . . I see a day when the farmer will no longer be a drudge and his wife a bond slave, but happy men and women who will go singing to their pleasant tasks upon their fruitful farms."

These "I have a dream" remarks come from Ida Wilbur, a Des Moines–based Grange circuit lecturer, as she visits with farmers in Rock County, Iowa, in the 1870s. The fictional Miss Wilbur, in Hamlin Garland's *A Spoil of Office* (1892), urges the nonpartisan Grangers to band together and understand their shared purpose.

Midwestern farmers had suffered from periodic recession, droughts, and plagues of pests and insects that devalued their crops. They were increasingly vulnerable to the monopolistic practices of railroad and banking interests. Eastern financial institutions had encouraged many farmers to invest in machinery and acquire more land; when crops failed, farms went into bankruptcy.

Hamlin Garland (1860–1940) had been raised in rural Wisconsin and Iowa. He dedicates his well-received 1891 book of short stories about the Midwest, *Main-Travelled Roads*, to his parents, "whose half-century pilgrimage on the main-travelled road of life brought them only toil and deprivation." For their struggles farmers blamed mortgage companies, merchants, grain elevator operators, railroads, land speculators, manufacturers of farm equipment, and, of course, politicians.

Miss Wilbur and Grange organizers in the 1870s preached that farmers had to make their complaints known and had to develop a common voice. The Grange, a political movement organized in the 1860s, was focused on social activities such as community picnics to help transcend the isolation farm families experienced. It had been intentionally designed as nonpartisan. After recessions in the 1870s the Grange experimented with cooperative processing plants and marketing systems. Most failed. A few states did respond to Grange requests to regulate warehouse and railway fees.

Hamlin Garland's first novel, *A Spoil of Office*, tells the story of how Iowa farmers finally realized that Grange social activities were inadequate in addressing their political and public policy needs. Nor, they learned, was the Republican Party any longer of much use to them: this novel contends that the party of Lincoln had become sadly corrupted by its embeddedness in state capitals. (Winston Churchill's *Mr. Crewe's Career*, discussed earlier, echoes this sentiment in describing a New England state.)

Spoil is a fictional account of the politicization of Iowa farmers. Garland's novel portrays how Grangers left the Republican Party, formed farmers' alliances, and eventually drew major political support to the People's Party, also called the Populist Party. *Spoil* "illustrates and analyzes, as no other novel does, crucial intellectual movements in American life, specifically the birth and ideological core of the Populist movement. . . . [The novel] beautifully captures the tenor of Western life in these years, especially the social activities of the Grange and offers a prescient blueprint for the coming success and failure of the Populist Party."[2]

Garland yearned for *Spoil* to be accepted as respected literature; yet it was generally viewed, correctly, as an amalgam of literature, muckraking, and political advocacy. One historian even called it more of a social tract than art. Garland admits it was written hastily and under deadlines from the magazine in which it was first serialized.

The novel is a combination of political storytelling and pamphleteering. Garland, who went on to be a prolific writer and winner of a Pulitzer Prize, had a political agenda. He was a disciple of Henry George's single-tax proposal. Although he does not use this novel to advance that policy, he fully embraces the spirit of populism, the need for a new political party, and for women's suffrage. Garland was greatly influenced by the commoner spirit as expressed by Walt Whitman and the realism of William Dean Howells.

His storytelling in *Spoil* begins with a young farmhand, Bradley Talcott, who is mesmerized by the touring or circuit-riding Grange lecturer Ida Wilbur. He falls in love with her message, her oratorical style, and eventually Ida herself. Moved by her prophetic call, Talcott decides to save up money to attend a local school. He knows that to be a valuable member of the Granger movement, he needs to upgrade himself and especially to learn to speak in public. Garland, who was a lifelong student of oratory, became a professor of public speaking in Boston, and a lecturer of note around the country.[3]

Talcott is humiliated in his first days at school because his clothes are ragged and he is much older than his peers, but Miss Wilbur's dream motivates him. A fellow classmate also comforts him just as he'd resigned himself to quit. A popular student named Radbourn shares classic Horatio Alger Jr. advice with Talcott: "Yes, you can. You think you can't, but you can. A man can do anything if he only thinks he can and tries hard. You can't afford to let a little thing like that upset your plans."

Talcott, with the encouragement of this mentoring peer, gets a new haircut and a new suit, and he goes back to school with renewed confidence. He dedicates himself to learn, compete, and develop his speaking and debating skills. Inspired by Ida's galvanizing speeches, he develops an inchoate yearning to persuade, inspire, and guide people toward new ideas, new principles, and higher fulfillment.

Protagonist Bradley Talcott lives in a Republican county in a thoroughly Republican state. His region had supported Lincoln and the Union cause. Locals were schooled to believe that while all Democrats were not thieves, "all thieves were Democrats."

Local lawyer Judge Brown, whose Jeffersonian and Jacksonian Democratic views make him an anomaly in the region, adopts Talcott. Brown and his wife give the young man a room, provide employment, and introduce him to the study of law and contrarian ideas about public policy.

Young Talcott begins to contemplate a more ambitious career. "He dared," our narrator says, "to hope that he might be a lawyer, and an orator, which meant also a successful politician to him." Politics, he thought, was an appropriate career, even a calling. He dreamed of Washington, D.C., as a mecca with its shining dome, as a beacon: "To go to Washington was equivalent to being born again."

Talcott, guided by Brown, gets involved with local farmers who feel disenfranchised by the mortgage bankers and city folks who monopolize county politics. He is initially an independent Republican, but he and his colleagues are unsuccessful.

Talcott, motivated by his mentor, moves to Iowa City to study law for a couple of years. He becomes a disciplined student of the law and begins to understand the emerging unrest in the region—especially the disquietude toward the monopolistic practices of railroads and big banks and the corruption of public officials in this so-called Gilded Age. He slowly gets imbued with the evolving populist spirit of his times.

The Grange had successfully brought farmers together, but its aversion to partisan politics limited its ability to encourage policy changes that would aid the farmers. As the Grange faded, activist farmers drifted either to the Democratic Party or to emerging farmers' alliances that were forming.

Talcott's political views continue to evolve, in part due to his muse Ida Wilbur, who has grown more militant on both feminist and economic inequality issues. His mentor, Judge Brown, and Brown's unapologetic Democratic views, also shape Talcott's political evolution. Talcott moves back to Rock River, becomes Brown's junior partner, and allows Brown to engineer his nomination as a candidate for state legislature.

Even as Bradley Talcott accepts his nomination, he pledges not only to represent local farmers but also to help resolve larger fundamental economic inequities.

> I'm going to run this campaign in the farmers' interest, because the interests of this county and of the state are agricultural, and whatever hurts the farmer hurts the state. There is no war between the town and the county. The war is between the people and the monopolist wherever he is, whether he is in the country or in the town. It is not true that the interests of the town dweller and of the farmers are necessarily antagonists; the cause of the people is the same everywhere.

Talcott relishes the campaigning and unites a coalition of dissidents who are yearning for change and tired of special-interest politics. This momentum steers him to victory in this state house election.

So the principled Mr. Talcott, like the protagonist in the later iconic Hollywood film *Mr. Smith Goes to Washington*, joins the political fray in Des Moines and is fired up with ideals of righting wrongs and fighting for justice. Talcott's idealism is immediately tested when he observes how his fellow legislators—from both political parties—are preoccupied with retaining their seats more than advancing progressive legislative policies.

Veteran legislators laugh at him, joking about his kind "coming down to save their country. They'll learn to save their bacon before the term is up. That young feller looks like one of those retrenchment and reform cusses, one of the fellers who never wants to adjourn—down here for business, ye know." Such jeers as well as unsavory overtures from the railroad interests embolden his resolve to fight the privileged interests and speak up on behalf of the common people.

Talcott then meets up again with ever-proselytizing Ida Wilbur. He tells her of his dream to reform the Democratic Party and get them to be more aggressive in fighting for average people. She startles him, however, by condemning both the traditional parties as broken-down and virtually useless vehicles of progress. Ida advises:

> I began to believe that we must wait 'till a new party rises out of the needs of people, just as the old free-soil party rose to free the slaves. Don't deceive yourself about your party in this state. It is after the offices, just the same as the party you have left. They juggle with the tariffs and the license question, because it helps them. They will drop any question and any man when they think they are going to lose by retaining him. They will drop you if you get too radical. I warn you.

She also warns the earnest Talcott that her brand of reformism and idealism would be a political liability for him: "My counsel does not keep men in office. I belong to the minority. I am very dangerous."

Ida, for Talcott, combined a personal, if austere, beauty with a zealous passion for justice. It was irresistible. He was indebted to her as a counselor and in love with her as a person: "You've taught me to think. . . . You gave me my first ambition to do something."

His legislative friends warn him that she is one of the infernal heretics and suffragists—an advanced woman: "She is a great woman but she is abnormal." Readers are never sure whether Talcott is so smitten with Wilbur that he obsequiously accepts her or whether he is wooed by her policy views. Garland, perhaps with poetic license, portrays their bonding as ideological, though a bit surreal.

Talcott slogs on at the state legislature but is disgusted by the endless corruption and impurities of both his colleagues and the political process. He takes some pride in speaking out against the railroad practices. He also gives a major speech on behalf of woman's suffrage. He knows his views will not bring about significant change and will likely hurt his reelection chances; yet he is resolved to do what is right despite the consequences. He begins to question whether this type of politics is worth it. He even wonders whether he should give up and walk away from politics.

But his mentor, Judge Brown, has other plans for him. He is now engineering Talcott's nomination for the U.S. House of Representatives. In quick order, he wins the nomination and then the general election and is off to Washington, D.C., as a Democrat from Iowa. He has transformed in just a decade from a farmhand to a congressman—an American Dream come true.

As in Des Moines, the drinking, obscene talk, and self-serving behavior of his fellow national legislators disgusts him. Party leaders are bloated, swaggering, unscrupulous, "treacherous tricksters." According to our narrator, Talcott "found that while he had less religion than these men, they had infinitely less reverence for the things which he considered sacred."

Representative Talcott continues to rail against monopolies and special interests. But he soon pays the price for his strong, progressive positions: he gets "primaried" by conservative interests when his local nominating convention occurs. His defeat is due, it is explained, to his advocacy of "cranky notions"—more specifically, his rabble-rousing about inequity. A local paper in his district calls him out as an anarchist and a socialist.

Meanwhile, Ida Wilbur continues to barnstorm around the Midwest, but now as a spokesperson for the budding Farmers' Alliance political movement. Talcott moves politically left with her, joins her movement, and wins her as his wife (presumably his one spoil of office). He returns to D.C. to finish his term in Congress, or so Garland reports, and catches a version of Potomac fever. Talcott has developed a fondness for the beauty and culture of Washington. And with both Judge Brown and Ida Wilbur as his mentoring muses, he is now definitely enjoying and perhaps even addicted to his new role as a principle-driven political maverick.

Garland highlights an enduring paradox of political life: our protagonist despises conventional politics while yearning to be agent for political liberation and empowerment for the common man. Talcott considers himself a failed politician; yet he navigates his way first through Republican ideologies, next into the Democratic Party, and finally into the politics of the Farmers' Alliance and the nascent Populist Party. On several occasions our protagonist considers quitting, but he understands the need for at least a few good political leaders to champion causes that many people believe are lost causes but which he believes are causes yet to prevail.

On the one hand, Talcott claims, "I'm sick of it. I don't believe I'm a politician. I'm sick all through with the whole cursed business." On the other hand, he relishes trying to win converts to his principles. Talcott had developed a growing love for how an orator could persuade people. "He hungered to lead men," Garland writes. "Notwithstanding his fits of disgust and bitterness he loved to be a part of the political life of his time. It had a powerful fascination for him. The deference which his old friends and neighbors paid him as things due a rising young man, pleased him."

And as *Spoil* unfolds, Talcott's mere being in the arena, if not really being politically influential, becomes a sufficient aphrodisiac to win him his cherished "spoil of office," his Ida as a wife.

Talcott, Ida, and novelist Garland acknowledge that politics is a bruising and messy enterprise; yet they yearn for a new politics, a new political party, and principled political alliances. They dream that a new party can come into existence as a redeeming force and help the American political experiment live up to its idealistic principles.

Literary critics have said that a majority of the political novels written in the 1870 to 1900 era are better described as social tracts and more propaganda than art. This is true of *Spoil*. It is a proselytizing narrative that describes and celebrates the emerging prairie populism of the time. However, the merit of this particular novel is that it beautifully captures local mores, local political yearning, and shares representative stump speeches and Act I and Act II campaign practices in the politically vibrant Midwest of the 1870s and 1880s. *Spoil* is a bottom-up portrait of the Gilded Age. It is a welcome companion and contrast to Twain's *Gilded Age* (1873) and Adams's *Democracy: An American Novel* (1880), novels written a few years earlier but which focused primarily on the nation's capital.

Hannibal Hamlin Garland, born in rural Wisconsin in 1860, was named after Abraham Lincoln's Republican running mate in the election that year. Garland liked to say truth was a higher quality than beauty. Spreading the ideals of justice, he believed, was a writer's central goal.

Garland was initially distrustful of the Farmers' Alliance. But he went out to Iowa and Kansas and interviewed its leaders, such as Mary Elizabeth Lease, Congressman Jerry Simpson, and former Greenback Party presidential candidate General James B. Weaver. "When I got among the farmers and really got an understanding of their position," Garland lost any previous qualms and became a full-throated supporter. "They are not pig-headed and reactionary." On the contrary, their populist Farmers' Alliance people "are alive to new ideas and willing to be set right if it can be shown they are wrong." They even listened sympathetically to Garland's advocacy of Henry George's single-tax reforms. "So I have cut loose from the old moorings and have thrown myself heart and soul into the farmers movement."[4]

There is much to fault in this novel. The hero and heroine are so noble, dedicated, and persevering that their "do-gooder" purity strains belief. Talcott's infatuation with Miss Wilbur, which leads to their marriage, is cartoonish and, as noted, surreal. *Spoil* suffers from cliché prose and overwrought regional sentimentalism that, at times, distracts from its narrative. Garland's depictions of the electioneering process are superficial. He rarely dives into detailed ideological policy debates, and as a storyteller, he leaves too much for the reader to imagine.

Yet there are useful insights about success in local politics. An aspiring politician needs mentors, communication skills, and stalwart policy advisors. They must learn, like Talcott, to adapt to changing community moods: our protagonist navigates these rituals and, remarkably, is a young leader in three distinct political parties. Talcott's ideological evolution mirrors what happened in Iowa, Kansas, and a few neighboring states in the 1870s and 1880s.

Garland's novel captures the local politics and populist movement of his time. His narrative explores the origins of the People's Party, a movement that would have its heyday in the 1880s with dozens of their members winning election to Congress and governorships. In 1892 People's Party presidential candidate General James B. Weaver won twenty-two electoral college votes. The party would fade fast, as it failed to become inclusive of more whites and blacks, North and South, men and women, but it incubated some of the evolving policy views later refined by William Jennings Bryan, Teddy Roosevelt, Eugene Debs, and Woodrow Wilson. Garland's story has its roots in Jeffersonism, Jacksonianism, Greenbackism, and a variety of antimonopoly crusades, and it brings alive the brooding spirit and this era's passionate uprisings of farmers.

Noteworthy, too, in *Spoil* is the celebration of feminist leadership and the struggle for woman's suffrage. Indeed, it is the crusading Ida Wilbur who provides an early version of memorable later exhortations by Eugene Debs and Steinbeck's Tom Joad. Thus, she exhorts:

> Wherever a man is robbed, wherever a man toils and the fruits of his toil are taken from him; wherever the frosty lash of winter stings or the tear of poverty scalds, there the principle of our order reaches. . . .
>
> The heart and center of this movement is a demand for justice not for ourselves, but for the toiling people wherever found. If this movement is higher and deeper and broader than the Grange was, it is because its sympathies are broader . . . it is no longer a question of legislating for the farmer; it's a question of the abolition of industrial slavery.

This same message is taken up anew in Sinclair's *The Jungle*, Stein-beck's *In Dubious Battle* and *Grapes of Wrath*, as well as in John Dos Passos, Robert Penn Warren, Howard Fast, John Nichols, and others. The struggle of how to achieve representation for the disenfranchised "little guy" is a persisting narrative in both American fiction and American politics.

Garland, in the preface to his 1897 edition of *Spoil*, said his was an effort to explain the origins and political impulses of the Grange, the Farmers' Alliance, and the People's Party. "They came as impulses with mightiest enthusiasms," and they all "died out like waves upon a beach." But Garland predicts, "The power which originated them did not die; it will return in different forms again and again, so long as the love of liberty and the hatred of injustice live in the hearts of men and women." His was a foreshadowing of later campaigns by Huey Long, Upton Sinclair, Henry Wallace, and Bernie Sanders.

Hamlin Garland's *A Spoil of Office* was a prime example of a novel written to urge Americans to imagine and move toward a more altruistic, egalitarian Republic.

FOR THE SOUL OF
THE DEMOCRATIC PARTY[5]

"Pardoning John, they called him, and he grinned back and continued to pardon. Wherever there was a reasonable doubt, wherever a man had been framed, a poor damned woman railroaded, a worker condemned with only a mockery of a trial, a homeless, unemployed wretch dragged into court and tried and convicted to clear an embarrassing blotter, a labor organizer beaten up and jailed for assault, he used the power of executive pardon. [Illinois governor John Peter Altgeld] did it because it made those who hated him scream with rage and anger and demand his impeachment, but he also did it because he could not live without groping for the essence of right and wrong, and because a long time ago certain men, whom he never mentioned now, had [wrongly] died upon a gallows."

Governor John Peter Altgeld, the Democratic governor of Illinois from 1893 to 1897, is the celebrated progressive hero in Howard Fast's (1915–2003) historical fictional treatment, *The American: A Middle Western Legend*.

Fast's novel can be read as a sequel to Hamlin Garlin's *A Spoil of Office* (1892) in that it describes the populist and progressive unrest taking place within the conventional political parties of the day, especially in the

Midwest. In many ways, *The American* uses the literary technique Michael Shaara would successfully use in writing his best-selling *The Killer Angels* (1975). The technique here is to write about real people and real events—as Shaara does about the battle of Gettysburg—but the novelist has to invent the dialogue and build off of public statements or occasional newspaper accounts. Fast does this effectively.

Fast's *The American* is a third invaluable examination of Chicago-area politics in the late nineteenth and early twentieth centuries and is thereby a literary companion to Upton Sinclair's *The Jungle* (1906) and Richard Wright's *Native Son* (1940).

The Altgeld story is a political coming-of-age and political-awakening narrative. Our hero was born in Germany and brought to the United States as a three-month-old infant. He was raised on a farm in Ohio. He served in the Union Army in Northern Virginia, and that experience together with a few teachers in Mansfield, Ohio, may have been the crucial Horatio Alger–esque mentoring that motivated Altgeld to push on first to a short career as a teacher and then a longer career as an attorney, judge, and eventually governor of Illinois and, briefly, the leader of the progressive wing of the national Democratic Party. It should also be mentioned that, similar to the earnest, restless, and striving young Abe Lincoln, Altgeld migrated westward to improve his lot and escape a difficult father-son relationship.

Altgeld became famous, or infamous, when he pardoned three men who had been accused of anarchism and mayhem at the Haymarket riots in Chicago (1886). He had long questioned the fairness of the trials that convicted eight men on that occasion. He was not alone in these views. Nearly half of the people in Illinois had misgivings or doubts about those trials and the capital punishment verdicts for four of the accused.

After he became governor, Altgeld read and reread every word in that trial. He decided that the jury was rigged and framed: "He came to the conclusion that Judge Gary, who had tried the case, was the most deliberate judicial murderer in all civilized history." He carefully studied the forged testimony, the perjury, the lies of hired spies, and the confused and incoherent statements of thugs and concluded that it was his moral responsibility to educate the public about the travesty of justice. "There were long hours when he thought of democracy, what it meant, what it might be. There was a theory that no one had ever tried, except perhaps Tom Jefferson, long, long ago and sometimes it seemed to him that another could try it, take democracy and make a fight of it."

This experience of reexamining the injustices done in the aftermath of the Haymarket riot transformed Altgeld. He had been a rather conventional politician who had been backed by both the Chicago political machine and labor unions.

A lynching of an African American in Decatur, Illinois (downstate), also jolted him. "This," he said, "is not civilization, not decency, but barbarism." The shame, he declared, is on all of us.

Altgeld sent out a proclamation to the people of Illinois, after he had been advised that a clamoring mob "broke down the doors of the jail at Decatur, overpowered the officers of the law, took from his cell a Negro confined there, dragged him out and killed him by hanging him to a post nearby." He denounced this as a "cowardly and diabolical act . . . not only murder under our laws, but as a disgrace to our civilization and a blot upon the fair name of our State."

Altgeld, who had already allied himself with the unions and similar workingmen alliances, began to fight more rigorously for the eight-hour workday and the rights of strikers. He regularly clashed with corporate titans such as George Pullman, Cyrus McCormack, and Phil Armour, and also with President Grover Cleveland, who sent in troops to quell strikes in Illinois. Altgeld also embraced the proposed graduated income tax and the populist crusade for free-silver coinage.

The *Chicago Tribune* and similar newspapers across the nation vilified Altgeld as a socialist, communist, and anarchist sympathizer. He, however, viewed himself in the tradition of Paine, Jefferson, Jackson, and Lincoln. His opponents tried to paint him as un-American. "He has apparently not a drop of true American blood in his veins," editorialized the *Chicago Tribune*. "He does not reason like an American, not feel like one, and consequently does not behave like one."

Altgeld was acutely aware that he was not born in America, but he would passionately define himself as an American who cared for and fought for the rights of working-class Americans. He especially fought for Americans accused of being foreigners or agitators.

"I am in the habit of calling this my land, my own native land. This is not entirely correct, but almost so. Perhaps in no other country would a foreigner be justified in referring to himself as a native, but that has always seemed to me to be one of the unique distinctions of America," said Altgeld. "This is my land; it has been so for as long as I can remember, and I think it will be so for whatever time is left to me. It is my land because it made me, shaped me, it nourished me. The thoughts I think came from this land, and the dreams I dream came from this land."

Altgeld was disturbed, later in life, as a defense attorney for some immigrant workers, when the prosecutors accused them of being foreigners.

"Their actions are called foreign actions." But former governor Altgeld argued their struggles were for basic human rights, for bread and warmth and for life itself. Altgeld continued:

> Well, Your Honor, I would not insult your intelligence . . . by reiterating the old saw about no white man being native to these states. We know only too well that the wealth and the goodness of this land came about through successive waves of immigration. Is there a land on earth that did not give us its blood, its people, its culture, its legends . . . its way of work and play, and the knowledge of how to earn liberty and keep it? How can I define America except to say that it is a place where these things jelled, where the many techniques of liberty were put to good use?

An emotionally worked-up Altgeld asked, "What insanity has brought us to a condition where all men who work with their hands are suddenly un-American." He added that plenty of foreign-born men like himself fought in the American Revolution and the Civil War to preserve the Union. He likewise pointed out that no one ever accused Andrew Carnegie, who had been born in Scotland, of being a foreigner or un-American.

Altgeld excoriated the unprincipled, greedy corporate leaders like Pullman, Armour, Field, Gould, and Rockefeller, who took unfair advantage of their workers. He called out bankers, lawyers, and judges who sold out the interests of the working class. In the process, Altgeld became a folk hero among the farmers, labor union members, and especially among labor union leaders, who became his chief allies. Many of these believed he should run for the American presidency, until reminded that he didn't meet the "natural born" requirement.

As governor and as the leader of the anti–Grover Cleveland faction at the Democratic Convention of 1896, Altgeld sided with the unions, the farmers, and the populists. His actions and platform ideals were the seeds of the Progressive era, especially Wilson's New Freedom. He backed William Jennings Bryan because of Bryan's eloquent campaign against the gold standard.

Fast's biographical novel does much more than eulogize a pioneering progressive. It captures the political machinations of Chicago politics in the 1880s and 1890s. It also brings to life the memorable election of 1896, which in many ways defined the class and partisan political clashes of the next fifty years.

Altgeld took to politics. He had won elections as a prosecutor in the small town of Savannah, Missouri, while still in his early twenties. But restlessness pushed him to move to Chicago. There he practiced law and acquired property. He ran unsuccessfully for Congress in 1884, but he was soon elected as a judge in the Cook County Superior Court.

He was backed early on by labor groups. But he also had to "play ball" with the political machine that was graft ridden and heavily influenced by big business. This Chicago machine is similarly described in Lewis's *The Jungle* and Wright's *Native Son*. Altgeld painfully knew that young lawyers and judges, shades of Harper Lee's older Atticus Finch in *Go Set a Watchman* (2015), had to befriend patrons and get on the "right political bandwagon."

As a young lawyer he wrote a book called *Our Penal Machinery and Its Victims*. Altgeld presciently faulted the penal system as a travesty for its brutal conditions, for its gratuitous humiliations, and for its failure to rehabilitate those incarcerated for any kind of decent future. This book won him praise from union leaders, but it earned him a scolding from corporate titans such as Phil Armour, "the great pork and beef king." "Jesus God," Armour told Altgeld, "there's no point attacking jail. It won't help your career to become a damned reformer . . . when you attack the very foundation of society, there you sound damn like a communist." Armour, sounding off like Nixon and Trump much later would, went further:

> Law and order. That's what I refer to, law and order. When we make a judge, we [the business elites of Chicago] expect him to stand up for law and order. When we break him, it's because he doesn't stand for those things. There's a lot of talk about you being a radical. We [presumably meaning Big Business] don't like that kind of talk.

Altgeld didn't like what he was becoming. He was widely admired as a brilliant lawyer and earned respect as a hardworking and reflective judge. He had also become wealthy—an honest wealth, we are told—through several shrewd real estate investments. Still, "he was," he felt, "a dirty, cheap political climber in a rigged political system."

Republicans had controlled the Illinois governorship for the previous four decades. Friends of Altgeld's along with labor and farmers' alliances—which had developed surprising strength throughout the Midwest—promoted Altgeld as the Democratic Party's candidate for governor in 1892. He agreed to run, and he self-funded his campaign from his personal wealth.

The Chicago business elites and political machine probably didn't think Altgeld had a chance and, in any event, were mostly preoccupied with controlling Chicago and Cook County. So, when they weren't really looking, this principled and progressive reformer won election as governor of Illinois. Business leaders would later regret this, as Altgeld evolved to become a pioneering fighter for workers' rights and champion of the underdogs—especially when oligarchical corporate cabals exploited them. Altgeld invested $100,000 of his own money in the election, thereby mostly freeing himself from indebtedness to special interests of various kinds.

His progressive policy views and pardons almost guaranteed he would not win reelection four years later. But that didn't concern him. He would do what was right, not what was politically expedient. That's why a leftist novelist like Howard Fast adopted him as a subject. Fast had earlier written, among many other books, a novel glorifying Tom Paine.

In 1896, Altgeld went down to defeat along with Democratic Party presidential nominee William Jennings Bryan. He had initially backed Bland of Missouri for that nomination, but then campaigned enthusiastically for Bryan that fall.

Altgeld, together with prairie populists and crossover supporters from the People's Party, essentially wrested the Democratic Party from the Grover Cleveland Eastern elites. They united Midwestern southerners and Rocky Mountain state politicians to challenge the establishment of both parties.

Politicians, Altgeld declared,

> are not the leaders of our progress and of our civilization. As a rule they do not gaze into the firmament or measure the stars; their vision is limited to the weather vane on public buildings. They never give the order for advance on any great question, they wait to be commanded to move, and then they hesitate until assured that it is the voice of the majority calling to them. They wait until the leaders of thought have captured the stronghold of a wrong, and then they try to plant their flag over the ramparts that were stormed by others.[6]

The establishment politicians and the newspapers hated Altgeld; yet, as noted, workers and farmers idolized him. He was an Act II politician in the traditional world of Act III politicos. He was portrayed by both Chicago and national business elites as a pernicious agitator.

Bryan and Altgeld gave voice and conscience to the have-less and have-not economic classes. The election of 1896 was a case of economic forces and economic classes in conflict. It was in this fervor that Altgeld said the "American people are called on this year to make a new Declaration of Independence for mankind."

Fast's novel fails to make clear how close the election of 1896 turned out to be. Republicans enjoyed a war chest about ten times larger than the Democrats. Many business owners reportedly threatened their workers that there might be no work if they voted for Bryan and Bryan won.

The Democratic Populists won at least half the states—from Florida to Washington State and from Texas to Virginia. They garnered nearly 47 percent of the popular vote but eventually lost to the Mark Hanna–managed McKinley campaign. A change of only fourteen thousand votes in six states such as California and Oregon would have resulted in a Bryan victory.

Altgeld said his party was

> confronted by all the banks, all the trusts, all the syndicates, all the corporations, all the great papers. It was confronted by everything money could buy, that boodle could debauch, or that fear of starvation could coerce. . . . It was confronted by a combination of forces such as had never been united before and will probably never be united again, and worse still, the time was too short to educate the public.[7]

A year later Altgeld was encouraged, with little resistance from him, to run as an independent third-party candidate for mayor of Chicago. He knew it was an uphill long shot, but he threw himself into the campaign.

"This is a graft-ridden city—I know," said the former judge and governor. "I played ball with the local politicians. I talk from experience and I don't claim absolution from guilt. But I say," he now proudly boasted, "that if elected mayor—I intend to clean up this city." Alas, Altgeld came in a distant third as the Democrats once again took City Hall.

Altgeld understood the unsentimental realities of politics. On the one hand, he was embarrassed by the vote-buying, vote-selling, and tawdry aspects of politics—especially Chicago machine politics. Yet he also knew that political progress, and desirable public policy changes, mainly came about when people like him are willing to get into the political arena. That's why Jefferson, Jackson, and Lincoln were role models for him. But Altgeld also understood, as pointed out by his accurate depiction of politicians, quoted above, that conventional politicians have to be pushed or led by coalitions of principled activists and that the role of Act I and Act II political leadership is crucial to the emergence of effective Act III leadership. In his case, Grangers, farmers' alliances, labor unions, and "Workingmen for Altgeld" and other such activists provided him the encouragement and political energy that enabled the pioneering progressive he became.

Howard Fast was a member of the Communist Party when he wrote this fictional account of the former governor of Illinois. He disowned that party in 1956 when he became disillusioned with Joseph Stalin's terrorism and the spread of anti-Semitism in the Soviet Union. Fast had refused in the early 1950s to cooperate with the House Un-American Activities Committee and thus served three months in federal prison for contempt of Congress.

Fast never tries to make Governor Altgeld into a Communist, or even a socialist. But his is an elegy for a Midwesterner who condemned racism, corporate greed, political machines, and criminal justice malpractices. Altgeld, in Fast's telling, was an American who not only imagined a more just and robust republic but also fought for both the soul of his political party and eliminating barriers in the workplace, so others could, like him, enjoy the fruits of their hard work. Fast's Altgeld was a real-life as well as fictional profile in courage. He was an immigrant American who fought in Lincoln's fight to free the slaves and developed a passionate commitment that American workers—both those born here and those who immigrated—deserved the right to unionize, decent wages and working conditions, and the right to strike if conditions warranted such action.

Altgeld shared the same American Dream that Horatio Alger wrote about in that very same period in the late nineteenth century. Altgeld lived the American Dream. His was a classic up-from-the-bottom example of hard work, striving, ambition, and determination. He was a self-made man. Yet he dedicated himself to fighting entrenched establishment interests he believed were thwarting working-class people who were trying to achieve their own modest American Dreams. Altgeld believed that those who had already made it were creating too many barriers for those who were trying to make it.

Fast's choice of telling Altgeld's story as a patriotic American story—and boldly proclaiming him as "The American"—is a telling and at times inspirational story. Even a superficial reading of other accounts of Altgeld's career suggests that Fast may have, if anything, understated Altgeld's courage and idealism.[8]

Fast was prolific and had an uncommon ability to write best-selling historical fiction. He championed leaders of unpopular causes. His selection of John Peter Altgeld and his specifically titling his novel *The American* underscores Fast's convictions that one can stand and fight for the Jeffersonian version of the American Dream, even if you were not born here.

There have been many other principled governors in America—people like Davis Waite, Ralph Carr, and Dick Lamm of Colorado; Earl Warren and Pat Brown of California; David I. Walsh and Leverett Saltonstall of Massachusetts; Tom McCall of Oregon; and Dan Evans of Washington. But even among these, John Peter Altgeld deserves the praise Fast gives to him. I'm grateful to novelist John Nichols for bringing this novel to my attention. Nichols praised it as among the novels that inspired him when he was young. This is another example of novels no longer read or even remembered. Neither Altgeld nor Fast has become legendary, although it should be noted that Barack Obama did part of his community organizing service in the Altgeld Public Housing project (built in the 1940s and named to celebrate Altgeld), which is located on Chicago's far South Side. Still, *The American: A Middle Western Legend* captured the politics of an important place and time and foreshadowed the fight for the soul of the Democratic Party that continues to be fought in our own time. Altgeld and Fast imagined a more egalitarian and tolerant America, and they yearned for a more advanced and mature constitutional republic.

ELEGY FOR AN AGING BIG-CITY BOSS[9]

"My decision [to run once again for mayor] represents a submission to the will of the populace," says Mayor Frank Skeffington, "and is against my every personal desire." Edwin O'Connor's fictional protagonist in *The Last Hurrah* reflects:

> I had hoped, at the end of my current term, to retire to a well-earned rest, but one look at the names of those who have declared themselves a candidate for this office forced me to change my decision. Why, the mind positively boggles at the presumption of these men! . . . This is the time for experience, for leadership; I cannot abandon this fine city to the care of such fumbling hands. And so, dutifully, if reluctantly, I submit my name to you once again, realizing full well that while my own health and rest are important, it is far more important that the city of ours should not be allowed to revert to Government by Pygmies!

Fictional seventy-two-year-old, long-term mayor Skeffington and twice-former governor, concealing an ailing heart, once more throws his hat into the political ring.

Pulitzer Prize winner Edwin O'Connor's (1918–1968) *The Last Hurrah* is a thinly disguised fictional account of Boston's legendary rogue boss James Michael Curley and his defeat in a 1950s mayoral race. Curley, amazingly, was mayor in four distinct decades from the 1910s through the 1940s. He had been an alderman, state representative, four-term U.S. Representative, governor, a candidate for U.S. Senate, and was famously once reelected from jail.

The Last Hurrah is rightly praised as the best American novel about urban and Irish American politics. Some critics complain O'Connor's tribute to Skeffington (or Curley) is overly sentimental and downplays the unscrupulous graft the real mayor employed. Yet novelist O'Connor masterfully shows us several sides of his politically crafty Skeffington.

Skeffington is the ethnic upward striver, motivated to run for office because other professions had been closed off to immigrant families like his. Achieving political success would enable him to gain power and recognition for first- and second-generation Irishmen, those whom the long-entrenched upper-class Yankee establishment had deemed a troublesome minority. A generation or so earlier Yankee businessmen were known to post signs that read, "No Irish need apply." At one point in *Hurrah*, Skeffington tells his nephew, "The main reason I went into politics was because it was the quickest way out of the cellar and up the ladder . . . the only way out was through politics, it was only when we gained a measure of political control that our people were able to come up for a little fresh air."

Skeffington brought to office deep-seated grudges against Yankee elites from earlier in his life; chief among them was against the Caleb and Amos Force family, who owned Boston's establishment newspaper. The publisher had humiliated his immigrant mother after she was fired while working as a maid in his Brahmin household. "Maids and cooks," Skeffington recalled, "were paid next to nothing; when they went home at night to their families, they'd sometimes take a banana or two with them. Everybody did, everybody knew about it," but the family Skeffington's mother worked for decided to make an example of her, publicly besmirching her and the family name. The mayor had an excellent memory, and in his case revenge was one of the factors fueling his political career.

Skeffington loved political life. He had an extraordinary gift for storytelling and public speaking. He loved doing favors, large and small, for his supporters and for those who might vote for him. He delighted in improving local health and recreational facilities for the working classes. And even business leaders applauded him for his slum-clearance programs. He loved the attention and the competitive aspects of politics. Yet in his later years he would recount to nephew Adam Caulfield that although it was a rewarding and exciting profession, it might not necessarily be a desirable one for someone of the nephew's generation:

Long hours, hard work, at the beck and call of every lunatic with a vote in his pocket, and in the end, unless you're lucky, you have a splendid chance of winding up with the assassins on your back, and nothing in your purse. I don't say this is necessarily so: I've done fairly well, for example, but there are a number of reasons for that we needn't go into now. Anyway, it's the exception that proves the rule. And of course when I began, it was long ago, and the situation around here was a bit different. I had no education to speak of, and a good many roads were closed to our people, and politics seemed to be the easiest way out. I can't complain. But today that's all changed, and on the whole I'd say a young man like yourself is far better out of it.

Beyond his identity as a rising first-generation American and ethnic underdog, a second portrait of Skeffington paints him as a ruthless political boss. O'Connor's "Boston" was a city of distinctive wards, neighborhoods, and ethnic and religious clans; Skeffington was skilled in milking each of these groups for as much political utility as possible. Over his career, Skeffington devised a powerful political machine: a hierarchy of devoted supporters and businesses who benefited from being in his inner circle and helped sustain his power. Skeffington's brand of politics was based on the transactional quid pro quo. His machine was built and reinforced by favors, contracts, and handouts. The goal was to make friends and dependents who would deliver the vote on election day. Boston's growing Irish clan served as his machine's base, but Skeffington worked hard to win support from the Polish, the Italians, and Jews. One of his top counselors was Sam Weinberg, an expert on ward politics.

The real Mayor Curley was an infamous dealer in what machine politicians oxymoronically called "honest graft." Construction companies, who built roads, bridges, libraries, and playgrounds, had to "pay to play," offering bribes or "kickbacks" to receive coveted government contracts. The system was such that Curley's red-brick mansion in one of Boston's fashionable neighborhoods came to be known as "the house Boston contractors had built." Upkeep of his Valhalla went far beyond his means. Indeed, the "care and feeding of the house made Curley a perennial candidate who could not afford to be out of office."[10]

Skeffington understood, as noted, that his political base consisted primarily of Irish Catholic neighborhoods, and he cleverly exploited ethnic and religious antagonisms whenever it helped. "I'm not just an elected official," Skeffington says. "I'm a tribal chieftain as well. It's a necessary kind of dual office-holding, you might say; without the second, I wouldn't be the first."

Skeffington used his spacious home as a kind of Grand Central Station every morning, where, at 9:45 a.m., he would welcome scores of constituents petitioning for jobs, contracts, or assistance of one kind or another. He loved dispersing favors or helping with recommendations. Similar lines of constituents would form outside his City Hall office every afternoon. He also took full advantage of wakes and neighborhood gatherings to press the flesh and exchange the blarney.

Still another Skeffington picks fights with the leading bankers, the newspapers, the Brahmin community, members of the exclusive Plymouth (Somerset) Club, and even the "lace-curtain" (upper-crust) Irish, including the local cardinal. His many opponents disapproved of the mayor's political practices, including intimidation, "featherbedding," wastefulness, and polarizing tactics. They envied his political genius but deplored his audacity. His adversaries unite behind a well-educated political newcomer, attorney Kevin McCluskey, and raise the necessary funds to help him run a modern, "high tech" television campaign; television was a new, emerging, and politically disruptive medium at the time. Skeffington sticks to his old person-to-person and machine-based politics, but this time, they fail him.

Skeffington's "last hurrah" election ends with a landslide defeat. His age and health have taken their natural toll. Also, as O'Connor makes clear, Roosevelt's New Deal had helped to undermine political machine bosses around the nation. Social security, unemployment insurance, and similar federal programs measurably weakened the "handout" politics of city leaders.

Frank Skeffington may have dominated his city for nearly half a century, but his supporters had grown older and perhaps complacent. Many of those he had helped had died off. Others were susceptive to new-styled television candidates and their ads showing their happy families with their "rented dogs."

O'Connor, and "Boston," give Skeffington a splendid funeral. "It followed a three-day wake which had seen thousands of mourners file into the big house on the Boulevard." The senior U.S. senator is there, as are the governor, several justices and judges, scores of policemen and firemen, delegates from the countless lodges and associations to which he had belonged: the Knights of Columbus, the Ancient Order of Hibernians, the Sons of Italy, the Eagles, the Elks, the American Legion, the Veterans of Foreign Wars, the Friendly Sons of Saint Patrick, and many more. "All had come for this last farewell to Frank Skeffington."

To his friends and supporters, the boss was the greatest man in the world—a larger-than-life humanitarian who cared about the little people and made his city a much better place for most of the people. To his opponents, especially the "Boston Brahmins," he was an utterly unprincipled thief, a rascal schemer, and a maneuverer who would do almost anything for a vote.

Skeffington's entire political career, said one aging Yankee, seemed dedicated to "the contravention of the law."

> He thought of buildings erected and roads constructed unnecessarily and at three times their normal cost; he thought of contracts skillfully diverted to political friends; he thought of tax rebates handed out in wholesale lots to campaign contributors; he thought of the endless jobs given to old pals, of the time when the entire city payroll seemed to be supporting nothing but a host of indolent comedians; he thought of the gerrymandering, the featherbedding.

O'Connor's genius is that he offers us a likable and seductive rogue. He gets us to adopt "Uncle" Frank Skeffington as a lovable, aging Don Quixote, forever waging the noble battle against greedy businessmen, prejudiced Brahmins, and kindred political snakes. Yet even O'Connor gradually, if subtly, questions the undemocratic and unethical code, and the favoritism and patronage, by which Skeffington and his machine operate. His mayor became corrupted in the relentless pursuit of and quest to retain power.

We are treated to a politics that is, all at the same time, insurgent, nostalgic, melancholy, and corrupt. Our aging political happy warrior entertains us and at the same time makes us question his overly personalized and graft-based transactional machine. Our attraction to Skeffington is partially, if unsubtly, reinforced because his opponents are depicted as irredeemably dislikable; the popularity contest in this novel is stacked in Skeffington's favor. In the end our "hero" loses, and we are left feeling conflicted about his legacy. What motivates politicians? How do politicians operate with different moral codes than their constituents? Should our judgments of their morality be based on altered standards? Isn't there a better way to govern our big cities? How might we reform politics without losing vital, attractive candidates? Also, is a machine-free system possible, or even desirable?

Some political realists contend governments cannot function well unless political machines or something like them exist. Jonathan Rauch, for example, suggests that "political machines" provided informal networks and relationships that enabled politicians to reach accommodations, reward and protect supporters, and bring about coordinated results. "Good government" ideas, he contends, may be overrated. So some aspects of the old machine style of governing may have encouraged useful ways for politicians to hammer out deals.[11]

The real Boston actually flourished in the immediate post-Curley years. Mayors John Hynes, Kevin White, Ray Flynn, and Tom Menino, among others, helped guide the city of Boston during an impressive renaissance. Each relied on some of the old economic and cultural tribalism of ethnic politics that flourished under Curley—but the post-Curley era was one of increasing professionalism, less patronage, and more good-government innovations.

Similar economic and cultural progress took place in Chicago during those same decades, and a well-greased political machine (the Daley family), similar to the Curley/Skeffington machine ascribed in *Hurrah*, ran Chicago.

One of the gifts Edwin O'Connor gives in *Hurrah* is his colorful descriptions of Skeffington's local supporters. There is, for example, Footsie McEntee, who voted for Skeffington seventeen times in the span of a day, "all by 3PM." There is a body-man goffer named Ditto Boland, who earned his nickname because he so closely adapted all of Skeffington's habits of dress, speech, and mannerisms. There is the infamous Knocko Minihan wake turned into a political rally.

O'Connor also captures the loneliness of his aging pol. Skeffington's wife had died, and their only child, "Junior," seems to immature with age. Skeffington pours out his thoughts to his young nephew, Adam Caulfield, and these reflections indicate melancholy blues, cynicism, nostalgia, and ethnic and family pride.

In the end, however, the Boss has been humiliated and his machine repudiated. His heart gives out and his era ends. O'Connor's *Hurrah* is an elegiac celebration of an old political warhorse. It is also a lament on the politics of insurgency. But it is not a uniformly celebratory account. A minority report is shared, especially through the views of Amos Force, the newspaper publisher, the cardinal, and other old-guard Bostonians.

Hurrah succeeds because of its fine writing, its shrewd insight on the very human aspect of urban politics, and because its themes are universal, transcending the neighborhood of what everyone assumes is the Boston of the 1940s and 1950s.

O'Connor's *Hurrah* remains one of the more enlightening works on urban politics, and readers could profitably read it together with two later nonfiction classics: Robert Caro's *The Power Broker: Robert Moses and the Fall of New York* (1975) and Mike Royko's *Boss: Richard J. Daley of Chicago* (1988).

O'Connor gave us a charming, story-filled account of mid-twentieth-century city politics. It was justifiably hailed as an instructive book about the ethnic politics of its time and place. Boston's Skeffington/ Curley political machine had failed on many fronts. Racism was not seriously addressed. The educational system was inadequate. Public-private partnerships had yet to be formed that would later help encourage innovative start-up companies and transform the economy of that city and its region.

Skeffington, however, was a political type that often emerged in many American cities where teeming and restless new waves of immigrants were yearning to gain acceptance and respect. *Hurrah* captures that important American narrative, and it masterfully raises probing questions about the American political experiment.

MACHIAVELLIAN CAMPAIGN OPERATIVE[12]

"Everybody is always scared of something, after a while you get good at finding out what it is. Sometimes I can find out what it is without pushing very hard. Sometimes the guy doesn't even know what I'm doing. Sometimes you have to push harder," says Stanford University student Mike Freesmith to his roommate and fellow California surfing buddy Hank Moore.

"Freesmith," his roommate notes with some concern, "you're so lacking in morals yourself that you can always spot immorality in someone else." Freesmith dismissively responds that he is just interested in how things work, what motivates people, and (similar to Mrs. Lee in Henry Adams's *Democracy*) how the political system functions as it does.

Freesmith's opinion of human nature was guided by these principles: everyone is always scared of something or someone. People are hateful. Tough, fearless people get ahead. They exploit fear and hate in others. "There is one thing that the masses know: real authority. And a real authority is someone who can satisfy their desire to hate and their fear." "A good authority works the two [hate and fear] . . . together," he adds. "He plays on 'em like they're an organ."

Burdick's (1918–1965) shameless protagonist in *The Ninth Wave* (1956) isn't interested in reforming "the system," much less human nature, nor is he interested in social justice. He is fixated instead, channeling Machiavelli, on how power is acquired and exercised. This is a novel of manipulative campaign politics in a California governor race, presumably in the 1950s. Central figure Mike Freesmith becomes a ruthless, intimidating, and mean authoritarian operative.

Literary critic Gordon Milne rightly sees Burdick's novel as a study about power and how power shapes its wielders.[13] Mike Freesmith operates on power-hungry maxims: "The tough people get ahead, the masses love a man who humbles them, the masses yield to the authority who can satisfy their fundamental desires to hate and fear, the masses are so many 'lemmings.'"

Freesmith, an irreverent and unapologetic badass, becomes a merciless manipulator, finding an outlet for his ambition in his attempt to steer John Cromwell into the California governorship and more broadly to dominate California politics.

Stanford grad, Navy vet, and now a young attorney, Freesmith stirs up fear and hate whenever it works to his and his candidate's advantage. He embraces the political axiom that your candidate doesn't have to win so much as your rival has to lose. He propagates McCarthy-esque Communist smears and guileful whispering campaigns against opponents. His is a "whatever it takes to get his man elected" attitude.

Freesmith is a data wonk who prioritizes votes into strategic categories. "The really important ones," he concludes, "are the eight or ten percent that're scared. They're the real independents, the people whose vote can be changed." "Scared people," Freesmith says, "don't look *for* something, they vote *against* something or somebody . . . they vote their fears." His methods are akin to the political realism of Machiavelli, Hobbes, and legendary political machine bosses, and they bear some resemblance to Trump's 2016 election fearmongering about illegal immigrants, Muslim terrorists, China, and Washington, D.C., elites.

Freesmith's candidate is wealthy attorney John Cromwell, who faces several challenges in his quest for election. He is a superb speaker and has considerable personal wealth; yet, in Freeman's eyes, he isn't ambitious or ruthless enough. Also, he drinks too much. Moreover, he doesn't want to be influenced or "bought" by wealthy special interests. "Not me," Cromwell says. "I'm not going to sell out to the Montgomery Street [San Francisco] and Spring Street [Los Angeles] boys just to get their money. I'll go to the people. I don't need the bribes of the big-money boys."

One of Cromwell's would-be contributors tells Cromwell he has to become more politically pragmatic:

> John, you're a strange sort of politician. You've been around a lot, but not in real politics. You've got to learn that you have two platforms. One is the official platform. That's public and your party will talk about it and it will go out to the newspapers and so make up a pamphlet on it.

> The voters don't pay any attention to it, but you have to do it anyway.
> . . . The second platform is the private one. That's the important one.
> That's what you really do. They're watching, John, to see what your
> private platform is.

When Cromwell asks who this "they" are, he is told "they" are the
people investing in offshore drilling, or wanting highway construction contracts, or concerned about gasoline and liquor taxes, and so on. "They" are
the ones who pull strings and who stand to benefit from favorable subsidies,
or regulations or tax arrangements.

Meanwhile, Mike Freesmith deviously wheels and deals with any
organized interests he can; he attracts them with his stock in trade: fear
and hatred. He was a strategist motivated by a singular goal: victory. *Ninth
Wave* sets up a compelling dynamic between a ruthless campaign manager
and his more genteel boss, the former striving to convince the latter what is
necessary. This relationship encourages the reader to consider what means
are justifiable in the rigorous campaigning process.

Freesmith gets Cromwell, as noted, to use a spurious Joe McCarthy–
style innuendo about a vulnerable Stanford University professor, among
other hateful or fearmongering ploys. Note that Burdick is writing right
after the heyday of Republican U.S. senator Joe McCarthy's red-baiting
scare harangues.

Freesmith's underdog Cromwell wins the Democratic primary. Everyone is surprised except Freesmith. He had mastered what would later
be called "microtargeting," the sending of messages to interest groups with
appropriate cues whipping up their fears about Cromwell's opponents.
Modern campaigns devote great attention to developing algorithms that
presume to identify the psychological predisposition of most voters; see,
for example, Daniel Kreiss, *Prototype Politics: Technology-Intensive Campaigning and the Data of Democracy* (New York: Oxford University Press, 2017).

Freesmith's mantra, as noted, is "Scared people don't vote for something, they vote against something or somebody. They vote their fears."
Following this precept, Freesmith crafted letters addressed to senior citizens
that raised doubts about Cromwell's chief opponent, suggesting he "might
not be for old-age pensions." Freesmith became adept at doing whatever
was needed to advance his candidate's interests—and if this meant "throwing people under the bus," he didn't hesitate.

Freesmith is next challenged with convincing Golden State general
election voters that nominee Cromwell is better qualified than the more
popular, heavily favored Republican. He immediately decides to scare "big

money" interests into supporting Cromwell by suggesting that their businesses may be compromised if they do not support his candidate. This tactic aligns with Freesmith's default mode of subtle but serious fearmongering.

Freesmith is nothing if not certain and self-assured. "He's absolutely sure of himself; completely confident; utterly assured," says his old friend and now physician Hank. "Everybody else knows there's a line you can't cross, but not Mike."

But then *Ninth Wave* has its "Moby Dick" moment. Hank invites Mike to take some time off to go surfing again, something the two had not done for more than a decade. As one huge "ninth" wave approaches, Hank warns Mike not to ride it. Ninth waves, according to surfing lore, are choice, juicy, adrenaline-rushing waves. And the ninth ninth wave, the eighty-first, is supposedly the mother of all prize, or perhaps fateful, waves. Freesmith, the political intimidator, won't back down and is done in by this fatal tidal wave off the Southern California coast.

Burdick is tantalizingly murky in what happens next: "Let it go. It's too big for you; you can't ride it." Yet our undaunted rogue protagonist rejects Hank's suggestion. Freesmith is quickly overwhelmed by the velocity of the water and hurtled beneath the sea and ultimately crashes against unforgiving rocks.

Burdick teases us with some "what if" explanations. But in the end, Hank unexpectedly takes responsibility for the drowning: "I had to do it. No one else was doing anything. So I had to." It may be, too, that Mike let him do it. Readers have to decide for themselves.

Burdick's narrative implies Freesmith's death was almost certainly a killing or an assassination, not unlike Dr. Adam Stanton's assassination of the power-intoxicated Governor Willie Stark (discussed earlier in *All the King's Men*), and not unlike Raymond Shaw (in *The Manchurian Candidate*) killing his mother and U.S. Senator Johnny Iselin.

Both Hank and candidate Cromwell had come to believe that Mike Freesmith was right about a lot of things—that average citizens were often afraid, irrational, frightened, and misinformed. "They're also wise, courageous, steady," Cromwell reflects. "Sometimes they're vicious and sometimes they're generous. They're everything." Similar to *Advise and Consent* (to be discussed), Burdick suggests in *Wave* that people and politicians can rarely be distilled down to reductive labels of "good" and "bad."

Burdick suggests, through his characters, that people are full of contradictions. Yes, people admire individuals who are fearless and certain, and Freesmith had those qualities, even as he lacked conventional moral qualities: "It's the one thing you can't fake. You have it or you don't. The people look up, sniff around. . . . They smell out the man with certainty. And if you have it, they'll believe you. They'll behave as you tell them."

Mike Freesmith's abbreviated eulogy might have read as follows: He was compulsively self-assured and had an uncanny ability to play upon people's fears and uncertainties—perhaps because people had so little faith in themselves. Yet power tripping can become addictive, intoxicating, and can come back to destroy the brash, driven power wielder.

How is society able to protect itself from this type of bullying authoritarianism? Cromwell eventually loses the general election because he no longer follows the Machiavellian script Freesmith prepared for him. Once Mike dies, Cromwell apologizes for his past misdeed, grows mellow, and becomes a mere conventional candidate.

How do people protect themselves from the Mike Freesmiths? Hank asks this of the now remorseful and relieved Cromwell. Cromwell replies that protection or checks come "because there are always some who disbelieve. At some point the disbelievers come together and fight the believer. . . . Sometimes the disbelievers fight alone." "Hank, you were a lonely disbeliever who disbelieved," says Cromwell, "so much that you drowned him."

Burdick's *Wave* captures many of the realities and calculations involved in political campaigning. It captures the constant struggle between competing notions of what tactics are justified in a campaign and what is necessary. It also depicts the type of self-confident, driven political operative all too regularly found in key behind-the-scenes roles in modern politics. Finally, it is a warning about how power—specifically financial and political power—can threaten principles of fairness. It ends with a defeated candidate and a drowned political strategist—not an especially uplifting conclusion. Readers are left to puzzle unanswered questions.

Wave is seldom considered a first-rate or important political novel. The plot is sometimes slow moving and spends an inordinate amount of time early in the novel discussing surfing and the rituals of undergraduate life at Stanford. Nonetheless, in its second half it raises important and enduring concerns about how to be effective in political life without losing sight of the declared purposes of politics.

This cult novel raises useful warnings. Beware the great simplifiers, Burdick says. Beware people who claim they know it all with their certitudes. See through political campaign imposters who are simply involved to manipulate people, power, and the system. Beware a politics divorced from ethical means and sensible purposes. Understand that politics is the interplay between coalitions, activists, and well-organized interest groups trying to capture and use government for their particular interest. Understand, too, that strong politicians and strong campaign operatives are undesirable unless their policy objectives are fair and their political methods are constitutional, democratic, and civil.[14]

Ninth Wave was a Book-of-the-Month Club selection and sold more than 1.5 million copies. Burdick gained even more fame as coauthor of two later political novels, *The Ugly American* (1958) and *Fail-Safe* (1962).

Rhodes scholar Eugene "Bud" Burdick was a Stanford University grad and a navy vet, like his fictional Freesmith. He was also a close student of the American political process and political psychology. He wrote and edited a number of nonfiction political science works and was a popular professor of political science at the University of California at Berkeley. *Wave* exemplifies his professional interests and is in the long tradition of political novels promoting civic awareness. He unmasks the motives that drive at least some political operatives and many would-be politicians. He urges us to examine means-ends relationships. We need to ask why candidates are running for office. What inspires them? Who's backing them and for what reasons? Are they truly committed to helping us achieve commonly shared and laudable aspirations? Do they use democratic and constitutional means? In the end, Burdick joins many fellow novelists in encouraging politicians and political practices that will advance and enrich constitutional democracy.

ELECTION YEAR FEVER MEETS POTOMAC FEVER[15]

"He was such a frightening paradox. He was an absolute patriot, unselfish about giving his time and energy to his country. And yet, so determined to get where he had to go, that he would stoop to any tactics that would advance his progress." This is how our narrator describes John Thurston, the apparently brilliant deputy secretary of defense, potential vice president of the United States, and someday presidential aspirant.

Andrew Tully (1914–1992) had served as a war correspondent in World War II and a Washington reporter covering the White House. He wrote this gossipy, mistitled political thriller, *Capitol Hill* (1962), around the time of the Nixon-Kennedy election of 1960. The novel is not so much about Capitol Hill, but rather about what a driven, ruthless subcabinet member is willing to do to further his career in the direction of becoming president of the United States.

Tully's fictional president is Warren P. Aldrich, a benign (yet apparently lazy) fellow who was winding down his largely uneventful two terms in the White House. The "Old Man" is described as "not very bright, but he looks sincere as hell. Everybody's kind of old uncle." He never works hard, but he loves hunting quail and fishing. This apparently doesn't much affect our celebrity-in-chief in the polls. He is as beloved as Eisenhower was liked. In one instance the Washington press corps follow him while he fishes for trout one day and diligently documents the fish he catches.

Thurston doesn't understand his president: "The Old Man doesn't seem to be *interested* in the job. He doesn't seem to be excited about being President of the United States. He seems to treat it as though it were just another job." Thurston himself, however, would love to be president. He would be, he believes, a different, consequential president. But first he must back the person who will become the next president and wait his turn—perhaps eight years from now.

A further note about President Aldrich: He understands people and politics, and he says, "I've learned that there are certain levers you have to use to get things done in Washington." But he is happy to leave the political heavy lifting to a few cabinet and cabinet deputies like the crafty John Thurston.

A primary fight for the presidential nomination heats up, pitting a handsome, wealthy U.S. senator from Tennessee against a popular liberal New York State governor, Dan Williams, who was described as half FDR and half Jim Farley (FDR's savvy political advisor and campaign strategist). Governor Dan Williams, we learn, is the consummate politician. He kisses babies, shakes hands, and makes promises he most likely will not be able to keep. His positions on civil rights are remarkably liberal for the time, and he is especially well connected among progressives. Williams, for example, is backed by most of the liberal interests, including the NAACP. He campaigns in the style of FDR, and he is intent on rebuilding the FDR political coalition.

Tennessee senator Philip Church Douglas is the underdog and presents himself as the more pragmatic and centrist candidate for his party's presidential nomination. He is for integration and the rights of African Americans to be treated equally; yet he urges gradual measures rather than a new Reconstruction Era–style federal imposition on southern and border states, like his own Tennessee. Douglas is the younger of the two candidates, and, like John F. Kennedy, who won in 1960, he is Harvard educated with a wealthy father.

Douglas predictably faults his rival, Dan Williams, for promising too much and for being too liberal. Douglas claims he would be the better coalition builder and the type of president who could earn support in Congress from both liberals and conservatives. Douglas is also a charming deal maker determined to go to Chicago and make it a contested convention.

Our protagonist, Deputy Secretary of Defense John Thurston, is an invaluable counselor to the president. He works hard, generally discreetly, to ingratiate himself with his party's front-runner Dan Williams. Williams confides in him and regularly asks for advice.

John Thurston's ruthlessness is not without at least some principles and ideals. He warns that limited aggression could grow into a war of annihilation. Yet he warns Congress, and anyone who will listen, that Western weakness in its capacity to fight limited and conventional war invited an imbalance the Communists might take advantage of.

This belief is his guiding philosophy, and he pursues it relentlessly. And he is willing to use questionable political means to force a leading congressman to support his doctrine. In this instance, Thurston calls one of the congressman's major donors to "talk some sense" into the representative. What Thurston does, which may be typical of his style of politics, may seem ugly to many people, but effective political operatives, it is suggested here, are those unafraid to get their hands dirty in pursuit of the greater good. (See these same themes in Klein's *Primary Colors* and Nye's *The Power Game*.) So, Tully suggests, readers may regard Thurston as evil or perhaps an unapologetic utilitarian, or both.

Thurston's obsession with becoming secretary of defense under the next president flounders because of several personal developments. First, both he and his wife, Anne, are involved in long-standing love affairs with other partners. His wife wants a divorce; yet she gamely goes along with being Mrs. Thurston to protect John's "reputation." Second, John's mistress insists that Thurston marry her now, not later. A frustrated Thurston tries to explain: "But, Alicia, you do understand that we will have to wait? You must know that any—oh, scandal—would be very dangerous. To put it plainly, I want to be defense secretary and I think I'll get it. But I've got to keep my private life sanitary." Neither wife nor mistress is pleased.

Further, he finds himself being blackmailed by the wife of a former Defense Department official Thurston had recently fired. This blackmailer had caught Thurston's wife in the midst of one of her many rendezvous with her boyfriend, Charles, at a New York hotel. Thurston tries in vain to squash her accurate, yet damaging, exposé. Soon his secretary and probably the White House know his situation. To make matters worse, his candidate, Dan Williams, is being outdueled by Senator Phil Douglas in the presidential race. Williams calls on Thurston to try to win endorsement from the popular, yet still neutral, incumbent president. He also asks Thurston to come to the national convention in Chicago to lend him substantive policy prestige. Thurston, until now, had tried, as most Defense and State Department officials regularly try, to remain publicly detached from overt presidential campaign politics. Indeed, President Aldrich had gently warned him, "I know I don't have to tell you to keep the Pentagon out of politics."

But Thurston's ambition takes over and propels him to fulfill Governor Williams's requests. He solicits the president's endorsement. And he flies to Chicago "to be seen" with Governor Williams. He deludes himself in the moment that he will soon have to decide between the vice presidential nomination and a promotion to a cabinet post.

Meanwhile, his blackmailer has "influenced" him to award a key Defense Department contract to a friend of his blackmailer. This becomes Thurston's undoing. It is such a dramatic switch that it arouses suspicions—especially in the White House.

President Aldrich is puzzled and skeptical of Thurston's reversal on this big contract. The president asks, "What could cause a man of Thurston's brilliant mind and sharp perception and hard-boiled realism and tough respect for facts and figures to make such a blunder?" Had something happened to John Thurston? the president wonders, and follows up.

The president eventually discovers Thurston's motives and becomes furious at his long-trusted national security advisor: "To be willing to sacrifice his country's welfare to his own career. To forget principle and his nation's safety because he wanted to be Secretary of Defense or Vice President. If war came, the decision to switch to Newport would mean defeat for the United States."

The president, upon further confirmation of Thurston's compromised decision, makes two decisions: He overrules Thurston's contract policy switch, and he suddenly decides to endorse Senator Phil Douglas for the presidential nomination, an endorsement at this crucial late stage that virtually guarantees Douglas, and not Dan Williams, the party's coveted nomination. Defeat for Williams dooms John Thurston's hopes for becoming secretary of defense.

Things get even more complicated. As Thurston learns of his "backing the wrong horse" for president, he also learns that his wife, Anne, has died from an overdose of sleeping pills at her New York hotel. Both his family and career have crashed.

Author Andrew Tully doesn't tell us what happens next, but his *Capitol Hill* conveys the clear message that politics in the nation's capital can be an uncomfortable mixture of unprincipled decisions and complicated personal lives, with the two intersecting at awkward times.

Tully's own views about politics as a profession are undoubtedly echoed in the words of newly minted presidential nominee Phil Douglas, who says:

> Yes, I'm Ivy League. If that's something bad, very well. But I'm also something else . . . I'm a very tough politician. You learn a lot of things in those books at Harvard. . . . And from these professors with their pipes and their tweeds and their gentle airs. If you're interested at all in a political career and have any kind of brain, you learn that politics is a tough and ruthless cutthroat business . . . I found out that George Washington and Thomas Jefferson and even little Jimmy Madison and all the rest of the really worthwhile politicians were worthwhile because they were tough and because when they had to they could kick and scratch and bite and gouge with the toughest of them.

Tully's Thurston lives a complicated life indeed, complications that get magnified by presidential election-year politics and his protagonist's Potomac-fever ambitions. Bright people make mistakes in every walk of life, but the glare of the limelight makes it hard to cover up corrupt double dealing in public life—especially as people try to ascend what the British often call the "greasy pole" of leadership.

Politics is a rough profession. It tests character. It magnifies strengths and it magnifies weaknesses, as we later saw in presidents like LBJ, Nixon, and Trump.

Tully raises critical questions about politics and political leadership. He reminds us that it is usually the tough, persevering political wheeler and dealer who gets elected. Family wealth also helps, as does an appeal to moderates. But citizens in a constitutional republic also want elected leaders and their advisors to do the right thing, to be honest and to serve the public interest. How do you navigate getting there and being good? How does one properly balance ambition, family, principles, loyalties, and integrity?

Capitol Hill made the *New York Times* best-seller list, as several of Tully's books did; yet it was much less successful financially and as literature than *All the King's Men*, *Advise and Consent*, and *Primary Colors*. Still, it is representative of post–World War II fictionalized political investigative exposés. *Capitol Hill*, along with *Advise and Consent*, could help comprise a Washington, D.C., reading course—which might also include Henry Adams's *Democracy*, Gore Vidal's *Washington, D.C.*, Knebel and Bailey's

Seven Days in May, Ward Just's *Echo House*, and Joe Nye's *The Power Game*. Finally, the questions Tully raises about election-year advising remain as relevant today as they were in the 1950s.

Tully later said his best seller lost him both sources and friends in Washington. Washington insiders, he said in 1964, were afraid to be seen with him for fear of having their sins or unorthodox relationships exposed. This is the price our fiction-writing unmaskers have to pay, and why it is that sometimes only fiction can do justice to the truth.

ROCKY ROAD TO THE WHITE HOUSE[16]

"Only certain kinds of people are cut out for the work—and, yeah, we are *not* princes. . . . Two-thirds of what we do is reprehensible. This isn't the way a normal human being acts," says fictionalized southern governor and 1992 presidential candidate Jack Stanton. "We smile, we listen. . . . We fudge. . . . We tell them what they want to hear—and when we tell them something they *don't* want to hear, it's usually because we've calculated that's what they really want. We live an eternity of false smiles—and why? Because it's the price you pay to lead."

Joe Klein's *Primary Colors* is a tour de force fictional account about how politicians often have to grovel for high office in a nation that disdains politics and politicians. It is well written, honest, earthy, entertaining, and instructive. It is about politicians who yearn to take the high road but find it hard to resist going negative.

This novel gives us a memorable southern governor, Jack Stanton, who is running for the Democratic Party's 1992 presidential nomination. His message, style, and foibles are strikingly similar to real-life Arkansas governor William Jefferson Clinton, who came from behind and surprisingly won his party's nomination that year. Stanton, like Clinton, was a magnetic, larger-than-life personality whose personal life was, to put it politely, roughish.

Veteran political reporter Joe Klein (1946–) covered the 1992 campaign. He published *Primary Colors: A Novel of Politics* anonymously for fear of losing access to the Clintons, their advisors, and other top politicians. He may also have, like novelist Henry Adams more than a hundred years earlier, feared lawsuits.

His novel is a probing account of what motivates politicians, what motivates campaign volunteers, and the often chaotic twists, turns, and unethical temptations that characterize national campaigns.

Klein's governor Stanton lives in a confusing world with moments of political brilliance and stretches of character lapses. He yearns to be a good person and a good leader—a person who wants to make people's lives better—yet his craving for affection, sex, and winning become shadowy demons.

The novel is told from the perspective of Henry Burton, an African American aide who becomes Stanton's "body man" and serves as a de facto assistant campaign manager. Burton's perception of the governor teeters between awe of Stanton's political prowess and worries about his promiscuous past and sometimes unchecked ambition. In our introduction to Stanton, Burton recalls, "I have seen better speakers and heard better speeches, but I don't think I'd ever heard . . . a speaker who measured his audience so well and connected so precisely." However, once reporters begin probing into Stanton's past, Henry and his fellow aides find themselves in a minefield of unpleasant surprises.

His fellow campaign aides call Burton a "true believer." He is, at least initially, able to overlook lies and fakery because he wants "to work for a man who fights the really good fight" on behalf of the American people. He'll stick with Stanton, with all his baggage, over someone who doesn't really care about the people.

Bill Clinton biographers suggest that his, like Stanton's, was a career constructed on the paradox of parallel lives. Pulitzer Prize–winning biographer David Maraniss suggests:

> One of the paradoxes of Bill Clinton is that he was drawn to a profession that promises constant tension and anxiety, conditions hardly conducive to keeping old demons at bay. Politics by its very nature demand parallel lives to some degree. It is the rare politician who can always say, in every situation, what he really believes or behave as he really is, and that politician is unlikely to get elected president. Politics makes it difficult for even the most secure and grounded people to feel integrated in mind, body and soul.[17]

Governor Stanton convinces himself, like many in politics, that what he can do for his party and his country is better than what his rivals can do. Klein submerges us into the world of campaign managers, aides, and consultants. Through Burton, the reader follows Stanton from town halls to radio interviews to televised debates. Scandals and surprise contenders make us doubt the success of the campaign and question Stanton's character and merit.

Klein's governor Stanton loves politics and is an uncommonly talented empathizer. He knows politics is a high-stakes game that involves issues, theater, and relentless pragmatism. "You need," he says, "someone who knows the emotional part of the game, the symbols, the theater, how to use the power. And you also need someone who *really* knows the issues . . . [Also] someone who knows what's doable."

Primary Colors depicts Stanton and his wife as incredibly caring and well-meaning, yet ultimately flawed, individuals. They are driven to toxic cover-ups and negative tactics, motivated by their drive to make history and change the world.

One of the compelling parts of *Colors* is how Klein makes his Stanton a likable rogue. Early on we root for his success and are drawn in by his compassionate narrative. The governor repeatedly uses the "stick with me and together we will make history and change the world" refrain. Here he is in New Hampshire pleading for the endorsement of a local official:

> It would mean the world to me here in New Hampshire. You have it in your power to make the next president of the United States, and I know you don't take it lightly. I don't take it lightly. Everyone knows the respect that people have for you here. But listen, Barry: We are going to do great things. We are going to make history.

Then Stanton tries to close the sale:

> You want to be part of that next year in Washington, after we win. We'll make a place for you, an important place. I'm not the sort who forgets who brung him to the dance. We take care of our friends, Barry. You know what that means, right?

Candidate Stanton talks about how things can be better, passionately presenting himself as the best person for the job, and regularly trying to portray opponents in an unfavorable light. He recognizes that it is a game. He understands he has to become a bullshitter but rationalizes, "This ain't the Boy Scouts. . . . Bullshit'll grease a lot of doors." He is the one, he boasts, who knows how to go through which doors to make the progress America needs.

However, as the novel develops, both narrator and reader are forced to question their allegiance to Stanton. He, like Bill Clinton with Gennifer Flowers in the 1992 election, is embarrassed by a previous affair that gets caught up in a media frenzy.

One of Stanton's defeated rivals asks how the governor keeps on going when the media and everyone is trying to "tear you apart." Exactly "how do you wake up in the morning . . . when they were pulverizing you?" "I don't rightly know," says Stanton:

> There just doesn't seem to be any other option for me—nothin' else I really *can* do. And yeah, I'm sure a part of it—a big part of it—it's ego sickness. You called it an addiction. You're right. But that's not *all* of it. I do *love* it—the part you talked about, moving a crowd. And the strategy, too, the game of it. But I don't think I'd be baring my butt for random whipping by that self-righteous, hypocritical pack of shitbirds if I didn't believe that you can make people's lives better. I know it sounds corny, but I still get excited when I come across some program we've done that actually works.

Klein's novel captures modern-day campaigning better than any other fictional work in recent times. He has an uncanny insider's sense of the strategies used by candidates, consultants, reporters, and even the hangers-on. He captures the highs and lows of a campaign, the fakery as well as the unscripted authentic joyous moments. His plot is strong and features the unexpected twists and turns most campaigns take.

Primary Colors is part raw journalism, part biography, part political satire, but in large part an exercise in political "junkie-ism." We are thrown into the world of the campaign—motel rooms at 3 a.m. filled with coffee cups, soda cans, and doughnuts, press conferences with swarms of cameras and questions, and call centers with devoted volunteers and lowly interns. Klein is especially good at depicting how campaigns invariably attract an odd collection of zealots, hard-to-define "hangers-on," and weirdos. Klein may have been closely covering the campaign, but he says he could only imagine the behind-the-scenes conversations and possible tantrums between candidate and spouse and inner-circle aides. These are rich. Klein later acknowledges this: "It was what I imagined might be happening on the other side of the wizard's curtain."

Klein seems equally amused and disturbed by the inspiring, yet sometimes crass, Stanton. In a subsequent work of nonfiction, *Politics Lost*, Klein acknowledges that he likes political rogues and is even a "pro-peccadillo" journalist. He is attracted, he writes, to the Clintons, the McCains, and Gingriches, who go off script or fail, fall down, and scramble to get back up again.

In this sense, Bill Clinton was a gift sent from central casting. He was fun to cover—both for the reporter and for the novelist. The real Clinton was, writes Klein, "a world-class baloney slicer who was a brilliant policy wonk" and "a womanizer of desperately bad taste." "He ran as who he was:

a big, smart, sloppy guy who loved talking to people, loved talking policy, and wanted desperately to be loved in return."[18]

Another complicated character in Klein's novel is Stanton's unexpected opponent, Fred Picker. Picker first enters the plot when he endorses Stanton's opponent Lawrence Harris. Harris beat Stanton in his home state primary in New Hampshire. As the race travels down the East Coast Harris is gaining momentum, propelled by Stanton's embarrassing reckoning with a former mistress, who publicly reveals tapes of their affair. However, when Harris suffers a heart attack, Picker, who had developed a close relationship with the candidate and his wife, is asked to continue the campaign.

Although Picker had mysteriously dropped out of politics a decade before, the former Florida governor shows he hasn't lost his campaigning prowess or tact. He begins his campaign surrounded by his family and Harris's wife, delivering a heartfelt tribute to Harris's vision and adding his own homespun convictions. He announces he will donate blood in honor of Harris, and blood donations throughout the country soar in the next week.

The media and the American public fall for Picker. Stanton and his staff watch as Picker's numbers climb and as he makes one successful speech after the other. In one particularly raucous rally, however, the new candidate discusses his discomfort with the nation's obsessive mood swings:

> This is a really terrific country, but we get a little crazy sometimes . . . I guess the craziness is part of what makes us great, it's part of our freedom. But we have to watch out . . . there's no guarantee we'll be able to continue this—this highwire act, this democracy. If we don't calm down, it all may just spin out of control. I mean, the world keeps getting more complicated and we keep having to explain it to you in simpler terms, so we can get our little oversimplified explanations on the evening news. Eventually, instead of even trying to explain it, we just give up and sling mud at each other—and it's a show, it keeps you watching . . . it's fake, it's staged, it doesn't mean anything. Most of us don't hate our opponents; hell, we don't even know 'em.

Klein makes Picker an oddly modest, yet appealing, politician. Candidate Picker is dismayed by the campaign circus and distances himself from normal campaign operations. This earns Picker increased respect from voters.

Meanwhile, in the Stanton camp, our allegiance to his campaign falters once more. In a last effort to save the campaign, Stanton assigns Henry and loyalist Libby Holden—a riotous and poignant character herself—to go to Florida to investigate Picker's past. Alas, they eventually dig up enough dirt, drug addiction, and a brief homosexual encounter that, if they could somehow leak this information, would doubtless take their chief rival down. When Libby and Henry present the evidence to the governor and his wife, the Stantons, despite their long-stated, high-minded rhetoric about running a positive campaign, eagerly consider how they will put this new ammunition to use.

Libby and Henry advise—even urge—the Stantons not to use this "dirt" against their rival. Libby knows Jack Stanton's flawed character; yet she reminds him that years ago he had committed himself to end the negative politics of dirty tricks. She recalls him telling her back in 1972, "Our job is to make it clean. Because if it's clean, we win—because our ideas are better."

That "was a long time ago," Stanton lamely replies.

Stanton's wife, Susan, rationalizes that "we didn't know [back then] how the world worked. Now we do." And if they don't deploy this dirt to encourage their rival to stand aside, then the press or the Republicans would invariably find out and the Democrats and the public will be the losers. Shades of Willie Stark and Mike Freesmith.

Libby doesn't waver. She is the Socratic gadfly trying to remind the Stantons of the central reason for their campaign: "Honey, you may be right, but it just ain't who we're supposed to be." She stands by her moral objection to this type of sleazy politics.

Libby considers Stanton's reaction an utter failure to pass this character test. "You have never paid the bill," she tells him. "Never. And no one ever called you on it. Because you're so completely fucking SPECIAL. Everyone was always so PROUD of you. And me, too. Me the worst."

An obviously dismayed and apparently distraught Libby Holden walks out, and our new moral hero—a tragic hero in this case—commits suicide later that night. A bewildered Henry Burton decides he is going to resign: "I just don't feel comfortable about this anymore."

A conflicted Governor Stanton considers taking himself out of the race but decides first he'll meet with Governor Picker to share the file of negative research his aides have compiled against him. He persuades the reluctant Henry to join him.

In a strange turn of events, Picker tells Stanton that he, too, has decided to get out of the race, a decision now reinforced by the revelations of his past now in Stanton's possession. Stanton allows that he will not use this information. But Picker breaks down emotionally and, in effect, insists Stanton remain in the race. Picker drops out. Stanton stays in. Henry is stunned and disgusted.

But Henry, who is now the most conflicted political advisor in American fiction since Jack Burden in *All the King's Men*, desperately wants out: "I have no idea who I am anymore." He has lost his moral compass *and* his appetite for national politics.

"Don't leave me now," says Stanton. "We've worked so hard—*together*, Henry—to get here. . . . And it's there for us now. It's right there. We can do incredible things. We can change the whole country."

The ethically challenged Stanton tries to reframe his case by saying, "I thought you got it Henry. I thought you understood. This is about the ability to *lead*. It's not about perfection," and then he sheepishly confesses, "Okay, I probably would have leaked the file to someone—and I'da felt slimy about it, but you know what? The bottom line wouldn't be any different. Picker was going down. It was only a question of when."

Then Stanton pleads with Burton to stand with him: "You're still with me, aren't you? Say you are. Say you are. *Say it* . . . Aw c'mon Henry. This is ridiculous: you've *gotta* be with me."

The novel ends there, leaving the reader to decide: Should Henry stay and help Stanton win the Democratic nomination? Can his moral doubts be offset by Jack's electability, progressive vision, and leadership promise? And how about you? Would you have remained as an aide to the talented, yet flawed, Stanton?

Klein's campaign novel raises useful questions about American elections. Is it possible to recruit, and can we find, effective politicians who are also truly good people to run for the White House? How do the requirements of fund-raising, stamina, and the superficiality of campaigns affect candidates? Does the drive, ambition, and cunning necessary to run encourage a form of temperament that is detrimental to being a balanced national leader? Finally, what is the price leaders have to pay for getting elected—and for leading?

Klein's book largely ignores the debilitating "money-chase" involved in presidential campaigns. But he does an especially good job of getting inside the mind of senior campaign aides. He captures the frantic and often chaotic pace of their mind-numbing schedule. He has some fun riffs about campaign staffers, the inevitable campaign groupies, and the ever lurking and often lazy press—derisively called "scorps" by campaign staffers.

Little Rock in the novel becomes Mammoth Falls. New York governor Mario Cuomo becomes Governor Ozio, campaign strategist James Carville becomes Richard Jemmons, and "girlfriend" Cashmere McLeod is the novel's stand-in for Gennifer Flowers. Klein had a lot of fun both on the campaign trail and in inventing his parallel fictional story of what he watched in Bill Clinton's surprising and often turbulent 1992 campaign for the White House.

Legendary campaign reporter Teddy White wrote a series of prize-winning nonfiction treatments of presidential elections in the 1960s and early 1970s. His books, *The Making of the President* series, celebrated and idealized each winner. Not so in *Primary Colors*. Klein portrays both candidate and the election system as imperfect. Still, the author is beguiled by the political artistry of his Jack Stanton. And his narrator Henry, like most Americans, wants his candidate and his president to be honest, consistent, and a forthcoming, transparent role model—yet he also wants his president to be elected so he can enact needed public policy changes. Ultimately, however, Burton is appalled by the ethical lapses and the toll the campaign takes on nearly everyone's character.

Colors was considered by some people as an attack on Clinton and his character. This was understandable. Klein, however, saw it as a positive portrayal of larger-than-life politicians. Candidates, he implied, invariably have weaknesses entangled with their obvious strengths. "It seemed obvious that a larger-than-life leader was preferable to one who was smaller-than-life." Clinton was mesmerizing and maddening; yet Klein concludes in the end, reflecting on his two terms of service in the White House, that President Clinton conducted a serious, substantive, and largely successful presidency.[19]

The real Clinton is in several ways a Shakespearean character. He was a popular two-term president who probably might have been (and would have liked to have been) elected to a third term. He presided over a robust economy and both balanced the budget and created millions of jobs in his second term. However, Clinton's FBI director rendered this scathing assessment of Clinton: "With Bill Clinton, the scandals and rumored scandals, the incubating ones and the dying ones, never ended. Whatever moral compass the president was consulting, it was leading him in the wrong direction. Worse, he had been behaving that way so long that the closets were full of skeletons just waiting to burst out."[20]

Clinton understood the role of paradox and dialectics as well as anyone else in politics. Even as a high school student he had reflected, "I am a living paradox—deeply religious, yet not as convinced of my exact beliefs as I ought to be; wanting responsibility, yet shirking it; loving the truth but often giving way to falsity . . . I detest selfishness, but see it in the mirror every day."[21]

Clinton's self-awareness and understanding of the contradictory nature of politics is also revealed in a talk he once gave at the University of

Arkansas. He was, he said, aware of how life is often a struggle between sunlight and shadows, pessimism and optimism. He talked of Robert Penn Warren's Willie Stark and other fictionalized politicians and concluded they were, paraphrases biographer David Maraniss, "powerful combinations of darkness and light—the darkness of insecurity, depression, family disorder. In great leaders, he told them, the light overcame the darkness."[22]

Klein's Stanton shines an invaluable light on Bill Clinton and perhaps even more on the realities of election politics in America. His is yet another example of how fiction can often be even more revealing than nonfictional analysis in doing justice to the truth. His is also a reminder that politics is much like real life because it is real life.

A first reading of *Colors* encourages disdain for all the fakery, hypocrisy, manipulation, and masks of electoral politics. A second reading explains the gamesmanship of politics and the "hardball" requirement of competitive politics—even making a case for occasional Machiavellian tactics if larger, positive ends are being served. But Klein dodges giving us a single moral or lesson. He triggers more conversations than he ends.

This is the case as Klein helps us better understand the limits of politics and the imperfections of party and electoral systems. Here, and in subsequent writings as a columnist for *Time*, Klein yearns for a high-minded leader, the kind who will tell constituents what they may not know and what they probably do not want to hear, things polls and political consultants do not provide.[23]

Part of imagining a great republic is wanting elections that transcend fakery and will nominate candidates who will balance optimism with reality, resoluteness with integrity. Klein reminds us that this is a rarely satisfied aspiration.

Many of us wish Klein would have written a companion volume to *Colors* describing the bizarre election of 2016, once again involving the Clintons. Bill Clinton, for all his strengths and earlier successes, proved more liability than asset in his wife's presidential campaign, and, alas, a "bad boy" rogue even larger than Jack Stanton eclipsed Hillary Clinton in the Electoral College in 2016. That election, to many people, seemed more novel than real.

What the works in this and the next chapter have in common is that they use fictional storytelling to help us understand the challenge and paradoxical realities of politics in a variety of settings.

7

THE NOVELIST AS
POLITICAL ANTHROPOLOGIST

Anthropologists study human behavior and our cultural development. Political anthropologists examine how we come together to cope with challenges and work with one another to satisfy human wants and yearnings. The novelists treated in this chapter teach us about who we are, what we believe in, and how our social and political practices shape our identity, our dreams, and our political behavior.

Three of these novels focus on political activity in the nation's capital. But most of them capture various realities of political life elsewhere in America. There is one novel, or novella, not based on American soil: Melville's *Billy Budd*. I include it in part because it was written by one of America's greatest fiction writers, and also because it is a majestic story addressing one of the enduring challenges for any political, civic, or military organization.

Several of these novels, especially *Gone with the Wind*, *Advise and Consent*, and Horatio Alger's works, were huge best sellers. But even the less commercially successful novels have much to teach us about politics, politicians, and the idea of America.

Enjoy.

HORATIO ALGER'S AMERICA[1]

Horatio Alger Jr. (1832–1899), a defrocked Unitarian minister and semi-ostracized Harvard-educated Bostonian, escaped to New York City in the 1860s and reinvented himself as a "dime novelist," celebrating examples of upward mobility and the American Dream for teenaged orphans in Gilded Age America.

Most of his more than a hundred readable short novels describe how, with perseverance, honesty, courage, and a little bit of luck and help, at least some impoverished youths can raise themselves up to satisfying levels of respectability and even modest prosperity.

America is now, according to French economist Thomas Piketty, in a second Gilded Age. Inequality in the United States now rivals that of the original Gilded Age and the early decades of the twentieth century. Dreams of upward mobility are being doubted. In this new era of globalization, disruptive technologies, and wage stagnation, can perseverance, honesty, courage, and a little bit of luck still provide the Alger-ian yellow brick road to the middle or upper-middle class?

Millions of young people cheered candidate Bernie Sanders when he said that the American system of capitalism was "rigged" to benefit the wealthy 10 percent and to penalize the other 90 percent. Millions of other voters cheered Donald Trump when he blamed trade pacts, globalization, wasteful overseas commitments, and illegal immigrants for "ruining" America.

Neither politicians nor economists have given us easy or acceptable remedies for inequality and the lessening of upward mobility. The stock market crash of 1929 and a combination of New Deal and World War II policies reduced the inequality of the original Gilded Age. Few look to these kinds of global shocks as likely remedies these days. Economic growth is likely to be slow in the coming years, which probably means that economic inequality will increase.

But back to Horatio Alger and the first Gilded Age. We don't read Alger anymore; his era is long past. The "Horatio Alger Legend," however, remains a vital part of our vocabulary and political culture.

"Save your money, my lad, buy books, and determine to be somebody, and you may fill an honorable position." This is the advice given by a prosperous New York businessman, Mr. Whitney, to a poor young street urchin, "Ragged Dick" Hunter. Alger's story, *Ragged Dick, or Street Life in New York with the Boot-Blacks* (1868), describes how the penniless young lad follows the advice he is given, quits smoking and gambling, and begins a campaign of self-improvement. He "gains something more valuable than money. He had studied regularly every evening, and his improvement had been marvelous. He could now read well, write a fair hand, and had studied arithmetic as far as interest."

Alger understands that some of his young readers may find it hard to believe his hero Dick had made so much progress. However, Dick "knew that in order to grow up respectable, he must be well advanced, and he was willing to work." Alger adds:

> But then the reader must not forget that Dick was naturally a smart boy. His street education sharpened his faculties, and taught him to rely upon himself. He knew that it would take him a long time to reach the goal which he had set before him, and he had patience to keep on trying. He knew that he had only himself to depend upon, and he determined to make the most of himself—a resolution which is the secret of success in nine cases out of ten.

Horatio Alger was born in Chelsea, Massachusetts, to a family of modest means. He had an overbearing and apparently unloving Protestant minister father. While he could trace his lineage to the Pilgrims and relatives who fought in the Revolution, his parents were not Boston Brahmins. He was a scholarship and "work-study" student at Harvard College, later earning a graduate degree from Harvard's Divinity School. He drifted around in various prep school teaching posts and in an ill-fated experience as a Unitarian minister in Brewster, Massachusetts. That job ended abruptly when he was accused of molesting youths and was essentially run out of town and out of his profession.

After moving to New York City, Alger found a second calling—or perhaps a "second ministry." He was already a skilled poet and magazine writer. But now he turned his talent to writing about young, fatherless boys who had to deal with being poor, uneducated, and having to struggle to eke out a minimal existence by doing menial jobs such as bootblack, newspaper boy, part-time school janitor, luggage boy, street musician, peddler, or errand boy.

A few of Alger's novels were about adults and a handful had women heroines, but the rest of his novels—called "dime novels" because they were cheap "juvenile fiction," adventure and moral uplift stories written for and about teenagers—were about male youths between the age of thirteen and sixteen. His novels could be bought at the local "Five and Dime" general stores of the day—perhaps another reason they are called "dime novels."

Alger hung out with teenage boys at the Newsboys' Lodging House on Fulton Street, Manhattan. He interviewed and mentored countless youths and, like an anthropologist, studied their habits, their travails, and their occasional triumphs. He was a clever and gifted storyteller. Snarky critics say he used the same formula to tell his "hero boy" stories over and over again. There is some truth in this statement; yet the fact that his novels sold twenty-five million or more (some claim he sold one hundred million), and were among the most borrowed library books for two or three generations, is testimony to his writing ability, his wit, and his ingenious (if sentimental) characterizations.

Young "Ragged Dick" lived a meager existence shining shoes near City Hall in New York. Bullied by rival toughs, he was repeatedly tricked and robbed. But Alger tells us that in spite of this existence, Dick had a strong moral character. He did not lie or steal. He listened when his customers told him that "honesty is the best policy." Most important, he developed his own ethic of hard work and perseverance.

When luck and opportunity arise, Ragged Dick is prepared. He jumps off a ferryboat to save the life of a drowning youth and is rewarded by the youth's father, who gives the poor young bootblack a decent-paying job in an accounting firm. Ragged Dick's courage and be-prepared diligence lead to modest upward mobility: he achieves some financial success, and, more important, he realizes his dream of becoming respectable. "Henceforth," Alger has Dick forecast, "he meant to press onward, and rise as high as possible."

All of Alger's young heroes are virtuous, manly, and brave. They work hard, answer emergency challenges, get assisted by mentor figures or surrogate fathers, and journey upward in the business world. None go into politics, sciences, the arts, or the clergy. Alger is all about business.

Most Alger novels also feature a condescending, conceited, mean-spirited bully. This antagonist, usually the same age as Alger's hero, may be the spoiled son of the town's bank president or town squire, who specializes in taunting, insulting, and stigmatizing Alger's struggling hero.

Alger's usual plots—a humble, struggling lad versus a haughty "affluenza"-addicted bully—are shamelessly contrived. Alger made no pretense to literary grandeur. His novels are devoid of distinctive literary style. But his calling card was readability—mixed with just enough adventure and suspense to hook his teenage audience. He succeeded: his novels were like a Harry Potter staple for a fifty-year period.

Is Alger a propagandist for capitalism and the American Dream of rugged individualism? He surely celebrates individual perseverance, courage, ambition, and self-reliance. His themes find resonance with the ideals celebrated by the Boy Scouts, Junior Achievement, Rotary Clubs, and Chambers of Commerce in America. But there is more nuance in Alger's novels than is conveyed in the poor-boy-makes-good Algerian legend.

Alger does not say that hard work alone will lead to social and economic mobility. He knows well that most of those born into poverty will *not* transcend their bleak situations. He may be an optimist about human nature, but he also understood the economic inequalities of the Gilded Age. He rails against bullies, prejudice, and corrupt political business schemes that penalize the poor. He favors fair wages, the right to unionize, and laws against usury.

While he celebrates the individual's desire for self-improvement, Alger also emphasizes the importance of benefactors and getting adopted by mentors and patrons. Ragged Dick "depicts several forms of outside aid—material and maturating—as absolutely essential to igniting the beneficiary's ambition," notes David K. Shipler. "Without the generosity of others, none of Dick's smart diligence would have propelled him out of the street, and without his initiative, no generosity would come his way."[2]

It is the combination of personal character, tenacity, *and* assistance from outside benefactors that forms the equation for success. In *Struggling Upward* (1890), the boy-hero Luke Larkin is virtuous and sturdy, and he works hard to help support his impoverished mother, but he attains success only when two complete strangers suddenly come along to adopt him, give him jobs, and pave his wave to becoming respectable. The equation is: *preparation and ambition + benefactors providing opportunities = personal and monetary success.*

Alger makes no reference to it, but his young heroes have a lot in common with Alexander Hamilton. Illegitimate and abandoned by his father, Hamilton was a fourteen-year-old orphan serving as a clerk in the British West Indies until some generous patrons recognized his promise and sent him off to New York City to get an education. But neither patronage nor hard work alone explained Hamilton's success—it was the combination thereof. A wonderful rap line from Lin-Manuel Miranda's Broadway musical *Hamilton* suggests an Algerian theme: "The ten-dollar founding father without a father/got a lot farther by working a lot harder,/by being a lot smarter,/by being a self-starter."[3]

Alger's novels are not in the Jack the Giant Killer fairy-tale tradition. His young heroes do not become rich tycoons; they do not go from "rags to Rockefeller" or "rags to Henry Ford." The hero's success is mostly about going from "rags to respectability."

Literary critic Malcolm Cowley notes that every popular novel is, on one level or another, a fairy tale or myth, and most have a long lineage. The Alger stories, he suggests, parallel and may have been inspired by the Greek myth of Telemachus, the supposed orphan who, forced to leave home, sets out in search of his warrior father, Odysseus. "It is the father's power, not his own, that restores him to his rightful place." In Alger's version of the myth, the struggling boy-hero "is always fatherless and is always a boy of noble principles. Though he plays the part of a bootblack, a newsboy, or a fiddler, his open and prepossessing features betray his princely nature."[4] Typically the boy is subject to prejudice and is bullied and often exploited. Then the day comes when he performs some noble deed—rescues a child from drowning or helps thwart a robbery—and his knightly quest is rewarded by being granted new opportunities.

Alger's stories are part of a long tradition, from Homer to Don Quixote, Napoleon and Beethoven, John F. Kennedy, *Star Wars*, and numerous other tales of the hero's journey. Mythologist Joseph Campbell has advanced the notion of a "monomyth" structure "in which a hero answers a call, is assisted by a mentor figure, voyages to another world, survives various trials and antagonists, and emerges triumphant."[5] Alger is undeniably in this tradition, and his own youthful love of the classics informs his narratives.

Political scientist Carol Nackenoff offers an intriguing alternative interpretation. She believes Alger's studies of Latin, Greek, and the classics at Harvard, perhaps combined with his Whiggish Unitarianism, influenced him to see his fictional heroes as engaged in challenges not dissimilar to the struggles of the coming-of-age American republic. Alger, she writes, was a cultural by-product of the emerging Gilded Age of American capitalism. He understood its benefits and abuses, its promise and its side effects.

Yes, Alger celebrates self-reliance and moral character, but he also is concerned with justice, equal opportunity, and the challenges associated with an increasingly industrialized America. His stories, Nackenoff suggests, are "about the youth's rite of passage serving as an allegory of the adolescent republic, in which individual and collective pilgrimages, sacred and secular meanings were indistinguishable."[6] Alger's underprivileged orphans had to become disciplined, energetic, and creative networkers to become part of the productive and prosperous community. And so the American republic also had to reinvent itself as a nation not only for the goal of individualism but also for social justice and equality of opportunity. Realistically, as Alger knew, for every boy-hero who was beginning to "make it" there were many more who remained destitute, or were sent to jail, or who were held back by drinking, gambling, or laziness, not to mention the color of their skin or their disabilities.

Nackenoff's thesis is in part a response to political scientist Louis Hartz's *The Liberal Tradition in America* (1955). Hartz suggests that Alger's stories helped bridge the gap between the elitist, capitalist, and Whiggish probusiness ethic of Hamilton and a more Jeffersonian egalitarianism that emphasized both the common man and equality of opportunity. Alger, according to Hartz, was a convenient mixture of Hamiltonian and Jeffersonian thinking, celebrating the idea of "democratic capitalism" and promoting an American Dream that emphasized the possibility of upward mobility.

The Alger "romance of business possibilities" was that nearly anybody could make it in America. All that was needed was honesty, energy, self-discipline, a dedication to learning, courage—and a little luck—and you, too, might become somebody, somebody on the road to respectability and personal security. We didn't need a progressive revolution. We just needed to celebrate character, moral fiber, and an ethic of hard work and encourage those who were already successful to lend a helping hand so the promise of America could be realized by as many as possible.

It was the genius of Alger that he could inspire teenagers, and perhaps even Gilded Age political leaders, to imagine an America in which everything is possible and no personal victory was beyond even a poor orphan's reach.

The political right in America has long embraced Alger-esque thinking. America is seen as both a promise and a destiny. Thus Ronald Reagan, who read Alger in his youth, could proclaim in his 1981 inaugural address, "Can we doubt that only Divine Providence placed this land, this island of freedom, here as a refuge for all these people in the world who yearn to breathe freely?"

Today there is a thriving Horatio Alger Association of distinguished Americans, a foundation that honors the accomplishments of outstanding business and civic leaders "who have reached success despite adversity." Donald Trump's dad, developer Fred Trump, was one of those Alger honorees several decades ago. The group honors success stories and raises scholarship funds, supported by Safeway stores, for disadvantaged youths.

The noted African American educator Booker T. Washington wrote an Alger-esque memoir titled *Up from Slavery* (1901). Barack Obama's best-selling memoir *Dreams from My Father* (1995) also had echoes of Alger—and Reagan. "In no other country on Earth," Obama says, "is my story possible."

In Alger's defense, both the American political experiment and the American republic are dreams. They are aspirational, just as the Declaration of Independence and FDR's Second Bill of Rights are aspirational. Every tribe has its myths and its dreams. Nothing great or bold happens unless it is first imagined.

The political left has sometimes mocked the Alger narrative. Yet, from Jefferson to the Bernie Sanders, progressives have fought for measures to encourage equality of opportunity. Jefferson fought to eliminate primogeniture laws. Lincoln and his colleagues fought not only to emancipate slaves but also to provide for land-grant colleges and homesteading. Much of Wilson's New Freedom, FDR's New Deal, and Lyndon Johnson's War on Poverty initiatives were intended to lessen America's inequality and encourage upward mobility.

Most Americans today understand that you cannot have political liberty without at least some degree of economic equality or equality of opportunity.[7] What threatens the American Dream of Horatio Alger is the fact that today, the possibility of upward mobility has stalled for so many, and economic inequality has increased to levels not seen since the first Gilded Age.

Politicians, political institutions, and elections are seldom discussed in Alger's novels. But at least a few of his books can be described as social purpose or even consciousness-raising fiction. Alger's *Phil, The Fiddler; or the Story of a Young Street Musician* (1872) is as close to a political novel as any. This novel, in the tradition of Harriet Beecher Stowe or Charles Dickens, appeals to public opinion to shame the Italian "padrones" whose business was importing teenage Italian youths for virtual slavery.

These young boys were forced to be street musicians and beg for money and then turn this money over to the "padrone" each evening. Failure to bring back enough earned a flogging. His despicable "padrone," said young Filippo (Phil), "cared more for the money than me." Life in the streets was miserable. But life in the boarding lodge was even worse. "Here were nearly forty boys, subjected to extreme fatigue, privation, and brutal treatment daily, on account of this greed of one man." "If I were only a man," Phil thought, "I would wrench the [flogging] stick from his hand, and give him a chance to feel it." Things only get worse when a bully steals Phil's fiddle. Filippo finally escapes to New Jersey, where he is rescued and adopted by surrogate parents who view him as a god-sent gift, replacing a son lost a few years earlier.

In common with most Alger juvenile novels, *Phil, the Fiddler* has melodrama and a contrived plot. But it was also an example of Alger railing against unfair, inhumane business practices. He was probusiness but antiexploitation. The novel is also an example of Alger's sympathy toward minorities. Alger mistakenly claimed that this novel led to the breaking up of the abusive "padrone" system. His novel may have helped, but, unfortunately, the "padrone" system continued for at least another decade.

In 1874, Alger published *Only an Irish Boy; or Andy Burke's Fortunes.* The hero here is a fatherless Irish immigrant who is subjected to derision and ridicule by the local WASPs. Andy is regularly scorned and bullied by the affluent Godfrey Preston, who calls him "only an Irish boy," a good-for-nothing beggar. But our Andy here is once again a wholesome young boy-hero. He is willing to work hard, study hard, and make something of himself. The more he gets bullied, the more he dedicates himself to self-improvement. His triumphant moment comes when he shows up at the scene of an attempted robbery at the home of the town's local squire and courageously foils the robbery. The squire happens to be the father of Andy's bully nemesis, but the father is now indebted and exceedingly grateful to young Andy. The squire bequeaths $5,000 to Andy and provides a mortgage for a house for Andy's struggling widowed mom.

The story is more complicated by Algerian melodrama. But here once again is a happy ending. Andy becomes a co-owner of a local business and wins the esteem of his fellow citizens. "His success, aided, indeed by good fortune, has served to demonstrate the favorable efforts of honesty, industry, and good principles, upon individual success." Alger adds that young Andy Burke "is not the first, nor will he be the last, to achieve prosperity and the respect of the community though beginning life as 'only an Irish boy.'"

Critics speculate that Alger, a defrocked minister and lapsed Unitarian, may have sublimated his homosexuality into a more secular ministry, one dedicated to the welfare of underprivileged, fatherless boys. Some also imagine, that like his young orphan boy-heroes, Alger himself may have been in search of respect, success, and a loving father.

In the preface to *Ragged Dick*, Alger urged his readers to help the underprivileged and orphaned children of New York and other cities, and appealed to them to contribute to the Children's Aid Society to "ameliorate their condition." His pleas foreshadowed the laudable and ubiquitous United Way and local community foundation campaigns of today.

Like Lincoln, Alger grew up with Whiggish political leanings. And like Lincoln, he became a lifelong Republican. Though not an abolitionist, he was antislavery, and he cheered on the Unionist cause by writing war ballads and poems celebrating those who went to war. He himself failed his army physical (he was a short 5'2" with bad eyes).

Alger's politics were more implicit than explicit. He was anti Tammany Hall and antagonistic to welfare programs, favoring private charitable efforts over government programs. Along with warning against smoking, drinking, and gambling, he also warned his young readers against Wall Street speculators. He had no praise for politicians or city hall—his heart and his pen rooted for the newsboy, the bootblack, the luggage attendant, and the Irish and Italian street kids, and his stories helped a large audience of teenagers to imagine an America where there was hope for the underdogs.

Alger accepted both the Hamiltonian notion of capitalism and competition and the Jeffersonian, Lincolnian conviction that the system must foster equal opportunity in order to sustain a strong middle class. In his personal life he regularly supported Republican candidates for president and was delighted to learn that a relative of his, Russell A. Alger, served as governor of Michigan and as an 1888 Republican presidential candidate and later served in President McKinley's cabinet. Like many Whigs, he probably shared James Fenimore Cooper's and Henry Adams's concern about how constitutional democracy might be weakened by too rapid an expansion of the suffrage.

Alger's Republican loyalties are clearly evident in his nonfiction biographies of James Garfield and Abraham Lincoln. These were written for young people, and Alger made clear they were not the result of original research but rather a synthesis of existing works on these presidents. He conveniently turns these two assassinated presidents into Alger-esque heroes—men who pulled themselves up from poverty, got themselves adopted by mentors, and made something of themselves.

From Canal Boy to President, or The Boyhood and Manhood of James A. Garfield (1881) describes how young Garfield worked as a canal boy guiding mules along the Erie Canal, and that he then worked his way through school as a janitor, a carpenter, and bell ringer. He was a raw country boy; yet he pushed himself to excel as a debater and student. He won a scholarship to Williams College, where he was befriended by legendary educator Mark Hopkins, and graduated in the Class of 1856.

A few years later Garfield became an officer in Ohio's 42nd Regiment and, in familiar Alger words, "was not a man to shirk from the call of duty." Indeed, in Alger's inspirational telling, Garfield "becomes a hero at the Battle of Chickamauga and elsewhere."

This leads Garfield to be elected as the youngest member of Congress and later as president of the United States. A humble boy who worked hard and was a disciplined striver becomes America's highest public official. Unlike the novels, however, Garfield's career ended unhappily with his assassination. Alger concludes his Garfield biography:

Had this been a story of the imagination, such as I have often written, I should not have dared to crown it with such an ending. In view of my hero's humble beginnings, I should expect to have it severely criticized as utterly incredible, but reality is often times stranger than romance, and this is notably illustrated by Garfield's wonderful career. (296–97)

Alger glosses over Garfield's disapproval of unions and his opposition to women's suffrage and the proposed eight-hour workday. Indeed, so conventional or conservative was Garfield that he still believed in property qualifications for voting. But such a political analysis would have distracted from Alger's more blissful biography.

Ten years later, Alger penned a hagiographic Lincoln biography for juveniles: *Abraham Lincoln, The Backwoods Boy; or, How a Young Railsplitter Became President* (1883). He recounts Lincoln's splitting rails for fences and lifelong self-improvement efforts. Alger doesn't go quite so far to say (as the old joke has it) that "Lincoln was born in a log cabin he built with his own hands," but he comes close. We learn that no man seems to have been more clearly designated as the instrument of Providence than Lincoln. "It seems strange," Alger writes, "that a rough youth, born and raised in the backwoods, without early educational advantages, homely and awkward, and with no polish of manner save that which proceeded from a good heart should have been selected as the guide and Savior for a great nation."

Alger, reflecting his own Whig beliefs, offers this benign interpretation of Lincoln's evolutionary attitudes, which later lead to his being honored as the man who freed the slaves. Notice Alger's praise for a steady, slow, determined style of leadership:

He was never an extreme man, and he was never classed with the Abolitionists—that intrepid band who worked early and late and for years without hope, against the colossal system of wrong when life seemed so intertwined with the life of the republic that it looked as if both must fall together. Abraham Lincoln moved slowly. He wasn't an impulsive man, but took time to form determination. (148)

Lincoln is both a boy-hero and a man-hero—and he becomes, in Alger's depiction, the martyred savior of America's democratic passion play.

Alger's only other political biography was about the New England Whig Daniel Webster: *From Farm Boy to Senator; Being the History of Daniel Webster* (1882). Alger wrote that he wished to revive the memory of the notable civic leadership of Senator Webster and acquaint young people with his public service.

But Alger found biographies difficult as well as time consuming to write. He preferred fiction. He liked to make up stories based loosely on his studies of the youths he befriended. His comfort zone was as a moralist and teacher. Some see his stories as veiled criticism of the excesses of the Gilded Age. But his concerns pale compared to the hard-hitting nonfiction *How the Other Half Lives* (1890) by Jacob Riis. Riis captures the squalor of people living in New York City's tenements and the nativist inhospitality of New Yorkers to its most recent newcomers. Compared to Riis, Alger sounds like the Chamber of Commerce, or the Harvard Club of New York (Alger's favorite club).

Alger's books sold moderately well during his lifetime and enjoyed huge sales soon after his death. Writers such as Theodore Dreiser, Upton Sinclair, Jack London, and Richard Wright acknowledge his influence on them. Countless businessmen and politicians said they grew up loving the Alger books in their youth. Presidents Gerald Ford and Ronald Reagan were both teenage fans of the Alger novels.

Alger had plenty of critics. He was faulted for contrived plots, wooden dialogue, cardboard one-dimensional characters, pious preaching, and un-realistically happy endings. His harshest critics accuse him of Pollyannaish optimism and of creating a misleading myth of upward mobility. These critics take direct issue with Alger's mantra that "in this country poverty in early life is no bar to a man's advancement."

As early as 1875 Mark Twain wrote "The Story of the Good Little Boy," a snarky parody of Alger's *Ragged Dick*. Twain's young Jacob Blivens has all the Alger-esque qualities of honesty and a hard work ethic, but he perishes in an iron foundry. Nathanael West's *A Cool Million* is another withering ridicule of Algerism. John Steinbeck's *The Grapes of Wrath* and Richard Wright's *Native Son* are additional examples where young Americans in search of upward mobility cannot achieve the American Dream. These novels are, in effect, reverse Alger narratives. Upton Sinclair's *The Jungle* and Toni Morrison's *Beloved* are still other politically themed stories that defy Alger-esque optimism. Filmmaker Michael Moore in 2003 proclaimed "Horatio Alger must die" because, Moore suggested, his message undercut the populist and redistributive programs America desperately needed.

But despite the many criticisms and parodies of his stories, Alger's aspirational themes are alive and well in America. Upward mobility is still the American Dream. A majority of Americans want to believe that anyone who works hard and perseveres can make it to higher social and economic status. Alger stories and the Alger dream, even if his books are unread nowadays, have acquired a life of their own.[8]

Policy experts such as Thomas Piketty point to the growing divide in America between rich and poor. Racism, unemployment, and family instability are obvious barriers for those at the bottom economically. Poor children who live in the worst neighborhoods and attend the worst public schools have the highest risk of unemployment and incarceration. "These disadvantages typically compound each other, with low income households, unstable families, and struggling parents living in the most hollowed-out communities containing the worst schools, with the fewest social and institutional supports for those in need," writes Brookings Institution analyst Richard V. Reeves. The barriers to upward mobility are growing, along with the risks of getting stuck at the bottom of the American ladder.[9] In fact, social mobility is greater in Canada and several European countries than in the United States.

All this makes Horatio Alger seem dated, quaint, or even delusional. And because virtually nobody reads his work today, his novels are essentially literary museum pieces. It is true, of course, that he was writing about a time and place that are different from our own. He was also writing almost exclusively about a Caucasian male world.

But Alger's dreams about making it in America are deeply ingrained. We may cherish liberty, freedom, and individualism, but we also want equality of opportunity, equality before the law, and as much political equality as might be possible.

American political and business leaders try to provide upward mobility by improving public schools, early childhood education, and making college education affordable and accessible. We want to believe that education is the equalizer. We yearn for "no child left behind" programs, even as we know the rich can afford private schools, tutoring, and abundant extracurricular activities. Education, we still like to believe, is the best ladder of opportunity, the best investment we can make in helping young people escape the vicious cycle of poverty. "Abandoning Alger—giving up on the American Dream—is not an option," concludes Richard Reeves. "The ideal of merit-fueled mobility is a fixed feature of American politics and ideology. It comes, almost literally, with the territory."[10]

People invariably read into the Horatio Alger stories what they want. Liberals generally, if perhaps too readily, dismiss his quaint narratives as a failure to understand racism, poverty, disability, and the limits of upward mobility in America. Conservatives see Alger as championing self-reliance and free enterprise and the charitable instincts of good Americans.

Novelist Richard Wright praised Alger's novels as stories of what America stood for, at least aspirationally, especially in contrast to the collectivism of the Soviet Union. "Alger," wrote Wright in 1945, "was perhaps American capitalism's greatest and most effective propagandist. He was an utterly American artist, claimed by his culture, and the truth of his books is the truth of the power of wish."[11] What is notable about Wright is that he grew up as a fatherless orphan in rural Mississippi, but he also discovered and was inspired by Alger stories. Wright later became a Communist Party member in Chicago. His novel *Native Son* won him great praise, fame, and income. Later he rejected Communism, and he seemed to reject America as well, becoming an ex-patriot in Paris, where he felt less ostracized. Still, ironically, Wright's life of hard work, self-improvement, and enormous success was in some ways an African American Horatio Alger story.

Others have been bemused because, although Horatio Alger has become a sainted apostle of American business values and success, his own story was one of going from modest means to that of a struggling writer who had to take on tutoring jobs in the homes of the wealthy or magazine assignments to get by. Alger was never a businessman, and he enjoyed only modest financial success. His books became best sellers, as noted, mainly after his death.

His canonization as an American success mythmaker largely occurred after he had died. "Money in the Alger novel is chiefly a symbol of other things," writes Malcolm Cowley, "emotional security . . . affection, and manly power." "The real theme of the Alger novel is not pecuniary but filial and paternal." Alger, insists Cowley, "is revenging himself on his own father three times: first he kills him before the story opens by making the hero an orphan; then he gives Horatio Sr.'s worst traits to the wicked squire; and finally he provides the hero with a father-by-choice to love and understand."

Cowley concludes that the larger Horatio Alger is paradoxical indeed:

> What I cannot understand is how the author of the message—that timid bohemian, that failure by his father's standards and doubly failure by his own, since he neither wrote a great novel nor amassed even a modest fortune—should come to be regarded as a prophet of business enterprise. Nor why the family melodrama he wrote and rewrote for boys like himself should be confused with the American dream of success.[12]

The real Horatio Alger Jr. was quiet, short, dumpy, balding, and "unmanly." He was not especially proud of his career or his writing. He wanted, his biographers tell us, to write significant contributions to literature.

Still Horatio Alger lives. Horatio Alger's America is one of heroes, the spirit of struggling upward, and the idea that hard work and perseverance can pave the way for opportunity and living the American Dream. There may have been a decline in recent years of those who still believe in this possibility, but it is very much a part of aspirational America. That's why we regularly hear "Yes, we can" or "Let's make America great again" campaign slogans.

People are motivated by myth, fairy tales, and inspirational and aspirational narrative. Horatio Alger was a clever storyteller and captured a large audience. He left an indelible mark on American political thinking—the image of America as we all would like it to be. Like Jefferson, Lincoln, FDR, and Ronald Reagan, Alger imagined a more prosperous and more egalitarian America.

ON COMMANDING AND LEADING[13]

"Who, in the rainbow, can show the line where the violet tint ends and the orange tint begins? Distinctly we see the difference of the colors, but when exactly does the one first blindingly enter into the other? So," says the invisible narrator in Melville's *Billy Budd*, "with sanity and insanity."

American novelist Herman Melville (1819–1891) offers a riveting case study of leadership under pressure. Captain Edward Fairfax Vere must navigate the troubled waters of the war between England and France and try to administer "justice" in a case where his personal sympathies run counter to his instincts of how to maintain order and obedience to the law.

Melville's wartime novella questions whether Vere may have been simultaneously a dutiful captain and an inadequate leader. Did the "fog of war" and his understandable fear of mutiny unhinge this seemingly unflappable commander? Or did he courageously set aside his personal and emotional beliefs to carry out his military responsibilities? Melville keeps us guessing.

Vere is a forty-year-old bachelor and book lover who is thoughtful, yet meticulous about enforcing rules. He has earned esteem for naval accomplishments. Vere is, we gather, a Burkean conservative, favoring British constitutional practices, especially in contrast to the revolutionary principles being experimented with in France. "But," Melville's narrator explains, "though a conscientious disciplinarian [Vere] was no lover of authority for mere authority's sake." The same narrator notes, however, "between you and me now don't you think there is a queer streak of the pedantic running through [Captain Vere]?"

Melville's narrative compels us to place ourselves in the captain's shoes. We participate with Vere and his senior deputies in a hastily arranged drum-head court trial and question easy assumptions about right and wrong, law and order, the rights of man, and leading and misleading. Melville pushes us to fathom the hard choices that commanders must make in war. He asks us, as in his rainbow metaphor, to discern between what is mostly right and partially wrong, or partially right and perhaps partially wrong. When and how can or should our values subtly shift, our principles slightly bend?

He makes us understand that, especially in times of crises, easy answers are elusive. This, Melville may be suggesting, was as true for the late nineteenth-century American political experiment as for the would-be leaders on the British frigate *Indomitable*. As Nicholas Warner writes in an essay on Melville's *Moby Dick*, "this is a writer for whom life and leadership at sea exist in significant parallel with life and leadership ashore."[14]

Billy Budd: Sailor (An Inside Narrative) was an unfinished novella at the time of Melville's death in 1891 in New York City. It remained unpublished until 1924, when *Moby Dick* and Melville's other writings enjoyed an unexpected revival.

Billy is a nineteen-year-old sailor on a British merchant ship, the *Rights of Man*. In 1797 he is impressed (forcibly drafted by the British Royal Navy) to serve on a man-o-war, the *Indomitable*. When he stepped onto the *Indomitable* (which in some editions is called the *Bellipotent*), Budd bid farewell not only to the *Rights of Man* but also to many of his own rights—including, perhaps, the right to justice. (Ironically, his rights on this merchant ship were, at least to an extent, protected by the very British naval fleet to which he was being impressed.) His youthful energy, natural grace, and superior seamanship are immediately evident on the war vessel. He is blessed with an irresistible good nature and "in the nude might have posed as a statue of young Adam before the Fall." Billy is a symbol of innocence, kindness, and obedience—characteristics that Melville sometimes associates with naïveté. He is honest, earnest, and wanting to appease his captain and shipmates. However, Billy has a flaw—an untimely and debilitating stutter.

Billy's goodness and likability soon clash with a symbol of evil: master-at-arms John Claggart. Claggart is the ship's chief disciplinarian, who takes sadistic pleasure in provoking quarrels and meting out punishment. Claggart is "one in whom was the mania of an evil nature." His innate cruelty is an example of what Plato describes as "a depravity according to nature."

Melville discusses the moral differences and motivations behind Budd and Claggart's characters. He employs a narrative voice that discloses more than the events of the story—it endeavors to describe how basic emotions like envy and animosity function: "Now envy and antipathy, passions irreconcilable in reason, nevertheless in fact may spring conjoined like Chang and Eng [Siamese twins]." Far from presenting overly simplified versions of good and evil, Melville seeks to explain and complicate their motives. The excerpt above speaks to the soured admiration that Claggart feels for Billy—a strange mixture of feelings no doubt derived from jealousy of Budd's innocence.

Claggart has a "magnetic" revulsion for Budd: "If askance he eyed the good looks, cheery health and frank enjoyment of . . . Budd, it was because these went along with a nature that, as Claggart . . . felt, had in its simplicity never willed malice or experienced the reactionary bite of that serpent." The reference to the serpent evokes parallels between Claggart and Satan, and Budd becomes linked to human innocence and "the fall of Man." Melville rewrites the biblical creation story, however, adding a concluding twist that causes us to reconsider the fine lines we draw between good and evil.

The sailors all fear the master-at-arms, except for Billy, who displays goodwill toward everyone, Claggart included. Unable to comprehend this fearlessness—or perhaps frustrated by ill-defined homoerotic feelings—Claggart accuses Billy of planning a mutiny. This is false. Billy is unambiguously loyal. Upset and stuttering, Billy cannot defend himself verbally in front of his accuser and his captain. He lashes out at Claggart and strikes a single fatal blow. "I did not mean to kill him. Could I have used my tongue I would not have struck him."

Melville's narrative thus far contrasts Billy's unworldly goodness with Claggart's repulsive, inhuman evil. This contrast—including Billy's extreme popularity and Claggart's unpopularity among the crew—makes Vere's decision all the more agonizing. Killing an officer is a crime punishable by death. The *Indomitable* was sailing at the time of the British war with Revolutionary France; fears of mutiny in the face of battle were high. Nearby French ships off the coast of Spain posed an immediate danger. Captain Vere's duty, owed to king and country, is to ensure that the *Indomitable* is battle ready.

Vere admires Billy from a distance and understands that Claggart may have lied about Billy's mutinous intentions. He understands that Billy intended no harm but was overwhelmed by Claggart's accusation and incapacitated by his stutter. What to do? Vere's fatherly heart yearns to protect Billy ("Billy's face before the killing was a crucifixion to behold"), but his captain's mentality urges him to follow the law. Vere prematurely exclaims prior to the drum-head trial, "Struck dead by an angel of God! Yet the angel must hang."

Vere convenes an improvised drum-head court to determine Billy's fate. The ship's senior officers, perhaps unexpectedly, oppose sentencing Billy to death. The ship's surgeon, we are told, worries that Vere might be somewhat unhinged. The narrator sympathizes with the surgeon's questioning and allows that "no more trying a situation is conceivable than that of an officer subordinate under a captain whom he suspects to be, not mad indeed, but yet not quite unaffected in his intellect." Ships at sea are a closed environment in which captains, especially in times of war, rule with an iron fist. The surgeon knew that to disagree with Vere "would be insolence. To resist him would be mutiny."

Vere's position of administering justice is made all the more difficult by the fact that he happened to be the sole witness of Billy's fatal blow to Claggart. In the drum-head trial, he must act as the judge, the chief witness, and the ship's captain charged with maintaining order and efficiency—an unenviable task, especially considering that impartiality is essential to a court ruling. Vere recognizes the officers' hesitancy to indict Billy, a hesitancy "proceeding . . . from the clash of military duty with moral scruple—scruple vitalized by compassion."

Vere reframes the trial to emphasize military and ship security instead of the moral question: Does Billy deserve to die for killing Claggart? Compassion collides with the dictates of admiralty law. How reasoned or impartial can a court be when obedience, security, and order are prioritized?

The paradoxes of leadership at sea were a Melville specialty. He had spent several years at sea on whaling ships, as well as briefly on the U.S. naval brigade *United States*. One of Melville's cousins was a naval officer and had served on a drum-head court on a U.S. ship in the 1840s.

Melville is justly celebrated for his allegorical novel *Moby Dick* (1851). The *Pequod*'s Captain Ahab in *Moby Dick* is eccentric, defiant, heroic, domineering, and obsessed. In Melville's telling, Ahab becomes a heroic, yet tragic, figure. The search for the great white whale becomes a microcosm of the world, as Melville deconstructs human nature, the irrational, and the abuse of power.

Ahab is motivated by a complex mix of revenge, narcissism, and shadowy demons. He is a solitary individual; yet he inspires his crew to a state of frenzy in the pursuit of Moby Dick. His vision and madness are a source of power on the ship, but they end in fanaticism and fatalism as Ahab tries unsuccessfully to conquer nature, in this case symbolized by the whale and the sea.

The *Moby Dick* epic is a story of "human delusions of grandeur," writes Buckard Sievers. It portrays the yearning "for godliness and immortality" and is a fictional metaphor for how leaders and colleagues can "destroy ourselves and others if we are not able to acknowledge, mourn, and recover from the losses, injuries and humiliations of an inner world other than by projecting them onto the outer world and retaliations against those who appear to be threatening."[15]

Billy Budd, *Moby Dick*, and other Melville writings offer detailed explorations of how individuals—especially leaders—navigate difficult social and political decisions. "Melville's fiction," Lawrence Buell notes, "is acutely conscious of the anomaly of shipboard authoritarianism in a supposedly equalitarian society."[16]

In the drum-head court on the *Indomitable*, the ship's senior officers agonize over the decision of what to do about Billy's crime. The officers sense that Vere is not himself and has become obsessed with honoring martial law rather than seeking justice according to natural law. Captain Vere, in turn, notes, as mentioned, the officers' "troubled indecision" and "troubled hesitancy." But he argues that they should "let not warm hearts betray heads that should be cool." He asks, "Tell me whether or not, occupying the positions we do, private conscience should not yield to that imperial one formulated in the code under which alone we officially proceed?" His officers must not flinch, he insists, at this exacting moment of truth.

The cowed officers are forced to align with their captain. Billy is formally convicted and sentenced to hang the next morning. The ship's crew, who hated Claggart and revered Billy, are assembled on deck to witness the execution. They are shocked to see Billy headed for the noose. Now they really want mutiny. However, in a stark, heart-wrenching moment, just before he dies, Billy cries out in a firm voice, "God save Captain Vere!" as if it was an enigmatic pardon of the dutiful, yet hapless, Vere. His cry probably has the effect of preventing a riot against the captain.

Billy becomes a legend. Vere is overwhelmed by grief and guilt and dies shortly afterward. Soon after Budd's hanging, a French man-o-war opens fire on the *Indomitable*, further diffusing what might have been a mutiny. The men return to their posts.

Melville's narrative about the "fated boy" has much in common with a Greek tragedy. Readers know Billy meant no harm. Almost immediately after Billy's lashing out, we realize his fate but can do nothing to prevent it. The narrator and reader alike admire Billy's acceptance of his fate. But where does this acceptance come from? He does little to defend his murder besides describing his anger and inability to speak after hearing Claggart's false accusation. To accept capital punishment in this way, Billy has some primitive confidence in Captain Vere's ability to administer justice. His unquestioning faith suggests to readers that he is a Christ-like figure, sacrificing himself for the good of the ship and their mission. But there is a nagging question: Is such unquestioned obedience justified?

Among Melville's noteworthy digressions is a visit by the ship's chaplain to the condemned man. Billy listens to the chaplain with a "certain natural politeness." Billy doesn't fear death, and his pure innocence is oblivious to thoughts about salvation. The chaplain concludes that Billy's innocence "was even a better thing than religion wherewith to go to Judgment." And then, "stooping over, he kissed on the fair cheek his fellow man, a felon in martial law, one who though on the connes of death, he felt he could never convert to a dogma; nor for all that did he fear for his future."

Melville's narrator puzzles over why the chaplain, who had been apprised by a senior officer of Billy's innocence, "lifted not a finger to avert the doom of such a martyr to martial discipline." Indeed, if the crew, officers, chaplain, and Vere himself are convinced of Billy's purity at heart, why do none protest this capital and fatal punishment? Why is the chaplain even there? Is it not ironic that this minister of the Prince of Peace functionally lends legitimacy to the God of "brute force" and war? Melville makes us uneasy about acts that can be justified—and convictions that can be nullified—in war.

It is tempting, as noted, to liken Billy to Christ, and Claggart to Satan. Melville's characters, however, are more complex—more human. Vere's decision, captaincy, and leadership have long been debated. Many contend Vere was an honorable, earnest military administrator forced to perform a distasteful duty. He was fulfilling his military responsibility and abiding by his oath of office.

Melville biographer Andrew Delbanco writes that attitudes for and against Captain Vere's final decision often reflect changing times and competing schools of political thought. Thus, "at times of high regard for constituted authority, Vere tends to come off as a heroic figure who, with tragic awareness of his responsibilities, sacrifices an innocent for the sake of the state." However, when there is greater distrust of central governments, Vere is condemned as a despot who callously goes by the book and follows the letter of the law rather than considering true justice.[17]

Those critical of Vere argue that he acted both improperly and imperially—as witness, prosecutor, judge, and executioner. He misread the applicable statutes, committed procedural errors, belittled the counsel of his senior officers, interjected in their deliberations, and intellectually and psychologically intimidated his drum-head court.[18]

Vere's leadership can also be questioned because he appears to have been fully aware of the problematic Claggart but did little to investigate how the master-at-arms was abusing his authority and creating debilitating morale problems among the crew. Claggart was hated. He was undermining the effectiveness of the ship. Yet Captain Vere remains aloof, safe in his study, immersed in his books, insufficiently alert to the increasingly dysfunctional human dynamics on his battleship. Why does Vere fail to be proactive? Why does his become a primarily cramped "by the book" leadership?

Others fault Vere because he shrank from courage and leadership. Unlike the sainted and more self-assured Lord Horatio Nelson, who had transcended mutinous attempts and fought side by side with his men, Vere nervously rushes to judgment and exhibits managerial rather than leadership ability. "Our vowed responsibility is this," Vere intones, "however pitilessly that the law may operate in any instance, we must nevertheless adhere to and administer it." Shades of the heartless bureaucrats in Heller's classic, *Catch-22*?

Did Vere find solace in obedience rather than justice? He had options he failed to explore. He could have postponed the trial or the sentencing until they were ashore. He could have mitigated the penalty. He could have explained the matter to his crew. He could claim Claggart died of an accident, which was the case. Instead, he tells his fellow officers that "in receiving our commissions we in the most important regards ceased to be natural free agents." Going by the book, for him, overrides free agency judgment. Melville hints that this was probably an abdication of responsibility. Yet Melville tries to leave it for his readers to decide.

Melville symbolically discusses the "fog of war" context: "The greater the fog, the more it imperils the steamer." "It is precisely [Vere's] conscious awareness of the necessity of making moral compromises," writes Joel Porte, "that defines his tragedy."[19]

Vere is confronted with competing obligations: to honor the rights, integrity, and life of a young man he may well have regarded as a son, and to fulfill his sworn duties as a military officer in service to his country and king. Civil and military laws, Melville suggests, though supremely important, are, like men, perishable and transient. But doesn't our ideal of justice, in contrast, transcend man-made laws and speak to the very depths of the human soul? Melville's reflections on the human condition, here, as in *Moby Dick*, are often submerged in a tapestry of symbolism.[20]

Melville viewed himself as a storyteller and a question raiser, not a reformer or agitator. Still, he compels his readers to reflect on leadership, power, authority, and human nature. He understood the dialectic between freedom and order outlined in the competing ideologies of Thomas Paine and Edmund Burke. Melville was well aware also of the debate between individual rights and the need for law and enduring governing institutions. He appreciated that each had valid points, and he understood, as did Machiavelli, that wartime and tumultuous events test character and everyone's sense of justice.

In wartime, rights necessarily get diminished. Battleship democracy is impossible. Is war the ultimate villain? "War," Melville has Vere say, "makes a mockery of justice." But Melville suggests there are lessons here for peacetime, for civil society, and for his contemporaries. Toward the end of *Budd*, Melville writes that "truth uncompromisingly told will always have its ragged edges." No narrative, he adds, can ever fully capture reality.

Melville is compelled to write *Budd* because the official British version of the legend held that Billy was in fact a mutinous dissident who had vindictively stabbed the master-at-arms. A British naval chronicle concluded that "the criminal paid the penalty of his crime" and that the execution was a valid contribution to both the ship's and the British navy's effectiveness. Melville's fictionalized narrative (which he explicitly called "An Inside Narrative" in some of his drafts), based on naval storytelling legends, yearns to clarify or even rectify this false version of events, doubtless the result of government spin.

Melville discounts this "official" account of Billy Budd by revealing the perspective of Billy's fellow sailors, who knew Billy as neither a murderer nor a mutineer. They understood that Billy accidentally killed a man in a moment of justified anger and fear. They likewise understood that Billy should not have been put to death for his actions. They admired his natural leadership. Billy's acceptance of his fate and forgiveness of Vere suggested to fellow sailors that he was a heroic martyr, sacrificing himself for them, for the good of the ship and their country. "To them a chip of [the spar from which Billy was hanged] was a piece of the cross," and the legend of Billy Budd spread from ship to ship wherever British and American sailors sailed. A much-traveled ballad, "Billy in the Darbies," memorialized him.

Budd is ultimately a parable of the exacting and often excruciating challenge of leadership. A ship at war is a rarefied environment, under the command of a single leader, but also dependent on the character and humanity of crew members. Melville suggests, says biographer Delbanco, that each of us has to live our lives on our own terms, guided not by official rules and commands but ultimately by our own principles and values: "But if Billy has re-enacted the death of Christ in this tale of sacrifice and redemption, Vere is no Pilate. He is Abraham performing the sacrifice of Isaac, torn to the depths of his soul by the conflict between love and duty—except that in Melville's reprise of the father-and-son story from Genesis, there is no intervention by a merciful God. There is no God at all."[21]

With his striking portraits of Billy, Claggart, and Vere, Melville sucks us into the harsh realities of leadership—the agonizing decisions that must be made and a bitter acceptance that human nature contains both good and evil, the desire for honor and loyalty.[22]

Critics are divided over Melville's intended meaning in this unfinished novella. Some detect Melville's pessimistic acceptance of the inevitability of evil and tragedy, an attitude at odds with the rebellious and even patriotic spirit manifest in his earlier writings. Such critics understand Melville as disillusioned, despairing, and fatalistic about life. Others more persuasively read *Budd* as a testament to resistance, a warning that we must transcend the inadequacies of man-made law.

Billy, because of his seamanship, innocence, and magnetic masculine beauty, oddly becomes the main rival to Captain Vere. Billy, not Vere, is the person on this seventy-four-man ship who commands the hearts and loyalties of his shipmates. Melville's denouement of Vere killing off his chief rival, his "love son," echoes, in certain ways, the classical narratives of Greek tragedies, adapted in Melville's time by Freud's Oedipus complex.

Robert Penn Warren contends that *Billy Budd* is a father-son story, an Abraham-Isaac story. It is, he writes, the story of the search by the son for the lost father. "Here the son finds the father, and the father recognizes the son. That is the scene that Melville did not—or could not—write. It is the encounter behind the locked door of the Captain's Cabin." Penn Warren asks, "Is this the dream of reconciling and of the search for the father that Melville, the son, never found in life?" Could it also be, Warren speculates, the dream of reconciliation that Melville, the father, wanted to have had with his own two troubled, deceased sons?[23]

Warren suggests *Billy Budd* is a narrative of reconciliation. It is a story, at least in part, of the groping movement toward maturity. Billy and Captain Vere reconcile behind the captain's door. "The Oedipal conflict is overpassed: Billy is initiated into the world of manhood, the 'father' offers both 'love' and 'law,' and now Billy, in accepting the 'doom' of the world, can bless the father."[24]

This is a provocative, yet plausible, reading.

What about the failed leadership of the ship's three senior officers? Vere was commander. But they were his deputies. Surely they knew how the *Indomitable* was being poorly led by Vere and ill managed by Claggart. Why didn't they intervene? Why, when they all disagreed with Vere's coercive and intimidating conduct at the drum-head court, did they falter and acquiesce? Melville suggests these officers, along with the ship's surgeon and chaplain, were so frightened by Vere's authoritarian style that their ability to advise was severely handicapped. What kind of leadership team is that? Another noted American novelist, Herman Wouk, has his officers on the World War II *Caine* (in his novel *Caine Mutiny*) relieve their commanding officer in an emergency situation, though Wouk later raises the question of whether those officers may have failed their captain.

Biographer Delbanco contends *Budd* may reflect Melville's populist distaste with what was going on in New York and in the United States at large; industrialists and "robber barons" trampling on workers' rights and protesters and strikers being brutally put down. As Melville wrote *Budd*, says Delbanco:

> He had seen his country go from being the vanguard nation of what he had once called "divine equality" to a nation deeply divided between poverty and wealth. He had seen the party of abolition become the party of big business. He had witnessed the principle of inalienable rights perverted into a legal rationale by which great corporations secured inviolate rights for themselves.[25]

Was *Budd* a proclamation for resistance (perhaps along the lines of Upton Sinclair's soon-to-be-written *The Jungle*) for better conditions for seadogs and impressed workers? Did Melville hint at this populist reasoning when he compares Billy to "a young horse fresh from the pasture suddenly inhaling a vile whiff from some chemical factory"?

A populist reading of *Budd* is plausible, if not entirely persuasive. Melville had been born to a prosperous family, even if his father's bankruptcy abruptly ended that prosperity in his youth. He went—not to college—but to sea, all over the world. He capitalized on his sailing experiences by becoming a shrewd anthropologist and storyteller about life at sea.

His life as a writer, his biographers say, was often lonely and unrewarding. He was apparently subject to melancholy and depression. He unsuccessfully sought a diplomatic assignment like his sometime-friend Nathaniel Hawthorne. When this failed and his writings failed to pay his bills, he served for more than twenty years as a lowly customs inspector in New York City, where he was obliged, unhappily, to pay patronage "dues" to the state Republican Party and witness petty corruption of various kinds.

Melville was not a political activist. In his youth he had optimistically applauded the aspirations of Jacksonian democracy and the New America movement. But this novel, written in Melville's retirement years, shares somber messages. The "Insider Narrative" of his subtitle implies one should not always believe the stories put out by the authorities. Beware, he seems to be saying, the bluster of hopefulness as well as the shallowness of cynicism.

Literary critics believe Melville became more a pessimist than an optimist and that he valued a certain amount of counterpoint to the juvenile hopefulness personified in the best-selling dime novels by his fellow New Yorker of the time, Horatio Alger. *Billy Budd* was, as noted, unfinished at the time of Melville's death. Melville's family and others tried to get the manuscript in shape for publication. This took thirty-three years. The original had ragged edges and unclear allusions. Later writers have expanded on Melville's tale and produced plays, films, and operas, often filling in his story with dialogue not in the original. These later works have failed to duplicate the crucial nuances of Melville's narrator, whose intricate musings are indicative of Melville's own voice.

Melville acts as a political anthropologist as he reminds us that human and political events are complicated interactions of multiple forces and counterforces. Leadership is nearly impossible to understand without acknowledging the blurred lines of good and evil, the imperfections of man and institutions. Melville's writings thrive on paradox, dilemma, and ironic contrasts. The novelist-poet Robert Penn Warren believes the Melville message is that "life is a tissue of polarities, ironies, contradictions, and its tragic nature derives from the fact that in this realm of ambiguity we must, in the end, act."[26]

Melville reminds us that the natural rights described by Rousseau and Paine will always be in tension with the necessity of some system of Burkean and Hamiltonian law and order. Budds and Claggarts cannot lead. Captain Edward Fairfax Vere tried diligently to discern the right course. He was a dutiful captain, if a flawed, failed, and inadequate leader of men—as so many political leaders are.

Melville ingeniously omits several crucial details and gives us a hard-to-understand and somewhat inscrutable protagonist in Captain Vere. The

Vere he gives us acts with his crew's and his country's best interest in mind. Whether he does the right thing is debatable. Many readers conclude that his leadership backfires in the end and that the execution of Billy was in fact more a murder than the killing of Claggart that prompted it. The challenge for the ideal leader is to find that perfect, if indistinct, spot on the rainbow where the orange and the violet intersect. That is the challenge for every leader in America's political experiment. He would have agreed with Justice Oliver Wendell Holmes's observation that the American Constitution "is an experiment, like all of life is an experiment." Melville would add—as leadership in exacting circumstances, especially in wartime, will always be a challenge.

Each reader has to grapple with their assessment of what they would have done if they were in Vere's place. And each reader has to consider what they would have done if they were a senior officer or merely a sailor on the *Indomitable*. The great novelist provokes and compels us to think—and in this Melville triumphs.

DEFIANT SOUTHERN DAUGHTER PERSEVERES[27]

"I love you Scarlett, because we are so much alike, renegades, both of us, dear, and selfish rascals. Neither of us cares a rap if the whole world goes to pot, so long as we are safe and comfortable." So declares Captain Rhett Butler, one of Katie Scarlett O'Hara's lovers, as he belatedly goes off to fight the Yankees in the waning months of their "Lost Cause" Civil War.

Butler returns a year later and woos and marries O'Hara, but their hopes and fantasies clash, and he once again leaves her with this dramatic farewell: "We are both scoundrels, Scarlett, and nothing is beyond us when we want something. We could have been happy, for I loved you, Scarlett, down to your bones in a way that Ashley [her longtime romantic obsession] could never know you. And he would despise you if he did know. . . . But no, you must go mooning all your life after a man you cannot understand. And I, my darling, will continue to moon after whores." She protests and urges reconciliation, to which he famously replies, "My dear, I don't give a damn." (In the film version, it is "Frankly, my dear, I don't give a damn.")

Margaret Mitchell's (1900–1949) famous, controversial, readable, slavery-affirming, best-selling Civil War–era epic is, among other things, "a war novel, a historical romance, a comedy of manners, a bitter lamentation, a cry of the heart and a long, cold hearted look at the character of this one lovely Machiavellian Southern woman," Katie Scarlett O'Hara Hamilton Kennedy Butler.[28] It also is a compelling fictional recollection of the bloody Civil War and tumultuous Reconstruction politics seen from both a southern and a female perspective. It is often a very human story of hardships and injustice. At times, too, it is a celebration of rugged individualism, tenacity, and capitalism.

Gone with the Wind, known widely as *GWTW*, is a remarkable example of societal and cultural storytelling. Mitchell credits her grandmother, Annie Fitzgerald Stephens, who was apparently very southern and very Irish, with sharing her vivid, partisan "Southern fried" remembrance of living through the Civil War and Reconstruction. *GWTW* was also doubtless influenced by her mother, who was a feisty suffragette, and her father, who had a passion for Atlanta and Georgia history. Other relatives supplied their embittered perspectives of what they viewed as the horrors imposed on them by the North. Mitchell was a true-gray Georgian.

Mitchell's biographer, Anne Edwards, writes that Mitchell's early years were filled with remembrances and stories of the Civil War: "She was taught the name of the battles, along with the alphabet, and her [mother's] lullabies were doleful Civil War stories."[29]

> And family reunions were dominated by honoring relatives who had fought in the war. She heard about battle wounds and the primitive way they were treated, how ladies nursed in hospitals, the way gangrene smelled, what measures were taken when the blockade got too tight for drugs and food and clothing had to be brought in from abroad. She heard about the burning and looting of Atlanta and the way refugees from the town had crowded the roads and the trains to Macon. And how her grandfather Mitchell had walked nearly fifty miles after the Battle of Sharpsburg with two bullet wounds in his skull. She heard about Reconstruction, too. In fact, she heard all that was to hear about the Civil War except that the Confederates had lost it.[30]

Mitchell's blockbuster classic is known for its seeming acceptance, if not glorification, of antebellum Georgia plantation society and the idealization of the Confederacy and slavocracy.

This novel, though not ostensibly a political novel, deserves a political reading, for it shares extended stories of Yankees versus Confederates, Lincoln versus Davis, Republicans versus Democrats, blacks versus whites, ideologues versus pragmatists, slaves, fugitives, blockade runners, a bipartisan brothel, scalawags, carpetbaggers, and countless political intrigue.

Ignoring the rich and instructive political anthropology of her novel would be like overlooking *The Iliad* and *The Odyssey* when trying to understand the political history and character of Greece and Troy. Novelist Pat Conroy is persuasive when he suggests that *GWTW* was *The Iliad* with a southern accent. "It is," he writes, "the song of the fallen, unregenerate Troy, the one sung in lower key by the women who had to pick up the pieces of fractured society when their sons and husbands returned with their [lost] cause in their throats."[31]

Novelist Mitchell had a genius for developing memorable, multidimensional characters. Her central character, Scarlett O'Hara, we immediately learn, "was not beautiful, but men seldom realized it when caught by her charm." She is also spoiled, willful, difficult, romantic, bullheaded, resourceful, unscrupulous, superficial, racist, anti-Semitic, and politically and socially ruthless. "You're so brutal to those who love you Scarlett. You take their love and hold it over their heads like a whip," says Butler. "You've wanted just two things," Butler tells her as they break up: her childhood dream beau, Ashley Wilkes, and "to be rich enough to tell the world to go to hell." Scarlett also had intense "love affairs" with her father's charmed cotton plantation, Tara, as well as with the dashing and iconoclastic Rhett Butler.

Mitchell's Rhett Butler is similarly unforgettable—indeed, one of the largest "larger-than-life" fictional male rogues in American literature. The Charleston-born, West Point and Charleston–expelled cynical realist is, among other things, a speculator, blockade runner, brothel owner, scamp, heavy-drinking reprobate, rascal, mercenary, "black hearted wretch," "consciousless scamp," and dashing romantic heartthrob. He accurately predicts that the South has no chance to win the Civil War and sets out to handsomely profit from this latest wreckage of civilization. "Why all we have," he tellingly notes, "is cotton, slaves and arrogance."

Butler, in Mitchell's hands, is a complicated hybrid of James Bond, Frank Underwood, Michael Corleone, John Galt, Rudolph Valentino, and, as it turns out, Mitchell's first husband, "Red" Berrien Kinnard Upshaw (a U.S. Naval Academy dropout who was a star athlete turned abusive and alcoholic spouse). He is a thoroughly clever, dandy "bad boy" who makes himself indispensable to Atlanta, Scarlett, and whomever he needs to advance his career and fortune. He becomes a skunk, a drunk, and a romantic hero. Butler is even more unscrupulous than Scarlett. He exploits every crisis and avoids going to war until he can gain political credit for serving safely and briefly. He exploits Republicans and Democrats as it suits his expedient interests, astutely reading the political situation.

A third Mitchell character is a debonair, iconic southern gentleman named Ashley Wilkes. Scarlett O'Hara loves him from age sixteen, when *GWTW* begins, through age twenty-eight, when the novel ends. Wilkes is the personification of the genteel, handsome, thoughtful, caring, well-mannered, and (unfortunately for Scarlett) elusive beau ideal: "All she could think of was that she loved him—everything about him, from the proud life of his gold head to his slender dark boots, loved his laughter even when it mystified her, loved his bewildering silences. Oh, if only he would walk in on her now and take her in his arms." But, alas, this never happens.

Wilkes marries Miss Melanie Hamilton, loyally goes off to war, and is as psychologically defeated by the war as the South is ingloriously humiliated. Scarlett's antebellum love fantasies never fade even as Ashley's and her own world are turned upside down by the war and the chaos of Reconstruction. He remains faithfully married to Melanie but is such a broken human being (his plantation and wealth were lost in the war) that he has to hire on as a manager of one of Scarlett's lumber mills. So, in a way, she has won Ashley's service, if not his heart.

Mitchell's novel is politically complex. Her storytelling narrative recounts fictional southerners giving at least a robust two cheers for the Confederacy and its defining practices such as loyalty, magnolia chivalry, plantation life, and, of course, unequivocal states' rights. Surprisingly, however, her three main characters question the Confederacy's political legitimacy.

Even the ever-loyal Ashley Wilkes regrets that he is a soldier fighting for a dubious lost cause. He writes to his wife from a battlefield that "we have been betrayed by our arrogant Southern selves, believing that one of us could whip a dozen Yankees, believing that King Cotton could rule the world. Betrayed, too, by words and catch phrases, prejudices and hatreds coming from the mouths of those highly placed, those men whom we respected and revered." Wilkes acknowledges that it was not states' rights, cotton, or slavery that motivated him to fight. What little motivation he had, he admits, was nostalgic remembrance for the good old plantation society days, days he now realizes were built on illusions, not to mention slavery—days that he now knows, even in the midst of the war, "are now gone forever." He even understands that they had to end. Gone, presumably, with the wind.[32]

Scarlett pretends to believe in and support the cause, but the "war didn't seem sacred to her. The war didn't seem to be a holy affair, but a nuisance that killed men senselessly and cost money and made luxuries hard to get." Scarlett volunteers in an Atlanta hospital assisting the wounded, joins sewing circles, and participates in charity balls, which raise money for "the Cause." But, remarkably, Mitchell has her heroine Scarlett conclude, "Oh Rhett, why do there have to be wars? It would have been so much better for the Yankees to pay for the darkies (which was among Lincoln's ideas as well)—or even for us to give them the darkies free of charge than to have this happen."

Butler explains that there will always be wars because men love wars. Wars, he explains, are invariably about money, and, invoking Napoleon, he adds that God is always on the side with the greatest battalions. "Scarlett," Butler insists, "our Southern way of living is as antiquated as the feudal system of the Middle Ages. The wonder is that it's lasted as long as it has. It had to go and it's going now."

Cotton was America's most valuable export, and it was a huge part of the American economy. It was, of course, grown and picked by plantation-exploited slaves. At the time of secession, the wealthiest states ranked in terms of wealth per white person were all southern states such as Georgia and South Carolina, states at the heart of *GWTW*.[33]

Scarlett's Irish-born, risk-taking father had prospered handsomely from both his own hard work and the cheap labor slavery provided. His Tara plantation "employed" around one hundred slaves before the war, and this funded an especially privileged life for Scarlett and her siblings. His fictional plantation is located near Jonesboro, Georgia, in Clayton County—about twenty-five miles southeast of Atlanta. Mitchell's own grandparents had a similar plantation in the same area.

Gerald O'Hara understandably bought into the southern political thinking that was part Jeffersonian and even more framed by John Calhoun's theories of states' rights and the doctrine of nullification—which called for the ability of states to go their own way rather than being forced to comply with unwanted, interfering federal laws.

There is more than a little irony in Gerald O'Hara's political evolution. He was born in Southern Ireland, where he and his fellow Catholic tribesmen were ruled over, manipulated, and exploited by the hated English. He was, we are told, a rebel against that system and indeed fled to America because of killing an English absentee landlord's rent agent. Now, ironically, the British are the prime market for his cotton, and he, as plantation owner and boss, is ruler and exploiter because of the "convenience" of slavery. All of this within just a couple of generations: from Irish peasant and rebel at age twenty-one to pious and patriarchal Confederate landlord in his forties and fifties. Quite a number of his fellow Irish immigrants famously fought with valor on the Union side, as was the case of Thomas Francis Meagher, brigadier general of the Irish Brigade from New York.

Scarlett loved her parents and the gala glory days of her family's Tara plantation. She was raised a devout Roman Catholic but developed an obsession with fancy dresses, being courted by local handsome suitors, and especially the balls held on nearby plantations that let her show off her gowns and dancing—and her flirting. To paraphrase Orwell: Such, Such were those days! And this is when Scarlett, just sixteen years of age, falls in love with Ashley Wilkes. Scarlett disliked school and enjoyed growing up spoiled, privileged, and courted. This the Civil War would devastatingly change.

Scarlett's political mind, limited as it was, became torn by her father's practices and the obvious self-interest of cotton plantation owners and those such as Rhett who realistically understood the national and regional transformations then underway.

So why, if Mitchell's three central characters (Scarlett, Rhett, and Ashley) were more or less heretical when it came to the Confederate Cause, is Mitchell's nostalgic ode to the old South considered such a triumphalist celebration of that region and its complicated past? There are several reasons.

First, her Scarlett O'Hara is an incredible symbol of resilience, survival, and tenacity. She is remarkably candid about her love and affection for her father, her mother, her lovers, and the land. She develops a fierce determination to overcome challenges. She vows in the midst of the South's humiliating defeats that she will never again go hungry. She will do whatever it takes to retain and rebuild her father's plantation and prosper. She will rise again, and so will her beloved Tara and Atlanta.

Politics and business, her mother had advised, were for men. But as much as Scarlett revered her mother, Scarlett loved to wheel and deal with men in both the political and the entrepreneurial worlds. And she would, while still in her youth, do whatever was needed to succeed, and in the process she becomes a feminist avatar.

Hers is a coming-of-age story when the age was about as tumultuous as could be imagined. Hers, Mitchell liked to explain, is a story of perseverance, survival, and hustle. *GWTW* is a beguiling story about what a person has to do to adapt to political and economic adversity.

Moreover, the fact that both Scarlett and Rhett shoot and kill a Yankee doubtless also endeared this novel to southerners. Still, the two of them never gave their hearts to the cause. They lived by their wits and didn't let the Yankees deny them their livelihoods or their dreams.

Dreams of the old South died hard. Part of that dream came from a love of liberty and private property and a fierce desire to be free from political interference from the national government. It was the dream of self-determination, decentralization, and local, home rule—all well-developed themes associated with both the American Revolution and the American political experiment.

Scarlett and Rhett flagrantly violated their region's code. Mitchell says this code was simple: "Reverence for the Confederacy, honor to the veterans, loyalty to old forms, pride in poverty and open hands to friends and undying hatred of Yankees."

These renegades may have defied this old code, but in some ways they were transcending this code and reframing a new, more realistic, pragmatic and entrepreneurial South. They were contrarians; yet they also understood political and financial realities of the emerging order. They became, in Mitchell's storytelling, symbols of courage, oomph, and enterprise.

Mitchell's novel has been long criticized for its acceptance and romanticizing of slavery. Many slaves are depicted in *GWTW* as happy and well cared for by reasonable slave owners. Tara, Twelve Oaks, and other plantations are described as blissfully pastoral settings. You can practically hear Beethoven's Sixth Symphony in the background.

Uncle Tom's Cabin, *Beloved*, *The Underground Railroad*, and countless slave narratives such as *Twelve Years a Slave* have educated us about slave abuses, broken families, mercurial and mean-spirited slavocratic owners, concubines, whippings, and the revolting and degrading realities of slavery. Missing from *GWTW* is the fact that many southerners had by 1860 grown to oppose and detest slavery and all the dissembling and disingenuous politics that tried to defend it. Even Ashley Wilkes, as noted, had come to this view as he went off to fight for the southern cause.

Scarlett O'Hara is an unapologetic racist who exploits, intimidates, and slights the blacks who had made her life mostly one of indulgence and luxury. Scarlett slaps one of her slaves. She threatens to use the whips and break anyone who would undermine her ownership of Tara. Mitchell too readily celebrates her authoritarianism as feisty individualism and "gumption." Moreover, Mitchell portrays most of the blacks as ignorant and childlike. A number of anti-*GWTW* books have been written, including the effective *The Wind Done Gone*, a parody of it through the eyes of slaves written by Alice Randall.

Mitchell at one point mocks the images of slavery suggested in Harriet Beecher Stowe's *Uncle Tom's Cabin*. *Beloved* and Harper Lee's two novels *To Kill a Mockingbird* and *Go Set a Watchman* share an entirely different South than *GWTW*.

In Mitchell's telling, the North terrorized the South with unrealistic and unfair Reconstruction policies. Southern states like Georgia were treated as military provinces. Elections were rigged, she implies, to favor Republicans. "Trainloads of Negroes had been rushing from town to town," and the voting period was extended to a three-day event in order to swell the vote.

Reconstruction, contrary to Mitchell's telling, did have some successes. Many blacks were educated. Some gradually became farm owners. And blacks began the long, if very uneven, march toward greater equality in politics, in the courts, and in education.

There is plenty of fault to go around as to why Reconstruction was less of a success than it should have been. But again, in Mitchell's novel, Reconstruction programs were tantamount to terrorism, and the terrorism was due, not surprisingly, to Yankees, carpetbaggers, scalawags, and even ungrateful blacks.

One of the understandable indictments of *GWTW* is that Mitchell embellishes the view that the South, with its (in her view) benevolent forms of slavery, would have been just fine if ignorant and moralistic interfering Yankees hadn't come along and ruined things. She ignores the reality that thousands and thousands of slaves jumped to escape and large numbers gladly joined with the Union forces to fight the Confederates. Indeed, Lincoln's long-delayed and reluctant decision to arm and let blacks join the Union Army, and their willingness to do so, was among the turning points that helped the North defeat the South.

Mitchell's depiction of the chaotic Reconstruction era is a revealing, yet misleading, part of her political anthropology. True, federal Reconstruction policies were often incoherent and poorly implemented. This was partly the case because Lincoln had died and had unfortunately replaced his pro-abolition vice president with a pro-southerner from Tennessee, Andrew Johnson, who proved inept in his strategies as well as unwilling to build upon Lincoln's legacy.

Emancipating slaves without providing for education, land, and appropriate guidance proved to be an enormous challenge in the late 1860s. Mitchell ignores all this and, as noted, relentlessly blames the carpetbaggers, Republicans, and blacks for fomenting troubles the South should not have had to endure.

Several historians have contradicted Mitchell's fictionalized account of Reconstruction. Historians such as Eric Foner and Douglas R. Egerton describe the profoundly moral and forward-looking programs aimed at educating blacks, encouraging positive black citizenship, and even black ownership of farms. American society would have greatly benefited had Reconstruction been properly funded and administered. But President Andrew Johnson—often considered both a racist and an alcoholic—was the wrong person for the job.

Some radical Republicans may have overplayed their hand. But it was the rise of the Ku Klux Klan and kindred vigilante groups in the South that undermined Reconstruction at almost every opportunity. Blacks who tried to exercise their new rights were intimidated, and sometimes murdered. Lawlessness, primarily by nostalgic and bitter "Lost Causers," paralyzed Reconstruction.

Abraham Lincoln is mentioned in passing just a few times, usually pejoratively, in this long novel. But, strikingly, no mention is made of his assassination in April 1865 by a Confederate-loving fanatic who was motivated by his fear that Lincoln would preside over the granting of political suffrage to black males.

Mitchell mistakenly implies that this right was to be granted by the Thirteenth Amendment. And she seems, even in writing her novel in the early 1930s, to share the attitude of antipathy toward this idea of her grandmother's generation. At times, indeed, much of the storytelling has the feel of "hand-me-down tales" passed along by her grandmother. President Jefferson Davis and Confederate Vice President (an Atlanta native) Alexander Stephens are, perhaps understandably, favorably portrayed in *GWTW*.

It may be unfair to criticize Mitchell for not treating the Lincoln story in greater detail. But *GWTW* readers need to know that this most tortured period in American history was influenced, more than by any other person, by a man whose political views were those of a gradualist on the issue of slavery and the Confederacy. Lincoln loathed slavery personally, but he was so committed to saving the American political experiment that he was willing in 1860 to let the South keep its slaveocracy as a price of keeping the fragile union together. He had even supported the Fugitive Slave Laws that allowed escaped slaves to be pursued, recaptured, and sent back to their masters. He also favored the deportation of freed slaves and at various times favored compensating southern plantation owners who would free their slaves.

Frederick Douglass, perhaps the foremost black leader in the nineteenth century, became a friend and celebrator of Lincoln. But he eloquently reminded Gilded Age Americans in 1876 that

> [Lincoln] was preeminently the white man's President, entirely devoted to the welfare of white men. He was ready and willing at any time during his first years of administration to deny, postpone, and sacrifice the rights of humanity in the colored people to promote the welfare of the white people of this country.[34]

Lincoln shifted from presiding over a limited to a total war, from gradual, compensatory emancipation to universal emancipation, "from opposition to the arming of blacks to enthusiastic support of it . . . from the colonization of freed slaves to the enfranchisement of black soldiers and literate blacks."[35] Lincoln adapted to the necessities of his times.

The Lincoln story may be ignored in *GWTW*, but it is the crucial backstory that has to be understood to finally locate this epic in the world of American storytelling. Later novels—*Native Son*, *To Kill a Mockingbird*, *Go Set a Watchman*, and *Beloved*, to name just a few, treated elsewhere in this book—help provide balance to many of Mitchell's embroidered southern epic storytelling.

None of this novel's flaws, however, should discourage people from reading this iconic page-turner of a novel or from viewing the Hollywood film based on "Peggy" Mitchell's novel. That film won a record ten Oscars, and the author fondly embraced it.

Biographies say Mitchell was a conservative Democrat in the 1930s (as typical of middle- and upper-class white Georgians at the time) and had only a superficial interest in politics. But politics was in her blood. Her relatives had seen their lives transformed by what southerners still like to refer to as the War between the States. Her mother, as noted, was a firebrand suffragette.

She and her husband initially supported FDR; yet they turned more conservative the longer he was in office. Her growing conservatism was also apparent in the pleasure she took in learning that liberals and "leftists" disliked her book.

Mitchell's older brother snarkily dismissed *GWTW* as a "psychiatric novel" about "juvenile love." But Mitchell's epic is much more than that. It is, among many things, a provocative fictionalized political celebration of how some people want to remember nineteenth-century Georgia and its survivors.

GWTW has been criticized for its length, its repetition, and being "middlebrow" literature. But it has become one of the best, if not *the* best, selling American novels. And even if Scarlett and Rhett broke countless southern traditional norms, this has become a much-beloved and inspirational story in the South—especially among the Caucasian southerners.

Mitchell's novel can also be read as an only slightly veiled feminist manifesto. It celebrates a strong-willed female who invents her own rules, declares her independence from her religion and local norms, and wills herself to become a fierce, competitive businesswoman. Indeed, Margaret Mitchell gives us at least four portraits of industrious, capitalistic hustle—Gerald O'Hara, Rhett Butler, Scarlett, and, to a lesser extent, the brothel-operating Belle Watling. They are, in each of their distinctive ways, Randians (as in *Atlas Shrugged*).

Mitchell was killed by a drunk driver when she was only forty-nine. She was crossing Peachtree Street in downtown Atlanta, a street that ironically is much mentioned in *GWTW*. *GWTW* helps, despite its flaws, in our understanding of a political mind-set of an extraordinarily important time in a distinctive region of the country. Hers is uncommonly gifted storytelling and an indelible sharing of "local knowledge" and local political folklore.

U.S. SENATORS AT WORK[36]

"Why does politics have to be so dirty?" asks a U.S. senator's daughter. Her boyfriend, the son of another U.S. senator, answers that there are many fine people in politics, adding, "I know lots of people I don't think are dirty" politicians. "Don't you?" "I suppose so," the girlfriend allows, "but they never seem to win." But, he counters, "They win a good deal of the time. It seems to balance out in the long run."

Allen Drury's best-selling melodrama about a controversial U.S. Senate confirmation hearing for a prospective secretary of state arrives at a similar verdict. Politics is complicated—it has the good, the bad, and the dispiriting. Yet Drury, a conservative former journalist for several newspapers, the UPI, and the *New York Times*, concludes that the U.S. Senate can rise to the occasion and do the right thing.

Mark Twain's *Gilded Age* (1873) and Richard Condon's *Manchurian Candidate* (1959) had previously provided instructive and entertaining fictionalized accounts of the U.S. Senate. But neither these novels nor subsequent fiction have done as splendid a job as Drury in capturing the human dimension of Washington political and social life and deal making in the Congress.

Drury says he was inspired to reveal a more human insider's account of congressional-presidential politics than is provided in political science textbooks. Indeed, Drury's narrator boasts, "They told you [in civics classes] about the machinery, but they never let on that human beings were what made it run."

Drury's fictionalized Washington has its vain, pompous, and ambitious officials. It even depicts unscrupulous operatives in all three branches. Yet it also has compassionate, hardworking, and conscientious senators dedicated to doing the right thing.

Drury (1918–1998), like other skilled political novelists, is fascinated by how politics shapes character and how politicians deal with moral ambiguity. He is at his best sharing rich portraits of personal lives, friendships, anxieties, and the multiple cross-pressures that influence U.S. senators.

Drury's long, blockbuster, Pulitzer Prize–winning novel compresses its whole story to a period of just two weeks. Here is how he sets the stage:

> Like a city in dreams, the great white capital stretches along the placid river from Georgetown on the west to Anacostia on the east. It is a city of temporaries, a city of just-arrives and only-visitings, built on the shifting sands of politics, filled with people passing through. They stay fifty years, they may love, marry, settle down, build homes, raise families, and die beside the Potomac, but they usually feel, and frequently they will tell you, that they are just here for a little while.

Advise and Consent was written in the mid-1950s in the middle of the Cold War; yet the events are set some time in a post-Eisenhower future. We are introduced to a hypothetical, unnamed president who had already been in office seven years. This president had served in the House of Representatives and as governor of California. In his race to win the White House, he made certain questionable, yet obviously coalition-enlarging, deals—with big business, big labor, and other well-organized interests. He promised his vice presidency to a strategically located governor of Michigan and the secretary of state post to an equally well-located governor of Ohio. This deal-making style became his standard operating practice, on full display in the heated contest to confirm his proposed secretary of state.

The president is sixty-two and in ill health. Still, he is a competitive activist who remains reasonably popular within his party. Like most politicians, he loves getting credit for achievements and is doing his best to postpone lame duckness and fortify his legacy. He decides, unexpectedly, to force out his secretary of state (the former governor of Ohio) and nominate a new one. He chooses Robert A. Leffingwell, a well-known, proven administrator who is popular with the media. Leffingwell is bright and articulate, yet somewhat enigmatic—perhaps a bit like Illinois governor Adlai Stevenson. He has many supporters. Like every cabinet department nominee, however, he must first win confirmation in the U.S. Senate.

The challenge is that Leffingwell is viewed by some senators as too liberal toward the then greatly feared Soviet Union. These concerns are held by conservative Democrats as well as Republicans. In any event, senators jealously cherish their constitutional prerogative of advising as well as consenting on top presidential nominees. Lame-duck presidents regularly learn this. Some higher-ups within Washington, including a few senators, speculate that Leffingwell might, under the next president, become an overly liberal and semi-pacifist "power behind the throne." The stage is set for a challenging confirmation hearing.

Leffingwell is asked at his confirmation hearing whether in his earlier days he was a member of a Marxist study group in Chicago. He denies it but apparently lies under oath. He continues to be grilled by other senators. Much of the novel revolves around how senators react to Leffingwell (and vice versa) and his chief supporter, the president.

Drury's narrative is shaped by the Cold War era's fears of the growing military might of the Soviet Union and related fears of Soviet espionage in the United States. Joseph McCarthy, a senator from Wisconsin, had exploited these fears in his exaggerated accusations of Russian double agents in the government. A decade before Drury's novel there was the famous Alger Hiss case where Hiss, a one-time high official in the Department of State, was accused of having given classified information to Soviet agents. Hiss was never prosecuted for this, though he was convicted of perjury.

Drury's characterization of Leffingwell hints of the Hiss and Hiss-related incidents. There are implicit suggestions here and there in the narrative, perhaps reflecting Drury's own political views, that the United States may be falling behind its Soviet counterparts both in military preparedness and in the space race.

Drury's president has done good things in his two terms, but he is characterized here as a vain, credit-hogging blackmailer, willing to break any promise and ruin reputations to get his way. Drury respects the presidency but at the same time gives us an especially conniving and narcissistic executive who seemingly combines the worst flaws of Nixon, LBJ, and FDR (and this is before LBJ and Nixon won office).

We understand and even expect presidents will negotiate, bargain, and try to persuade reluctant senators to support them, but Drury's president crosses the line. He collaborates in blackmailing a U.S. senator, he makes promises he doesn't keep, and, in a last-ditch effort to save his flawed nominee, he promises his endorsement in the next presidential election to an old rival in exchange for that senator's confirmation vote.

The Senate majority leader Bob Manson appoints the senior senator from Utah, Brigham Anderson, to chair the Foreign Relations Committee hearings on the Leffingwell confirmation.

Drury shares an intimate, even affectionate portrait of the thirty-seven-year-old Anderson. Anderson was born into a prominent Mormon family. He excelled as a star student and football star both in high school and at Stanford University. He was regularly elected to leadership positions in his schools and his Stanford fraternity. He is blond, popular, and in love with Stanford and the Bay Area (as Drury, Stanford Class of 1939, was).

He joins the Air Force and becomes a pilot in World War II. He wins promotions and medals for valor. After the war he goes to Stanford Law School, again serving as president of his class and editor of the law review. He then joins his father's Salt Lake City law firm, marries a young, attractive Provo woman, and two years later runs for and wins a U.S. Senate seat at thirty years old.

The confirmation hearings become testy as seventy-five-year-old Senator Seabright "Seab" Cooley of South Carolina raises character and policy objections to Leffingwell. Cooley carries an old grudge against Leffingwell for some condescending slight from a decade ago. "I'm going to raise all the hell I can," says the southern conservative Cooley when he hears of Leffingwell's nomination, adding, "and you know that's a mighty lot."

Cooley not only relentlessly prods Leffingwell but also produces a former student from Leffingwell's teaching days at the University of Chicago. This witness, Howard Gelman, recalls a Communist cell group Leffingwell and Gelman were in and says he therefore opposes Leffingwell's confirmation to be secretary of state. "I don't believe he is a loyal citizen of the United States." Both Leffingwell and his allies try to dispute Gelman's testimony by pointing out a few of his mental health breakdowns as well as discrepancy in his testimony. But Gelman's testimony and some further sleuthing by Seab Cooley about fellow cell members from that old Chicago study group diminish Leffingwell's support.

Senator Anderson decides to oppose the Leffingwell nomination. Senator Anderson does not fault Leffingwell for exploring Communism in his earlier career, but he is troubled by Leffingwell's lying under oath during the Senate hearing. He, based on principle as well as his conscience, tells his majority leader and his president that he cannot support Leffingwell's confirmation. The president tries to cajole Anderson to change his mind. But Anderson, a much-liked "rising star" in the Senate, sticks to his earnest and evidently principled decision.

Then things get ugly. A justice on the Supreme Court, who is pro-Leffingwell, is given material that links Brigham Anderson to a homosexual affair he had during his military service. This gets passed on to the majority leader and eventually to the president. The president is so determined to win this confirmation battle that he is willing "to do what it takes" to change Anderson's mind. The unscrupulous president works with the equally, if not more, unscrupulous Senator Fred Van Ackerman of Wyoming to threaten to "out" Anderson as gay if he is not willing to back nominee Leffingwell.

Drury's moving portrait of the conflicted Anderson is one of the best sections of the novel. The Texas-born, Stanford-educated Drury was a lifelong bachelor. He deftly describes Anderson's wartime affair (which lasted a month during R&R leave in Honolulu) and his confusion and conflict. Anderson's colleagues sense something wrong is happening. Cooley is so moved by Anderson's apparent plight and so upset at the character assassination by the president and Van Ackerman that he telephones Anderson, right before Anderson shoots himself, to say he'll do anything—including dropping his opposition to Leffingwell—to come to Anderson's assistance. Cooley's empathy is heartfelt:

> I have decided that much as I despise Mr. Robert-A.-Leffingwell, and much as I despise that being in the White House, and much as I would dearly love to get them both, the pleasure is not sufficient if it is really going to mean harm to you. No, sir, it isn't sufficient if that's what it means. I am quite an old man, Brigham . . . and I know by now when a fine young man comes to the Senate, and I suspect that as much as it might satisfy my ego to get them, an old man's ego isn't worth a young man's career and happiness. I truly suspect it isn't. I don't know what they have to fight you with, but I don't like the sound of it. I don't like the sound of it at all. I think you could be most severely hurt. I think this would be a real tragedy for you, and for the country, and for the Senate. I think you are worth a hundred times any satisfaction I might get from beating Mr. Leffingwell. I gen-u-inely do.

Other colleagues also call with sympathy and support—but too late. Drury's treatment of Anderson, his homosexuality, and his support from his fellow senators were remarkably more enlightened than prevailing attitudes in the 1950s. Still, the tormented Anderson shoots himself in his Senate office on a Sunday—as Wyoming senator Lester Hunt had in 1954, presumably because of allegations about a son's homosexuality.

Drury describes another fictionalized senator whose vote the president is desperately trying to win. This is Senator Orrin Knox. Seven years earlier Knox had lost in his party's presidential nomination fight with the now incumbent president. He is a model senator, family man, and patriot. His Senate colleagues admire his integrity and judgment.

Knox privately opposes the Leffingwell nomination but still has aspirations for the White House. Drury's ever wily president knows this, and he plays upon Knox's obvious ambition. The president promises Knox he will endorse him as their party's nominee—provided Knox casts a supporting vote in the Leffingwell nomination. "There is a price for everything, in this world," the president tells Knox. "You're no less immune to paying for it than any other ambitious man. Are you?" Knox enigmatically responds, "Perhaps, and perhaps not."

Knox leaves the White House and agonizes over his conundrum. Drury dramatizes Knox's plight as a compromise of conscience versus an enticing shot at becoming president of the United States. Knox is no friend of the president. He dislikes the president's deviousness and "too much going around the back alley just for the sake of going around the back alley," but, as noted, he also dearly yearns to succeed him.

Knox lets the president temporarily seduce him with the tantalizing offer. Knox is confident he could be a splendid president; all he needs to do is accept this Faustian bargain. Drury milks this dramatic dilemma for all, and perhaps for more than, it is worth. Will, alas, the imperatives of ambition triumph over the dictates of integrity and conscience? Senator Knox, in his "High Noon" moment, rejects the president's offer and sticks to his conscience.

Drury leaves little doubt that the president has badly overplayed his hand, cruelly in the Brigham Anderson case and insidiously in the Orrin Knox episode. The president and his chief senatorial ally violate honor, civility, and decency. Leffingwell, Drury almost proudly tells us, is denied confirmation by a vote of 73 to 23.

The president soon dies of a heart attack. His vice president assumes the presidency, and, in one of his first acts, he nominates our new principled hero Senator Knox as secretary of state. The former veep and new president also announces he will not run for president when his short term expires.

Politics is neither as good nor as evil as most people believe, says a senator's wife in this novel. No, she says, it is usually somewhere in between, "with aspects of both, on occasion one or the other predominates, as it had now."

Drury's novel, as noted, gives us the good, the bad, and the ugly of insider politics. The "good" consists of the senators like Orrin Knox, Brigham Anderson, and perhaps Seab Cooley, who are dedicated patriots and hardworking legislators. He characterizes others, the "bad," as lazy, or showboating playboys. Among the "ugly" is a Senator Joseph McCarthy (R-Wisconsin) type who happens in this case to be on the left. Senator Fred Van Ackerman (D-Wyoming) smears a fellow senator and is depicted as a thoroughly unlikable excuse for a public servant. The Senate ultimately censors him, just as the Senate eventually censored the infamous

Joe McCarthy. Yet, in contrast to the dishonorable Van Ackerman and the scheming president, Drury shares mostly admiring portraits of several key senators.

Indeed, *Advise and Consent* portrays the U.S. Senate as its collective hero. Drury doesn't get Pollyannaish about the Senate. Still, his is a more rational and deliberative group than we are given in most fictional works. Drury's Senate with stalwarts such as Anderson, Knox, and Cooley encourage the view that the Senate can play a positive role in constitutional governance.

Sure, bad apples can from time to time get elected, but Drury implies that this is rare: "Every once in a while the electoral process tosses to the top someone smart and glib and evil, someone lacking in basic character and principles. They can be on either the liberal or the conservative side, but the essential personality pattern is the same: a gambler, thug, and scumbag."

What does Drury teach us about politics? He teaches that politics can be incredibly personal; that friendships and civility can count for as much as, if not more than, partisanship or ideology. He, as noted, gives us good guys. Yet he also reinforces negative stereotypes about the profession. His president is worse than our stereotypes, and the self-serving games some of the senators play are on par with our pessimistic expectations of elected officials.

Drury takes pride in providing "insider" axioms that seldom find their way into generally lifeless textbooks. He has his LBJ-styled Senate majority leader intone that in legislative politics, the shortest distance between two points is seldom a straight line: "If you wish A to do something, for instance, you frequently are well advised to go to B, who knows him intimately, or even to C, who is an old pal of B, to start the wheels in motion." Who asks whom to do what can be crucial: "The whole future of a bill, the whole course of the committee action, the whole completion of a debate, can frequently be changed entirely by the personality of the man who sets it in motion."

Advise was a major best seller (on the *New York Times* best-seller list for more than one hundred weeks), later a play, and still later a successful Hollywood film directed and produced by Otto Preminger. Reviewers hailed it as the "most intimate" and "most gripping" novel about Washington political life. Russell Baker of the *New York Times* blurbed that *Advise and Consent* "was authentic, readable, and done with great technical skill." Liberal *Washington Star* columnist Mary McGrury hailed it as a "Washington novel worthy of the name and city . . . it has all the sweep of great events and the sparkle of telling detail, brilliant characterization and lively dialogue" (comments from the book's jacket cover).

Its detractors, however, called *Advise* too long, too slick, journalistic, and melodramatic. Its president seems, even with our more recent imperial-minded chief executives, too clumsy a Machiavel. Its treatment of love and women are weak. And "Drury's people," writes novelist and literary critic Thomas Mallon, "fare better at making speeches than conversation."[37] Its anti-Communism themes and homosexuality side plot are dated nowadays.

This novel reminds us again about the personal temptations and dilemmas that come with political life. We learn, as gifted storytellers have long instructed, that political leaders are, like the rest of us, flawed and subject to self-doubts, vanity, and greed. Senators, like people they represent, are, unsurprisingly, a mixture of good and evil, of idealism and pragmatism and cynicism.

Drury's is, as noted, a more sympathetic depiction of congressional politics than is found in most novels. His fiction should be read alongside political scientist Donald Matthews's excellent nonfiction *U.S. Senators and Their World*, written around the same time. Readers might also compare *Advise and Consent* to Robert Caro's multivolume biography of LBJ, which includes an instructive history of the U.S. Senate and a vivid portrayal of Lyndon Johnson's years inside it. For a more "noir" perspective, LBJ aide Bobby Baker's memoir *Wheeling and Dealing* provides a decidedly bleaker view of the Senate.

Advise remains the best fictional account of the U.S. Senate. It is a quintessential Washington political novel. Before *West Wing* and *House of Cards* captivated television audiences there was *Advise and Consent*. It helped spawn dozens of subsequent Washington novels, including those by Andrew Tully, Fletcher Knebel and Chuck Bailey, Gore Vidal, Ward Just, Joe Klein, and Thomas Mallon, and several television series.

If Drury's account of the U.S. Senate is triumphant in the end, it remains a very human institution—vulnerable, venerable, and valuable. Drury's Washington has its snakes and its heroes. He succeeds, as noted, in showing that personal relations can matter just as much and sometimes more than partisan allegiances. He also captures the ideological debates and anxieties of the Cold War and how they shaped politicians, the press, and political institutions. Drury doesn't conceal his skepticism about the liberal press or his opposition to those who object to hard-power military preparedness. Some of these themes were prophetic in telegraphing major campaign positions in the 1960 presidential election. Both Richard Nixon and John Kennedy read and praised the novel.

Drury soon retired from journalism and became a full-time novelist, eventually writing twenty novels and five works of nonfiction—yet none had the impact of this classic. He lived most of the rest of his life in bucolic Tiburon, California. The never-married Drury was intensely private. He died on his eightieth birthday and gave his personal papers to the conservative Hoover Institution at his beloved Stanford University.[38]

SOME OF THE WAY WITH "LBJ" FENSTEMAKER[39]

"You do what you *have* to do, Neil. I shouldn't have to tell you that. You need to make the best of a not-so-bad bargain. Give a little, take a little. . . . The first principle is that you've got to learn to rise above principle." Governor Arthur Fenstemaker advises his wavering mentee and possible candidate for U.S. Senate, Neil Christiansen:

> Your job is to get elected and stay elected. That's the first consideration. When that's assured, you get good enough, mean enough, you learn to fend off the bill collectors [big donors]. They come around wanting the moon you give 'em green cheese and make 'em think that was what they were lookin' for all the time. *That's* what you do. That's what a professional *has* to do.

Billy Lee Brammer (1929–1978) served as a young aide and speech-writer for U.S. senator Lyndon B. Johnson in the late 1950s. Brammer had been an Austin, Texas–based political reporter prior to his brief career in Washington. He set out in this novel to portray a political pragmatist, and he does so by inventing a fictional Texas governor, Arthur "Goddam" Fenstemaker. His colorful and politically masterful protagonist acts, looks, and sounds like LBJ.

The title *The Gay Place* was used before the word *gay* took on its later common usage referring to same-gender preference. Its use here refers to the political and social life, including Gatsby-esque parties, drinking, and bacchanalia that surrounded his fictional governor, U.S. senator, and their friends around the Texas capital. These politicos and their lobbyist friends have a gay old time talking politics, doing politics, and trying, at least in this case, to keep the then moderate wing of the Texas State Democratic Party in office. Brammer doesn't give us perfect politicians because he understands that they do not exist. He gives us pragmatic dealmakers whose motivations are a mix of ambition, vanity, and ideals. Pragmatism almost always wins over idealism, Brammer instructs; yet this pragmatism requires a dose of idealism in order to properly function.

Gay Place was a commercial failure and remains a neglected, obscure work. Yet it has a cult following, especially in Texas and among writers with a sympathetic bent toward politicians. Indeed, despite the fact that LBJ never spoke to the author after the publication of this book, Brammer claimed his novel was mostly sympathetic toward the politicians it portrayed. It has, over the years, been hailed as one of the more insightfully descriptive novels about American politics. Brammer unmasks what motivates politicians to act as they do. He writes with humor about the behind-the-scenes personal stories of politicians and their aides.

He is an analyst here, though not an especially judgmental one. *Place* is a trilogy of interrelated novellas, each with Fenstemaker as the canny, master politician on center stage.

The first and longest novella, *Flea Circus*, describes the way the governor maneuvers bills through the Texas legislature. Brammer is a shrewd storyteller, describing local legislators in action, in both their public and their private lives. Governor Fenstemaker proudly "greases the skids" as he gets legislation passed, rewards his allies, and diminishes his opponents. In a wonderful mimic of vintage LBJ speak, Brammer has his governor tell a reluctant legislator, "Looky heah, Alfred, wooden you much rathuh git haff uh loaf than none at all? Then whyn't year git behind me on this heah legislation."

Brammer has one of his "good" legislators reflect on why some legislators take bribes and others don't:

> I was just trying to see it from his point of view. The everyman politician with a cause. Most politicians accommodate themselves this way. One damn self-administered absolution after another—ends and means. But there's a limit to how far you can go. The good ones know this. They realize—certainly Alfred must've been *aware* of it—that you can only go so far. If you carry your justifications any farther, it's a risk, and it's wrong. I mean if you're Rinemiller, you know it's a risk. If you're Giffen [another legislature], you just know it's wrong. If you're [Governor] Fenstemaker . . . well. The good ones know there are limits. The really great ones don't even have to think about it—it's instinctive.

Brammer leaves little doubt that his governor is a LBJ parallel. The governor's wife is "Sweet Mama Fenstemaker" instead of Lady Bird Johnson, and his younger brother is "Hoot Gibson Fenstemaker" (for LBJ's real brother, who was named Sam Houston Johnson). Fenstemaker, like LBJ, has daughters, likes women and drink, is vain, loves politics, and has heart problems. He is called Arthur "Goddam" Fenstemaker, a name he himself embraces because he regularly uses this adjective, as in it's a "hell of a goddam country."

Fenstemaker understands that politics can be unsavory, but he also understands that politicians can make good things happen—build more hospitals, improve public schools, and work toward a more inclusive society. He also understands that nothing gets done unless you work through existing institutions and practice the art of compromise.

Fenstemaker is not above manipulative practices. In one instance he encourages a friendly journalist to oppose a bill he is attempting to get passed. The governor's ploy is that conservative legislatures will be more favorably disposed to passing a measure that the liberal press is unhappy about.

> "Oppose the goddam bill! But, just a little bit, understand? Don't get real ugly about it."
>
> "I don't understand," Willie [the journalist] said.
>
> "Those fellows in the Senate—they think this is all I want, they'll give it to me. But if somebody's runnin' around whoopin' about how good this is, settin' precedents and havin' a foot in the door and braggin' on how much more we'll get next year, then all my support'll get skittish and vanish overnight."
>
> "I see," [said Willie].
>
> "Only don't oppose it too much, either. You raise hell and *your* bunch [the liberals] won't go along. They'll introduce their own bill askin' for the goddam aurora borealis. I need their votes, too. Just oppose it a little bit—oppose it on *principle!*"

Fenstemaker isn't about heroics or purity; his political mantra is "somethin's better than nothin." He appreciates that politics can be messy and untidy; yet it is the art of making doable and possible good things happen. Yes, you need to have vision, ideas, and a sense of purpose, but you also need to persuade people, bargain, and put coalitions of like-minded people together.

Room Enough to Caper is Brammer's second novella. This involves a recently appointed U.S. senator from Texas (appointed by Governor Fenstemaker) trying to decide whether to run for election to a real six-year term. Senator Neil Christiansen is not sure he wants to run, but the governor essentially decides for him.

Christiansen frets that he might not be able to win. He is concerned, he says, "that I'll be murdered. I don't much like that feeling." "Nobody does," Fenstemaker says. "But nothing ventured, nothing by god gained."

> And you can take that bastard. I *know* you can. Hell! I just didn't pick you in a lottery. Hell and damn! I looked all over for someone I thought could take that sonofabitch. He ran against me once, you know. And by god he was the favorite in the early polls. But I stuck him—I *harpooned* him. And I think you can. He panics in the stretch.

State senator Owen Edwards, to Christiansen's political right within the Democratic Party, declares he will run for the party nomination. Sounding like later Texas politicians Rick Perry and Ted Cruz, Edwards calls for a return to "constitutional government." He blasts the tax-and-spend Congress, foreign-aid giveaways, and "rabble invading our shores." He chides the appointed Christiansen by saying "and our unelected representative in Washington" never raises "his voice in protest" against the horrible things happening in Washington, D.C.

The hesitating Christiansen likes the Senate. "It's a nice place, full of good and occasionally extraordinary men struggling with a hopeless and possibly unattainable noble ideal. The fact that the ideal might be impossible to realize doesn't undignify the effort."

Fenstemaker was eager for Christiansen to run, and he believed he would win. But he first had to motivate the vacillating Christiansen to commit to the race. So Fenstemaker deviously leaks to state senator Owen Edwards information about a few of Christiansen's associates who have had Communist ties. (This is the 1950s.) Owen publicly blasts Christiansen for associating with several known Communists, using Joe McCarthy–era language, impugning his patriotism and integrity. This does, as Fenstemaker believed, get Christiansen mad and motivated. He fights back against these charges.

> Fenstemaker steps in as well, and comes out swinging at Christiansen's opponent: . . . And what you've also seen today, my friends, is an example of the kind of vicious, poisonous, witch burning, hate-mongering demagoguery that has *always* characterized the campaigns conducted by Owen Edwards. . . . His kind of hatefulness reached a new low today— a new low even for the man who just about *invented* hate—he got so low down in the gutter today he'll *never* get out! I'll tell you folks, and I know you know without my saying, that *that old horse don't run no more* . . . that old dog won't fetch no bones.

Fenstemaker raises a ton of cash from "career contributors," the type that always yearn to be on the winning side, and he shrewdly guides Christiansen to reelection victory.

A third story, *Country Pleasures*, is the shortest and thinnest of these interrelated novellas. We get more of Fenstemaker's politicking and travels around Texas, especially in South Texas. Brammer writes more about deal making, complicated personal lives, and carnival-style political sideshows. There are some rather coarse descriptions of Hispanics and other minorities in this pre–civil rights and –voting rights era, when Texas was still a reliably blue, conservative Democratic stronghold. The novel is similarly sexist, with women in decidedly secondary and submissive roles.

There is a bizarre story of a Hollywood movie being made in the middle of Texas. Fenstemaker is, rather improbably, asked to play a role in it. He also falls for a voluptuous, sensual femme fatale movie queen who, small world, is the estranged wife of his chief of staff. "Miz Vicki" and another attractive associate on the governor's staff help enliven a grand reelection party for old Fenstemaker at his Hill Country estate.

Governor Fenstemaker dies of a heart attack at his Hill Country ranch under suspicious circumstances. But, and here is where *Gay Place* differs from most American political novels: politicians are generally viewed positively. Good guys regularly emerge. Good guys win office. Good politicians care about serving the public interest *as well as* staying in office. And, or so we are led to believe, political pragmatists do their best as they cope with the realities of human nature and an always imperfect and gradualist-based political process.

Brammer raises one disturbing issue about civil rights. An African American had been beaten to death in one Texas community—essentially a lynching. Segregationist officials are pressing no charges against the perpetrators. But federal officials at the Department of Justice are threatening to intervene and come investigate. Fenstemaker, concerned with his reelection, tries to postpone the federal investigators—until after his reelection. This is a case where he believes, doubtless rationalizing, that doing the wrong thing right now will be for the greater good later on, because he—rather than his more prosegregationist states' rights opponents—would be able to fashion the more sensible form of accommodation and administration of justice. He has the governor explaining, "I'm ready, willing and able to do the right thing—in sixty days." Brammer raises this issue but leaves it muddled. It is a case, to paraphrase an old LBJ election slogan (and later the name of a Broadway play and HBO documentary)—"Some of the way with LBJ."

Brammer's cult novel will likely remain unheralded even if it was briefly hailed as one of the best novels about American politics and favorably compared to Robert Penn Warren's *All the King's Men*. Its chief achievement is giving us the Johnsonian Fenstemaker, who navigates Texas politics as an earthy, savvy, old happy warrior more often than not on the side of the good guys than against them.

Fenstemaker loved politics and was a clever, if sometimes devious, wheeler-dealer. He is a curious mix of "virtues and sins, and righteousness and vanity," just like LBJ, who, as journalist Christopher Lehmann notes, "masterminded both the [Vietnamese era] Gulf of Tonkin Resolution and the Civil and Voting Rights Acts."[40]

Brammer's novel is an instructive fictional counterpart to Robert Caro's prize-winning nonfiction biography of Lyndon Johnson. Caro's invaluable writings capture LBJ's masterful legislative achievements as well as his vanity and vindictiveness.[41] It is also a companion to Bobby Baker's *Wheeling and Dealing*—the confessions of a top LBJ senate aide who would have been a staff colleague of Billie Lee Brammer.[42]

Gay Place will be a fictional footnote to Caro's work, and it will be judged less noteworthy than the more celebrated political novels of Robert Penn Warren, Allen Drury, Joe Klein, and Ward Just. Still, it remains an entertaining read for political junkies, and it is an example of political anthropology of a special place and era. It captures the way politicians talk to one another. It captures that some politicians can find the magical sweet spot between being idealistic and pragmatic. It describes lesser politicians who are in the game but lack a well-defined sense of purpose.

Brammer is more skilled as a storyteller than as a writer. His portrait borders on trivializing the art of politics and policymaking, especially with its emphasis on partying, drinking, and affairs. Still, his stories teach us about hardball politics, coalition building, and the flaws and quirkiness of political practitioners.

Brammer also teaches us about the limits of politics and the imperfect people and institutions that make up our governing processes. Somehow, however, Brammer's storytelling narrative affirms the inevitability and desirability of politics. Politics is a means of getting important things done. Politicians are flawed like the rest of us; yet there are Fenstemakers, Brammer tells us, who believe in the common good and figure out ways to move us in the direction of a responsible republic. His politicians understand that compromises and deal making are the oxygen of constitutional democracy.

Brammer's writings about a fictional Texas governor reminds me of another novel that focuses on a second fictional Texas governor. What makes this similarly overlooked novel of special interest is that this was coauthored by a popular three-term governor of Colorado. Richard Lamm and Arnold Grossman's *1988* tells the story of a conservative Texas governor, Stephen Wendell, who decides to run for the U.S. presidency as an independent. Wendell was a popular governor, but he had grown impatient with his Democratic Party—a party he perceived as too dominated by unions, teacher's associations, and various "special interests." He believed he could forge a middle, more moderate and sensible, path between the two major parties. One of his major issues would be upgraded border security (sound familiar?) and limiting the flow of undocumented workers into the United States.

Wendell hires veteran Democratic media consultant Jerry Bloom, and Bloom proceeds to craft Wendell's strategy and media campaign. Both the candidate and the "hired gun" media wonk worry over whether some of their fearmongering ads went too far—as indeed a few of George H. W. Bush's did in 1988 and Donald Trump's did in 2016.

One of Bloom's ads has brown-skinned refugees swarming over and maiming the revered Statue of Liberty in New York harbor—with an announcer saying:

> Stephen Wendell has fought to protect our cherished way against the crushing tide of illegal immigration . . . a tide that steals jobs from our people and creates crime in our streets.
> We must continue the fight in the name of liberty.

The screen has Wendell's name together with the words LET FREEDOM RING AGAIN, followed by the striking of a large bell, and this ringing lingers until the end of the campaign commercial.

What is compelling in *1988* is the confessional agonizing of the campaign aide. Coauthor Grossman provides some of the best descriptions available in political fiction of the joys, excitement, and darker forebodings of a campaign strategist. He witnesses and participates in a campaign for the White House that is cursed with questionable influence peddlers, seductions, druggings, cover-ups, and an assassination.

Governor Lamm, it seems, provides commentary of what it is like to be a candidate and on the state of the Democratic Party at that time and on the atmospherics and messiness of a real campaign.

Their book is part political thriller and part political anthropology. Their novel has a few too many twists and turns; yet, like the Brammer stories, it is a delight for political junkies. It entertains and informs about the workings of campaign politics. It also presciently anticipated the later campaigns of maverick independent Ross Perot of Texas and the populist Trump campaign.

Neither the Brammer nor the Lamm-Grossman novels are likely to enjoy a literary revival; yet they merit a place on recommended reading lists for courses on American poli-lit.

SHOWDOWN AT GETTYSBURG[43]

"General, I want you to make this attack. . . . General, I need you," Robert E. Lee tells General James Longstreet.

Longstreet sees a disaster in the making; yet, like so many others in the American Civil War, he reveres Lee. "Sir, I have been a soldier all my life. I have served from the ranks on up. You know my service. I have to tell you now, sir, that I believe this attack will fail. I believe that no fifteen thousand men ever set for battle could take that hill, sir."

"That's enough," said Lee. "General, we all do our duty. We do what we have to do." Longstreet was right, and Lee (fifty-seven years old), who had earned iconic status in his recent military triumphs at Fredericksburg and Chancellorsville, was wrong. His sense of invincibility, together with incipient heart troubles, apparently clouded his judgment in these early July days of 1863. Perhaps it was because, compared to Longstreet, he was outdated in his traditional tactics? Perhaps his blunder stemmed from a nagging personal need to refute an earlier reputation as risk averse and too cautious? Or perhaps the Confederates would lose because shrewder Union commanders had earlier secured the strategic high ground? Or perhaps some of his officers had let him down? The fact they were undermanned had not hurt them before, but it may have here—especially on "enemy" territory.

The Battle of Gettysburg was the bloodiest and most consequential few days in the long war (1861–1865) between northern and southern American states. Well over forty-five thousand soldiers died or were wounded, captured, or missing in action that week. Historians tell us that about sixty-five thousand Confederates, serving in the Army of Northern Virginia under Lee, faced off that week against eighty-five thousand from the Army of the Potomac, which is what that part of the Union army was called. This marked the farthest north the Rebels ever came and, together with Grant's victory at Vicksburg (the same week), it marked the slow beginning to the end of the American Civil War. General Lee overruled his second in command and the Confederates suffered a humiliating defeat.

Michael Shaara's (1928–1988) *The Killer Angels* is a brilliant novel about war, history, leadership, and politics. It focuses exclusively on the Battle of Gettysburg, depicting the carnage and bloodshed from the point of view of leading officers on both sides.

It is a political novel because, as Prussian general Clausewitz pointed out, war is politics by other means. War is a means to an end, and the ends are invariably political. Soldiers fought and died in Gettysburg because neither the framers of the U.S. Constitution nor leading members of Congress could resolve the slavery issue and related states' rights matters through conventional political deliberations.

Killer Angels describes and tries to unpack this key battle in the most traumatic political conflict in American history. The country was so divided over political issues that the division probably could only, unfortunately, be settled by violence. *Angels* is in many ways a political anthropology novel, exploring why men fight and die. The "why" in war is always a political question. It is also, as will be discussed, an instructive novel about effective and ineffective styles of leadership.

Michael Shaara was the son of an Italian immigrant father (from clan Sciarra) and a southern-bred mother who traced her roots back to pre-Revolutionary Virginia. One of her grandfathers was injured at the Battle of Gettysburg fighting with the 4th Georgia Infantry.

Shaara was raised in New Jersey, graduated from Rutgers University, served as a sergeant in the 82nd Airborne Division prior to the Korean War, and admired Hemingway and Shakespeare, among others. He taught writing for more than a decade at Florida State University and wrote science fiction and about sports. He was an accomplished short story writer before moving to novels. Young writers will savor that *Angels* was turned down by at least a dozen publishers before being published in 1974 and winning the Pulitzer Prize for Fiction in 1975.

Shaara tells readers in a foreword that Stephen Crane had written his acclaimed *The Red Badge of Courage* because reading the cold history was inadequate. Crane wanted us to know what it was like to be there, the weather, and what men's faces looked like. Shaara wrote *Killer Angels*, he says, for the same reasons. He tried to rely as much as possible on the words of the men themselves, their letters, documents, and memoirs. But the "interpretation of character is my own," says Shaara.

Shaara's clever device is to tell the Gettysburg story through the reflections or musings of a handful of generals and colonels. Abraham Lincoln and Jefferson Davis are almost entirely offstage. Lincoln's freshly appointed commanding general, George Gordon Meade, is present, yet at a distance.

It is a character-driven novel. Shaara relied heavily on several memoirs, especially on those of General James Longstreet and a visiting British officer named Arthur Fremantle, who had traveled with and admired the Rebels and went home and wrote about them. He also relied on letters and related historical material. But Shaara had to imagine much of what these men said to one another and what they thought about war, and what they believed the conflict was about.

Shaara won high praise from leading historians for re-creating this momentous battle. Noted Civil War historian James M. McPherson praised *Killer Angels* as his favorite historical novel and credited Shaara for helping us understand what the war meant to those who were fighting.

Most readers, even those who are usually bored by military history, agree that this novel succeeds in bringing the Civil War to life and liken it to the writings of Hemingway and Stephen Crane. Historian Stephen Oates called it the best Civil War novel and its description of combat was incomparable, conveying "not just the sights but the noise and smell of battle." Oates adds, "Shaara has managed to capture the essence of the war, the divided friendships, the madness and heroism of fratricidal conflict." Prize-winning documentary filmmaker Ken Burns said the book changed his life. He later directed and produced an award-winning PBS series on the Civil War.[44]

Back to General Robert E. Lee. Lee was a Virginia aristocrat who had gone to West Point and fought with distinction for the U.S. Army in the Mexican War. He later served as superintendent at West Point. As the South seceded from the Union in 1861, he was asked to serve as a commanding general of the U.S. Army. He agonized over the choice he had to make, but he ultimately withdrew from the U.S. Army and took up arms as the leading officer of the Northern Army of Virginia in rebellion against the United States.

Some historians suggest he did not have to do this. Many of his fellow Virginian officers remained with the Union. And Lee, at least in theory, was not a supporter of slavery. But Lee viewed himself as a Virginian first, and he at least tacitly accepted the right of his fellow southerners to own and sell black Americans and to take slaves to the western territories.

"If he'd been successful in the central task of his life (in Gettysburg and the larger Civil War), he would have preserved and prolonged slavery," writes David Brooks. Lee "fundamentally believed the existence of slavery was, at least for a time, God's will."[45]

Shaara wrongly informs readers in a preface that Lee neither owned slaves nor believed in slavery. Lee and his wife were in fact slave owners. But Shaara was right in saying Lee believed in God and "he love[d] Virginia above all." Lee was the ultimate southern gentleman and, in many ways, along with George Washington, among America's preeminent generals.

Shaara captures a reflective and melancholy Lee, who, in a soft, slow tone of voice, turns to General Longstreet and shares, perhaps as a Shakespearean character might share, that "soldiering has one great trap."

> To be a good soldier you must love the army. But to be a good officer you must be willing to order the death of the things you love. This is . . . a very hard thing to do. No other profession requires it. That is one reason why there are so very few good officers . . .
>
> We don't fear our own deaths, you and I. We protect ourselves out of military necessity, not fear. You sir, [he says to Longstreet] do not protect yourself enough and must give thought to it. I need you. But the point is, we are afraid to die. We are prepared for our own deaths and for the deaths of comrades. We learn that at the Point. But . . . we are not prepared for as many deaths as we have to face, inevitably as the war goes on.

Victory celebrations, Lee acknowledges, are a hallowed event for a few.

> But the war goes on. And the men die. The price gets even higher. . . . We are prepared to lose some of us. . . . But never all of us. Surely not all of us. But . . . that is the trap. You can hold nothing back when you attack. You must commit yourself totally. And yet, if they all die, a man must ask himself, will it even have been worth it?

Lee had hoped this battle would be the war's last. If they had won this battle, the pressure on Lincoln would have been great to enter into peace settlements with the South. It might also have led to Lincoln being defeated in the 1864 elections.

The novel's title *Killer Angels* comes from a brief discussion of Yankee Colonel Joshua Lawrence Chamberlain's recalling how he once recited a speech by Hamlet to his father: Hamlet had said, "What a piece of work is man . . . in action how like an angel!" to which Chamberlain's father quipped, "Well, boy, if he's an angel, he's sure a murderin' angel," doubtless in reference to Hamlet. This oxymoronic title, the joining of incongruous terms, recalls Hamlet's infamous line that "I must be cruel . . . to be kind." Is this what Shaara had in mind? Or perhaps it was a reference to the biblical "angel of death." In the New Testament, Michael leads God's armies against Satan's forces and defeats Satan.

Shaara's "Killer Angel" reference may in addition suggest, in this dubious battle, that noble, idealistic, and often well-educated men on both sides, sometimes men who had been classmates at West Point, or fellow officers in the Mexican War, and sometimes even members of the same family, all may have been remarkable pieces of work. Shaara's strength is in his depictions of remarkable and often inexplicable courage and valor—yet these same men were also killers, with killer instincts.

Confederate troops at Gettysburg, despite their losses from desertion and disease, were fired up with high morale to defeat their Federal rivals. Some likened it to a holy war, to a crusade for a special way of life.

Southern troops sometimes said they were fighting for states' rights. Others were fighting for glory and because they had a contempt for the Yankees, whom they had crushed in the recent battles in Virginia. Still others fought for "honor," their own honor, and the honor of their region and its customs and traditions.

The visiting British Fremantle believed the South was fighting for aristocratic values, for chivalry, and because southerners worried that the new polyglot North would destroy their [*Gone with the Wind*] older, traditional, more genteel way of life. Lee's deputy, General Longstreet, more accurately knew the war was primarily about slavery. At least half of the Confederate officers were slave owners.

Longstreet understood the political reasons that motivated southern independence. Confederate vice president Alexander Stephens unequivocally rejected notions that slavery was wrong and that it would somehow fade away: "Our new [Confederate] Government is founded upon exactly the opposite ideas; its foundations are laid, its cornerstone rests, upon the great truth that the negro is not equal to the white man; that slavery, subordination to the superior race, is his natural and moral condition. This, our new government, is the first, in the history of the world, based upon this great physical, philosophical and moral truth." Stephens's unsugarcoated and misguided case for slavery may have been a rallying cause for some southerners, but in the longer run it was a political gift for Lincoln and the North.[46]

Longstreet also knew that he could never forgive General Lee for ordering Pickett's Charge on July 3, 1863, named after General George E. Pickett, who led more than twelve thousand in the ill-fated attack against the much better positioned blue coats atop Little and Big Round Tops. He almost immediately lost 60 percent of his soldiers.

Lee, after the fact, accepted the Confederate defeat in Gettysburg as his fault. A few weeks later he even wrote President Jefferson Davis asking to be relieved of his command: "No blame can be attached to the army for its failure to accomplish what was projected by me . . . I alone am to blame, as perhaps expecting too much of its prowess and valor." (Historians and biographers point out, however, that Lee later tried, at least partially, to blame the defeat on some of his officers.) Longstreet wanted to resign as well. He didn't think he could go on leading his troops: "To die. For nothing."

Shaara's fictional treatment of Longstreet is decidedly more favorable than his treatment of Lee. This is in part due to the fact that Gettysburg was Lee's greatest blunder. It may also be the case because Shaara heavily relied on Longstreet's memoirs.

Longstreet, remarkably, stayed loyal to Lee and the southern cause right up to the end of the war in the spring of 1865. The historical Longstreet, despite his wartime loyalty to Lee and despite being wounded severely in 1864, later earned the enmity of southerners, especially from the writers of the "Lost Cause" school, for publicly faulting Lee in his misleadership at Gettysburg—and for becoming a Republican in 1865 in an effort to work with those trying to bring the South constructively back together with the Union. He endorsed Grant in the 1868 presidential election and attended his inauguration. He had years earlier, before the war, attended Grant's wedding to a fourth cousin of his. Longstreet and Grant had been at West Point and in the U.S. Army together. He won several White House patronage positions, including serving as U.S. ambassador to the Ottoman Empire. Only later in life (he lived to eighty-three) was he belatedly recognized in the South for his frank and visionary military leadership.

An unlikely hero in Shaara's *Killer Angels* is Colonel Chamberlain, who had taken a leave of absence from being a humanities professor at Bowdoin College. He led a brigade of Maine volunteers, the 20th Maine. He had fought in losing battles in Virginia before moving north under the Army of the Potomac to defend Gettysburg.

Chamberlain was a brilliant student and teacher who mastered several languages and was steeped in poetry and classics. He would later become a major general and a right-hand man for General Grant at the end of the war, despite having been severely wounded on several occasions. After the war he was three times elected governor of Maine and later still became the president of Bowdoin College.

His role at Gettysburg was to defend the high ground, just south of Gettysburg, from repeated attacks from the more confident and experienced Rebels. "Most of us soldiers had volunteered to fight in the Union." Some came because they were bored at home and this looked exciting. "Some came because they were ashamed not to." Others came, Chamberlain believed, because they believed, like him, that it was the right thing to do.

Union political principles are wonderfully laid out in Shaara's depiction of the youthful, handsome, and poetic Joshua Chamberlain. His Chamberlain believes in the Union cause and the aspirations of the larger American political experiment. He is morally opposed to slavery. He also fears that the southern planation system, if further enabled and extended west, would create a new aristocracy rather than a more egalitarian America.

Chamberlain makes a speech to a group of fellow Maine troops who had been imprisoned when they had recently mutinied because they wanted to quit and be allowed to go home to Maine. (They, like John Yossarian in Heller's *Catch-22*, had had enough. Like Yossarian, they say, "I done my share.") These "prisoners" are assigned to Chamberlain's regiment with orders from the top of the Union Army that he could shoot them if need be.

Chamberlain knows he cannot and will not shoot fellow Mainers. He also knows his diminished regiment badly needs more troops. His regiment, formed in Maine the previous year, once had a thousand men and now had just three hundred. So he listens to their complaints; shares that he understands their needs, hurts, and yearnings; and tells them he will look into helping them get free and back to Maine in due course. (Heller's Yossarian never had an officer like this.)

He pleads with the 120 men, formerly with the 2nd Maine, to join ranks with his 20th Maine as they try to defend Gettysburg and everything the Union stands for. Shaara's Chamberlain explains that while other men have gone to war for loot or new territory, the Union Army fights for something new and more noble: they fight to set other men free. "This is free ground. All the way from here to the Pacific Ocean. No man has to bow. No man born to royalty. Here we judge *you* by what you do, not by what your father was. Here you can be something. Here's a place to build a home. It isn't the land—there's always more land. It's the idea that we all have value."

Chamberlain had been raised to believe this was the first place on earth where the men mattered more than the state. Slavery was antithetical to this dream. Shaara's Chamberlain develops a Periclesian-Lincolnian voice, perhaps with a Gregory Peck pose, as he tries to inspire these erstwhile mutineers: "I've been ordered to take you with me. I've been told if you don't come I can shoot you. Well, you know I won't do that. Not Maine men. I won't shoot any man who doesn't want to fight. Maybe someone else will, but I won't. So that's that."

He lays it out. He will take them along—under guard if necessary. But he tells them, "We can sure use you." He tells them they can have their rifles back, and if they want to fight alongside him, he will be grateful: "When this is over I'll do what I can to see that you get fair treatment. Now we have to move out . . . I think if we lose this fight the war will be over. So if you choose to come with us I'll be personally grateful. Well. We have to move out."

One hundred and fourteen of these 120 deserters were motivated enough by Chamberlain's inspiring words to rejoin the battle alongside him. Novelist Shaara does not dwell on this, but one can appreciate that this Chamberlain-esque character and leadership may help, at least in part, to explain what happened in those sweltering, muggy "High Noon" days in Gettysburg.

Chamberlain was later awarded the Congressional Medal of Honor for his and his unit's defense of Gettysburg's Little Round Top. Chamberlain and his men held their ground against the Rebels. And when they ran out of ammunition Chamberlain directed them, in an act of courageous desperation, to charge down the hill with swords and bayonets, and this had the desired effect of scaring Confederates to flee.

Shaara, perhaps reflecting his northern upbringing and his mother's southern roots, is relatively balanced in his portrayal of Confederacy valor versus courageous Union troops in this ultimate battle of cannons and even bayonet charges. Yet he portrays the Union's political cause in a more sympathetic light. There is no equivalent Chamberlain principled rally talk on the Confederate side.

Killer Angels reads like an adventure novel—ample action, blood, gore, and tragedy. But it is also an illuminating study of leaders, paradoxes of leadership, and the idea of America.

Leaders on both sides understood they were fighting fellow countrymen. In some cases their best friends were now on the other side (as was the case with the South's General Lew Armistead and the North's General Winfield Scott Hancock).

General Lee said it was exceedingly painful personally trying to fight troops he had once commanded. Senior officers on both sides knew they were supposed to have the killer instinct, but most were conflicted. Many had their doubts about the real purpose of the war and whether this endless carnage was justified. (Note that, as discussed, many of novelist Margaret Mitchell's *Gone with the Wind* rebel soldiers, and even her Scarlett O'Hara and Rhett Butler, shared these conflicted "in dubious battle" attitudes.)

Lincoln and his new commanding general were not popular. Even Lincoln's Emancipation Proclamation (now revered) was unpopular among many northerners at that time. There was widespread pressure to negotiate a peace deal, and there was mounting opposition to newly adopted conscription policies. The nation was divided, and so also were many of its leaders.

Loyalty is essential for a well-functioning army. But desertion plagued both sides. Shaara alludes to this concept but understates it. Lee's army, historians tell us, was divided not only between Virginians and non-Virginians but also, and more important, between those who had favored secession and those who did not, and between those who championed slavery and those who had their doubts about slavery.

Historian David Blight adds that Union army officers may have been just as conflicted. These were "the 'McClellanite' Democrats, devoted to the discredited and fired General George B. McClellan, who sought a limited war that would never threaten the racial order, and those Republicans of a New England antislavery stripe who really did believe the war must destroy slavery."[47]

Shaara discusses at length how fiercely loyal Confederate troops were to General Lee. He had led the Army of Northern Virginia to repeated success, and he had a regal manner and a commanding presence that mesmerized his soldiers of all ranks. His men whooped and hollered and saluted whenever he rode by. But, and this Shaara emphasizes, Lee's celebrated success and bravery may have led to his vulnerability in Gettysburg. As a good leader, he asked for and demanded blunt advice. "I rely on you always to tell me the truth as you see it," he says to Longstreet. And his chief deputy James Longstreet provides this. But Lee does not, as discussed, heed this advice. In this "fog of war" moment, Lee may have believed Longstreet's love of his own troops was making him too cautious. Lee was willing, as top military leaders often have to, to engage in greater risk taking. In any event, Lee digs in, becomes stubborn in the face of both Longstreet's contrarian advice and perhaps the data, and, in Shaara's telling, makes a fatal military decision.

Students of Gettysburg also explain that Lee had just lost, to death, his all-star attack-fighting General Stonewall Jackson. He missed Jackson enormously, especially now. Jackson, it is thought, may have sided with Lee rather than with Longstreet, but in any event he would have helped Lee think things through. Lee was also disadvantaged by the inexplicable absence of General Jeb Stuart, whose failure to provide accurate information about the whereabouts of the Union troops hampered the Confederates.

Moreover, Lee was in the process of regrouping his own senior staff with some new officers. All of this may have impaired Lee's judgment.

Longstreet is depicted as uncommonly loyal to Lee but torn between that loyalty and his hardheaded analysis of how Lee's decision will probably lead to disaster.

Should Longstreet have been even more forceful in getting Lee to do the right thing? In Herman Wouk's novel *Caine Mutiny* the second in command believes his captain is so unhinged that he relieves him of command. Herman Melville's senior crew in the novel *Billy Budd* may have wanted to do the same with their Captain Vere. But the South's General Longstreet permits Robert E. Lee to make what many consider the greatest military blunder of the Civil War. Union forces, as noted, loved neither Lincoln nor General Meade. They had loved the popular McClellan, but Lincoln had relieved him.

Colonel Chamberlain, the professor who becomes our patriot-hero warrior, muses that there are two crucial responsibilities an officer must perform to lead men in battle: "You must care for your men's welfare. [And] you must show physical courage." Chamberlain does these things, and his citizen-soldiers from Maine triumph at Gettysburg. This is obviously one of the messages Shaara gives us.

Jefferson Davis and Robert E. Lee had military credentials superior to those of Lincoln and his rotating band of commanders, and, as Sharra points out, they generally had better morale and unity; yet experience, credentials, and morale don't always produce victory.

Longstreet understood, painfully, that morale, however important, was no match for what his and Pickett's troops faced on July 3, 1863. Longstreet knew, also painfully, that the war was about slavery more than most of the Rebels would admit, and that the cause of preserving slavery was not something they could use to inspire most of their troops. Ironically, historians point out, there may have been ten thousand slaves accompanying the southerners in their Gettysburg encampments to do cooking, laundry, and related menial tasks. There were apparently no known black soldiers on either side at Gettysburg.

Angels is used as an instructional reading at many military academies and leadership education programs.[48] It is used in part because it dramatizes that even the best of generals make mistakes. It also offers several useful case studies about the crucial role clear communication and explicit instructions play in war, as well as in complex organizations.

Killer Angels instructs, even if it is fictional storytelling, that military leaders have to be proficient at considering multiple and paradoxical perspectives in order to make sense of the complexities of war. Moreover, the role of obedience, loyalty, and dutifully carrying out the orders of superiors may be a cardinal rule in the military, but not every order should be carried out. General Dwight Eisenhower once said, "I need officers who know what orders to disobey." Chamberlain chose to inspire rather than punish the mutineers handed over to him. Longstreet dutifully goes along with Lee's flawed orders, although his "Lost Cause" critics believe Longstreet's delays and lack of complete commitment may have impaired Lee's strategy.

Shaara makes no pretense of being a leadership scholar; yet his novel is full of rich political and leadership questions. Did this war have to be fought? Why did these American families fight and kill one another? Which officers at Gettysburg provided the most desirable leadership? How do military officers balance their conflicting responsibilities? And is Shaara's novel, as some readers believe, a compelling case study about the senselessness of war? Finally, the "why" in war is always a political question, and why here was central to the idea of America—that all men are created equal and that there should be liberty and justice for every American.

One matter not explicitly covered in *Angels* helps put this riveting novel in the larger political context. Abraham Lincoln clashed with his famous Union general George B. McClellan because Lincoln believed McClellan lacked *the killer instinct* and had let too many opportunities slip through his fingers. So strained were relations between Lincoln and his top general that at one point in 1862 Lincoln famously quipped, "If General McClellan isn't going to use his army, I'd like to borrow it for a time." McClellan was a West Point graduate, experienced, talented, handsome, and popular with his troops, who had dubbed him "Young Napoleon." But Lincoln replaced him. McClellan responded later by entering politics and running against Lincoln in the 1864 presidential election.

If the battles of Gettysburg and Vicksburg had gone the other way, Lincoln would likely have been sent packing in late 1864, and Democrat George McClellan might have become the seventeenth president of the United (or dismantled) States of America.

Because it focuses exclusively on Gettysburg, this novel is unable to describe the significant roles that Lincoln, William Seward, U. S. Grant, W. T. Sherman, and perhaps as many as two hundred thousand black Americans, who would fight in the Union Army, also played in winning the larger Civil War.[49] It is also, understandably, unable to note the important role that world opinion and leaders in other nations played in this conflict.[50]

Killer Angels, however, is invaluable military and political storytelling about America's armageddon. It reminds us again about the enduring challenges of sustaining constitutionalism and a democratic republic. It also celebrates courage, character, and the soul of exemplary leaders at the same time it shines a beacon on fundamental American political values.

SLAVERY REMEMBERED[51]

"Where I was before I came here, that place is real. It's never going away. Even if the whole farm—every tree and grass blade of it dies. The picture is still there and what's more, if you go there—you who never were there—if you go there and stand in the place where it was, it will happen again; it will be there for you, waiting for you."

So Margaret "Sethe" Garner warns her surviving daughter Denver: "You can never go there. Never."

Sethe Garner, the protagonist in Toni Morrison's remarkable *Beloved*, is an African American woman who became a fugitive in 1856 when she fled from a hostile, woefully misnamed "Sweet Home" Kentucky plantation. Sethe made a harrowing near-fatal escape across the Ohio River to Cincinnati. She gave birth to a second daughter, Denver, just before she crossed the Ohio. Sethe and her newborn, with the almost miraculous help of the Underground Railroad in the area, make it to a relative safe haven.

Sethe, we learn, is strong willed, independent, and a proud protective mother at a time when many, if not most, blacks, including her, never knew their mother.

The U.S. Fugitive Slave Act of 1850 permits her Kentucky owner to track her down and reclaim her and her children (she now had four—two daughters and two sons) as property. That infamous act made it legal for a slave owner to go into states like Ohio, where slavery was not allowed, and it legally obligated local law enforcement officers and citizens to aid in the recapturing and reslaving of fugitives.

Her sadistic former owner and his nephew, aided and abetted by the local Cincinnati sheriff and a slave hunter, come to her mother-in-law's borrowed house on the outskirts of the city to take her back to the Kentucky plantation where she had been whipped, raped, used, and abused.

Sethe is defiant. She is so physically and psychologically spent that she is willing to do anything to prevent the reslaving of her family, so much so that she kills her older daughter, age two, and attempts to kill her other children. "That's how I had to get all my children out," she explains. "No matter what."

Morrison neither condemns nor approves of this infanticide, and later in the book she writes, "This is not a story to pass on." But her novel *Beloved* does force the reader to deal with emotionally painful moral ambiguity. One scholar puts the reader's challenge this way:

> We do not want to encounter this event shorn of our ethical orientations: we insist on the furnishing needed to moralize the deed. Thus Sethe's killing of Beloved has been read as the twisted and sinful consequence of the pressure of slavery enforced on her, as her resistance to that pressure (a sort of jamming of its machinery) as a moment of unthinking violence (nearer to manslaughter than to premeditated murder), and as many other things as well.[52]

Readers yearn for an explanatory closure on this shocking episode, but Morrison resists. Morrison's novel tries to get us to understand how a mother's love could have nurtured her killing of her child. Sethe did it freely and swiftly. If "I hadn't killed her she would have died and that is something I could not bear to happen to her." Her options were all bad, and she went with the one she believed she had to choose. But "it's at the same time," writes Weinstein, "a chosen act she cannot live with, one where traumatic revelations haunt her thereafter."[53]

Sethe's "boldness" successfully scares off the slave-catching posse that had come to reslave her and her children. But she is jailed by the local sheriff and spends three months with her infant daughter in jail. Meanwhile, the black community in Cincinnati shuns her in part because of her pride and in part because they are shocked. Some local white abolitionists are more sympathetic and use her case as yet another reason to repeal the Fugitive Slave Act and abolish slavery.

Once Sethe is released, she returns to her mother-in-law's home (loaned to them by the Bodwins, an abolitionist family) at 124 Bluestone Road. She is haunted by what she has done, and her dead daughter, whom she renames "Beloved," several years later revisits her in a supernatural way. Eventually she and her other daughter welcome this mysteriously (yet physically) real Beloved back to live with them: "Come on. Come on. You may as well just come on." Maybe the person is another person. Perhaps it is Beloved's ghost. Morrison purposely confuses us here. But Sethe believes and acts as if Beloved is her resurrected daughter.

Beloved "joins" them at 124. It is now in the 1870s. She "lives" with them, bewilders, and drains them. She is, most critics believe, an allegorical figure, mentally age two—the age she was slain—yet physically now nineteen to indicate what her age would be if she had been with the family all along.

Morrison's imaginary Beloved doubtless represents both the haunting memory of the slain daughter and the repressed memory of all those who died because of slave-trading and American slavery. Sethe embraces "the visitor" and wants to believe it is her murdered child.

> Beloved, she my daughter. She mine. She come back to me of her own free will. And I don't have to explain a thing. I didn't have to explain before because it had to be done quick. Quick. She had to be safe and I put her where she would be. But my love was tough and she back now. I knew she would be.

Is this a mother's imagination or rationalization? Readers are understandably puzzled. Morrison weaves a plausible story that either Beloved came back to life or a coincidental stray youth arrives at the doorstep, a possible case of mistaken identity, and takes on a presence that serves as a metaphorical stand-in for Beloved.

Meanwhile, Sethe's two boys have fled their haunted house, and her mother-in-law dies at the Bluestone house. The mother-in-law, Baby Suggs, was sixty years a slave and ten years freed; yet in her late years, especially after the infanticide and the shaming of Sethe by the black community, she was a physically broken woman in Cincinnati. Suggs's son Halle, Sethe's husband, had let his "Sweet Home" master rent him out for five years of Sundays so he could purchase his mother's freedom.

Morrison's flashback parable about Baby Suggs is especially magical. When the Garner family of Sweet Home plantation finally frees her in the late 1840s, she gets to Cincinnati, where she is barely able to stand. But with emancipation comes rejuvenation. And in Morrison's telling, Baby Suggs, on the north side of the river, becomes "an unchurched preacher." "Uncalled, unrobed, un-anointed, she let her great heart beat" in the presence of those who could use it.

Suggs's communal gatherings and dances in the clearing revitalize the spirit of her fellow blacks. She understood what happens when people lose their pride and self-confidence. She tells them to "love your flesh" and love your bodies because in order to ever think about getting better, you have to love yourself.

Morrison's endearing Baby Suggs gets children laughing, men dancing, women crying, and everyone loving what minor blessings they have: "She did not tell them to clean up their lives or to go and sin no more. She did not tell them they were the blessed of the earth, its inherited meek or its glory-bound pure." Baby Suggs instead tells them the only grace they could have was the grace they could imagine. "That if they could not see it, they would not have it."

Her daughter-in-law Sethe lives imagining that she did the right thing, that she stood up to racism and slavery. But Baby Suggs is unable to deal with the infanticide and declines rapidly. Moreover, her people rebuke Sethe, writes Morrison. She lives eighteen years of disapproval and a near solitary existence. This is in the free state of Ohio and mostly after the Confederacy has been defeated. But her defiant act of "tough" or "thick" love is incomprehensible even in her own black community. "Your love is too thick," an old friend tells her. Sethe replies somewhat like Sophocles's Antigone's love for her brothers: "Love is or it ain't. Then love ain't love at all." She ekes out a minimal existence as a restaurant cook and by taking in sewing. But no one visits her, and she and Denver, her remaining daughter, are treated as virtual aliens in their own community.

There is some hint that the black community could have and should have warned Sethe soon after she escaped that the slave master and bounty hunters were en route to 124 Bluestone. Why was this? This may have been due to some hard-to-understand jealousy toward her and her mother-in-law. It isn't entirely clear. In any event, the house at Bluestone Road is haunted by this communal rebuke and haunted again, repeatedly, by the ghost of Beloved. Morrison wants us to believe that America is and should be equally haunted by America's cursed slave trade and practices.

Morrison's novel is obviously not just about what Sethe Garner wants to remember or forget but also about the memory of a nation and the de-humanizing atrocities that happened in the Middle Passage, the slave trade across the Atlantic, and in the course of slavery in America. It isn't just about the garish killing of a child—it is the story of a nation that had made countless bad choices and lost its morale compass.

At one point, Sethe's friend Paul D. asks a fellow who helps out on the Underground Railway, "Tell me something, Stamp. Tell this one thing. How much is a nigger suppose to take? Tell me. How much?" "All he can," said Stamp Paid. "All he can."

Sethe Garner had taken all she could bear. She would not return as a slave with her sadistic Kentucky slave master. And she would not allow her children to be dragged back across the Ohio. She did what she believed she had to do. Yet she is haunted by it, and a central part of Morrison's narra-tive is that Sethe is simultaneously haunted by both her enslaved servitude at Sweet Home and her taking a handsaw to her older daughter's throat.

Morrison has the ghost of this daughter come back to question and pass judgment on Sethe. Sethe wants desperately for her child to understand that she tried to kill her children out of a profound love—and that they would thereby be saved from the horrors of slavery. But the murdered Beloved does not forgive. She instead comes back and torments her mother.

> Sethe assumes Beloved will forgive her. She does not. For Beloved, her mother's protection became the act of possession that led to her own death, which was murder. Beloved becomes mean-spirited and exploits her mother's pain. Sethe gives Beloved story after story of her love and devotion to her. She tells her how nothing was more important than getting her milk to her, how she waved flies away from her in the grape arbor, how it pained her to see her baby bitten by a mosquito, and how she would trade her life for Beloved's. Sethe tries to impress upon her how slavery made it impossible for her to be the mother she wanted to be.[54]

If Beloved is unforgiving, Morrison suggests, none of us can forget the tragic practices of the American past.

Morrison had been raised in Ohio by parents who had come from the Deep South. She had been fascinated by a newspaper story of a real Margaret Garner who had in fact committed infanticide. But Morrison wanted to invent and create a larger narrative in order to relate this case to contemporary issues about freedom, responsibility, and the place of women in society.

Morrison was well acquainted with scores of slave narratives such as Frederick Douglass, *The Narrative of the Life of Frederick Douglass* (New York: Signet, 1968), and Harriet Jacobs, *Incidents in the Life of a Slave Girl*, edited by Jean Fagan Yellen (Cambridge, MA: Harvard University Press, 1987). But she knew that even these slave narratives often understated the more dehumanizing and emasculating aspects of slavery. Her *Beloved* pulled no punches. There are repeated accounts of horrible rapes—rapes aboard the ships crossing the Atlantic, rapes and whippings at Sweet Home, men who were forced to share their wives with their master's sons, male slaves forced to fellate their white guards, and women repeatedly raped by masters.

Morrison's point is that rape was regularly used to dehumanize enslaved people and that the larger tragedy, politically, was that the enslavers were the creators of a system that undermined the integrity of the country.

At one point Sethe suggests to Baby Suggs that maybe they should move from their obviously haunted house. "What'd be the point?" asked

Baby Suggs. "Not a house in the country ain't packed to its rafters with some dead Negro's grief." Morrison is suggesting that there is no escape for Sethe, and no escape or forgetting for the rest of us as well.

Morrison's storytelling in this work is capacious, exhausting, lyrical, and richly packed magical realism with biblical symbolism. She turns the tragic human interest story into a gripping description of slavery, the practice of the fugitive slave laws, and the confused mid-nineteenth-century American mind. Hers is also a story of love, forgiveness, and redemption. And although it makes no mention of this, it is a compelling refutation of *Gone with the Wind* fantasies of plantation life and slaveocracy. Morrison's description of slave plantations and fugitives could not be more distant and contrarian than Margaret Mitchell's historical fiction set at the same time.

Morrison does this in several ways. She provides flashbacks to slave life at the "Sweet Home" Kentucky plantation where Baby Suggs and Sethe Garner had been enslaved. Morrison also does it in her vivid descriptions of Sethe's friend and sometime lover Paul D.'s eighteen-year odyssey around the South during antebellum, Civil War, and Reconstruction-era America.

Morrison's sidebar narrative of Paul D.'s bitter travels throughout the South, especially his dehumanizing Georgia-based chain gang experiences (note to Margaret Mitchell that this was in her beloved Tara land), help the author capture the misery and brutality of southern misanthropy toward African Americans.

Paul D. was sold by his "Sweet Home" masters for $900. This was, Morrison writes, the "dollar value of his weight, his strength, his heart, his brain, his penis, and his fortune." He never found a white who would comfort or protect him. He fled from one menace to the next—in Georgia, Alabama, and eventually Delaware. Morrison's descriptions are about as antithetical to Mitchell's happy North Georgia life for blacks, at exactly the same time, the 1850s and 1860s, as is imaginable. Morrison poignantly adds "And in all these escapes [Paul D.] could not help being astonished by the beauty of this land that was not his."

Morrison's goal was for Americans, especially black Americans, to revisit and try to understand a past that most wanted to forget and repress. She makes her readers travel an unforgiving journey through black trauma and the dysfunctional American political nightmare of mid-nineteenth century. "*Beloved*, like the slave narrative tradition it invokes, explores the effects of slavery's many deprivations (legal or otherwise), and none so prominently as its interference with the capacity for healthy expressions of love and the development of love relationships," writes African American studies scholar Lovalerie King. "Such conditions breed desire, and Morrison's spiteful title character is the essence of insatiable desire, distilled from the extreme deprivation and abuse that emanate from slavery."[55]

Beloved is, as noted earlier, dedicated to "Sixty Million and more," a reference to the Africans and their descendants who died as a result of the Atlantic slave trade and the institution of slavery in America. In her foreword Morrison writes, "I wanted the reader to be kidnapped, thrown ruthlessly into an alien environment as the first step in a shared experience with the book's population"—slaves, fugitives, and used-to-be slaves. She succeeds.

Morrison's style is understated descriptive storytelling. There are multiple flashbacks, and readers are sometimes confused by shifting time periods and different narrative voices, and especially by the ethereal symbolism and reincarnation of Beloved. At least one critic faulted her for sensationalism, for writing an alternative holocaust novel and for one too many attempts at biblical grandeur. Nearly everyone else, however, has called *Beloved* a dazzling, magical masterpiece.

The novel ends with a ritual exorcism rendered by thirty black women in the community. They come to pray for Sethe and cast out what they assume is the demonic ghost in her haunted life. Some in the community have developed guilt at not being there for this troubled neighbor. Now they come to 124 Bluestone Road to pray, and they seek to exorcise Beloved from the house. They succeed. They also stop a startled Sethe from mistakenly stabbing the kindly Mr. Bodwin, who was coming in his wagon to pick up Denver for her new job. Sethe had feared the white male visitor might have been her old slave master. It is the power of locals coming together (a form of communitarianism), perhaps a bit too conveniently at the close of the novel, that gives Morrison's character the redemptive strength to move on. Sethe can now share her house with Paul D., who had been forced to flee by the domineering Beloved, Denver finds employment and even the promise of college, and the community can transcend its intolerance and ghosts real and imagined.

In the end Sethe comes to terms with her life. It is Morrison's hope that with her remembrances, Americans can similarly come to terms with, yet never forget, these unspeakably harsh political realities as America continues to try to live up to its constitutional aspirations.

Morrison's novel is a warning to those who would forget history, and perhaps in the same breath an apology to those who cannot. "Generations pass on history, pain and power. The African-American community is still trying to find its personal, political, and communal power after years of having it stripped from them, but the first step in any sort of recovery comes from acknowledging the problem, and remembering where it came from."[56]

Philip Brendese concludes that *Beloved* speaks to a still-divided America "that has not come to terms with the haunting memory of slavery and its untranslated legacy in racial politics."[57] Morrison joined Richard Wright and Ralph Ellison, author of another classic, *Invisible Man*, in reminding Americans that African Americans have long struggled to be seen, recognized, accepted, and granted full agency in this land of the free and brave.

This novel of vivid and thick description was intentionally written to disturb the peace and inform the present. Morrison had told a BBC interviewer in 1982 that the best art "is political and you ought to be able to make it unquestionably political and irrevocably beautiful at the same time." *Beloved* did that.[58] Hers is simultaneously a protest novel, a consciousness-raising novel, and a wondrously crafted work of political anthropology. It is a poetic, musical, luminous literary as well as political triumph and was so recognized when it earned a Nobel Prize for Literature in 1993.

SPECIAL AGENT HARRY HUBBARD[59]

"In our Judeo-Christian culture, therefore, difficulties arise. . . . Manipulation is Machiavellian, we say, and are content to let the name judge the matter. Yet if a good man working for his beliefs is not ready to imperil his conscience, then the battlefield will belong to those who manipulate history for base ends. This is not an inquiry into morality, so I pursue the matter no further than to say that a visceral detestation of manipulation is guaranteed to produce an incapacity to find agents and run them."

These are mentoring words, part of a series of inspirational lectures to younger CIA agents, of legendary counterespionage agent Hugh Montague, widely known in the Agency by his code name "Harlot." Harlot is the godfather role model, boss, and essentially the spiritual "rabbi" in the coming-of-age odyssey of Herrick "Harry" Hubbard. Hubbard revered Harlot, both for his distinguished covert operations in World War II and because he was "my master in the only spiritual art that American men and boys respect"—machismo. "He gave life courses in grace under pressure."

Most of Mailer's lengthy historical novel *Harlot's Ghost*, about the U.S. Central Intelligence Agency in the 1950s and 1960s, tells the story of a fictionalized clandestine operative. His well-bred WASPy Harry Hubbard grows up in a wealthy New York socialite family, with summers on

Maine's chic Mount Desert Island and prep school at "St. Matthews" (a fictionalized composite of St. Mark's, St. Paul's, Groton, and Andover). His mother is wealthy and unlikable. His father, divorced, is a dashing, daring veteran of the OSS and one of the CIA's most famous and infamous clandestine operatives. His father would spend the early 1960s trying, unsuccessfully, to eliminate Fidel Castro.

Hubbard is the novel's narrator and protagonist. We learn of his prep school years—sermons, sports, camaraderie, and occasional homosexuality. We watch him pass through Yale, join ROTC, and graduate a semester early so he can jump-start a CIA career. He is fascinated, apparently like Mailer, with intrigue and the macho exhilaration of the Agency.

Hubbard endures the arduous boot camp training at the CIA's Camp Perry (the "Farm"), along with the requisite and boring anti-Communist courses. He wonders out loud if all Communists are bad but is essentially silenced by his instructors. Hubbard comes to see the work of the Agency as an ambiguous, yet strategically necessary, force for good in the United States' magisterial fight against totalitarianism.

His mentor, Harlot, reminds him that the true force of the Russians has less to do with their military strength than with their ability to merchandize their ideology: "For the Russians are able to get their licks in on whatever is left of the Christian in many a rich swine. It goes so deep—this simple idea that nobody on earth should have too much wealth."

"That's exactly what's satanic about Communism," says Harlot. "It trades on the noblest vein in Christianity. It works great guilt in us." We're rich and we're drenched in guilt. "The Reds, not us, are the evil ones, and so they are clever enough to imply that they are in the tradition of Christ." Harlot explains his deep faith:

> Our spiritual offering is finer, but their marketing of ideas proves superior. Here those of us who are serious tend to approach God alone, each of us, one by one, but the soviets are able to perform the conversion en masse. That is because they deliver the commonweal over to man, not God. A disaster. God, not man, has to be the judge. I will always believe that . . .
>
> I also believe that even at my worst, I am still working, always working, as a soldier of God.

Hubbard's first assignment is as a junior officer in Berlin, where he helps with operating a tunnel under the Berlin Wall and trying to recruit sources. He is constantly learning about himself—in what amounts to a lifelong search for understanding his own identity (akin, no doubt, to Mailer's own journey). He has the first of what will seem like a score of sexual affairs, and learns from a tough taskmaster of a boss.

Hubbard leaves Berlin and goes to Montevideo, Uruguay, where he works as a midlevel employee. The day-to-day work of espionage and clandestine operations is lonely and usually boring. Hubbard wonders whether it all matters. Exactly what is the mission? Why do interagency rivalries and interdepartmental feuds take as much time and energy as going after the bad guys? Good information, as all agents learn, sometimes comes from bad guys, and many of their "sources" and "recruits" are unsavory.[60]

Mailer captures the spirit of the Cold War in the 1950s. In *Harlot's Ghost*, some of his finest writing, he develops several disjointed narratives. Mailer (1923–2002), who was one of the twentieth century's brilliant as well as belligerent writers, boasts that "plot is the enemy of the great novel." He adds, "I'm interested in plots that do not have a resolution. Life is like that."[61] His novel is a sprawling, wandering, geopolitical sweep through the Cold War years, with portraits of both real and fictional figures who manned the barricades in America's war against totalitarianism.

Reviewers were divided. Salman Rushdie and Christopher Hitchens hailed it as a masterpiece. Others criticized its incoherent structure and complained it lacked serious editing. One critic suggested there were a few hundred pages of powerful writing in *Harlot's Ghost*—implying that most of it was forgettable. The lengthy section about Uruguay earned special criticism.

New York Times reviewer John Simon wrote that Mailer deploys just about all known and even some unknown forms of fiction writing: "Bildungsroman, epistolary novel, diary novel, phone-call novel, gossip-column novel, philosophico-political novel, pornographic novel and adventure story rotate into our field of vision."[62]

One of the strangest interior narratives consists of dozens of letters Hubbard exchanges with Harlot's wife, Hadley Kittredge Gardiner Montague. Hubbard had been a frequent dinner guest, and he subsequently becomes godfather to Harlot and Kittredge's son and later becomes Kittredge's lover. Hubbard and Kittredge correspond as philosophical and gossipy soul mates.

Kittredge also works for the CIA, specializing in psychological operations. Her big idea (brought up throughout the novel) is that all of us have within ourselves two competing forces, which she calls the Alpha and the Omega. These two forces are essentially two different psyches: "Alpha and Omega originate from separate creatures. One is descended from the sperm cell, Alpha; Omega from the ovum." They coexist, suggests Kittredge, like

Siamese twins, inside each person, and they ceaselessly vie with one another in guiding our actions. The Alpha connotes force, pessimism, and routine. The Omega is optimistic and spontaneous. "The male side can be full of the so-called female qualities, whereas Omega can be an outrageous bull of a woman, just as virile and muscular as a garbage collector," Kittredge explains. "Each self can borrow from the other, and do, because they are wed like the corporal lobes of the brain."

Hubbard wonders why Kittredge's theory seems to describe an "endless capacity for strife" in everyone's psychological makeup. She replies that this is the reality of human nature. That's what comes with free will. "Free will amounts to giving the Devil equal opportunity," she explains. Moreover, she proudly notes, this is how spies "are able to live with the tension of their incredible life-situations."

Some of Mailer's friends and biographers believe Kittredge's theories reflected Mailer's own existential notion that all of us have two separate personalities. Critics rightly complained that the lengthy discussion of these psychological theories confuses more than informs and that it distracts as well as weakens the book.

Hubbard's long letters to Kittredge describe not only his professional life but also his serial love affairs in Montevideo. Mailer's exhaustive case study on Hubbard seeks to explain what motivates CIA types, exposing the "covert mind" of America.

Much of the last half of the book is about the Bay of Pigs fiasco and the chaotic October 1962 Cuban Missile Crisis. Hubbard and his father, "Cal" Hubbard, become partners in these episodes. Hubbard is assigned at one point to have an affair with a woman who is simultaneously having affairs with John F. Kennedy and a Chicago Mafia boss. He willingly does so (following in the footsteps of his father, who had a reputation for such exploits). He describes these affairs at length, improbably, in letters to Kittredge.[63]

Mailer's fictionalized accounts are strikingly close to subsequent journalistic and political analyses of these liaisons. (Mailer claims he read nearly a hundred books on these and related CIA operations.) He goes into detail about the Agency's miscalculations and mistakes, the Kennedy brothers' antipathy toward Fidel Castro, and the CIA's bungled attempts to assassinate Castro. He offers a picture of endless internecine bureaucratic struggles among the FBI, the State Department, presidential advisors, and the CIA.[64]

Ghost was a surprise to many of Mailer's longtime readers. He had earned a reputation as an especially talented writer who was also an antiestablishment lefty, regularly criticizing what he saw as the increasingly totalitarian culture of America. He was an early admirer of the machismo of Hemingway, and as a young man he took up boxing, tried drugs, and began a lifelong fascination with existentialism. He had championed socialism when he was younger, and variously celebrated "hipsterism," anarchism, and even violence as the appropriate response to racism and statism. He earned a reputation, much cultivated, as a rogue "bad boy" political provocateur.

Yet he also craved recognition in the literary community and in elite New York social circles. He was, as a friend put it, "hungry for fame." He loved interviewing and writing about celebrities like John F. Kennedy, Henry Kissinger, or Muhammad Ali. He covered several national political conventions as a journalist, and wrote books about Marilyn Monroe and Lee Harvey Oswald.

In 1969, he ran for the Democratic nomination for mayor of New York City. He ran for mayor on a ticket with reporter Jimmy Breslin, who ran for city council president. Their main pledge was "No More Bullshit." Another slogan was "Throw the Rascals In." Mailer called for New York City to become the fifty-first state, and for political power to be devolved to the neighborhoods. He was an inept campaigner, and his campaign was miserably disorganized. Mailer lost his cool and his dignity on several occasions. Mailer and Breslin came in fourth out of the five primary contenders. For most of the campaign, friends say, Mailer was the only one who thought he had a chance.

Biographers say Mailer, the provocateur of the 1950s and 1960s, mellowed as he grew older. He had a handful of wives and a flock of children. He had won fame and acclaim, including the Pulitzer Prize and the National Book Award.

Mailer did years of research for *Harlot's Ghost*. Somewhat unexpectedly, he came to respect many of the CIA leaders like Allen Dulles and Richard Helms, and his novel is brilliant political anthropology, providing "thick descriptions" of this often mysterious and dark side of America's foreign policy. He "portrays the Cold War C.I.A. in loving detail, seemingly uncritical of its history of deception, murder, and worse."[65] He came to believe the Agency was an essential and necessary part of government, even if it sometimes had to do questionable or illegal things. This may have been, for Mailer, his Machiavellian awakening, or something akin to this. In some later editions Mailer's publisher provided this novel with a subtitle, so it read *Harlot's Ghost: A Novel of the CIA*.

Mailer's fascination with the clandestine operatives and their lifestyles both recognizes and minimalizes the extent to which CIA elites transcended the law. One CIA biographer put it more bluntly:

> During the Cold War, these men considered themselves so important to the survival of our country that they thought ordinary rules did not apply to them. That sort of elitism has haunted the CIA throughout its entire history. A feeling of exemption from rules and regulations is the norm.[66]

Ghost sees things through the eyes of Harry Hubbard, who took to espionage because he believes that any "mischief we could work on evil opponents [the Communists] left us clearly on the right side. I think that was the allure of tradecraft." Moreover, perhaps sounding like the irrepressible rouge-child within Mailer, Hubbard asks, "Is there any state more agreeable than living and working like a wicked angel?"

In a flash-forward sequence, Mailer gleefully relates an incident during the Warren Commission hearings on the Kennedy assassination, in which Chief Justice Earl Warren asks former CIA director Allen Dulles during the Kennedy assassination hearings that led to the famous *Warren Report*, "The F.B.I. and C.I.A. do employ undercover men who are of terrible character?" Dulles, "in all the bonhomie of a good fellow who can summon up the services of a multitude of street ruffians, replied, 'Yes, terribly bad characters.'"

Why the title *Harlot's Ghost*? The "ghost" part comes from Hubbard trying to understand whether the CIA or others knocked off Montague— or whether he may have defected to Russia. The "harlot" may have been borrowed from Balzac, who compared whores and political intelligence agents. The harlot, after all, inhabited the world of *as if*, Mailer explained to one of his biographers: "You paid your money and the harlot acted for a little while . . . as if she loved you, and that was a more mysterious proposition than one would think, for it is always mysterious to play a role. It is equal in a sense to living under cover."[67] CIA agents, he is saying, must live with multiple identities and must, like the harlot, become an actor or actress, and live a life of masks and pretense.[68]

Mailer called his novel an "antispy" novel because the goal was to demythologize as well as celebrate the life and work of spies. He wished to explain why and how they do what they do. His left-wing friends felt this novel made him an apologist for the Agency, but he denied this, saying he was merely trying to understand this hard-to-understand, though important, part of American political culture.

Ghost was widely read by members of the CIA. Some agents complained he exaggerated the Agency's mistakes and went on unnecessarily and excessively about agents' sexual activities. Still, six months after the publication of the novel, Mailer (who, in his younger days, as noted, had been a militant critic of governmental operations such as the CIA) was invited to Langley, Virginia, and honored by the CIA. He received several standing ovations as he spoke to five hundred or more of the CIA brass at their headquarters.

Biographers say Mailer loved the drama and romance of spying and intelligence work. Part of Mailer was doubtless fascinated by the rogue double lives of agents like Hubbard. He also came to feel that several of the top CIA officials in the 1950s and 1960s were as consequential in American politics as anyone save the president. He increasingly accepted the CIA's role in guaranteeing national security and advancing U.S. interests. This did not mean he approved and admired all CIA undertakings. *Ghost* describes their mistakes and satirizes some of their stereotypical cloak-and-dagger rituals.[69]

This thinly veiled account of the daring and often arrogant clandestine exploits of Allen Dulles, Richard Helms, Richard Bissell, Desmond FitzGerald, Tracy Barnes, and Frank Wisner is fiction as history or historical fiction. "I have looked to avoid exaggeration," Mailer said in his author's note. "If I have succeeded, *Harlot's Ghost* will offer an imaginary C.I.A. that will move in a parallel orbit to the real one, and will be neither an over- nor under-estimation of its real powers." Good fiction, he claimed, could be "more real" and "more nourishing to our sense of reality than nonfiction."

Mailer self-servingly contends *Ghost* will be more helpful for those who want to understand the CIA and Cold War America than the histories, biographies, and political science that will emerge. This argument, much like Mailer's whole life, is brash and provocative; yet, for those who carefully read *Ghost*, his contention has merit. He does indeed "take us in" to covert operations and the political psychology that inspired presidents, CIA directors, and midlevel clandestine operatives. His novel is a sweeping account—almost Homeric, or Thucydidean in its breadth—of an unusual time and place in the American experiment.

Longtime *Washington Post* reporter David Ignatius has written a series of novels about espionage and on intelligence agencies. They are a useful follow-up to Mailer. See, for example, David Ignatius, *The Director: A Novel* (New York: Norton, 2014).

One has to remember that, like Mailer and Ignatius, the historian Thucydides had to make up or invent speeches and events for which he had no documents, no press releases, no firsthand observations. But we profit from his recollections of what probably happened in the long and unhappy Peloponnesian wars. Mailer's fictionalized CIA accounts may be no match for the great Thucydides, but his claim is a compelling one.

Mailer adds in an author's note:

> My hope is that the imaginary world of Harlot's Ghost will bear more relation to the reality of these historical events than the spectrum of facts and often calculated misinformation that still surrounds them. It is a sizeable claim, but then I have the advantage of believing that novelists have a unique opportunity—they can create superior histories out of an enhancement of the real, the unverified, and the wholly fictional.

GOVERNMENT TOWN—USA[70]

"He doesn't know anything about Washington," Adolph said. "He's never lived here. He doesn't know the way we do things. He won't know who counts. He won't know how to preside over the Senate. He's too green. These outsiders always muck things up."

So spoke Midwestern U.S. senator Adolph Behl, a high-ranking, safe-seat Democratic U.S. senator, who had just been rudely (and wrongheadedly, in his view) passed over for his party's nomination as vice president. The outsider selected in his stead was a baby-faced Midwestern governor.

The novel *Echo House* is a multilayered, three-generation analysis of Washington, D.C., as "Government Town," full of powerbrokers, shadowy intrigues, ghosts, payoffs, cemeteries, and unrequited egos.

Echo House is a lavish mansion overlooking beautiful Rock Creek Park, slightly northwest of the Georgetown neighborhood, that Adolph Behl purchased in 1916. The family would have preferred, we are told, a stately home on Lafayette Square across from the White House, but the home they wanted (presumably Henry Adams's old house) is not available.

The house they buy, Echo House, is also historic. Lincoln and McClellan had met there in the early 1860s, and Cleveland and FDR had dined there. Senator Adolph Behl, his son Axel Behl, and grandson Alec Behl live and work in Echo House as the nation's capital grows and changes over a span of almost eight decades.

Novelist Ward Just (1936–) retired from journalism at age thirty-six to write fiction. He had been an admired reporter for *Newsweek* and the *Washington Post*. He won accolades as a Vietnam War correspondent, and had concluded early on that the Vietnam War was unwinnable. Ward shifted from faction to fiction because journalists, he said, can tell only part of the story. "Truth," he said, "wears many masks."

Just's novels, many of them about Washington and politics, include *In the City of Fear* (1982), *The American Ambassador* (1987), *Exiles in the Garden* (2009), and *American Romantic* (2014). He says Flaubert, Henry James, F. Scott Fitzgerald, and Hemingway influenced him as a writer.

Echo House (1997) draws inspiration from Henry Adams's novel *Democracy*, and is, in part, a sequel to that classic in its goal of trying to understand how democracy and American government work. (A first edition of Adams's *Democracy* is a prized volume in the Echo House family library.) Just's *Echo House* is not exactly a political thriller, nor a political exposé; yet it is a sweeping portrait of twentieth-century Washington, of a Gatsby-esque, John LeCarre–like vortex of networking, loyalties, deal making, and grand as well as petty crusades.

Just believed fiction was better able than journalism to explore a person's character and unmask political deal making. What is it that motivates a person, especially people in politics and government, to do the things they do despite the sometimes dire consequences?

Ward Just came from a Midwestern Republican background. His father published the *Waukegan News-Sun* in Illinois. Just had a brilliant career as a journalist. But he walked away from journalism for the bigger and broader canvas of fiction writing. It may also be, and this is speculation, that just as he lost confidence in the U.S. war-making efforts in Vietnam, Just may also have lost his faith in the ability of Washington or the nation's capital to live up to the aspirational promises of constitutional democracy. As he documents the decline of the Behls, at least from being center stage in Washington, D.C., he also suggests America may be in decline from its heyday of the post–World War II era when it had enjoyed unrivaled superpower status.

Senator Adolph Behl, the family patriarch, had come ever so close to winning his party's nomination as vice president. He was passed over, as noted, in favor of a popular young governor who had never served in Washington. Behl, his family, and his buddies learn the harsh lesson that "in politics, runners-up don't count." Nobody cares about past "gallant efforts."

The senator's son, Axel, is unable to forget how his father's political fortunes came to a crashing and humiliating halt. Instead of choosing an overtly public career himself, he migrates to the shadows and becomes a clandestine intelligence operative with the OSS, later with the CIA, and perhaps also with the State Department.

His career, both inside and outside of government, is described in mysterious code. During the Cold War, he and his cabal apparently fight the Soviets in a variety of European and other foreign venues. Their enterprises are secret and off the radar, morally ambiguous, and perhaps illegal—including bribery, blackmail, and checkbook diplomacy. (Their secretive crusade and financial subterfuge may remind some readers of the Iran-Contra White House and CIA dealings in the 1980s.) In an ironic twist, Axel narrowly escapes being exposed by the Joe McCarthy "anti-Communist" hearings. Our narrator, presumably Just, shares Axel's elliptical view of his profession:

> He saw his chores literally as bridges, elaborate spans of iron and cable soaring into the sky as gracefully as a hawk in flight. A bridge took you from one frontier to another. Axel identified with the agile and imperturbable New York Indians, the Mohawks who balanced on the foot wide beams . . . placing the rivets just so, wielding them into place, scratching your own signature on the underside of the beam where no one would ever see it. . . . If you were successful your labor and the elegance with which you went about it were noticed only by your fellow aerialists, those who shared the heights, the danger was a given. And the danger was not the point. The bridge was the point, and the applause, when it came, would never be heard by the spectators below. That was the point.

At one point, Axel Behl spends some time with his son, Alec, at an election-eve gathering in Illinois. Adlai Stevenson has just received news of his defeat. Axel Behl is bitter. Adlai's biggest problem? "He's not a prick. You have to be a prick in this business and he's not."

After he retires from the intelligence work, Axel Behl becomes an influential behind-the-scenes player in Washington politics, quietly influencing foreign policy, supporting certain administration appointments, fixing problems, and raising money for Democratic candidates. He uses his family name and wealth, and Echo House, to further his political fortunes. He and a gang of aging cohorts live in a complicated Cold War world. His domain is deliberately opaque and nontransparent, nuanced and oblique, and in it he becomes a legend.

What motivates the fierce Cold Warrior Axel Behl? Ward Just can't resist a somewhat sappy Hollywood moment. Once a month, often at midnight, the wounded Axel limps to his garage, climbs into his black Packard, and makes a pilgrimage to the Lincoln Memorial. Here he contemplates America's brooding sixteenth president:

He [Lincoln] had preserved the Union, but his knowledge of the terrible price cast an eternal shadow on his soul, an ocean of blood to secure an idea, a free, liberated, and undivided nation. Abraham Lincoln had known the cost to the last corpse, and still he persevered. The identical task awaited Lincoln's successors. The demands differed and the price varied with the demand, but it was always paid in blood. The task in the present decade was no less sublime and the cost would be as high.

Behl is pleased this memorial is in Washington and will remind each generation, every day, that America's challenge is to know itself, its principles, and remain resolute. "Thus consoled, Alex Behl put his car in gear and went home."

A third-generation Behl family member is Alec, who foregoes elective politics and formal governmental service of any kind. Instead, he goes to law school and joins a lobbying firm in Chicago. But he soon returns to Washington, D.C., and, of course, to Echo House. Alec learns who and what counts in Washington. He also learns that much of what goes on in the nation's capital is done behind the scenes, sometimes in the alleys.

In the shadow of such real-life venerables as Tommy Corcoran (FDR aide), Clark Clifford (Truman aide), and high-profile criminal defense attorney Edward Bennett Williams, young Alec Behl cuts deals, influences appointments and government contracts, and fixes problems. At one point he mediates between Congress and Nixon to stave off a criminal prosecution of the president. Alec Behl becomes even more influential than his father or grandfather; he becomes a power-brokering fixture: "the man to see in Washington." One of his specialties is getting the right people off the hook with as little collateral damage as possible.

Most of this is a novel about unelected political players. Members of Congress come and go. Presidents and White House staffers come and go. These politicians may be temporarily in the political limelight, but there are, as this novel reveals, many others, who may have come as children of elected officials or as young staffers, or who may have retired from civil service, who flourish outside the defined roles of representative government. And, Just suggests, this growing legion of behind-the-scenes players are at least as consequential as elected representatives.

Novelist Just contrasts the three generations of Behls and their missions. The grandfather, Senator Adolph Behl, is a man of the Midwest, part of the idealistic progressive Wilson era. His son, Axel Behl, is a much decorated, battle-scarred, and curmudgeonly intelligence operative, committed to defending the United States against fascism, and later against the Soviets.

Indeed, Axel Behl, in the eyes of his friends, was a pivotally consequential agent in winning the Cold War. Grandson Alec Behl plays the ultimate insider's game seemingly for its and his own sake. His is an increasingly consequential form of politics; yet it does not require election or civil service.

Just makes his readers puzzle about a decline of moral purpose, a decline of idealism, and a decline in political transparency from the Progressive Era to the modern-day Washington politics.

Axel Behl, for all his manipulating and scheming, did, after all, help to defeat both Hitler and the Soviets. He and his cronies were crusading Cold Warriors, with a clear, if messianic, mission. He worries that the newer generation of players lack any cause greater than themselves. The young generation, he complains, have turned Washington into a self-absorbed, money-obsessed citadel of egoism and political opportunism. Is it, he wonders, merely a game for them, a game played mostly for the sake of personal and pragmatic quid pro quo self-interest?

The younger, more pragmatic generation of Washington players, writes Just, reject the nostalgia of their elders, viewing their stories as unreliable Cold War propaganda, "a loud fart from another time altogether." Moreover, the meddling of these old "venerables" led the United States into unwinnable wars and dubious alliances and interventions. (Just's book was written before the Iraq and Afghanistan wars would consume additional blood and treasure.) Readers are left to wonder which point of view is true—or perhaps whether both are true.

Echo House investigates generational changes through its clear portrayal of the Behl men. Each generation gravitates further away from traditional electoral politics. Of course, as one of Just's characters rightly notes, if you live in Washington, you're part of politics and government. But it is Axel Behl, more than anyone, who is at the heart of this political novel.

At the novel's end, Echo House is jammed with Washington notables who have come to celebrate Axel's birthday and his career. The U.S. president has come to confer on him the Presidential Medal of Freedom. Both the president and many of his acquaintances cannot precisely recall why Axel has become an "eminence grise," for so many of his contributions to the nation had been "sub rosa, made many years before and dubious even then, not precisely illegitimate but surely on the margins of the law." He was an unelected, though consequential, political actor, and the president and many others had come to pay their respects to the aging and wheelchair-bound Echo House hero.

Even the president can't quite remember Axel's precise contributions, so his remarks come across as well-worn bromides of a very generic kind:

> Let us praise the character of Americans who choose the life in the arena. Let us praise their passion for politics and government despite its many disadvantages, the slanders, the misinterpretations, the pettifoggery and the condescension, the unwholesome criticism of the critics. You need the hide of a rhinoceros and the mind of Copernicus!
>
> A patriot, an exemplary Washingtonian, a Washingtonian of principle, honor, and vision, one of us through and through, a true man of state.

Just is satirizing inflated celebratory presidential rhetoric; yet he knew firsthand the hardships and ridicule that dogs thousands of hardworking, dedicated public servants exemplified in Axel Behl.

Alas, the honored guest suffers a stroke, and his wheelchair comes crashing down the grand staircase at Echo House just as the president and Axel's admirers are toasting him and as the president is about to present the Presidential Medal. Chaos ensues. The Secret Service agents are alarmed by the noise of what sounded like shots. They rush the president and his wife away in their cavalcade. The press is banging on the door to learn what happened. Alec and a few friends are left to make sense of what had just happened—and to puzzle about the ghosts and perhaps the curse of Echo House.

We are left, unhappily, with a Washington of shadowy grayness and political constipation, a city populated by multiple layers of unelected transactional politicians who are the new decision makers. Just's Washington is a somber city, personified by Alec Behl and his friends, preoccupied with who knows whom, who counts, and who can be bought or persuaded—rather than with wistfully remembered presumably grand causes and the Jeffersonian and Lincolnian aspirational principles of the American democratic experiment.

Echo House "echoes" the disillusionment with Washington experienced a hundred years earlier by Madeleine Lightfoot Lee in Adams's *Democracy*. In Adams's novel, as discussed, Mrs. Lee tries to find out how Washington works, but eventually, disgusted with greed and corruption, she flees the capital city. So, too, in Just's story, Sylvia Behl, wife of Axel Behl (and mother of young Alec), eventually flees Echo House for Cape Cod, leaving behind the deceits and intrigues of Washington, D.C. Novelist Just himself long ago escaped to Martha's Vineyard, where in comfortable exile he has written a shelf of excellent novels.

The Behl family in Just's *Echo House* are a clever literary device. This is not a character-driven novel, unless the character is Washington, D.C. Just probably asks: What is the character of the nation's capital? Some see

Washington, D.C., as a passionate "ballet of force"; others see the city-states of Genoa and Venice.

But, as Just suggests, it is a city where almost everyone is from somewhere else and there are a lot of lonely, flawed people. Indeed, the relationships in this book are deeply problematic—affairs, divorces, fights, family resentments. *Echo House*, along with Tully's *Capitol Hill* and Vidal's *Washington, D.C.* and Nye's *The Power Game*, portray a Washington that is a taxing place for everyone, especially married couples.

The new Washington, D.C., Just implies, seems claustrophobic, self-absorbed, and lacking a commitment to larger purposes beyond personal self-interest. Ward Just, as his many novels about Vietnam attest, knew well that ideological causes could be dangerous and could end dangerously.

Just laments the loss or at least the diminution of political activism of the earlier generation. He also laments an apparent decline in the commitment to democratic politics. Political scientist Michael Nelson reflects on this:

> During the long course of [the Echo House story], Washington is transformed from a "dull Southern village . . . just another glum city of government, like Albany or Sacramento" into a national center of money, media and power. (But . . . by century's end, Just writes, Washington "had become a self-infatuated money-grubbing iron triangle of stupefying vulgarity, vainglory, egoism, and greed, worse than Rome because at least in Rome there was lively sexual license, orgies and the like.") Side by side with the story of Washington's material ascent and moral decline is the ebbing in importance of the rough and tumble of elections and . . . democracy.[71]

Echo House is an important and clarifying novel about American politics. It introduces us to the faces and hearts behind the masked individuals who populate the often gray and murky facades of the nation's capital. It is partly a novel about the disillusionment and limits of politics. It is also very much a story about the complex ironies and paradoxes of politics.

Just seems at times to be yearning for a simpler past before the corrupting influences of Vietnam, Nixon, dark money, and globalization. But Ward Just understands the importance of good leadership, the importance of Lincoln and principles, and the importance of hardball politics if we are to achieve a better constitutional republic.

Kudos to Ward Just and *Echo House*. There will never be a novel that can fully explain our national capital. But *Echo*, read together with Henry Adams, Allen Drury, Richard Condon, Knebel and Bailey, and Joe Nye, goes a long way in helping us to unmask the complicated people and political culture of America's "Government Town."

BITING THE APPLE OF POWER[72]

"I was not made for life in this city where ruining people is considered sport," was the haunting suicide message left by Clinton White House aide Vince Foster in the mid-1990s. Author Joseph Samuel Nye Jr.'s (1937–) semi-autobiographic *roman à clef*, *The Power Game*, is almost as fatalistic as the Foster message it invokes in its early pages. It examines how the forces of personal ambition can make for decidedly complicated and cutthroat public policymaking relationships in Washington, D.C. Friendships and loyalties, he writes, can never be taken for granted. That's why Washingtonians regularly say, "If you want a friend in this town, buy a dog."

Rhodes Scholar Joe Nye is a Harvard University political scientist who served in top national security positions in the Carter and Clinton administrations and advised John Kerry and Barack Obama. He has advised presidential candidates and has also been a foreign policy consultant to various countries and multinational corporations. His writings on diplomacy, especially on the creative use of persuasive "soft" power, have made him among the most prominent foreign policy scholars.

His illuminating *The Power Game: A Washington Novel* is told through the eyes of fictional Princeton University international relations professor Peter Cutler. An old Princeton classmate recruits Cutler to serve as a policy advisor to rising star and presidential candidate U.S. senator Wayne Kent, a Democrat from Montana. Cutler thrives in his new role but admits that he is wary of the political compromising and deal making he begins to see up close. Still, he confesses, "Now I had bit the apple of power and my appetite grew with the eating." The once reluctant academic slowly evolves into a real-time Washington insider before our eyes.

"Politicos ain't angels, but don't knock 'em. Somebody's got to do the hard work of putting a coalition together," his old friend, Jim Childress, who is helping to run Kent's campaign, tells Cutler. "Otherwise there'd be anarchy. Like the Balkans and the Middle East." Cutler learns, "Straight talk that pleases one group scares the hell out of another." Thus, "We need politicians who can blur people's differences if we're going to get anything done." Democracy works "when there's politicians who can overcome our differences."

What was presidential candidate Kent like as a person? "Good man . . . Wants to make this country a better place," says Childress. "But deep down, I don't think anyone knows him. For all their surface friendliness, politicos are lonely people. He keeps a big part of himself fenced off. Working for him is like being invited onto the front porch for a drink, but never into the house."

Cutler gets to meet Senator Kent. He briefs him on international hotspots and terrorism threats. Cutler sympathetically laments the negative ads and exhausting nature of the campaign. Candidate Kent tries to put it in perspective: "It's a hard business. Everything is fair game from your economic plan to your mother's sex life." "Negative ads work. You have to drive up the other guy's negatives." "Define him before he can define you." "Then why'd you want to do it?" asks Cutler. Kent laughs and says, "If I don't [run], somebody else will, who'll be worse. I like to think I can make a difference. That's part of it." Cutler notes that a candidate also loses his privacy, and that everywhere you go people recognize you. Kent smiles and, tellingly, adds, "I'd worry a helluva lot more if they didn't. That's the other part of the answer."

Kent wins and Cutler is subsequently recruited to serve as undersecretary of state for security affairs. Preventing nuclear proliferation and terrorism become his priorities. But interdepartmental and interagency personnel and bureaucratic politics become as consuming as any of his policy projects. He learns to insist on getting the needed top-secret documents, whether or not he is technically privy to them. He learns to seize the initiative by making colleagues and rivals work from *his* paper drafts. He learns to meet the key players privately "so everything is wired before you can get into the big room." He learns to cultivate the key allies, especially at the White House. He learns that it is who you know *as well as* what you know that counts. He learns to deal discreetly with the media. In short, he is slowly becoming a hardened bureaucratic operative.

Professor Cutler learns also, albeit slowly, that clashing egos and ambitions, elements central to the Washington power game, are changing *him* more than his idealism and diplomacy are changing Washington. "Come home, Peter," his wife, Kate, urges, "Washington is changing you."

Cutler becomes an absentee husband and father, as his family remains in Princeton, and he also becomes entangled in a high-stakes sexual affair. He loses touch with his parents as they are dying. He is agonizingly torn between moral ideals and the often-brutal political forces that drive the making of national foreign policy relations. Cutler is knowingly intoxicated by the adrenaline rush that comes with his high-level policy responsibilities;

yet he is increasingly perplexed by the taxing and emotional roller-coaster ride his exacting schedule and political role demand. And in the process, Cutler makes some miscalculations, which prove costly.

Cutler's ultimate downfall occurs when he is caught leaking a warning to an old Princeton buddy from graduate school who now works as a nuclear engineer for the Pakistan government. Cutler learns there will be a U.S. missile strike at the power facility where Ali, his old friend, works. Cutler's leak, a serious national security indiscretion, leads to many deaths, and also to Cutler's firing.

Upon being fired, Cutler's self-regard and self-confidence are so jolted that he instinctively retreats to Cathedral Lake in Maine, his favorite fishing place. He seriously contemplates suicide and reflects that it would be poetic to die there, in a place so paradoxically untouched by greed and competitive entanglements that so define the capital's power game.

He thought of the many times he had drifted and fished out there and "how different life seemed then." "I thought of my father and his favorite quote about being filled with awe by the moral law within man and the starry heavens above him." Has Cutler lost faith in the moral law within man? Has he become uncertain of the moral ideals that drive him—and the society at large? He lays his shotgun aside, tries to pray, and paddles back toward shore and his family cabin. In less than a year or so he has lost his wife, his dad, his job, several of his friends, and much, if not all, of his self-esteem.

We are left to wonder about the price politicians and their advisors pay to participate in these ruthless tug-of-war power games. Is it possible for good people to become "players" in the high-stakes game of professional politics? Is ruining people's reputations and demonizing one's rivals an inevitable part of politics? How does one balance idealism and personal and patriotic loyalties with pragmatism?

Are cunning, deception, and wheeling and dealing just part of the price we pay for leadership? Peter's old Princeton buddy, Jim Childress, the one who went to work as a White House aide, has become a utilitarian, if not Machiavellian, political actor. Bargaining, deal making, and seizing the initiative were all fair play. The "pursuit of the perfect," Jim adds, "must not defeat achievement of the good." Which is, of course, a variant of an old Washington, D.C., maxim, "Purity is the enemy of victory."

Childress, in at least some ways, emerges as the model Washington operative. Is Nye holding him up as the prototype exemplar for younger professionals? Or is his merely an equivocal compliment?

Another Princeton buddy, Abe Klein, who intentionally remains in the ivory tower, cautions that though it is possible, it is hard for someone to both be a good person and do good things in politics. Cutler retorts to "clean-hands Abe" that high-minded purity seldom works in the real world and recalls their old graduate school joke about Kant: "His hands were so clean that he had no grip on anything." But, Abe replies, Kant "had a grip on his integrity."

Storyteller Nye had himself tried to navigate the bureaucratic, tangled political swamps of Washington, D.C. He had enlisted in high-level administration politics confident that it is possible to do good and be good at the same time. He knew it wouldn't be easy. Politics can be messy; yet, as Peter Cutler's White House friend puts it, "It's also a way to do good on a large scale." What Nye's protagonist learns, often the hard way, is that what too often counts in Washington is the ability to project power, look the part, and play the game. His fictional Peter Cutler slowly learns the often devious and combative tactics that he believes will enhance his influence and power position. He also learns that pursuit of the perfect can undermine accomplishing anything.

The novel's despairing argument is that Washington, D.C., attracts good people; yet it changes them, and sometimes it unfortunately ruins them. *The Power Game* is part exposé and part a reflective commentary on high-level bureaucratic politics. Heroes are hard to find. Politics and policy fights at the highest level can be brutal. At least in Nye's Peter Cutler, it proved impossible to do good and remain the person he wanted to be.

Nye, the storyteller, successfully uses fiction to provide an insider's view of high-stakes politics. He captures the excitement senior officials experience. But he also unmasks the temptations, deceptions, minefields, and sand traps that come along with high-profile public service.

Nye's nonfiction political science writings on foreign policy, power, and leadership offer more optimism about the possibilities in active politics and creative, effective leadership. In his long and distinguished career at the Harvard JFK School of Government, Nye was a champion mentor to thousands of young people preparing for careers in politics and public service. His teaching and mentoring have been primarily that of an optimist. But his experiences, as recounted in this fictional work, also make him a realist and pragmatist. Policymaking, politics, and foreign policy reform, he is warning, are not for the meek, the short winded, or inflexible policy purists. He is also warning that service to one's country may (or must?) override loyalty to one's friends.

One of Joe Nye's former Harvard colleagues, Michael Ignatieff, had a similar bruising experience at the highest level of Canadian politics. He had been drafted to head up the Canadian Liberal Party and stand as their leader in the next parliamentary elections. He was smoked. He came away chastened by the Canadian power game, but he offers this more upbeat interpretation:

> I may have come into politics with an unacknowledged condescension toward the game and those who played it, but left with more respect for politicians than when I went in. The worst of these—the careerists and predators—you find in all professions. The best of them were a credit to democracy. They knew the difference between an adversary and an enemy, knew when to take half a loaf and when to insist on the whole bakery, knew when to trust their judgment and when to listen to the people.[73]

But, as is the case with Nye's fictional State Department official, Peter Cutler, Ignatieff also "found myself wondering what political life was doing to me." He concludes, like Cutler, and perhaps Nye, "I had made myself into a politician, and I didn't much like what I was becoming."[74]

Just as Ignatieff limped back to Harvard after striking out in high-stakes Canadian politics, Nye's Peter Cutler limps back to his Princeton University professorship with the disheartening sense that the power game in Washington and the way practitioners of the game lived there too often privileged gamesmanship and appearances over principled substance.

Has Nye, the veteran and chastened Washington realist, told us what it is "really like"? His story is less triumphant than those of George Marshall, Henry Kissinger, Brent Scowcroft, or James Baker, but Nye's practical anthropology of top-level bureaucratic politics is, I believe, an instructive, if semi-chilling, analysis of life on the national political stage, a step or two below *Meet the Press* Washington.

Critics faulted Nye for his "middling" fiction writing, one-dimensional characters, and lame sex scenes. The near-exclusion of women from Nye's novel is puzzling, especially since we have had three women secretaries of state and a few women national security advisors at the White House, and even a woman presidential candidate (who won the popular vote) in recent years. His one "femme fatale" is described as "the type that uses her looks to jerk guys around." Alexa Byrnes is the ultimate power gamer as she flaunts her intellect and her attractiveness to get her men and to get ahead.

Nye's novel was a risky venture for a high-profile foreign policy counselor and a highly respected social scientist. Yet his impressive high-level public service enhanced the credibility and the value of his story—and in many ways his is a much more refreshing and authentic contribution than the large library full of unctuously self-serving and self-congratulatory memoirs written by people with similar public service experience.

We turn next, in the epilogue, to a discussion of concluding propositions that emerge from reading these celebrated political novels.

EPILOGUE

Conclusions and reflections have been sprinkled through the previous chapters. Here I will highlight and discuss a few of the thematic propositions that have emerged from my political reading of these works.

- Most of these novelists, even as they shine their spotlights on the many imperfections of the American political experiment, are optimists. They understand the possibility of their storytelling as a means of pointing the way to a more desired future. To paraphrase Toni Morrison's beloved Baby Suggs character, they believed that if they could not imagine a better country, neither they nor we would be able to achieve it.
- Most of these novelists likewise understood the paradoxes of politics—that, on the one hand, politics is a messy, semi-cursed business and, on the other hand, it is inevitable, necessary, and urgent if people want to achieve their common aspirations and a shared humanity. Political storytelling at its best puts us inside the minds of others and gives us the gift not only of seeing the world through their eyes but also of hope, courage, and redemption.
- Most of these novelists are simultaneously realists as well as optimists—they understand human nature, self-interest, and the natural inclinations toward prejudice and pride, as well as that humanitarian and communitarian political leadership is monstrously hard to exercise in a nation of competing ideological narratives, not to mention all the Madisonian public and private sector checks and balances. Yet writers understand their lamps must do more than illuminate the dark corners of life—they can also help educate their readers and

help readers imagine a more idealistic way of people living together and solving collective problems.

- Most of the novelists understand, better than most of us, that the American political experiment, and constitutionalism in general, are simultaneously exceptional in scope *and* fragile. The history of the world is full of glorious city-states and empires that flourished in their golden eras but floundered and lost their way in overreach and decay. Our system is always being tested. What happened elsewhere, to contradict the title of Sinclair Lewis's novel, "can happen here." Citizen vigilance, civic engagement, and a continually alert moral compass are only a part—yet a crucial part—of the price we regularly must pay for preserving and improving the American republic.

- The founding of America was primarily a male-dominated enterprise; yet many of our best political novelists have been women, such as Stowe, Lee, and Morrison, and American political fiction has given us plenty of strong women.

- Finally, political fiction may be produced by many introverts who necessarily have to do their creative work in solitary venues; yet their imaginations and writing can change lives, change events, and can be a form of political activism. The paradox here is that while writing may be a passive activity, what is written—whether it is agitational, consciousness raising, satirical, or merely investigative— can set off alarm bells, bring people together, and change the way we think and act politically.

Most of these political novelists, regardless of their primary narrative theme, are optimists. I mean this in the sense that most of them are artists who are gladly confronting mendacity and hypocrisy and seeking in their own way to speak truth to power.

Most writers discussed here wrote so that people would care more for others and care more deeply for the cherished aspirations of the republic. Writers such as Steinbeck, Jackson, Stowe, Garland, Fast, Lee, Nichols, and Grisham wrote on behalf of the dispossessed and the disadvantaged. Novelist John Nichols explained that he and the other novelists he admired wrote to find hope even in the darkest situations. Despair, he noted, is a betrayal, not a solution. Let's rejoice, Nichols added, at the possibilities of literature carving out, and helping lead us to, a more desirable future.

Wright, Jackson, Bradbury, Ellison, and Morrison wrote to remind us of past and future policies that degraded human beings—yet they yearned for a more educated and enlightened citizenry, and for a liberated America that transcended racism, prejudice, and enslavement of any kind.

Most of these novelists understood politics. Yes, it is messy, rough, and rightly characterized as a "hardball" enterprise pitting groups against groups, and regions against regions, but they also knew that politics and politicians are indispensable to a people who want freedom and democracy.

Political fiction is very good at mocking and even loathing politicians, such as U.S. Senator Johnny Iselin in Condon's *The Manchurian Candidate* and U.S. Senator Fred van Ackerman in Drury's *Advise and Consent*. Sinclair Lewis, Nathanael West, and Philip Roth gave us dreadful national political leaders. Mark Twain, Henry Adams, and Gore Vidal gave us politicians we learned to despise. Yet, as discussed, these novelists agree that giving up on politics is not an option. Politics and steadfast political engagement are the price we have to pay for bringing about better public policies and a better republic.

Churchill's *Mr. Crewe's Career* and Nichols's *The Milagro Beanfield War* make this case. Hamlin Garland's *A Spoil of Office* celebrates the earnest politics of 1880s populism even if it had its limitations. Joe Klein and Edwin O'Connor celebrate the messy and imperfect American election processes even if they revealed flawed individuals that play a central role in them.

Robert Penn Warren and Herman Melville, two of our greatest novelists, again and again teach us that our leaders live in a world of complicated irony, contradiction, and paradox. Humans—including our elected and appointed political leaders—have to act and make choices in an imperfect world full of ambiguity and tugging polarities. Still, people need to come together, organize, and reconcile differences. Liberty, equality, and justice are the aspirations—politics is the non-negotiable means by which we can strive to attain them.

It is easy to satirize politics and the political. It is much harder to make the case that the absence of politics and political courage gave us the world Stowe, Jackson, Morrison, Wright, Sinclair, and Lee depicted—or the world Lewis, Roth, Bradbury, and Knebel and Bailey wrote about as a possibility.

Most political novelists also help us understand that politics is a team sport. Too many Hollywood films and popular myths pay excessive tribute to "great men" as if solo individuals singularly caused victory or transformational political change. Lincoln saved the union. Patton won the war. Jefferson Smith saved democracy. Harrison Ford, on Air Force One, saved civilization.

Storybook leadership narratives sell popcorn—hero, drama, me versus the machine. But crucial groundwork politics takes place in the Act I and II phases of politics—often underreported and underappreciated. The spotlight cameras are far more attuned to Act III political actors. Our best political fiction reminds us that useful political change is achieved when persistent people not only in the early stages of politics but also in countless scenes and communities act together and collaborate in sustained ways to bring about shared purpose. Michael Shaara's novel *The Killer Angels* makes this clear, as do John Nichols, Billy Brammer, Joe Klein, Winston Churchill, and Hamlin Garland.

Effective political leadership in a democracy seldom comes from the top down, and it rarely comes from a single person. In the case of civil rights it came about because of Rosa Parks, Thurgood Marshall, Martin Luther King Jr., Earl Warren, and countless thousands of preachers, lawyers, teachers, marchers, and caring activists who—over a long period of time—pressed on with the case Harriet Beecher Stowe and the abolitionists had made generations earlier.

Those who favor advancing humanity but are impatient with politics and political mobilization are people who, to paraphrase Frederick Douglass, want crops without plowing up the ground, and who want rain without thunder and lightning.

Politics is, in sum, a team sport and a long-distance test of commitment and endurance.

Politics is almost always frustrating. Positive political change seldom happens quickly. We forget the American Revolution took nearly eight years. Abolishing slavery took generations; the right to vote for women took even longer.

It is tempting indeed for people, in the manner of Thoreau, to walk away and disdain politics. Politics can be exceedingly polarizing—setting people into divided partisan and geographical camps.

Our novelists like Steinbeck and Grisham remind us that rich people enjoy a much louder voice than the average person. That, too, is alienating. Our novelists also describe how politics and political power can deform those in office. Condon, West, Vidal, Tully, Drury, Adams, and Warren all give us driven politicians who develop swollen and defective egos. Their novels urge us to beware of savior figures or political gurus all too willing to sacrifice cherished political principles for personal political advancement.

Several political novelists educate us about the potential vulnerability of constitutionalism and republican practices. Sinclair Lewis, Nathanael West, Ray Bradbury, and Philip Roth all famously warned about the possibility of authoritarianism and fascism taking root in America. Condon's brilliant *The Manchurian Candidate* warns us to beware of fearmongering and conspiracies. Robert Penn Warren educates us about the double sidedness of power—how it can liberate while also having an intoxicating effect on power wielders. Burdick's *The Ninth Wave* alerts us to the authoritarian personalities who are attracted to electoral politics and the work of political strategy. Churchill's *Mr. Crewe's Career* and Knebel and Bailey's *Seven Days in May* entertain us, yet also invaluably enlighten us about the necessity for civic and patriotic vigilance.

Even though politics in America has usually, until recently, been a male-dominated activity, political fiction celebrates many strong and effective female political operatives. First there have been distinguished women novelists, including several treated at length in this volume such as Harriet Beecher Stowe, Helen Hunt Jackson, Margaret Mitchell, Harper Lee, Ayn Rand, and Toni Morrison. Each was a powerful storyteller and a best-selling author. Jackson gave us the courageous Ramona. Harper Lee gave us the perceptive and caring Scout. Ayn Rand gave us the formidable Dagny Taggart, Morrison the unforgettable Sethe Garner and her mother-in-law Baby Suggs. And Mitchell gave us the tenacious indomitable Scarlett O'Hara.

Male writers have also given us stalwart women politicos. Garland's Ida Wilbur is a hero, as are Nichols's Ruby Archuleta and Buckley's Pepper Cartwright.

Steinbeck gave us the Joad family matriarch in Ma Joad. Mary Bird plays a small, yet powerful, role as the wife of a state senator in *Uncle Tom's Cabin*. Madeleine Lee plays the leading role in Henry Adams's *Democracy: An American Novel*. Laura Hawkins is a politically shrewd femme fatale in Mark Twain's *Gilded Age*. Anne Morrow Lindbergh plays a valorous, if cameo, role in *The Plot Against America*. And then there is the infamous Ellie Iselin, the despicable powerbroker and villain in *The Manchurian Candidate*.

It is also true, however, that some male novelists have done an especially poor job in developing their female characters. Hunter S. Thompson and Joseph Heller head that list. And Gore Vidal, Eugene Burdick, Horatio Alger, Andrew Tully, Allen Drury, and Edward Abbey were not especially good in this regard.

The sad reality is that too many political novelists have either underestimated or been inconsiderate of the role that women have played in politics. Women politicians have been much more favorably featured in contemporary television series. Women will surely be more central in forthcoming American political literature—and that literature will be the richer for it.

Political fiction writing can be a form of political activism and is indisputably a form of politics. Thus John Grisham and Christopher Buckley, among the most entertaining novelists discussed here, also splendidly educated us about the importance of an independent judiciary at the state and national level. Upton Sinclair, John Steinbeck, and Harriet Beecher Stowe called America's attention to injustices—and their novels were read from City Hall to the White House. These writers had as much impact (if not more) as most political officials of their day.

Ayn Rand may never have run for elected office, but she became the intellectual guru and galvanizing publicist for a distinctive political ideology. She became, as was discussed, the inspiration for countless libertarian and free-market conservative politicos. Edward Abbey similarly celebrates Act I and Act II environmental activists and denigrates the Act III power brokers of his era.

Mitchell's *Gone with the Wind* may have been a retro celebration of pre–Civil War Georgia, but it was also an unapologetic political manifesto, championing states' rights and defending an alternative history of her grandparents' way of life. Her narrative may be viewed as misguided; yet she gave us a semi-Tolstoyian treatise on the political chaos of that special time and place.

Most people would not consider Horatio Alger's novels as political novels. They were primarily inspirational homilies intended as entertaining pep talks for teenage males. It was a form of redemptive chaplaincy as well as a way for Alger to earn a living. Yet his message-sending "purpose stories" celebrated individual initiative and philanthropy, and called for nongovernmental strategies for dealing with poverty and inequality. In this sense his were political novels and his—just as much as Hamlin Garland or Upton Sinclair—were putting forth and celebrating a political approach for the Gilded Age he lived in.

Debates about the American Dream and inequality course through much, if not most, of this political fiction, and those themes will inevitably continue to be revisited, redebated, and relitigated. Horatio Alger did not invent the notion of the American Dream. It is more of a 1930s term. But that dream lives. It survived and persisted through the Great Depression of the 1930s, and virtually every politician well into the twenty-first century has to pledge he or she will dedicate themselves to creating more and better jobs and more and better educational opportunities so every American can live a "better, richer, and fairer" life. Americans may be cynical about much in politics and life, but the dream of social and economic mobility and of a postclass and postracial America still is a luminous yearning.

Americans similarly yearn for peace even if the history of America is marked by many prolonged and draining wars. Mailer, Nye, Just, Shaara, and coauthors Knebel and Bailey discuss war and peace, the role of intelligence agencies, and the critical importance of civilian control over the military in a constitutional democracy. Readers of these works learn about bureaucratic politics and military realities in a way that voters are rarely educated on during presidential elections.

Chilean novelist Isabel Allende said she was motivated to write in the hope that it would encourage people to love one another more. "We [writers] dare to think humanity is not going to destroy itself," Allende said. We have, she adds, "the capacity to reach an agreement not only for survival but also to achieve happiness. That is why we write—as an act of human solidarity." As I stated in an essay titled "Writing as an Act of Hope," "We want to change the rules, even if we won't live long enough to see the results. We have to make real revolutions of the spirit, of values, of life. And to do so we have to begin dreaming them."

The best of our political fiction reminds us that politics is important and matters. These stories force us to reevaluate our assumptions and political attitudes. Invariably, too, they remind us of the necessity for a tough-minded optimism combined with patient, persistent civic engagement. American political fiction also reminds us of three enduring lessons: Little of consequence can be accomplished alone. And we cannot love our country unless we first love our fellow Americans. And finally, constitutional democracy can only work if large numbers of citizens learn and understand state and national public policy issues. Only if this happens, and it is too seldom, can we begin to hold elected officials accountable and boast of ours being an effective participatory democracy and republic.

We are a democracy, but we have little right to claim ours as the model or a finished product. Our best fiction writers remind us of the work to be done.

NOTES

PREFACE

1. This is a consistent theme in historian David McCullough's biographies and lectures. See his *The American Spirit* (New York: Simon & Schuster, 2017).

CHAPTER 1

1. Richard Cavendish, introduction to *Legends of the World* (New York: Shocken Books, 1982), 11.

2. *The Man Who Shot Liberty Valance* (1962), a John Ford–directed Hollywood classic.

3. See Dixon Wecter, *The Hero in America: A Chronicle of Hero-Worship* (Ann Arbor: University of Michigan Press, 1941).

4. David Guterson, "Looking Back, Warily, But with Affection," *American Scholar* (Spring 2014): 97.

5. Joseph Campbell, *The Hero with a Thousand Faces* (Princeton, NJ: Princeton University Press, 1949), 11.

6. Campbell, *The Hero with a Thousand Faces*, 382.

7. James A. Morone, *The Devils We Know: Us and Them in America's Raucous Political Culture* (Lawrence: University Press of Kansas, 2014), 63 and 66. Note, however, that contemporary reviewers in Mark Twain's time did not necessarily see the Huck Finn story as the heartwarming narrative of racial reconciliation that we do today. See Andrew Levy, *Huck Finn's America* (New York: Simon and Schuster, 2015).

8. E. L. Doctorow, "The Case for the Writer as a Politician," *Washington Post*, May 28–June 3, 1990 (weekly edition), 25.

9. Christopher Lehmann, "Why Americans Can't Write Political Fiction," *Washington Monthly*, October/November 2005 (online).

10. Dos Passos and Wolfe quoted by Henry Steele Commager, *The American Mind* (New Haven: Yale University Press, 1950), 275–76.

11. From her introductory notes, *Atlas Shrugged* (New York: Plume, 1999), xiv.

12. Quotes in Grace Lichtenstein, "Edward Abbey, Voice of Southwest Wilds," *New York Times*, January 20, 1976, 24.

13. Edward Abbey, *One Life at a Time, Please* (New York: Holt, 1988), 177.

14. George Orwell, "Why I Write," in George Orwell, *A Collection of Essays* (San Diego: Harcourt, 1981), 312 and 314.

15. Aleksandr Solzhenitsyn, Nobel Address, 1970.

16. Rand, foreword to *The Fountainhead*, centennial edition (New York: Signet, 1993), xi.

17. Edward Abbey, *Desert Solitaire* (New York: Ballentine, 1968), 149.

18. Richard Chase, on Melville's motivations, in *The American Novel and Its Tradition* (Garden City, NY: Doubleday, 1957), 91.

19. Toni Morrison, *Beloved* (New York: Random House, 1987), xiii.

20. Solzhenitsyn, Nobel Address, 1970.

21. Ernest Hemingway quoted in George Plimpton, "An Interview with Ernest Hemingway," *Paris Review* (Spring 1958).

22. John Steinbeck, *America and Americans and Selected Nonfiction*, edited by Susan Shillinglaw and Jackson J. Benson (New York: Viking, 2002), 390.

23. I adapt here from earlier writing on the character of political leadership. See Thomas E. Cronin, *On the Presidency* (Boulder: Paradigm Publishers, 2009), chapter 3, and Thomas E. Cronin and Michael A. Genovese, *Leadership Matters* (Boulder: Paradigm Publishers, 2012), chapter 8.

24. Mary McCarthy, "The Lasting Power of the Political Novel," *New York Times*, January 1, 1984.

25. George Orwell, "Politics and the American Language," *A Collection of Essays*.

26. Robert Penn Warren, introduction to Ernest Hemingway, *A Farewell to Arms* (New York: Charles Scribner's Sons, 1949), xxxv.

27. "Bruce Springsteen: American Idol," in *Rolling Stone*, February 12, 2015, 17 (a flashback interview).

28. Steinbeck, *America and Americans*, 390.

29. Morris E. Speare, *The Political Novel* (New York: Oxford University Press, 1924), 305.

30. Orwell, "Politics and the American Language," *A Collection of Essays*, 316.

31. I have written on this elsewhere: Thomas E. Cronin, "Laughing at Leaders," *Leadership and Humanities* 2, no. 1 (2014): 27–43.

32. See, among his many works, Clifford Geertz, *The Interpretation of Cultures* (New York: Basic Books, 1973) and *Local Knowledge* (New York: Basic Books, 1983).

CHAPTER 2

1. Arthur M. Schlesinger Jr., "America: Experiment or Destiny?" *American Historical Review* (June 1977): 512. See also Gordon S. Wood, *The Idea of America* (New York: Penguin, 2011).

2. Mark Twain, *The Autobiography of Mark Twain* (New York: Harper & Row, 1959), 360.

3. For two contrasting nonfictional accounts of these positions, see Edwin J. Feulner and Brian Tracy, *The American Spirit: Celebrating the Virtues and Values That Make Us Great* (Nashville: Thomas Nelson, 2012), and Donald L. Barlett and James B. Steel, *The Betrayal of the American Dream* (New York: Public Affairs, 2012). Yet see in general the excellent summary, *The American Dream: In History, Politics and Fiction* by political scientist Cal Jillson (Lawrence: University Press of Kansas, 2016). See also David McCullough, *The American Spirit: Who We Are and What We Stand For* (New York: Simon & Schuster, 2017).

4. Quoted in "The Prophet of Decline," *The Economist*, January 23, 2016, 25.

5. David K. Shipler, in his introduction to a reissued edition of Horatio Alger Jr.'s *Ragged Dick; or, Street Life in New York with Boot-Blacks* (published originally in 1868; New York: Modern Library, 2005), xi.

6. Dick Cheney and Liz Cheney, *Exceptional: Why The World Needs a Powerful America* (New York: Threshold Editions, 2015), 1.

7. See the analysis in Carol Nackenoff, *The Fictional Republic: Horatio Alger and American Political Discourse* (New York: Oxford University Press, 1994).

8. See Richard V. Reeves, "Stuck," *Esquire*, December/January 2015/2016, 154–58 and 170.

9. See Jacob S. Hacker and Paul Pierson, *American Amnesia: How the War on Government Led Us to Forget What Made America Prosper* (New York: Simon and Schuster, 2016).

10. Schlesinger, "America: Experiment or Destiny?" 521.

11. Ralph Waldo Emerson, *Essays* (New York: Charles E. Merritt Co., 1907), 83 and 90.

12. Kathryn Schulz, "Pond Scum: Henry David Thoreau's Moral Myopia," *The New Yorker*, October 19, 2015, 41.

13. Schulz, "Pond Scum," 43.

14. See Betsy Gaines Quammers, "The War for the West Rages On," *New York Times*, January 30, 2016, A21.

15. Irving Dillard, *Mr. Justice Brandeis: Great American* (St. Louis, MO: The Modern View Press, 1904), 42.

16. See Richard Hofstadter, *The Paranoid Style in American Politics and Other Essays* (New York: Knopf, 1965), chapter 1.

17. Neil Gaiman, introduction to Ray Bradbury's *Fahrenheit 451* (New York: Simon and Schuster, 2013, 60th-anniversary edition).

18. Abraham Lincoln, Speech at Springfield, Illinois, June 26, 1857, *Collected Works of Lincoln*, ed. R. P. Basler (New Brunswick, NJ: Rutgers University Press, 1953), vol. 2, 406.

19. See the book *Just Mercy: A Story of Justice and Redemption* by Bryan Stevenson (New York: Spiegel and Grau, 2014).

CHAPTER 3

1. Edward Abbey, *One Life at a Time, Please* (New York: Holt, 1988), 163.

2. Nobel Prize in Literature Talk, 1970.

3. Harriet Beecher Stowe, *Uncle Tom's Cabin* (Boston: John P. Jewitt, 1952).

4. The minority political status of, and hardship faced by, northern abolitionists are documented persuasively in Eric Foner, *Gateway to Freedom: The Hidden History of the Underground Railroad* (New York: W. W. Norton, 2015).

5. Charles A. Madison, *Critics and Crusaders* (New York: Holt, 1947), 25.

6. James McPherson, *Battle Cry of Freedom* (New York: Oxford University Press, 1988), 91.

7. Joseph L. Blotner, *The Political Novel* (Garden City, NY: Doubleday, 1955), 11.

8. Andrew Delbanco, summarizing critics such as James Baldwin, in *Required Reading: Why Our American Classics Matter Now* (New York: Farrar, Straus and Giroux, 1997), 64. See also, for example, Claire Oberon Garcia, Vershawn Ashanti Young, and Charise Pimentel, eds., *From* Uncle Tom's Cabin *to* The Help*: Critical Perspectives on White-Authored Narratives of Black Life* (New York: Palgrave, 2014).

9. Roxana Robinson, "The Right to Write," *New York Times*, June 29, 2014.

10. Lawrence Buell, *The Dream of the Great American Novel* (Cambridge, MA: Belknap, 2014), 227.

11. Buell, *The Dream of the Great American Novel*, 227.

12. *The Jungle* by Upton Sinclair (New York: Doubleday, 1906).

13. Christopher Phelps, introduction to *The Jungle* (Boston: Bedford/St. Martin's, 2005), 1.

14. Eric Dallesasse, an Illinois native, suggested this, March 2017.

15. Upton Sinclair, *I, Candidate for Governor: And How I Got Licked* (Pasadena: published by the author, 1935).

16. John Dos Passos, *The 42nd Parallel* (New York: Random House, 1930).

17. See, in general, Stuart A. Scheingold, *The Political Novel: Re-Imagining the Twentieth Century* (London: Continuum, 2010). On the American Dream and its limits, see Jennifer Hochschild, *Facing Up to the American Dream: Race, Class, and the Soul of the Nation* (Princeton, NJ: Princeton University Press, 1995). Also helpful is Cal Jillson, *The American Dream: In History, Politics, and Fiction* (Lawrence: University of Kansas Press, 2016). In addition, see the Dos Passos–inspired nonfiction narrative by George Packer, *The Unwinding: An Inner History of the New America* (New York: Farrar, Straus and Giroux, 2013).

18. Robert C. Rosen, *John Dos Passos: Politics and the Writer* (Lincoln: University of Nebraska Press, 1981), 144 and 145. See also the helpful biography by Virginia Spencer Carr, *Dos Passos: A Life* (Garden City, NY: Doubleday, 1984).

19. Sinclair Lewis, *It Can't Happen Here* (New York: Penguin, 1935).

20. Mark Schorer, *Sinclair Lewis: An American Life* (New York: McGraw Hill, 1961).

21. Roosevelt's views are shared by his advisor, Rexford G. Tugwell, *The Democratic Roosevelt* (Baltimore: Penguin, 1969), 349.

22. John Steinbeck, *The Grapes of Wrath* (New York: Viking Press, 1939).

23. Quoted in Maxwell Geismar, *Writers in Crisis: The American Novel* (London: Secker and Warburg, 1947), 240.

24. Emphasized in John H. Timmerman, *Searching for Eden: John Steinbeck's Ethical Career* (Macon, GA: Mercer University Press, 2014), 66.

25. Steinbeck, Nobel Prize Speech, December 10, 1962, reprinted in John Steinbeck, *America and Americans and Selected Nonfiction*, eds. Susan Shillinglaw and Jackson J. Benson (New York: Viking, 2002), 173.

26. Steinbeck, Nobel Prize Speech, 173.

27. James MacGregor Burns, *The Crosswinds of Freedom* (New York: Knopf, 1989), 142.

28. See Upton Sinclair, *I, Candidate for Governor: And How I Got Licked* (Pasadena: published by the author, 1935).

29. Quoted in Susan Shillinglaw, *On Reading* The Grapes of Wrath (New York: Penguin Books, 2014), 98. See also the introduction to *Portable Steinbeck* by Lewis Gannette (New York: Viking, 1966), xxiv.

30. Steinbeck, in a letter to Herbert Sturz in 1953, republished in the *New York Times*, August 6, 1990.

31. Shillinglaw, *On Reading* The Grapes of Wrath, 35.

32. Shillinglaw, *On Reading* The Grapes of Wrath, 107.

33. Richard Wright, *Native Son* (New York: Harper and Brothers, 1940).

34. Robert Butler, *Native Son: The Emergence of a New Black Hero* (Boston: Twayne Publishers, 1991).

35. Irving Howe, "Black Boys and Native Sons," in *A World More Attractive: A View of Modern Literature and Politics* (New York: Horizon Press, 1963), 100–101.

36. Ta-Nehisi Coates, *Between the World and Me* (New York: Spiegel and Grace, 2015), 17.

37. Butler, *Native Son: The Emergence of a New Black Hero*, 116–17.

38. Butler, *Native Son: The Emergence of a New Black Hero*, 52.

39. Martin Luther King Jr., "Letter from Birmingham Jail," 1963.

40. I am in debt to Henry Baldwin for bringing these lyrics to my attention. And I am grateful also to Evan Miyawaki for suggestions in my discussion of this novel.

41. Andrew Delbanco, *Required Reading* (New York: Farrar, Straus and Giroux, 1997), 187.

42. *Atlas Shrugged* by Ayn Rand (New York: Random House, 1957; New American Library, Plume, 1999).

43. Paul Ryan told an interviewer in 2014 that Rand's writings sparked his early interest in economics: "I adored her novels when I was young." However, "as a devout, practicing Catholic, I completely reject the philosophy of objectivism." Ryan interview with Jim Rutenberg, *New York Times*, September 14, 2014, 12.

44. Stephen Prothero, "You Can't Reconcile Ayn Rand and Jesus," *USA Today*, June 6, 2011. See also Jennifer Burns, *Goddess of the Market: Ayn Rand and the American Right* (New York: Oxford University Press, 2009).

45. Leonard Peikoff, *Objectivism: The Philosophy of Ayn Rand* (New York: Meridian, 1993), 377.

46. Ayn Rand, introduction, centennial edition, *The Fountainhead* (New York: Signet, 1993), vii.

47. Edward Abbey, *The Monkey Wrench Gang* (New York: HarperCollins, 1975).

48. Abbey quotes from his life chronology, summarized in an appendix of the HarperCollins 2006 edition, 8.

49. Abbey journal notes, quoted in Jack Loeffer, *Adventures with Ed: A Portrait of Abbey* (Albuquerque: University of New Mexico Press, 2002), 107.

50. So Abbey is described by historian Douglas Brinkley, in an introduction to the 15th-anniversary publication of *The Monkey Wrench Gang*, xvi.

51. Jim Fergus, "The Anarchists Progress," *Outside*, November 1988, 54.

52. Abbey anecdote cited in Jack Loeffer, *Adventures with Ed*, x.

53. Loeffer, *Adventures with Ed*, 123.

54. See, for example, Brian Allen Drake, *Loving Nature, Fearing the State* (Seattle: University of Washington Press, 2013).

55. James Surowiecki, "Bundynomics," *The New Yorker*, January 25, 2016, 23.

56. David Gessner, *All the Wild That Remains: Edward Abbey, Wallace Stegner, and the American West* (New York: Norton, 2015), 284.

57. Gessner, *All the Wild That Remains*, 285.

58. From Abbey's lecture notes, about 1976, used at the University of Montana and elsewhere. Located in Special Collections, University of Arizona Library, 2–3.

59. Patricia Nelson Limerick, *Desert Passages* (Albuquerque: University of New Mexico Press, 1985), 163.

60. Abbey lecture notes, 3–4.

61. Philip Roth, *The Plot Against America: A Novel* (New York: Houghton Mifflin, 2004).

CHAPTER 4

1. Mark Twain and Charles Dudley Warner, *The Gilded Age: A Tale of Today* (Hartford, CT: American Publishing Co., 1873).

2. Marin Felheim, introduction to the Meridian reproduction of *The Gilded Age*, 1994, x.

3. Twain recalls some of this in *The Autobiography of Mark Twain*, ed. Charles Neider (first published in 1873, New York: HarperCollins, 1966).

4. Phillip S. Foner, *Mark Twain: Social Critic* (New York: International Publishers, 1958), 102.

5. See, in general, Bryant Morey French, *Mark Twain and the Gilded Age* (Dallas, TX: Southern Methodist University Press, 1965).

6. Henry Adams, *Democracy: An American Novel* (New York: Harmony/Crown, 1981 edition). Originally published in 1880.

7. Helen Hunt Jackson, *Ramona* (Boston: Roberts, 1884).

8. Helen Hunt Jackson, *A Century of Dishonor: A Sketch of the United States Government's Dealings with Some of the Indian Tribes* (New York: Harper and Brothers, 1881), 3.

9. Allan Nevins, "Helen Hunt Jackson: Sentimentalist vs. Realist," *American Scholar* 10, no. 3 (Summer 1941): 278.

10. Jackson's letter to her friend William Ward, November 1, 1876, quote in Kate Phillips, *Helen Hunt Jackson: A Literary Life* (Berkeley: University of California Press, 2003), 202–3.

11. Jackson in a letter to her friend Moncure Conway, quote in Evelyn Banning, *Helen Hunt Jackson* (New York: Vanguard, 1973), 149.

12. Quoted in William Safire, *Safire's Political Dictionary* (New York: Oxford University Press, 2008), 412.

13. Helen Hunt Jackson and Abbot Kinney, *Of the Condition and Needs of the Mission Indians of California* (Colorado Springs, Colorado, July 13, 1883). It can be found in the appendix of most editions of *A Century of Dishonor*.

14. Douglas Monroy, "Ramona, I Love You," in *The Borders Within* (Tucson: University of Arizona Press, 2008), 93.

15. Denise Chávez, introduction to Helen Hunt Jackson, *Ramona* (New York: Modern Library edition, 2005), xv and xix.

16. Nevins, "Helen Hunt Jackson: Sentimentalist vs. Realist," 281. See also its historical and emotional impact on historian Douglas Monroy in *The Borders Within*, chapter 3.

17. Peter Matthiessen, foreword to Oren Lyons et al., *Exiled in the Land of the Free: Democracy, Indian Nations and the U.S. Constitution* (Santa Fe: Clearlight Publishers, 1992), xii.

18. Quoted in most of the biographies of Jackson. See, Antionette May, *Helen Hunt Jackson: A Lonely Voice of Conscience* (San Francisco: Chronicle Books, 1989), 132.

19. See, for example, Donald L. Fixico, *The Invasion of Indian Country in the Twentieth Century: American Capitalism and Tribal Natural Resources* (Niwot, CO: University Press of Colorado, 1998), and Lyons et al., *Exiled in the Land of the Free*.

20. Frank Waters, *People of the Valley* (New York: Farrar and Rinehart, 1941), republished (Chicago: Swallow Press, 1969), 177. See also by Waters *The Man Who Killed the Deer* (1942) and *The Woman at Otawi Crossing* (1966).

21. (American) Winston Churchill, *Mr. Crewe's Career* (New York: Macmillan, 1908).

22. See the useful book by Robert O'Kell, *Disraeli: The Romance of Politics* (Toronto: University of Toronto Press, 2013).

23. See the similar verdict of Morris Edmund Speare, *The Political Novel* (New York: Oxford University Press, 1924), 306–21.

24. Robert Penn Warren, *All the King's Men* (New York: Harcourt, Brace, 1946).

25. David Brooks, "Really Good Books, Part I," *New York Times*, May 23, 2014, A19.

26. Brooks, "Really Good Books, Part I," A19.

27. T. Harry Williams, *Huey Long* (New York: Bantam, 1970), xi.

28. Williams, *Huey Long*, 829.

29. See Richard D. Wright, *Kingfish: The Reign of Huey P. Long* (New York: Random House, 2006).

30. Quoted in Joseph Blotner, *Robert Penn Warren: A Biography* (New York: Random House, 1997), 151.

31. V. O. Key Jr., *Southern Politics* (New York: Vintage, 1949), 164.

32. See, for example, Robert Penn Warren, ed., *Selected Poems of Herman Melville: A Reader's Edition* (New York: Random House, 1970) and *A Robert Penn Warren Reader* (New York: Random House, 1987).

33. See Blotner, *Robert Penn Warren*.

34. Harper Lee, *To Kill a Mockingbird* (Philadelphia: J. B. Lippincott, 1960) and *Go Set a Watchman* (New York: HarperCollins, 2016).

35. Carolyn Jones, "Atticus Finch and the Mad Dog," in Harold Bloom, ed., *Harper Lee's* To Kill a Mockingbird (Philadelphia: Chelsea House, 1999), 113.

36. Charles J. Shields, *Mockingbird: A Portrait of Harper Lee* (New York: Holt, 2006), 121.

37. Shields, *Mockingbird*, 121. See additional views and personal evaluations in the useful Wayne Flynt, *Mockingbird Songs: My Friendship with Harper Lee* (New York: HarperCollins, 2017).

38. Marja Mills, *The Mockingbird Next Door* (New York: Penguin, 2014).

39. I have borrowed a few paragraphs here from Thomas E. Cronin and William Kim, "Say It Ain't So, Atticus," *Denver Post*, July 19, 2015, 1D and 6D.

40. Key, *Southern Politics*, 665.

41. Randall Kennedy in his review "Tarnished Hero," *New York Times* Book Review, August 2, 2015, 8.

42. Margaret Eby, *South Toward Home: Travel in Southern Literature* (New York: Norton, 2015), 135.

43. See, for example, Angie Debo, *The Road to Disappearance: A History of the Creek Indians* (Norman: University of Oklahoma Press, 1979—earlier edition 1941).

44. Fletcher Knebel and Charles W. Bailey II, *Seven Days in May* (New York: Harper and Row, 1962).

45. See Dick Cheney and Liz Cheney, *Exceptional: Why the World Needs a Powerful America* (New York: Threshold Editions, 2016), and Jeffrey Goldberg, "The Obama Doctrine," *The Atlantic*, April 2016, 70–90.

46. John Nichols, *The Milagro Beanfield War* (New York: Holt, 1974).

47. See, for example, Miriam Pawel, *The Crusades of César Chávez* (New York: Bloomsbury, 2014).

48. Rudolfo Anaya, *Bless Me, Ultima* (Berkeley, CA: TQS Publications, 1972; reissued as a Warner Books Paperback, 1994), 98.

49. John Nichols, *Dancing on the Stones: Selected Essays* (Albuquerque: University of New Mexico Press, 2000).

50. John Nichols, *An American Child Supreme: The Education of a Liberation Ecologist* (Minneapolis: Milwaukee Edition, 2001), 110. See also his comments on himself in Bill Whaley, ed., *Taos Portraits* (Taos, NM: Hondó Mesa Press, 2012), 78.

51. Nichols, *Dancing on the Stones*, 90.

52. John Nichols, *The Magic Journey* (New York: Holt, 1978).

53. Cronin, notes from conversation with John Nichols, September 16, 2016, Guadalajara Grill #3, Taos, New Mexico.

54. Nichols, *An American Child Supreme*, 86.

55. John Nichols, talk at Antler's Hotel, Colorado Springs, Colorado, April 12, 2003. He was accepting the Frank Waters Award (mimeo copy shared by Nichols with the author).

56. Quoted in Nichols's talk, Colorado Springs, Colorado, 2003, 7.

57. John Grisham, *The Appeal: A Novel* (New York: Doubleday, 2008).

58. In most other states, an advisory panel nominates judges and justices, from which the governor selects them. Then, after a set number of years, they must have retention elections for still longer terms. The goal of such systems is to remove as much political corruption as is possible.

59. Sandra Day O'Connor, "Take Justice Off the Ballot," *New York Times* (*Times* Week in Review), May 23, 2010, 9.

60. This is echoed in Lexington, "The Trouble with Electing Judges," *The Economist*, August 23, 2014, 26.

61. Lincoln Caplan, "Justice for Sale," *American Scholar* (Summer 2012): 25.

CHAPTER 5

1. I have drawn here from my article "Laughing at Leaders," *Leadership and Humanities* (2014): 27–43.

2. Hugh Henry Brackenridge, *Modern Chivalry: Containing the Adventures of Captain John Farrago, and Teague O'Regan, His Servant (1792–1815)*, Volumes I and

II, published in Philadelphia, John M'Culloch, subsequent volumes published in Pennsylvania by other publishers.

3. James MacGregor Burns and Susan Dunn, *George Washington* (New York: Times Books, 2004), 12.

4. Vernon L. Parrington, *The Colonial Mind* (New York: Harcourt, Brace and World, 1927), 397.

5. John Dos Passos, *The Ground We Stand On* (New York: Harcourt, Brace and Co., 1941), 388.

6. Alexander Cowie, *The Rise of the American Novel* (New York: American Book Company, 1948), 56.

7. Carl Van Doren, *The American Novel, 1789–1939* (New York: Macmillan, 1940), 7. An earlier edition was published in 1921.

8. Parrington, *The Colonial Mind*, 396.

9. Nathanael West, *A Cool Million* (New York: Farrar, Straus and Giroux, 1934).

10. Horatio Alger Jr. (1832–1899). His most famous novel was *Ragged Dick or Street Life in New York with the Boot-Blacks*, first published in 1868 (New York: Modern Library, 2005). Most of his narratives have a young orphan who is forced to leave home and to work at menial jobs as a means of making friends and money, and he has noble principles and pluck and luck on the path to success.

11. Jay Martin, *Nathanael West: The Art of His Life* (New York: Farrar, Straus and Giroux, 1970), 227.

12. Martin, *Nathanael West*, 232–33.

13. A useful, yet probably too harsh, criticism of *A Cool Million* is found in Kingsley Cridmer's *Nathanael West* (Boston: Twayne, 1982), chapter 3.

14. Richard Condon, *The Manchurian Candidate* (New York: McGraw Hill, 1959).

15. Michael A. Genovese, *Politics and the Cinema: An Introduction to Political Films* (Needham Heights, MA: Ginn Press, 1986), 25. See also the 2016 Hollywood film, *Trumbo*, on the life of screenwriter Dalton Trumbo.

16. Joseph Heller, *Catch-22* (New York: Simon and Schuster, 1961, 2011).

17. For more on his life and the context in which he wrote, see Tracy Daugherty's excellent *Just One Catch: A Biography of Joseph Heller* (New York: St. Martin's Press, 2011).

18. Robert Brustein, "The New Republic," November 13, 1961, reprinted at the end of the 50th-anniversary edition of *Catch-22*.

19. John W. Aldridge, "The Loony Horror of It All," *New York Times* Book Review, October 2, 1986, reprinted at the end of the 50th-anniversary edition of *Catch-22*, 512.

20. Quoted in Christopher Buckley's introduction to the 50th-anniversary edition of *Catch-22*.

21. Gore Vidal, *Washington, D.C.: A Novel* (New York: Random House, 1967).

22. Jay Parini, *Empire of Self: A Life of Gore Vidal* (New York: Doubleday, 2015), 405.

23. Parini, *Empire of Self*, 174. See also Heather Neilson, *Political Animal: Gore Vidal on Power* (Clayton, Victoria; Australia: Monash University Press, 2014).

24. Hunter S. Thompson, *Fear and Loathing in Las Vegas: A Savage Journey to the Heart of the American Dream* (New York: Random House, 1971).

25. Robert C. Sickels, "A Countercultural Gatsby: Hunter S. Thompson's Fear and Loathing in Las Vegas, the Death of the American Dream and the Rise of Las Vegas, USA," *Popular Culture Review* 11 (November 1, 2000): 67.

26. Kevin T. McEneaney, *Hunter S. Thompson: Fear, Loathing, and the Birth of Gonzo* (Lanham, MD: Rowman & Littlefield, 2016), 104.

27. Interview with Hunter S. Thompson, August 26, 1997, reported in *Ancient Gonzo Wisdom*, edited by Anita Thompson (Cambridge, MA: Da Capo Press, 2009), 240.

28. Juan F. Thompson, *Stories I Tell Myself* (New York: Knopf, 2016), xii. See also the useful biography by Paul Perry, *Fear and Loathing: The Strange and Terrible Saga of Hunter S. Thompson* (New York: Thunder's Mouth Press, 1992), and Peter O. Whittmer's *When the Going Gets Weird: The Twisted Life and Times of Hunter S. Thompson* (Chelmsford, MA: Courier Corporation, 2000).

29. Thompson, *Stories I Tell Myself*, 179.

30. From an essay by Colorado College student Alex Peebles-Capin: "Hunter S. Thompson's American Nightmare," April 13, 2015. Alex shared other ideas I used here and was a valued editor on this work.

31. Evan Oxman, "The American Dream in Fear and Loathing in Las Vegas," paper presented at the Western Political Science Association, Las Vegas, Nevada, March 2015, 18.

32. Hitchens interview with Thompson in *Ancient Gonzo Wisdom*, xx.

33. Interview with Adam Bulger, March 9, 2014, in *Ancient Gonzo Wisdom*, 362.

34. See Acosta's own novel, for which Thompson writes an introduction, *The Revolt of the Cockroach People* (San Francisco: Straight Arrow Books, 1973), reissued by Vintage Books in 1989.

35. McEneaney, *Hunter S. Thompson*, 242.

36. I am grateful to Tracy Santa at Colorado College for helpful suggestions on this section.

37. Christopher Buckley, *Supreme Courtship: A Novel* (New York: Twelve, 2008).

38. Illustrative political and constitutional reformers are Erwin Chemerinsky, *The Case Against the Supreme Court* (New York: Viking 2014), and Sanford Levinson, *Our Undemocratic Constitution* (New York: Oxford University Press, 2006).

39. Alexandria Wolfe, "Christopher Buckley," *Wall Street Journal*, November 21–22, 2015, C19.

CHAPTER 6

1. Hamlin Garland, *A Spoil of Office: A Story of the Middle West* (Boston: Arena Press, 1892).

2. Quentin E. Martin, "'This Spreading Radicalism': Hamlin Garland's *A Spoil of Office* and the Creation of True Populism," *Studies in American Fiction* 26, no. 1 (Spring 1998): 31.

3. Keith Newlin, *Hamlin Garland: A Life* (Lincoln: University of Nebraska Press, 2008).

4. Hamlin Garland, "Urges Democrats to Leave," *Chicago Tribune*, January 29, 1892, 3, discussed in Newlin's *Hamlin Garland: A Life*, 164.

5. Howard Fast, *The American: A Middle Western Legend* (New York: Duell, Sloan and Pearce, 1946).

6. Altgeld, quoted in Matthew Josephson, *The Politicos (1865–1896)* (New York: Harcourt, Brace, 1938), 616–17.

7. Josephson, *The Politicos*, 206.

8. See, for example, Josephson, *The Politicos*, and Charles A. Madison, *Critics and Crusaders: A Century of Protest* (New York: Henry Holt, 1947), 366–94.

9. Edwin O'Connor, *The Last Hurrah* (Boston: Little, Brown, 1956).

10. Gerard O'Neill, *Rogues and Redeemers: When Politics Was King in Irish Boston* (New York: Crown Publishers, 2012), 73.

11. Jonathan Rauch, *Political Realism* (Washington, D.C.: Brookings Institution, ebook, 2015).

12. Eugene Burdick, *The Ninth Wave* (Boston, MA: Houghton Mifflin Co., 1956).

13. Gordon Milne, *The American Political Novel* (Norman, OK: University of Oklahoma Press, 1966), 116–17.

14. Two other political novels that raise equally important questions are Richard Lamm and Arnold Grossman, *1988* (New York: St. Martin's Press, 1988), and Stuart Stevens, *The Innocent Have Nothing to Fear* (New York: Knopf, 2016).

15. Andrew Tully, *Capitol Hill* (New York: Simon & Schuster, 1962).

16. Joe Klein, *Primary Colors: A Novel of Politics* (New York: Random House, 1996).

17. David Maraniss, "Beyond a Biographer's Reach," *Washington Post* National Weekly Edition, July 12–18, 2004, 23.

18. Joe Klein, *Politics Lost* (New York: Doubleday, 2006), 110.

19. Joe Klein, *The Natural: The Misunderstood Presidency of Bill Clinton* (New York: Doubleday, 2002), 27 and 216.

20. FBI director Louis Fried quoted in David E. Rosenbaum, "In New Book, Ex-Director of the F.B.I Fights Back," *New York Times*, October 15, 2005, A14. See a similarly scathing account of Clinton's early postpresidency years, Todd S. Purdum, "The Comeback Id," *Vanity Fair*, July 2008, 76–82, 127–31.

21. Bill Clinton, *My Life* (New York: Knopf, 2004).

22. Clinton, quoted in Maraniss, "Beyond a Biographer's Reach," 22.

23. Klein became a regular feature writer for *Time* for many years. His *The Running Mate* was in part a sequel to *Primary Colors*, but it attracted little attention.

CHAPTER 7

1. See Horatio Alger Jr., *Only an Irish Boy* (Chicago: Donahue, 1874); *Phil, the Fiddler* (Chicago: Donohue, 1872); *Ragged Dick* (Boston: Loring, 1868); and *Struggling Upward*; or, *Luke Larkin's Luck* (1890) republished in Russell Crouse, ed., *Struggling Upward and Other Books* (New York: Bonanza Books, 1955), also the helpful Alger bibliography in Carol Nackenoff, *The Fictional Republic: Horatio Alger and American Political Discourse* (New York: Oxford University Press, 1994), 337–41. See also the excellent biography *The Lost Life of Horatio Alger Jr.* by Gary Scharnhorst with Jack Bales (Bloomington: Indiana University Press, 1985).

2. David K. Shipler, introduction to a more recent printing of *Ragged Dick* (New York: The Modern Library, 2015), xvi.

3. *Hamilton: An American Musical*, book, music, and lyrics by Lin-Manuel Miranda, Richard Rodgers Theater, New York City, 2015.

4. Malcolm Cowley, "The Real Horatio Alger Story," in Cowley, *New England Writers and Writing* (Hanover, NH: University of New England Press, 1996), 102.

5. "Star Wars, Disney and Myth-Making," *The Economist*, December 19, 2015, 13.

6. Carol Nackenoff, *The Fictional Republic: Horatio Alger and Political Discourse* (New York: Oxford University Press, 1994), 269.

7. Symposium, *Foreign Affairs* (January/February 2016).

8. See Norman W. Provizer, "The Horatio Alger Jr. Novels and Their Impact on Political Discourses," paper presented at Western Political Science Association Meetings, March 2015, Las Vegas, Nevada. This paper especially informed my reading of Alger's works, and I am indebted to Professor Provizer for his guidance.

9. Richard V. Reeves, "Saving Horatio Alger: Equality, Opportunity, and the American Dream," Brookings Institution eBook essay, 2014, 26.

10. Reeves, "Saving Horatio Alger," 32. Thanks also to the insights in Norman W. Provizer, "The Horatio Alger Jr. Novels."

11. Quoted in Shipler, introduction, xii–xiii.

12. Shipler, introduction.

13. Herman Melville, *Billy Budd: Sailor (An Insider Narrative)* (New York: Simon and Schuster, completed in 1891). First published in 1924.

14. Nicholas O. Warner, "Of 'Gods and Commodores': Leadership in Melville's *Moby Dick*," in Joanna B. Ciulla, ed., *Leadership at the Crossroads* (Westport, CT: Prager, 2008), 4.

15. Buckard Sievers, "Leadership and Monomania: Herman Melville's *Moby-Dick*," in Jonathan Gosling and Peter Villiers, *Fictional Leaders* (New York: Palgrave, 2013), 80. See also Warner, "Of 'Gods and Commodores.'"

16. Lawrence Buell, *The Dream of the Great American Novel* (Cambridge, MA: Harvard University Press, 2014), 370.

17. Andrew Delbanco, *Melville* (New York: Knopf, 2003), 313.

18. See discussions by Tom Goldstein, "Once Again Billy Budd Stands Trial," *New York Times*, June 10, 1988, and by Christopher J. Sterritt, "Ode to 'Billy Budd,'" *Federal Bar News and Journal*, May 1991, 208–12.

19. Joel Porte, *The Romance in America* (Middleton, CT: Wesleyan University Press, 1969), 188.

20. John Whalen-Bridge, *Political Fiction and the American Self* (Urbana: University of Illinois Press, 1998). He argues there is a distinctive, though submerged, political novel in *Moby Dick*, one that deals with authority and political rebellion.

21. Delbanco, *Melville*, 314.

22. Thoughts suggested in Thomas J. Scorza, *In the Time Before Steamships* (DeKalb: Northern Illinois University Press, 1979), xxiv, and Milton R. Stern, ed., *Billy Budd, Sailor* (Indianapolis: Bobbs-Merrill, 1925), xix–xx. See also Catherine H. Zuckert, *Natural Right and the American Imagination* (Savage, MD: Rowman & Littlefield, 1990).

23. Robert Penn Warren, introduction to *Selected Poems of Herman Melville* (New York: Random House, 1967), 62–63.

24. Warren, introduction, 88.

25. Delbanco, *Melville*, 305.

26. Warren, introduction, 87.

27. Margaret Mitchell, *Gone with the Wind* (New York: Macmillan, 1936).

28. Pat Conroy, from a preface written for a 1996 edition of *GWTW* (New York: Pocket Books, 1996), v.

29. Anne Edwards, *Road to Tara: The Life of Margaret Mitchell* (New Haven: Ticknor and Fields, 1983), 21.

30. Edwards, *Road to Tara*, 22–23.

31. Conroy, preface, v–vi.

32. The *gone with the wind* phrase is used in the novel in the following passage as Scarlett is desperately trying to fight her way back to her family's plantation home after the fall of Atlanta: "Was Tara (her family's cherished home and plantation) still standing? Or was it gone with the wind, which had swept through Georgia? She laid the whip on the tired horse's back and tried to urge him on while the waggling wheels rocked them drunkenly from side to side."

33. See, for example, Edward Baptist, *The Half Has Never Been Told: Slavery and the Making of American Capitalism* (New York: Basic Books, 2014).

34. Frederick Douglass, "Oration in Memory of Abraham Lincoln," April 14, 1876, in *The World's Great Speeches*, edited by Lewis Copeland and Lawrence W. Lamm (New York: Dover Publications, 1973), 811.

35. James M. McPherson, *Ordeal by Fire: The Civil War and Reconstruction* (New York: Knopf, 1982), 477.

36. Allen Drury, *Advise and Consent* (Garden City, NY: Doubleday, 1959).

37. Thomas Mallon, "'Advise and Consent' at 50," *New York Times* Book Review, June 25, 2009, 23.

38. I benefited from reading Gordon Milne, *The American Political Novel* (Norman: University of Oklahoma Press, 1966, chapter 9); Cord Meyer, "Melodrama on the Hill," *The Kenyon Review* (Spring 1960): 327–31; Jonathan Karl, "An Eavesdropper in the Smoke-Filled Room," *Wall Street Journal*, May 24–25, 2015, C11; and Mallon's "'Advise and Consent' at 50."

39. Billy Lee Brammer, *The Gay Place* (Boston: Houghton Mifflin, 1961; reissued in 1986 by Random House, New York).

40. Christopher Lehmann, "Why Americans Can't Write Political Fiction," *Washington Monthly*, October/November 2005 (online).

41. See especially Robert A. Caro, *The Passage of Power* (New York: Knopf, 2012).

42. Bobby Baker with Larry L. King, *Wheeling and Dealing: Confessions of a Capitol Hill Operator* (New York: W. W. Norton, 1978).

43. Michael Shaara, *The Killer Angels: Four Days in Gettysburg* (New York: McKay, 1974). Its subtitle was twice changed by its marketers to "A Novel of the Civil War" and later still to "The Classic Novel of the Civil War."

44. These citations of praise came from blurbs on the Ballantine paperback edition.

45. David Brooks, "The Robert E. Lee Problem," *New York Times*, June 26, 2015, A23.

46. Stephens's quote and this interpretation is shared in Don H. Doyle, *The Cause of All Nations: An International History of the American Civil War* (New York: Basic Books, 2015), 36 and 37.

47. David W. Blight, "That a Nation Might Live," *New York Times* Book Review, June 30, 2013, 13.

48. See how Larry Taylor and William E. Rosenbach used this novel in their Creative Leadership Development program based in Gettysburg, discussed in Robert L. Taylor and William E. Rosenbach, eds., *Military Leadership*, 6th edition (Boulder: Westview Press, 2009), chapter 22. I am also grateful to Bill Rosenbach for additional insights on this topic.

49. *Killer Angels* readers should also read the prize-winning nonfiction works of James M. McPherson, *Battle Cry of Freedom* (New York: Oxford University Press, 1988); Stephen W. Sears, *Gettysburg* (Boston: Houghton Mifflin, 2003); and Allen Guelzo, *Gettysburg: The Last Invasion* (New York: Knopf, 2013).

50. See Don E. Doyle, *The Cause of All Nations* (New York: Basic Books, 2015).

51. Toni Morrison, *Beloved* (New York: Vintage, 1987).

52. Philip Weinstein, "'Dangerously Free': Morrison's Unspeakable Territory," in Adrienne Lanier Seward and Justine Tally, eds., *Toni Morrison: Memory and Meaning* (Jackson: University Press of Mississippi, 2014), 13–14.

53. Weinstein, "'Dangerously Free,'" 14.

54. Carl Plasa, *Toni Morrison, Beloved* (New York: Columbia University Press, 1998), 63.

55. Lovalerie King, "Property and American Identity in Toni Morrison's *Beloved*," in Seward and Tally, eds, *Toni Morrison*, 161.

56. John Henry Williams, a research assistant, Colorado College, May 2016.

57. P. J. Brendese, *The Power of Memory in Democratic Politics* (Rochester, NY: University of Rochester Press, 2014), 89.

58. Novelist Colson Whitehead's *The Underground Railroad* (New York: Doubleday, 2016) speaks to similar themes and is one of the best sequels in the Morrison tradition. Oprah Winfrey, who had earlier both produced and starred in the film version of *Beloved*, made Whitehead's novel a Winfrey book club pick.

59. Norman Mailer, *Harlot's Ghost* (New York: Random House, 1991).

60. There is a long shelf of good books on the life and service of CIA agents. Two useful ones are Henry A. Crumpton, *The Art of Intelligence: Lessons from a Life in the CIA's Clandestine Service* (New York: Penguin, 2012), and Kai Bird, *The Good Spy: The Life and Death of Robert Ames* (New York: Crown, 2014).

61. Norman Mailer quoted in J. Michael Lennon, *Norman Mailer: A Double Life* (New York: Simon and Schuster, 2013), 614.

62. John Simon, "The Company They Keep," *New York Times*, September 29, 1991.

63. Mailer acknowledged his debt to Kennedy mistress Judith Exner, *My Story* (New York: Grove, 1977), for his "imaginations" here.

64. Joseph Trento, *The Secret History of the CIA* (Roseville, CA: Prima Publishing, 2001).

65. Mary V. Dearborn, *Mailer: A Biography* (Boston: Houghton Mifflin, 1999), 409.

66. Trento, *The Secret History of the CIA*, xiii.

67. Personal letter to Michael K. Glenday, December 10, 1993, quoted in Michael K. Glenday, *Norman Mailer* (New York: St. Martin's Press, 1995), 133.

68. Mailer's accounts of Mafiosi being recruited and hired by the CIA, the strange interconnections of the CIA, the Kennedy mistresses, and mobsters are amusing and entertaining, yet amazingly accurate. See the detailed later corroborations of these hard-to-believe-but-true events in Evan Thomas, *The Very Best Men: Four Who Dared: The Early Years of the CIA* (New York: Simon and Schuster, 1995), and Seymour M. Hersh, *The Dark Side of Camelot* (Boston: Little, Brown, 1997).

69. For valuable nonfiction biographical treatments of several of these CIA legends, see Evan Thomas, *The Very Best Men*, and Stephen Kinzer, *The Brothers* (New York: Times Books, 2013).

70. Ward Just, *Echo House* (Boston: Houghton Mifflin Co., 1997).

71. Michael Nelson, "Ward Just's Washington," *Virginia Quarterly Review* (Spring 1998), online edition, 80.

72. Joseph S. Nye Jr., *The Power Game: A Washington Novel* (New York: Public Affairs, 2004).

73. Michael Ignatieff, "Letter to a Young Liberal," *The New Republic*, November 24 and December 8, 2014, 33. See his larger book on his successes and failures in Canadian politics: *Fire and Ashes* (Cambridge, MA: Harvard University Press, 2013).

74. Ignatieff, *Fire and Ashes*, 81.

SELECTED BIBLIOGRAPHY

Blotner, Joseph L. *The Political Novel*. Garden City, NY: Doubleday, 1955.

Buell, Lawrence. *The Dream of the Great American Novel*. Cambridge, MA: Belknap Press of Harvard University Press, 2015.

Chase, Richard. *The American Novel and Its Tradition*. Garden City, NY: Doubleday, 1957.

Cowie, Alexander. *The Rise of the American Novel*. New York: American Book Company, 1948.

Delbanco, Andrew. *Required Reading: Why Our American Classics Matter Now*. New York: Farrar, Straus and Giroux, 1997.

Haas, Elizabeth, Terry Christensen, and Peter J. Haas. *Projecting Politics: Political Messages in American Films*, second edition. New York: Routledge, 2015.

Howe, Irving. *Politics and the Novel*. New York: Horizon Press, 1957.

Jillson, Cal. *The American Dream in History, Politics and Fiction*. Lawrence: University Press of Kansas, 2016.

Milne, Gordon. *The American Political Novel*. Norman: University of Oklahoma Press, 1966.

Monroe, N. Elizabeth. *The Novel and Society: A Critical Study of the Modern Novel*. Chapel Hill: University of North Carolina Press, 1941.

Nackenhoff, Carol. *The Fictional Republic: Horatio Alger and American Political Discourse*. New York: Oxford University Press, 1994.

Nafisi, Azar. *The Republic of Imagination: America in Three Books*. New York: Viking, 2014.

Speare, Morris. *The Political Novel: Its Development in England and in America*. New York: Oxford University Press, 1924.

Van Doren, Carl. *The American Novel*. New York: Macmillan, 1921.

Zuckert, Catherine. *Natural Right and the American Imagination*. Savage, MD: Rowman & Littlefield, 1990.

THANKS

This was a challenging new venture for me, and I was fortunate in having many friends, colleagues, and students offer help and advice along the way.

Colorado College and the McHugh Chair of American Institutions and Leadership provided indispensable financial help. Colleagues in the Colorado College community who shared their counsel included Bob Loevy, Timothy Fuller, Barry Sarchett, Lisa Hughes, Bill Hochman, Doug Monroy, Tracy Santa, Katrina Bell, and Joe Barrera.

Friends in the Whitman College community provided helpful ideas and nominated important novels to be considered. Special thanks to Patrick Henry, Mary Anne O'Neil, John Desmond, Elizabeth Vandiver, Kathy Ketchum, and Patrick Keef. Leadership scholar William Rosenbach shared valued advice.

Political scientists Michael A. Genovese and Norman W. Provizer shared inspired advice and valued encouragement.

Several Colorado College students served as outstanding research assistants for this project, especially Andy Post, Alex Peebles-Capin, Robbie J. Caseria, William Kim, and John Henry Williams. I also profited from productive discussions with dozens of students who wrote papers on some of the novels treated in this book. I especially thank Jess Ayers, Khris Grant, Evan Miyawaki, Ian O'Shaughnessy, David Trevithick, and Ty Wagner.

Jessica Pauls, our Department of Political Science administrative assistant and office coordinator extraordinaire, provided invaluable help in typing, editing, and manuscript preparation. Rhonda Van Pelt also shared editorial advice and typed early chapters.

Senior executive editor Jon Sisk, acquisitions editor Kate Powers, senior production editor Patricia Stevenson, and copyeditor Desiree Reid at Rowman & Littlefield transformed the manuscript into this book. I am grateful to them and their colleagues, especially Jon for his enthusiastic support for this project.

Special thanks to novelist John Nichols, who discussed his books with me and shared his views on several other novels I discuss here.

Above all, I am indebted to Dr. Tania Z. Cronin, who was my greatest muse, editor, and cheerleader for this novel project.

Tom Cronin
Colorado Springs
Tom.cronin@coloradocollege.edu

INDEX

ABOUT THE AUTHOR

Thomas E. Cronin is McHugh Professor of American Institutions and Leadership at Colorado College. He served as president of Whitman College from 1993 to 2005 and acting president of Colorado College in 1991.

He has authored or coauthored best-selling books on American politics and the American presidency and other books on leadership, elections, and public policy. He has won awards for teaching, advising, and his research and writings, including the Best Leadership Book Award of 2013 and the American Political Science Association's Charles E. Merriam Award for his early writings on the American presidency. He has written for several dozen journals and magazines and is a guest columnist for state and national newspapers.

Cronin has held visiting scholar appointments at the Brookings Institution, the Hoover Institution at Stanford, the Aspen Institute, and the Center for the Study of Democratic Institutions. He also served as a visiting professor of politics at Princeton University.

He served as one of the founding presidents of the American Political Science Association's Presidency Research Group, as president of the Western Political Science Association, and on the Executive Council of the American Political Science Association.